Employment Guide
2010

Employment Guide
2010

First published in 2002

This revised edition published in 2010 by
EEF
Broadway House
Tothill Street
London SW1H 9NQ
www.eef.org.uk

In association with Profile Books Ltd
www.profilebooks.com

10 9 8 7 6 5 4 3 2 1

Copyright © EEF 2010

All rights reserved. Without limiting the rights under copyright reserved above, no part of this publication may be reproduced, stored or introduced into a retrieval system, or transmitted in any form or by any means (electronic, mechanical, photocopying, recording or otherwise), without prior written permission of both the copyright owner and the publisher of this book.

Text design by Sue Lamble

Typeset in FS Albert by MacGuru Ltd
info@macguru.org.uk

Printed and bound in Great Britain by Bell & Bain Ltd, Glasgow

A CIP catalogue record for this book is available from the British Library

ISBN 978 1 905715 50 3

Disclaimer

The *Employment Guide 2010* is intended to give general guidance only. It does not purport to be comprehensive or to give specific legal advice. The *Employment Guide* relates only to the laws of England and Wales and of Scotland.

Although EEF has endeavoured to ensure the content of the *Employment Guide* is accurate and up to date:

- Users should always seek advice before taking or refraining from any action, including making use of any documents provided within the Guide.

- EEF does not accept liability, including liability for any negligence, for the content of the *Employment Guide*.

- EEF does not accept responsibility for the content of any website to which a reference or link is provided in the *Employment Guide*.

Contents

Section 1 Starting the relationship ... 1

1.1 Recruitment ... 3

Overview 3; Defining the job 5; Defining the person 6; Inviting applications 8; Receiving applications 11; Shortlisting for interview 14; Conducting the interview 15; Selection tests 17; Supporting information 18; Candidate assessment 25; Making the job offer 26; Monitoring recruitment 28; Keeping records 29; Induction 30; Probationary periods 31

1.2 Contracts ... 32

Overview 32; Forming the contract 33; Express terms 34; Implied terms 43; Documenting the contract 47; Enforcing the contract 52; Employment status 55; Fixed-term contracts 61

Section 2 Rights during employment ... 67

2.1 Pay ... 69

Overview 69; Contractual issues 71; Documenting pay 73; The national minimum wage 75; Discrimination in pay 82; Deductions from pay 94

2.2 Family rights ... 99

Overview 99; Contractual rights 100; Health and safety 101; Maternity leave 104; Returnng from leave 112; Legal protection for pregnancy and maternity 114; Maternity checklist 117; Paternity leave and pay 121; Adoption leave 125; Parental leave 131; Requests for flexible working 137; Time off for dependants 141

2.3 Working time ... 144

Overview 144; Health and safety 145; Contract terms 147; Discrimination issues 148; Working Time Regulations 149; Working week limit 154; Night work 156; Rest breaks and periods 160; Holidays 163; Non-statutory leave 169; Part-time working 170; Time off for public duties 172; Time off for young people for study and training 175

2.4 Pension rights — 177

Overview 177; Types of pension schemes 178; Pension benefits 181; Basic legal framework 182; Taxation 183; Contractual issues 183; Discrimination in pensions 184; Information on pensions 190; Consultation on pension changes 193; Rights of employee trustees 196; Resolving disputes 197; Stakeholder pensions 198

Section 3 Managing the relationship — 201

3.1 Equal opportunities — 203

Overview 203; Defining discrimination 204; Direct discrimination: some common principles 209; Indirect discrimination 211; Disability discrimination 215; Reasonable adjustments 222; Victimisation 224; Types of workers covered 225; Types of discriminatory act 226; Exceptions to the principle of non-discrimination 228; Employer liability for discrimination 231; Positive action 237; People with criminal records 239

3.2 Managing performance — 241

Overview 241; Performance appraisal 241; Managing absence 251; Sickness absence 255; Managing sickness absence 260; Following a fair sickness absence procedure 264

3.3 Handling discipline and grievances — 273

Overview 273; Discipline: some general principles 274; Making the standards clear 278; Operating a disciplinary procedure 284; Investigating the conduct 287; Holding a disciplinary hearing 292; Choosing the sanction 300; Dealing with appeals 305; Keeping records 309; Dealing with grievances 310; Protection for 'whistleblowers' 318; Asserting legal rights 321; Responding to health and safety concerns 322

Section 4 Terminating employment — 325

4.1 Terminating employment — 327

Overview 327; Dismissal 328; Resignation 337; Mutual agreement 340; Retirement 340; Task or purpose contracts 341; Frustration 341; Fixed-term contracts 342; Termination of apprenticeships 344; Written reason for dismissal 345; References 345; Post-employment restrictions 347; Recovering training and other costs 349; Retaining employment records 350; Settlements 350; Tax 351; Social security considerations 351; Pensions 352; Exit interviews 352; Labour turnover 354; Succession planning 356

4.2 Unfair dismissal 358

Overview 358; Eligibility to claim 360; Establishing the dismissal 363; The reason for the dismissal 364; Did the company act reasonably? 368; Capability 371; Qualifications 373; Conduct 373: Redundancy 374; Legal restriction 375; Some other substantial reason 375; Retirement 376

Section 5 Change and reorganisation 379

5.1 Changing contracts of employment 381

Overview 381; Does the change affect employees' contracts? 383; Express terms requiring flexibility 386; Implied flexibility 388; Change through agreement 388; Imposed change and its dangers 390; Offering new contracts 393; Avoiding unfair dismissal 394; Collective consultation 398; Documenting change 398

5.2 Redundancy, lay-off and short-time working 401

Overview 401; Company procedures on redundancy 403; Defining redundancy 405; Considering alternatives 409; Warning and consultation 410; Notifying BIS 418; Volunteers and early retirement 418; Identifying the pool for selection 420; Choosing the selection criteria 421; Applying the selection criteria 424; Consultation 425; Disabled employees 426; Appeals 426; Considering alternative employment 427; Terminating employment 431; Time off during notice period 431; Redundancy payments 432; Alternatives to redundancy 436; Redundancy and insolvent companies 439; Apprentices 440; Redundancy Ready Reckoner 443

5.3 Transfer of undertakings 444

Overview 444; When do the Regulations apply? 445; Informing and consulting the workforce 448; Transfer of employees 453; Protection from dismissal 460; Effect on collective bargaining 461; Special rules for insolvent employers 462; Government contracts 463

Employment Guide 2010

Section 6 The collective dimension — 465

6.1 Trade union members — 467

Overview 467; Discrimination on trade union grounds 468; Protection for non-members 471; Rights to time off 472; Check-off arrangements 476

6.2 Collective bargaining — 478

Overview 478; Recognition considerations 479; Statutory procedure for recognition 482; Recognition agreements 488; Resolution of disputes 490; Collective agreements 491; Right to bargaining information 494

6.3 Industrial action — 498

Overview 498; Types of industrial action 499; Avoiding industrial action 500; Responding to industrial action 501; Union liability for industrial action 502; The position of individual employees 511; Unfair dismissal protection 511; Contractual issues 515; Employer responses 516; Lay-off and redundancy 519

6.4 Employee involvement — 522

Overview 522; Benefits of employee involvement 524; Methods of employee involvement 524; Reporting on employee involvement 527; General duty to inform and consult 527; Consultation by trans-European employers 532; Redundancies and business transfers 536; Health and safety 538; Training 543; Legal rights of representatives 543

Section 7 Employment tribunals and remedies — 547

7.1 Employment tribunals — 549

Overview 549; The membership of employment tribunals 550; Bringing a claim 550; Responding to a claim 551; Settling a claim 552; Mustering the evidence 553; Preliminary hearings 554; The main hearing 555; The decision 557; Remedies 558; Restrictions on publicity 559; Costs and expenses 559; Reviews and appeals 560

7.2 Enforcing employment law — 562

Overview 562; Late claims 563; Breach of contract 564; Remedies for discrimination 565; Remedies for unfair dismissal 567; Recoupment 572; The ACAS arbitration scheme 572; Table of employment rights 573

Appendices 579

Appendix 8.1 Calculating qualifying periods 581
Overview 581; Calculating continuous employment 581

Appendix 8.2 Calculating a week's pay 584
Overview 584; Employees with normal working hours 585; Employees without normal working hours 586; New employees 586; Appropriate hourly rate 586; The calculation date 587

Appendix 8.3 Data protection 588
Overview 588; The information covered 589; Conditions for fair and lawful processing 590; Additional conditions for sensitive data 591; Fair processing information 592; Processing for a lawful and specified purpose 593; Information must not be excessive 593; Information must be accurate 593; Obsolete information should not be retained 594; Respecting the rights of individuals 594; Safeguarding information 594; Transferring information outside the EEA 594; Subject access rights 595; Automated decision-making 596; Enforcement 596; Notification 597; Compliance checklist 597

Appendix 9 Useful information 599
Recruitment 599; Contracts of employment 600; Pay and related matters 601; Family rights 602; Working time 603; Pensions 604; Equal opportunities 604; Managing performance 606; Handling discipline and grievances 606; Changing contracts of employment 607; Redundancy, lay-off and short-time working 607; Transfer of undertakings 607; Union members 608; Collective bargaining 608; Industrial action 608; Employee involvement 609; Employment tribunals and remedies 609; Data protection 610; Other organisations and government bodies 610

Appendix 10 Model documents 611

About EEF 612

Index 614

section 1

Starting the relationship

1.1

Recruitment

Overview

1.1.1 There are few legal restrictions on employers' freedom to recruit. The Trade Union and Labour Relations (Consolidation) Act 1992 does, however, prohibit an employer from basing its recruitment decision on whether or not an applicant is a trade union member. And the Sex Discrimination Act 1975 requires that the recruitment process should not be affected by a person's sex, gender reassignment or status as a married person or civil partner. For these purposes, discriminating against a job applicant because she is pregnant or will need maternity leave is automatically viewed as sex discrimination. Racial discrimination in recruitment is also outlawed, by the Race Relations Act 1976. More recently, the Employment Equality (Religion or Belief) Regulations 2003 and the Employment Equality (Sexual Orientation) Regulations 2003 and the Employment Equality (Age) Regulations 2006 have made it unlawful to discriminate on those grounds.

1.1.2 The discrimination legislation prohibits indirect as well as direct discrimination. This means that it is not only unlawful to base a recruitment decision directly on a person's sex, race, age, religion or sexual orientation (see 3.1.7), but also unlawful for any aspect of the recruitment process to put people of a particular sex, race, age, religion or sexual orientation at a particular disadvantage, unless the employer has objective justification for designing the process in that way (see 3.1.37). The ways in which indirect discrimination might arise are highlighted in the discussion of the specific stages of the recruitment process that follows.

1.1.3　　　Disability discrimination in recruitment can also be challenged. The Disability Discrimination Act 1995 makes it unlawful for a company to reject a disabled job applicant on the grounds of the person's disability. It is also unlawful for an employer to reject a disabled applicant for a reason relating to the candidate's disability, unless it has objective justification for doing so (see 3.1.67). A company may also be under a legal duty to make adjustments to the recruitment process to accommodate not only disabled applicants but also disabled people who have notified the company that they are considering applying for the post. This duty applies if the company either knows or could reasonably be expected to know that the applicant or potential applicant is disabled and is likely to be put at a disadvantage by the company's usual recruitment arrangements (see 3.1.70). Government funding from the Access to Work scheme (see 3.1.82) may be available for some adjustments.

Codes of Practice

1.1.4　　　Much of the guidance in this chapter is based on the recommendations of the Codes of Practice issued under the sex, race and disability discrimination legislation (see 9.1.1) and the Immigration, Asylum and Nationality Act 2006. Although it is not in itself unlawful to ignore these Codes, it is unwise to do so for two reasons.

1.1.5　　　An employment tribunal that hears a discrimination claim must take into account whether the employer has complied with these Codes when deciding whether discrimination has occurred. It must also take into account whether an employer has followed the Codes when deciding whether the employer should escape liability for discrimination in the recruitment process because it had taken 'such steps as were reasonably practicable' to prevent the discrimination occurring (see 3.1.109).

Training

1.1.6　　　All the Codes emphasise how important it is that those involved in the recruitment process should be given training in how to avoid discrimination. If an unsuccessful applicant complains of discrimination to an employment tribunal, one of the first questions interviewers are likely to be asked is whether they have received training in how to avoid discrimination. If the answer is no, the employer will be at a serious disadvantage in defending the claim.

Small businesses

1.1.7   The discrimination Codes acknowledge that small companies may not have the resources to carry out their recommendations in full. However, small employers would nevertheless be well advised to ensure that their practices are consistent with the Codes' general intentions. That means identifying the skills and experience required for the job, matching candidates objectively against those requirements and recording how candidates met or did not meet them.

Data protection

1.1.8   Recruitment involves the gathering of personal information on candidates, and recruiters must therefore ensure that they comply with the requirements of the Data Protection Act 1998 in the way they obtain and handle this information. The Information Commissioner has issued a Code giving guidance for employers on how to comply with the law, and this chapter refers to the part of the Code that deals with recruitment and selection (see 9.1.1). Although there is no express legal requirement to comply with this Code, it could be referred to as evidence should the Commissioner decide to take legal action against an employer for failing to comply with data protection principles.

Defining the job

Drawing up a job description

1.1.9   Since the content of the job to be filled forms the basis of the whole recruitment exercise, the first stage of the process should be to draw up an accurate job description. This need not be an elaborate exercise – all that is necessary is to summarise the main duties and responsibilities of the post. If the job description is later to be incorporated into the successful applicant's contract, it should make clear that the duties it specifies are not exhaustive and that the jobholder may also be required to carry out other duties that may prove necessary for the proper performance of the job (see 1.2.24).

1.1.10   An accurate job description is also useful as a basis for job evaluation (see 2.1.59), identifying training needs and assessing performance (see 3.2.3).

Disability discrimination

1.1.11   Employers are under a legal obligation to consider reasonable adjustments to their recruitment arrangements and the terms on which they offer employment, in order to accommodate disabled applicants or potential applicants (see 3.1.69). It is therefore important for recruiters to be open to the possibility that, in an individual case, a job description may need to be revised to remove or amend duties that are relatively minor but effectively exclude an otherwise well-qualified disabled person from being considered for the job.

Defining the person

Drawing up specifications

1.1.12   Once an accurate job description has been drawn up (see 1.1.9) it should be possible to identify the skills, experience and knowledge that will be required in the successful candidate (sometimes termed the 'person specification' or 'job specification' for the post). Some of these are likely to be essential requirements and some merely desirable attributes.

Specifying race, sex, religion or sexual orientation

1.1.13   In some strictly limited circumstances, it is lawful for employers to specify that applicants for a post must be people of a particular race, sex, religion or sexual orientation, because that is a genuine occupational qualification or requirement for the post (see 3.1.96, 3.1.99). These circumstances are, however, tightly defined – covering, for example, jobs requiring dramatic authenticity or the provision of personal services – and are unlikely to be relevant to the engineering, manufacturing or construction sectors.

Retirement age

1.1.14 Due to an exemption in the age discrimination legislation, it is lawful for an employer to discriminate on the ground of age against a job applicant who is either already over the employer's normal retirement age or, if the employer does not have a normal retirement age, over 65, or who will be over that age within six months from the date of the application to the employer. (The normal retirement age for a job is the age at which employees in the employer's business who hold that kind of job are normally required to retire.)

Indirect discrimination

1.1.15 It is important for recruiters to be aware when drawing up person specifications of the potentially indirect discriminatory effect of some requirements or preferences (see 3.1.37). For example, it may be necessary for an employer to justify these requirements, which have a bigger impact on women as a group than on men:

- requiring candidates to be flexible in hours or place of work;
- requiring candidates to work full-time or refusing to consider a job-share;
- imposing an upper age limit, especially where this is linked with possession of a specified number of years' experience.

1.1.16 Likewise, some requirements have a disproportionate impact on certain racial groups, and so may need to be objectively justified. One example would be requiring candidates to possess qualifications awarded by academic or vocational bodies based in the UK, and not recognising equivalent qualifications from overseas bodies. Another example would be requiring candidates to possess a certain level of educational qualifications or competence in spoken or written English.

1.1.17 Certain requirements may be indirectly discriminatory on the ground of age. It may, for example, indirectly discriminate against younger applicants to require candidates to have a certain minimum length of experience.

Justifying requirements

1.1.18   In order to show that a particular requirement is objectively justified, a company must do more than assert that it is part of the way it has always operated. The company must be able to prove that the requirement is appropriate and necessary to meet its business objectives, and that the requirement's discriminatory effect is outweighed by the company's business needs. For example, a company may be able to justify refusing to allow a job to be done on a job-share basis if it can show that it has a real business need to maintain continuity of contact with its customers. It will, however, need to prove that it has objective grounds for saying that it is necessary for the job to be done by one person if that continuity is to be provided.

Overseas qualifications

1.1.19   It may also be justifiable to refuse to recognise qualifications from an overseas body if the company has no means of assessing the weight it should give to that qualification. It should be noted, however, that employers are required to recognise certain educational, professional and vocational qualifications obtained in other Member States of the European Union. Further information can be obtained from the Department for Children, Schools and Families (see 9.1.1).

Specifications and disability

1.1.20   Person specifications may also need to be revised in order to avoid disability discrimination (see 3.1.73) or to meet the company's duty to make reasonable adjustments to accommodate disabled candidates (see 3.1.69). Employers should therefore ensure that they do not require applicants to have any skills, experience or qualifications that are not necessary for the performance of the job but exclude disabled applicants.

Inviting applications

1.1.21   Where and how a vacancy is advertised will have a significant effect on the success of a recruitment exercise, and may also have legal repercussions. As a guiding principle, the more widely a vacancy is advertised, the more likely it is that indirect discrimination (see 3.1.37) will be avoided.

Where to advertise?

1.1.22	If a company's workforce is currently dominated by one or other sex or by a particular racial group, recruiting by word of mouth or internal advertising is likely to reinforce that dominance. This can therefore lead to unlawful indirect discrimination against the under-represented group, unless the use of that method can be objectively justified. One of the major advantages of these recruitment sources is that they save advertising costs. But cost considerations alone cannot justify a failure to externally advertise posts that are suitable for free placement with Jobcentres.

Notifying fixed-term employees

1.1.23	Under the Fixed-term Employees (Prevention of Less Favourable Treatment) Regulations 2002, a company's fixed-term employees must be given the same opportunity as its permanent employees to apply for permanent vacancies in the company, unless the company can justify treating them differently. (The Regulations are explained in more detail in 1.2.90.) Further, fixed-term employees have the right to be informed of all permanent vacancies, either by being given a reasonable opportunity of reading the job advertisement while at work (such as by displaying it on a notice board) or by being notified of the vacancy in some other way (such as by e-mail).

Briefing external agencies

1.1.24	Companies should ensure that any external recruitment agency they use knows that suitably qualified candidates will be considered regardless of their sex, gender reassignment, marital or civil partner status, race, age, disability, religion, sexual orientation or trade union membership. Instructing an agency to discriminate on those grounds would be in breach of discrimination law. For example, it would be unlawful to ask an agency to send only female candidates for a receptionist post.

Content of advertisements

1.1.25 A job advertisement is not an offer of employment, but the contents of an advertisement may end up being referred to later if there is a dispute about the terms of the successful candidate's employment contract. For example, a statement in an advertisement that the job carries access to a bonus could be used as evidence that the bonus is a contractual entitlement rather than merely a discretionary benefit. Care should therefore be taken in ensuring that the details of the terms and conditions on offer are accurate.

Drafting advertisements

1.1.26 It is unlawful for a company to place an advertisement that indicates, or might reasonably be understood as indicating, an intention to discriminate on the grounds of gender, sexual orientation, religion or belief, age, gender reassignment, marital or civil partner status, disability or race. It is therefore advisable to draft any advertisement in a way that makes clear that no assumptions are being made about these aspects of the successful applicant.

1.1.27 If one sex or racial group is under-represented in a particular type of work in a company, then the law permits, but does not require, the company to encourage people of that sex or racial group to apply for a vacancy to do that work (see 3.1.124). A company in this situation could therefore lawfully state in a job advertisement that it positively encourages applications from the under-represented group.

1.1.28 Since discrimination in favour of disabled people is lawful, a company is entitled, if it wishes, to include a statement in a job advertisement encouraging applications from disabled people. On the other hand, discrimination against disabled applicants is unlawful (see 3.1.51).

1.1.29 In particular, recruiters should ensure that advertisements are not drafted in a way that indicates that the successful applicant will not be disabled, or that the company is unwilling to make reasonable adjustments to accommodate disabled applicants. It is therefore worth avoiding using closed statements such as 'Our premises are not wheelchair accessible' in advertisements.

Union membership

1.1.30   It is unlawful to refuse somebody a job because:

- they are or are not a trade union member; or
- they are unwilling to join or leave a union; or
- they are unwilling to make payments in lieu of union subscriptions.

1.1.31   If an advertisement suggests that there is a union requirement of this kind, then the law assumes that any unsuccessful applicant who does not meet the requirement was refused the job for that reason. This will be so even if the company can produce evidence that the candidate was in fact rejected because he or she was not the best-qualified applicant for the post. It is therefore advisable not to mention union membership at all in a job advertisement.

1.1.32   If an employer has an arrangement or practice that it will offer employment only to individuals put forward or approved by a trade union, then the law assumes that an unsuccessful candidate who is not a union member was refused the job for that reason.

Data protection legislation

1.1.33   In order to meet the requirements of the data protection legislation, the Data Protection Code advises employers to ensure that individuals who respond to job advertisements know to whom they are providing their information and how it will be used. An advertisement should therefore not ask potential applicants to provide even their names and addresses to an unidentified answering machine. Where a recruitment agency rather than the employer places the advertisement, no personal data should be passed from the agency to the employer without the individual's knowledge.

Receiving applications

1.1.34   There are several legal and practical advantages in candidates submitting their application on a standard application form rather than by curriculum vitae (CV).

Using application forms

- If candidates supply information on a standard form, it is easy for the recruiter to locate and compare the relevant information when deciding whether they meet the person specification (see 1.1.12), so saving the recruiter a substantial amount of time.

- An application form can be designed in a way that ensures that irrelevant information such as marital status or nationality is not included, so avoiding the possibility of an allegation of discrimination on those grounds.

- Since candidates are not obliged to disclose adverse information about themselves unless it is specifically requested, an application form can be used to request information of particular relevance to the job. It is worth noting, however, that criminal convictions that are 'spent' under the Rehabilitation of Offenders Act 1974 need not be disclosed (see 3.1.127). The Data Protection Code advises employers to make this clear.

- An application form can include a statement that informs applicants about the purposes for which the personal information they are giving will be used and explains any checks that may be made on the information they provide, so meeting data protection requirements.

- If the company decides to monitor the results of its recruitment practices to ensure that they are not influenced by unlawful discrimination, a monitoring form can be appended to the application form (see 3.1.119).

Adjustments for disabled applicants

1.1.35   It may be necessary for companies to accept applications in alternative formats, such as on CD or by email, in order to meet their duty to make reasonable adjustments to the recruitment process for disabled applicants (see 3.1.69).

Online applications

1.1.36 If applications are accepted online, the Data Protection Code advises employers to ensure that a secure method of transmission is used.

Application form content

1.1.37 An application form might usefully include:

- basic biographical facts;
- education and training, including qualifications;
- work experience, as an employee, trainee or volunteer;
- a statement of why the applicant considers that he or she is qualified for the job;
- availability, including reasons for leaving any existing job;
- personal interests;
- current and previous health record.

The Data Protection Code

1.1.38 The Data Protection Code advises employers not to seek personal information that is not necessary to enable a recruitment decision to be made. Applicants should be told if information about them is to be obtained from other sources. Any checks that are to be undertaken to verify the information on the application form (see 1.1.60) should be explained. If checks reveal discrepancies, applicants should be given the opportunity to explain them. If sensitive information, such as information on health or trade union membership, is sought, applicants should be told how this will be used. Information about criminal convictions should be asked for only if this can be justified in terms of the job on offer, and applicants should be informed that 'spent' convictions (see 3.1.127) need not be disclosed.

Information for applicants

1.1.39 Prospective applicants may find it helpful to receive copies of the job description (see 1.1.9) and person specification (see 1.1.12), so that they can tailor their application to make clear how they meet the requirements.

1.1.40 An employer's duty to make reasonable adjustments to the recruitment process for disabled applicants or potential applicants (see 3.1.69) may involve supplying this information in different formats, such as in large print or other appropriate media.

Shortlisting for interview

Shortlist criteria

1.1.41 Any shortlist for interview should be drawn up by reference to criteria that are linked to the person specification (see 1.1.12). In some cases, no one candidate will meet all the requirements and this process will consist of finding those who are the best fit. If no candidate meets even the majority of the criteria, it may be necessary for the employer to reconsider the person specification, perhaps to look for someone with the potential to respond to training. Any 'moving of the goalposts' in this way must be done for clearly defined reasons and must involve reconsideration of all candidates against the new criteria. Otherwise it will be difficult to explain if the recruitment process is later alleged to have been discriminatory. The Data Protection Code also advises employers to ensure that personal information is used in shortlisting in a consistent way.

Guarding against bias

1.1.42 Where practicable, shortlisting decisions should not be made by one person alone, but should at least be checked by another person, in order to guard against conscious or unconscious bias.

1.1.43 The reason for rejecting candidates who do not make the shortlist should be recorded, even if only by a brief note on the top of their application form or CV, in case it later becomes necessary to defend a discrimination claim.

Conducting the interview

Legal and practical considerations

1.1.44   Most employers still use interviews to select the person they will appoint. When planning an interview, there are several legal and practical considerations to bear in mind.

> **Planning an interview**
>
> - It is sensible to let candidates know not only when and where the interview is to take place but also how long it is likely to last.
>
> - The office where the interview is to be held should be quiet, and steps should be taken to ensure that there are no interruptions.
>
> - If any of the candidates to be interviewed is disabled, it may be necessary to consider whether any adjustments to the interview process need to be made (see 3.1.69), such as holding the interview in a brightly lit or wheelchair-accessible room, or providing a sign-language interpreter. (Government funding through the Access to Work scheme may be available to meet the costs of adjustments to the interview process (see 3.1.82).)
>
> - In order to avoid allegations of any kind of unlawful discrimination, it is advisable to have two representatives of the company present at the interview, wherever practicable, to minimise the possibility of conscious or unconscious bias.
>
> - If two people are to interview, it should be agreed in advance which areas are to be covered by which interviewer.

Interview questions

1.1.45   In planning the questions that they intend to ask, interviewers should identify what information they already have about the candidates and what further information they need. If the job requires specialist knowledge, this area in particular may need to be probed.

1.1.46   In order to avoid discrimination, it is advisable to ask broadly the same questions of each candidate, but individualised questions may also be needed to follow up on unsatisfactory answers or to address the particular circumstances of an applicant. In order to encourage the applicants to talk, interviewers should avoid closed questions, which elicit 'yes' or 'no' answers, unless the intention is merely to confirm some piece of factual information. Rather, questions should be open, giving the candidates the opportunity to express themselves fully. Candidates should also be given the opportunity to ask questions about the post and the company. As a rule of thumb, interviewers should aim for the candidates' contribution to take up 80 per cent of the interview time.

1.1.47   Interviewers should ensure that questions are relevant to the candidates' suitability for the job and do not stray into irrelevant personal details. In particular, asking female candidates about their marriage plans, intention to have children or childcare arrangements is inviting a sex discrimination complaint. Even if the same questions are asked of male candidates, an employment tribunal will recognise the sex-based assumptions behind them. A candidate's ability to meet a job requirement can be tested by a direct question. If, for example, an interviewer wants to confirm with candidates that they are able to meet the extensive travel requirements of the job, that could be done by saying to all candidates: 'This job involves a considerable amount of travelling. Will you have any problem in meeting that requirement?', rather than by asking female candidates only: 'Who is going to look after your children if you have to go away on business?'

1.1.48   Questions to disabled candidates about their impairment should be asked only if they are relevant to their ability to do the job or the scope of any possible reasonable adjustment (see 3.1.69). The interview may be a good opportunity to explore with a disabled candidate what reasonable adjustments could be made to the job or the working environment to enable him or her to do the job effectively.

Record keeping

1.1.49   It is advisable to keep notes of what is said at interview, in order to help make the decision on whom to recruit. A written record should also be made of why each applicant was or was not appointed. Written records will make it easier to defend any subsequent allegation that the recruitment exercise was discriminatory.

1.1.50 The Data Protection Code makes the point that personal information collected and recorded in an interview should be relevant to the job and not in excess of what is needed for the purpose of making a recruitment decision or defending the recruitment process against challenge. Under the data protection legislation the interviewee may have the right to see the interview notes (see 8.3.21), so care should be taken to avoid recording irrelevant comments that might be taken to indicate discrimination.

Contractual repercussions

1.1.51 Since a contract of employment can be formed by the oral offer and acceptance of a job, interviewers should ensure that they do not use words that could be construed as an offer, unless this is what they intend. In most cases, and particularly where the job offer is to be made subject to conditions such as satisfactory references, it is advisable for an interviewer to say no more than that he or she will recommend that an offer be made. Interviewers should also bear in mind that promises made to successful candidates at their interview can end up as part of their contract of employment. Statements made at interview can also be used as evidence of the terms of the contract if there is subsequently a dispute about its content.

Selection tests

1.1.52 It is common practice for companies to ask candidates to complete a test that can objectively confirm that they have the abilities required for the job. For example, applicants for secretarial posts are often asked to complete a typing test to confirm that they can type with the required speed and accuracy.

1.1.53 Some companies also use more sophisticated testing mechanisms, such as assessment centres and psychometric and aptitude testing. As long as these mechanisms are well constructed and operated by people who are qualified to administer and interpret them, they can provide valuable additional information on candidates.

Monitoring tests

1.1.54 In order to avoid unlawful discrimination, companies that use these tests as part of their recruitment procedure should ensure that the tests relate directly to the measurement of applicants' ability to do the job in question. Tests should be monitored regularly to ensure that they remain relevant and free from unlawful bias, either in content or in the scoring mechanism.

1.1.55 The content of all tests and the way in which they are administered or assessed may also need to be revised in order to make reasonable adjustments for disabled candidates (see 3.1.69).

Data protection

1.1.56 The Data Protection Code reaches similar conclusions. It advises employers to ensure that if psychological or other tests based on the interpretation of scientific evidence are used, they are carried out and interpreted only by those who are qualified to do so.

Supporting information

1.1.57 There are various legal issues to bear in mind when requesting or assessing information in support of a job application. (Note that, if it is a company's practice to seek supporting information only after it has offered the applicant the job, it should make the job offer conditional on that information being satisfactory (see 1.1.90).)

Security clearance

1.1.58 Some jobs may require special security clearance. For example, certain work for the government requires special clearance under the Official Secrets Act. Where this is relevant, employers should seek further advice from us.

Data protection

1.1.59 When deciding what supporting information they need and when they should obtain it, employers should bear in mind the advice in the Data Protection Code. Personal information should be obtained only when necessary for a fair recruitment decision to be made. An employer may not need to obtain some information on an applicant, such as banking details, until it has decided to offer him or her the job.

1.1.60　The Code accepts that employers are justified in making reasonable checks on the information that applicants have given. However, the Code advises that applicants should be told the nature and extent of those checks. If the employer intends to ask a third party for information about the applicant, the applicant should be asked for his or her written consent to this. If checks reveal discrepancies, the applicant should be given an opportunity to explain them.

Fit for work

1.1.61　A company may wish to confirm that candidates are able to comply with the mental and physical requirements of the job. In particular, where the job involves night work, the company will need to check that candidates are fit for this type of work (see 2.3.54).

1.1.62　For most purposes, it will be adequate for candidates to complete a section in the application form on their medical history or a brief medical questionnaire. However, if the information they provide indicates that they may not be fit for the job, either because of the duties involved or because of the environment in which it is carried out, it may be necessary to follow this up with a GP's report or even a full medical examination.

1.1.63　Fuller information may also be necessary for the purposes of the employer's occupational pension scheme. However, it should be borne in mind that it is likely to be unlawful to reject a disabled candidate simply because he or she is not eligible to join the pension scheme, rather than because he or she is not the best-qualified candidate for the job.

Medical questionnaires

1.1.64　If a company uses medical questionnaires or asks for medical reports on candidates, it should ensure that this policy is not confined to disabled candidates. There is usually no reason to assume that a disabled candidate will be any more or less healthy than a non-disabled applicant, and singling all disabled candidates out in this way is therefore likely to amount to unlawful discrimination (see 3.1.51). If, however, it appears that a candidate, whether disabled or otherwise, has an impairment that may affect his or her ability to do the job, then it is perfectly lawful to question the applicant further about this. It is also lawful to reject a disabled applicant on the grounds that the applicant's impairment would have a substantial adverse impact on his or her ability to do the job and that no reasonable adjustment (see 3.1.69) could be made to overcome that.

1.1.65　Medical questionnaires must be carefully drafted. Their aim is to obtain proper disclosure of the applicant's health, both past and present. They need to be precise and unambiguous. It may also be useful to include a 'sweep up' question calling for disclosure outside the questions asked; for example 'Is there anything else in your history or circumstances which might affect our decision to offer you employment?'

Medical reports

1.1.66　If the company decides to obtain a medical report on a candidate from his or her GP, then it must comply with the Access to Medical Reports Act 1988. In summary, the Act requires employers to obtain written consent from job applicants before they ask their GP for a report on them. The applicants have the right to see a copy of the report before it is sent to the employer and can ask for it to be amended. Further information on the Act and detailed advice on obtaining and using medical reports can be found at 3.2.60 and 3.2.66.

Data protection

1.1.67　The Data Protection Code (9.8.3) points out that information on workers' health is sensitive personal data, and employers are entitled to collect it only where one of the conditions for holding such data is met. These include where the information is necessary for the employer to fulfil a legal obligation, such as the duty not to discriminate on grounds of disability or to protect health and safety, or the job applicant has expressly and freely consented to providing the information. A job applicant should be told why health information is being asked for and how it will be used. Once obtained, the information should be kept secure, and retained only for as long as is necessary (see 1.1.100–1.1.102). While the Code accepts that a decision as to whether an applicant is suitable for a particular job is a management one, it advises that any health information that the applicant provides should be interpreted by a suitably qualified health professional.

Conditional offers

1.1.68   A job offer can be made conditional on the company receiving a medical report that it considers to be satisfactory. The job offer should indicate that if the successful applicant starts work before the report is received and the report then proves unsatisfactory, the company might decide to terminate the employee's contract. If this happens during the first month of employment, then the company can terminate the contract without notice, unless the contract states otherwise. After one month, the company must give at least one week's notice of termination. The job offer and contract of employment should make this position clear.

The right to work in the UK

1.1.69   Under the Immigration, Asylum and Nationality Act 2006 it is a criminal offence for an employer to recruit anyone who does not have the right to work in the UK. However, the employer has an absolute defence to such a charge if it did not know that the applicant did not have the right to work in the UK. In order to establish this defence, the employer must be able to show that, before the person's employment began, it saw and either retained or copied certain documents, specified in the legislation, which indicated that the person did have the right to work in the UK. The employer must also satisfy itself that the documents appear to relate to the individual producing them, in particular by checking that the individual resembles any photograph the documents contain and is of an age that corresponds with the date of birth given in the documents.

1.1.70   Certain documents are sufficient in themselves to show the right to work in the UK. These include a passport showing that the holder is a British citizen, or a national passport or national identity card showing that the holder is a national of a country in the European Economic Area or Switzerland. Alternatively, an individual must produce two specified documents in a specified combination. These include, for example, a document giving the person's permanent name and National Insurance number, such as a P45 or P60, together with a full UK birth certificate that includes the names of the holder's parents. If the individual's name differs between these documents, he or she must also produce a document, such as a marriage certificate, to explain the difference. (Full details of the documents that are acceptable can be obtained from the Home Office UK Border Agency (see 9.1.1) or us.)

1.1.71 In order to avoid committing a criminal offence under the Act, a company would be well advised to ensure that it sees, checks and copies the required documents before offering an applicant a job. Employers also need to bear in mind that these requirements apply to all recruits, regardless of their racial or national origin. Asking only those applicants who have 'foreign'-sounding names or do not speak with an 'English' accent to produce the necessary documentation would be an act of unlawful racial discrimination. The Home Office has produced a Code of Practice on how to avoid racial discrimination while seeking to prevent illegal working (see 9.1.1). The Code advises employers to give all the specified documents equal weight.

Worker Registration Scheme

1.1.72 Employers must meet an additional requirement if they wish to recruit a national of the Czech Republic, Estonia, Hungary, Latvia, Lithuania, Poland, Slovakia or Slovenia. As well as checking the individual's right to work in the way set out above, the employer must check whether the new recruit needs to register with the Home Office's Worker Registration Scheme within one month of starting work. Also, Bulgarian and Romanian nationals that wish to work for an employer in the UK may require prior permission from the Home Office to do so.

1.1.73 Further information on the Immigration, Asylum and Nationality Act 2006, the Worker Registration Scheme and authorisation, including exemptions, for EEA nationals can be obtained from the Home Office (see 9.1.1). Employers can obtain information on the immigration points based system for overseas applicants from us or from the UK Border Agency (see 9.1.1).

Criminal record checks

1.1.74 A company may wish to check whether a prospective employee has a criminal record.

1.1.75 In general, it is unlawful to refuse to employ someone because of a criminal conviction that is 'spent' under the terms of the Rehabilitation of Offenders Act 1974. Only certain types of work specified under the legislation, such as jobs involving the administration of justice or contact with children or vulnerable adults, are exempt from this principle.

Spent convictions

1.1.76   A conviction becomes spent after a specified period of time that depends upon the sentence given for the offence and the individual's age at the time of conviction. A conviction that led to the individual being sentenced to between 6 months and 30 months in prison, for example, becomes spent after 10 years if the individual was 18 or over when convicted, whereas a conviction leading to an absolute discharge becomes spent after 6 months.

1.1.77   Applicants are under no obligation to disclose spent convictions, even in response to a direct question about whether they have a criminal record. If a company obtains information about spent convictions, for example from an applicant's referee, it is unlawful for the company to act on that information, such as by dismissing the person.

Abuse of access rights

1.1.78   Some employers require job applicants to use their subject access rights under the data protection legislation to obtain a copy of their criminal record from the police. The Information Commissioner regards this practice as an abuse of individuals' access rights. It is also unsatisfactory because police computer records may not differentiate between spent and unspent convictions.

Criminal conviction certificates

1.1.79   Currently only certain registered organisations with the consent of the individual concerned can obtain disclosure of criminal records from the Criminal Records Bureau in exchange for a fee. This service is available in Scotland through Disclosure Scotland (see 9.1.1).

1.1.80   Further information on employing ex-offenders can be obtained from the National Association for the Care and Resettlement of Offenders (see 9.1.1).

Working with children and vulnerable adults

1.1.81   The Safeguarding of Vulnerable Groups Act 2006 creates a unified system aimed at protecting children and vulnerable adults. It establishes a vetting and barring process, run by the Independent Safeguarding Authority (ISA), to prevent unsuitable people, whether paid or unpaid, working with children and vulnerable adults. The Act is being implemented in phases over a number of years, leading to full registration of all those working with children and vulnerable adults.

1.1.82   Since October 2009, it has been a criminal offence for individuals barred by ISA to work or apply to work with children or vulnerable adults in a wide range of posts, and a criminal offence for employers to employ a barred person across a wide range of posts. Employers are also under a duty to refer to ISA relevant information about individuals working with children and vulnerable adults where they consider them to have caused harm or pose a risk of harm. More information is available from the Independent Safeguarding Authority.

Taking up references

1.1.83   A company may wish to obtain references on candidates, perhaps from present and past employers. References can be used to obtain another view on an applicant's suitability for the post, or to check the accuracy of information that the applicant has given, such as dates of employment and attendance records. In general, employers are under no obligation to give a reference. However, if they choose to give one, they have a legal duty to the subject of the reference (the job applicant) and to the recruiting employer who relies on it, to exercise reasonable care in compiling it. Referees may state that they are providing the reference on the basis that they do not accept any legal responsibility for loss the recipient may be caused by relying upon it.

1.1.84   Individuals may seek access to references that the recruiting company has received, under the subject access provisions of the data protection legislation (see 8.3.21). The company may be entitled to refuse access if this is necessary to protect the identity of a third party, such as the author of the reference. Disclosure is lawful, however, if the third party has consented to the disclosure or it is reasonable in all the circumstances to disclose the information despite the lack of consent. The supplementatry guidance to the Data Protection Code (see 9.8.3) suggests when it would be reasonable to withhold the reference.

1.1.85   If references have not been received at the time when the job offer is made, then the offer can be made conditional on the company receiving references that it considers to be satisfactory. The offer should also indicate that if the successful applicant starts work before references are received and these then prove to be unsatisfactory, the company might decide to terminate the employee's contract. If this happens during the first month of employment, then the company can terminate the contract without notice, unless the contract states otherwise. After one month, the company must give at least one week's notice of termination. The job offer and contract of employment should make this position clear.

Candidate assessment

1.1.86   When deciding who should be offered the job, recruiters should make an objective assessment of the applicants' strengths and weaknesses, as demonstrated in the recruitment process.

Avoiding discrimination

1.1.87   In order to avoid discrimination claims, recruiters should put aside any positive or negative assumptions they may have made about candidates' suitability based on sex, gender reassignment, marital or civil partnership status, race, age, disability, religion, sexual orientation or union membership. It is advisable for two people to make or agree the decision on who to appoint, to minimise the possibility of conscious or unconscious bias. In order to be in a position to counter any subsequent allegation of discrimination, companies should clearly identify and record the reason why candidates were successful or unsuccessful.

1.1.88   The law recognises that direct evidence of discrimination is rarely available. So the discrimination legislation requires the employment tribunals that adjudicate on discrimination claims to draw inferences from the surrounding circumstances, where appropriate. For example, if one candidate for the job fared worse than another candidate who was of a different race but had similar qualifications, the tribunal will expect the employer to be able to explain why. If a credible, non-discriminatory explanation is not forthcoming, the tribunal is required to infer that the decision was based on the candidate's race. In particular, if a decision was based wholly or partly on the recruiter's view of what type of person would 'fit in' within the company, the tribunal may well conclude that the selection was influenced by a desire to avoid disrupting the status quo by appointing someone who was different from the established workforce in terms of sex, race, age, religion, sexual orientation or disability.

Unsuccessful candidates

1.1.89   It is good practice to inform unsuccessful candidates as soon as possible in a polite and constructive manner, and is commonplace to give them feedback on the reason for their failure if asked to do so.

Making the job offer

Legal implications

1.1.90   A contract of employment is formed as soon as the successful candidate accepts the offer of the job. (The skeleton of an offer letter is available on the EEF website: see page 607. This will need to be modified to meet the requirements of the company and the circumstances of the individual applicant.) Two important legal points arise from this:

1. If a job offer is intended to be conditional on certain conditions being met, such as the receipt of satisfactory references, medical reports, security clearance or proof of the right to work in the UK, then the company must make that clear when the offer is made.

2. The job offer must set out, or make reference to, all the contractual terms that an applicant is being asked to accept. Ideally, therefore, all the documents that contain terms that the company intends to be binding on the employee, such as details of benefit schemes or collective agreements, should be sent to the applicant at the time the offer is made (see 1.2.17). In practice, where a large number of collective agreements apply, employers may choose merely to list the agreements and their subject matter.

Additional documents

1.1.91   If the candidate is sent a document, such as an employee handbook, that contains some terms that are intended to be part of employees' contracts but other terms that are not, care should be taken to point out which terms are contractual. The company may, for example, wish its disciplinary procedure not to be contractual, so that it has freedom to alter it in line with operational or legislative developments.

Telephone offers

1.1.92   A company may need to act swiftly to secure a successful candidate, and so may decide to make the initial offer by telephone, in order to find out whether the candidate is in principle interested in accepting. If so, it is important to make clear that the full terms of the offer will be set out in writing.

Applicant's conditions

1.1.93   The applicant may simply accept the offer as it stands. On the other hand, he or she may want to discuss the terms of the offer or may accept the offer but subject to his or her own conditions, such as receiving assurances about salary reviews. If so, these issues should be dealt with promptly and in any event before the applicant starts work, in order to clarify and confirm unconditionally the terms on which the applicant is being recruited.

Unconditional acceptance

1.1.94   A job offer cannot be withdrawn once the applicant has accepted it – that is, once the applicant sends or orally communicates his or her unconditional acceptance of the offer. If the applicant accepts the offer, he or she has a contract of employment and the company must then give the employee proper notice of termination if it wishes to withdraw from the contract, even if the employee has not yet started work. If the company decides to withdraw from the contract for discriminatory or inadmissible reasons (see 4.2.32), then it will be liable for discrimination or unfair dismissal.

Existing employers' rights

1.1.95   In accepting a job offer, an applicant may be acting in breach of contractual obligations towards his or her existing employer by, for example, leaving without giving proper notice of resignation, or acting in breach of some form of restriction on his or her subsequent employment. If the recruiting company knows this but deliberately induces a breach, it should be aware that it could be liable to pay the applicant's existing employer compensation for inducing the applicant to breach his or her contract.

Monitoring recruitment

Codes of Practice

1.1.96   The Discrimination Codes of Practice recommend that employers should monitor their recruitment practices by sex, race and disability to ensure that they are not operating in a discriminatory way (see 3.1.119).

1.1.97   Monitoring involves checking whether the proportion of job applicants, shortlisted candidates and successful candidates who are from a particular sex or racial group or who are disabled is roughly equivalent to the proportion of that group in the particular labour market from which the employer is recruiting. (The labour market may well differ according to the job at issue.) Monitoring need not be a complex process. In small companies, monitoring can be carried out from personal knowledge and visual identification.

Reviewing practices

1.1.98   Gathering monitoring information is not an end in itself. The aim is to identify whether there is a marked disparity between the number of applications or successful appointments from a particular group, and the number that could be expected in the light of that group's representation in the relevant labour market. If there is, the company should review its recruitment practices in order to decide whether they are being affected by direct or indirect discrimination. Action should then be taken to end any discrimination that is discovered.

1.1.99 Employers who are considering including a commitment to monitor in their equal opportunities policy should bear in mind that effective monitoring takes time. If an employer has said it will monitor but then fails to do so, an employment tribunal hearing a discrimination claim against the employer may form an unfavourable view of its commitment to equal opportunities.

Keeping records

Period of retention

1.1.100 In order to respect the principles of data protection law, the documentation relating to a recruitment exercise should be retained no longer than is necessary. The paperwork may need to be used in evidence should an unsuccessful candidate allege discrimination. Although discrimination claims must normally be brought within three months, late claims are possible. It is therefore advisable to retain the paperwork for at least a year. If records are maintained for management analysis, such as to monitor for unlawful discrimination (see 3.1.119), then that should be done in a way that does not enable individuals to be identified.

Applicants' information

1.1.101 Where information has been obtained for the purpose of verifying details supplied by applicants, the Data Protection Code advises employers not to use that information for any other purpose, and to destroy it once checking is complete. Information about criminal convictions should be deleted once it has been verified by the Criminals Records Bureau or Disclosure Scotland. If the employer intends to hold on to the details of unsuccessful applicants so that it can consider them should a vacancy arise in the future, then applicants should be advised of that and given an opportunity to object.

1.1.102 The interview notes, job offer and any other correspondence with the successful candidate may need to be retained to form the basis of the employee's personnel file. The Data Protection Code advises, however, that not all information about the candidate should be retained. Information that is not relevant to the appointee's employment, such as details of his or her former salary, should be deleted.

Induction

Induction programmes

1.1.103   Putting new recruits through an induction programme is good business practice. Introducing the employee to the job and the work environment, including work colleagues, the physical environment and work procedures, including disciplinary and grievance procedures, ensures that the employee becomes a productive member of the workforce as soon as possible. It is important to explain health and safety procedures at an early stage, in order for the company to meet its health and safety obligations.

Data protection requirements

1.1.104   Certain data protection requirements must also be addressed early in an employee's employment. The Data Protection Code advises employers to inform newly appointed employees of what information will be kept about them, where it was obtained, how it is to be used, and to whom, if anyone, it may be disclosed. The Code also advises that employees should be provided annually with a copy of any personal details that might change, such as their home address, so that they can check whether they are still accurate.

Special attention

1.1.105   Certain new recruits may need special attention:

- It may be necessary to discuss special arrangements, facilities or safety arrangements with disabled recruits.

- School leavers may be unfamiliar with even simple and routine business practices, and so may need extra guidance.

- Women returning to work after a period spent caring for a family may need extra support and updating.

- Staff turnover amongst management trainees will be reduced if they are offered a development programme that fulfils their expectations.

Probationary periods

Purpose of probation

1.1.106   Companies may wish to consider designating the first few weeks or months of a new recruit's employment as a probationary period, during which time his or her performance will be closely assessed. The purpose of this period will be not only to ensure that the employee's performance meets the required standard but also to identify any training and support that is needed.

Monitoring performance

1.1.107   It is important that there should be regular monitoring of performance and conduct during this time, and the employee should be clearly informed if he or she is failing to meet the required standard. Remedial steps can then be agreed and a timetable set for improvement. If shortcomings are not brought to employees' attention, they may legitimately argue that they have successfully completed their probation. This may make it difficult for the employer to maintain that it is acting reasonably if, after a year, it dismisses an employee for poor performance. If an employee narrowly misses the required standard and the employer decides to extend the probationary period, it is advisable for this to be confirmed in writing and signed by employee and manager.

Failing probation

1.1.108   It is advisable for the employee's contract to state that it may be terminated if the probationary period is not satisfactorily completed, and it should specify the notice of termination that will be given. It should also be made clear that the company's usual disciplinary or performance procedures, which may be incorporated into the employee's contract, do not apply in these circumstances. It would be advisable, however, to follow a simple fair dismissal procedure even when terminating the employment of a probationer with less than one year's continuous service.

1.2

Contracts

Overview

1.2.1 An employee's contract of employment is the foundation stone of his or her relationship with the employer, and gives the employee many important legal rights. These contractual rights may be more generous than the rights that the employee is given by employment legislation. For example, many employees are entitled under their contracts of employment to sick pay that is better than that laid down by statute.

1.2.2 Although contractual rights can build upon statutory rights, they cannot undercut them. For example, if a contract specifies that an employer is entitled to terminate the contract by giving one week's notice, but the employment legislation sets down a minimum period of two weeks' notice, then the legislation prevails. And if a worker is entitled to the national minimum wage, that overrides any lower rate of pay set out in his or her contract.

1.2.3 This chapter sets out the legal principles that apply to how employment contracts are formed (see 1.2.7). It then goes on to describe the content of employment contracts. The employer and employee will expressly agree many important terms of the contract (see 1.2.10), but there are other significant terms that will be implied (see 1.2.37).

1.2.4 A contract of employment does not need to be in writing to be legally valid and enforceable. An employer does, however, have a legal obligation to give its employees written information about the main terms and conditions of their employment, and this chapter explains what is required (see 1.2.47).

1.2.5 Because a contract of employment is a legally enforceable agreement, there are legal consequences where the employer or the employee fails to abide by the contract's terms, and this chapter sets out what they are (see 1.2.59).

1.2.6 This chapter explores the distinction between those who work for their employer under a contract of employment and those who have some other form of contract with the employer, and explains the legal implications of that distinction (see 1.2.70). It also explains the protection that employees have from unjustified discrimination if they work on a fixed-term basis (see 1.2.89). Separate sections of the Guide set out the legal principles that apply where the original terms of a contract are amended (see Chapter 5.1) or where a contract is terminated (see Chapter 4.1) and to discrimination against part-timers (see 2.3.83)

Forming the contract

1.2.7 A contract of employment is formed when a job applicant accepts the employer's offer of the job. There is no need for a contract of employment to be in writing, so the offer can be made and accepted orally, perhaps in a telephone conversation. Alternatively, the employer may set out the offer fully and formally in a letter and ask the applicant to confirm in writing that he or she accepts the terms. In practice, it is preferable for a job offer to be made in writing, to ensure that the terms of the offer are clear.

Prior conditions

1.2.8 Once the job applicant has unconditionally accepted an unconditional job offer, he or she has a contract of employment, even if he or she has not yet started work. Therefore, if the offer is intended to be conditional on certain events occurring, such as the employer receiving satisfactory references or medical reports, then the employer needs to make that clear. The contract will then not take effect unless and until those conditions are met. But if the employer allows the employee to start work before the conditions are met, it could be argued that the conditions no longer apply. The employee is working under a contract of employment, and the employer must give proper notice to terminate it.

Benefits of a written contract

1.2.9 Many employers choose to give employees a written contract of employment. Although not essential, this is advisable for these reasons:

- A written contract provides a record of the rights and responsibilities of the employer and the employee, making it less likely that disputes will arise later about what the terms of their relationship are. In particular, the contract can clarify which of the company's policies and procedures, if any, are intended to be part of the employee's contractual terms.

- While an employer does not need to issue an employee with a written contract of employment, it is under a legal obligation to give the employee written information on the main terms and conditions of his or her employment (see 1.2.47). If the employer supplies the employee with a written contract containing the necessary details, it meets that obligation.

- Where relevant, a written contract can provide the authorisation needed for certain deductions from the employee's pay (see 2.1.92).

Express terms

1.2.10 In theory, employer and employee freely agree the express terms of an employment contract. In practice, it is usually the employer who decides what the express terms will be, although a job applicant with substantial bargaining power, such as an applicant with scarce and highly desirable skills or experience, may be able to influence or even dictate the terms.

Drafting terms

1.2.11 Since a company is usually in a strong position to decide the express terms of the contract, it should take advantage of this and draft the contract terms carefully. If the company later finds that the contract's terms as originally drafted do not meet its business needs, it will need the employee's consent to alter them (see 5.1.4). Companies can obtain advice on drafting their contracts of employment from us.

Guiding principles

1.2.12   In drafting the contract, two guiding principles may be useful:

1. The terms should be clear. Legal terminology should be avoided unless both employer and employee fully understand the words and phrases used. If an employee's rights depend upon the employee meeting certain conditions, such as eligibility criteria or notification requirements, that should be spelt out.

2. The terms should reflect the company's current and future operational needs. A draft contract obtained 'off the shelf' from a legal or personnel publication can be a useful starting point. (A statement of main terms and conditions that could be used as the basis for drafting a written contract is available for download from EEF's website.) But each company and employee is unique, and the drafter must identify the issues that his or her particular company needs to cover in the contract. A broad range of issues may need to be addressed, from payment systems through to the organisation of working time, disciplinary issues and the protection of confidential information. In particular, the drafter must ensure that the contract gives the company the flexibility it needs over the content of the employee's work and where and how it is to be performed. (This issue is explored further below in the context of specific terms that may be included in the contract.)

Discretionary benefits

1.2.13   A company may want certain benefits in the contract, such as sick pay and bonuses, to be payable at the company's discretion. Making a benefit discretionary means that the employee cannot insist upon receiving it as a matter of right. It is therefore important for the contract to make clear when a benefit is discretionary.

1.2.14   The drafter should consider whether or not to specify the factors that the company will take into account when exercising that discretion. The advantage of doing so is that both employer and employee are clear about how the discretion will be used, which should reduce the likelihood of a dispute if the benefit is withheld. The disadvantage is that the company must then exercise its discretion by reference to the specified factors, or it will be acting in breach of the employee's contract. Even where no guiding factors are specified, however, it would be a breach of contract for a company to withhold a discretionary benefit irrationally, that is, in circumstances where no reasonable employer would have done so.

Incorporating documents

1.2.15 Some conditions of employment may be laid out in detail in some other document, such as a collective agreement with a trade union, a company policy or procedure, or an employee handbook. If a company wants to make any of these terms part of an employee's contract, the other document must be incorporated into the contract. This is explained further below (see 1.2.17).

Legal constraints

1.2.16 Although companies usually have the power to control the express terms of their employment contracts, there are two legal constraints that should be noted:

> **1.** Under the discrimination legislation, any term in a contract that directly or indirectly discriminates on the ground of sex, age, race, religion or sexual orientation is unenforceable. A term is indirectly discriminatory if it puts people of a particular sex, age, race, religion or sexual orientation at a particular disadvantage, unless the employer can prove that the term is necessary to meet its legitimate business needs (see 3.1.37). For example, contract terms requiring employees to be prepared to change their working hours or work location may be potentially indirectly discriminatory against women, because a much larger proportion of women than of men have responsibility for childcare and are less flexible in their hours or place of work as a result. A company using those contract terms would therefore need to be able to show that the flexibility was needed for operational reasons and could not be achieved in another, less discriminatory way. Also any term in a contract that is unlawful because it is in breach of the Disability Discrimination Act is void and so unenforceable.
>
> **2.** Every contract of employment contains implied terms that can in some circumstances limit the way in which an employer uses its express

contractual powers. In particular, an employer is under implied obligations not to act in a way that breaches the trust and confidence that is integral to any employment relationship, and to take reasonable care for the health and safety of its employees (see 1.2.45). For example, an employer could be acting in breach of contract if it used an express power to relocate an employee without giving the employee any opportunity to make the necessary personal arrangements for the move, or used an express power to require an employee to work overtime to such a degree that it damaged the employee's health.

Incorporating terms

1.2.17 Many employment conditions, particularly those offered by larger employers, are complex. They may, for example, involve benefits that are dependent on employees meeting certain eligibility criteria or notification requirements, or they may involve procedures with several different steps or stages. Because they are complex, these terms are likely to be set out in detail in a document of their own, such as:

- a sick pay or company car policy;
- a disciplinary or grievance procedure;
- the rules of a pension scheme; or
- an employee handbook.

In a company that negotiates terms and conditions with a trade union, there may also be collective agreements that deal with terms and conditions of employment (see 6.2.47, 6.2.51).

Incorporation by reference

1.2.18 As a first step, an employer will need to decide whether it wants all or any of the terms set out in these documents to be part of an employee's contract. The employer may decide, for example, that it does not want its disciplinary or grievance procedures to be contractual, since it could then face a breach of contract claim if it did not follow them or changed them unilaterally.

1.2.19 Even if an employer does not want its disciplinary procedure to be contractual, it would be well advised to include in the contract a power to demote or suspend the employee, if these are disciplinary sanctions it may want to impose.

1.2.20 If any of the documents are to be contractual, then it is advisable for the employee's contract expressly to incorporate them, by referring to them. This process is sometimes called 'incorporation by reference'. It is also possible for a document to be incorporated into a contract by implication, where the employer and employee act in a way that indicates that they accept the document's contents as a legally binding part of their relationship. Nevertheless, it is preferable to include an express term in the employee's contract dealing with incorporation, to avoid any uncertainty or dispute.

Changing content

1.2.21 If the employer wants to change the content of the document that is incorporated, the term incorporating the document should make clear that the contract will include any amended version as well. For example, a clause incorporating permanent health insurance cover might read: 'You are entitled to the benefit of a permanent health insurance scheme. The current terms of the scheme are set out in the booklet which has been given to you, but the rules and benefits of the scheme may be altered from time to time.' A clause incorporating a collective agreement might read: 'Your hours of work are as set out in the collective agreement on working time between the company and the ABC Union that is in force from time to time.' It is worth noting that an individual's contract can validly incorporate a collective agreement, even if the individual is not a member of the union.

Incorporation of part

1.2.22 Particular care is needed when incorporating only part of a document. A company may wish, for example, to incorporate into an employee's contract the sections of an employee handbook that deal with sick pay and parental benefits but not the section that deals with disciplinary rules and procedures. If so, the contract must make that clear. If it refers to the employee handbook in general, the employee could argue that the whole of the handbook is incorporated, including the disciplinary procedure, so that if the employee is disciplined or dismissed without the procedure having been used, he or she could claim breach of contract or wrongful dismissal (see 1.2.59, 4.1.21).

Suitability for incorporation

1.2.23 Some documents are not capable of being incorporated into an individual's contract because they do not deal with individual terms and conditions of employment. For example, an agreement between an employer and a union that the employer will give the union certain facilities or information cannot be a term of an individual employee's contract. The courts have accepted, however, that equal opportunities policies and redundancy selection procedures are capable of being incorporated, although whether they have in fact been incorporated in a particular case will depend on the issues discussed above.

Job content

1.2.24 In order for the employee's job performance to be effectively managed, the employee will need to be aware of the main duties and responsibilities of the job. It is not essential, however, for these details to be given in the contract, which could simply state the job title. Alternatively, the contract could incorporate a job description (see 1.1.9) by reference (see 1.2.19). It is important, however, to ensure that any contractual term or job description is not overly detailed, as it may then limit the company's power to ask the employee to change what he or she is doing in even minor ways. In addition, the company may wish to consider whether it needs to include within the contract a power to ask the employee to move to different work temporarily or permanently, or to take on duties that are reasonably incidental to the main job but have not been expressly listed in the job description. We can advise on drafting job descriptions.

Job location

1.2.25 When drafting the contract terms on job location, the company should consider whether it needs the power to move the employee to a different place of work. If it has that power, then it will not have to pay a redundancy payment if it needs to relocate the employee but the employee refuses to move. On the other hand, a relocation clause for which the employer has no business need could be indirectly discriminatory against women and so unenforceable (see 3.1.37). If a relocation clause is included, it should set out the area within which the employee may be expected to move. Thought should also be given to the terms on which an employee may be asked to move. The company may want to leave this to be decided at the time. Alternatively, it may be prepared to commit itself in the contract to giving a specified period of advance notice and relocation expenses, or at least commit to considering these.

Conditions on pay

1.2.26　Certain parts of an employee's wages or salary may be payable only if certain conditions are met. If so, the conditions need to be made clear. If, for example, a bonus is dependent upon the employee meeting certain targets, the contract may need to specify what those targets currently are and how they will be set in the future. If the employee is given an entitlement to an annual pay review, the company may wish to confirm that this will not necessarily result in a pay increase. Where relevant, it is advisable for the contract to state that deductions may be made from an employee's pay in certain circumstances, to enable the company to make those deductions without facing an allegation that it has made an unlawful deduction from the employee's wages (see 2.1.92).

Sick pay

1.2.27　If the company intends to provide occupational sick pay, the contract should make clear the amount and duration of the pay and what conditions apply. It may be, for example, that employees are not entitled to company sick pay unless they notify the company that they are ill by a certain time or in a certain way and provide certain evidence of their incapacity. The company may want to retain the right to refuse to pay occupational sick pay if it considers that there are grounds for believing that the employee is not ill. It would also be advisable to specify what happens if an employee is ill during a holiday, in terms of both payment and notification requirements (see 2.3.74).

Lay-off and suspension

1.2.28　Most employees are not entitled to be provided with work to do (see 1.2.45). They are, however, entitled to their wages or salary, provided that they are ready and willing to work. Therefore if the company wants the right to suspend an employee from work without pay, perhaps as a disciplinary sanction, or to lay an employee off without pay because of a shortage of work, then it must include that power in the contract. (Lay-off is discussed in 5.2.127.)

Working time

1.2.29 The contract should specify what an employee's working hours will be, but can also include flexibility for the employer to change those hours. The contract should also set out any terms on overtime, including whether the employee is obliged to work overtime or has the right to do so (that is, whether the overtime is voluntary, compulsory or guaranteed), and what additional payment, if any, will be made for it. The Working Time Regulations 1998 set out some limits on working time. (Working time is discussed in more detail in Chapter 2.3.)

Holidays

1.2.30 The contract will need to explain how much holiday entitlement the employee has, including any entitlement to public holidays, and how holiday pay is calculated. There are rules on how holiday pay must be calculated for the minimum holiday to which the employee is entitled under the Working Time Regulations 1998. For the purposes of the Regulations, holiday pay may in some cases need to reflect bonus and overtime payments. If any holidays in excess of the statutory minimum are to be paid on a different basis, the contract will need to say so. It is also advisable to state any restrictions on when and how holiday should be taken, including annual shutdowns and rules on carrying forward holidays into the next holiday year. (Holiday entitlement is discussed in more detail in 2.3.71.)

Confidential information

1.2.31 During the course of his or her employment, an employee is under an implied legal obligation not to disclose the employer's confidential information (see 1.2.46). If the information is of such a highly confidential nature that it amounts to a trade secret, the employee remains under a duty not to disclose it even after leaving the company's employment. Nevertheless, where an employee has access to confidential information during his or her employment, it is advisable for the company to identify clearly, in the contract or elsewhere, what that information is, in order to ensure that the employee is aware of his or her duty not to disclose it.

Restrictions on departing employees

1.2.32   In some cases, an employer may want to restrict the ability of a departing employee to work for a rival company, set up in competition or poach the company's customers, suppliers or employees. These forms of restriction, often referred to as 'restrictive covenants', are legally enforceable only if they are protecting the company's legitimate business interests, rather than merely preventing competition, and the restraints they impose are no broader than is necessary. It is therefore advisable for a company to obtain advice from us when drafting restrictive covenants. It is also important to bear in mind that if a company dismisses an employee in a way that breaches his or her contract, as, for example, where the company does not give the proper notice of termination, the company will not be able to enforce any restrictive covenants in the contract (see 4.1.84).

Notice of termination

1.2.33   A contract should specify what notice the employer and the employee must give to terminate the contract. Minimum notice periods are laid down by law (see 4.1.16), but the contract can lay down longer periods. In most cases, an employer is entitled to ask an employee not to come into work during the notice period (usually referred to as giving 'garden leave'). There are some employees, however, who have a right to be provided with work (see 1.2.45). If an employer wants the option of asking these employees to take garden leave, it needs to include a clause in their contracts giving the company that power.

1.2.34   The company may also want to give itself the option to terminate an employee's contract without notice (known as a 'summary dismissal') and instead make a payment to the employee equivalent to the contractual benefits he or she would have received during the notice period. This is usually referred to as a 'payment in lieu of notice' clause. (Reliance on this type of clause is not necessary where the employee is in serious breach of contract, since the employer is then entitled to dismiss the employee without notice or payment in lieu (see 4.1.12).)

1.2.35 The advantage of a 'payment in lieu' clause is that the company can terminate the contract with immediate effect without being in breach of contract, so enabling it to enforce any restrictive covenants there might be in the employee's contract. The disadvantage of this type of clause for the company is that the employee has the right to his or her full contractual benefits for the notice period, even if he or she immediately gets another job or makes no effort to find alternative employment. That would not be the case if the employee were summarily dismissed without a payment in lieu clause. The disadvantage of the clause to the employee is that the payment made under it is taxable, whereas any payment in lieu that is not made under a contractual term is tax free up to a certain limit (see 4.1.93).

Management prerogative

1.2.36 There is no need to include within the contract rules of conduct, including disciplinary rules, or methods of working. These are within the area of management prerogative and can be changed at management discretion (see 5.1.12). For example, an employer that asks employees to move from working on paper-based systems to working with computers is unlikely to be altering employees' contractual terms.

Implied terms

1.2.37 Some contractual obligations of employers and employees flow not from the terms that they expressly agree, but from terms that are implied in the contract. Terms can be implied in order to fill gaps in the terms that have been expressly agreed (see 1.2.39) or from custom and practice (see 1.2.41). In addition, some terms have come to be implied into every contract of employment as a result of court decisions over the years (see 1.2.45, 1.2.46).

Filling gaps

1.2.38 If the employer and employee have failed to reach any express agreement on a particular aspect of the employment relationship, a term may need to be implied in order to make the contract workable. For example, if a contract includes a relocation clause, a further term may need to be implied that the employer will not ask the employee to move beyond commuting distance without giving sufficient notice to enable the employee to make the minimum necessary personal arrangements.

1.2.39   A term may also be implied because, although no express agreement was reached on it, it is obvious from the relationship between the employer and the employee and all the surrounding circumstances that the term was intended to be included in their agreement. For example, if the employer and employee have not expressly agreed on the employee's place of work, it is likely to be implied that the workplace is the location where the employee reports for work each day.

1.2.40   If there is a dispute over issues covered by implied terms of this nature, it will ultimately be for a court or employment tribunal to decide what the terms are. Since the outcome of litigation is unpredictable, it is obviously preferable for companies to ensure that all the necessary issues are covered by express terms.

Custom and practice

1.2.41   In some limited circumstances, terms can be implied into a contract as a matter of custom and practice. In order for this to happen, the contract term must be reasonable, clearly and precisely defined and widely known in the industry or in the particular workplace involved. If the term meets these criteria, then it will be implied into an individual employee's contract even if he or she was not aware of its existence. Because it is difficult to assess with any certainty whether these criteria are met, it is not advisable to rely on custom and practice as a source of contract terms; express terms are always preferable.

1.2.42   It is important to note that a term does not become part of a contract as a matter of custom and practice simply because the employer or employee has acted in a particular way over a period of time. The litmus test is whether the company or the employee was acting in that way because they viewed themselves as under a legal obligation to do so.

1.2.43   Take, for example, a company that operates from a working assumption, set out in an internal management policy document, that it will make redundancy payments in excess of the statutory minimum when it implements redundancies. Each time there is a redundancy exercise, it reviews that assumption to ensure that the company can afford to make the enhanced payments. Over the course of several years, it makes the enhanced payments, but there then comes a time when it decides it can afford only the statutory minimum. The company is unlikely to be breaching the contracts of those who are dismissed by paying them the minimum, because it never intended that the enhanced payments should be a contractual entitlement, and never indicated to the workforce that they were.

1.2.44   Companies can obtain advice from us on the contractual status of company policies.

Employer's implied obligations

1.2.45   Over the years, the civil courts have decided that some terms should be implied into all contracts of employment. These terms continue to evolve, but currently the most important implied obligations on an employer are:

> ### Employer's implied duties
>
> - **Duty to pay.** The employer has a duty to pay the employee, provided the employee is ready and willing to work. In general, an employer is not obliged to provide an employee with work. There are two exceptions to this, where an employer *is* under an obligation to provide work. One is where the employee's earnings depend on work being done, such as in the case of pieceworkers or those paid on a commission basis. The other is where the employee's position in the labour market is dependent on him or her continuing to work, because lack of work leads to immediate loss of reputation or skills. The courts have accepted that this could apply to traders in the financial markets in the City of London, so it could also extend to other employees with specialist knowledge or expertise that quickly loses its value if it is not used.
>
> - **Trust and confidence.** The employer has a duty not to act in a way

that is likely to destroy or seriously damage the relationship of trust and confidence between the employer and the employee, unless it has a reasonable and proper reason for doing so. This is an important implied term, which has been applied and developed in many recent court cases. It is breached, for example, where an employer fails to support an employee who is being bullied or harassed. In some circumstances, it can have the effect of limiting the employer's ability to exercise its express powers under the contract. For example, a company could be in breach of this implied term if it used an express power to move an employee to different work without giving the employee sufficient support or training in the new role.

- **Health and safety.** The employer is obliged to take reasonable care for the health and safety of the employee. The employer has similar duties under the law of negligence and the Health and Safety at Work etc Act 1974.

Employee's implied obligations

1.2.46 The employee also has implied duties, the most important of which are:

Employee's implied duties

- **Co-operation.** The employee is obliged to co-operate with the employer, including obeying the employer's lawful and reasonable instructions. Whether an instruction is lawful and reasonable will depend in part on the express terms in the employee's contract dealing with job duties.

- **Loyal service.** The employee is also obliged to give loyal service to the employer. This term may mean that the employee should not be involved in competing activities or work for a competitor in his or her spare time, if this poses a clear risk that the employer will be substantially harmed. The term certainly means that the employee should not disclose confidential information that he or she comes across in the course of work.

Contracts

> - **Trust and confidence.** Like the employer, the employee is under a duty not to act in a way that breaches the relationship of trust and confidence between them, unless he or she has reasonable and proper cause for doing so.
> - **Health and safety.** The employee is also under an implied duty to take reasonable care for his or her own health and safety and that of fellow employees and to exercise reasonable care and skill in his or her work.

Documenting the contract

1.2.47 Although there is no legal requirement for a contract of employment to be in writing, the law does require an employer to give its employees written information on their main terms and conditions of employment, and to update this information if the details change (see 5.1.57). This information is often referred to as a 'statement of employment particulars' or a 'written statement of main terms and conditions of employment'. It is also sometimes referred to as a 'statutory statement' or a 'section 1 statement', because the duty to provide it is set out in section 1 of the Employment Rights Act 1996.

Consequence of failure to provide the information

1.2.48 If an employer fails to provide the required information, the employee is not entitled to compensation for that failure alone, although he or she can ask an employment tribunal to rule on what the information should have been. However, if the employee succeeds in some other claim to a tribunal, such as an unfair dismissal or unlawful deductions claim, and the tribunal also finds that the employer has not met its obligation to provide the information, the tribunal must award the employee between two and four weeks' pay as compensation for that failure.

Timing

1.2.49 The information must be given to every employee who is with the company for one month or more, and must be supplied within not more than two months of the employment beginning. If the employee is due to work outside the UK for more than a month within two months of starting work, then the information must be supplied by the time the employee leaves the UK.

Status of statement

1.2.50   The information is not in itself a contract of employment, it is merely the employer's version of the contract's terms. So a company cannot assume that the employee agrees that the written information it provides accurately reflects the contract's terms, unless the employee has expressly said so. This is one reason why some companies choose to offer new recruits the job on the basis of a written contract of employment or offer letter that includes all the details that need to be included in the written information, thereby meeting their obligation to provide the information and ensuring that the terms are agreed.

1.2.51   Employees must be provided with information on some terms, such as disciplinary procedures, that the employer may not intend to be part of their contract of employment. A company that is meeting its obligation to provide information by issuing a written contract will therefore need to make clear which terms, if any, are not contractual.

Content

1.2.52   The law lays down in detail what terms should be included in the written information and how those details should be provided. If any of this information changes, the employer must notify the employee (see 5.1.57). (A statement of terms and conditions is available for download from EEF's website.)

1.2.53   The information that an employer must provide is listed below. The details should be accurate as at a specified date not more than seven days before the information is given. If there are no relevant details to give, then the information should make that clear. For example, if the employer does not provide a pension, the information should say so.

- The names of the employer and the employee.

- The date the employee's employment began.

- The date the employee's period of continuous employment began. This may need to take into account any previous employment with the same company or with another employer that counts towards the employee's continuous employment (see 8.1.3).

- If the employment is not intended to be permanent, the period for which it is expected to continue. This might be, for example, until a specific task is completed or until a specified event occurs.

- If the employment is for a fixed term, the date when it is to end. Employment is for a fixed term if it is possible to identify at the time when the contract begins the exact date on which it will end.

- The employee's job title and/or a brief description of his or her work.

- The scale on which or rate at which the employee is paid, or the method of calculating pay. This may involve, for example, giving details of any piecework scheme and overtime or bonus payments.

- The intervals at which the employee is paid. This is likely to be either weekly or monthly.

- Any terms and conditions relating to hours of work, including normal working hours. This should include not only the number of hours but also when they are worked, including details of any shift system or flexitime. Details of overtime arrangements should also be given.

- The employee's place of work. If the employee is required or permitted to work at various places, then that should be stated and the employer's address should be given.

- Any terms and conditions relating to holidays, including public holidays, and holiday pay. The details must be sufficient to enable the employee's entitlement, including entitlement to accrued holiday pay on termination of employment, to be precisely calculated.

- Any terms and conditions relating to incapacity for work due to sickness or injury, including details of any sick pay scheme that the company operates.

- Any collective agreements that directly affect the terms and conditions of the employment, including, where the employer is not a party to a collective agreement, the persons by whom the agreement was made. This will entail listing the dates, title or subject matter and parties to any domestic, local or national collective agreements dealing with terms and conditions that are incorporated into the employee's contract.

- If the employee is required to work outside the UK for more than one month:

    – the period for which he or she is to work outside the UK;

    – the currency in which he or she is to be paid while working outside the UK;

    – any additional remuneration payable to the employee, and any benefits to be provided to or in respect of him or her, because he or she is required to work outside the UK; and

    – any terms and conditions relating to the employee's return to the UK.

- The length of notice the employee is obliged to give and entitled to receive to terminate his or her contract.

1.2.54   The information must also include a note of the following:

Notes to be included

- Any disciplinary rules that apply to the employee, and reference to any procedures relating to discipline or dismissal. This may include reference to a redundancy procedure and any other procedure providing for dismissal, as well as to the disciplinary procedure. The disciplinary procedure should comply with the ACAS Code of Practice on discipline and grievance (see 3.3.8). The note should refer to the person to whom the employee can apply if dissatisfied with any decision to discipline or dismiss him or her, identified by job title or by name or in some other way. The way in which the appeal should be made must also be specified. Details should also be given of any steps that follow on from the appeal. Disciplinary rules and procedures relating to health and safety issues do not need to be included.

- The person to whom the employee can apply with any grievance relating to his or her employment, identified by job title or name or in some other way. The manner in which the application should be made – which would normally be 'in writing' – should also be specified, as should any steps that follow on from the application. Details on how to lodge grievances relating to general health and safety issues need not be included, but, if the company has a bullying and harassment procedure, reference should be made to this. The grievance procedure should comply with the ACAS Code of Practice on discipline and grievance procedures.

- Any terms and conditions relating to pensions and pension schemes, including a statement of whether a contracting-out certificate under the Pension Schemes Act 1993 is in force in respect of the employment (see 2.4.20).

Format

1.2.55 The information can be given in any form, provided it is in writing. It could, for example, be set out in an offer letter, a contract of employment or a dedicated statement. The legislation does, however, lay down some rules on the format in which the information must be provided. Some of the most important aspects must be covered in a single statement. These are:

- the names of employer and employee;
- the date employment and continuous employment began;
- terms on pay and the intervals at which it is paid;
- terms on hours of work and holidays;
- the job title and/or description; and
- the place of work.

Although these details need to be brought together in a single statement, that requirement could be met by stapling separate documents together. The other information can be given in separate instalments if the company wishes to do so.

Other documents

1.2.56   For certain details, the written information can refer the employee to other documents, if the company so chooses. These details are:

- sick leave and pay;
- pensions;
- disciplinary rules; and
- disciplinary, dismissal and grievance procedures.

1.2.57   However, this option is available only where the other documents are reasonably accessible to the employee, either because he or she has a reasonable opportunity of reading them in the course of employment or in some other way. Referring the employee to a pension scheme booklet that is pinned to a notice board or kept in the personnel department at the employee's workplace might be acceptable. Referring the employee to documents kept at head office 20 miles away would not, unless, for example, the document was also available on an office intranet to which the employee had access while at work.

1.2.58   For details of terms on notice, the company may choose to refer the employee to the law (the Employment Rights Act 1996 lays down minimum periods of notice – see 4.1.16) or to a collective agreement that is reasonably accessible to the employee.

Enforcing the contract

1.2.59   Because a contract of employment creates legal rights, there are legal consequences if the employer or the employee does not respect its terms, or, to use the legal terminology, acts 'in breach of contract'. The potential consequences are:

- the employer or the employee may make a claim for damages (see 1.2.60);
- the employer or the employee may apply for an injunction (see 1.2.63);

- the employee may bring a claim that there has been an unlawful deduction from his or her wages (see 2.1.92);

- the employee may resign and claim unfair or wrongful constructive dismissal (see 4.1.35); or

- the employer may dismiss the employee, in which case the employee may claim unfair or wrongful dismissal (see 4.1.21 and Chapter 4.2).

Damages

1.2.60 If the employer breaches the contract, the employee can claim compensation, or 'sue for damages', for the loss he or she has been caused by that breach. This type of claim can be made to a civil court, which will usually be the local county court in England and Wales or the local sheriff court in Scotland. In certain cases where the employee's employment has ended, he or she can bring a claim for damages for breach of contract to an employment tribunal (see 7.2.11). Whether the employee brings the claim in a court or in a tribunal, the employer is entitled to make a counter-claim for damages for any breach of contract by the employee.

Amount of damages awarded

1.2.61 When deciding the amount of damages to award, the court or tribunal will aim to put the employee in the position he or she would have been in had the contract terms been followed. For example, if the employer has failed to pay the employee a contractual bonus, the damages will be equivalent to the bonus that the employee should have received, net of tax and National Insurance contributions.

Employee breach

1.2.62 Where it is the employee who has breached the contract it is, in theory at least, possible for an employer to sue the employee for damages. But these types of action are rarely brought, because it will usually be difficult to identify and quantify in financial terms the loss that the employer has been caused by the employee's breach of contract. Even if an award of damages is made against the employee, he or she may not be able to pay it.

Injunctions

1.2.63   Another option for the employee whose employer is in breach of contract is to apply to a civil court for an order requiring the employer to comply with the terms of the contract. This type of order is usually known as an 'injunction' in England and Wales and an 'interdict' in Scotland.

1.2.64   Applications for an injunction are much rarer than claims for damages, and the court has discretion as to whether to grant an injunction. In particular, it will not grant an injunction if it considers that an award of damages would provide adequate compensation. It has no power to grant an injunction compelling the employee to work or to attend at a particular place for the purpose of working.

1.2.65   An employee is most likely to apply for an injunction if the employer has indicated that it intends to breach the contract but has not yet done so, or where the breach of contract will not cause the employee any quantifiable financial loss. An example might be where the employer has indicated that it will be moving the employee's place of work, even though there is no relocation clause in the employee's contract, but the employee's travel-to-work expenses will be the same.

1.2.66   An employer can also apply for an injunction to require the employee to meet his or her obligations under the contract. This is commonly done to keep an employee to his or her contractual obligations during his or her period of notice of resignation. This is also done to ensure that the employee abides by any restrictive covenants (see 1.2.32) in his or her contract after employment has ended, often with the aim of preventing the employee going to work for a competitor. In other circumstances, an employer is more likely to discipline or even dismiss an employee who fails to meet his or her contractual obligations, rather than apply for an injunction.

Unlawful deductions

1.2.67   Where an employer's breach of contract involves a failure to pay the employee some sum that is properly payable under his or her contract of employment, then the employee has the option of bringing a claim that the employer has made an unlawful deduction from his or her wages (see 2.1.92). Unlike a claim for breach of contract, this type of claim can only be brought to an employment tribunal, and can be heard by the tribunal even if the employee is still in the employer's employment.

Dismissal actions

1.2.68   If the employer is in very serious breach of contract, the employee may choose to resign and claim that he or she has been constructively dismissed (see 4.1.35). The employee can then allege that the dismissal is unfair (see Chapter 4.2) and wrongful (see 4.1.21).

1.2.69   Where it is the employee who is in breach of contract, the employer may decide to dismiss. If the breach is very serious, the employer is legally entitled to dismiss without having to meet its usual obligation to give notice of termination. This is known as a 'summary dismissal'. Although a summary dismissal is not in breach of the employee's contract in these circumstances, it may still be challenged as unfair.

Employment status

1.2.70   A person's employment rights depend to a substantial degree on whether or not he or she is an employee. Those who do not have a contract of employment (sometimes referred to as a 'contract of service') or a contract of apprenticeship (see 1.2.84) are excluded from many important employment rights given by legislation, such as the right to claim unfair dismissal, the right to a redundancy payment and parental rights. They also cannot rely on the significant terms that are implied in all contracts of employment (see 1.2.45). It is therefore important for employers to be aware of which members of their workforce meet the legal tests for employee status, summarised in 1.2.72.

1.2.71   It should also be borne in mind, however, that some employment rights given by legislation extend to many workers who are not employees. The legal position of these workers is summarised in 1.2.74–1.2.88.

Employee status

1.2.72   Over the years, many different courts and tribunals have had to consider the issue of employee status. From their decisions, some guiding principles can be gleaned:

- The more the employer controls the work that the worker does, in terms of how it is done, where it is done and when it is done, the more likely it is that the worker will be viewed as an employee.

- If an employer is under no obligation to provide work and the worker is under no obligation to accept it if it is offered (as may be the case for some casual workers), then there are insufficient mutual obligations to create a contract of employment.

- The label that the employer and the worker apply to their relationship does not dictate its legal status. The fact that an employer categorises a worker as self-employed does not mean that he or she is in fact self-employed.

- The tax status of a worker does not determine his or her employment status. The mere fact that the Inland Revenue has not challenged an individual paying tax on a self-employed basis does not prevent the individual from claiming before an employment tribunal that he or she is an employee (although workers who knowingly manipulate their tax status in this way may find that tribunals are not prepared to enforce their employment contracts, on public policy grounds).

- The economic realities of the relationship are important. If the worker runs the direct risk of losing money if the job is not done well and stands to gain if the job is done efficiently, then he or she may well be self-employed.

- Another way of looking at it is to ask whether, in the light of all the surrounding circumstances, it can realistically be concluded that the worker is in business on his or her own account – that is, genuinely self-employed – rather than merely working to further the employer's business. It may be relevant to examine whether the worker also works for other employers, whether the worker also employs people, and whether the worker supplies his or her own tools and equipment to do the work.

- A contract of employment involves personal obligations between employee and employer. If the relationship is such that the worker is not obliged to do the work himself or herself, but is allowed to supply replacements when he or she is not available, the worker is unlikely to be working under a contract of employment.

1.2.73 In assessing the nature of an employment relationship, no one of these guiding principles gives the answer. They should all be taken into account in painting the overall picture.

Company directors are office holders under company law but they may also, depending on the circumstances, be employees.

The self-employed

1.2.74 Even workers who are genuinely self-employed and in business on their own account will have a contract with the company for which they are working (sometimes referred to as a 'contract for services') that gives them legal rights and defines their obligations. The contract is likely to specify, for example, what work has to be done and by when, what they will be paid and on what conditions, and what notice each side has to give to terminate the contract.

1.2.75 Self-employed people working under contracts that require them to carry out the work personally also have the right not to be discriminated against on the grounds of sex, gender reassignment, married or civil partner status, race, religion, sexual orientation or disability. This includes the right not to be discriminated against in the pay and benefits that they receive.

'Workers'

1.2.76 Several of the employment rights that have been created by legislation over recent years have been extended to many workers who cannot establish that they are employees. Workers qualify for these rights if they contract with an employer to perform personally any work or services, provided that the contract does not make the employer the client or customer of a profession or business undertaking that the workers are running. As a result, these workers are not only covered by the discrimination legislation but also have:

- the right not to have unlawful deductions made from their wages (see 2.1.92);

- the right to paid holiday and limits on their working time (see 2.3.20);

- the right not to be discriminated against on the ground that they work part-time (see 2.3.85);

- the right not to be discriminated against on grounds of union membership or activities (see 6.1.7);

- the right to be accompanied at disciplinary and grievance hearings (see 3.3.80);

- the right to be protected from retaliation if they make a 'protected disclosure' under the Public Interest Disclosure Act 1998 (see 3.3.142); and

- the right to receive the national minimum wage (see 2.1.22).

Where a company employs a worker who in turn employs another worker who works on the company's premises, then the company shares legal responsibility for ensuring that the sub-contracted worker receives the national minimum wage.

Agency workers

1.2.77 Some companies use temporary workers supplied by an employment agency. These companies have a contract with the agency for the agency to supply the workers, and pay the agency a fee for the workers' services. The workers do not usually have a contract of any description with companies where they work. It is possible, however, that a court or tribunal in certain circumstances might imply that the worker is the company's employee, but an employment contract will only be implied between the agency worker and end user when it is necessary to do so in order to explain the work undertaken by the worker for the end user. We can provide further advice on the issue.

1.2.78 Agency workers do have some sort of contract with the agency, although not necessarily a contract of employment. It is the agency that is nearly always responsible for ensuring that these workers receive at least the national minimum wage. We can provide further advice on the issue.

1.2.79 Although agency workers are not usually the employees of the company where they work, that company is still under a legal obligation not to discriminate against them on the grounds of their sex, sexual orientation, gender reassignment, married or civil partner status, race, religion, or disability. In particular, companies may in some circumstances be legally obliged to make reasonable adjustments for disabled agency workers who are supplied to work for them (see 3 1.78). Agency workers are also protected from retaliation for making protected disclosures under the Public Interest Disclosure Act 1998 (see 3.3.142).

1.2.80 New rights for agency workers are expected to come into force in October 2011. The key right in the proposed legislation is for agency workers to be entitled to equal treatment in relation to certain defined basic and working employment conditions (including pay) after a qualifying period of 12 weeks. The new rights will not, however, affect the employment status of an agency worker.

Temporary workers

1.2.81 Most workers that a company recruits on a temporary, casual or seasonal basis are likely to be its employees, at least for the time that they are working for the company.

Nevertheless, these workers may find it difficult to qualify for those employment rights, such as protection from unfair dismissal, that depend upon building up a particular period of continuous employment (see Appendix 8.1). It is possible that some of these workers will have ongoing contracts of employment with the company that continue to exist even when they are not working, so allowing them to build up their period of continuous employment. And even if these workers have contracts of employment only during their periods in work, they may in some circumstances be able to count the periods between the contracts towards their period of continuous employment (see 8.1.4).

1.2.82 Some temporary workers are given fixed-term contracts, to last for a specified period such as a week, a month or a year, or until a specified date. Others may have a contract to work until a particular task, such as a construction project, is completed or a particular event occurs. In general, an employee working under this type of contract has the same statutory rights as any other employee. It is also important to note that if a contract of this type comes to an end and the employer decides not to renew it, the employee is viewed as having been dismissed for unfair dismissal and redundancy payment purposes (see 4.2.13, 5.2.115). Further, it is unlawful for an employer to discriminate against an employee with this type of contract on the ground of his or her contractual status, unless it has objective justification for doing so (see 1.2.92).

Homeworkers

1.2.83 An employee's legal rights are not affected by being asked, or requesting, to work from home. The more traditional type of homeworkers, who are paid to carry out manual tasks on a piecework basis, may not always be able to establish that they have contracts of employment with the company that uses them. They may nevertheless qualify for the statutory rights that extend to workers who have contracts to carry out work personally (see 1.2.76). Whether or not they are under an obligation to carry out their work personally, homeworkers are entitled to the national minimum wage (see 2.1.22) and to protection from retaliation for making a protected disclosure under the Public Interest Disclosure Act 1998 (see 3.3.142).

Trainees and apprentices

1.2.84 Various different types of work relationship may be covered by the terms 'trainee' and 'apprentice'.

1.2.85 Under a traditional contract of apprenticeship, the apprentice agrees to work for the employer for a fixed period, during which the employer is responsible for training the individual to a standard that qualifies him or her to pursue his or her chosen trade. Legislation gives traditional apprentices the same statutory employment rights as employees. The rules on the termination of contracts of apprenticeship are, however, different from those that apply to the termination of employment contracts. A contract of apprenticeship should be in writing.

1.2.86 In contrast with traditional apprentices, modern apprentices usually work under a tripartite arrangement, under which they obtain their work experience from their employer but a third-party training provider or college provides them with the more theoretical aspects of their training. Depending on the circumstances, a modern apprentice may be working under either a traditional contract of apprenticeship or a contract of employment. If the documentation establishing the relationship uses the terminology of apprenticeship and the employer agrees to provide the worker with an extended period of training to reach a recognised qualification, the contract is likely to be one of apprenticeship, even if it is agreed that most if not all of the theoretical side of the training will be provided by a college or other training provider.

1.2.87　Sometimes new recruits are labelled 'trainees', to indicate that they are in the early stages of doing the job and are still learning their duties. This does not affect their employment rights: 'trainees' of this kind are in fact employees.

1.2.88　Individuals working for an organisation on an unpaid basis, in order to acquire work experience rather than to produce productive work for the company, are neither employees nor apprentices. They are, however, protected by the legislation that outlaws disability discrimination.

Fixed-term contracts

1.2.89　Most contracts of employment are open-ended: they do not specify an end date and will last until either the employer or the employee terminates the relationship. Some contracts, however, are intended from the outset to be of a limited duration. They may be 'task' or 'specified purpose' contracts, which state that they will end when a particular task, such as a construction project, is completed or a specified event occurs. Or they may be fixed-term contracts, which specify the period for which they will last (such as 'one year from 1 January 2007') or the date on which they will end ('This contract will run from 1 January 2007 until 31 December 2007'). Fixed-term contracts may be short, so an employee working under a contract for a day, a week or a month that is renewed on a rolling basis is also a fixed-term employee.

1.2.90　Employees who work under these types of contracts of limited duration are protected by the Fixed-term Employees (Prevention of Less Favourable Treatment) Regulations 2002. Under the Regulations, 'fixed-term' employees include not only those working under a fixed-term contract but also those working under a task or specified purpose contract.

1.2.91　Traditional apprentices (see 1.2.85) are not covered by the Regulations. Nor are employees on schemes that are designed to provide them with training or work experience to help them find work and that are provided under arrangements made with the government or are EC-funded. Employees who are on work-experience placements of up to one year as part of a higher education course are also excluded.

Equal treatment principle

1.2.92 Under the Regulations, employers must not treat fixed-term employees less favourably than permanent employees on the ground of their fixed-term status, unless they can objectively justify doing so. This principle applies, for example, to fixed-term employees' terms and conditions of employment (see 2.1.88, 2.3.19, 2.4.49), their access to training, their opportunity to apply for permanent vacancies in the company (see 1.1.23, 5.2.96) and their dismissal, including redundancy (see 5.2.78).

Basis of comparison

1.2.93 In order to claim the protection of the Regulations, the fixed-term employee must be able to show that he or she has been treated less favourably than a comparable permanent employee. A permanent employee is comparable if he or she does the same or broadly similar work and has a similar level of the qualifications and skills that are relevant to the treatment in question. In companies with various sites, if there is no comparable permanent employee at the fixed-term employee's workplace, then a comparison can be made with a comparable permanent employee at another site.

1.2.94 In deciding whether a fixed-term employee has been less favourably treated, the pro rata principle should be applied in appropriate cases. So, for example, a fixed-term employee on a six-month contract is not being treated less favourably than a permanent employee if he or she is given only half the permanent employee's annual holiday entitlement.

Objective justification

1.2.95 An employer can lawfully treat a fixed-term employee less favourably than a permanent employee if it can objectively justify doing so. According to the government guidance on the Regulations (see 9.1.2), less favourable treatment of fixed-term staff is justified if it is a necessary and appropriate way of achieving a genuine business objective.

1.2.96   It may be possible, for example, to give a fixed-term employee a benefit on a pro rata basis, rather than exclude the employee from the benefit altogether. So, for example, if a company offers employees a loan to buy an annual season ticket, an employee on a fixed-term contract of six months could be offered a loan to buy a six-month ticket. In other cases, however, it may be disproportionately expensive to provide a fixed-term employee with the same benefit as a permanent employee. The government guidance gives the example of where a fixed-term employee is on a contract of three months and a comparable permanent employee has a company car. The employer may be justified in not offering the fixed-term employee a car, it suggests, if the cost of doing so would be high and the employee's work travel needs could be met in some other way.

1.2.97   The Regulations state that it is justified to treat a fixed-term employee less favourably in respect of any contractual benefit, provided the employee's contract, taken as a whole, is no less favourable than that of a comparable permanent employee. (For examples, see 2.1.90 and 2.4.50.)

Statement of reasons

1.2.98   A fixed-term employee who believes that his or her employer is not respecting the right to equal treatment can write for an explanation of the way in which he or she is being treated. The employer's response can be used as evidence in any claim the employee may then make to an employment tribunal to enforce his or her rights under the Regulations. If the employer fails to provide a statement of reasons or the statement it provides is evasive or unclear, the tribunal is entitled to draw whatever conclusions it considers fair to draw, including that the employer has breached the Regulations.

Successive fixed-term contracts

1.2.99   The Regulations also limit the extent to which employers can use successive fixed-term contracts. Fixed-term employees who have their contracts renewed, or who are offered a new fixed-term contract, when they have already been employed on a fixed-term basis for four continuous years or more, will be treated as working under a permanent (that is, open-ended) contract from the date the contract is renewed or the date the new contract is entered into. The law does not restrict the length of the initial fixed-term contract. (The rules on calculating continuous employment are explained in Appendix 8.1.) The contract will not be converted into a permanent one, however, if the employer can objectively justify continuing to use a fixed-term contract.

1.2.100 A company can amend or replace these rules by reaching a collective agreement with its recognised trade union or a workforce agreement aimed at preventing the abuse of fixed-term contracts. (Workforce agreements are explained in 2.3.34.) The agreement can achieve this aim in one or more of the following ways:

- by fixing a maximum period for which an employee may be employed on a fixed-term basis (which could be more or less than the four years set out in the Regulations);

- by limiting the number of fixed-term contracts or the number of times a fixed-term contract may be renewed; or

- by specifying objective grounds on which the renewal of a fixed-term contract or use of successive fixed-term contracts may be justified.

Written statement

1.2.101 An employee who believes that he or she has become a permanent employee as a result of these rules is able to ask the employer for a written statement confirming that. The employer must either confirm the employee's permanent status or explain why the contract remains fixed-term. If the employer considers that it is justified in continuing to employ the employee on a fixed-term basis, it will need to state why.

1.2.102 If the employer fails to reply, or the employee does not accept the employer's reply that his or her contract remains fixed-term, the employee can ask an employment tribunal to decide whether he or she is in fact a permanent employee. Any reply that the employer gave can be used as evidence in that claim. If the employer failed to reply, or the reply it gave was evasive or unclear, the tribunal is entitled to draw whatever conclusions it considers fair from that.

Victimisation

1.2.103   It is unlawful for an employer to penalise an employee for asserting or enforcing his or her rights under the Regulations, or for supporting someone else in bringing a claim. It is also automatically unfair to dismiss an employee on these grounds, regardless of the employee's age or length of service. This protection does not apply where an employee has alleged that his or her employer has breached the Regulations and the allegation was not only false but also not made in good faith.

section 2

Rights during employment

2.1

Pay

Overview

2.1.1 This chapter of the Guide covers the law and good practice on pay. In general, employers are free to decide what their workforce is paid, but there are some legal constraints. One of the most significant is the need to respect employees' rights under their contract of employment. This chapter explains the contractual principles that underlie how employees are paid (see 2.1.6). It also describes employers' duties to provide employees with written information on their pay details when they are first recruited, and itemised pay statements each time they are paid (see 2.1.18 and 2.1.20).

2.1.2 Another important legal consideration is that most workers must be paid at least the national minimum wage. This chapter outlines who qualifies for the minimum wage and how it is calculated (see 2.1.22).

2.1.3 Although employers have a large degree of freedom in how they set pay rates, the law prohibits employers from allowing a worker's pay to be affected by his or her sex, race, age, religion, sexual orientation or disability. It is also unlawful to pay a worker less because he or she works part-time or on a fixed-term basis, unless the employer has objective justification for doing so. This chapter summarises how discrimination law affects payment systems (see 2.1.51).

Deductions

2.1.4   There are many reasons why an employer may make deductions from a worker's pay, from tax and National Insurance contributions through to loan repayments. The law prohibits employers from making deductions from workers' pay, or receiving payments from them, unless certain conditions are met. This chapter explains these rules (see 2.1.92), and how deductions can include shortfalls and non-payments. Finally, the section summarises the circumstances in which an employer may be under a legal duty to make deductions from a worker's pay (see 2.1.105).

Other legislation on pay

2.1.5   Various pieces of employment legislation require employers to pay employees in certain specific situations. These are covered in other chapters of the Guide:

- paid annual holidays (see 2.3.72);

- statutory sick pay (see 3.2.38);

- statutory maternity pay (see 2.2.47), paid time off for antenatal care (see 2.2.12) and paid maternity suspension (see 2.2.22);

- statutory paternity pay (see 2.2.95);

- statutory adoption pay (see 2.2.113);

- guarantee payments (see 5.2.132);

- paid time off for trade union officials (see 6.1.30), health and safety representatives (see 6.4.78), workforce representatives (see 6.4.79) and pension fund trustees (see 2.4.59);

- paid time off for study and training (see 2.3.102);

- payment during notice of dismissal (see 4.1.18); and

- paid time off during notice of redundancy to look for other work or arrange training (see 5.2.111).

Contractual issues

2.1.6　The right to be paid is a fundamental component of any employee's contract of employment. Background information on how a contract of employment is formed and what its contents are can be found in Chapter 1.2.

2.1.7　A written contract is likely to state the employee's basic rate of pay or salary and the intervals at which it will be paid.

Pay reviews

2.1.8　Some contracts also give employees the right to an annual pay review. An employer may wish to state what the basis of the review will be. The review might, for example, be based on the individual's performance in the job, or the rise in the cost of living over the past year or the coming year, or a combination of these factors. The advantage of including these details is that both employer and employee are clear about the basis on which the review will be conducted, and that should reduce the likelihood of a dispute about the result. The disadvantage is that the company must then conduct the review within the framework of the factors it has specified, or it will be acting in breach of the employee's contract. Therefore, if a review were stated to be dependent on the increase in the cost of living, it would be a breach of contract for the employer to refuse to pay it because it was dissatisfied with the employee's performance.

2.1.9　It would also be a breach of contract for an employer to act irrationally or perversely in reviewing an employee's pay. Therefore, if a company reaches a decision on a pay review that no reasonable employer could have reached, it is acting in breach of contract. If the intention is that a pay review will not necessarily result in a pay increase, the contract should make that clear.

Methods of payment

2.1.10　A written contract is also likely to state how an employee's wages or salary will be paid, whether by credit transfer into the employee's bank account, by cheque or in cash.

Incorporating other documents

2.1.11 Payment systems can be complicated, often including elements linked to individual or group performance or company profit. Where employees are entitled to these types of payments, it may not be practicable to include full details in the main body of their written contract: their contract may need to refer to and incorporate some other documents where the detail can be found (see 1.2.17). A contract could, for example, incorporate another document that sets out in detail how shift premiums are calculated.

If a company wants the flexibility to amend these aspects of an employee's pay, it needs to ensure that the contract makes clear that the details may be amended from time to time. This could be done in the body of the written contract or in any document that is incorporated into it by reference.

2.1.12 If an employee's pay rate is set by collective bargaining, then his or her contract is likely to incorporate the pay agreement that the company reaches with its recognised union from time to time. For clarity, it is advisable for the contract to include an express incorporation clause, although it is also possible for collective agreements to be incorporated into employees' contracts on an implied basis (see 6.2.92).

Discretionary payments

2.1.13 A company may want a particular payment, typically a bonus or an increase after a pay review, to be within its discretion. Making a payment discretionary means that the company can decide whether or not it is paid and how much it should be, and the employee has no legal right to insist on a payment. It is, therefore, important for the contract to make clear when a benefit is discretionary and what part or parts are discretionary. For example, with a bonus scheme, the term discretionary may be attached to the decision whether to pay a bonus at all, to its calculation or to the amount.

2.1.14 The contract may spell out the factors that the company will take into account when exercising its discretion. The advantage of including those details is that both employer and employee are clear about how the discretion will be used, which should reduce the likelihood of a dispute if the benefit is withheld. The disadvantage is that the company must then exercise its discretion within the framework of the factors it has specified, or it will be acting in breach of the employee's contract. Therefore if a discretionary bonus is stated to be dependent on the employee's performance, it would be a breach of contract for the employer to refuse to pay it in order to keep within budget on its pay bill.

2.1.15 It would also be a breach of contract for an employer to act irrationally or perversely in deciding whether to make a discretionary payment. So, if a company refuses to make a discretionary payment in circumstances where no reasonable employer would have done so, it is acting in breach of contract.

Breach of pay rights

2.1.16 A company should be clear about its contractual position before withholding a payment from, or reducing a payment to, an employee. Courts and tribunals view employees' pay rights as fundamentally important. If an employer fails to respect those rights, a court or tribunal is likely to take the view that the employee is entitled to resign and claim that he or she has been constructively dismissed (see 4.1.35).

2.1.17 In addition, an employer that reduces or withholds a payment that is properly payable to an employee may face a claim for damages for breach of contract (see 1.2.60) or a claim that it has made an unlawful deduction from the employee's pay (see 2.1.92).

Documenting pay

2.1.18 When employees are first recruited, they are entitled under section 1 of the Employment Rights Act 1996 to written information on the main terms of their employment. The content of this information and its legal status are explained in detail in 1.2.47.

Written information

2.1.19 In relation to pay, the information must include:

Employment Guide 2010

> ### Information on pay
>
> - The scale or rate of the employee's pay or the method by which it is calculated. This should include, for example, details of piecework rates and overtime pay, commission and bonuses, performance- and profit-related pay.
>
> - How frequently the employee will be paid, whether weekly, monthly or at some other interval. The employee may, for example, receive a basic monthly salary, a commission payment every quarter and an annual bonus payment.
>
> - Any entitlement the employee has to holiday pay or sick pay.
>
> - If the employee will be required to work outside the UK for more than one month, the currency in which he or she will be paid and any additional payments and benefits he or she will receive for working abroad.
>
> - Details of any collective agreements that affect the employee's employment, including those relating to pay.

Itemised pay statement

2.1.20   Employers are also required by the Employment Rights Act 1996 to give their employees a written itemised pay statement. This must be provided at or before the time the wages or salary are paid, and must set out these details:

- the gross amount of the wages or salary;

- the amount of any fixed or variable deductions from pay, and the reason for them (such as tax, National Insurance contributions, loan repayments and so forth);

- the net amount of wages or salary;

- if the wages or salary are paid in different ways – such as partly through a credit transfer and partly in cash – the amount and method of each part-payment.

Fixed deductions

2.1.21 If several fixed deductions are made, the employer may prefer to take up the option of giving the employee a separate written statement of them, rather than setting them out on every pay slip. In that case, the statement must detail the amount of the deductions, how often they will be made, and what they are for. This statement can be amended from time to time by adding or deleting deductions or altering their details. It must, however, be reissued at least annually.

The national minimum wage

2.1.22 Most workers are entitled to be paid at least the national minimum wage (NMW). The legislation that underpins the NMW – principally the National Minimum Wage Act 1998 and the National Minimum Wage Regulations 1999 – is complex, and not every detail is covered here. More information on the NMW can be found in a detailed guide produced by the Department of Business, Innovation and Skills (BIS) or from us or the BIS helpline (see 9.2.1).

Who qualifies?

2.1.23 A company is obliged to pay the NMW to most workers that it directly employs. It is not only employees who are entitled to the NMW. The NMW also covers workers who contract with a company to perform personally any work or services, unless they are dealing with the company as a part of a profession or business undertaking that they are running.

Agency and homeworkers

2.1.24 Homeworkers and agency workers are also entitled to the NMW. The person responsible for ensuring that agency workers receive the NMW is the person with whom they have their contract, or, if the contractual position is not clear, the person who pays them. In the case of workers placed with a company on temporary assignments through an employment agency, that will usually be the agency.

Exclusions

2.1.25 Certain workers are excluded from the NMW. These include trainees on certain government-funded training programmes, including the New Deal programmes, unless they are entitled to receive wages for the work they do. Those participating in the Entry to Employment, Get Ready for Work and Skillbuild schemes are also excluded.

Apprentices

2.1.26 There are special rules for apprentices. For NMW purposes, apprentices include those who have traditional contracts of apprenticeship (see 1.2.85), and those taking part in Apprenticeships, Advanced Apprenticeships, Modern Apprenticeships or Foundation Modern Apprenticeship programmes. In Scotland, apprentices include those taking part in Skillseekers or Modern Apprenticeship programmes leading to a National Vocational Qualification Level 2 or 3 or a Scottish Vocational Qualification Level 2 or 3.

Apprentices aged 16 to 18 are not entitled to the NMW. Apprentices aged 19 and over are not entitled to the NMW in the first year of their apprenticeship, but become entitled in the second year of their apprenticeship and beyond. However, there is a minimum contractual payment fixed by law of £95 per week for apprentices.

What is the rate?

2.1.27 The various rates of the NMW are reviewed from time to time. Currently (from October 2009) the standard rate of the NMW stands at £5.80 per hour. Workers aged 18 to 21 are entitled to £4.83 per hour and those aged 16 and 17 are entitled to £3.57 per hour. (Although these rates discriminate on the ground of age, they do not breach the age equality legislation, which contains a specific exemption to allow employers to pay workers who are under 22 less than the standard rate of the NMW.)

The pay reference period

2.1.28 A worker must be paid an average of the NMW over his or her pay reference period. A worker's pay reference period is generally the interval at which he or she is paid, whether daily, weekly or monthly. But the maximum period is one month, so a worker who is paid quarterly has a pay reference period of one month.

The payments that count

2.1.29 In order to assess whether a worker has received an average of the NMW in a particular pay reference period, it is necessary to identify what payments count towards the NMW for that period.

2.1.30 Any payments made to the worker in the period are taken into account, as is any pay earned in the current period but not paid until the next. This could include, for example, overtime or commission that a monthly-paid worker receives in the month after the one in which it is earned. Most of an annual bonus is counted in the pay reference period in which it is paid. A proportion can, however, be allocated to the previous period. For example, one-twelfth of an annual bonus can be allocated to the previous period for a monthly-paid employee.

Calculating the payments

2.1.31 Broadly, the amount that counts towards the NMW is the result of this calculation:

1. Take gross basic wages or salary, including performance-related pay and bonuses (apportioned where relevant, as explained above).

2. Deduct any premium element for overtime or shift working (that is, the difference between the rate paid for overtime or shift working and the worker's basic rate of pay).

3. Deduct any special allowances, such as allowances for unsocial hours, 'on call' duties or location allowances, if these are not consolidated into basic pay.

If an employer provides accommodation, that counts towards the NMW. The amount that counts is £4.51 multiplied by the number of days in the reference period for which accommodation is provided. Accommodation is the only benefit in kind that can be counted towards the NMW.

Hours that count

2.1.32 The hours for which the NMW must be paid depend upon the way in which the worker is paid for the work he or she does. There are four different categories of work:

- time work;
- salaried hours work;
- output work;
- unmeasured work.

Time work

2.1.33 This is work that is paid according to the number of hours the employee works, but the employee is not paid an annual salary. In practice, most workers who are expected to be at work for a set number of hours (such as 40 hours a week) or at set times (such as 8 am to 5 pm from Monday to Friday) will be time workers, unless they are on an annual salary.

2.1.34 All the hours when a time worker is required to be available for work are taken into account, but rest breaks are not. Time when the worker is 'on call' at or near the workplace counts, but time when the worker is 'on call' at home does not. If a worker is permitted to sleep at or near the workplace during specifically allocated hours and is provided with suitable sleeping facilities, those allocated hours do not count as time work unless and until the worker is called on to work. Travelling during normal working hours can be counted but travel between home and work cannot. Time spent on training during normal working hours also counts, as does training outside normal working hours if done at the worker's normal place of work. Time when the worker is on holiday, sick leave or maternity leave does not count, but any payment the worker receives for those absences is also left out of the calculation of whether he or she has received the NMW.

Salaried hours work

2.1.35 This covers time where an employee receives an annual salary, paid in equal instalments, for a basic minimum number of hours in a year. Those basic hours may be expressed as an annual total, as in an annualised hours contract, or as a weekly or monthly figure, such as 35 hours a week. Most office workers and non-manual workers with large companies are likely to be salaried hours workers.

2.1.36   In the main, hours count for salaried hours workers on the same basis as for time workers. However, hours of absence, including rest breaks, holidays, sick or maternity leave, are counted as salaried hours work, but only if the worker is paid his or her normal pay during those hours and they count towards the worker's basic hours. Broadly, the salaried hours that must be taken into account in a pay reference period are the basic hours that must be worked in the year divided by the number of times the worker is paid in the year.

Output work

2.1.37   This is work that is paid according to output, whether that be the number of things the employee makes or processes, the number of sales the employee achieves or the number of transactions the employee completes. So, a homeworker who is paid by the piece or a worker who is paid on the basis of commission is doing output work, unless his or her hours are fixed, in which case he or she is doing time work.

2.1.38   The hours of an output worker are assessed in one of two ways. One method simply involves counting the number of hours spent by the worker in producing the type of piece or performing the type of task concerned during the pay reference period. Another method applies, however, if the work is 'rated output work', as explained below. Whichever method applies, if the output worker is a homeworker who has to travel to an employer's premises to pick up and deliver work, that travelling time also counts as output work for which the NMW must be paid.

Rated output work

2.1.39   Work can be rated output work only if the worker's contract does not set any normal, minimum or maximum working hours, the employer does not in practice decide what hours the worker must work, and the employer has calculated the mean hourly output rate for the piece or task involved. The employer can calculate this mean rate by testing the output of its other output workers doing the same work in similar circumstances. Alternatively, the employer can estimate the rate, by reference to the rate at which its other output workers produce pieces or perform tasks that are reasonably similar to those in question, or produce pieces or tasks that are the same as those in question but in different working circumstances.

2.1.40 Where a worker is engaged on rated output work, the number of hours that count for NMW purposes is 120 per cent of the number of hours that a worker working at the mean rate would have taken to produce the number of pieces or perform the number of tasks that the worker in question produced or performed.

2.1.41 An employer must give rated output workers a written notice containing certain specified information. In particular, the notice must explain what their mean hourly output rate is and how it was calculated, and give the telephone number of the NMW Helpline.

Unmeasured work

2.1.42 This covers all work that does not fit into one of the other three categories already mentioned. It would include work where the worker has certain tasks to do but no specified hours or times when they must be done, or where the worker is required to work only as and when needed.

2.1.43 There are two ways of assessing the amount of unmeasured work that counts for the NMW. One is for the worker and the employer to come to a written agreement on a realistic average number of hours that the worker is likely to spend each day doing the work. If no 'daily average' agreement is reached, then the actual hours worked during the pay reference period are the ones that count.

NMW calculation

2.1.44 To calculate whether a worker has been paid the NMW, take the payments that count in the pay reference period, divide them by the hours of work that count in that period, and compare the result with the rate of the NMW that applies to the worker concerned.

Salaries close to NMW

2.1.45 Complications can arise where an employee who does salaried hours work works longer than the basic annual hours before the end of the year. In this case the employer will need to ensure that the employee is paid the NMW for any hours he or she works in excess of the basic annual hours in the pay reference period when he or she first starts working them, and for the remaining reference periods in the year. Likewise, an employer may need to adjust the final salary payment to a worker who leaves its employment having worked more than the basic annual hours, or the basic hours for the part of the year that he or she has worked. The government guide to the NMW (see 9.2.1) gives guidance on how to make these calculations.

2.1.46   In practice, these calculations will usually be necessary only where a worker is paid a salary that is close to the NMW or works substantially longer than basic hours.

Record keeping

2.1.47   All employers are required to keep records that show that they are paying at least the NMW. If they have reached a training agreement or a daily average agreement with a worker, they must keep a copy. If they employ rated output workers, they must also keep a copy of the notice they have given to the workers explaining their mean hourly output rate (see 2.1.41) and a copy of the data they used to calculate that rate and the rate to be paid for each piece produced or task performed. It is a criminal offence for an employer not to keep adequate records or to falsify its records. Another good reason for keeping adequate records is that, if there is a dispute, it is up to the employer to prove that it has paid the NMW.

2.1.48   The legislation does not specify what records have to be kept. However, the closer to the NMW a worker's pay is, the more detailed the records will need to be on hours worked and payments received. The records can be kept in any form, but the employer must be able to produce them for a particular worker in relation to a particular pay reference period in a single document.

Retention of records

2.1.49   The NMW legislation requires records to be retained for only three years from the end of the pay reference period following the pay reference period that the records cover. Nevertheless, a worker has six years in which to bring a claim that he or she has not been paid the NMW and it would therefore be advisable for employers to retain their records for at least six years.

Access request

2.1.50   Workers who reasonably believe that they are not receiving the NMW are entitled to see their pay records and to copy them. A worker must put any request for access in writing, and the employer must produce the records within 14 days or within whatever further time is agreed with the worker. When inspecting the records, a worker is entitled to be accompanied by any person of his or her choice. HM Revenue and Customs, which is responsible for enforcing the NMW, is also entitled to see employers' records.

Discrimination in pay

2.1.51   The principles of discrimination law, outlined in Chapter 3.1 of this Guide, apply just as much to payment systems as they do to any other aspect of an employer's personnel practices. The broad principles are that an employer must not discriminate against an employee directly or indirectly on the grounds of sex, race, age, religion or sexual orientation. Nor must an employer treat a disabled employee unfavourably on the grounds of his or her disability or for a reason that relates to his or her disability unless, in the latter case, it has objective justification for doing so. Unjustified pay discrimination against part-timers and fixed-term employees is also unlawful (see 2.1.79 and 2.1.88).

2.1.52   It is important to remember that the discrimination legislation protects not only employees but also agency workers and other workers, including the self-employed, who have a contract with an employer to carry out work personally. The legislation on part-timers covers employees and anyone else who has a contract with a company to carry out work personally, although it does not cover self-employed workers who are contracting with a company in the course of their profession or business. The protection from discrimination on grounds of fixed-term status covers employees only.

Sex discrimination in pay

2.1.53   Under the Equal Pay Act 1970, men and women who are employed on equal work are entitled to equal terms and conditions, including pay, unless their employer can demonstrate that the difference in their terms is not due to the difference in their sex. This summary of how the Act works assumes that the person claiming equal pay is a woman, although the legislation also outlaws pay discrimination against men.

Bringing a claim

2.1.54 In order to bring a claim, a woman must be able to identify a male colleague in the same employment, usually referred to as her 'comparator', who is employed on work that is equal to hers but is entitled to better terms than she is. Her claim could relate to any term of her comparator's contract. So her claim could just as well be based on sick pay or holiday entitlement or access to a bonus as on basic pay. (It would also be possible for her to allege that she had been discriminated against in relation to non-contractual terms, but that type of claim would be brought under the Sex Discrimination Act 1975 rather than the Equal Pay Act.)

Choosing a comparator

2.1.55 The comparator the claimant chooses could be an employee. He could also be any other person who has a contract with the company personally to carry out any work. He must, however, be employed by the same employer as the claimant or by an associated employer (see 8.1.9), such as another company in the same corporate group. The claimant can choose a comparator at the same workplace as her. She can also choose a comparator who works elsewhere, provided broadly the same terms and conditions of employment apply at both workplaces.

Equal work

2.1.56 The comparator and the claimant are employed on equal work if:

- His job is the same or broadly similar in nature to hers. It is the content of the job that is important here, not the job title, and what is done in practice, not what the job descriptions say.

- His job has been rated as equivalent to hers under the employer's job evaluation scheme.

- His job is of equal value to hers in terms of the demands it makes in relation to factors such as effort, skill and decision-making.

Equal value claims

2.1.57 It is 'equal value' claims that probably have the most potential for disrupting employers' established payment systems. Successful equal value claims have, for example, been brought by a cook claiming equal pay with a painter, a thermal insulation engineer and a joiner; a clerk claiming equal pay with a storeman and a caretaker; a group personnel and training officer claiming equal pay with a divisional sales trainer; and a packer claiming equal pay with a labourer.

2.1.58 It is for the employment tribunal that hears an equal value claim to decide whether two jobs are of equal value. The tribunal can decide the issue on its own or with the help of an independent expert. Broadly speaking, a job will be evaluated by identifying the demands made on the jobholder (such as effort, skill and decision-making), assessing the size of those demands, and then giving them more or less weight according to their importance to the organisation.

Job evaluation schemes

2.1.59 An equal value claim will be thrown out at an early stage if the employer's own job evaluation scheme has given the woman's job a lower rating than her comparator's. This has led some employers to adopt job evaluation schemes. Further information on job evaluation is given in the box below.

Job evaluation systems

Job evaluation involves assessing the relative value of the jobs within an organisation. There are several reasons why a company might wish to introduce job evaluation:

- to establish pay equity within the organisation as a basis for introducing a new pay and benefits structure;
- to ensure that the company provides equal pay for men and women for equal work;
- to assist career management by clarifying possible progression routes, particularly lateral ones;

- to clarify and rationalise the organisation's structure after a merger;
- to support and complement other human resource initiatives such as performance management;
- to benchmark salaries and benefits either nationally or internationally.

Types of scheme

Job evaluation schemes may be analytical or non-analytical. Analytical schemes break jobs down into defined core components or factors and compare them on that basis. These schemes can be designed for a specific employer. Alternatively, they may be proprietary schemes that are capable of being applied to many organisations with minimal adjustment, which are usually provided by management consultancies. Using a proprietary scheme can be useful when benchmarking salaries.

Non-analytical schemes examine jobs as a whole and compare them on that basis. Because they do not break jobs down into their constituent demand factors, non-analytical schemes are not capable of providing a defence to an equal value claim (see 2.1.60). There are three types of non-analytical schemes:

- job ranking – which ranks the jobs in an organisation in order of perceived importance;
- job classification – which assigns jobs to pre-defined grades;
- paired comparison – which compares pairs of jobs to assess whether they are more, less or equally demanding, and develops a ranking from those results.

2.1.60   In order to be able to block an equal value claim, a scheme must meet certain requirements. It must analyse jobs by their constituent demand factors, as a tribunal would do in an equal value claim, rather than evaluating the jobs as a whole. In other words, the scheme must be 'analytical'. Further, the scheme must not be directly or indirectly discriminatory on grounds of sex. The

Equality and Human Rights Commission has produced guidance on ensuring that job evaluation schemes are free of sex bias (see 9.2.1). Finally, the scheme must be 'suitable' to be relied upon, which implies that it must be regularly reviewed to ensure that it is up-to-date.

Employer's defence

2.1.61   Once the claimant has established that she and her comparator are employed on equal work, she is entitled to the same terms of employment as him, unless their employer can show that the difference in their terms is genuinely due to some factor other than the difference in their sex.

2.1.62   In order to establish this defence, the employer must be able to show that the reason for the difference in terms is not directly or indirectly discriminatory. Direct discrimination involves treating a person less favourably on the ground of his or her sex. So, for example, an employer would have no defence if a manager had recruited the woman on a lower salary than her comparator because he had made a conscious or unconscious assumption that she was working for 'pin money' whereas the comparator needed to earn a 'family wage'.

Indirect discrimination

2.1.63   An employer's pay practice will be indirectly discriminatory if it has the effect of disadvantaging a higher proportion of one sex than of the other, unless it can be objectively justified by a clear business need (see 3.1.48). For example, assume that the woman claiming equal pay is in a category of workers that is predominantly made up of women and has no access to a productivity bonus. Assume that her comparator is in a category of workers that is predominantly made up of men and does have access to a bonus. In order to defend her claim that she should receive a bonus, the employer will need to explain why it is not feasible or appropriate to offer the category of workers to which the woman belongs any reward for productivity. Likewise, if an employer excludes part-timers from its sick pay scheme and the majority of those part-timers are women, it will need to show clear business reasons for that rule, other than solely the desire to save money. (Part-timers of both sexes also have specific protection from discrimination in pay and conditions, as explained in 2.1.79 and 2.1.80.)

Questionnaires

2.1.64   It is important to be aware that an employee has the right to question her employer about the difference in pay between herself and a potential comparator, in order to establish the extent of any difference and the reasons for it. There is a potential penalty if the employer deliberately and without reasonable excuse fails to reply to her questionnaire, or replies in a way that is evasive or unclear: an employment tribunal hearing any equal pay claim she may later bring is entitled to draw whatever inferences it considers just to draw from the employer's conduct, including an inference that the difference in pay is due to unlawful sex discrimination.

Code of Practice

2.1.65   The Equality and Human Rights Commission (EHRC) has produced a Code of Practice on eliminating sex discrimination in pay systems (see 9.2.1). Employment tribunals must refer to this Code when they are hearing equal pay claims, if they consider it relevant to the issues they have to decide. It is therefore advisable for employers to bear the contents of the Code in mind when setting up or reviewing payment systems.

Equal pay review

2.1.66   At the heart of the Code is a recommendation that employers should carry out a pay systems review, an essential first step in establishing whether any unlawful sex discrimination exists.

2.1.67   The EHRC has published checklists and a toolkit for carrying out an equal pay audit (see 9.2.1) to give employers guidance on conducting an equal pay review. In summary, a review involves the following steps:

   1. Decide the scope of the review and identify the data required.

   2. Identify where men and women are doing equal work – that is, like work, work rated as equivalent or work of equal value. In some cases, this may

involve introducing a job evaluation scheme, or reviewing an existing job evaluation scheme to ensure that it is not sex-biased. The Kit gives some guidance on estimating equal value if the employer does not have a job evaluation scheme.

3. Collect and compare pay data to identify any significant pay gaps between men and women doing equal work.

4. Establish the causes of any significant pay gaps and assess whether the gaps are justifiable.

5. Where the gaps are not justifiable, develop an Equal Pay Action Plan to close the gaps and change the policies and practices that contributed to them. Where the gaps are justifiable, review and monitor pay practices to ensure that they continue to be non-discriminatory.

2.1.68 The checklists and toolkit include detailed guidance notes on the legal framework, gathering data, analysing statistics, reviewing job evaluation schemes for sex bias, estimating whether jobs are of equal value, and reviewing payments systems, policies and practices. (The EHRC has also produced more basic guidance, aimed at small businesses without in-house personnel specialists, on how to carry out an equal pay review (see 9.2.1).)

2.1.69 An Action Plan to deliver equal pay may involve changes to rules or practices, including those in collective agreements, that have led to discrimination. Chapter 5.1 of this Guide discusses the legal and practical issues involved in changing employees' terms and conditions, including terms originating in collective agreements.

Racial, religious and sexual orientation discrimination

2.1.70 It is unlawful for an employer to discriminate directly or indirectly on the ground of race, religion or sexual orientation in the way it pays its employees.

2.1.71 It is direct discrimination for an employer to pay an individual less than it pays or would pay an employee of another race, religion or sexual orientation, if it does so on grounds of race, religion or sexual orientation. For example, it would be unlawful for a company to give an employee a minimal or nil annual pay increase, if the manager carrying out the performance appraisal on which the increase was based was influenced in his or her appraisal by conscious or unconscious racial prejudice against the employee.

2.1.72   Indirect discrimination can arise if one category of workers made up predominantly of one racial group is paid less than another category made up predominantly of a different racial group and the employer cannot justify that practice. For example, if workers on one shift are predominantly of Asian ethnic origin and are excluded from anti-social hours payments, but workers on another shift, who are predominantly not of Asian ethnic origin, are entitled to those payments, the employer will need to show why the type of working involved in one shift justifies the extra payment while that involved in the other does not.

Age discrimination

2.1.73   It is unlawful for an employer to pay one employee more than another on the ground of the employee's age, unless it has objective justification for doing so. It is also unlawful for an employer to discriminate indirectly on the ground of age, by adopting pay practices that put people in a particular age group at a disadvantage and that are not justified.

2.1.74   On the face of it, a practice of basing benefits, such as pay rates and holidays, on length of service is likely to amount to indirect discrimination, as it puts younger employees at a disadvantage compared with older employees. The age equality legislation provides a partial exemption, however, for this type of discrimination. Basing benefits on length of service is lawful for the first five years of an employee's service. After that, it remains lawful to base benefits on length of service, if it reasonably appears to the employer that the way in which it uses the criterion of length of service fulfils a business need, such as encouraging the loyalty or motivation, or rewarding the experience, of workers.

Benefits for partners

2.1.75   Some employers extend some benefits, such as private healthcare cover, to the partners of their employees. In order to avoid breaching the legislation on sexual orientation discrimination, employers must either restrict benefits to married partners and civil partners (that is, same-sex couples who have officially registered as civil partners) or extend the benefits to all partners, including same-sex partners.

Disability discrimination

2.1.76   There are three ways in which an employer can contravene the Disability Discrimination Act 1995. One is by treating a disabled employee unfavourably on the grounds of his or her disability (see 3.1.48). Another is by treating the employee unfavourably for a reason relating to the employee's disability, without having objective justification for doing so (see 3.1.49). The third is by failing to meet its duty to make reasonable adjustments to its employment practices to accommodate a disabled employee (see 3.1.54).

2.1.77   These principles apply just as much to payment systems as to any other aspect of employment, as this example from the Code of Practice issued under the Act illustrates:

> A disabled home-worker, who is paid a fixed rate for each item he produces, has a reduced output rate because he or she does not have the right equipment to do the job to the best of his or her ability. It is likely to be a reasonable adjustment for the employer to provide that equipment, possibly with funding or advice from the Access to Work scheme, to improve the disabled worker's output and consequently his or her pay.

2.1.78   Disability discrimination in pensions is dealt with in 2.4.44 and 2.4.45.

Part-timers

2.1.79   Since women make up the majority of the part-time workforce, pay discrimination against part-timers may amount to indirect sex discrimination against women (see 2.1.53 and 3.1.74).

2.1.80   All part-timers, whether male or female, also have protection from being treated unfavourably because they are part-timers under the Part-time Workers (Prevention of Less Favourable Treatment) Regulations 2000. The broad principle established by these Regulations is that part-timers must be treated in the same way as full-timers, unless their employer has objective grounds for treating them differently. According to government guidance on how to comply with the Regulations (see 9.2.1), treating part-timers less favourably than full-timers is justified on objective grounds if the employer can show that it is necessary and appropriate to achieve a legitimate business objective. For the purposes of the Regulations, full-timers and part-timers are workers who are paid wholly or in part by reference to the time they work and who are identifiable as full-time or part-time from the employer's custom and practice.

Comparable full-timers

2.1.81   In order for it to be possible to establish that a part-timer has been treated less favourably than a full-timer, he or she must work under similar types of contract. For example, it is not possible to make a comparison between the terms and conditions of a part-time 'worker' (see 1.2.76) or traditional apprentice (see 1.2.85) and those of a full-time employee. Comparisons are possible, however, between employees working under fixed-term contracts and employees with open-ended contracts. The comparison must also be between workers doing the same or broadly similar work, taking into account, where relevant, their level of qualifications, skills and experience.

2.1.82   A different comparison applies for part-time workers whose hours have been reduced from full-time, or who were full-timers but have returned to work on part-time hours after a period of under 12 months' absence from work. They are entitled to the same terms as they had while full-timers, unless their employer can objectively justify treating them otherwise.

Equal treatment

2.1.83   In the context of pay, the upshot of the Regulations is that part-timers should be on the same basic rate of pay as full-timers, and should be given the same premiums for working shifts and anti-social hours, unless their employer has some objective justification for paying them differently. They should also receive the same hourly rate of overtime as full-timers. The Regulations expressly permit employers not to pay part-time workers premium overtime rates until they have worked normal full-time hours.

2.1.84   The same principle of equal treatment applies to all contractual terms, although a part-timer's entitlement will reflect the hours he or she works, where relevant. Therefore if a full-timer who works 38 hours a week is entitled to 65 working days' occupational sick pay and a Christmas bonus of £100, a part-timer on 19 hours a week should be entitled to 32.5 days' sick pay and a bonus of £50, unless the employer can objectively justify giving the part-timer less. (In this example, both full-timer and part-timer would get 13 weeks' sick pay, but the full-timer would receive five days' sick pay each week and the part-timer two and a half days' sick pay each week.)

2.1.85 If a benefit cannot be reduced pro rata, as in the case of health insurance or a company car, the employer may be able to justify not extending that benefit to part-timers on the grounds that it would involve the company in disproportionate cost. The government's guidance on the Regulations suggests that an employer might nevertheless consider, as a matter of good practice, calculating the financial value of the benefit and applying that pro rata to the part-time employee.

Written reasons

2.1.86 Part-timers who believe they may have been discriminated against because of their part-time status can ask their employer for written reasons for their treatment. If an employer fails to respond to a request without reasonable excuse, or provides a response that is evasive or unclear, and the part-timer then brings a claim under the Regulations, the employment tribunal that hears that claim is entitled to take the employer's conduct into account when deciding whether it has complied with the Regulations.

Victimisation

2.1.87 It is unlawful for an employer to penalise a worker for asserting or enforcing his or her rights under the Regulations, or for supporting someone else in bringing a claim. It is also automatically unfair to dismiss an employee on these grounds, regardless of the employee's length of service. This protection does not apply where a worker has alleged that an employer has breached the Regulations and the allegation was not only false but also not made in good faith.

Fixed-term employees

2.1.88   Under the Fixed-term Employees (Prevention of Less Favourable Treatment) Regulations 2002, employers must not give fixed-term employees less favourable pay and benefits than comparable permanent employees, unless they have objective justification for doing so. The Regulations are summarised in 1.2.90.

2.1.89   The Regulations require in particular that any service qualification for a benefit must apply to fixed-term employees in the same way as to permanent employees. So, for example, if employees are entitled to an increase in their pay rate after a year's service, that must apply to those who have been working on a fixed-term basis for a year as well as those who have a year's service under a permanent contract.

Valuing the overall package

2.1.90   The Regulations state that one of the ways in which it is possible to justify treating a fixed-term employee less favourably in respect of any contractual benefit is to show that the employee's contract, taken as a whole, is no less favourable than that of a comparable permanent employee. The government guidance on the Regulations (see 9.1.2) says that, when assessing the value of an employee's contract as a package, benefits should be given their objective monetary worth, rather than the value the employer or employee perceive them to have. So, for example, it would be justified to give a fixed-term employee four weeks' holiday entitlement when a comparable permanent employee gets five weeks, if the fixed-term employee's salary was greater than the permanent employee's by the equivalent of one week's holiday pay.

2.1.91   An employer may still be justified in giving a fixed-term employee a less favourable overall package than a permanent employee, if the difference between the two packages is one or more terms that the employer can objectively justify not providing to the fixed-term employee.

Deductions from pay

2.1.92   Employers make many deductions from employees' pay, from tax and National Insurance contributions through to deductions for union subscriptions and repayment of loans. There is, however, a general legal rule set out in the Employment Rights Act 1996 that an employer is not entitled to make a deduction from a worker's pay unless certain conditions are met. The rule specifies which workers and sums are protected (see 2.1.94 and 2.1.95), which deductions are covered (see 2.1.96–100) and the conditions that must be met for a deduction to be lawful (see 2.1.101). Payments from workers to employers are regulated in the same way.

2.1.93   It is important to note at the outset that, for the purposes of this rule, a deduction can include a shortfall in, or a complete failure to pay, any sum that is due to the worker.

Scope of protection

2.1.94   This protection is not limited to employees. It also applies to workers who contract with a company to perform any work personally, provided that they are not dealing with the company as part of a profession or business undertaking that they are running. Therefore many casual workers, self-employed labourers and homeworkers will be protected, even if they are not employees.

Which deductions?

2.1.95   The legislation regulates not only deductions from a worker's wages or salary, but also deductions from many other payments, including bonuses, commission, holiday pay, statutory sick pay, statutory paternity pay, statutory adoption pay and statutory maternity pay. Benefits in kind are included only if they have a fixed monetary value and can be exchanged for money, goods or services. Shortfalls in a loan or an advance of wages, a payment of expenses or a redundancy payment are not, however, covered.

What is a deduction?

2.1.96   An employer is viewed as having made a deduction from a worker's pay if it has paid the worker less than what was properly payable under the worker's contract. So the legislation covers shortfalls and complete non-payments as well as deductions that an employer is making for a specific purpose such as the repayment of a loan. It could apply, for example, where an employer has unilaterally reduced a worker's pay. It could also apply where an employer has failed to pay a bonus or any other payment that is due to the worker, even if this was because the employer misunderstood the worker's contractual rights. However, a shortfall that is due to a mathematical error of calculation by the employer is not viewed as a deduction.

Recovering overpayments

2.1.97   Deductions to recover overpayments of wages or expenses are not covered by this legislation. It would nevertheless be advisable for a company that intends to recover an overpayment by deducting it from a worker's pay to agree a timetable for repayment with the worker and not to deduct more than a reasonable proportion from each pay packet. If it did not do so, the employer could face an allegation that it was acting in breach of its implied obligation not to act in a way that destroyed the trust and confidence between itself and the employee (see 1.2.45).

2.1.98   If a company decides to ask a worker to repay an overpayment, rather than make a deduction from his or her pay, the worker may have a defence to that claim. But the defence would apply only if the worker had no reason to believe that he or she was not entitled to the original payment and the worker had changed his or her position on the basis of the payment by, for example, taking on additional financial commitments.

Industrial action deductions

2.1.99   Deductions that are made from a worker's pay because the worker has taken part in industrial action are not covered by this legislation. It could not, therefore, be used to challenge an employer that decided not to pay a worker for any days when he or she was not ready and willing to work because he or she was taking part with others in industrial action. The worker could nevertheless sue the employer for breach of contract if the employer made an excessive deduction from the worker's pay in these circumstances. (An employee's entitlement to pay during industrial action is explained in more detail in 6.3.63–6.3.69.)

Check-off

2.1.100   A company may have agreed with a trade union that it will deduct members' subscriptions from their wages or salary and pay them over to the union. This is usually referred to as a 'check-off' arrangement. Provided the worker has agreed in writing to the arrangement, deductions made under it are outside the scope of this legislation. They are, however, regulated by separate legislation on 'check-off' (see 6.1.46).

Lawful deductions

2.1.101   It is lawful for an employer to make a deduction from wages if one of these conditions is met:

- The deduction is required or authorised by legislation. This covers deductions for tax and National Insurance contributions and attachment of earnings orders made by courts.

- The deduction is required or authorised by a term of the worker's contract. The term may be express or implied, oral or in writing, but the employer must have given the employee a copy or a written explanation of the term before the deduction is made.

- The worker has agreed in writing to the deduction before it is made, and the deduction relates to an event that has not yet occurred.

New term or consent

2.1.102   If a company wants to make a deduction but the worker's contract does not currently authorise it to do so, it may decide to introduce a new term into the worker's contract or ask for the worker's agreement to the deduction. But any new term or consent cannot validly authorise a deduction that relates to anything that happened before the new term was introduced or the worker gave his or her consent. For example, if an employee crashes a company vehicle and is only then asked to agree in writing to the cost of repairs being deducted from his or her wages, the deductions will be unlawful. It is also important to remember that the introduction of a new contract term requires the employee's consent (see 5.1.4).

Contract terms

2.1.103 In the light of this, it is advisable for a company to include in its contracts of employment from the outset a term authorising any deductions that it envisages making from its employees' pay. In order to be effective, the term should clearly state the payment from which the deduction may be made, such as, for example, basic pay and commission. It should also set out what the deductions may relate to, such as recovery of loss or damage caused by the employee's failure to take proper care in carrying out his or her job duties. Alternatively, an employer may choose to obtain an employee's specific written consent to deductions, provided these relate to events that are yet to happen. For example, an employee could be asked to agree in writing to the repayment of a season ticket loan through deductions from his or her basic pay, at the time when the loan is first agreed but before it is made.

Recovery of training costs

2.1.104 Some employers include terms in their employment contracts allowing them to recover training costs in certain circumstances, often where the employee leaves the company within a certain period after completing the training. These terms are likely to be legally valid provided the amount to be recovered is a genuine estimate of the loss caused to the company by the employee's departure. The amount should not, therefore, exceed the costs that the employer has incurred in providing the training. It should also reduce over time, to take into account the service that the employee has provided after receiving the training and before leaving the company. Further advice on using this type of clause can be obtained from us.

Other deductions from pay

2.1.105 There are various other deductions that an employer may be required to make from an employee's wages by law. (These do not fall foul of the legislation on deductions from pay (see 2.1.92) because either they are viewed as authorised or they are expressly excluded from that legislation.) They include:

Deductions from pay

1. *Income tax.* Employers are responsible for deducting income tax from employees' pay and accounting for it to HM Revenue and Customs, under the Pay As You Earn system. The Revenue sends employers detailed information on the system each year.

2. *National Insurance contributions.* Employers are also required to deduct National Insurance contributions from employees' pay. The annual information pack sent to employers by HM Revenue and Customs includes information about this.

3. *Employees' contributions to a stakeholder pension scheme* (see 2.4.79).

4. *Attachment of earnings orders, earnings arrestments and deduction from earnings orders.* Employers may be required to deduct money from employees' pay under an order from a court, a local authority or the Child Support Agency. These orders are made to recover judgments

   relating to debts, fines, council tax arrears and maintenance payments from an employee's pay. When an order is sent to an employer it will usually be accompanied by information on the employer's obligations and rights. The employer must, for example, notify the employee of the deductions it is making, and must let the relevant body know if the employee leaves. Employers are entitled to deduct an extra £1 from the employee's wages along with each deduction, to offset the cost of administering the order.

5. *Repayment of student loans.* Employers may be required to make deductions from the pay of employees who have a student loan to repay. Employers will know that they need to make these deductions if they receive a 'start notification' from HM Revenue and Customs or if a new employee has a 'Y' marked in the Student Loan box on his or her P45. Repayments are based on the employee's income. Further information on collection of student loans is available from the Revenue (see 9.2.1).

2.2

Family rights

Overview

2.2.1   This chapter of the Guide deals with family rights in the workplace. Many employers give their employees family rights under their contracts of employment (see 2.2.6) but the bulk of this chapter describes the rights given to employees by legislation.

2.2.2   Initially, it was only mothers who had family rights, in the form of maternity leave (see 2.2.25) and maternity pay (see 2.2.47). More recently, family rights have been introduced that apply to fathers and same-sex partners as well as mothers. Both men and women, including adoptive parents, may be entitled to parental leave (see 2.2.128). Further, employees who have or adopt a child may be entitled to paternity leave and pay (see 2.2.85) or adoption leave and pay (see 2.2.103).

2.2.3   Many employees find it difficult to combine their work and family responsibilities. In recognition of this, the law gives employees the right to ask their employer to change their hours or place of work in order to enable them to care for their children aged 16 or under, or 18 if disabled, and to care for certain adults (see 2.2.150).

2.2.4   All employees, not just parents, have the right not to be unreasonably refused unpaid time off work to deal with emergencies involving their dependants. Although the dependant may be a child, he or she could also be the

2.2.5 employee's partner, elderly relative or even, in certain circumstances, neighbour. This chapter concludes with a summary of this right (see 2.2.161).

2.2.5 The government has announced that it will introduce additional paternity leave that will apply to children born on or after 3 April 2011. Under these proposals, mothers who have returned to work will be able to transfer up to six months of any remaining leave to the father. The earliest start date will be 20 weeks after the child's birth. Any part of the father's additional paternity leave that falls within what would have been the mother's maternity pay period will be paid at the same rate as her statutory maternity pay. Any additional transferred leave will be unpaid. There are similar proposals for parents who adopt children. Contact us for details.

Contractual rights

2.2.6 It is important to remember that employers may provide employees with benefits under their contracts of employment that are more favourable than the rights guaranteed by employment legislation.

Exceeding statute

2.2.7 It is common, for example, for larger employers to offer maternity pay that is more generous than the statutory minimum. Many employers also give paternity pay based on normal wages or salary and allow some time off with pay to deal with family emergencies, and in particular bereavement. Even small employers may find that it suits their business requirements and their employees' personal needs not to operate within the confines of the legislation.

2.2.8 In all these cases, employees' family rights are contractual, based either on their contracts of employment or on the specific agreement that they have reached with their employer. For these employees and their employers, the complexities of the employment legislation are relevant only insofar as the employees' contractual rights cannot fall below the level provided by the legislation in any respect.

Family rights

Conditions

2.2.9 To the extent that its family benefits are more generous than the statutory minimum, an employer can make those benefits dependent on the employee meeting certain conditions. It is common, for example, for companies that provide generous maternity pay to make it conditional on the employee completing a certain period of service after her return to work, failing which she will be required to repay whatever she has received in excess of statutory maternity pay.

2.2.10 It is important for an employer to make clear any conditions that apply to contractual family benefits.

Health and safety

2.2.11 Perhaps the most important legal issue facing the employer of a woman who is pregnant or has recently given birth is the need to meet its duty to protect the health and safety of the employee and her child. There are two aspects to this: the employer must respect the employee's right to time off for antenatal care (see 2.2.12); and the employer must take whatever steps are necessary to deal with the specific risks to health and safety that the employee may face in the workplace as a pregnant woman or new mother (see 2.2.17).

Antenatal care

2.2.12 Under the Employment Rights Act 1996, any pregnant employee, regardless of her length of service with her employer, has the right not to be unreasonably refused paid time off during working hours to receive antenatal care.

2.2.13 Antenatal care can include exercise and relaxation classes and may also include parentcraft classes. The appointment must be made on the advice of the employee's doctor, midwife or health visitor. After the first appointment, the company can ask the employee to produce a certificate confirming her pregnancy and written evidence, such as her appointment card, that the appointment has been made.

2.2.14   An employee is entitled to sufficient time off to enable her to keep her appointment. So she may need to be allowed travelling time to and from the appointment and waiting time when she gets there, as well as time for the appointment itself.

Reasonable right to time off

2.2.15   An employee does not have an absolute right to time off, only the right not to be unreasonably refused it. If, for example, she works only part-time hours and could arrange her appointment for outside working hours without much difficulty, it may be reasonable to refuse her time off. On the other hand, a company does not have the right to ask an employee to alter her working hours so that the appointment falls outside her normal work time, or to make up her time off at another time.

2.2.16   It is automatically unfair for an employer to dismiss a woman for claiming her right to time off for antenatal care, or to select her for redundancy for that reason, regardless of her length of service. Dismissing a woman, or treating her unfavourably in any other way, because of this right to time off is also likely to amount to sex discrimination.

Health and safety risks

2.2.17   All employers are under a legal obligation, under the Management of Health and Safety at Work Regulations 1999, to carry out an assessment of the risks to health and safety in their workplace. Using this assessment as a basis, the employer must then plan what steps it needs to take to protect its workforce from those risks.

Risks to new or expectant mothers

2.2.18   If an employer employs any women of childbearing age, its assessment must include any risk that might be posed to the health and safety of a 'new or expectant mother'. This means a woman who is pregnant or breastfeeding or who has given birth within the previous six months.

2.2.19   If the assessment reveals a risk to an individual employee who is a new or expectant mother, the employer's first step should be to take whatever

Family rights

preventive or protective action is required by any specific legislation that covers the hazard concerned.

2.2.20   For example, a pregnant woman is at particular risk from manual handling injuries. It may be that this risk could be adequately addressed by implementing the requirements of the Manual Handling Operations Regulations 1992. But if that would not be enough to avoid the risk, then the employer must alter the woman's working conditions or hours of work to protect her. That might mean, for example, adjusting her job duties so that she is not involved in the heavier of the manual handling operations that would normally be included in her work.

Alternative work

2.2.21   If altering a woman's working conditions or hours of work would not be reasonable or would not avoid the risk, then the Employment Rights Act 1996 requires her employer to consider whether it would be possible to offer the woman suitable alternative work. If it is, then the work must be offered, and on terms and conditions that are broadly similar to those that apply to the employee's normal job.

2.2.22   If no suitable alternative work is available, or if the woman refuses an offer of alternative work, then the employer must suspend the employee from work for as long as is necessary to avoid the risk. An employee who is suspended on maternity grounds is entitled to her usual pay during her suspension, unless she has unreasonably refused an offer of suitable alternative work, in which case she can be suspended without pay.

Night workers

2.2.23   There is a special rule for night workers. If a new or expectant mother does night work, and she has a certificate from her doctor or midwife that shows that it is necessary for her health and safety that she should not work at night for a specified period, then the employer must consider whether it would be possible to offer her suitable alternative day work. If the woman is transferred to day work, she is entitled to terms and conditions that are broadly similar to those that apply to night work. If a transfer to day work would not be possible,

Employment Guide 2010

or if the employee refuses an offer of day work, then the company must suspend the woman from work, as explained in 2.2.22.

Guidance

2.2.24　The Health and Safety Executive has produced useful guidance on the known risks to new and expectant mothers and what employers must do to comply with the law (see 9.2.2). The guidance also sets out some aspects of pregnancy that employers might want to take into account in considering their working arrangements and policies, even though these are not required by law.

Maternity leave

2.2.25　All women, however short their length of service, have the right to maternity leave. The details of this right are set out in the Employment Rights Act 1996 and the Maternity and Parental Leave etc Regulations 1999 (as amended). A woman has the right to maternity leave if she gives birth to a living child, however premature, or she has a stillbirth after 24 weeks of pregnancy.

2.2.26　All employees are entitled to 26 weeks' ordinary maternity leave and 26 weeks' additional maternity leave making 52 weeks in all.

Timing of leave

2.2.27　Generally, a woman can choose when her maternity leave begins, although this cannot be before the beginning of the eleventh week before her expected week of childbirth. But the start of an employee's leave can be triggered by two events. One is the birth of her baby. The other is her absence from work wholly or partly because of pregnancy in the last four weeks before her expected week of childbirth. In these circumstances, her leave begins the day after her pregnancy-related absence occurs or on the day after the baby is born.

2.2.28　If an employee is off work with a pregnancy-related illness in those four weeks, her leave can be triggered, even if she had planned to carry on working until just before her baby was due and had informed her employer of that. If it suits the employer and the employee that the woman's leave should not be triggered in this way, there is nothing to prevent them agreeing that her leave will begin on the date she planned, although it would be advisable to put that agreement in writing. If the woman is off work sick in the relevant period with an illness that is not connected with her pregnancy, her maternity leave is not triggered.

Length of leave

2.2.29 Ordinary maternity leave lasts 26 weeks and additional maternity leave runs for a further 26 weeks after that. A woman does not have to take her full leave entitlement, but it is a criminal offence for an employer to allow a woman to do any work in the two-week period after she gives birth, or in the four weeks after the birth if she works in a factory.

Notice requirements

2.2.30 In order to claim maternity leave, the employee must let her employer know the week in which her baby is due and the date she wants to start her leave. She must give the notice in or before the fifteenth week before her expected week of childbirth. She can change the date her leave begins, provided she gives her employer notice at least 28 days before the date she originally gave or the new date she wants her leave to start, whichever is the earlier. If for some reason it is not reasonably practicable for a woman to meet these deadlines, she must give notice as soon as it is reasonably practicable. The employer is entitled to ask her to put her leave date in writing.

2.2.31 If the woman's leave has been triggered because of a pregnancy-related absence in the four weeks before the baby is due, or by the birth of the baby, she must let her employer know as soon as she can that she is absent for that reason and give the date on which her absence began. The employer can ask her to put this in writing.

2.2.32 The employer is entitled to ask the employee to produce a certificate from a doctor or midwife confirming her expected week of childbirth. The doctor or midwife can issue this certificate from 20 weeks before the week the baby is due. The maternity leave legislation gives no time limit for the employee to produce the certificate, although, in order to protect her right to statutory maternity pay (see 2.2.48), she will normally have to do so by the end of her third week of maternity leave.

Confirmation of return date

2.2.33   Once a company receives notice from a woman that she is intending to take maternity leave, or if it hears from her that her maternity leave has been triggered by a pregnancy-related absence or the birth of her baby, it must write to her within 28 days, confirming the date by which she must return to work. If it does not do so, it will be restricted in its ability to postpone her early return to work or to discipline her for failing to return on time (see 2.2.68, 2.2.73 and 2.2.76). If the employee changes her mind about the start date of her leave, the employer must write to her again, within 28 days of the start of her leave, to confirm her amended date for return. The Department of Business, Innovation and Skills has produced a model letter that employers can use to confirm an employee's return date (see 9.2.2).

Entitlement to protection

2.2.34   It is important to note that women who do not meet their notice obligations do not lose all their employment rights.

2.2.35   If an employee fails to give proper notice before going on leave, she is not entitled to have her terms and conditions during ordinary maternity leave protected (see 2.2.38) and she could be viewed as being on unauthorised absence. But a woman who does not meet the notice requirements is still entitled to the protection of sex discrimination law and, if she has a year's service, unfair dismissal law.

2.2.36   An employer should therefore ensure that it does not treat a woman who fails to meet the notice requirements for maternity leave more severely than it would deal with any other employee who did not meet the notice requirements for a period of absence from work. If it is inclined to dismiss a woman who fails to meet the notice requirements, it must ensure that it has followed a fair procedure before doing so.

2.2.37   Because of the dangers of liability for unfair dismissal and sex discrimination, a company that is considering disciplining or dismissing an employee for failing to meet the notice requirements is strongly advised to contact us for advice before taking any action.

Rights during maternity leave

2.2.38   A woman on maternity leave (both ordinary and additional) is entitled to all her usual terms and conditions apart from 'remuneration'. For example, she continues to accrue any rights she has to service-related benefits, and she retains any rights she has to a company vehicle, unless it is solely for business use. 'Remuneration' is defined in the legislation as 'sums payable to an employee by way of wages or salary'. It is unclear whether this covers payments that the employee has opted to take in place of other benefits such as a car allowance. The specific issue of bonuses is discussed in 2.2.45.

2.2.39   Companies that are unclear as to whether a certain payment should be maintained during a woman's maternity leave are advised to obtain advice from us. Although the employee is not entitled to her normal pay during maternity leave, she is likely to be entitled to statutory maternity pay instead during the majority of her leave (see 2.2.50).

2.2.40   While on maternity leave, the employee is bound by all her usual obligations under her contract, except those that are inconsistent with her right to be absent on maternity leave. So, for example, she is still obliged to give proper notice if she decides to resign.

Pensions

2.2.41   The Social Security Act 1989 requires that during any period when an employee is receiving contractual or statutory maternity pay, she must be treated for pension purposes as if she were working normally and receiving her normal pay. The pension contributions that the employee is obliged to make, on the other hand, must be based on the pay she is actually receiving.

Holidays

2.2.42   Any entitlement that an employee has to paid holiday both under the Working Time Regulations 1998 (see 2.3.71) and her contract is unaffected by the fact that she may be on maternity leave for part of the leave year. An employee may lose her entitlement to holiday if she is not able to take it before the end of the holiday year. This area of law is complex and companies with particular problems should contact us.

Sex discrimination

2.2.43 As a general principle, a woman who is given the rights outlined above is not entitled to claim that she has been discriminated against on the ground of her sex, even if, as is likely, she is on less generous pay than her colleagues who are still at work. However, in order to avoid breaching the Equal Pay Act 1970 or the Sex Discrimination Act 1975, her employer must still ensure that it does not unduly penalise her for being on maternity leave.

2.2.44 A woman on maternity leave is entitled to have her pay rate reviewed or increased on the same date as it would normally be. Therefore, if she is receiving contractual maternity pay that is based on her normal rate of pay, her maternity pay should be increased at that time. (The special rule on how pay rises affect statutory maternity pay is explained in 2.2.51.)

2.2.45 A woman on maternity leave should also receive any bonus that is paid to everyone else in the workforce, if the bonus is based simply on being on the payroll – as, for example, a Christmas bonus may be. On the other hand, a bonus that is based on the work the employee has done over a period, either individually or through her contribution to group or company performance, can lawfully be reduced to reflect the proportion of the relevant period when the woman was on maternity leave. If a bonus is based on performance targets, the targets may need to be reduced to reflect the period of leave. For these purposes, the two- or four-week compulsory period of maternity leave (see 2.2.29) and any periods of absence prior to maternity leave for pregnancy-related reasons should be treated as a period when the woman was at work. Employers who need more detailed guidance may wish to contact us.

Continuous employment

2.2.46 A woman's contract of employment continues throughout her maternity leave, so she continues to build up continuous service for the purposes of any employment rights that depend on continuous employment (see Appendix 8.1), such as unfair dismissal and redundancy rights.

Statutory maternity pay

2.2.47 Statutory maternity pay (SMP) is a social security benefit administered by employers, who are responsible for making payments to eligible employees. The main pieces of relevant legislation are the Social Security Contributions and Benefits Act 1992 and the SMP (General) Regulations 1986 (as amended). HM Revenue and Customs produces a clear and detailed manual on the calculation and payment of SMP (see 9.2.2).

Main features of SMP

2.2.48 In order to be entitled to SMP, a woman must meet the following conditions:

- She must have been continuously employed for 26 weeks by the end of the fifteenth week before the week her baby is due.

- She must have normal weekly earnings in the eight weeks ending with that fifteenth week (the calculation period) of at least the lower earnings limit for SMP (which is reviewed annually and is currently £97 from April 2010).

- She must give at least 28 days' notice of her maternity leave or, if that is not possible, as much notice as she can. Her employer is entitled to ask her to put this in writing.

- She must supply medical evidence from her doctor or midwife of the week when her baby is due. This evidence, usually on Form Mat B1, must be supplied before the end of the third week of her maternity leave, or before the end of the thirteenth week of her leave if there is good reason for the delay.

2.2.49 An employee who meets these qualifying rules is entitled to be paid SMP even if she has no intention of returning to work or resigns when she goes on maternity leave. She will also continue to be entitled to SMP even if she is dismissed after qualifying for it, regardless of the reason for her dismissal.

SMP rate and payment period

2.2.50   SMP is paid for up to 39 weeks. For the first 6 weeks, SMP is equivalent to 90 per cent of the woman's normal weekly earnings. This is referred to as higher-rate SMP. For the remaining 33 weeks, SMP is paid at a flat rate or 90 per cent of the employee's normal weekly earnings, whichever is lower. The flat rate is reviewed annually. From April 2010, it is £124.88 per week.

2.2.51   If a woman receives a pay increase that takes effect at any time from the beginning of the calculation period used to calculate her normal weekly earnings until the end of her maternity leave, the rule is that the increase must be treated as if it had applied throughout the calculation period. This rule may result in low-paid women qualifying for SMP because their earnings are lifted to the lower earnings limit or above. The rule will also affect the amount of an employee's higher-rate SMP, since that is based on her normal weekly earnings. Her employer will need to recalculate how much her higher-rate SMP should be and make up any shortfall in the SMP she has already been paid.

2.2.52   SMP should be paid in the same way as the employee's normal wages or salary, with tax and National Insurance contributions deducted.

Recouping SMP

2.2.53   Employers are entitled to recoup 92 per cent of any SMP that they pay out, by deducting it from their National Insurance payments. Small employers whose annual National Insurance bill is £45,000 or less can recoup their SMP in full, plus an additional 4.5 per cent of that sum to compensate for administration and other costs.

2.2.54   Women who do not qualify for SMP may be entitled to maternity allowance, which they can claim direct from their local Social Security office.

Temporary cover

2.2.55   An employer may decide to recruit an employee on a temporary contract to cover for a woman on maternity leave or an employee on parental or adoption leave. If it does, it should bear in mind that the temporary employee will acquire unfair dismissal protection if he or she ends up being employed for a year or more.

2.2.56   It would therefore be advisable to ensure that the employee is fully aware from the outset that he or she is being employed to provide temporary cover only.

2.2.57   When the other employee returns from family leave, the company should consider whether it has any other work it could offer the temporary employee before deciding to terminate his or her contract. The company should follow a fair procedure and act reasonably in all the circumstances including offering the employee a right to appeal, if the employee's contract is being terminated.

2.2.58   If the other employee does not return to work after family leave but the company does not consider that the replacement is suitable for a permanent job, the company should still follow a fair procedure and act reasonably in all the circumstances before deciding to dismiss the temporary employee. For example, if his or her competence is in doubt, he or she should be given an opportunity to improve before a decision is made to dismiss.

2.2.59   Regardless of the length of time the temporary employee has been with the company, he or she is entitled to protection from unjustified discrimination on the ground of his or her fixed-term status (see 1.2.89).

2.2.60   It should also be noted that the temporary employee has the right to be notified of any permanent vacancies that may arise in the company (see 1.1.23).

'Keeping in touch days' during maternity leave

2.2.61   A woman on maternity leave may undertake up to 10 days' work for her employer during her maternity leave period without bringing her leave to an end. However, there is no requirement for an employee to undertake work during her maternity leave neither is there any requirement for an employer to provide such work. Work for this purpose is broadly defined to include any work not only under the contract of employment but also training and any other activity undertaken for the purposes of keeping in touch with the workplace. These 'keeping in touch days' are entirely voluntary but can be of benefit to both employers and employees.

Returning from leave

2.2.62   The legislation imposes certain notice requirements on women who want to return from maternity leave early (see 2.2.63) and specifies the terms and conditions that apply to returners (see 2.2.67). There are also legal considerations for an employer to bear in mind if an employee fails to return to work after her leave (see 2.2.70). The legal position of employees who want to change their working hours or place of work when they return from maternity leave is discussed separately below (see 2.2.150).

Notice of early return

2.2.63   If an employee takes her full maternity leave entitlement, she does not have to give her employer any notice of her return to work. The company must assume that she will come back to work at the end of her maximum possible leave. But if the employee wants to return to work early before the end of the full maternity leave period or if having fixed a return date she wishes to change it, she must give the company 8 weeks' prior notice. This notice need not be in writing.

2.2.64   If an employee returns early without giving any notice or sufficient notice, the company can postpone her return to a date that will ensure that it has the appropriate notice of her return, and it need not pay her until that date. The company cannot, however, postpone her return beyond the end of what would have been her maximum maternity leave. An employer has no right to postpone an employee's return in this way if it did not confirm to her the date on which she was due to return to work (see 2.2.33).

The job on return

2.2.65   Broadly speaking, an employee returning to work after maternity leave is entitled to return to the same job as she was doing before she went away. However, if she is returning from additional maternity leave and it is not practicable to allow her to return to her original job, she can be given a suitable alternative, provided the status and terms and conditions of the new job are as good as those of her old job.

2.2.66   A company that wants to take up this option should first ensure that it has grounds for maintaining that it was not practicable to keep the woman's original job open for her. Larger employers may find it difficult to show that it was not possible to make arrangements for cover. The offer of suitable alternative work can also come from an associated employer (see 8.1.9).

2.2.67   On her return to work, an employee's terms and conditions must be as good as those that would have applied to her had she not been away.

2.2.68   There are complicated rules on the position of an employee who returns to work after a combination of consecutive periods of family leave. The rules that apply where an employee takes a period of parental leave after her maternity leave are set out in 2.2.143. Companies who need advice on other situations should contact us.

Failure to return

2.2.69   It is important to note that, once an employee's maternity leave is over, she remains an employee. If she does not return to work, she should not be viewed as having resigned unless there is clear evidence that she has, such as a letter or a telephone call from her saying that she will not be coming back. If she telephones with that news, it would be advisable to ask her to put her resignation in writing.

2.2.70   An employer should treat a woman who does not return to work after maternity leave in the same way as it treats other employees who fail to return to work after a period of authorised absence. If it does not do so, it may face allegations of unfair dismissal, sex discrimination or unfavourable treatment linked to pregnancy and maternity (see 2.2.72). In particular, if a woman is ill at the end of maternity leave, she should be dealt with in a way that takes no account of any periods of absence linked to her pregnancy or maternity leave.

2.2.71   Once a woman's maternity leave is over, all her usual contractual terms come back into force. So if she is unable to return to work because of illness, she may be entitled to sick pay.

Legal protection for pregnancy and maternity

2.2.72   Employees have legal protection from being treated unfavourably (see 2.2.73) or dismissed (see 2.2.74) because they are pregnant or have taken up their maternity rights. Women on maternity leave have special protection if they are affected by redundancy (see 2.2.79). A woman who is dismissed while she is pregnant or on maternity leave must be given written reasons for her dismissal (see 2.2.83). And there is special protection for the pay of women who are given notice of dismissal while on maternity leave (see 2.2.84).

Unfavourable treatment

2.2.73   The Employment Rights Act 1996 makes it unlawful for an employer to penalise an employee in any way or put her at any disadvantage in the workplace because of her pregnancy or maternity. In particular, it is unlawful to discipline a woman for failing to return to work on time if the employer did not confirm to her when her leave was due to end (see 2.2.33) and the employee reasonably believed that her leave had not ended, or if the employer gave her less than 28 days' notice of the date on which her leave would end and it was not reasonably practicable for her to return on the due date.

2.2.74   Treating a woman unfavourably on the grounds of pregnancy or maternity is also automatically unlawful sex discrimination, contrary to the Sex Discrimination Act 1975. For example, it would be unlawful for an employer to:

- reject a job applicant because she was pregnant; or
- refuse to train or promote an employee because she would need to take maternity leave; or
- leave a woman out of a redundancy or other consultation exercise because she was on maternity leave.

Unfair dismissal

2.2.75   An employee who is pregnant can be dismissed for good reason in the same way as any other employee, although, if the employee has at least one year's service, the employer must follow a reasonable procedure, before dismissing her in order to avoid liability for an unfair dismissal. It is automatically unfair, however, to dismiss a woman for reasons connected with her pregnancy or maternity, regardless of her length of service, whilst she is pregnant or during her maternity leave. This means that it is unfair to dismiss a woman for a pregnancy-related sickness absence.

2.2.76   It is also automatically unfair to dismiss a woman for failing to return to work on time if the employer did not confirm to her when her leave was due to end (see 2.2.33) and the employee reasonably believed that her leave had not ended, or if the employer gave her less than 28 days' notice of the date on which her leave would end and it was not reasonably practicable for her to return on the due date.

Sex discrimination

2.2.77   It is also automatically sex discrimination to dismiss a woman for reasons relating to her pregnancy or maternity. For example, it would be sex discrimination, as well as unfair dismissal, to dismiss a woman for a poor attendance record on the basis of pregnancy-related absences during her pregnancy.

2.2.78   An employee's automatic protection from sex discrimination ends at the end of her maternity leave. It is not, therefore, sex discrimination for an employer to dismiss a woman for an unacceptable level of sickness absence after maternity leave, even if the absence is due to a pregnancy- or childbirth-related illness, provided the employer has left out of account any such absences the employee had during her pregnancy and maternity leave, and treated her as it would any other employee with the same level of sickness absence.

Redundancy

2.2.79   If a woman is selected for redundancy for reasons relating to her pregnancy and maternity, that automatically amounts to sex discrimination and unfair dismissal, regardless of her length of service. For example, if an employer is selecting employees for redundancy on the basis of attendance record, it should ensure that it leaves out of account any absences for pregnancy-related reasons, including pregnancy-related illness, and any periods of maternity leave.

2.2.80   In any redundancy situation, employers should routinely consider redeployment as an alternative to redundancy, in order to avoid unfair dismissal (see 5.2.95). However, women on maternity leave have special rights to be redeployed. Where it is impracticable to continue to employ a woman on maternity leave because of redundancy, she must be offered any suitable alternative work that is available with her employer or any associated employer (see 8.1.9). The offer must be made before the end of the employee's original contract, and the new contract must take effect immediately, and on terms and conditions that are broadly similar to those of her original contract. If suitable alternative work is available but is not offered to the employee, her dismissal will be automatically unfair, regardless of her length of service.

Acting reasonably

2.2.81   Like any other employee dismissed for redundancy, an employee who is made redundant while pregnant or on maternity leave is entitled to complain of unfair dismissal if the employer does not act reasonably in handling the redundancy (see 5.2.3). The employer should therefore ensure that it has chosen and applied objective selection criteria, warned and consulted with the employee, and considered whether it has any other work it can offer her, whether or not that work is objectively suitable for her. The employer will also need to ensure that it has followed a fair procedure including allowing her the right to appeal against dismissal.

Redundancy payment

2.2.82   Weeks when the employee is on maternity leave and receiving no pay or less than her normal pay are discounted when calculating the size of her statutory redundancy payment (see 5.2.114). However, if an employee has been offered suitable alternative employment and has unreasonably refused it, she loses her right to a redundancy payment (see 5.2.103).

Written reasons

2.2.83   If an employee is dismissed while she is pregnant or during her maternity leave, she must be given written reasons for her dismissal, regardless of her length of service and even if she does not ask for the reasons. This right usually applies only to employees who have at least one year's continuous service and have asked for written reasons for their dismissal.

Pay during notice

2.2.84   An employee who is dismissed or resigns with notice while on maternity leave may have the right to be paid her usual pay during her period of notice. This is the case even if that falls during a time when she would otherwise be receiving less than her full pay or no pay at all. Employees have this right if they are entitled to no more than six days more than the minimum notice of dismissal required by the Employment Rights Act 1996 (see 4.1.16). The minimum notice by the employer is, broadly speaking, one week for each year that the employee has been employed, up to a maximum of 12 weeks. The employee has to give one week of notice.

Maternity checklist

When first informed

1. Inform yourself about maternity rights by reading this Guide. If you need further information, read the BIS guide to maternity rights (*Pregnancy and work*) and the Revenue's employers' help book (*E15: Pay and time off work for parents*).

2. Consider whether there are any risks to the employee's health and safety that need to be addressed. Are any alterations needed to her working conditions? Is it necessary to move her to alternative work? If so, is any available? Might she need to be suspended from work with pay?

3. Meet with the employee to discuss how her leave will be managed and what her rights are. When you meet:

   – Ask the employee when her baby is due. Explain to her how long her leave can last.

- Explain to the employee her right to time off for antenatal care and ask her to show you her appointment card after she has had her first appointment.

- Tell the employee that she needs to notify you by the 15th week before her expected week of childbirth (EWC) of the date she intends to start her leave. Ask for the notice to be given in writing.

- Explain to the employee that she cannot start her maternity leave before the 11th week before her EWC (unless the baby is born before that date). If she changes her mind about her start date she must give you at least 28 days' notice before the original start date or new start date, whichever is earlier.

- Explain to the employee that if the baby is born before she starts her maternity leave, the birth will automatically trigger her maternity leave period. In this case, she should contact you as soon as reasonably practicable and tell you the date the baby was born. If she works on into the four weeks before her baby is due and she is away from work for a pregnancy-related reason in those weeks, she should also inform you of this in writing. At that point you will discuss with her whether the absence has automatically triggered her maternity leave.

- Consider working through a pregnancy/maternity timetable that establishes the important dates for the employee (for example, the 11th and 15th weeks before the EWC). It may be helpful to use the Business Link website (www.businesslink.gov.uk) to establish the likely timetable.

- Ask the employee if she has any provisional plans for how much leave she will be taking.

- Explain to the employee that she must give you 8 weeks' notice if she wants to come back to work early. Ask for the notice to be given in writing.

- Establish whether the employee is entitled to SMP, and explain to her how much this is and how it will be paid.

- Ask the employee to give you her MAT B1 form as soon as she receives it, and explain that her right to statutory maternity pay may be put at risk if she does not do so.

- If the employee qualifies for parental leave, or will do so while she is off on maternity leave, discuss with her whether she plans to tack any parental leave on to the end of her maternity leave.

- Discuss with the employee any health and safety concerns that she or you may have, and any alterations to her work that may be necessary.

- Explain about any arrangements for 'keeping in touch days' that you operate.

4. After the meeting, write to the employee summarising her legal rights and notice obligations.

5. If the employee is not entitled to SMP, give her form SMP1, *Why I cannot pay you SMP*.

6. Consider whether a temporary replacement should be recruited to cover for the employee while on maternity leave, or what other cover arrangements need to be made.

7. Within 28 days of receiving the employee's notice of her intended start date, write to her confirming the last day of her maternity leave. If the employee changes her mind about her intended start date, you will need to write to her again because the last day of her maternity leave will have changed. You must write to her within 28 days of the start of her maternity leave.

During employee's leave

1. Ensure that the employee's terms and conditions are observed, according to the statutory rules.

2. Keep in touch with the employee and ask her to let you know when the baby is born. Ensure that she does not do any work for you in the two-week period after she gives birth, or in the four weeks after the birth if she works in a factory. However, confirm details of any arrangements for 'keeping in touch days'.

3. If the employee changed her mind about the start date of her maternity leave (or it was automatically triggered by pregnancy-related absence or the birth of the baby), and you have not already done so, write to her within 28 days of the start of her leave to advise the last day of her maternity leave.

4. Confirm arrangements for the employee's return.

5. If the employee requests flexible working arrangements on her return, ask her to complete an application form under the Flexible Working Regulations and then follow the statutory procedure (see 2.2.150–2.2.155).

Managing maternity cover

1. If you decide to recruit a temporary replacement for the employee on maternity leave, consider whether to recruit a temporary employee or use agency staff. If you decide to recruit an employee, put the job offer in writing, and state clearly that it is a temporary job to cover maternity leave. Explain that the job may be extended if the employee decides to take parental leave or holiday.

2. While the employee is on maternity leave, confirm whether she intends to return to work and discuss the situation with the temporary replacement.

3. If a permanent vacancy arises in the company during maternity cover, you must notify the temporary employee of it.

4. If the employee is not intending to return to work, consider whether to offer the temporary replacement the job on a permanent basis. If you decide to do so, confirm this in writing to the replacement. If you decide not to do so, remember that, if the replacement has one year's service, he or she will have the necessary service to bring an unfair dismissal claim. You should therefore follow a fair procedure and act reasonably in all the circumstances before deciding to dismiss the temporary employee and you must treat him or her as you would any other employee.

5. If the employee is intending to return to work after maternity leave, you should consider whether the temporary replacement could be offered other work, and put any offer of alternative work in writing. Again, if there is no alternative work, you should follow a fair procedure.

Paternity leave and pay

2.2.85   Under the Employment Rights Act 1996, an employee whose partner is having a baby may be entitled to paternity leave in order to care for the child or support the mother. Where a couple is involved in adopting a child, one of the couple may be entitled to adoption leave (see 2.2.102) and the other may be entitled to paternity leave. An employee is entitled to paternity leave in respect of a child who is born alive or who is stillborn after 24 weeks of pregnancy. The details of the right to paternity leave are set out in the Paternity and Adoption Leave Regulations 2002. (There are separate regulations that explain how the right applies where the child is adopted from overseas. We can advise you on the effect of these.)

Who qualifies?

2.2.86   Employees are entitled to paternity leave if they have completed 26 weeks' continuous employment (see Appendix 8.1) with their employer by the end of the fifteenth week before the week their baby is due, or by the end of the week in which the adoption agency confirms the adoption match.

2.2.87   Paternity leave is available to the child's biological father, provided he has responsibility for the child's upbringing. It is also available to an employee who is married to or the civil partner or partner of the child's mother or adopter and has the main responsibility (apart from the mother or adopter) for the child's upbringing. A 'partner' is someone who lives with the mother or adopter and the child in an enduring family relationship, but who is not a parent, grandparent, sister, brother, aunt or uncle of the mother or adopter. A partner may be of the same sex as the mother or adopter, and couples involved in an adoption may decide that the woman should take paternity leave while the man takes adoption leave. The employee taking paternity leave may therefore be a woman. This summary of the law is based on the more common situation where the employee taking paternity leave is a man.

Length of paternity leave

2.2.88   An employee can opt to take either one or two consecutive weeks' paternity leave. The statutory scheme does not allow for paternity leave to be taken in odd days or in two separate weeks, although there is nothing to prevent companies allowing this. (If they do so, however, they should note that the statutory paternity pay scheme reflects the statutory paternity leave scheme, so they will not be able to recoup any payment they make to the employee for odd days or the second of two separate weeks of leave (see 2.2.97).)

2.2.89   The maximum length of paternity leave is two weeks for each pregnancy or adoption arrangement, even if the mother has a multiple birth or more than one child is adopted at the same time.

Timing of paternity leave

2.2.90   The employee can choose to start paternity leave on the date of the child's birth or placement, or a specified number of days after the child is born or placed, or on any specified date later than the first day of the week the birth or placement is due. The employee can change his mind about the start date, but must give his employer notice of the change (see 2.2.92). If the employee planned to take leave from the date the child was born or placed and is at work on that day, his leave starts the next day. If the employee planned to take leave on a specified date but the child has not yet been born or placed by then, the employee will need to alter the start date.

2.2.91   Paternity leave must be taken within 56 days of the child's birth or placement. If the baby was born before the week in which the birth was due, the leave must be taken within 56 days of the beginning of the expected week of childbirth.

Notice requirements

2.2.92   There are various notice requirements that the employee must meet in order to qualify for paternity leave, and the employer can ask for these notices to be given in writing. If it is not reasonably practicable for the employee to meet these deadlines, he must give notice as soon as is reasonably practicable.

- *Intention to take leave.* For birth children, the employee must give notice of his intention to take paternity leave in or before the fifteenth week before the week the baby is due. The notice must specify the expected week of childbirth, the length of leave the employee will be taking and the date the employee wants the leave to start. For adoptive children, the employee must give notice within seven days of the adoption match being notified. The notice must specify the date the match was notified, the date the child is expected to be placed, the length of leave the employee proposes to take and the date the employee wants the leave to begin.

- *Changing the start date.* If the employee wants to change the date on which his leave is to start, he must give the employer notice of that fact 28 days before the new start date. Where the child has not been born or placed for adoption by the start date the employee originally notified, he must let his employer know the new start date as soon as reasonably practicable.

- *Notice of birth or placement date.* Once the child is born or placed for adoption, the employee must let the employer know the child's birth day or placement date, as soon as reasonably practicable.

- *Declaration of entitlement.* If his employer asks him to, the employee must confirm in writing that he is taking leave for the purpose of caring for his child or supporting the child's mother or adopter, and that he meets the eligibility requirements outlined in 2.2.86–7.

HM Revenue and Customs has produced a form that employees can use to apply for paternity leave and pay (see 9.2.2).

Rights during paternity leave

2.2.93 An employee on paternity leave is entitled to the benefit of all his usual terms and conditions of employment, apart from those relating to wages or salary. Likewise, the employee is bound by all his usual obligations under his employment contract, except for those that are inconsistent with his right to be away on paternity leave.

Pensions

2.2.94 The Social Security Act 1989 requires that an employee who is receiving statutory or contractual paternity pay must be treated for pension purposes as if he were working normally and receiving his normal pay. Any pension contributions he is required to make, on the other hand, must be based on the paternity pay he is actually receiving.

Statutory paternity pay

2.2.95   Employees may qualify for statutory paternity pay (SPP) during their paternity leave. The right to SPP is laid down in the Social Security Contributions and Benefits Act 1992 and the Statutory Paternity Pay and Statutory Adoption Pay (General) Regulations 2002. In order to qualify, an employee's normal weekly earnings in the eight weeks ending with the fifteenth week before the week their baby is due, or in the eight weeks before the week in which the adoption match is notified, must be at or above the lower earnings threshold. This is reviewed annually and is £97 from April 2010.

2.2.96   An employee must give his employer 28 days' notice of his intention to claim SPP or, if that is not possible, as much notice as he can.

2.2.97   SPP is paid at the same weekly rate as flat-rate SMP, that is, £124.88 from April 2010 per week or 90 per cent of normal weekly earnings, if that is less. Employers can recoup their SPP payments from their National Insurance contributions, in the same way as they do SMP (see 2.2.53).

Returning to work

2.2.98   On return from paternity leave, an employee is entitled to return to the same job, on the same terms and conditions as would have applied had he not been absent. If he wants to change his working hours or place of work to care for his child, he has the right to apply to do so (see 2.2.150).

2.2.99   There are complicated rules on the position of an employee returning to work after combining paternity leave with one or more consecutive periods of other family leave. Companies who need advice on this should contact us.

Protection from unfavourable treatment or dismissal

2.2.100   It is unlawful for an employer to treat an employee unfavourably for any reason connected with his right to paternity leave. Likewise, it is automatically unfair to dismiss an employee for a reason relating to paternity leave, including selecting the employee for redundancy on that basis, regardless of the employee's length of service.

Discrimination in parental rights

2.2.101   Although paternity rights are substantially less generous than maternity rights, men cannot bring a sex discrimination claim on that basis. The Sex Discrimination Act 1975 and the Equal Pay Act 1970 expressly allow especially favourable treatment for women in relation to pregnancy and maternity.

2.2.102   Employers should ensure, however, that any family benefits they offer that do not specifically relate to pregnancy and childbirth are extended to male as well as female employees. This could apply, for example, to financial help with childcare expenses.

Adoption leave

2.2.103   Employees who are adopting a child under the age of 18 may be entitled to adoption leave. The right to adoption leave is set out in the Employment Rights Act 1996 and the Paternity and Adoption Leave Regulations 2002 (as amended). (There are separate regulations that explain how the right applies where the child is adopted from overseas. We can advise you on the effect of these.)

2.2.104   Where a couple is adopting, they must decide which partner should take adoption leave. The other partner may then be entitled to paternity leave (see 2.2.85). An employee is entitled to only one period of adoption leave for each adoption arrangement, even if the arrangement involves more than one child.

Who is entitled?

2.2.105   An employee qualifies for adoption leave if he or she has been continuously employed (see Appendix 8.1) for 26 weeks by the end of the week in which he or she was notified of having been matched with the child.

Length of adoption leave

2.2.106   Adoption leave lasts up to 52 weeks. The first 26 weeks are called ordinary adoption leave; the next 26 weeks are additional adoption leave.

Timing of adoption leave

2.2.107 An employee can choose to start adoption leave on the date of the child's placement or up to 14 days before the placement is due. (The employee can alter the start date, but must give the employer notice of the change – see 2.2.109.) If the employee wanted to begin the leave on the date of the placement but is at work that day, the leave begins the following day.

2.2.108 If an employee begins adoption leave before the child is placed and the placement falls through, or if the child dies or is returned to the adoption agency, the employee's adoption leave will end eight weeks after the week in which that event occurs.

Notice requirements

2.2.109 In order to qualify for the right to adoption leave, an employee must meet certain notice requirements:

- *Notice of leave.* Within seven days of receiving notification of the match, the employee must let the employer know that he or she plans to take adoption leave. (If it is not possible for the employee to give notice by this time, he or she must give notice as soon as is reasonably practicable.) The notice must give the date the child is due to be placed and the date on which the employee wants to begin the leave. The employer can ask for this notice to be in writing.

- *Notice of change in leave date.* If the employee decides to alter the date of the leave, he or she must notify the employer at least 28 days in advance of the revised date or, if that is not possible, as soon as reasonably practicable.

- *Evidence of match.* If it wants to, the employer can ask the employee to provide evidence of the adoption agency's name and address, the date of notification of the match and the expected date of placement. (Copies of documents provided by the adoption agency should suffice.)

Confirmation of return date

2.2.110 When it hears from the employee that he or she intends to take adoption leave, the employer must write to the employee within 28 days confirming the date on which he or she will be due back at work. Likewise, if the employee changes the date on which he or she wants to begin leave, the employer must confirm the revised end date, within the first 28 days of the employee's leave. If the employer fails to do so, it will be restricted in its ability to control the employee's return to work (see 2.2.119) or to discipline the employee for failing to return on time (see 2.2.124). The Department of Business, Innovation and Skills (BIS) has produced a model letter that employers can use to confirm an employee's return date (see 9.2.2).

Rights during adoption leave

2.2.111 Employees' rights during adoption leave are similar to their rights during maternity leave. During adoption leave (both ordinary and additional), employees are entitled to all their normal terms and conditions of employment, apart from their wages or salary (although they may be entitled to Statutory Adoption Pay instead – see 2.2.113). They are also bound by all their usual employment obligations, except those that are inconsistent with their right to be absent on adoption leave.

Pensions

2.2.112 The Social Security Act 1989 requires that during any period when employees are on additional adoption leave and receiving any pay under their contract, they must be treated for pension purposes as if they were working normally and being paid their normal pay. Any pension contributions that the employees are obliged to make, however, must be based on the pay they are actually receiving.

Statutory adoption pay

2.2.113 Employees who take adoption leave may qualify for 39 weeks' statutory adoption pay (SAP). The right to SAP is set out in the Social Security Contributions and Benefits Act 1992 and the Statutory Paternity Pay and Statutory Adoption Pay (General) Regulations 2002. In order to qualify, an employee's normal weekly earnings in the eight weeks before the week in which the adoption match is notified must be at or above the lower earnings threshold. The lower earnings threshold is reviewed annually and is £97 from April 2010.

2.2.114   SAP is paid at the same weekly rate as flat-rate SMP, that is, £124.88 or 90 per cent of normal weekly earnings, whichever is less. Employees must give their employer 28 days' notice that they wish to claim SAP or, if that is not possible, as much notice as reasonably practicable, and provide evidence of the adoption match (see 2.2.109).

2.2.115   Employers can recover their SAP payments from their National Insurance contributions, in the same way as they recover SMP (see 2.2.53).

Entitlement to holiday

2.2.116   Any entitlement that an employee has to paid holiday under the Working Time Regulations 1998 (see 2.3.71) and their contract of employment is unaffected by the fact that he or she may be on adoption leave for part of the leave year.

Continuous employment

2.2.117   An employee's contract of employment continues throughout adoption leave, so the employee continues to build up continuous service for the purposes of any employment rights that depend on continuous employment, such as unfair dismissal and the right to a redundancy payment.

'Keeping in touch days' during adoption leave

2.2.118   An employee on adoption leave may undertake up to 10 days' work for their employer during their adoption leave period without bringing the leave period to an end. However, there is no requirement for an employee to undertake work during their adoption leave nor is there any requirement for an employer to provide such work. Work for this purpose is broadly defined to include not only work under the employment contract but also training and any other activity undertaken for the purposes of keeping in touch with the workplace.

These 'keeping in touch days' are entirely voluntary but can prove of benefit to both employers and employees.

Returning to work

2.2.119   The position of an employee returning from adoption leave is broadly the same as that of an employee returning from maternity leave. The company should assume that the employee will return to work at the end of his or her maximum adoption leave. If the employee decides to return to work early, he or she must give the employer eight weeks' notice of the return date. If the employee fails to give proper notice, the employer can postpone the employee's return for up to eight weeks, or until the date on which his or her additional adoption leave would have ended, whichever is sooner. The employer is under no obligation to pay the employee until the postponed date of return. If, however, the employer has not written to the employee confirming his or her return date (see 2.2.110), it has no right to postpone the employee's return in this way.

2.2.120   An employee who returns to work after up to 26 weeks' adoption leave is entitled to return to the same job. If the employee returns after more than 26 weeks, he or she is usually entitled to return to the same job. If the employer can show, however, that it is not reasonably practicable to allow the employee to return to the same job, it has the option of giving the employee a suitable alternative, provided the status and terms and conditions of the new job are as good as the old.

2.2.121   On return to work, the employee's terms and conditions must be as good as they would have been had he or she not been away.

2.2.122   There are complicated rules on the rights of employees who return to work after two or more consecutive periods of family leave. Companies who need advice on this should contact us.

Protection from unfavourable treatment or dismissal

2.2.123   It is unlawful for an employer to treat an employee unfavourably for any reason connected with the employee's right to adoption leave. Likewise, it is automatically unfair to dismiss an employee for this reason, including selecting the employee for redundancy on this basis, regardless of the employee's length of service.

2.2.124 In particular, it is unlawful for an employer to discipline or dismiss an employee for failing to return to work after additional adoption leave, if the employer did not meet its duty to confirm to the employee the date on which his or her leave was due to end (see 2.2.110) and the employee reasonably believed that the leave had not ended, or if the employer gave the employee less than 28 days' notice of the date on which the leave would end and it was not reasonably practicable for the employee to return on the specified date.

Notice pay

2.2.125 An employee who is dismissed or resigns while on adoption leave may have the right to be paid his or her usual pay during the period of notice. This is the case even if that falls during a time when he or she would otherwise be receiving less than full pay or no pay at all. This protection applies to employees who are entitled to no more than six days more than the minimum notice of dismissal required by the Employment Rights Act 1996 (see 4.1.16 – the minimum period of notice is, broadly speaking, one week for each year that the employee has been employed, up to a maximum of 12 weeks).

Redundancy during leave

2.2.126 Like an employee made redundant while on maternity leave, an employee who is made redundant during adoption leave is entitled to be offered any suitable alternative vacancy that may exist with the employer or an associated employer (see 8.1.9), on terms and conditions that are broadly the same as under his or her existing contract (see 2.2.80).

Written reasons for dismissal

2.2.127 Any employee who is dismissed while on adoption leave is entitled to a written statement of the reasons for his or her dismissal, without having to ask for it. This right normally applies only to employees who have at least one year's service and who request the statement.

Parental leave

2.2.128 Employees with responsibility for a child, including adoptive parents, may have the right to unpaid time off work to care for the child. The details of this right are set out in the Employment Rights Act 1996 and the Maternity and Parental Leave etc Regulations 1999.

2.2.129 The purpose of parental leave is to care for a child, which means not only physically caring for the child but also looking after the welfare of the child in a general sense and making arrangements for the child's good. Parental leave could therefore be used, for example, to check out new schools, to accompany the child on a stay in hospital, or to take the child to stay with grandparents.

Who qualifies?

2.2.130 An employee qualifies for parental leave if he or she has been continuously employed (see Appendix 8.1) for one year or more at the time when the leave begins. The employee must have, or expect to have, responsibility for a child. This covers:

- the child's birth mother;
- the child's biological father if married to the child's mother;
- the person registered as the child's father on the birth certificate;
- the child's adoptive parents; and
- anyone else who has acquired parental responsibility for the child under the Children Act 1989 or the Children (Scotland) Act 1995.

2.2.131 The right to parental leave is personal, so one parent cannot transfer his or her leave entitlement to the other.

Length of parental leave

2.2.132 Employees are entitled to a total of 13 weeks' parental leave in respect of each qualifying child for whom they have responsibility. Parents of a child who is entitled to disability living allowance are entitled to 18 weeks' parental leave.

2.2.133   A week's parental leave is equal to the time an employee would normally be required to work in a week. For example, an employee who works a two-day week will be entitled to a total of 26 working days off work as parental leave. Employers are not legally required to keep records of how much parental leave an employee has taken, but are likely to want to do so nevertheless.

Timing of parental leave

2.2.134   Parental leave must be taken:

- before the child's fifth birthday; or
- if the child is entitled to disability living allowance, before the child's eighteenth birthday; or
- if the child has been placed with the employee for adoption, before the fifth anniversary of the date on which the child was placed for adoption or the child's eighteenth birthday, whichever comes earlier.

Leave may be taken later if the employer postpones the dates of the leave, under the default rules explained in 2.2.137.

The mechanics

2.2.135   Employers have a degree of flexibility in deciding the mechanics of how parental leave is taken, provided this is done by agreement. This can be an agreement with the employee. It can also be a collective agreement with an independent trade union or, if the employer does not negotiate with a union, a workforce agreement, provided the collective or workforce agreement is incorporated into the employee's contract (see 1.2.17).

2.2.136   A workforce agreement is an agreement with employee representatives who have been elected by the workforce. If the employer has 20 or fewer employees, it has the alternative option of reaching a workforce agreement with a majority of the workforce. A workforce agreement must meet detailed conditions. Employers who are considering entering into a workforce agreement on parental leave should obtain advice from us.

Default rules

2.2.137 If no agreement is reached, then these default rules apply:

1. Parental leave must usually be taken in periods of a whole week or weeks. However, if the child is entitled to disability living allowance, the leave may be taken in shorter periods.

2. No more than four weeks' parental leave can be taken in any year. Each year runs from the date on which the employee first became entitled to parental leave for the child, or, if the employee joined the employer after first qualifying for parental leave, the date on which the employee first qualified for parental leave from this employment by completing one year's service.

3. The employee must produce any evidence reasonably required by the employer to show that the employee has legal responsibility for the child, the date of the child's birth or adoption, and, if relevant, the child's entitlement to disability living allowance. This could include, for example, a birth certificate or adoption papers.

4. The employee must notify the employer at least 21 days in advance of the date he or she wants the parental leave to begin, and give the dates on which the leave is to begin and end. This need not be in writing. Women on maternity leave who want to take parental leave after their maternity leave has ended should also give notice in this way.

5. If the employer considers that its operation would be unduly disrupted if the employee took parental leave between those dates, it can postpone the leave for up to six months, to a date fixed after consultation with the employee. The leave cannot be postponed beyond the child's eighteenth birthday. If the employer decides to postpone the leave, it must let the employee know in writing within seven days of receiving the request for leave, and must give the reason for the postponement and the dates on which the leave will now begin and end. For example, an employer may be justified in postponing parental leave if the work is at a seasonal peak, a significant proportion of the workforce has applied for parental leave at the same time, or the employee's role is such that his or her absence at the particular time would unduly harm the business.

6. If the employee is a father-to-be who intends to take parental leave from the date his baby is born, different rules apply. He must let his employer know he intends to take parental leave at least 21 days before the week the baby is due. He need not give the dates the leave is to begin and end, but must notify the employer how long he intends to take, and the week the baby is due. The employer cannot postpone the leave.

7. Different rules also apply if the employee is an adoptive parent who intends to take parental leave from the date the child is placed for adoption. The employee must let the employer know that he or she intends to take parental leave at least 21 days before the week the child is due to be placed for adoption, or as soon after that as possible. The employee need not give the dates the leave is to begin and end, but must let the employer know how long he or she intends to take, and the week the child is due to be placed for adoption. The employer cannot postpone the leave.

Employees are likely to take paternity leave rather than parental leave immediately around the time their child is born or placed for adoption, since they may qualify for statutory paternity pay, whereas parental leave is unpaid.

Collective agreement

2.2.138 It seems that a collective or workforce agreement can override any aspect of these default rules, but an agreement with an individual employee can depart from the default rules only if it improves upon them. For example, a collective agreement could stipulate that the shortest period for which parental leave can be taken is two weeks, whereas a similar term in an individual's contract would be overridden by the default rule of one week.

Rights during parental leave

2.2.139 During parental leave, the employee is bound by his or her implied obligation to act in good faith and by any of his or her terms and conditions that relate to notice of resignation, disclosure of confidential information, acceptance of gifts or other benefits or participation in any business. All of an employee's other terms and conditions will be suspended during parental leave, unless his or her contract of employment, or any agreement he or she has reached with the employer, states otherwise.

Pensions

2.2.140 Although an employer is not obliged to pay an employee any wages or salary during parental leave, some employers may give employees a contractual right to be paid for some or all of their leave. Under the Social Security Act 1989, during any period when an employee is on parental leave and receiving any pay under his or her contract, he or she must be treated for pension purposes as if he or she were working normally but being paid what he or she is actually receiving. The pension contributions that the employee is obliged to make must also be based on the pay he or she is receiving.

Entitlement to holiday

2.2.141 Any entitlement that an employee has to paid holiday under the Working Time Regulations 1998 (see 2.3.71) is unaffected by the fact that he or she may be on parental leave for part of the leave year. The employee is therefore likely to be entitled to at least the legal minimum paid holiday in addition to parental leave. Any contractual holiday entitlement over and above the minimum statutory entitlement will not accrue during parental leave unless the contract or some other agreement between the employee and employer says otherwise.

Continuous employment

2.2.142 An employee's contract of employment continues throughout parental leave, so the employee continues to build up continuous service for the purposes of any employment rights that depend on continuous employment, such as unfair dismissal and the right to a redundancy payment. Any weeks of parental leave when the employee was not paid, or received less than his or her usual pay, are disregarded when calculating the size of any statutory redundancy payment to which the employee may later be entitled (see 5.2.116).

Rights after leave

2.2.143   An employee returning from parental leave of four weeks or less is entitled to return to his or her original job, even if, in the case of a female employee, she has tacked the leave on to the end of her ordinary maternity leave.

2.2.144   The position is slightly different for an employee who has taken parental leave of four weeks or less immediately after additional maternity leave. If her employer can show that it would not have been reasonably practicable to allow her to return to her old job either at the end of her additional maternity leave or at the end of her parental leave, her employer or an associated employer (see 8.1.9) is entitled to offer her suitable alternative work. The status and terms and conditions of the employee's new job must be at least as good as those of her old job.

2.2.145   The employer also has that option if the employee is returning from parental leave of more than four weeks and it is not reasonably practicable to allow the employee to return to his or her original job.

2.2.146   Companies that need advice on the rights of employees returning to work after two or more consecutive periods of any other combination of family leave should contact us.

Terms and conditions on return

2.2.147   An employee returning from parental leave is entitled to return on terms and conditions that are as favourable as those that would have applied had he or she not been absent from work.

Protection from unfavourable treatment and dismissal

2.2.148   It is unlawful for an employer to dismiss an employee, select an employee for redundancy or treat an employee unfavourably in any other way on the grounds that the employee:

- has taken, or sought to take, parental leave;
- has refused to sign a workforce agreement on parental leave; or
- has acted as an employee representative or candidate for election in connection with a workforce agreement.

Family rights

For example, it would be unlawful to discipline an employee for a poor attendance record, if that were due to the employee's absence on parental leave.

2.2.149 An employee who is dismissed or resigns while on parental leave may have the right to be paid his or her usual pay during the period of notice. This is the case even if that falls during a time when he or she would otherwise be receiving less than full pay or no pay at all. This protection applies to employees who are entitled to no more than six days more than the minimum notice of dismissal required by the Employment Rights Act 1996 (see 4.1.16 – the minimum period of notice is, broadly speaking, one week for each year that the employee has been employed, up to a maximum of 12 weeks).

Requests for flexible working

2.2.150 Employees with children or who care for an adult may ask to change their working pattern in order to accommodate their responsibilities, perhaps by moving to part-time hours or a job-share arrangement or working from home. Employers receiving a request of this type need to bear two legal considerations in mind. One is that unjustifiably refusing such a request may amount to indirect sex discrimination. The other is that employers are under a specific legal obligation to give serious consideration to employees' requests for a change in hours or place of work, if they are asking for the change in order to care for their child or certain adults.

Sex discrimination

2.2.151 A much larger proportion of women than of men have primary responsibility for childcare and certain adults. It is therefore likely that an employer's refusal to allow part-time working, jobsharing or flexible working hours may have a bigger impact on the women in its workforce than on the men. This means that refusing a woman's request for this type of arrangement is likely to amount to indirect sex discrimination, unless the company can objectively justify its position on the basis of a real and demonstrable business need (see 3.1.37).

2.2.152 A refusal might be justified, for example, if the employee's job involves continuity of customer care, which would be prejudiced by part-time working or a job-share arrangement. Companies who need advice on justification should contact their local office.

The right to request flexible working

2.2.153 Employees of either sex are entitled under the Employment Rights Act 1996 to ask their employer to consider changing their hours of work or working times or allowing them to work from home, to enable them to care for their children and certain adults.

Who qualifies?

2.2.154 In respect of childcare, an employee qualifies to make such a request if he or she has been working for the company for 26 weeks by the time the request is made and has a child aged 16 or under or a disabled child under the age of 18. Biological and adoptive parents have this right, as do guardians and foster carers. Anyone who is married to or is the civil partner of one of these people can apply, as can anyone who is a 'partner' (of either sex) of one of these people. A partner is someone who lives with the person and the child in an enduring family relationship, but does not include parents, grandparents, siblings, aunts and uncles. In respect of adult care, the employee qualifies to make the request if the employee has been working for the company for 26 weeks by the time the request is made and is or will be the carer of an adult who is either their partner or is a relative or who is neither of these two but lives at the same address.

2.2.155 There are detailed procedural rules governing the way in which a request must be handled, set out in the Flexible Working (Procedural Requirements) Regulations 2002. These are summarised below. Further detail is available from us. In this summary, it is assumed that the employee making the request is a woman, but men also have the right to apply.

Procedure for flexible working requests

- The employee must put her request in writing, explain how she meets the qualifying conditions, and specify the change she wants and when she would like it to start. She should also suggest how any effect the change might have on the company could be dealt with. The

Department for Business, Innovation and Skills has produced a model letter that an employee can use to make her request (see 9.2.2).

- Within 28 days, the company must either agree to the request or hold a meeting with the employee to discuss it. (If the person who would normally deal with the application is on sick leave or holiday when the request is received, the time limit expires 28 days after that person returns to work or 56 days after the application is made, whichever is sooner.)

- If the employer then refuses the request, the employee has the right to appeal within 14 days, and the employer must hold a meeting with the employee to discuss the appeal.

- If the company refuses the request or any appeal, it must confirm to the employee in writing the grounds for its decision (see 2.2.156) and explain why it considers those grounds apply. If it agrees to the request, it must confirm to the employee in writing what change has been agreed and when it will take effect.

- An employee has the right to be accompanied by another worker employed by the company at the meeting at which her request is discussed and at any appeal meeting (see 3.3.80).

Grounds for refusal

2.2.156 The company is entitled to refuse an employee's request if it considers that one or more of these grounds applies:

- The change would involve additional costs.

- The company would be unable to recruit additional staff or re-organise work among existing staff.

- The change would have a detrimental impact on quality or performance or ability to meet customer demand.

- There would be insufficient work during the periods the employee wants to work.

- The change would not be compatible with planned structural changes.

2.2.157   The breadth of issues covered in this list shows that a company has substantial scope for refusing an employee's request, provided it bases its decision on correct facts. Thus although the tribunal is not entitled to look to see whether the employer acted fairly or reasonably in putting forward its rejection of the flexible working request, the tribunal is entitled to look at the ground which the employer asserts was the reason why the application was not granted and to see whether it is factually correct. It should be borne in mind, however, that the test of justification in sex discrimination law is relatively rigorous (see 3.1.48), so that a company that turns down a request may still find itself in breach of sex discrimination law, even if the ground for its decision falls within the list. In particular, cost considerations are included in the list but are unlikely in themselves to be sufficient justification for indirect sex discrimination.

2.2.158   Companies can obtain further advice from us on when they may have grounds for refusing a request.

Basis of the change

2.2.159   The legislation giving the right to request flexible working assumes that any change that is agreed will involve a permanent change in the employee's terms and conditions of employment. The company or the employee may wish, however, for the change to be on a trial basis or to last for a limited period only. The company may, for example, have grounds for refusing a permanent change but may be prepared to accept a temporary arrangement; or the employee may want to revert to his or her original working hours when his or her child reaches school age. In these circumstances, it would be advisable for the company and the employee to agree in writing when and on what basis the arrangement may be reviewed or brought to an end.

2.2.160   Where employees' hours are reduced, they remain contractually entitled to their other terms and conditions, including benefits (reduced pro rata where relevant). Further, the Part-time Work Regulations give them specific legal protection from being treated less favourably than when they were working full-time, unless their employer can objectively justify doing so (see 2.3.85).

Time off for dependants

2.2.161 All employees, regardless of their length of service or sex, have the right not to be unreasonably refused a reasonable amount of unpaid time off during working hours to deal with emergencies involving their dependants. This right is given by the Employment Rights Act 1996.

What is covered?

2.2.162 The employee is entitled to time off to take action that is necessary:

- to help a dependant who has fallen ill, given birth, or been injured or assaulted;
- to arrange for care to be provided to a dependant who is ill or injured;
- because of a dependant's death;
- because of an unexpected breakdown in a dependant's care arrangements, as where a childminder falls ill; or
- to deal with an unexpected incident involving the employee's child during a time when an educational establishment is responsible for the child, as where a child is suspended from school or injured on a school trip.

Time to take action

2.2.163 It is worth noting that the employee has the right to time off only to take the action that is necessary to deal with one of these unexpected emergencies. For example, time off to deal with a burst pipe or to wait in for a service engineer is not covered. If an employee's child falls ill unexpectedly, he or she is entitled to time off to arrange for a family member or friend to care for the child, but not to spend an extended period caring for the child himself or herself. (The employee may be entitled to take parental leave (see 2.2.128) for that purpose, if the employer's parental leave scheme allows for leave to be taken at short notice.) Furthermore the unexpected circumstances giving rise to the right are not limited to sudden events, although the longer the time available to make alternative arrangements the less likely it is that the employee can establish it was necessary to take the time off.

2.2.164 The government guide to time off for dependants (see 9.2.2) suggests that, while the amount of time off that is reasonable will vary according to the circumstances of the emergency, one or two days' leave should be sufficient in most cases.

Who is a dependant?

2.2.165 An employee's dependants include his or her spouse, children and parents. It also includes any person who lives in the same household as the employee, which could include, for example, the employee's partner, stepchild or grandparent. It does not include anyone who shares the household as the employee's employee, tenant, lodger or boarder.

2.2.166 In the case of time off to deal with illness or injury, a dependant also includes anyone who reasonably relies on the employee for assistance if he or she is ill, injured or assaulted, or to make care arrangements in the event of illness or injury. That could include, for example, an elderly neighbour. In the case of time off to deal with an unexpected breakdown in care arrangements, a dependant also includes any person who reasonably relies on the employee to make care arrangements.

Notification requirements

2.2.167 The employee must let the employer know as soon as possible why time off is needed and how long it will be. If circumstances change while the employee is off work so that he or she needs more time than originally envisaged, he or she must let the employer know as soon as possible why extra time is needed and how long the extension will be. If it is not possible for the employee to contact the employer before taking the time off, the employee must still let the employer know the reason for the absence when he or she returns to work.

Protection from unfavourable treatment and dismissal

2.2.168 It is unlawful for an employer to treat an employee unfavourably because he or she has taken, or sought to take, reasonable time off for dependants. It would also be automatically unfair for an employer to dismiss an employee or select an employee for redundancy for that reason, regardless of the employee's length of service.

2.2.169   If, on the other hand, an employer has good grounds for believing that an employee has abused the right to time off for dependants by claiming time off for a fictitious emergency, then it is entitled to discipline the employee for dishonesty. If the employer is considering dismissing the employee, it should ensure that it has followed a fair disciplinary procedure before doing so (see Chapter 3.3).

Contractual rights

2.2.170   Many employers offer time off with pay on a contractual or discretionary basis to employees who need to deal with family emergencies. This counts towards the employee's right to time off under the legislation, but cannot limit it. For example, an employer that gives employees one day's paid leave to attend family funerals may need to give a particular employee whose parent has died further unpaid time off to make the funeral arrangements.

2.3

Working time

Overview

2.3.1   This chapter of the Guide deals with working time, holidays and related legal issues.

2.3.2   These aspects of working time are regulated in detail by the Working Time Regulations 1998 (as amended), but when grappling with the detail of the Regulations it is important not to lose sight of the other legal rules that apply. Health and safety law (see 2.3.6), an employee's contractual rights (see 2.3.9) and the discrimination legislation (see 2.3.14) can all affect employers' freedom to regulate working time.

2.3.3   Some workers have the right not to be discriminated against because of the hours they work. This chapter outlines the protection that the law gives to part-time workers (see 2.3.82).

2.3.4   Finally, the chapter summarises the rights that employees have to time off work for various public duties (see 2.3.92) and for study and training (see 2.3.102).

Further rights

The following rights to time off work are dealt with elsewhere in the Guide:

- Maternity leave (see 2.2.25).
- Time off for antenatal care (see 2.2.12).

- Paternity leave (see 2.2.85).
- Adoption leave (see 2.2.103).
- Parental leave (see 2.2.128).
- Time off for dependants (see 2.2.161).
- Time off during notice of redundancy to find another job or retrain (see 5.2.111).
- Time off for trade union duties and activities (see 6.1.27).
- Time off to accompany a worker to a disciplinary or grievance hearing (see 3.3.90).
- Time off for employee representatives (see 6.4.76).
- Time off for pension scheme trustees (see 2.4.74) and representatives consulted on pension changes (see 2.4.79).

2.3.5 The law and good practice on managing absenteeism and sickness absence are covered elsewhere in this Guide (see 3.2.20), as are matters relating to short-time working (see 5.2.127) and parents' right to request a change in their working hours (see 2.2.150).

Health and safety

2.3.6 The most important legal consideration for an employer in structuring the working hours of its workforce is health and safety law. Employers are under a duty, under a term that is implied in every contract of employment and in the law of negligence, to take reasonable care for the health and safety of their employees. They are under a similar duty under the Health and Safety at Work etc Act 1974. These duties involve providing a safe system of working, which includes working hours.

Deciding hours

2.3.7 In deciding on the number of hours that employees will be required to work, when those hours will be worked, and how many rest breaks they will be given, employers must ensure that they do not endanger the health and safety of their workforce. If employees are asked to work long hours for an extended period, it may not only be their own physical and psychological health that is at risk. If their performance is affected by fatigue, they may also put at risk the safety of others, including their fellow employees and members of the public.

Employee characteristics

2.3.8 The steps that an employer needs to take to fulfil its duty to protect an employee's health and safety depend in part on the characteristics of that employee. Therefore special care may need to be taken to monitor the working patterns of vulnerable groups such as young workers and pregnant women and new mothers (see 2.2.18). The Working Time Regulations 1998 also make special provision for young workers, who are those below 18 but above 15 and compulsory school age, as summarised in the following box.

> ### Extra protection for young workers under the Working Time Regulations 1998
>
> - Eight-hour limit to the working day.
> - Forty-hour limit to the working week, with no possibility of averaging or 'opting out'.
> - Subject to several exceptions, no working between 10pm and 6am.
> - Health and capacities assessment before assignment to night work. Adults get health assessment only.
> - Thirty-minute rest break in each period of more than four and a half hours, rather than the adult entitlement of a rest break in each period of six hours.
> - Daily rest of 12 consecutive hours rather than the adult entitlement of 11 consecutive hours.
> - Weekly rest of 48 hours, rather than the adult entitlement of 24 hours.
> - Not covered by 'unmeasured working time' or 'special cases' exceptions.
> - Not covered by exceptions to daily and weekly rest breaks for shift workers changing shifts.
> - No scope to modify or exclude entitlement to rest breaks or daily and weekly rest periods by collective or workforce agreement.

Contract terms

2.3.9 Most written contracts of employment stipulate the number of hours that an employee will be required to work over a given period, and when those hours must be worked. There are also likely to be contract terms covering rest breaks, including details of their length and whether they are paid or unpaid. An employer that operates a shift system is likely to include details of the system in employees' contracts, either directly in the contract itself or by incorporating into the contract a collective agreement or other document where the detail can be found.

2.3.10 Even if they do not have a written contract of employment, all employees must be given a written statement of their terms and conditions relating to hours of work, including any terms and conditions on normal working hours (see 1.2.47).

Flexibility over hours

2.3.11 Many employers operate contracts of employment that give them flexibility over working hours. It is common, for example, for employers to have the power to require employees to alter their working hours by changing the shift that they work, or to extend their working hours by working overtime.

Overtime

2.3.12 Overtime can be of various types. It may be voluntary overtime, which the employee can choose whether or not to work. It may be guaranteed overtime, which the employer must provide. Or it may be compulsory overtime, which the employee must work if asked to do so by the employer but which may or may not be guaranteed. There may be conditions attached to an employer's power to require overtime working, such as a requirement that the employer should give the employee a certain number of hours' notice. Commonly, overtime is paid at a premium rate of pay or attracts the right to time off in lieu.

Implied terms

2.3.13 It is important to bear in mind that the flexibility that an employer has to regulate employees' working time may in practice be limited by implied terms in their employment contracts. For example, the courts have ruled that if an employer asks its employees to work such long hours that they become ill, it is breaching its implied duty to protect their health and safety, even if it has an express power in their contract to require them to work overtime.

Discrimination issues

2.3.14 Some employment terms relating to working hours have the potential to be challenged on the grounds that they are unlawfully discriminatory.

Sex discrimination

2.3.15 An example of potential unlawful sex discrimination is a term in a woman's contract giving her employer power to require her to work overtime without advance notice. Fewer women than men are able to comply with a term of this type, because more women than men have family and childcare responsibilities that limit their flexibility. If this particular employee cannot comply with the term, it amounts to unlawful indirect sex discrimination against her (see 3.1.37), unless her employer can show a clear business need for it.

2.3.16 An employer may find it difficult to justify a requirement that an employee must be prepared to work overtime without notice, if there is evidence that, by efficient management planning of its staffing needs, the employer could have avoided the need for any overtime working or at least have given the employee advance notice.

Religious discrimination

2.3.17 Most religions have festival days that followers are expected to observe. The Advisory Conciliation and Arbitration Service (ACAS) has produced guidance on the religious discrimination legislation that includes details of the festivals of the most widely followed religions (see 9.3.1). Companies should try to accommodate employees' requests to take their holiday entitlement at these times, where this is compatible with business needs, both as a matter of good practice and in order to avoid indirect religious discrimination. Likewise, it would be advisable for employers, where practicable, to accommodate employees' requests for time off during the working day for religious observance, perhaps by allowing employees to take their rest breaks at a different time. Companies who would like further advice on accommodating their employees' religious beliefs may wish to consult us or the ACAS guidance.

Disability discrimination

2.3.18   Disability discrimination law can also affect the organisation of working time. Employers have a duty under the Disability Discrimination Act 1995 to consider whether there are any reasonable adjustments that they might make to accommodate disabled job applicants or employees (see 3.1.69). The possible adjustments listed in the legislation include altering a person's working hours. For example, if an employee with impaired mobility finds it difficult to use public transport during the rush hour, it may be reasonable for a company to consider altering the employee's normal working hours to allow him or her to travel outside peak times. Likewise, employees with certain impairments may find night work difficult, so their employers may need to consider whether it would be reasonable to transfer them to day work.

Part-time workers and fixed-term employees

2.3.19   Under the Regulations on part-time and fixed-term work, employers must ensure that they do not treat part-time workers any less favourably than full-time workers, or fixed-term employees any less favourably than permanent employees, unless they can objectively justify doing so. (The Regulations are explained in more detail in 2.3.82 and 2.3.85.) This principle applies to terms and conditions relating to working time, including, for example, access to flexible working arrangements and holiday entitlement.

Working Time Regulations

2.3.20   The Working Time Regulations 1998 lay down detailed rules on:

- weekly working hours (see 2.3.35);

- the length of night work and health assessments for night workers (see 2.3.43);

- daily and weekly rest periods and in-work rest breaks (see 2.3.60); and

- annual holidays (see 2.3.71).

The Regulations give additional protection to young workers under 18 (see 2.3.8).

2.3.21 The requirements of the Regulations are summarised here, but companies that need more detailed guidance should contact us. The Department for Business, Enterprise and Regulatory Reform (now BIS) has also produced guidance on complying with the Regulations (see 9.2.3).

Scope of the Regulations

2.3.22 The Regulations apply to more people than just employees. They also apply to other workers who have a contract to carry out work for a company personally, unless they are contracting with the company in the course of their profession or business. The tribunals have adopted a wide interpretation of who is covered by the Regulations and they are willing to look at the substance of the relationship rather than just how it is expressed in the written contract. The Regulations will therefore cover many casual workers, self-employed labourers and homeworkers who are not employees. Those who are receiving work experience or training are covered even if they are not company employees, unless the work experience or training is being provided on a course run by an external trainer or educational institution. The Regulations therefore apply to those on National Traineeships or participating in the New Deal. Agency workers are also covered, but in this case the agency is likely to be responsible for ensuring that the Regulations are applied, rather than the company that is using the agency workers.

Compensatory rest

2.3.23 In some cases where workers are excluded from the Regulations, they must be given 'an equivalent period of compensatory rest'. The compensatory rest must be a continuous period and should be given as soon as is practicable, rather than being accumulated. Where, in exceptional circumstances, it is not possible for objective reasons to give a worker compensatory rest, the employer must take 'appropriate' steps to protect the worker's health and safety. It is unclear what this means. The Health and Safety Executive suggests that it could in some cases involve changing or restricting the worker's duties.

Entitlements and obligations

2.3.24   The requirements of the Regulations in relation to holidays, rest breaks and rest periods are expressed as entitlements. If a worker freely chooses not to take up these entitlements, the employer is not acting unlawfully. On the other hand, it is a criminal offence for an employer to fail to comply with its obligations in relation to limits on working time, and night work and health assessments for night workers.

Disadvantage and dismissal

2.3.25   It is unlawful for an employer to put a worker under any form of disadvantage for asserting or exercising his or her rights under the Regulations. Further, it is automatically unfair for an employer to dismiss a worker or select an employee for redundancy for that reason, regardless of the employee's length of service.

Keeping records

2.3.26   An employer must keep adequate records to show that it has complied with the weekly working time and night work limits and the requirement to provide health assessments for night workers. This includes keeping a record of those workers who have 'opted out' of the 48-hour working week. These records need to be available to the Health and Safety Executive and the local authority, which enforce these parts of the Regulations. In many cases, records kept for other purposes, such as pay records for hourly-paid workers, will be adequate to show compliance with the working time limits. Although the Regulations require records to be retained for only two years, employers may want to retain them for at least three years, in case they are needed to defend a personal injury claim.

Definition of working time

2.3.27 For the purposes of the Regulations, working time includes any period during which a worker is working, at the employer's disposal, and carrying out his or her activity or duties.

2.3.28 Time spent travelling may count as working time where this is part of the job, but travelling between home and work does not. 'On call' time counts as working time if the worker is required to be at the workplace during that time. However, 'on call' time does not count if the worker is not required to be at the workplace and is free to carry out other activities unless and until called upon to work. Time when the worker is receiving work experience or training counts as working time, except where it is provided on a course run by an external trainer or educational institution.

Excluded workers

2.3.29 Various groups of workers are excluded from some parts of the Regulations. For example, some, but not all, drivers are covered by some aspects of the Regulations. (The rules on drivers' hours are complex, and differ according to the type of vehicle that is being driven; we can provide details.)

2.3.30 Workers whose working time is not measured or predetermined or who can decide the length of their working time themselves, are covered only by the Regulations' requirements relating to annual holiday, night work assessments and workers under 18. For example, senior managers who are genuinely free to decide when and how long they work are excluded from most of the Regulations.

Other special cases

2.3.31 The Regulations' requirements on night work limits, daily and weekly rest periods and in-work rest breaks for adult workers do not apply to the categories of workers listed in the box below.

> ### Special cases
>
> 1. Workers whose activities are such that their home is distant from their workplace, or who have different places of work that are distant from each other.
> 2. Workers involved in security and surveillance work, where a permanent presence is required to protect property and people.
> 3. Workers involved in activities that require continuity of service or production, including industries where workers cannot interrupt their work on technical grounds.
> 4. Where there is a foreseeable surge in activity.
> 5. Where the worker's activities are affected by an unusual or unforeseeable occurrence beyond the employer's control, or an exceptional event that could not have been prevented by the employer taking proper care, or an accident or the imminent risk of an accident.

Nevertheless, these workers must usually be given a period of compensatory rest that is equivalent to the in-work rest break or daily or weekly rest that they have not received. In exceptional cases where it is not possible for objective reasons to allow the workers compensatory rest, they must be given appropriate protection for their health and safety.

Flexibility by agreement

2.3.32   Employers have some flexibility in the way in which they implement the Regulations. Certain details can be fixed through collective bargaining with an independent trade union, or through a 'relevant agreement' or a 'workforce agreement'.

2.3.33   A relevant agreement is a written, legally binding agreement between the employer and the worker (such as a term in a worker's written contract of employment), a collective agreement that is incorporated into the worker's contract (see 1.2.17) or a workforce agreement.

2.3.34   A workforce agreement is a written agreement signed by elected representatives of the workforce. In order for the agreement to be valid, the representatives must have been elected in a specified way. If an employer has 20 or fewer workers, it has the alternative option of reaching a workforce agreement with a majority of its workforce, rather than elected representatives. A workforce agreement can last up to five years. A workforce agreement cannot cover workers whose terms and conditions are provided for in a collective agreement. Because of the detailed requirements that apply to workforce agreements, a company that is considering entering into one should contact us for advice.

Working week limit

2.3.35   The broad principle behind the Working Time Regulations 1998 is that workers should not be required to work more than 48 hours on average in a week unless they have agreed in writing to do so. The Regulations specify how the average must be calculated and lay down the conditions that must be met if a worker is validly to 'opt out' of the weekly limit (see 2.3.41). For young workers under 18, there is an absolute limit of 40 hours on the working week and 8 hours on the working day, with no possibility of averaging or 'opting out' (see 2.3.8 and 2.3.42).

Taking reasonable steps

2.3.36   Employers must take 'all reasonable steps' to ensure that these limits are met. The government guidance assumes that the limits apply to work from whatever source, and suggests that employers may wish to ask their workers if they have other jobs. If an employer knows that a worker has another job that may take him or her over the 48-hour limit, the employer can then agree an opt-out with the worker. On the other hand, if a worker is taken over the limit because he or she has another job that the employer does not know about and could not reasonably have discovered, it is extremely unlikely that the employer would be found to have breached the Regulations.

Calculating the average

2.3.37   The first step in calculating whether a worker has exceeded the 48-hour limit is to identify the reference period over which the average has to be calculated.

2.3.38 The starting point is that the reference period is 17 weeks. This is a rolling period of any 17 weeks in the course of the worker's employment, unless a relevant agreement specifies successive fixed periods of 17 weeks (such as, for example, each successive 17-week period beginning on 1 January 2007).

2.3.39 For new recruits who have not yet worked for 17 weeks, the reference period is the period for which they have been employed. The reference period can be increased to up to 52 weeks by a collective or workforce agreement, if there are objective or technical reasons or reasons concerning the organisation of work that justify doing so. For the workers referred to as 'special cases' (see 2.3.31), the reference period is 26 weeks.

Certain days in the reference period are called 'excluded days'. These are days when the worker is taking annual holiday entitlement under the Regulations or is on sick leave or maternity, paternity, adoption or parental leave, and any days covered by the worker's agreement to 'opt out' of the 48-hour week (see 2.3.41).

2.3.40 In order to calculate the average:

1. Take the number of hours the worker has worked during the reference period.

2. Add the number of hours the worker has worked in the first X days after the reference period when the worker has worked, where X is the number of 'excluded days' in the reference period.

3. Divide the result by the number of weeks in the reference period.

Opting out

2.3.41 A worker can opt out of the 48-hour limit by agreeing in writing, in advance, to work longer hours. An opt-out agreement can relate to a specified period, or apply indefinitely. It can include a term requiring the worker to give up to three months' notice to terminate the agreement. If there is no notice clause in the agreement, the worker need only give seven days' notice in writing to terminate an opt-out. An opt-out agreement is available for download from EEF's website.

Young workers

2.3.42   For workers under 18, there is an absolute limit of 40 hours on the working week and 8 hours on the working day, with no possibility of averaging or 'opting out'. These limits can be exceeded if the young worker is needed to maintain continuity of service or production or to respond to a surge in demand, provided no adult is available to do the work and the work would not adversely affect the young worker's education or training. It is also lawful to exceed the limits if the young worker is needed to work immediately because of unusual and unforeseeable circumstances or exceptional events, provided the work is only temporary and no adult is available to do it. The young worker must be given an equivalent period of compensatory rest within the following three weeks.

Night work

2.3.43   Although the Health and Safety Executive does not consider that night work in itself poses a risk to workers' health or safety, night work can lead to health problems for employees with particular medical conditions. These include diabetes, heart or circulatory disorders, stomach or intestinal disorders, conditions that cause difficulties sleeping, chronic chest disorders, and medical conditions that require medication to a strict timetable. In order to meet their general health and safety duties, employers may need to consider transferring workers off night work if they have or develop any of these conditions.

Legal regulation of night work

2.3.44   The law also specifically acknowledges the particular nature of night work in two ways. First, night workers who are pregnant, breastfeeding or who have recently given birth may be entitled to be moved to day work, or to be suspended from work on full pay if no day work is available, if they have a certificate from their doctor or midwife stating that it is necessary for their health or safety that they should not work at night for a specified period (see 2.2.23). Second, the Working Time Regulations 1998 impose limits on the length of night work (see 2.3.47) and require employers to carry out health assessments on night workers (see 2.3.53) and to transfer them to day work when necessary to protect their health, where possible (see 2.3.58). Young workers under 18 must not usually work at all at night (see 2.3.52).

Defining night workers

2.3.45   For the purposes of the Regulations, a night worker is a worker who works at least three hours of his or her daily working time during night-time, as a normal course. This definitely covers workers who work at least three hours at night on a majority of their work days. It could also cover others. A court has held that a worker who worked at night for one-third of her working time was a night worker. The government guidance suggests that workers work at night 'as a normal course' if they do night work on a regular, as opposed to occasional, basis. A worker is also a night worker if he or she is likely to work at night for at least the proportion of his or her annual working time specified in a collective or workforce agreement (see 2.3.34).

2.3.46   Night-time is also defined in the Regulations. It must include the hours between midnight and 5 am. The other hours can be fixed by a relevant agreement (see 2.3.33), but if they are not, night-time is 11 pm to 6 am.

Night work limits

2.3.47   Under the Working Time Regulations 1998, employers must take 'all reasonable steps' to ensure that night workers' normal hours of work do not exceed an average of 8 hours in each 24-hour period. As with the limits on weekly working time, the employer may need to take into account work that an employee does for another employer when assessing whether the employee is exceeding this limit. The night work limits can be modified or excluded entirely by a collective or workforce agreement, provided the workers concerned are given compensatory rest or, in exceptional cases where that is not possible, other protection for their health and safety.

Calculating average hours

2.3.48   A worker's average hours are calculated over a reference period of a rolling period of any 17 weeks in the course of the worker's employment, unless a relevant agreement specifies fixed successive periods of 17 weeks (such as, for example, each successive 17-week period beginning on 1 January 2007). For new recruits who have not yet worked for 17 weeks, the reference period is the period for which they have been employed.

2.3.49 In order to calculate a worker's average hours, it is first necessary to identify what his or her normal working hours are. This will include looking at his or her working pattern over time, including overtime. To work out the average:

1. Take the number of days in the reference period.

2. Subtract the number of hours the worker has spent on weekly rest entitlement under the Regulations (see 2.3.68) divided by 24.

3. Divide the number of normal working hours in the reference period by the resultant figure.

Special hazards

2.3.50 There are stricter limits for night workers involved in work that involves special hazards or heavy physical or mental strain. Employers must ensure that these workers do not work more than 8 hours in any 24-hour period.

2.3.51 A worker's job definitely falls into this category if it is identified as involving special hazards or strain in a collective or workforce agreement that takes account of the specific effects and hazards of night work. A job also falls into this category if the employer has recognised that it involves a significant risk to health or safety in a risk assessment under the Management of Health and Safety at Work Regulations 1999. Work may be especially hazardous even if it has not been identified in one of these ways.

Young workers

2.3.52 Workers under 18 are prohibited from working between 10 pm and 6 am. If their contract requires them to work beyond 10 pm, then the restricted period is 11 pm to 7 am. It is lawful to employ a young worker in this period only if he or she is needed to work immediately because of unusual and unforeseeable circumstances or exceptional events, the work is only temporary, and no adult is available to do it. The young worker must be given an equivalent period of compensatory rest within the following three weeks.

Health assessments

2.3.53 An employer must not assign a worker to night work unless the employer has first given the worker the opportunity to have a free health assessment. There is no need to offer an assessment if the worker had an assessment when assigned to night work on a previous occasion and the employer has no reason to believe that the original assessment is no longer valid.

2.3.54 Employers must also ensure that night workers have an opportunity to have their health reassessed at regular intervals, without cost to themselves. The frequency of this must depend on what is appropriate in a particular worker's case, in the light of the type of night work the worker does, its duration and the worker's age and state of health. Employers may need to obtain advice on this from a healthcare professional. The government guidance on the Regulations says that in many cases an annual assessment may be appropriate.

2.3.55 An employer has a similar duty to ensure that workers under 18 who are asked to work at any time between 10 pm and 6 am have the opportunity to have a free assessment of their health and capacities, before they are assigned and then at regular intervals. This should take into account whether the young workers' physique, maturity and experience make them suitable for night work. There is no need to offer an assessment if the work that the young worker is assigned to do is of an exceptional nature.

Health questionnaires

2.3.56 The government guidance to the Regulations suggests that a health assessment can usually be limited to asking the worker to complete a questionnaire that asks specific questions about health that are relevant to the type of night work the worker will be doing. A medical examination will be necessary only where the questionnaire leaves the employer in some doubt about the worker's fitness to do night work. The guidance also suggests that employers should get help from a suitably qualified health professional when devising and assessing the questionnaire.

Disclosure

2.3.57   The Regulations prohibit the disclosure of an assessment to anyone other than the worker unless the worker has consented to the disclosure in writing, or the disclosure is simply a statement that the worker is fit to do night work. If the employee's own doctor produces a medical report for the assessment, the employee will have a right under the Access to Medical Reports Act 1988 to see the report before it is supplied and to refuse to allow it to be disclosed (see 3.2.67).

Transfer to day work

2.3.58   If a doctor has advised an employer that a worker is suffering from health problems that the doctor considers to be connected with working at night, the Working Time Regulations require the employer to transfer the worker to suitable day work, where that is possible.

2.3.59   If a transfer to day work involves a change in a worker's contract terms, such as a reduction in pay, the employee's consent may be required. The issue of securing changes in employees' contractual terms is dealt with in Chapter 5.1 of this Guide.

Rest breaks and periods

2.3.60   Under the Working Time Regulations 1998, workers are entitled to rest breaks during the working day (see 2.3.62), rest periods between periods of work (see 2.3.66) and weekly rest periods (see 2.3.68). All of these requirements can be modified or excluded, in so far as they apply to adult workers, by a collective or workforce agreement. However, the workers must then be given an equivalent period of compensatory rest or, in exceptional cases where it is not possible for objective reasons to allow the workers compensatory rest, appropriate protection for their health and safety.

2.3.61   The Regulations also state that the worker must be given adequate rest breaks if the pattern by which the work is organised puts the worker's health and safety at risk. This covers in particular where the work is monotonous or the work-rate is predetermined.

Breaks during work

2.3.62 If a worker's daily working time is more than six hours, he or she is entitled to a rest break during that period. This requirement could be met, for example, by giving the worker a meal break.

2.3.63 The length of the break and whether it is paid or unpaid can be set by a collective or workforce agreement (see 2.3.34). In the absence of an agreement, the worker is entitled to an uninterrupted rest break of at least 20 minutes, which can be spent away from the workstation, if the worker has one. The Regulations do not require the rest break to be paid, although many workers have the right to be paid during rest breaks under their contracts of employment.

2.3.64 Workers under 18 are entitled to a 30-minute rest break if their total daily working time, for one or more employers, is more than four and a half hours. An employer can ask a young worker to work during his or her rest break if no adult is available to do the work and it has to be performed immediately, it is temporary and it has arisen from unusual and unforeseeable circumstances or exceptional events. The young worker must be given an equivalent period of compensatory rest within the following three weeks.

Rest facilities

2.3.65 Although the Working Time Regulations leave much of the detail of rest breaks to be set by agreement, it is worth noting that the Workplace (Health, Safety and Welfare) Regulations 1992 require employers to provide 'suitable and sufficient' rest facilities. Rest facilities for pregnant women and breastfeeding mothers should be close to toilets and include the facility to lie down.

Rest between periods of work

2.3.66 A worker is entitled to a rest period of at least 11 consecutive hours in each 24-hour period. This does not apply to shift workers when they change shift and cannot take 11 hours off between the end of one shift and the start of the next. Nor does it apply to workers whose work is split up over the day, such as cleaning staff. However, these workers must usually be given an equivalent period of compensatory rest. In exceptional cases where it is not possible for objective reasons to allow the workers compensatory rest, they must be given appropriate protection for their health and safety.

2.3.67   If a worker is under 18, he or she is entitled to daily rest of 12 consecutive hours. However, this rest period may be interrupted if the job involves periods of work that are short or split up over the day. An employer can also ask a young worker to work during the daily rest period if no adult worker is available to do the work and the work has to be performed immediately, is temporary and is due to unusual and unforeseeable circumstances or exceptional events. The worker must be given an equivalent period of compensatory rest within the following three weeks.

Weekly rest periods

2.3.68   An adult worker is entitled to an uninterrupted rest period of at least 24 hours in each seven-day period. Alternatively, the employer can give two rest periods of 24 hours or one rest period of 48 hours in each 14-day period. Workers under 18 are entitled to 48 hours uninterrupted rest in each seven-day period.

2.3.69   The entitlement to a weekly rest period is additional to the entitlement to a daily rest break. However, for adult workers, the two may overlap if there is an objective or technical reason, or a reason concerning the organisation of work, that justifies them doing so. For workers under 18, the weekly rest period may be interrupted if their periods of work are short, or split up over the day. The length of their rest period may also be reduced, but only where this is justified for technical or organisational reasons, and the rest period does not fall below 36 hours.

2.3.70   Adult shift workers are not entitled to the weekly rest break when they are changing shift and cannot take a weekly rest period between the end of one shift and the start of the next. Adult workers whose work is split up over the day, such as cleaning staff, are also excluded from the weekly rest break entitlement. However, these workers must be given an equivalent period of compensatory rest or, in exceptional cases where it is not possible for objective reasons to allow the workers compensatory rest, appropriate protection for their health and safety.

Holidays

2.3.71   The two main legal issues that employers need to bear in mind in relation to holiday entitlement are employees' contractual terms on holidays and the need to comply with the minimum holiday entitlement laid down by the Working Time Regulations 1998 (as amended). There are also some more specific issues that may arise in relation to employees who are on maternity, adoption or parental leave (see 2.3.76).

Contract terms and the Working Time Regulations

2.3.72   Employees' holiday entitlement is likely to be spelt out in their written contract of employment, if they have one. Even an employee who does not have a written contract must be given a written statement of his or her holiday rights, including entitlement to public holidays and holiday pay (see 1.2.47). The detail must be sufficient to enable the employee to work out his or her exact entitlement, including any entitlement to accrued holiday pay when his or her employment ends.

2.3.73   When drafting contract terms on holidays, employers need to ensure that the terms meet the requirements of the Working Time Regulations 1998. However, if an employer gives more generous holidays than the Regulations require, it is free to decide the terms of that extra entitlement. If a company wants those terms to differ from the terms of entitlement to holidays under the Regulations, such as in relation to the calculation of holiday pay, it should make that clear in the contract. It is also useful to remember that many of the requirements of the Regulations can be modified by a written contract of employment, which counts as a 'relevant agreement' (see 2.3.33).

2.3.74   When drafting contract terms on holidays, employers will need to cover some or all of the following issues:

  1. *The number of days holiday to which the employee is entitled.* Employers need to decide:
     - what holiday entitlement to give;
     - whether entitlement should rise with length of service; and

- how entitlement is affected by periods of maternity, adoption and parental leave (discussed further below in 2.3.76).

The minimum is set by the Regulations, which provide that all workers are entitled to 5.6 weeks' holiday each year. A week's holiday should allow the worker to be away from work for a week. For example, someone working a five-day week is entitled to 28 working days off work a year, with a pro-rata basis for part-timers. In principle, awarding employees more holidays the longer their length of service could amount to indirect age discrimination. The age equality legislation provides a limited exemption, however, for service-related benefits of this type (see 2.1.74).

2. *The timing of the holiday year.* Employers would be well advised to stipulate in the contract when the holiday year begins. The Regulations allow for the worker's leave year to be set by a relevant agreement (see 2.3.33). However, if there is no agreement, then it runs from the date when the worker's employment began or, if he or she started work before 2 October 1998, from 1 October. Specifying the holiday year in the worker's contract allows the employer to operate one holiday year for the entire workforce.

3. *Carry-over of holidays.* Employers may wish to decide whether any holiday entitlement not used in one leave year can be carried forward and if it can, on what terms. Under the Regulations, a worker must be allowed to take their statutory leave in the year it is due. However, if the sole reason why that leave has not been taken is sickness absence (or family leave other than parental leave), you should allow them to carry it forward. But there is nothing to prevent an employer agreeing with an employee to carry over any additional contractual leave entitlement into the following year.

4. *Payment in lieu of holidays.* Employers may want to consider whether there are any circumstances where they would want the power to require the employee to accept a payment in lieu of holiday. Under the Regulations the statutory holiday entitlement cannot be replaced by a payment in lieu except at the end of the worker's employment.

5. *Public holidays.* The contract will need to state whether the employee is entitled to any public holidays and what happens if a public holiday falls

on a day when the employee would not normally be working. There is no legal obligation on an employer to allow its workforce time off on a public holiday, although many employers choose to do so. Any public holidays that a worker is given count towards his or her holiday entitlement under the Regulations. The government gives details of public holidays for the current and future years in England and Wales (see 9.2.3). Information on public holidays in Scotland can be obtained through the Scottish Executive (see 9.2.3). This information is also available from us.

6. *Notice of holiday dates.* Employers will wish to make clear what notice employees must give of their holiday dates. The Regulations allow this to be set by a relevant agreement. If there is no agreement, then the worker must give the employer notice at least twice as many days before the holiday begins as the holiday is to last. For example, if the employee wants to take a fortnight's holiday, he or she must give the employer at least four weeks' notice. The employer can respond by requiring the employee not to take holiday on those days, as explained below.

7. *Annual shutdowns and peak periods.* Some companies may wish to stipulate that employees will be required to take holiday at a certain time, such as over Christmas and the New Year or during an annual shutdown. It may also be necessary to make clear that there are periods when holiday cannot be taken, such as at busy times in the production cycle. The Regulations allow an employer to control when holiday is taken. If an employer wants a worker to take holiday on certain dates, it must give the worker notice that is at least twice as long as the holiday is to last. For example, if a company wants a worker to take 10 days' holiday over Christmas and the New Year, it must give the worker at least 20 days' advance notice. (This is the notice required by the Regulations – it would, of course, be good practice to give the workforce as much notice as possible of an annual shutdown of this type.) Where an employer wants to prevent a worker taking holiday on certain dates, it must give the worker notice that is at least as long as the period over which the worker must not take leave. For example, if a worker has given the company notice that he or she wants to take two weeks' holiday but the company is unable to spare the worker for the first week of that period, the company must let the worker know that he or she cannot take

that week at least one week before the holiday was due to begin. These notices do not need to be in writing, although it would be advisable for them to be. (Again, it would be good practice to give employees as much notice as possible of periods when they cannot be released.) Employers that do not allow employees to take leave during certain periods should bear in mind that they may need to establish that these policies meet objective business needs, in order to avoid indirect race or religious discrimination (see 2.3.17). The position of employees on family leave is dealt with at 2.3.78.

8. *Calculation of holiday pay*. Under the Regulations, a worker is entitled to be paid a week's pay for each week's leave. A week's pay is calculated according to the rules laid down in the Employment Rights Act 1996, explained in Appendix 8.2 of this Guide. If an employer wants pay for days of contractual holiday in excess of the statutory minimum to be calculated on a different basis, this needs to be made clear in the worker's contract.

9. *Illness and holiday*. Employees are now entitled to reclassify working time holiday as sick leave if they fall ill whilst on prearranged working time holiday. This means that they are entitled to take the working time holiday they have missed at a later date. If they are unable to take the rest of their statutory holiday that holiday year they can carry it over to the next holiday year. If you offer more than 5.6 weeks' holiday a year, you do not have to allow an employee to reclassify any additional (contractual) holiday as sickness absence. However, you will have to ensure that they can take their full working time holiday at other times. If you pay contractual sick pay, you can minimise the scope for abuse by making contractual sick pay in these circumstances contingent on the employee notifying you on the first day of illness that they are ill and, possibly, requiring them to provide a medical certificate from day 1. For further advice, contact us.

Employees who are on sick leave can ask their employer to re-classify their absence as statutory holiday in order to receive holiday pay. If an employee on sick leave does not want to take their outstanding statutory holiday before your current leave year ends, they should be permitted to carry it over into the next leave year. Employees returning from sick leave can take their statutory holiday entitlement for the current year on their return, but if there is insufficient time for them to take it, they should be allowed to carry it forward to the next leave year.

10. *Calculation of an employee's holiday entitlement in the first and last year of employment.* It would be advisable for a worker's contract to clarify his or her holiday entitlement in the first and last year of employment. This could simply follow the scheme in the Regulations. This says that workers who begin employment after the leave year has begun are entitled to a proportion of their annual entitlement, rounded up where necessary to the nearest whole day. The Regulations limit when workers can take their leave entitlement in their first year of employment. They can take only the amount of their entitlement that has accrued by the time they want to take leave. They accrue one-twelfth of their annual entitlement at the beginning of each month, rounded up where necessary to the nearest half day. Employees who have not taken their entitlement under the Regulations by the time of leaving employment are entitled to a payment in lieu of the holiday not taken. The amount of that payment can be set by a relevant agreement. If it is not, it will equal the holiday pay due for the proportion of the holiday year that has passed, less any holiday already taken. If employees have outstanding leave from previous years, contact us.

11. *Recovery of overpayment of holiday pay.* The contract should make clear that if an employee takes more holiday than he or she is entitled to during the course of a leave year, the company will be entitled to recover the overpayment of holiday pay by deducting it from the employee's wages or salary. It is advisable for the company to consult with the employee before making the deduction, in order to avoid an allegation that it is acting in breach of its implied obligation to maintain trust and confidence between itself and the employee (see 1.2.45). The Regulations say that a relevant agreement can require a departing worker who has taken more holiday than was due to compensate the employer by making a payment, undertaking additional work, or in some other way. If there is no relevant agreement, then an employer is not entitled to recover the overpaid holiday pay.

2.3.75   Since there may be many details to cover, employers may prefer not to spell out holiday terms in the body of an employee's written contract, but rather to refer in the contract to some other document where the detail can be found, such as a staff handbook, collective agreement or holiday policy.

Impact of family leave

2.3.76   The entitlement that an employee has to paid holiday under the Working Time Regulations 1998 is unaffected by the fact that he or she may be on maternity, paternity, adoption or parental leave for part of the leave year. The employee, therefore, is entitled to at least 5.6 weeks' paid holiday in addition to these forms of family leave. When calculating holiday pay under the Regulations (in accordance with the rules on a week's pay explained in Appendix 8.2), any weeks when an employee is on family leave and receiving no pay or less than normal pay are disregarded.

2.3.77   Any contractual holiday entitlement that an employee has, over and above the 5.6-week statutory minimum, is not affected by maternity or adoption leave or paternity leave, because the legislation preserves an employee's terms and conditions during that period (see 2.2.42, 2.2.111 and 2.2.93). It is advisable for employers to make clear in the contract how holiday entitlement is affected by parental leave. She must, however, be allowed the 5.6-week entitlement in order to meet the requirements of the Working Time Regulations.

2.3.78   An employee's contract may state that holidays must be taken on certain days in the year, such as public holidays or an annual shutdown. If these happen to fall while the employee is on family leave, he or she is not entitled to other days off in lieu. All employees must, however, be allowed to take at least their 5.6 weeks' leave under the Working Time Regulations.

2.3.79   If an employee is on family leave for a substantial part or even the whole of the holiday year, it may be difficult or even impossible to ensure that the employee also takes his or her holiday entitlement. The legal position is still unclear about precise entitlements but detailed advice depending on the particular circumstances is available from us.

Non-statutory leave

2.3.80 Although not legally obliged to do so, employers may wish as a matter of good practice to give employees time off work for reasons not covered by the employment legislation:

1. *Time off to keep appointments.* If an appointment to visit the doctor, dentist, optician, hospital or clinic cannot be made outside working hours, employers may wish to consider allowing employees time off to attend them, as a matter of good practice.

2. *Compassionate leave.* Under employment legislation, employees have a right to a reasonable amount of unpaid time off work to take action that is necessary as the result of the death of a dependant (see 2.2.161). Employers may wish to consider whether to grant additional leave to cover a broader range of situations including, for example, the death of family members not covered by the statutory right to time off.

3. *Extended leave.* Employers may be prepared to grant extended leave in some circumstances, such as where an employee wishes to undertake training or visit relatives in a distant country. In these cases, it is advisable to put the terms on which leave is granted in writing. If an employee does not attend for work at the end of a period of extended leave, he or she should be dealt with in the same way as any other employee who takes unauthorised absence. That could include, where appropriate, applying the disciplinary procedure.

4. *Breaks from work.* If an employee wants to take a substantial period off work, it may be more appropriate for him or her to resign, although the company may be willing to offer the employee a job if one is available when he or she is ready to return to work. It would be highly advisable to confirm this type of arrangement in writing, to ensure that the company makes clear the extent of its commitment to offer re-employment. If the company does not want an employee to continue to build up his or her period of continuous employment (see Appendix 8.1) during a break from work, it should confirm in writing that it does not view the employee as continuing in employment for any purpose during the break.

2.3.81   Employers who choose to give extra leave can do so on a discretionary basis or by giving employees additional rights in their contracts of employment. Even if leave is non-contractual and granted on a discretionary basis, it is advisable for those considering a request for leave to have some form of internal management guidelines on the issues that should be taken into account in deciding whether to grant leave. This will help to ensure a consistent and objective approach to requests, and avoid the danger of discrimination. The guidelines might also cover whether any conditions should be applied to leave that is granted. An employer may, for example, be more inclined to allow time off if the employee is prepared to make up the time at some future date.

Part-time working

2.3.82   There has been a substantial growth in part-time work in recent years. The government has issued guidance on best practice in the use of part-time workers, covering issues such as widening access to part-time work and making part-time work more accessible (see 9.2.3).

2.3.83   Employers who differentiate between full-time and part-time workers in their employment practices need to bear in mind two aspects of the law. One is indirect sex discrimination. The other is the need to comply with the Part-time Workers (Prevention of Less Favourable Treatment) Regulations 2000.

Indirect sex discrimination

2.3.84   A large majority of part-time workers are women. Employers who limit the benefits or opportunities available to part-timers may therefore be indirectly discriminating against their female employees on the ground of their sex, unless they can objectively justify their position (see 3.1.37).

Part-time Workers Regulations

2.3.85   The broad principle established by the Part-time Workers (Prevention of Less Favourable Treatment) Regulations 2000 is that an employer must treat part-timers of either sex equally with full-timers, unless it can objectively justify treating them less favourably. Treating part-timers less favourably is justified only if the employer can show that the treatment is aimed at achieving a legitimate objective, it is necessary to achieve that object and it is an appropriate way of achieving that objective.

2.3.86　In order for a comparison to be possible under the Regulations between a part-timer and a full-timer, they must work under similar types of contract. For example, the Regulations do not allow a comparison between the terms and conditions of a part-time 'worker' (see 1.2.76) or traditional apprentice (see 1.2.85) and those of a full-time employee. Comparisons are possible, however, between employees working under fixed-term contracts and employees with open-ended contracts. The comparison must also be between workers doing the same or broadly similar work, taking into account, where relevant, their level of qualifications, skills and experience.

2.3.87　A different comparison applies for part-time workers whose hours have been reduced from full-time, or who were full-timers but have returned to work on part-time hours after less than 12 months off work. They are entitled to the same terms as they had while full-timers, unless their employer can objectively justify treating them otherwise.

Equal treatment principle

2.3.88　The principle of equal treatment applies to all terms and conditions of employment, although a part-timer's entitlement may need to be reduced to reflect the hours he or she works, where relevant. For example, if a full-timer who has normal hours of 38 hours a week is entitled to 65 working days' occupational sick pay, a comparable part-timer on 19 hours a week should be entitled to 32.5 days' sick pay, unless the employer can objectively justify giving the part-timer less. (In this example, both full-timer and part-timer are entitled to 13 weeks' sick pay, but the full-timer receives five days' sick pay each week whereas the part-timer receives two and a half days' sick pay each week.) It is lawful, however, not to pay part-timers an overtime premium until they have exceeded full-time hours. Pay discrimination against part-timers is discussed in 2.1.79.

Protection against disadvantage

2.3.89　The Regulations are not limited to contractual terms. They also require employers not to put part-timers at any other type of disadvantage compared with full-timers, unless they have objective justification for doing so.

Government guidance therefore recommends that, in order to comply with the law, employers should ensure that part-time staff are not excluded from training opportunities simply because they work part-time, and that training should be scheduled so far as possible so that all staff, including part-timers, can attend. Similarly, part-time status should not of itself be a barrier to promotion. And part-timers should be treated in the same way as full-timers in a redundancy situation, on the basis of selection criteria that are objectively justified.

Providing written reasons

2.3.90   Part-timers who believe they may have been discriminated against because of their part-time status can ask their employer for written reasons for their treatment. If an employer fails to respond to a request without reasonable excuse, or provides a response that is evasive or unclear, and the part-timer then brings a claim under the Regulations, the employment tribunal that hears the claim is entitled to take the employer's conduct into account when deciding whether it has complied with the Regulations.

Victimisation

2.3.91   It is unlawful for an employer to penalise a worker for asserting or enforcing his or her rights under the Regulations, or for supporting someone else in bringing a claim. It is also automatically unfair to dismiss an employee on these grounds, regardless of the employee's length of service. This protection does not apply where a worker has alleged that his or her employer has breached the Regulations and the allegation was not only false but also not made in good faith.

Time off for public duties

2.3.92   Employees involved in public duties of various types have the right to time off work to carry out those duties. The Employment Rights Act 1996 gives the right to time off to serve on various public bodies (see 2.3.93). Time off for jury service is covered by the Juries Act 1974 (see 2.3.96). There is also separate legislation covering the position of members of the Volunteer Reserve Forces (see 2.3.99).

Service on public bodies

2.3.93   Under the Employment Rights Act 1996, a company must allow employees who are magistrates or members of certain public bodies a reasonable amount of unpaid time off work to perform their duties. The relevant public bodies are currently these:

- Justice of the Peace.
- Local authorities, including the Common Council of the City of London, National Park authorities and the Broads Authority.
- Police Authorities.
- Statutory tribunals (such as employment tribunals).
- Monitoring boards of prisons.
- Certain health bodies.
- Certain education bodies.
- The Environment Agency and the Scottish Environment Protection Agency.
- Scottish Water or a Water Customer Consultation Panel.

More precise details are available from us.

2.3.94   In deciding how much time off to allow and under what conditions, an employer is entitled to take into account how much time off for public duties or for trade union duties and activities the employee has already had, and the impact the employee's absence will have on the running of the business.

2.3.95   A company is under no legal obligation to pay an employee during time off spent on public duties. The employee may be entitled to allowances or expenses from the body on which he or she serves.

Jury service

2.3.96   An employee who is 18 or over may be required to attend for jury service, under the Juries Act 1974. It is possible for an employee to put off jury service to a later date if, for example, it clashes with work commitments or holiday dates, but this can be done only once. A form to apply for a deferral accompanies the jury summons. Employers are not obliged to pay employees for time spent on jury service, but employees can claim expenses and compensation for loss of earnings for their attendance at court from the Court Service.

2.3.97   It is unlawful for an employer to penalise, dismiss or select an employee for redundancy on the ground that he or she has been summoned for or undertaken jury service. This protection applies regardless of the employee's age or length of service. If the employee's absence on jury service would cause substantial damage to the employer's business and the employee unreasonably refuses to apply to be excused jury service or have it deferred, then it is not automatically unfair for the employer to dismiss the employee or select the employee for redundancy on the ground of jury service. In order to avoid a finding of unfair dismissal, however, the employer must still follow a fair dismissal procedure and act reasonably in all the circumstances before deciding to dismiss.

2.3.98   Further information on jury service can be obtained from the Court Service (see 9.2.3).

Volunteer Reserve Forces

2.3.99   Employees who are members of the Volunteer Reserve Forces are usually required to attend a continuous 15-day training period each year, in addition to occasional weekend and evening training. Employers will need to decide whether to give additional leave for this purpose or require that some or all of the leave should be taken from the employees' annual holiday entitlement. Although reservists receive allowances and pay for attending annual training, it is good practice to ensure that they do not lose out financially because of their duties.

2.3.100 Reservists may be called out for permanent service in the event of national emergency or war, and for peacekeeping and humanitarian operations. The Reserve Forces (Safeguard of Employment) Act 1985 requires employers to offer reservists their old job back, or one that is reasonably equivalent, on their return from call-up, if this is reasonably practicable. The Act also makes it an offence to dismiss someone for being liable to be called out.

2.3.101 If the absence of a reservist would cause serious harm to its business and staffing cover is not available, the employer has the right to apply for the employee to be exempt from the call-out or for the call-out to be deferred. Employers can also apply for compensation for the additional costs they incur as a result of an employee being called out. Further information on the Volunteer Reserve Forces is available from the National Employer Advisory Board for the Armed Forces (see 9.2.3).

Time off for young people for study and training

2.3.102 Under the Employment Rights Act 1996, employees who are 16 or 17 and have not reached a certain level of educational achievement must be given a reasonable amount of paid time off work to study or train for qualifications to reach that level. Employees who are 18 but began the study or training before reaching that age also qualify.

2.3.103 The relevant standard of achievement is defined in detail in the Right to Time off for Study or Training Regulations 2001 and the Right to Time off for Study or Training (Scotland) Regulations 1999. Broadly, the standard is:

- five GCSEs at grades A* to C; or
- Scottish Qualifications Authority Standard Grades at grades 1 to 3 in five subjects; or
- one Intermediate level GNVQ; or
- one General Scottish Vocational Qualification at level 2; or
- one National Vocational Qualification at level 2; or
- one Scottish Vocational Qualification at level 2.

In deciding what time off to allow, an employer is entitled to take into account its business circumstances and the impact the employee's time off will have on the running of the business.

2.3.104 More details of this right are available from the Department of Children, Schools and Families (see 9.2.3).

The right to request time off for training and study

2.3.105   From 6 April 2010, all employees with more than 26 weeks' continuous employment who work for an organisation where there are 250 or more employees are entitled to request time off for study or training. The training should improve business performance and the employee's effectiveness in the employer's business. From 6 April 2011, the right will apply to employees working in all organisations of all sizes.

2.3.106   The right to request time off for training or study is closely modelled on the right to request flexible working. The employer must consider the request carefully, but can turn down the request on specified business grounds. The employer is not required to pay for the time off or the training. The online version of the *Employment Guide* will be updated with more details of this right when the regulations are finalised.

2.4

Pension rights

Overview

2.4.1 For a variety of reasons, access to an occupational pension is an increasingly significant benefit of being in work. Employers who can afford to offer an occupational pension are aware of its importance in recruiting and retaining staff. This chapter of the Guide outlines the various types of pension schemes (see 2.4.7) and pension benefits that are available (see 2.4.22), and the legal (see 2.4.23) and taxation (see 2.4.26) frameworks within which they operate. It then goes on to summarise the main employment law issues that arise from pension provision.

2.4.2 One of the most important legal issues for employers to consider is how they should frame employees' pension rights in their contracts of employment (see 2.4.28). In deciding who should be entitled to a pension and on what terms, there are some important principles of discrimination law that need to be borne in mind (see 2.4.32).

2.4.3 In order to foster employee involvement in pensions, the law requires pension fund trustees and managers to provide information on the pension scheme and the benefits it provides (see 2.4.52). Further, an employer with a workforce of 50 or more that was contemplating making certain changes to its pension scheme is required to consult with the active and prospective members of the scheme (see 2.4.61). Also, pension scheme members are entitled to nominate and select at least a third of the trustees who are responsible for running their pension scheme. Pension trustees who are employees have the right to paid time off work to carry out their duties, and are protected from being penalised or dismissed for carrying out their role (see 2.4.74).

2.4.4 Given the complexities of pension schemes, disputes about entitlement may arise. The law requires all pension schemes to have an internal procedure for dealing with disputes between members and the scheme's trustees or managers (see 2.4.76).

2.4.5 Reflecting the importance that the government attaches to pension provision, even employers that do not themselves provide occupational pensions may be under a duty to provide their employees with access to a stakeholder pension. This chapter explains which employers are covered by this obligation and what is involved in meeting it (see 2.4.79).

Other issues

2.4.6 Other parts of this Guide deal with:

- the special rules that apply to employees' pension rights during maternity, paternity, adoption and parental leave (see 2.2.41, 2.2.95, 2.2.112 and 2.2.140);
- ill-health early retirement (see 3.2.47);
- what happens to pension rights on the transfer of a business (see 5.3.56).

Types of pension schemes

2.4.7 Pension schemes are of various types, as outlined below. There are strict legal controls on who can give financial advice, and employers should therefore ensure that they do not advise employees on the best pension option for them. Employees cannot be required by their employer to join a particular scheme, or indeed any scheme. HM Revenue and Customs has produced a free leaflet giving information on pension options for employees and sources of further guidance and help (see 9.2.4).

2.4.8 There are two main types of company pension scheme: those that provide defined benefits and those that are based on defined contributions.

Defined benefit schemes

2.4.9 Defined benefit schemes provide pensions that are defined by reference to, generally, the employee's salary at or near retirement and how long the employee has been a member of the scheme. Commonly, employees accrue the right to a pension of one-eightieth or one-sixtieth of their salary at or near retirement for each year they are in the scheme. Therefore an employee with 40 years' service in a defined benefit scheme with an accrual rate of one-eightieth will retire on half his or her salary at or near retirement.

2.4.10 These schemes may require employees to make a contribution ('contributory schemes') or, less frequently, may be entirely funded by the employer ('non-contributory schemes'). The employer must make whatever contributions are necessary to fund the scheme adequately, based on actuarial advice. If the pension fund is in surplus, the scheme rules may allow the employer to reduce its contributions or pay no contributions for a period (sometimes referred to as taking a 'contributions holiday').

Defined contribution schemes

2.4.11 Some pension schemes are funded by specified contributions from the employer, and sometimes also from the employee, defined as a percentage of the employee's wages or salary. While the employer's liability to pay contributions is fixed, the size of the pension is not. It depends not only on the size of the contributions that have been paid into the fund by the employer and the employee, but also on how well those contributions have been invested, and what annuity rates are available when the employee reaches pension age.

Additional voluntary contributions

2.4.12 Employees who want to enhance their pension benefits can make additional voluntary contributions (AVCs). There are rules that apply to both occupational and personal pension schemes for people who want to pay more into their pension scheme.

Personal pensions

2.4.13   Employees cannot be forced to join an employer's pension scheme. They may prefer to take out a personal pension. Personal pensions are also an option for employees whose employer does not offer an occupational pension.

2.4.14   Personal pensions are operated by financial services companies, independently of employers. Employers can, however, arrange for personal pensions to be offered on a group basis (known as a 'group personal pension scheme'), so giving employees the benefit of the lower administrative charges that come with economies of scale.

Some employers choose to contribute to employees' personal pensions as an alternative to providing a pension scheme themselves.

Stakeholder pensions

2.4.15   Stakeholder pension schemes are operated by financial services companies rather than by employers. But certain employers must facilitate employees' access to a stakeholder pension, by choosing a scheme (after consulting with employees), providing employees with information on the scheme and deducting employees' contributions to the scheme from their pay if they choose to join. Stakeholder pensions are discussed in more detail later in this chapter (see 2.4.79).

The basic state pension

2.4.16   Occupational and personal pensions operate against the backdrop of the state retirement pension. Employees are eligible for the basic flat-rate state pension if they have paid, or been credited with, sufficient National Insurance contributions. Men need to have contributions for 44 years, women for 39, to qualify for the full pension. (Women will also need 44 years' contributions when the state pension age is equalised for men and women.) Those without full National Insurance contributions records may still be entitled to a reduced basic state pension.

2.4.17   The age at which the state pension becomes payable is currently 65 for men and 60 for women. A common retirement age of 65 is to be phased in over a 10-year period, beginning in April 2010. Women born before 6 April 1950 will continue to be able to claim their state pension at 60, but women born on or after 6 April 1955 will not be able to claim their pension until they reach 65. Women born between 6 April 1950 and 5 April 1955 will receive their pension at some age between 60 and 65, depending on their date of birth.

2.4.18 Those who do not qualify for a full basic state pension may qualify for a non-contributory pension once they reach the age of 80.

The State Second Pension and 'contracting out'

2.4.19 Between 1978 and 2002, the state administered a State Earnings-Related Pension Scheme (SERPS), which provided additional benefits based on earnings between the lower and upper National Insurance earnings limits. In April 2002, the State Second Pension was introduced. This provides a more generous additional state pension for low and moderate earners and certain carers and people with a long-term illness or disability.

2.4.20 If an employer's pension scheme meets certain conditions, it is entitled to 'contract out' of the State Second Pension by applying for a contracting-out certificate under the Pension Schemes Act 1993. Both employer and employee then make reduced National Insurance contributions, and the employee is no longer entitled to a State Second Pension in respect of the period that they are contracted out.

2.4.21 An employee with a contracted-in employer pension scheme, personal pension or stakeholder pension can also contract out of the State Second Pension if the pension meets the requirements laid down by the Department for Work and Pensions. Both employer and employee continue to pay National Insurance contributions at the usual rate, but the Inland Revenue makes a lump sum payment into the individual's pension account at the end of each year of an amount broadly equivalent to what would have been paid towards the State Second Pension. This rebate is applied on a sliding scale depending on the age of the member.

Pension benefits

2.4.22 The benefits that a pension scheme provides are likely to include one or more of the following:

- A pension payable from a certain age, known as the 'normal pension age'. It may be possible for the pension to be taken earlier or later than the normal pension age, in which case it is likely to be reduced or increased, to reflect the difference in the period for which the pension will need to be paid.

- A pension that is payable if the employee has to retire early on grounds of ill health.

- The possibility of converting (or 'commuting') part of the pension into a lump sum.

- The payment of a lump sum if the employee dies while still in service with the employer but before reaching normal pension age (often referred to as a 'death in service' benefit).

- The payment of a survivor's pension to the employee's husband or wife, or the payment of a pension to the employee's dependent children, in the event of the employee's death.

Basic legal framework

2.4.23   Many pension schemes operate through a trust. A trust is a legal mechanism whereby certain individuals, known as trustees, are given property on the understanding that they will hold, invest and dispose of that property in the interests of those who are intended to benefit under the trust – the 'beneficiaries'. In the case of a pension scheme, the employer gives money to the trustees of the pension scheme and the trustees are then under a duty to administer those funds in the interests of the scheme's members, that is, the employees, deferred members and pensioners.

Trust deed

2.4.24   A trust is set up by a trust deed, which sets out the powers that the trustees have and the broad framework within which they must operate. In the case of a pension scheme, for example, the trust deed is likely to contain a power for the trustees to amend the scheme and to wind up the scheme. The trust deed is accompanied by rules that set out who is eligible for benefits under the scheme and how benefits are calculated.

Other arrangements

2.4.25 Pension schemes that are not set up under a trust are established by some other form of agreement or arrangement, but will have similar rules on eligibility and benefits. They are operated by scheme managers rather than trustees.

Taxation

2.4.26 If a pension scheme meets certain conditions laid down by HM Revenue and Customs, it will have exempt approved status, which brings many tax advantages. Employers' and employees' contributions attract tax relief. The employers' contribution is not taxed as a benefit in kind in the hands of the employee. Capital gains earned on the pension fund are tax free, as are lump sum death benefits and lump sum retirement benefits. Pensions in payment are taxable as earned income.

2.4.27 A scheme must meet many detailed conditions to achieve approved status. In particular, there are upper limits on the benefits that approved schemes may provide, and upper limits on the contributions that attract tax relief.

Contractual issues

2.4.28 Employers who offer membership of a pension scheme to their workforce are likely to refer to entitlement to join the scheme in their employees' contract of employment. Because of their complexity, pension rights are unlikely to be set out in full in the body of the contract. Pension rights may become contractual by being incorporated by reference (see 1.2.17).

Drafting terms

2.4.29 When drafting contracts of employment, employers should take care to ensure that they are not committing themselves to providing pension benefits that they may not be able to maintain. Rather than stating that the employee is entitled to membership of a particular scheme, or to particular pension benefits, it may be preferable to refer in more general terms to the employee being entitled to be a member of any pension scheme the employer currently provides, on the terms and subject to the conditions laid down in the scheme's trust deed and rules. It may also be advisable to state explicitly that any scheme the employer provides may be amended or wound up, in accordance with the scheme's trust deed and rules.

2.4.30   If an employee's contract of employment does give the right to membership of a particular scheme, or to particular benefits, and the employer wishes to change that entitlement in some way, it will need to vary the employee's contract. The possible ways of approaching this are discussed in detail in Chapter 5.1 of this Guide. (It should be noted that if an employer with a workforce of at least 50 employees is proposing to make certain changes to its pension scheme, it must consult with the active and prospective members of the scheme before deciding whether to implement the change.)

Written statement

2.4.31   Whether or not employees have a written contract of employment, they are entitled to be given a written statement of the main terms and conditions of their employment, within two months of starting work (see 1.2.47). This information must include any terms and conditions relating to pensions, including whether or not their employment is covered by a contracting-out certificate under the Pension Schemes Act 1993 (see 2.4.20). If an employee's terms and conditions on pensions change, he or she must be notified in writing at the earliest opportunity and, in any event, not later than one month after the change.

Discrimination in pensions

2.4.32   As Chapter 3.1 of this Guide explains in detail, it is unlawful for employers to discriminate directly or indirectly on the grounds of sex, race, age, religion, sexual orientation or disability. Those principles apply to pension provision just as they do to every other aspect of employment. There are, however, certain specific legal provisions on sex, sexual orientation and disability discrimination in pension provision that need to be borne in mind. Employers also need to ensure that they do not breach the regulations that prohibit unjustified discrimination against those who work part-time or on a fixed-term basis.

2.4.33   The age equality legislation applies to pensions but it remains lawful to fix minimum and maximum ages for admission to a scheme, use age-related criteria in the actuarial calculations of benefits and contributions and set different rates of contributions for different ages in order to equalise benefits for members of different ages.

Sex discrimination

2.4.34   Under the Pensions Act 1995 and the Occupational Pension Schemes (Equal Treatment) Regulations 1995, pension schemes must not discriminate either directly or indirectly on the ground of sex. This principle applies to the terms on which people become members of a scheme. It also applies to the terms on which members are treated, but only in relation to pensionable service on or after 17 May 1990 (the date on which the European Court of Justice confirmed that occupational pensions are covered by the principle of equal pay for men and women).

2.4.35   The principle of equal treatment also applies to dependants' benefits, and trustees and managers must follow the principle when they use any discretionary powers that they have. Where the way in which an individual is treated by a scheme depends on his or her marital status, men and women of the same marital status must be treated in the same way.

This means that:

- The same eligibility criteria to join a scheme should be applied to men and women.

- Any eligibility criteria that exclude a greater proportion of one sex than of the other may need to be objectively justified.

- Men and women should be entitled to receive their pension at the same age.

- Men and women with the same earnings and the same length of pensionable service in a final salary scheme should receive the same pension, at least in respect of service on or after 17 May 1990.

- Dependants' benefits should be available on the same terms to the dependants of men and women.

Significant exceptions

2.4.36   There are some significant exceptions to the principle of equal treatment, where sex discrimination remains lawful. For example, men and women can be paid different pension benefits where this reflects their different pension ages in the state pension scheme. It is therefore lawful for schemes to offer 'bridging pensions', which give men between 60 and 65 a larger pension than women of the same age, to compensate for the fact that they are not yet receiving their state pension.

2.4.37   Furthermore, different actuarial factors can be used for men and women when calculating an employer's contributions to a scheme, if the factors reflect the differences between the average life expectancy of men and women and are set with a view to providing equal pension benefits for men and women. Different actuarial factors can also be used for men and women when calculating the size of certain benefits, including the lump sum into which a pension can be commuted, the pension that can be bought with a lump sum and money purchase benefits.

Equal treatment claims

2.4.38   The principle of equal treatment in pensions is framed in the same way as the right to equal pay for men and women, as explained elsewhere in this Guide (see 2.1.53). Therefore a woman is entitled to claim equal pension benefits with a man who is in the same employment as her and employed on equal work (her 'comparator'). Likewise, a man can claim equal pension benefits with a woman employed on equal work. The claim is made against the trustees or managers of the scheme, rather than against the employer. The employer is entitled, however, to appear before and to address the employment tribunal that hears the claim, and is obliged to provide the funds to secure the claimant's rights.

Resisting equal treatment claims

2.4.39   If they are to resist a claim for equal treatment, the trustees or managers must be able to show that the difference in pension benefits between the claimant and the comparator is genuinely due to some material factor other than the difference in their sex. A factor that directly or indirectly discriminates on the grounds of sex will not suffice to establish a defence. For example, the trustees of the scheme might argue that a particular employee is not eligible for membership because she works less than 12 hours a week. If that minimum hours' requirement excludes a considerably larger proportion of the women in the workforce than of the men, the trustees will need to show that it meets some objective business need.

2.4.40   A tribunal would not accept a desire to save money as justification. However, it might be possible to justify excluding those working only a small number of hours a week on the ground that the cost of administering those employees' membership of the scheme would outweigh the benefits they would receive from it.

Part-timers

2.4.41   It is also worth bearing in mind that part-timers of both sexes are protected from pensions discrimination by the Part-time Workers (Prevention of Less Favourable Treatment) Regulations 2000. These require an employer to treat a part-timer in the same way as a comparable full-timer, unless the employer can justify on objective grounds why the two should be treated differently. The Regulations are discussed in more detail in 2.3.85.

Restricting benefits to spouses

2.4.42   The legislation on sexual orientation discrimination allows employers to restrict survivors' benefits to married partners, provided they also extend them to civil partners (that is, same-sex couples who have officially registered as civil partners). On the other hand, if a scheme gives survivors' benefits to members' partners, whether or not they are married/civil partners, it must ensure that same-sex partners are covered.

Disability discrimination

2.4.43   The Disability Discrimination Act 1995 makes it unlawful for employers to discriminate against disabled employees or job applicants on the grounds of their disability. It is also unlawful for employers to discriminate against disabled people for a reason relating to their disability, unless there is objective justification for doing so. In addition, the Act places employers under a duty to consider whether they can make any reasonable adjustments to accommodate disabled employees and job applicants. The Act is considered in more detail in Chapter 3.1 of this Guide.

2.4.44   Trustees and managers of an occupational pension scheme are bound by the same principles of non-discrimination as employers, in relation to the terms on which people become members, and the way in which members are treated. Any discrimination by them would be treated as a breach of the scheme's rules, and a disabled person who was affected would be able to seek redress through the scheme's dispute resolution mechanisms, or could complain to OPAS (the Pensions Advisory Service) or the Pensions Ombudsman (see 2.4.78), as well as to an employment tribunal.

2.4.45   Regulations made under the Disability Discrimination Act make it lawful in certain circumstances to exclude disabled employees from a pension scheme, or to allow them access to the scheme only on certain conditions, or to reduce the amount of pension benefits that they receive. This applies only where an employee's disability and prognosis mean that the cost of providing benefits for him or her is likely to be substantially greater than it would be for a comparable person without that disability.

Disability Discrimination Code of Practice

2.4.46   As the Code of Practice issued under the disability discrimination legislation points out, discrimination against a disabled person in relation to pension benefits may be possible only when the employee is first considered for admission to the scheme. Once a member, the disabled person is covered by the scheme rules, and can be discriminated against only if the terms of the scheme allow for this. The Code of Practice also stresses the need for employers to satisfy themselves, if necessary with actuarial advice and medical evidence, that it would be likely to be substantially more expensive to provide benefits for the particular individual they are considering excluding from the scheme or from certain benefits. It is not enough to make a broad assumption that disabled people generally or people with a particular impairment or illness, will necessarily involve greater cost.

2.4.47   Even if a disabled person is excluded from a pension benefit, or is not entitled to receive the same amount of benefit as other employees, the employer can lawfully require him or her to pay the same rate of contribution as the other employees.

2.4.48 An employer's usual duty to consider reasonable adjustments does not apply in relation to any benefit under an occupational pension scheme. This means, for example, that where an employee works fewer hours for a reason relating to his or her disability, and so is paid less, it is lawful for his or her pension to be based on that lower pay rate.

Fixed-term employees

2.4.49 Under the Fixed-term Employees (Prevention of Less Favourable Treatment) Regulations 2002, employers must ensure that they do not treat fixed-term employees any less favourably than comparable permanent employees unless they have objective justification for doing so. (The Regulations are explained in more detail in 1.2.89.) The government guidance on the Regulations (see 9.1.2) suggests, for example, that an employer may be justified in excluding a fixed-term employee from its pension scheme if the contract is shorter than the vesting period for the pension scheme and admitting the employee to the scheme would be disproportionately expensive in comparison with the benefit that would be provided to the employee. If the employer was justified in excluding the fixed-term employee from the scheme, it would not need to provide an alternative, such as contributions to a personal pension, unless this option was offered to comparable permanent employees.

2.4.50 Another way of justifying the exclusion of fixed-term employees from a contractual benefit is to show that their package of benefits, taken as a whole, is no less favourable than that of comparable permanent employees. So, for example, it might be justifiable to exclude fixed-term employees from an occupational pension scheme if their pay was higher than that of permanent employees by an amount equal to the contribution the employer made to the pension scheme on the permanent employees' behalf.

2.4.51 It should be noted, however, that an employer that can justify excluding a fixed-term employee from its occupational pension scheme may still be obliged to offer the employee access to a stakeholder pension (see 2.4.79).

Information on pensions

2.4.52 Employees are entitled to written information on the terms and conditions relating to their pension when they first start work, and must be notified promptly of any changes to those terms (see 1.2.47, 5.1.58). In addition, the trustees or managers of a pension scheme must provide certain information about the scheme and the benefits paid under it, under the Occupational Pension Schemes (Disclosure of Information) Regulations 1996. The way in which information is provided may need to be modified for disabled employees, under the duty to make reasonable adjustments (see 2.4.43).

Disclosure of Information Regulations

2.4.53 The Disclosure of Information Regulations are very detailed, and employers who wish to check that their requirements are being met would be well advised to obtain a copy of them or to contact us for advice. The Regulations apply in full to tax-approved schemes (see 2.4.26); there are more limited obligations on schemes that are not tax-approved.

2.4.54 Much of the information covered by the Regulations must be given not only to members and prospective members of the scheme but also to their spouses, other beneficiaries under the scheme, and independent trade unions that are recognised for collective bargaining purposes in relation to members and prospective members of the scheme. In some cases, the information must be provided free. In other cases, a charge may be made for furnishing a copy of a document, but this must not exceed the expenses incurred in providing it.

Providing information

2.4.55 The key points to observe when providing information on pensions are as follows:

Pension information

1. On request, the trustees and managers must disclose the contents of the trust deed or other document that set up the scheme, and the scheme rules.

2. Certain basic information about the scheme must be given automatically to prospective members either before they join or, if that is not practicable, within two months of them joining. This information must also be made available on request to members or prospective members and their spouses, other beneficiaries and independent recognised trade unions. This basic information includes:

    - eligibility conditions;
    - how contributions are calculated;
    - what arrangements there are for making additional voluntary contributions;
    - what the normal pension age is; and
    - what benefits are payable under the scheme.

    Alterations to some of these details must be notified to members and beneficiaries before the change takes effect or, if that is not practicable, within three months of the change.

3. Individuals are entitled to information on their own benefit entitlement in certain circumstances. For example, a statement of entitlement must be given when benefits become payable because a member has retired or died; those who are members of money purchase schemes are entitled to an annual statement of contributions and benefits and an annual illustration of the pension benefits that are likely to be payable to them under the scheme; and final salary scheme members are entitled to request information on their entitlement once a year. (It is advisable for employers to issue an annual benefit statement to all employees. This should reduce the number of requests by individuals for information about their entitlements, and may also reveal inaccuracies in information that is being held.)

4. A copy of the scheme's annual report and audited accounts must be made available on request, as must actuarial valuations and the scheme's statement of investment principles.

Data protection

2.4.56 Employers and pension scheme trustees and managers are all bound by the requirements of the data protection legislation when they obtain, hold and pass on personal information for the purpose of administering pensions (see Appendix 8.3). Employers, trustees and managers are all data controllers, and so each is under a duty to notify the Information Commissioner that it is processing personal data.

2.4.57 The Data Protection Code (see 9.8.3) advises employers to ensure that they do not use personal information about an employee for general employment purposes, if it was provided for use by the pension scheme administrator or trustees. Exchange of personal information between the employer and the scheme provider should be limited to the minimum necessary for the effective operation of the scheme.

Scheme booklet

2.4.58 Given the legal requirement to provide information about pension schemes and the complexities of pension benefits, it is important for companies to provide well-presented, clear information about their pension scheme. Employers should check that the information they provide on their scheme, and the way in which it is provided, meets the requirements of the Disclosure of Information Regulations.

2.4.59 Employers may wish to consider producing a booklet that explains their pension scheme and the benefits of joining it. The contents of the booklet need to be easy to understand, so technical jargon is best avoided. It is also important to ensure that the booklet is kept up to date. If properly drafted, a booklet can meet the requirements of the Disclosure of Information Regulations.

Requests procedure

2.4.60 It is advisable for employers to develop a procedure for dealing with requests for information by individuals and recognised trade unions. This could:

- identify the person to whom a request for information should be made;
- state how quickly requests will be responded to;

- set out any charges that will be made for the provision of copy documents;

- explain how disputes over entitlement to information will be dealt with; and

- establish arrangements for recording requests for information. (This is especially important for companies that operate from various sites.)

Companies that operate from various sites may find it convenient to have copies of the documents that may need to be disclosed at each site. If more than one union is recognised for a particular class of employees, it may be useful to agree that one representative should act on behalf of them all.

Consultation on pension changes

2.4.61 Where an employer proposes certain changes to the terms of its pension scheme, or the trustees or managers of the scheme propose such a change, the employer may be obliged to consult with the active and prospective members of the scheme before the decision is finalised. This duty, set out in the Occupational and Personal Pension Schemes (Consultation by Employers and Miscellaneous Amendment) Regulations 2006, is complex, and a summary only is given here.

2.4.62 The duty to consult under these Regulations applies to businesses employing 50 or more people.

The relevant changes

2.4.63 An employer is obliged to consult if it proposes to make any of the following changes to its occupational pension scheme, or the trustees or managers of the scheme propose to make such a change:

- Increase the normal pension age.

- Close the scheme to new members.

- Stop future accrual of benefits under the scheme.

- Remove the liability to make employer contributions or, in the case of defined contribution schemes, reduce employer contributions.

- Introduce or increase members' contributions.

- In the case of defined benefit schemes, change the rate of accrual of benefits under the scheme or convert whole or part of the scheme into a defined contribution scheme.

2.4.64 If an employer offers employees access to a personal pension scheme to which it makes contributions, then it has an obligation to consult if it proposes to reduce or stop employer contributions or to increase members' contributions to the scheme.

Information

2.4.65 Where one of these changes is proposed, the employer must provide certain information to the affected members (that is, those people who are active or prospective members of the scheme and would be affected by the change) and to their representatives. The information must be in writing and must be provided before the consultation begins. It must describe the proposed change, the proposed timetable for its introduction and the likely effect on the scheme and its members. Any relevant background information must also be provided. The content of the information and the way in which it is presented must be such as to enable representatives to consider, conduct a study of, and give their views to the employer on, the impact of the change on the members they represent.

Mechanism for consultation

2.4.66 The way in which the employer consults depends upon whether it has pre-existing consultation arrangements in relation to the affected members. An employer who already has one or more of the following consultation partners must use them (although where more than one partner represents a particular affected member it may choose between them):

- Representatives of a trade union that it recognises for collective bargaining purposes.

- Elected or appointed information and consultation representatives under the Information and Consultation of Employees (ICE) Regulations 2004 (see 6.4.21)

- Representatives under a pre-existing arrangement recognised by the ICE Regulations

- The affected members themselves, where a pre-existing arrangement or negotiated agreement under the ICE Regulations provides for direct consultation with employees.

2.4.67 If none of the above are in place (or some of the affected members are not covered by them), but specific pension representatives have been elected in accordance with conditions set out in the pensions consultation legislation, the employer must inform and consult with them. If representatives do not already exist for the affected employees, then the employer can arrange for new elections to put them in place, but is not obliged to. Instead, it can consult the employees directly. The DWP's guidance recommends employers hold an election to appoint pension consultation representatives, but it is not mandatory to do so. The election of representatives must meet requirements that are very similar to those that apply to the election of representatives for consultation on redundancies and business transfers (see 6.4.55), the main difference being that here the employer must ensure that the interests of both active and prospective members are represented.

2.4.68 An employer contemplating pension changes may be under a duty to consult about its proposal under a negotiated agreement made under the ICE Regulations (see 6.4.30) or the fall-back provisions of those Regulations. The employer is released from this duty if it notifies its consultation partner in writing that it will be meeting its duty under these pension consultation Regulations instead.

Method of consultation

2.4.69 All those involved in the consultation process are under a duty to work in a spirit of co-operation, taking into account the interests of both sides. The employer must notify those consulted of any date set for the end of the consultation or for the submission of written comments. The consultation must continue for what the Regulations call 'an appropriate period', and must in any event last for at least 60 days. The employer (or the trustees or managers of the scheme if they proposed the change) must then consider the responses received during the course of consultation, before deciding whether to proceed with the proposed change.

Role of the Pensions Regulator

2.4.70 The Pensions Regulator has power to waive or relax the requirements of the Regulations, but only if he or she is satisfied that it is necessary to do so in order to protect the interests of the generality of the members of the scheme.

2.4.71 If an employer does not fulfil its duty to consult, a representative or affected member may complain to the Pensions Regulator, who has power to make an order requiring the employer to comply and to impose a penalty on the employer of up to £50,000.

Employee rights

2.4.72 Employees who are consultation representative under the Regulations are entitled to reasonable paid time off to perform their duties. It is automatically unfair to dismiss an employee, or to select an employee for redundancy, for these reasons: acting as a representative or candidate for election as a representative; exercising or enforcing the right to time off; complaining to the Pensions Regulator that the consultation requirements have not been met; voting in an election; influencing by lawful means the way in which others vote; or expressing doubt as to whether the election had been properly conducted. Likewise, it is unlawful to subject an employee to any disadvantage short of dismissal for these reasons. All of these protections apply regardless of the employee's age and length of service.

Rights of employee trustees

2.4.73 The Pensions Act 2004 requires that where a pension scheme is set up under a trust, the trustees must ensure that at least one-third of their number are nominated by the scheme's members. These member-nominated trustees are frequently employees who are members of the scheme.

Trustees' paid time off

2.4.74 Under the Employment Rights Act 1996, employees who serve as pension fund trustees of their employer's pension scheme have certain rights. They are entitled to paid time off work to perform their duties, and to take part in training that is relevant to those duties. The amount of time off that the employee is allowed, the purposes for which it is allowed, when it is allowed, and any conditions that apply, all depend on what is reasonable in all the circumstances. The circumstances of the employer's business and the effect the employee's absence will have on the running of the business can be taken into account. If the employee's pay does not vary with the amount of work he or she does, then he or she must be paid as normal during the time off. If the employee's pay does vary with the amount of work done, he or she must be paid at the rate of his or her average hourly earnings.

Protecting trustees

2.4.75 Employee trustees also have the right not to be put at any disadvantage because they have performed, or proposed to perform, their duties. It is automatically unfair to dismiss an employee, or to select an employee for redundancy, because he or she has performed, or proposed to perform, his or her duties as a trustee. This protection applies to all employee trustees, regardless of their length of service.

Resolving disputes

2.4.76 There are various routes by which an employee can raise a grievance in relation to his or her pension entitlement. Under the Pensions Act 2004 and Regulations, occupational pension schemes and stakeholder pension schemes must have an internal procedure for resolving disputes between the trustees or managers and the scheme's members and prospective members.

External bodies

2.4.77 If the employee is not satisfied with the way in which his or her complaint has been dealt with under the internal disputes procedure, he or she can contact TPAS, the Pensions Advisory Service, for help and advice (see 9.2.4).

2.4.78 The Pensions Ombudsman (see 9.2.4) is ultimately available to deal with complaints of maladministration in personal and occupational pension schemes, or disputes of law or fact in relation to pension entitlement. The Ombudsman will not usually take up an individual's case unless and until he or she has exhausted the scheme's internal dispute resolution procedure and TPAS has been unable to help resolve the problem.

Stakeholder pensions

2.4.79   The Welfare Reform and Pensions Act 1999 launched stakeholder pensions. Stakeholder pension schemes are run by financial services companies. Employees do not have to join a stakeholder pension scheme, nor do employers have to contribute to one. The legislation does, however, require employers to take certain steps to help employees who do want to join.

2.4.80   Employers need not facilitate access to a stakeholder pension if they already offer an occupational pension scheme that all their employees can join within a year of starting work, or if they offer a group personal pension scheme that meets certain conditions. They are also exempt if they have fewer than five employees. Employers do not have to provide access to a stakeholder pension for certain employees, including those whose earnings are below the National Insurance lower earnings limit or who have worked for the employer for less than three months. The Pensions Regulator provides an online 'decision tree' to help employers decide whether they are obliged to offer their employees access to a stakeholder pension (see 9.2.4).

Conditions for stakeholder schemes

2.4.81   A stakeholder scheme must meet certain conditions. There is, for example, a limit on the administration charges that it can make (up to 1 per cent of the fund value) and it must be prepared to accept contributions as small as £20. A scheme that meets these conditions can be registered with the Pensions Regulator. The register of schemes is available on the internet (see 9.2.4) or from the Regulator.

Employers' duties

2.4.82   The combined effect of the 1999 Act and the Stakeholder Pension Schemes Regulations 2000 is that employers must ensure that they do the following:

Employers' duties

- designate, or choose, a particular registered stakeholder pension scheme, after consulting with the employees and any organisations representing them, such as trade unions and staff associations;

- give employees the name and address of the scheme;

- allow representatives of the scheme reasonable access to the employees so that the scheme can be explained to them;

- if an employee so requests, deduct the employee's contributions to the scheme from his or her pay and pay them over to the scheme promptly;

- keep up-to-date records of the payments that have been made and send the records to the scheme provider; and

- provide employees with information on how they can request that deductions of stakeholder pension contributions should be made, varied or stopped, and how such requests will be dealt with.

2.4.83 Designating a particular scheme does not imply that the employer is making any judgement on the merits of joining the scheme, or on its past, present or future performance.

2.4.84 Employers who need more information about stakeholder pensions can contact us or the HM Revenue and Customs helpline, or consult the guide produced by the Department for Work and Pensions (see 9.2.4).

section 3

Managing the relationship

3.1

Equal opportunities

Overview

3.1.1 This chapter of the Guide covers the issue of equal opportunities in employment. It is unlawful for employers to discriminate against employees or job applicants on grounds of sex, race, age, religion, married or civil partner status, sexual orientation, gender reassignment or disability. This chapter explains how discrimination is defined (see 3.1.7). It then sets out the types of workers who are covered by the legislation (see 3.1.86), the types of discriminatory act that are unlawful (see 3.1.87) and the limited circumstances in which discrimination is permitted (see 3.1.93).

3.1.2 This chapter also explains how employers are liable for discrimination by their employees (see 3.1.103) and the 'reasonably practicable steps' defence (see 3.1.109). The Codes of Practice issued by the three original equality Commissions have particular practical importance in this area (see 3.1.116). Since October 2007, the Equality and Human Rights Commission has taken over responsibility for promoting equality and tackling discrimination in relation to sex, gender reassignment, disability, sexual orientation, religion or belief, age and race, as well as promoting human rights. The Commission (EHRC) brings together the work and powers of the original Commissions.

3.1.3 If a company intends to provide equality of opportunity, it will aim to do more than merely avoid liability for unlawful discrimination. It will want to take positive steps to identify and remove unnecessary barriers to participation in employment opportunities, and promote equal participation by all. The discrimination legislation sets some limits, however, on the positive action that companies can take, and this chapter explains what these are (see 3.1.123).

3.1.4   The law gives some, albeit limited, protection to ex-offenders from being discriminated against because of their criminal record. This chapter summarises the legislation on the rehabilitation of offenders (see 3.1.126).

3.1.5   Discrimination in pay is covered in 2.1.51 and discrimination in pensions is dealt with in 2.4.32. Other parts of the Guide deal with discrimination on trade union grounds (see 6.1.6) and discrimination against part-time workers (see 2.3.83) and fixed-term employees (see 1.2.89).

3.1.6   It is expected that the Equality Bill will receive Royal Assent in spring 2010 with most of its provisions coming into force in autumn 2010. The Equality Bill aims to consolidate existing legislation that outlaws discrimination in employment and, with the exception of the law on disability discrimination, standardises the approach to each form of discrimination. In some areas, it also aims to strengthen the law. For example, the prohibition on harassment is extended to all forms of discrimination, there are measures designed to increase pay transparency, and Employment Tribunals will have extra powers to deal with discrimination cases. There may even be a provision allowing individuals to bring claims of dual discrimination. This would enable someone to claim, for example, that they were discriminated against because they were a young woman, as opposed to being discriminated against on the basis of either their gender or age. There are also provisions which will impose duties on public authorities to tackle all forms of discrimination and promote equality. The Equality and Human Rights Commission will produce new guidance and statutory codes alongside the legislation. Contact us for details about this legislation and its implementation.

Defining discrimination

3.1.7   One of the most challenging aspects of discrimination law is the number of differing definitions of discrimination that exist. Take, for example, the definitions of direct discrimination. Direct discrimination on the grounds of sex, sexual orientation, race, religion, marital and civil partnership status and gender reassignment is defined in broadly the same way. It is treating someone less favourably on the prohibited ground. The definitions of disability and age discrimination, on the other hand, are different. In particular, while it is unlawful to discriminate against a person on most of the prohibited grounds, it is not unlawful for an employer to treat a person unfavourably on the ground of his or her age, if it is justified in doing so. Disability discrimination is even more complex: it may be lawful for an employer to discriminate against a person for a reason relating to his or her disability, if it has justification for doing so, but it is always unlawful to discriminate against the person on the ground of his or her disability itself.

3.1.8　There is another important difference between disability discrimination law and the rest of the discrimination legislation. Most of discrimination law includes the concept of indirect discrimination (see 3.1.37), which outlaws the use of unjustified barriers to employment opportunities that particularly disadvantage people of a particular sex, race, age group, religion or sexual orientation. The disability legislation does not include the concept of indirect discrimination. Instead, it imposes a duty on employers to make reasonable adjustments to their premises or working practices to accommodate disabled people (see 3.1.69). If an employer fails to meet that duty, that amounts to disability discrimination.

3.1.9　Because of the substantial differences between disability discrimination law and other areas of discrimination law, it is dealt with in a separate section below (see 3.1.51).

3.1.10　All areas of discrimination law have two concepts of discrimination in common: they make it unlawful to harass a person (see 3.1.88) or to victimise a person for bringing or supporting a discrimination complaint (see 3.1.84).

Sex

3.1.11　Under the Sex Discrimination Act 1975, it is unlawful for a company to discriminate against a person on the grounds of his or her sex.

Pregnancy and maternity

3.1.12 The same Act makes it unlawful sex discrimination for an employer to treat a woman who is pregnant or on maternity leave less favourably, on the ground of her pregnancy, than it would treat her were she not pregnant. Likewise, it is sex discrimination for an employer to treat a woman less favourably because she is taking, is seeking to take, or has taken maternity leave.

Married and civil partnership status

3.1.13 As well as outlawing discrimination on the grounds of sex, the Sex Discrimination Act 1975 prohibits discrimination against a person because he or she is married. So it would be unlawful for a company to refuse to promote a woman because she was married, if it would have promoted a single woman of similar skills and experience.

3.1.14 Although people of the same sex cannot marry, they can, through an official registration process acquire civil partnership status. It is unlawful under the Sex Discrimination Act for an employer to discriminate against a person on the ground that he or she is a civil partner.

3.1.15 Discriminating against a person because he or she is single is not contrary to the Sex Discrimination Act 1975. It could, however, potentially amount to indirect discrimination on the ground of sexual orientation, since a larger proportion of homosexual people than of heterosexual people are single.

Race

3.1.16 The Race Relations Act 1976 prohibits discrimination on racial grounds. 'Racial grounds' covers not only race but also nationality, colour and ethnic or national origins.

3.1.17 By including the concept of national origins, the legislation encompasses discrimination against those who are part of a nation that is not currently a separate nation state, but can be identified by historical or geographical factors. This means, for example, that a person who is discriminated against because he or she is English or Scottish can claim race discrimination. In this context, 'nationality' includes not only legal nationality, but also the national identity that a person has adopted or is perceived to have.

3.1.18   In order to be a racial group defined by ethnic origins, a group must have a long shared history and cultural traditions, and also share other characteristics such as a common geographical origin, common ancestors, and a common language, literature or religion. The courts have ruled that Sikhs and Gypsies are distinct racial groups defined by ethnic origins, but that Rastafarians are not. Muslims probably are not a racial group. (Sikhs, Rastafarians and Muslims would all, however, be protected from discrimination on the ground of their religion – see 3.1.24.)

3.1.19   Discrimination does not need to relate to an individual's own racial group to be unlawful. It would be race discrimination, for example, for an employer to dismiss a white employee because he or she objected to racist banter in the workplace, or refused to carry out an instruction to discriminate against customers of a certain race.

Age

3.1.20   Under the Employment Equality (Age) Regulations 2006, it is unlawful for an employer to discriminate against a person on the ground of his or her age, or apparent age, unless the employer can show the treatment is justified, that is, it is a proportionate means of achieving a legitimate aim. The Regulations apply not only on grounds of being too old but also on grounds of being too young.

3.1.21   The age discrimination legislation is unique in permitting direct discrimination on the prohibited ground if it is justified. In other cases, justification is only possible where the discrimination is indirect rather than direct. The test of justification is the same as that which applies in the context of indirect discrimination, and is discussed further below (see 3.1.48).

Sexual orientation

3.1.22   Discrimination on the grounds of sexual orientation is unlawful under the Employment Equality (Sexual Orientation) Regulations 2003. For these purposes, sexual orientation means sexual orientation towards people of the same sex, or people of the opposite sex, or people of the same sex and the opposite sex.

3.1.23   It is unlawful to discriminate against a person not only on the ground of his or her actual sexual orientation, but also on the ground of the sexual orientation he or she is perceived to have, even if that perception is false. Further, discrimination does not need to relate to an individual's own sexual orientation to breach the law. It would be unlawful, for example, for an employer to discriminate against a worker because of the sexual orientation of his or her relative or friend, or because the worker objected to homophobic jokes.

Religion

3.1.24   Religious discrimination is unlawful under the Employment Equality (Religion or Belief) Regulations 2003. For these purposes, religion or belief covers any religion, or religious or similar philosophical belief. The Advisory Conciliation and Arbitration Service has produced guidance on the Regulations (see 9.3.1). This suggests that the courts and tribunals will consider a number of factors when deciding what amounts to a religion, including collective worship, a clear belief system and a profound belief affecting the way of life or view of the world. Belief systems such as paganism and humanism could therefore be covered, as well as the more well-known religions. Case law has suggested that the test of whether views can properly be considered to fall into the category of a philosophical belief is whether they have sufficient cogency, seriousness, cohesion and importance, and are worthy of respect in a democratic society.

3.1.25   It is unlawful to discriminate against a person not only on the ground of his or her actual religion or belief but also on the ground of the religion or belief that he or she is perceived to have, even if that perception is false. Discrimination does not need to relate to an individual's own religion to be unlawful. It would be unlawful, for example, for an employer to discriminate against a worker because of the religion or belief of his or her relative or friend, or because the worker objected to anti-religious jokes.

Gender reassignment

3.1.26   The Sex Discrimination Act 1975 (as amended) outlaws discrimination against a person because he or she has undergone, is undergoing or intends to undergo gender reassignment.

3.1.27 Gender reassignment discrimination arises where an employer treats a person less favourably than it treats, or would treat, other people in the same, or not materially different, circumstances, and it does so on the grounds that the person intends to undergo, is undergoing or has undergone gender reassignment. In particular, it is discriminatory for an employer to treat an employee who is absent from work to undergo gender reassignment less favourably than it would have treated the individual if the absence were due to sickness or injury.

3.1.28 The Gender Recognition Act 2004 gives people who have changed their gender the opportunity to apply for a gender recognition certificate. The certificate entitles them to be treated as being of their acquired gender for most legal purposes, including employment. It is a criminal offence for an employer to disclose information about an employee or job applicant having applied for a certificate or about their previous gender, except in very limited circumstances.

3.1.29 The government has published a useful guide to the law and good practice in this area (see 9.3.1).

Direct discrimination: some common principles

Like for like comparison

3.1.30 In order to establish whether an employer has directly discriminated against a person, it is necessary to pose two questions, which in practice are often closely inter-linked. Using a case of alleged sex discrimination against a woman as an example, the first question is, has the employer treated this woman less favourably than it treats, or would treat, a man in the same, or not materially different, circumstances? The second question is, was the basis for that less favourable treatment the woman's sex or some other, non-discriminatory ground?

3.1.31 So, to illustrate, assume that an employer has shortlisted a man and a woman for a post. The candidates have the same or broadly equivalent skills, experience and qualifications for the job. Both have young children. The employer decides to recruit the man because it believes that women with young children are unreliable. The employer has therefore treated the woman less favourably than it has treated a man who has the same, or not materially different, relevant attributes, by recruiting him and rejecting her. The ground for that treatment was the employer's sex-based assumption that women with young children are unreliable but men with young children are not. The employer has therefore directly discriminated against the woman on the grounds of her sex.

Motive irrelevant

3.1.32   A common factor in all the definitions of direct discrimination is that they take no account of the employer's motive, purpose or intention in acting in the way that it did. For example, an employer that refuses to recruit women or black people because of a conscious or unconscious desire to 'protect' them from the sexist or racist language that they are likely to encounter in the workplace is acting just as unlawfully as an employer who rejects black and female candidates because of sexual or racial prejudice.

Proving discrimination

3.1.33   Another important practical point common to all types of direct discrimination relates to the way in which discrimination is established in an employment tribunal. It is up to the person who alleges discrimination to prove that it has occurred. Tribunals recognise, however, that direct evidence that an employer has based an employment decision on a person's sex, sexual orientation, age, race, religion or disability is rarely available. Few employers are likely to admit in evidence, or to record in their personnel documentation, that their actions were influenced in that way. Indeed, employers may be biased against certain job applicants and employees because of their sex, sexual orientation, age, race, religion or disability without even being aware that they are.

3.1.34   The legislation therefore gives some help to those who are alleging discrimination, by effectively relieving them of the need to prove all the aspects of their claim. To illustrate how this works, assume a woman has brought a claim of sex discrimination. It is up to her to put to the tribunal some evidence that could indicate that she has been less favourably treated than a man was, or would have been, treated in the same or not materially different circumstances. However, it is then up to the employer to prove that the woman's less favourable treatment was not on the grounds of her sex. If the employer cannot provide an adequate, non-discriminatory explanation for the way it acted, the tribunal must uphold the woman's claim.

3.1.35 The possibility that a tribunal may conclude that discrimination has occurred if an employer cannot provide a cogent explanation for its actions underlines the need for companies to ensure that they base their employment decisions on objective and non-discriminatory grounds and, wherever possible, record the reasons for their decisions.

Questionnaires

3.1.36 In order to help them discover whether they have been the subject of unlawful discrimination, individuals have the right to question employers about whether they have been less favourably treated, and, if they have, what the reason for that treatment was. If an employer deliberately and without reasonable excuse fails to reply to an individual's questionnaire within eight weeks, or replies in a way that is evasive or unclear, an employment tribunal hearing any discrimination claim that the individual may bring is entitled to draw whatever inferences it considers just to draw, including an inference that the employer has discriminated unlawfully.

Indirect discrimination

3.1.37 Indirect discrimination is unlawful under sex, race, age, sexual orientation and religious discrimination law.

3.1.38 Taking indirect race discrimination as an example, an employer indirectly discriminates against a person on the grounds of race if it applies to that person some form of provision, criterion or practice that it applies, or would apply, equally to people of other races, but:

- the provision puts people of that individual's race at a particular disadvantage compared with others; and

- the employer cannot justify the provision by showing that it is a proportionate means of achieving a legitimate aim.

Identifying a barrier

3.1.39 The initial key to recognising a possible indirect discrimination issue is identifying that there is a provision, criterion or practice being used. Even insisting that an employee should carry out the existing duties of his or her job can amount to a potentially discriminatory practice. So can including a particular term in a contract of employment, even if the employer has not yet relied upon that term.

Examples

3.1.40 Here are some examples of employment practices that might potentially be discriminatory, with a note of the groups that may be put at a particular disadvantage by them:

- Using a shortlisting criterion that candidates must have a GCSE at Grade A* to C in English Language (certain racial groups/people over a certain age).

- Applying a policy that employees will be considered for promotion only if they are flexible in the hours they will work (women).

- Restricting training opportunities to employees who work full-time (women).

- Requiring employees to work on a Friday after dusk or Sunday (followers of religions that forbid work at these times).

- Using employment contracts that allow the company to move an employee's place of work to any location in the country (women).

- Enforcing a dress code (followers of religions with rules on dress and appearance).

- Requiring job applicants to have a minimum length of work experience (younger people).

3.1.41 Since the definition of indirect discrimination covers 'practices' as well as absolute requirements, even preferences can be challenged as discriminatory. For example, a shortlisting criterion that was a 'desirable' characteristic rather than an 'essential' one could potentially amount to indirect discrimination.

Assessing the impact of the practice

3.1.42 A provision, criterion or practice is indirectly discriminatory only if it puts people of a particular sex, race, age group, religion or sexual orientation at a particular disadvantage. Unfortunately, the case law in this area does not give a clear picture of which group of people should be used as the basis for assessing the impact of a provision. It is also difficult to predict what an employment tribunal will accept as amounting to a 'particular disadvantage'. A tribunal is entitled to rely on its own general knowledge of the likely impact of the provision in question, however, and will not necessarily require statistical evidence on the point.

Accommodating differences

3.1.43 The practical solution to this uncertainty is for employers to be aware in a general sense that employment practices can pose indirect discrimination issues if they fail to accommodate those differences between people of different sexes, racial groups, age groups, religions and sexual orientation that can affect their working lives. We can give advice on this.

3.1.44 For example, women are more likely than men to have primary responsibility for childcare and are more likely than men to be the secondary earners within their family. This means that, as a group, they are more likely than men to have broken patterns of employment, they are likely to work shorter hours than men, their flexibility to work longer or changing hours is more limited than men's and they are less likely than men to be mobile. This indicates that employers need to be aware of the possible indirectly discriminatory effect of any employment practices that require employees to work full-time, flexible hours, that reward those who have built up certain periods of continuous periods of employment or experience, or that require employees to be mobile.

3.1.45 The differences between racial groups and religions that have occupational relevance are mainly linked to language, dress, religious observance, and the source and standard of educational qualifications. For example, employers need to be aware of the possible indirectly discriminatory effect of employment practices that require certain levels of competence in spoken or written English, impose dress codes or fail to accommodate the need of employees to take time off for religious observance.

3.1.46   In terms of age discrimination, employers should bear in mind that people in older age groups will have difficulty in meeting rules that reward recently-acquired qualifications whereas those in younger age groups will be adversely affected by rules that link any employment advantage to length of experience or service.

3.1.47   It should be emphasised, however, that employment practices that put certain groups at a particular disadvantage are not unlawful if they can be objectively justified.

Justification

3.1.48   In many cases of potential indirect discrimination, the crucial question will be whether the employer can justify adopting the provision, criterion or practice at issue. If it can, then it is acting perfectly lawfully, even if the requirement puts certain groups at a particular disadvantage. This is also the question that needs to be answered before it can be decided whether an employer has acted unlawfully in treating someone less favourably because of his or her age.

3.1.49   The provision or treatment at issue will be justified, and therefore lawful, if it aims to meet a legitimate business need, and it is an appropriate and reasonably necessary way of meeting that need. When deciding whether justification has been established, an employment tribunal will balance the reasonable needs of the employer against the discriminatory effect of the provision. An employer will find it difficult to justify a provision that has a marked impact on a particular group if it could achieve its objective by another means that has no, or a smaller, discriminatory effect.

3.1.50   Take, for example, an employer that does not extend its usual training and development opportunities to workers on the twilight shift. Assume that the twilight shift is made up predominantly of women, who find that they can combine those hours of work with their family responsibilities. Assume that the rest of the employer's workforce is made up predominantly of men. The employer needs to justify its policy of not giving workers on the twilight shift equal development opportunities. It will not be able to do so if it has been acting on the sex-based assumption that, since these shift workers are mainly women, they are working for pin money only and are not interested in developing their skills or progressing within the company.

Disability discrimination

3.1.51   The Disability Discrimination Act 1995 prohibits various forms of disability discrimination, as explained further below.

Defining disability

3.1.52   In order to be protected by the Act, however, a person has to fall within its complex definition of disability. The employment tribunals that adjudicate on disability discrimination claims will take into account official guidance that the government has published on the definition of disability (see 9.3.1). Employers who are in any doubt as to whether a particular individual meets the definition may find it useful to read this guidance or to seek advice from us.

3.1.53   In summary, a person has a disability if he or she has a physical or mental impairment that has a substantial and long-term adverse effect on his or her ability to carry out normal day-to-day activities. It is important to note that the definition covers most mental impairments except those listed below and so, for example, dyslexia can constitute a disability if it has a substantial long term adverse effect on a person's ability to carry out normal day-to-day activities which could include examinations and tests.

3.1.54   As an exception to the general rule, people with certain conditions automatically qualify as disabled, regardless of the effect their condition has on their activities. These are:

- people who have been certified as blind or partially sighted by a consultant ophthalmologist, or who are registered as such with their local authority;
- people with cancer;
- people who are infected with HIV; and
- people who have multiple sclerosis.

Excluded mental conditions

3.1.55 Certain mental conditions are expressly excluded from the definition of disability. Dependence on alcohol or any other substance does not count as a disability, unless it has resulted from taking drugs that were originally medically prescribed. Illness or disease that results from drug or alcohol dependency, such as liver or heart disease, may, however, qualify as a disability. Certain personality disorders are also excluded from the definition of disability. These are:

- a tendency to set fires;
- a tendency to steal;
- a tendency to physical or sexual abuse of others;
- exhibitionism; and
- voyeurism.

Medical treatment and aids

3.1.56 It is essential to note that, when assessing the effect that a person's impairment has, any medical treatment that he or she is receiving, or any aid or prosthesis that he or she is using, must be left out of account. For example, if a person is taking medicine and receiving counselling for clinical depression, the question is what effect the illness would have on the individual if those steps were not being taken. The only exception to this principle relates to people with sight impairments: the extent to which a person's sight could be corrected by the use of glasses or contact lenses is taken into account. In addition, if treatment of a person's condition has led to a permanent improvement, as in a case where a mobility impairment has been corrected through surgery, that treatment can also be taken into account.

Normal day-to-day activities

3.1.57 In order to be viewed as affecting a person's normal day-to-day activities, the impairment must affect the individual in one or more of these respects:

- mobility;

- manual dexterity;
- physical coordination;
- continence;
- ability to lift, carry or otherwise move everyday objects;
- speech, hearing or eyesight;
- memory or ability to concentrate, learn or understand;
- ability to perceive the risk of physical danger.

3.1.58 Government guidance states that, in deciding whether an activity is a normal day-to-day activity, 'account should be taken of how far it is normal for most people and carried out by most people on a daily or frequent and fairly regular basis'. So, an impairment that only affects a person's ability to carry out activities of a specialised kind, such as playing a musical instrument, or taking part in a particular hobby, may not amount to a disability.

3.1.59 It is important to bear in mind that it is the effect a person's impairment has on his or her day-to-day activities that is relevant, not the effect that it has on the individual's ability to do his or her job. For example, a warehouseman who has a heart condition that makes it impossible for him to continue doing the heavy manual lifting that is part of his job may not be disabled if his illness does not substantially affect his ability to move everyday objects. On the other hand, it is permissible to take into account the effect a person's impairment has on his or her day-to-day activities at work as well as at home, even if the work environment is unusual.

Assessing impairment

3.1.60 A person's impairment is viewed as having a 'substantial' effect on his or her activities if the effect is more than merely minor or trivial. Progressive conditions are viewed as disabilities as soon as they have any effect on an individual's activities, if the likely prognosis is that they will eventually have a substantial effect. (As noted in 3.1.54, people who have cancer, HIV or multiple sclerosis automatically qualify as disabled.) A severe disfigurement is also viewed as having a substantial effect on a person's activities, unless it consists of body piercing or a tattoo that has not been removed.

3.1.61   In order to be viewed as 'long term', a person's impairment must have already affected his or her activities for at least 12 months, or be likely to do so. If an individual has a condition that is subject to periods of remission or improvement, so that it sometimes has a substantial effect but at other times does not – as may be the case, for example, with arthritis – the impairment is treated as continuing to have a substantial effect during the periods of improvement.

Guidance on substantial effect

3.1.62   Government guidance on the definition of disability gives extensive examples on when an impairment should, or should not, be viewed as having a substantial effect on a person's day-to-day activities. For example, the guidance says that it would be reasonable to regard an impairment as having a substantial adverse effect on a person's mobility if it meant that he or she was unable to walk other than at a slow pace or with unsteady or jerky movements, or had difficulty going up and down stairs. It would not, on the other hand, be reasonable to regard the effect as substantial if the person had difficulty walking a distance of 1.5 kilometres unaided without discomfort or having to stop.

Direct disability discrimination

3.1.63   There are three forms of disability discrimination. The first is direct disability discrimination. This is where an employer, on the ground of a disabled person's disability, treats that person less favourably than it treats, or would treat, a person not having that particular disability whose relevant circumstances, including his or her abilities, are the same as, or not materially different from, those of the disabled person. So, for example, it would be unlawful for an employer to refuse to recruit a job applicant who is as well qualified as other applicants for the post, in terms of competency and employment history, but who has epilepsy, if the ground for the employer's decision is that the person has epilepsy.

Reason relating to disability

3.1.64 The second form of disability discrimination arises where an employer treats a disabled person unfavourably not on the ground of the person's disability itself, but for a reason relating to it.

3.1.65 This form of disability discrimination requires firstly that the disabled person shows that the employer's reason for the treatment was connected with the disability. The employer will only be liable if it knew or ought to have known that the person was disabled. Secondly, the disabled person must also show that the employer has treated the disabled person less favourably than the employer treats others to whom that reason does not or would not apply. The appropriate comparators are those without the disability. Thirdly, even in cases where it is established that the employer has discriminated by treating a disabled person unfavourably for a reason which relates to the person's disability, the employer can justify the discrimination and so avoid liability.

Justification

3.1.66 The test of justification in this context is different to that in cases of indirect discrimination (see 3.1.48), and is much easier to meet. All that the employer need establish is that it had a reason for treating the individual in the way that it did, and that the reason was relevant to the circumstances of the particular case and not merely minor or trivial.

3.1.67 *It is very important to note, however, that before an employer can establish justification, it must also show that it has met its duty to make reasonable adjustments (see 3.1.69).*

Code of Practice

3.1.68 The Equality and Human Rights Commission has a Code of Practice giving guidance on avoiding disability discrimination. This Code must be taken into account by employment tribunals when they are considering a disability discrimination claim, if it is relevant to the issue they are considering, and it contains a section that specifically deals with the issue of justification.

Duty to make reasonable adjustments

3.1.69 The third form of disability discrimination is where the employer fails to comply with the duty to make reasonable adjustments. The duty on employers to make reasonable adjustments to accommodate disabled people who are placed at a substantial disadvantage is, in practice, the most important aspect of disability discrimination legislation. If an employer fails to meet this duty, that in itself amounts to an act of disability discrimination. Furthermore, an employer cannot justify treating a person unfavourably for a reason relating to his or her disability unless it has first met its duty to take steps to reduce or prevent the disadvantage.

3.1.70 A company may owe this duty to its existing employees, whether they were disabled when they were recruited or have become disabled since they were employed. An employer may also owe the duty to a disabled person who has applied to it for a job, or has told the employer that he or she is considering applying for a job. The duty arises, however, only where the employer's policies or practices, or the physical features of its premises, put the disabled person at a disadvantage compared with non-disabled people. Furthermore, the disadvantage caused must be more than minor or trivial.

3.1.71 An employer is under no duty to make adjustments for an individual if it neither knows, nor could reasonably be expected to know, that the individual is disabled and is likely to be put under a disadvantage by the employer's current practices or premises. An employer that takes the appropriate steps may meet its duty to make reasonable adjustments, even if it is not aware that the individual is disabled.

3.1.72 If an employer does have information about a worker's disability, it should ensure that it complies with the requirements of the data protection legislation (see Appendix 8.3) and the related Code of Practice (9.8.3). This will involve ensuring that the information is restricted to those who need to know it in order to meet the employer's legal obligations. So, for example, it may be sufficient for those involved in implementing a reasonable adjustment for a disabled employee to know that the adjustment needs to be made, without being given details of the employee's disability.

Equal opportunities

Potential adjustments

3.1.73   If an employer has not met its duty to an individual to make reasonable adjustments, it will not normally be able to justify treating the individual unfavourably for a reason relating to his or her disability. The only exception to this is if the employer would have been justified in treating the individual unfavourably, even if it had complied with its duty. Take, for example, an employer that fails to make a reasonable adjustment to the recruitment process to accommodate a disabled applicant, and then rejects the applicant for a reason relating to his or her disability. The employer can justify rejecting the applicant if it can show that he or she would not have met the requirements for the job even if reasonable adjustments had been made.

3.1.74   The legislation lists some of the potential steps that an employer might need to take in relation to a disabled person to comply with its duty to make reasonable adjustments. These are shown in the following box.

Potential adjustments

- Adjusting premises to accommodate the disabled person, which could include adjusting fixtures, fittings, furniture, equipment, entrances and exits.
- Allocating some of the disabled person's duties to another person.
- Transferring the disabled person to another job, where there is an existing vacancy.
- Altering the disabled person's hours of work or training.
- Assigning the disabled person to a different place of work or training.
- Allowing the disabled person time off work for rehabilitation, assessment or treatment.
- Giving or arranging training or mentoring for the disabled person or any other person, such as a work colleague or manager.
- Acquiring or modifying equipment.
- Modifying instructions or reference manuals.
- Modifying procedures for testing or assessment.

- Providing a reader or interpreter.
- Providing supervision or other support.

Reasonable adjustments

3.1.75 It may not be necessary for an employer to take any of these steps. The duty is to take whatever steps are reasonable in the circumstances of the particular case. Many different factors may therefore need to be taken into account when assessing what adjustments, if any, are reasonable. Companies may wish to obtain advice on this issue from us.

3.1.76 The legislation says that the following factors in particular can be taken into account when considering what adjustments would be reasonable:

Factors affecting whether adjustment would be reasonable

- The effect that the adjustment would have on the disabled person's disadvantage. For example, it might not be reasonable to expect an employer to make an adjustment that would achieve only a small improvement in the output of someone who was significantly underproductive, especially if the adjustment would be costly or disruptive.

- The extent to which it is practicable for the company to make the adjustment. It might not, for example, be reasonable for an employer needing to fill a post urgently to have to wait for an adjustment to be made to allow a disabled person to be employed, unless a temporary adjustment or arrangement could be made until the permanent adjustment was in place.

- The cost to the employer of making the adjustment, which includes use of staff and other resources and disruption, as well as direct money costs. The Code of Practice says that it would be reasonable for an employer to spend at least as much on an adjustment to enable it to retain a disabled employee, including any retraining, as it might spend on recruiting and training a replacement.

> - The extent of the employer's financial and other resources.
> - What financial or other assistance may be available to the company to make the adjustment. The disabled person him- or herself is likely to be the most valuable source of advice on what adjustments would be appropriate, but advice and financial or other support may also be available from specialist agencies or the government (see 3.1.82).
> - The nature of the employer's activities and its size.

Health and safety requirements

3.1.77   It is worth noting that the Workplace (Health, Safety and Welfare) Regulations 1992 expressly require employers to equip rest rooms and rest areas with seating that is adequate for the number of disabled people they employ and suitable for them. Further, the Regulations stipulate that parts of the workplace used by disabled people must be organised in a way that takes their needs into account, particularly in relation to doors, passageways, stairs, showers, washbasins, lavatories and workstations.

Adjustments for agency workers

3.1.78   There are special rules on how the duty to make adjustments is split between the employer of an agency worker and the company to which the worker is sent to work, referred to here as the 'host company'.

3.1.79   If the contract worker is likely to be placed at a similar disadvantage by the arrangements or premises of all or most of the companies where he or she works, then it is the worker's employer who is responsible for considering what reasonable adjustments should be made. The host company is not responsible for taking any step that the worker's employer should be taking. On the other hand, it is the host company's responsibility to consider adjustments that arise from any aspects of its arrangements or premises that are different from the other companies where the worker works.

3.1.80 Whether it would be reasonable for a host company to make an adjustment depends on all the usual factors (see 3.1.76). These are likely to include the length of time for which the disabled person will be working for the company.

Government assistance

3.1.81 When a company is assessing how far it would be reasonable for it to go in making adjustments, it should consider the government assistance that is available to help employers accommodate disabled employees and job applicants.

3.1.82 Jobcentre Plus has Disability Employment Advisers, contactable through Jobcentres, who provide advice on employing disabled people. They can also put employers in touch with specialist advisers on the Access to Work scheme, which can help with the extra employment costs of employing a disabled person. The scheme could, for example, contribute towards the cost of a communicator at a job interview for a person with a hearing impairment, an adapted keyboard for a person with impaired manual function or alterations to a lift to accommodate a wheelchair user.

3.1.83 There is also a Job Introduction Scheme, which provides financial help for employers to take on a disabled person for a trial period, and a Workstep Scheme, which enable employers to give work opportunities to more severely disabled people.

Victimisation

3.1.84 In order to ensure that people are not deterred from bringing discrimination claims through fear of reprisal, the discrimination legislation makes it unlawful for an employer to victimise a person for bringing a claim or alleging discrimination. Likewise, it is unlawful to victimise a person for supporting someone else in claiming or alleging discrimination, by providing information or giving evidence. This protection also applies if the employer knows or suspects that a person intends to take one of these steps. A person is protected from victimisation even after leaving the company's employment.

3.1.85 The only circumstance in which a person is not protected from victimisation is where he or she made an allegation that was both false and not made in good faith. If a person makes an allegation that he or she believes to be true, the protection applies even if the allegation turns out to be unfounded.

Types of workers covered

3.1.86 A striking feature of discrimination legislation is the breadth of working relationships it covers. All of the following types of workers are protected from discrimination:

- Employees.

- Apprentices.

- Trainees.

- Anyone working for the company under a contract to carry out work personally. This includes self-employed contractors with personal contracts as well as casual workers or homeworkers who are not employees but whose contract with the company requires them to carry out the work assigned to them themselves.

- Contract workers who are supplied to a company through an employment agency or service company. Even though these workers do not have a direct contract with the company, it is unlawful for the company to discriminate against them.

- In relation to disability, age and sex discrimination, a person undertaking practical work experience for the purposes of vocational training.

- People who are applying to a company to work under any of the types of relationship set out above.

- Anyone who used to work for the company in any of the types of relationship set out above, if the discrimination arises out of and is closely connected with the employment relationship. This would cover, for example, a company that discriminated against an ex-employee by refusing to provide a work reference.

Types of discriminatory act

3.1.87 The discrimination legislation has been drafted to ensure that it outlaws discrimination in all aspects of employment. It is therefore unlawful for an employer to discriminate:

- in its recruitment practices, including where and how jobs are advertised, which selection criteria are used, how interviews are conducted and how the decision to appoint is made (the issue of how to avoid discrimination in recruitment is covered in detail in Chapter 1.1 of this Guide);
- in the terms on which it offers employment;
- in the way it decides which of its employees to promote, transfer or train, and on what terms;
- in the way it provides benefits, facilities and services to its employees;
- by subjecting an employee to any form of disadvantage in employment;
- by subjecting an employee to harassment (discussed further in 3.1.88);
- in deciding who to dismiss, including how employees are selected for redundancy; and
- by subjecting a former employee to any form of disadvantage or harassment, if the disadvantage or harassment arises out of and is closely connected to the employment relationship.

Harassment on discriminatory grounds

3.1.88 If an employee is harassed at work, that may be a breach of discrimination law if the grounds for the harassment are related to sex, race, age, religion, sexual orientation, disability or gender reassignment. The sex discrimination legislation also prohibits sexual harassment (that is, unwanted conduct that is sexual in nature) and makes it unlawful to penalise a person for rejecting or submitting to harassment. If one employee harasses another during the course of employment, the employer is legally liable for that conduct, unless it has taken all reasonably practicable steps to prevent it happening (see 3.1.103).

With regard to an employee harassed in the course of her employment by third parties, such as a customer, the employer will be liable unless it has taken reasonable practicable steps to prevent the third party acting in that way and the employer knows the employee has been subject to harassment on at least two previous occasions.

3.1.89　In order to amount to unlawful harassment under the discrimination legislation, the conduct at issue must be unwanted by the subject, and it must be committed on one of the prohibited grounds. Either the purpose or the effect of the conduct must be to violate the individual's dignity, or to create an intimidating, hostile, degrading, humiliating or offensive environment for him or her. Conduct is viewed as having the effect of violating a person's dignity or tainting his or her environment only if it should reasonably be considered as having that effect, taking into account all the circumstances, including the views of the subject.

Other harassment and bullying

3.1.90　Harassment that is not on one of the prohibited grounds is not unlawful discrimination. Therefore, a person who is simply harassed or bullied by an aggressive manager has no remedy under discrimination law. However, an employer that failed to deal with this type of harassment or bullying could find itself facing an unfair constructive dismissal complaint. An employee who is bullied can resign and claim that, by not tackling the issue, the employer has broken its implied contractual obligation to maintain the relationship of trust and confidence that is essential to the employment relationship (see 4.1.35).

3.1.91　Further, an employer will be liable to pay compensation under the Protection from Harassment Act 1997 to anyone harassed by its employee, if the harasser pursued a course of conduct during the course of his or her employment that he or she knew, or ought to have known, amounted to harassment. If an employee is so badly bullied or harassed that he or she suffers a foreseeable physical or psychiatric illness or injury as a result, there is also a possibility of the employee claiming compensation for negligence, on the basis that the employer failed to meet its duty to take reasonable steps to safeguard the employee's health and safety.

Employment Guide 2010

3.1.92 Companies considering what steps to take to prevent harassment at work may find it useful to refer to the bullying and harassment policy which is available for download from EEF's website.

Exceptions to the principle of non-discrimination

3.1.93 There are certain limited circumstances in which it is not unlawful for an employer to discriminate, and the most significant of these are set out here. In certain circumstances, it is also lawful for an employer to train or encourage applications from a particular group that is under-represented in its workforce, even though this amounts to discrimination against the majority group. This type of 'positive action' is discussed further below (see 3.1.123).

Job applicants over 65

3.1.94 The age discrimination legislation allows employers to discriminate on the ground of age in recruitment if the job applicant is within six months of, or older than, the employer's normal retirement age or, if the employer does not have a normal retirement age, the age of 65.

Retirement

3.1.95 It is also lawful for an employer to discriminate by dismissing an employee when he or she reaches age 65, if the reason for the dismissal is retirement. The legislation contains complex provisions that explain when the reason for a dismissal is to be viewed as retirement. The rules on lawful retirement are summarised at 4.2.60.

Sex as a genuine occupational qualification

3.1.96 The law acknowledges that some jobs may be more suitable for a particular sex, or, as the discrimination legislation puts it, there are some circumstances when being of a particular sex is a 'genuine occupational qualification' ('goq') for the post. In these cases, it is lawful for an employer, if it wishes, to consider only people of that particular sex when it recruits to the job, or decides who to promote or transfer into it, or who to train for it.

Defining a 'goq'

3.1.97 The circumstances in which a 'goq' applies are tightly defined. It is not enough, for example, that an employer thinks that a job should be done by a man because it needs physical strength or stamina, since both men and women can meet that criterion. The 'goqs' that are most likely to be relevant to the readers of this Guide are set out in the following box:

> ### Relevant 'goqs'
>
> - It is lawful to restrict a job to a particular sex if this is necessary to preserve decency or privacy, because the job involves working in circumstances where people of that sex are undressed or using sanitary facilities and they might reasonably object to the presence of someone of the opposite sex.
>
> - A job can be limited to a particular sex if the nature or location of the workplace means that the job holder must live on the premises, the premises lack separate sleeping accommodation and sanitary facilities for each sex, and it would not be reasonable for the employer to provide separate facilities.
>
> - A company may restrict a job to men if the post is likely to involve working in a foreign country whose laws and customs would make it impossible for a woman to perform the job effectively.
>
> - These 'goqs' can also be used to justify discrimination on gender reassignment grounds, but only if the employer can show that it is acting reasonably in all the circumstances. In gender reassignment cases, the 'goqs' can be used to justify dismissing someone from a job, as well as discriminating in recruitment, promotion, transfer and training.
>
> - There is an additional 'goq' that permits discrimination against a person at the stage when he or she is planning to undergo or is currently undergoing gender reassignment. This applies where the job involves living on the premises and it would be reasonable for other employees to object to sharing accommodation and facilities with a person who intends to undergo or is undergoing gender reassignment, and it is not reasonable for the employer to make alternative arrangements.

Employment Guide 2010

> ■ It should be noted, however, that an individual who has been issued with an official gender recognition certificate must be viewed for employment purposes as being of the sex the individual has acquired. It would therefore be unlawful for an employer recruiting to a job for which being a woman was a 'goq' to refuse to recruit an applicant with a gender recognition certificate confirming that she was now female, if the employer's decision was based on the ground that the applicant was formerly a man.

3.1.98   A 'goq' can apply where only some of the duties involved in a job fall within the specified circumstances. However, an employer cannot rely on a 'goq' if it already has existing employees of the relevant sex whom it would be reasonable for it to redeploy to the relevant duties, provided there are enough of those employees to meet its requirements without undue inconvenience.

Race, religion, sexual orientation or age as a genuine occupational requirement

3.1.99   The law also accepts that, in certain prescribed circumstances, employers may restrict certain jobs to people of a particular race, religion or sexual orientation, or require a person to possess a certain characteristic related to age. These exceptions apply only in very limited circumstances that are unlikely to be relevant to readers of this Guide.

Pregnancy and maternity

3.1.100   As a result of exceptions set out in the sex discrimination legislation, the fact that an employer may provide special, favourable treatment for women in relation to pregnancy and maternity cannot be challenged as sex discrimination against men.

Statutory authority

3.1.101   It is not unlawful for an employer to discriminate against a person on racial grounds or for reasons relating to the person's disability if it is doing so in order to meet its obligations under other legislation. For example, if an employer needs to modify its equipment to meet its obligation to protect the health and safety of its machine operators, it can lawfully do so, even if that makes it impossible for a particular disabled employee to operate the equipment, even with a reasonable adjustment.

Restricting benefits to spouses

3.1.102   Some employers extend certain benefits, such as private health insurance and pension benefits, to employees' legal spouses but not to unmarried partners. This puts gay and lesbian employees at a particular disadvantage because they are less likely to be married than their heterosexual colleagues. Nevertheless, the practice will not breach the sexual orientation legislation, provided employers also offer the benefits to employees' civil partners. On the other hand, if employers offer benefits to employees' partners it would be unlawful to exclude same-sex partners.

Employer liability for discrimination

3.1.103   Employers are liable for the discriminatory acts of the people they employ, if the acts are committed in the course of employment. This means that a company is legally accountable for any act of discrimination that an employee commits while at work, whether or not the employer knows about it or approves of it.

Liability outside the workplace

3.1.104   A company can even be liable for discrimination that occurs at a social event outside the workplace, if the event can properly be regarded as an extension of employment. Take, for example, a case where an employee is sexually harassed by a work colleague at a party to mark someone's retirement from the company, and the company has organised and funded the party. It is possible that an employment tribunal would conclude that the company was liable for that act of discrimination, even if the party took place outside the workplace and outside working hours.

Responsibility for contractors and agencies

3.1.105   It is also important to note that an employer is liable not only for the acts of its employees and apprentices, but also for the acts of any other person it employs under a contract to carry out work personally, including self-employed contractors.

3.1.106   It is unlawful for an employer to instruct another person to discriminate or to aid another person in discriminating. For example, if a company tells a recruitment agency to send only women candidates for a job as a receptionist, or not to send disabled people, it is acting unlawfully.

Employees' liability for discrimination

3.1.107   Employees who discriminate in the course of their employment are themselves acting in breach of the discrimination legislation. Claims of discrimination can be, and often are, brought against the individual who committed the act of discrimination as well as against the employer. If it upholds a discrimination claim, a tribunal can, and often does, order the individual as well as the company to pay compensation.

3.1.108   This is a point that companies may think it worth mentioning if they meet resistance when introducing new policies or procedures aimed at preventing discrimination in the workplace.

'Reasonably practicable steps' defence

3.1.109   Although the initial assumption is that a company is liable for the discriminatory acts of its employees, the company has a potential defence. It can escape legal liability if it can show that it 'took such steps as were reasonably practicable' to prevent the employee from doing the act, or from doing that type of act while at work. The defence will not apply if there were preventive steps that it was reasonably practicable for the company to take but it failed to do so, even if taking those steps would not actually have prevented the discrimination occurring.

Preventing discrimination

3.1.110 The steps that it is reasonably practicable for a company to take will depend on the nature of the act of discrimination and the circumstances of the company. For example, if a manager discriminated when recruiting, the employment tribunal hearing the discrimination claim is likely to be interested in knowing whether the company had made clear to the manager the importance of avoiding discrimination, and had trained the manager in how to draw up and apply objective selection criteria based on the requirements of the job and conduct any interview in a fair and objective manner.

3.1.111 Depending on the company's size and resources, the tribunal might also expect it to have adopted and publicised a formal equal opportunities policy, with top-level management support, in order to confirm the importance it attaches to avoiding unlawful discrimination. Further, it might expect the company to monitor the outcome of its recruitment practices by sex, race, age and disability, to identify whether they might be affected by conscious or unconscious bias (see 3.1.118).

3.1.112 Where an employee has been harassed at work, a company is unlikely to be able to avoid liability unless it can show that it had, as a minimum:

- made clear to its workforce what types of conduct would be viewed as harassment;

- made clear to the workforce its policy that harassment would not be tolerated in the workplace, and implemented that policy in practice; and

- provided employees with some accessible means of raising complaints of harassment.

Equal opportunities checklist

3.1.113 The following equal opportunities checklist summarises the steps that employers should consider in order to avoid liability for discrimination. A bullying and harassment policy and procedure is available for download from EEF's website.

Equal opportunities checklist

- Establish unequivocal support at the highest level of management for a policy that the company will not discriminate on the grounds of sex, race, age, religion, sexual orientation, gender reassignment or disability.

- Adopt a clear policy statement that sets out the company's commitment to equal opportunities, how this commitment will be implemented and who is responsible for its implementation.

- Publicise the policy statement to the workforce and to job applicants.

- Review the company's policies and procedures relating to recruitment, promotion and allocation of training and development opportunities, to ensure that:
    - decisions on who to appoint, promote or train are made on objective, job-related grounds, and are well documented to show that this is so; and
    - any unjustified barriers to full participation by all are identified, and modified or removed where this is compatible with the business's operational needs.

- Adopt and publicise a policy on harassment that:
    - sets out the types of behaviour that will be viewed as harassment; and
    - states unequivocally that harassment will not be tolerated in the workplace.

- Ensure that an effective procedure is in place to enable employees who are subjected to harassment to seek redress. Ensure that employees know about the procedure and that managers are trained in how to implement it.

- Ensure that discrimination, including harassment, is included as a disciplinary offence in the company's disciplinary rules.

- Deal firmly with employees who discriminate, including those who harass, by using the disciplinary procedure where appropriate.

- Monitor the operation of recruitment, promotion, training, performance appraisal, pay, redundancy and disciplinary policies and procedures by sex, race, age and disability, to ensure that their outcomes are not being affected by direct or indirect discrimination.
- Where monitoring reveals that a particular sex or racial group is under-represented in a particular category of work in the company, consider what action might be taken to encourage that group to apply for that work. Training could also be provided to improve that group's chances of obtaining the work.

The role of the Equality and Human Rights Commission

3.1.114   In October 2007, a unified Commission – the Equality and Human Rights Commission – replaced the three Equality Commissions. The new Commission's remit covers all the equality legislation, i.e., sex, gender reassignment, disability, sexual orientation, religion or belief, age and race as well as human rights. The new Commission is also responsible for enforcing anti-discrimination laws on sexual orientation, religion or belief and age, which were areas not covered by the original Commissions.

3.1.115   The Commission is available to give employers advice on all aspects of discrimination and on setting up effective policies and practices to ensure that discrimination does not occur in their workplace. It can give guidance, for example, on drawing up an equal opportunities policy, drafting a procedure to deal with harassment, and putting in place systems to monitor the current workforce and job applications to ensure that discrimination is not occurring.

The Codes of Practice

3.1.116   The original equality Commissions have published Codes of Practice giving guidance on how to avoid unlawful discrimination and these Codes remain in force (see 9.3.1). The UK Border Agency has also issued a Code, on avoiding racial discrimination while seeking to prevent illegal working (see 9.1.1). While it is not unlawful for an employer to disregard the recommendations in these

Codes, tribunals hearing discrimination claims must take the Codes into account where they are relevant to the issues before them. The Codes are likely to be particularly relevant when the tribunal turns to the issue of whether an employer had taken all steps that were reasonably practicable to prevent the discrimination occurring.

3.1.117 Companies may therefore find it useful to incorporate the guidance from these Codes when reviewing existing employment policies and procedures or introducing new ones. The disability Code is much more detailed than the sex and race discrimination Codes and is likely to be a particularly useful reference source. The Equality and Human Rights Commission will produce updated guidance ahead of the implementation of the Equality Act 2010.

Monitoring

3.1.118 While there is no express legal obligation to do so, the Codes of Practice recommend that employers should monitor their employment practices by sex, race, age and disability, in order to identify whether discrimination is occurring. The collection and analysis of monitoring information is also necessary in order for a company to assess the effectiveness of any equal opportunities initiatives that it may have taken. The Race Equality Code gives specific guidance on monitoring. It recommends that employers should monitor the following, by racial group: applications for jobs and success rates at each stage of the process; distribution of workers in the organisation by type of job, location and grade; applications for promotion, transfer and training and success rates for each; the results of performance appraisals; grievances and disciplinary action, including the results; and terminations of contract, for whatever reason.

3.1.119 An employer must ensure that the way it handles monitoring information complies with the requirements of the data protection legislation (see Appendix 8.3). The legislation classifies information on racial or ethnic origin, religious belief and disability as sensitive personal data (see 8.3.10), but allows for it to be processed if this is necessary in order to monitor equal opportunities. The Data Protection Code (see 9.8.3) advises that, where practicable, monitoring information should be collected in a way that does not enable individuals to be identified. The information should also be accurate and not excessive, so, for example, there should be sufficient categories of ethnic origin to enable employees to be properly categorised.

3.1.120 The easiest point at which to gather monitoring data is on recruitment. All job applicants can be asked to complete a form giving details of their sex, racial or ethnic origin and any disabilities. Applicants should be told why the information is being requested and how it will be used. It is advisable for the monitoring form to be kept separate from the application form, so that the information it contains does not influence the recruitment process.

3.1.121 Existing employees will need to be asked to submit a monitoring form. In order to maximise the number of forms returned, the employer should explain the purpose of the exercise and the importance of completing the form. In organisations where unions are recognised, it would be good practice to obtain union support for the monitoring exercise and union involvement in explaining its importance.

3.1.122 Employees should be given the opportunity to raise any concerns that they may have about the exercise, either with the employer or with their union representative. If an employee is not willing to complete a monitoring form, he or she should be advised that his or her immediate manager will provide the monitoring information, based on the manager's knowledge and assessment of the employee, and that the information provided by the manager will be placed on the employee's personnel file. If this proves to be necessary, the Data Protection Code advises that the record should make clear how the categorisation was made.

Positive action

3.1.123 Some employers may want to go beyond avoiding unlawful discrimination. They may decide to take positive steps to address the fact that people of a particular sex, age or racial group, or disabled people, are currently under-represented in their workforce. The discrimination legislation contains various exceptions designed to ensure that employers who choose to take such steps can do so without fear of being challenged for discrimination against the groups that are not benefiting from the action.

Lawful positive action

- Employers can lawfully discriminate in favour of disabled employees or job applicants. For example, a recruiter who wants to shortlist all disabled candidates who meet the minimum requirements of the job, or even to prefer a disabled candidate over a better-qualified non-disabled candidate, is free to do so.

- In certain circumstances, it is lawful for employers to expressly encourage people of a particular sex to apply for a job, whether through external recruitment or internal promotion. This applies if at any time in the past 12 months there has been no one of that sex doing the job, or the number of people doing the job has been comparatively small. Therefore a company that currently employs very few women engineers could lawfully state in a job advertisement for engineers that it would particularly welcome applications from women. The decision on who to recruit to the post must still, however, be based on objective factors, not on the applicant's sex.

- Where one sex is under-represented in a particular job, it is also lawful for employers to limit training opportunities for that job to that sex. For example, if a company has no, or few, women at senior management level, it is free to put on a management development course for women employees only.

- There are similar provisions in the race discrimination legislation. These allow employers to encourage people of a particular racial group to apply for a job at a particular workplace, or to offer training for that work at that workplace to a particular racial group. For these exceptions to apply, the employer must be able to show that the particular racial group is under-represented in the work and at the workplace in question. This should be either in comparison with that group's representation in the employer's workforce as a whole or in comparison with its representation in the labour market from which the company normally recruits to that workplace.

- It is lawful for employers to give people of a particular racial group facilities or services to meet their special educational, training or welfare needs. This means, for example, that a company is free to arrange language tuition for those of its employees who have English as their second language.

Equal opportunities

> - Employers may lawfully give only people of a particular age or age group access to training to fit them for particular work, or encourage people of a particular age or age group to take advantage of opportunities to do particular work, if it reasonably appears to the employer that the step prevents or compensates for disadvantages linked to age suffered by that age or age group.

3.1.124   Companies that are considering developing positive action measures may wish to obtain further advice from the Equality and Human Rights Commission or us.

People with criminal records

3.1.125   The law gives ex-offenders some protection from being discriminated against because of their criminal record. This protection is much less extensive than that provided by the discrimination legislation.

Spent convictions

3.1.126   The Rehabilitation of Offenders Act 1974 set up a system whereby people who have been sentenced for criminal offences are entitled to have those convictions disregarded, or treated as 'spent', after a certain period of time. The length of that period, known as the 'rehabilitation period', differs according to the type of sentence imposed and the age of the person when convicted of the offence. For example, the rehabilitation period for an offence for which the sentence was a fine is five years for a person who was 18 or over when convicted, and two and a half years for someone who was under 18 at the time of conviction. Convictions resulting in prison sentences of over 30 months never become spent.

3.1.127   The significance of this for employers is that, when applying for a job, an ex-offender need not disclose in most circumstances any conviction that is spent, even if directly questioned about his or her criminal record.

3.1.128   There may be legal consequences if an employer chooses to dismiss an existing employee because of his or her criminal record. If the conviction on which the employer's decision is based is 'spent' and the employee has at least one year's service, he or she will have a very strong argument that the employer had acted unreasonably in deciding to dismiss, and that the dismissal was therefore unfair.

Exemptions

3.1.129   Certain employment is exempt from the application of the Rehabilitation of Offenders Act, such as jobs concerned with the administration of justice or involving work with children, older people or other vulnerable groups.

3.1.130   Further legal and practical advice on the employment of ex-offenders is available from us or the National Association for the Care and Resettlement of Offenders (see 9.3.1).

3.2

Managing performance

Overview

3.2.1 Effective management of staff performance is crucial to the success of any business. This chapter of the Guide deals with the principles of law and good practice in this area, focusing in particular on handling performance appraisal and capability issues and the management of absence, including sickness absence.

3.2.2 In some cases, employees will be dismissed because of poor performance or unsatisfactory attendance records. This chapter summarises the legal issues involved in dismissing employees for these reasons. The general legal framework relating to termination of employment and unfair dismissal is covered in Chapters 4.1 and 4.2 of the Guide.

Performance appraisal

3.2.3 Many employers manage employees' performance through routine supervision. Others prefer to use a formal appraisal system, which gives both managers and those being managed a structure within which to address performance issues. Whichever approach is used, the objectives are the same:

- to ensure that employees are aware of the standards that are expected of them;
- to motivate employees to achieve or even exceed those standards;

- to ensure that employees have the appropriate training and support to do their job; and

- to identify employees' potential for development.

3.2.4 Some employers also choose to link pay to performance. There are various methods of doing this, based on individual, group or company performance. The methods based on individual performance range from individual payment by results and measured day work to individual performance-related pay, often referred to as merit pay. The aim of merit pay is to increase individuals' productivity by linking some or all of their pay to their performance in the job.

Adopting a formal appraisal system

3.2.5 A company that is considering adopting a formal appraisal system may find it helpful to obtain advice on which approach or scheme would be best suited to its needs and objectives and would best fit with its overall human resources strategy. The Advisory, Conciliation and Arbitration Service has produced a booklet on performance appraisal, which provides useful general guidance on drawing up and operating appraisal systems (see 9.3.2). Companies can also contact us for advice.

3.2.6 In order to be effective, an appraisal scheme needs to have the co-operation and commitment of managers and employees at all levels. It would therefore be highly advisable for a company to consult fully with employees and their representatives, both when first establishing the scheme and when operating it in practice. The establishment of any appraisal system is likely to involve the following steps:

Steps to establish an appraisal system

1. Define the jobs covered by the system (see 1.1.9), and agree the descriptions with the jobholders. Employees may already have fairly detailed job descriptions that could serve as a useful basis for this, provided they are accurate.

2. Set the standards to be achieved, based on past performance or some

other objective criterion. If performance is to be meaningfully assessed, standards must be sufficiently well defined to be capable of measurement. In order to motivate rather than demoralise, standards should be challenging but also achievable. Those giving advice on designing performance systems often refer to the need to ensure that objectives are SMART: specific, measurable, achievable, realistic and time-based.

3. Factors by which performance is assessed commonly include:

    - job knowledge/ability;
    - adaptability/flexibility;
    - productivity;
    - quality of work;
    - attitude to work;
    - originality/initiative;
    - interaction with others;
    - perception/ judgement/use of resources;
    - attendance and timekeeping;
    - safety awareness;
    - need for supervision;
    - supervisory ability; and
    - performance against set targets.

4. Decide how often performance will be appraised.

5. Draw up a procedure for the appraisal, which will usually consist of a written assessment of the employee's performance by the manager, followed by an interview between the manager and the employee to discuss the assessment, and an appeals procedure to deal with any disagreements.

6. Train appraisers on how to conduct appraisals effectively, including issues such as consistency of scoring and effective interview techniques.

> 7. Ensure that employees are aware of how their performance has been assessed. Where pay is linked to performance, the way in which performance affects pay should also be made clear.
>
> 8. Establish a procedure for dealing with poor performers (discussed further in 3.2.16).
>
> 9. Set up a mechanism to monitor the results of the appraisal system, to ensure that it is working fairly and consistently and in a way that does not unlawfully discriminate (see 3.1.118).

3.2.7   Companies that use performance appraisal need to be aware that if the system is not operated objectively and fairly, it may lead to allegations of discrimination on the grounds of sex, race, disability, religion, age or sexual orientation (see Chapter 3.1). In addition, an employee who is appraised in an unfair or arbitrary way could resign and claim unfair constructive dismissal, provided that he or she has at least one year's continuous service. The basis of the claim would be that the company had failed to meet its legal duty not to act in a way that undermined trust and confidence between itself and its employee (see 1.2.45).

Documenting appraisals

3.2.8   It is important for an employer to keep accurate records relating to performance appraisal. If an employee is dismissed for poor performance or believes that an appraisal has been carried out in a biased way, these records will be invaluable in defending an unfair dismissal or discrimination claim.

3.2.9   Information relating to appraisals is personal data that must be obtained, held and used in a way that complies with the Data Protection Act 1998 (see Appendix 8.3). The company is likely to be able to show that it has met the conditions for processing the data, either because the employee will have consented to the company holding them or because the company needs to hold them for the purposes of its legitimate business interests. Nevertheless, employees need to be notified in advance that the data are being held and the purposes for which they may be used. Only information that is relevant to the appraisal process should be recorded so that, for example, remarks about an employee's character should be omitted if not relevant to his or her work performance.

Monitoring and surveillance systems

3.2.10   Some companies monitor employees' performance by checking their e-mails, telephone calls or use of the internet, or by installing surveillance equipment. Monitoring and surveillance techniques of this nature raise several legal issues, which are outlined in 3.3.55.

Reasons for poor performance

3.2.11   Active supervision or formal performance appraisal will reveal whether individuals are performing their job adequately. If an employee's work performance has fallen below the required standard, there may be many reasons why. It is important for the company to establish the cause of the poor performance at an early stage, in consultation with the employee, to enable it to deal with the individual in the most effective way.

3.2.12   It may be, for example, that the employee needs more training, support or supervision. On the other hand, if the employee's work is not up to scratch because of lack of effort or care on his or her part, it may be appropriate for the company to take the disciplinary route. If this proves necessary, the company should maintain a clear distinction between any formal appraisal process that it uses and the disciplinary procedure. Appraisal interviews are a useful opportunity to provide constructive criticism of an individual's performance, and that would be undermined if the employee regarded the manager's remarks as akin to a disciplinary warning. If disciplinary action may be necessary, the appraisal process should be completed before the disciplinary procedure is used. Handling of disciplinary matters is dealt with in Chapter 3.3 of this Guide.

Underperformance and disability

3.2.13   Where individuals who underperform are disabled within the definition in the Disability Discrimination Act 1995 (see 3.1.51) and their performance has been affected by their disability, their employer is under a legal obligation to consider whether any reasonable adjustments could be made to reduce or eliminate the effect that their disability is having on their work. It is also unlawful disability discrimination for an employer to treat a disabled employee unfavourably for a reason relating to the employee's disability, such as a deterioration in performance, unless the employer can objectively justify its actions.

3.2.14   Even if an individual is not disabled within the meaning of the disability legislation, his or her performance could be affected by mental or physical illness or injury. This possibility should therefore be canvassed in the company's discussions with the employee. The effective management of sickness absence is discussed further below (see 3.2.51).

Breakdown in working relationships

3.2.15   An employee's work performance can also suffer if there has been a breakdown in the working relationship with managers or colleagues. It is important to establish if this is the case, since there may be an underlying issue that the company needs to address. If, for example, an employee is underperforming because he or she is being bullied or harassed, and the company does not deal with this adequately or at all, the employee may decide to resign and claim unfair constructive dismissal. The employee would argue that, by failing to deal with the bullying or harassment, the company had breached its implied duty not to act in a way that undermined trust and confidence between itself and its employee (see 1.2.45). If the bullying or harassment was linked to the employee's sex, race, disability, sexual orientation or religion, the company would also be liable for discrimination, unless it could show that it had taken whatever steps were reasonably practicable to prevent the bullying or harassment occurring (see 3.1.88, 3.1.109).

Dealing with poor performers

3.2.16   Where poor performance is due to lack of effort or carelessness on the employee's part, a disciplinary approach will be appropriate. The ACAS Code of Practice on discipline and grievance is relevant when considering this type of poor performance. The Code states that if employers have a separate capability procedure they may prefer to address performance issues under that procedure. If so the basic principles of fairness set out in the ACAS Code should still be followed , but they may need to be adapted. The ACAS Code says that when dealing with formal action about poor performance it is important to deal with the issue fairly and that there are a number of elements to this which are:

- Employers and employees should raise and deal with issues promptly and should not unreasonably delay meetings, decisions or confirmation of those decisions.
- Employers and employees should act consistently.
- Employers should carry out any necessary investigations, to establish the facts of the case.
- Employers should inform employees of the basis of the problem and give them an opportunity to put their case in response before any decisions are made.
- Employers should allow employees to be accompanied at any formal disciplinary or grievance meeting.
- Employers should allow an employee to appeal against any formal decision made..

3.2.17   The ACAS Code will be taken into account in any employment tribunal proceedings both in relation to whether the employer is liable or not and also when assessing compensation as the tribunal can adjust awards by up to 25 per cent if it decides that the Code has not been followed without good reason by the employer or employee. The conduct of disciplinary proceedings is discussed in detail in Chapter 3.3. The most effective way of bringing performance back up to standard is likely to involve the steps set out below. Taking these steps will also ensure that the company does not fall foul of unfair dismissal law, should it eventually prove necessary to dismiss the employee for poor performance.

Bringing performance up to standard

1. Establish the facts and ensure that the employee is aware of the standard that is expected, and check that the standard has been set at a realistic and achievable level.

2. Inform the employee of the issue and fix a date for a meeting. The notification should be in writing and contain sufficient information about the poor performance to enable the employee to prepare to answer the case. The employee should also be informed about the possible consequences of continued poor performance and should be advised about the right to be accompanied at the meeting.

3. At the meeting, identify in consultation with the employee the shortfall in his or her performance and a target for improvement. In some cases, it may be appropriate to set staged improvement targets.

4. Set a realistic timetable for the improvement required, and make arrangements for the individual's performance to be reviewed at the appropriate time.

5. Identify and provide any necessary training, support or supervision that the employee may need to meet the target set. If the employee is disabled, consider whether there are any reasonable adjustments that could be made to the physical work environment or the way that his or her work is organised to enable the employee to meet the target.

6. The outcome of this process should be a note for the employee (sometimes known as an improvement note) setting out the performance problem, the improvement that is required, the timescale for achieving the improvement, a review date and any support the employer will provide to assist the employee.

7. Warn the employee of the possible ultimate consequences of failing to meet the target, which could include demotion, transfer or dismissal.

8. Review the employee's progress as agreed and decide what further action, if any, is necessary. Depending on the circumstances, this could include confirming that the employee is now performing satisfactorily, arranging training or support, setting further targets for improvement and review dates, transferring or demoting the employee, or considering dismissing the employee on capability grounds. If the employee is making concerted efforts to improve and has the potential

to perform the job satisfactorily, it may be reasonable to give him or her several months to reach the required standard, structured around repeated performance reviews and revised targets. However, if the employee's performance is falling substantially below the standard required and he or she appears unable to improve to any significant degree, even when given clear targets and appropriate support and training, it may be reasonable to consider dismissing the employee after only a couple of rounds of target-setting and review provided that a final written warning has been issued.

9. If the employee has failed to meet the targets after being given a reasonable opportunity to do so, consider transferring the employee to another job, if there is work available that is more suited to the employee's capabilities. It is lawful to transfer an employee to another job only if the employee's contract allows for it or the employee agrees. If the employer has no contractual right to transfer or demote the employee and the employee refuses to move job, then it would be advisable to explain to the employee that dismissal is the only other option, to give the employee the opportunity to reconsider his or her position.

10. If transfer or demotion is a possibility, follow the same fair procedure as in the case of dismissal. So the company should write to the employee explaining that the company is contemplating transferring or demoting the employee because of his or her performance, and invite the employee to a meeting to discuss the situation. The employee has the right to be accompanied at the meeting by a work colleague or union official of his or her choice (see 3.3.80). If the decision is made to move the employee, he or she should be given the right to appeal.

11. If having issued a final written warning, the circumstances are such that dismissal appears the most realistic option, write to the employee explaining the situation and that the company is contemplating dismissing the employee because of his or her performance, and invite the employee to a meeting to discuss the situation. The employee has the right to be accompanied at the meeting by a work colleague or union official of his or her choice (see 3.3.80).

12. If the decision is made to dismiss, notify the employee of his or her right to appeal (see 4.2.45).

> **13.** If the company's practice is to implement the decision to dismiss without waiting to see whether an appeal is lodged, terminate the employee's contract by giving proper notice (see 4.1.12) or without notice but with a payment in lieu (see 4.1.27) and then deal with the appeal if it is made. If an appeal is upheld but the employee's contract has already ended, the employee can be reinstated. If the company's practice is not to implement the decision to dismiss until any appeal has been heard, hear the appeal and then, if the appeal is unsuccessful, terminate the employee's contract on notice or with a payment in lieu. (An employee who is covered by the EEF national procedural agreements is entitled to call for an external conference, and remain in employment until agreement is reached or the procedure is exhausted, or his or her notice expires if that is later.)

Disability discrimination

3.2.18   A disabled employee who is demoted, transferred or dismissed for poor performance can allege disability discrimination if the reason for the employee's poor performance was linked to his or her disability. However, the company will be able to defend that claim effectively if it can show that:

- it made whatever adjustments were reasonable in the circumstances to prevent the employee's disability affecting his or her performance, such as modifying equipment (see 3.1.69); and

- it was justified in demoting, transferring or dismissing the employee for reasons that were relevant to the circumstances of the individual's case, such as the impact that his or her performance was having on the business, and were not merely minor or trivial (see 3.1.66).

Sex discrimination

3.2.19   If an employee is demoted, transferred or dismissed for poor performance that is linked to the fact that she is pregnant or has had a baby, that is likely to be sex discrimination. It is also automatically unfair to dismiss an employee for poor performance connected with pregnancy or maternity, regardless of her length of service (see 2.2.72).

Managing absence

3.2.20　Employees may have the right, either under legislation or under their contract of employment, to be absent from work for several reasons. They may have the right under employment legislation, for example, to take time off to have a baby (see 2.2.25), to care for their children (see 2.2.128), to deal with family emergencies (see 2.2.161) or to carry out public duties (see 2.3.92). Although there is no statutory right to time off for illness or injury, many employers give their employees the right to some form of sick leave under their contract of employment. (The management of sickness absence is discussed further below (see 3.2.51).)

Flexible working practices

3.2.21　In addition, some employers find that they can minimise disruption to their business by operating flexible working practices that give employees time to attend to other personal matters. These range from providing flexible working hours to giving compassionate leave or authorising absence for medical appointments.

Unauthorised absence

3.2.22　Employees may also, however, be absent from work without a legitimate reason. They may take the odd day off work without authorisation, feign ill health to take advantage of the company's sick pay scheme or arrive late at work without good cause.

3.2.23　Whatever the reasons for employees' absence, high levels of absence within a company are costly. There may be substantial direct costs, in terms of lost or disrupted production and additional staffing costs to fund overtime working, sickness benefits or staffing cover. Indirect costs can also be significant, including low workforce morale and investment of management time to deal with the effects of the absence. It is therefore important for a company to manage employees' absences effectively.

Defining the problem and its causes

3.2.24   A company that is concerned about high levels of absence and wishes to take action to tackle the problem at an organisational level should begin by examining the evidence. For example:

- Is the problem a general one affecting the entire workforce, or do only a few employees or certain areas of the business have substantial levels of absence?

- Has management tolerance of slack attendance created a culture in which frequent absence is the norm?

- Are sickness absences long term or short term? Are they mainly covered by medical certificates or is there a large number of odd uncertificated days off, perhaps clustered around public holidays?

- Are there any discernible causes for the absences that are within the company's power to control, such as working conditions or management style?

Reducing absence levels

3.2.25   The Advisory Conciliation and Arbitration Service has produced an advisory booklet on managing attendance and employee turnover (see 9.3.2), which suggests that employers who want to reduce absence levels should ensure that they:

- provide good physical working conditions;
- take into account ergonomic factors when designing workplaces;
- maintain rigorous health and safety standards;
- provide sufficient training for new recruits, and especially young people;
- establish an ethos of teamwork;
- design jobs so that they motivate employees and provide job satisfaction;
- critically review training, career development and promotion policies, communication procedures and welfare provision, and improve them where necessary;

- adopt and implement policies on equal opportunities and procedures to prevent harassment; and

- ensure supervisory training is adequate and that supervisors take an interest in their employees' health and welfare.

3.2.26 Once a company has identified the nature and possible causes of its absence problem, it can develop a strategy to deal with it, whether that be through tackling the causes of absence or by taking tighter control of the management of it. The objective should not be to punish those with legitimate reasons for being absent, but rather to create a climate in which attending work regularly becomes the norm and those who are absent from work without good cause can expect to be challenged and, where appropriate, disciplined.

Monitoring absence levels

3.2.27 In order to manage absence effectively, a company needs to have a reliable system for recording and monitoring absence levels. While this can be done centrally, it is preferable to make it an integral part of the responsibilities of managers and supervisors, since it is they who are responsible for managing absence. Records should show who has been absent and why, and whether the absence was short term or long term.

3.2.28 These records can then be used as a basis for identifying patterns of absence at the level of the individual, the department or the company, and for picking up promptly levels of absence that are unacceptably high. Accurate absence records will also significantly enhance the company's ability to defend any allegation of unfair dismissal or disability discrimination, if an employee is disciplined or dismissed for poor attendance.

Data protection

3.2.29 Absence records are personal data that must be obtained, held and used in a way that complies with the Data Protection Act 1998 (see Appendix 8.3). The Data Protection Code (see 9.8.3) recommends that absence records should be kept separately from sickness records and should be made available only to those who need to see them in order to carry out their managerial responsibilities. (The handling of sickness records is discussed at 3.2.52.) The company is likely to meet the conditions for processing general absence records, either because the employee has consented to this or because the company needs to process the data to pursue its legitimate business interests.

3.2.30   Employees should be informed at the beginning of their employment that a record will be made of their absences and told the purposes for which the record may be used.

Clear rules and procedures on absence

3.2.31   A company is more likely to be in a position to manage absence effectively if it has clear rules and procedures for dealing with absence of whatever type, which are communicated to employees and which it applies consistently. For example, employees should be clearly informed of what procedure they should follow if they want to take holiday or apply for compassionate leave, and what requirements on notification and medical evidence they must meet in order to qualify for sick leave or pay.

3.2.32   All employees should be made aware of any company rules that treat certain types or levels of absence as disciplinary offences. If certain levels of absence have certain consequences, such as triggering a particular stage of the disciplinary or absence procedure, then employees also need to be aware of this.

Dealing with poor attendance

3.2.33   Where an employee's attendance record or timekeeping is giving cause for concern, the company's first step should be to discuss the situation with him or her, in order to establish the reason for it.

3.2.34   Where the employee's absences are due to illness or injury, the case should be dealt with as one of sickness absence, discussed further in 3.2.51. If the employee reveals another reason for the absences, such as harassment or bullying, then the company will need to take steps to deal with that issue. If the harassment is on grounds of sex, race, disability, age, sexual orientation or religion, the employee could allege unlawful discrimination. If the company takes no action to deal with the harassment or bullying, or the steps it takes are inadequate, the employee might decide to resign and claim unfair constructive dismissal.

Adjustments for disability

3.2.35 Where a disabled employee's attendance or timekeeping is poor for reasons relating to his or her disability, then the company will need to consider whether any reasonable adjustments are appropriate (see 3.1.69). An employee with impaired mobility might, for example, be frequently late for work because of difficulties in using public transport in the rush hour. It might be reasonable for the company to alter his or her working hours to allow travel at quieter times.

Disciplinary issue

3.2.36 If it appears that there are no legitimate reasons for the employee's poor attendance or timekeeping, then the company may decide to deal with the case through the disciplinary procedure. Handling discipline is dealt with in Chapter 3.3.

Sickness absence

3.2.37 There are two main aspects to managing sickness absence: ensuring that employees receive their proper entitlement to sick pay and other health-related benefits (see 3.2.38); and dealing with the impact of employees' absence on the business, by measures up to and including dismissal (see 3.2.51 and 3.2.79).

Statutory sick pay

3.2.38 All employers are under a legal obligation to pay a certain level of sick pay to employees who are off work through illness or injury, under the Social Security Contributions and Benefits Act 1992 and the Statutory Sick Pay (General) Regulations 1982. Statutory sick pay (SSP) is payable for up to 28 weeks, at a rate that is adjusted annually. From April 2009, the weekly rate is £79.15.

3.2.39 At the beginning of each tax year, HM Revenue and Customs sends all employers a free guide to SSP (see 9.3.2), which contains clear, detailed guidance on calculation of entitlement to and payment of SSP. The main features of the scheme are set out below:

- In order to qualify for SSP, a person must be an employee with average weekly earnings at or above the lower earnings limit for National Insurance contributions. This figure is adjusted each year. From April 2010, it is £97.

- In order to be entitled to SSP, the employee must be unable to work because of illness or injury for four or more calendar days in a row. This is referred to as a 'period of incapacity for work'.

- An employee is entitled to be paid SSP for his or her 'qualifying days'. These are usually the days the employee would normally be required to be at work, but the company can agree other days with the employee, provided there is at least one qualifying day each week.

- SSP is not payable for the first three qualifying days in a period of incapacity for work, referred to as 'waiting days'. However, where two periods of incapacity for work are separated by eight weeks or less, they are treated as one, so that there are no waiting days for the second period of absence.

- An employer is entitled to ask employees to observe certain rules on notifying the company that they are ill, and to withhold payment of SSP if those rules are not met and there was no good cause for the delay. Employees must be told what the rules are, and there are certain limitations:

    - if notification must be in writing, it must be treated as made on the day it is posted;

    - the company must accept notification made by a third party on the employee's behalf;

    - the company cannot insist on notification earlier than the end of the first qualifying day of sickness, or more than once a week; and

    - the notification need not be in the form of medical evidence or on a document supplied by the employer or a printed form.

- An employer is obliged to pay SSP only where an employee's absence is genuinely due to incapacity, and it is the company's responsibility to decide whether the employee is genuinely ill. The company may ask for reasonable evidence of incapacity. Many employers allow employees to self-certify for the first seven days of absence (that is, simply confirm in writing the reason for their absence) but require them to provide a doctor's certificate or other medical evidence for periods of absence after that.

- The maximum entitlement to SSP is 28 weeks in any one period of incapacity for work, or in any two linked periods. However, once an employee has been back at work for over 8 weeks, he or she qualifies for a further period of up to 28 weeks' SSP.

- SSP is treated as earnings and therefore tax and National Insurance contributions are deducted. The level of SSP that an employee receives for each qualifying day of his or her absence is the weekly rate of SSP (£79.15 from April 2009) divided by the number of qualifying days in the week.

- Employers dealing with high levels of sickness absence may be entitled to reimbursement of the SSP they have paid out above a certain level, under the Percentage Threshold Scheme. Full details of this are given in the Revenue SSP manual.

- Employees who are not entitled to SSP may be able to claim Incapacity Benefit. Employers must issue employees with the appropriate standard form to enable them to transfer to Incapacity Benefit from SSP, or to claim Incapacity Benefit because they are not entitled to SSP.

- Employers must keep a record of dates of sickness absence lasting four or more consecutive days and of the SSP payments they have made, and retain them for three years.

Company sick pay

3.2.40   Some employers choose to improve on the statutory minimum level of provision by offering sick pay at a higher level than SSP, or for a longer period of payment. Any terms and conditions on incapacity for work due to sickness or injury, including any provision for sick pay, must be included in the written information on main terms and conditions that employees should be given within two months of starting work (see 1.2.47).

3.2.41   Employers who offer contractual sick pay that is at least as generous as SSP do not have to administer SSP. If an employer pays contractual sick pay, that is offset against its liability to pay SSP.

Contractual status of company sick pay

3.2.42   Not all companies offer sick pay as part of employees' contractual terms – some make clear that sick pay is entirely discretionary. If sick pay is to be contractual, it can either be included in the body of the contract or it can be incorporated into the contract by reference to another document. This could be, for example, a staff handbook that gives full details of the amount and conditions of entitlement, including conditions on notification and evidence. Even if sick pay is contractual, the company may wish to stipulate that it may be withheld at the company's discretion in certain circumstances, such as where it has grounds for believing that the employee is not genuinely ill. Even if an employer has discretion as to whether it pays sick pay, it is under an implied contractual obligation to exercise that discretion rationally.

3.2.43   Importantly, if an employee is entitled under his or her contract to be paid sick pay or some other sickness benefit for a certain period, the company may be acting in breach of contract if it dismisses the employee for sickness absence before the benefit is exhausted. It is lawful to dismiss only if the employee's contract makes clear that the company has the right to terminate the contract, whether because of sickness absence or for other reasons, before the sickness benefit has been exhausted.

Drawing up schemes

3.2.44   When drawing up a sick pay scheme, an employer will need to make policy decisions on the following questions:

Drawing up a company sick pay scheme: key questions

- Should an employee be required to have a certain period of service before qualifying for company sick pay?

- Should any categories of employees be excluded? If the company decides to exclude certain categories of employees, it should check whether this has a

Managing performance

> disproportionate impact on a particular sex, racial or religious group, or group of individuals of a particular sexual orientation in the workforce, or excludes part-timers or those working on fixed-term contracts. If it does, then it must be able to objectively justify its decision to exclude those categories, in order to avoid falling foul of the law on discrimination on grounds of sex, race, religion or sexual orientation (see 3.1.37), part-time work (see 2.3.86) or fixed-term status (see 1.2.89).
>
> - What rules should there be for notifying sickness absence and providing evidence of incapacity for work?
> - Should the first days of sickness absence be viewed as 'waiting days' for which the employee does not qualify for sick pay and if so, how many?
> - At what level should company sick pay be set, and for what period should it be payable? Should sick pay be reduced after a certain period? If a maximum length of payment is to be set, should that be per calendar year or on a rolling-year basis?
> - If the employee is ill while on holiday, will you still pay contractual sick pay? Will you require a medical certificate from day 1?

3.2.45　When deciding how to approach these issues, the company needs to bear in mind that it is relieved from the obligation to administer SSP only if the rules of its contractual scheme are at least as generous as those governing SSP.

3.2.46　An employee's right to 5.6 weeks' paid holiday under the Working Time Regulations 1998 is unaffected by the fact that he or she may be off work sick for part of the year. If the employee is off work sick for the entire year, he or she may be entitled to take that leave in the following year. This issue is complicated; call us for detailed advice.

Long-term sickness benefits

3.2.47　Some employers offer permanent health insurance, ill-health early retirement or other benefits to cover the possibility that employees may have long-term sickness. It is important to note that, if an employee is contractually entitled to this type of benefit, the company may be acting in breach of contract if it dismisses the employee for sickness absence before he or she qualifies for the benefit or exhausts his or her entitlement to it. A dismissal in these circumstances is lawful only if the benefit is not contractual, or if the employee's contract clearly indicates that the benefit does not affect the company's right to terminate the employee's contract for sickness absence at any time. It is also important to ensure that the circumstances in which the benefits are payable are covered by any policy the employer has taken out with an insurance company to meet the cost of the benefits.

3.2.48   Due to an exception in the age discrimination legislation, if an employer arranges life assurance cover for employees who take early retirement on grounds of ill health, it is not unlawful for that cover to end when the employees reach their normal retirement age or, if they have no normal retirement age, when they reach 65.

Disabled employees

3.2.49   Some benefits for ill health, including ill-health early retirement, are contained in employers' pension schemes. Discrimination against disabled employees in relation to pension scheme benefits is unlawful, under the Disability Discrimination Act 1995.

3.2.50   Employers may arrange with insurance companies to provide their workforce with insurance-based employment benefits, including benefits payable for long-term ill health. In certain circumstances, it is lawful for these insurers to treat disabled employees less favourably than others, such as by refusing to provide them with cover or only offering restricted cover. The insurer must, however, be able to show that the treatment is based on reliable information. This information must be actuarial or statistical data or a medical report that is relevant to the assessment of the risk to be insured. The insurer is also required to prove that it is reasonable to treat the disabled person less favourably in the light of that information and 'any other relevant factors'.

Managing sickness absence

3.2.51   Illness and injury are two of the most common causes of absence from work. Some of the steps that an employer will need to take in order to manage sickness absence effectively have already been mentioned above in the general context of managing absence (see 3.2.24). In particular, employers need to ensure that they keep accurate records of sickness absence, regularly monitor and review sickness absence levels and take steps to tackle any causes of sickness absence that are within their power to control. The government plans, from 6 April 2010, to introduce a new version of the medical certificate which makes it easier for GPs to provide employers with information about whether an employee can do some work despite their illness or injury. The recommendations will not be legally binding.

Data protection compliance

3.2.52   Sickness absence records, health records and medical reports are personal data, so employers must ensure that the way they obtain, hold and use this information complies with the Data Protection Act 1998 (see Appendix 8.3). The Data Protection Code (see 9.8.3) gives detailed guidance on handling information about workers' health. The Code states that an employer who holds information on its workers' health should be clear about its purpose in doing so, and be satisfied that it will lead to real business benefits. The employer should tell its workers what information it is holding about their health and why. The Code also advises that, while it is management's role to make decisions about a worker's suitability for particular work, the interpretation of medical information should be left to suitably qualified health professionals.

3.2.53   It is important to note that the Data Protection Act classifies information about a worker's physical or mental health or condition as sensitive personal data, meaning that it can be processed only if one of the conditions for handling that type of information is met (see 8.3.10). Employers would be best-advised to rely on the condition that the processing is necessary to enable them to meet their legal obligations. In effect, this means that an employer should satisfy itself that it needs to process the information in order to meet its duty to safeguard workers' health and safety, to fulfil its duties under the disability discrimination legislation, to administer statutory sick pay or to ensure that any proposed dismissal of an employee for reasons relating to health would be fair. Although it is theoretically possible to process sensitive personal data on the basis that the employee has consented, the Information Commissioner takes the view that this condition will apply only in limited circumstances as, in order to be valid, the worker's consent must be explicit and freely given. An employer should not rely upon a worker's blanket consent given at recruitment.

Summary of the legal framework

3.2.54 In legal terms, the most important consideration for an employer managing the case of an employee who has an unacceptably high level of sickness absence is the need to avoid liability for discrimination and unfair dismissal. The relevant legal principles are summarised here, and a suggested procedure for dealing with sickness absence that reflects how these principles can be observed in practice is set out below (see 3.2.57):

- An employee is protected from disability discrimination if he or she meets the definition of disability in the Disability Discrimination Act 1995 (see 3.1.51) by virtue of having a mental or physical impairment that has a substantial and long-term effect on his or her ability to carry out day-to-day activities.

- If an employee is disabled, it is unlawful for the employer to treat him or her less favourably than it treats others for a reason linked to the individual's disability, unless it has justification for doing so. In other words, it must have a reason for acting as it did that is relevant to the circumstances of the particular case and is more than minor or trivial (see 3.1.67). It would therefore be unlawful for a company to dismiss an employee for a period of sickness absence that was linked to the employee's disability, unless it could show that the employee's absence was having an impact on the business. According to the Code of Practice issued under the disability legislation, an employer would not be justified in dismissing a disabled employee for taking 'very little more' time off for sickness than other employees.

- Before an employer can establish that it was justified in discriminating against a disabled employee, it must be able to show that it has met its duty to consider making reasonable adjustments to accommodate the individual (see 3.1.69). This could, for example, involve a company modifying its usual absence procedure so that it treated a certain level of absence as a trigger for action, such as a review. A company may also need to consider alterations to job content or adaptations to equipment, or redeployment to another job, as an alternative to dismissal.

- If an employee is dismissed for sickness absence after being continuously employed for a year or more, the company must be able to show that it acted reasonably in treating the employee's absence as a sufficient reason for dismissal, to avoid a finding of unfair dismissal. This includes:

- taking steps to consult with the employee about his or her illness and its impact on the business;
- obtaining medical evidence not only on the employee's current state of health but also on his or her prognosis;
- considering redeployment to other work;
- writing to the employee to explain that the company is considering dismissing the employee because of his or her absence and inviting the employee to attend a meeting to discuss the situation, at which the employee has the right to be accompanied (see 3.3.80);
- after the meeting, deciding whether it is practical to continue to employ the individual in all the circumstances; and
- informing the employee of the decision to dismiss and of his or her right to appeal.

- If an employee is dismissed wholly or mainly because of a period of sickness absence that relates to the employee's pregnancy, then her dismissal will automatically be unfair, regardless of her length of service. This principle applies whenever the dismissal occurred, so it is unfair to dismiss a woman for a pregnancy-related sickness absence even if it extends long after the end of maternity leave.

- It is unlawful sex discrimination to dismiss a woman for sickness absence linked to pregnancy or absence during maternity leave. It is not, however, discriminatory to dismiss a woman for a period of sickness absence that falls after the end of her maternity leave, even if her illness is pregnancy related, if any other employee would also have been dismissed for a similar amount of absence. To this extent, the protection provided by sex discrimination law is more limited than the unfair dismissal protection summarised above.

Frustration of contract

3.2.55   In theory, it is possible for an employment contract to be brought to an end by the operation of a legal principle termed 'frustration'. A contract is frustrated if the fundamental basis on which it was entered into has been destroyed by subsequent events. This could potentially apply where an employee has developed a serious illness or injury that makes it likely that he or she will be absent from work for a substantial period or even indefinitely.

3.2.56   Where the principle of frustration applies, the employee's contract is brought to an end by the operation of the principle rather than by dismissal. As a result, the employee is not entitled to claim unfair dismissal. It is difficult to predict with certainty, however, when the principle of frustration will apply. If the employee's contract itself provides for the payment of sickness benefits for a certain period, the contract is unlikely to be frustrated during that period at least. Even after that, it is difficult to know how long an employee's absence would have to be before an employment tribunal would be satisfied that the fundamental basis of the contract has been destroyed. It is advisable, therefore, for a company always to follow a fair procedure in dealing with an employee who is long-term sick, rather than relying on the principle of frustration.

Following a fair sickness absence procedure

3.2.57   The ACAS Code of Practice on discipline and grievance is not applicable to sickness absence issues. However, the key elements in the Code are useful guidelines on the fair handling of sickness absence issues. The key elements are:

- Establish the facts of each case
- Inform the employee of the problem
- Hold a meeting with the employee to discuss the problem
- Allow the employee to be accompanied at the meeting
- Decide on appropriate action
- Provide employees with an opportunity to appeal

Consultation with the employee

3.2.58 As the first stage of a fair sickness absence procedure, it is essential for employers to consult with employees about their sickness absence record as soon as this gives cause for concern. The purpose of this discussion is twofold: to let the employee know that his or her absence record is being reviewed, and to enable the employer to discover the reasons for it. Consultation also gives the employer an opportunity to alert the employee to the possibility that his or her future employment may be at risk if his or her sickness absence record does not improve.

3.2.59 If there are underlying reasons for the sickness absence that the company can control, this gives it an opportunity to deal with them. For example, if the employee reveals that his or her absence is due to stress caused by harassment or bullying, then the company will need to take steps to address that issue. If the harassment is on one of the grounds covered by the discrimination legislation, the employee could allege unlawful discrimination. If no action is taken to deal with the harassment, the employee could resign and claim unfair constructive dismissal.

Right to be accompanied

3.2.60 All workers have the right to be accompanied by a work colleague or trade union official of their choice at a disciplinary hearing, if they reasonably request this. This right is discussed in 3.3.80. For these purposes, a disciplinary hearing is defined as a hearing that could result in the employer giving the worker a warning or taking some other action in relation to him or her. A worker will not, therefore, have the right to be accompanied at any interview to discuss his or her sickness absence unless the interview could result in the issuing of a warning that forms part of the employee's disciplinary record, or the imposition of some other form of disciplinary sanction. Companies may nevertheless wish, as a matter of good practice, to allow an employee to be accompanied at this type of interview.

Obtaining medical evidence

3.2.61 In its discussions with the employee, the company should mention that it will be asking for the employee's consent to obtain medical information on his or her condition. An employer that dismisses an employee without having an adequate picture of his or her current condition and likely prognosis is very unlikely to be acting reasonably. A company will therefore need to obtain information on the effect that the employee's condition is having, and is likely to have, on his or her ability to work. Medical evidence may also be useful when a company is deciding whether any reasonable adjustments could be made to enable a disabled employee to return to work.

3.2.62 Medical information can be obtained from the employee's own GP or specialist, or the company may decide to ask its in-house occupational health physician or an independent doctor to examine the employee and prepare a report.

Company assessment

3.2.63 It is important to remember that the role of medical evidence is to inform the company's decision-making, rather than substitute for it. A doctor's opinion on whether an employee is fit to return to work is only one factor that the company will need to take into account when deciding how to manage the employee's case. Likewise, the question of whether an employee is disabled within the definition of the Disability Discrimination Act 1995 is a question of fact, and a doctor's view on this is not conclusive. While a doctor may be able to give valuable input on possible adjustments for a disabled employee, whether a particular adjustment is reasonable in all the circumstances is an assessment for the company to make.

Medical evidence in cases of intermittent absence

3.2.64 Where an employee is dismissed for intermittent absences, an employment tribunal may be prepared to accept that there was no need for the employer to obtain medical evidence if the employee had had a series of unrelated short-term absences of a day or two. This is because a doctor is unlikely to be able to provide useful information on the causes of these intermittent absences. It may therefore be fair for a company to dismiss an employee with a history of intermittent, short-term absences if it has:

- consulted with the employee about his or her attendance record;
- given him or her an opportunity to improve it;
- cautioned him or her about the consequences if attendance does not return to an acceptable level.

3.2.65 In the context of disability discrimination, however, an employer is under a duty to make reasonable adjustments for an employee if it either knows or could reasonably be expected to know that he or she is disabled. Therefore, in practice, it is always worth obtaining medical evidence, to ensure that an employee with a record of intermittent absences does not have an underlying condition that may amount to a disability, such as clinical depression or a back injury.

Obtaining the employee's consent

3.2.66 A company cannot obtain medical information about an employee, or require an employee to undergo a medical examination, unless the employee consents. An employee is entitled to refuse consent. The company then has no alternative but to make a decision on the basis of the information that it does have. This should be made clear to an employee who is inclined to refuse consent, but without pressurising him or her.

Written consent

3.2.67 If the company wants to obtain medical information from any doctor who is, or has been, responsible for the clinical care of the employee, such as a GP or consultant, it must meet the detailed requirements of the Access to Medical Reports Act 1988. This means that the employee must be notified in writing that a report is to be requested and must supply written consent to it being obtained.

3.2.68 When writing to the employee for consent, the company must also inform the employee that he or she has the following rights:

- to withhold consent to the company applying for the report;
- to have access to the report before it is supplied, and for six months after it is supplied;
- to ask the doctor to amend the report before it is supplied; and
- to withhold consent to the report being supplied after the employee has seen it.

The letter must also explain that in some circumstances, explained below, the doctor may not be obliged to give the employee access to all or part of the report.

Employee's access to report

3.2.69 If the employee gives consent to the company obtaining the report, the company can then write to the doctor requesting it. The letter to the doctor should confirm that the employee has given written consent to the report being requested. If the employee has said that he or she wants access to the report, the company must let the doctor know this when it applies for the report, as well as letting the employee know in writing that the report has been requested.

3.2.70 The employee then has 21 days in which to contact the doctor to make arrangements to see the report. If the employee does not contact the doctor by then, the doctor can supply the report to the company without the employee seeing it. Even if the employee did not originally say that he or she wanted access, he or she can contact the doctor to ask to see the report before it is supplied, and then has 21 days to make the necessary arrangements.

Withholding information

3.2.71 The doctor need not give the employee access to any part of the report that the doctor believes would be likely to:

- cause serious harm to the physical or mental health of the employee or others, or would reveal the doctor's 'intentions' in respect of the employee;

- reveal information about another person;

- reveal the identity of someone who has supplied the doctor with information about the employee, unless that other person has consented, or he or she is a health professional who has been involved in the care of the employee and the information was provided in that professional capacity.

If part of the report is withheld from the employee, the doctor must let the employee know. If the whole of the report is withheld, the doctor must let the employee know, and must not supply the report to the company unless the employee has given written consent.

Employee's comments

3.2.72 If, on reading the report, the employee believes it to be incorrect or misleading, he or she can write to the doctor and ask for an amendment. If the doctor refuses to amend the report, the employee can ask for a statement to be attached to the report reflecting the employee's views. Once the employee has had access to the report, the doctor cannot forward it to the company until the employee gives written consent. Therefore an employee who is not happy with the report can prevent it being supplied to the company.

3.2.73 The Access to Medical Reports Act does not apply to reports from doctors who have not had clinical care of an employee. 'Care' here includes examining, investigating or diagnosing the employee in connection with any form of medical treatment. Therefore the Act would not apply to reports from independent doctors who are asked to examine the employee and prepare a report on behalf of the company. Nor would it apply to reports prepared by in-house occupational health physicians, unless they have had care of the employee.

Requesting the information

3.2.74 In order to obtain useful medical information, the company should be specific about what it needs to know and supply the doctor with relevant contextual information. When it contacts the doctor, the company should:

- explain that it is reviewing the employee's sickness absence record;
- ask for the doctor's view on whether the employee is fit to do his or her current job;
- give the doctor a summary of the employee's duties and the physical environment in which they are performed;
- if the employee is not currently fit to do his or her job, ask the doctor when the employee will be fit to do it, and whether the doctor considers that any reasonable adjustments could be made to the job or the context in which it is carried out that would enable the employee to return to work;

- if the employee is not fit to do his or her job now or in the immediate future, ask the doctor whether the employee is now or may be fit to do any other work that the employer has available; and

- give the doctor a summary of the duties of alternative posts that might be available.

Assessing the information

3.2.75   Once the medical report has been received, the company will need to assess whether it gives sufficient information to make an informed decision on the employee's future employment. The report may not address the points that the company has asked it to address or it may be unclear. If so, the company may need to go back to the doctor for further information or clarification.

3.2.76   Where medical evidence is obtained from more than one source and it conflicts, the company is entitled to rely on the evidence that it believes to be the most credible, provided it has reasonable grounds for that belief. For example, if the company has obtained a report from an employee's GP and from its in-house occupational health physician, it may prefer the occupational health report because that doctor has a better idea of what is involved in the job and the type of working environment in which it is performed.

3.2.77   It is important for the company to discuss the medical evidence with the employee, to ensure that any comments that the employee has about its accuracy are taken into account.

Considering alterations or redeployment

3.2.78   The medical evidence may indicate that although the employee is not fit for his or her job as it currently stands, he or she may be able to do some form of work. The company will then need to consider, in consultation with the employee, whether alteration of the employee's job duties or redeployment is an option.

3.2.79   This is particularly important if the employee is disabled within the meaning of the Disability Discrimination Act 1995, in the light of the employer's duty under that Act to consider reasonable adjustments for disabled employees.

The Code of Practice that gives guidance on avoiding disability discrimination suggests:

> A newly disabled employee is likely to need time to readjust. For example, an employer might allow: a trial period to assess whether the employee is able to cope with the current job, or a new one; the employee initially to work from home; a gradual build-up to full time hours … additional job coaching may be necessary to enable a disabled person to take on a new job.

If no reasonable adjustment would enable the disabled employee to stay in his or her job, the Code states that it might be justifiable to move the employee to another job, even if that post is lower paid. According to the Code:

> it would be reasonable for an employer to have to spend at least as much on an adjustment to enable the retention of a disabled person – including any retraining – as might be spent on recruiting and training a replacement.

Deciding on dismissal

3.2.80 In some cases, the medical information will confirm that the employee is unlikely to return to work within a reasonable time, or will not be well enough in the foreseeable future to maintain a satisfactory attendance record. It may not be feasible to allow the employee to return to amended or alternative duties, even with reasonable adjustments. The company will therefore need to decide whether it can wait any longer for the employee to return to work, or for the employee's attendance record to improve, or whether it should consider dismissing the employee.

3.2.81 In its deliberations, the company will need to take into account all the relevant circumstances, including the length of the employee's absence from work and the organisational and financial impact that the employee's absence is having on the business and how other comparable employees have been treated. If, for example, the employee has a chronic condition with an uncertain prognosis and the company is having difficulty covering for his or her absences, it may be reasonable to dismiss. On the other hand, if the employee has been absent for an extended period but the company has established satisfactory cover arrangements and the employee is likely to be fit to return in the next few weeks, it is likely to be unreasonable to dismiss. Also, where the employer provides an enhanced pension on retirement through ill-health, the employer will be expected to take reasonable steps to ascertain, in long-term sickness cases, whether the employee is entitled to the benefit of ill health retirement before proceeding to dismiss the employee. The decision is a managerial, not a medical, one.

3.2.82　In any event, before deciding to dismiss, the employer must act reasonably which in practice requires following a procedure. This means that the employer must write to the employee explaining that it is contemplating dismissing the employee because of his or her sickness absence record and invite the employee to attend a meeting to discuss this. At the meeting, the employee has the right to be accompanied (see 3.3.80). After the meeting, the employer must notify the employee whether it has decided to dismiss and confirm that he or she has the right to appeal.

If the employee is covered by the EEF national procedural agreements, he or she is entitled to call for an external conference and to remain in employment until agreement is reached or the procedure is exhausted or his or her notice expires, if that is later.

Employee's entitlements on dismissal

3.2.83　If the employer decides to dismiss, it should give the employee whatever notice of dismissal he or she is entitled to under his or her contract (see 4.1.12) and ensure that he or she is paid any other benefits to which he or she is entitled, such as accrued holiday pay. An employee who is dismissed or resigns with notice while on sick leave may have the right to be paid his or her usual pay during the period of notice, even if that falls during a time when he or she would otherwise have received less than full pay, or no pay at all. Employees have this right if they are entitled to no more than six days more than the minimum notice of dismissal required by the Employment Rights Act 1996 (see 4.1.16 – the minimum notice that the employer has to give is, broadly speaking, one week for each year that the employee has been employed in the company, up to a maximum of 12 weeks).

3.2.84　The company may prefer to dismiss the employee with immediate effect. In that case, it should ensure that it makes the employee a payment in lieu of notice (see 4.1.27) that fully reflects the pay and other benefits the employee would have received during his or her notice period.

3.3

Handling discipline and grievances

Overview

3.3.1 If a business is to run efficiently, it must set and enforce appropriate standards of conduct and performance for its workforce and ensure that any grievances that employees may have about their employment are dealt with promptly and fairly. This chapter of the Guide covers the law and good practice on handling discipline and grievances with particular reference to the provisions of the ACAS Code of Practice on discipline and grievance procedures.

3.3.2 Employees who are guilty of serious or persistent misconduct may end up being dismissed. This chapter therefore summarises the legal issues involved in dismissing an employee for misconduct. Readers may also wish to refer to Chapters 4.1 and 4.2 of the Guide, which deal in more detail with the legal framework relating to termination of employment and unfair dismissal.

3.3.3 In this chapter, the term 'misconduct' includes poor performance caused by an employee's lack of attention or application. Some employees, however, fail to meet the required standard of performance through illness or incapability rather than a lack of effort, making a disciplinary approach inappropriate. Chapter 3.2 of this Guide discusses the management of performance where the employee is not 'at fault', including the management of sickness absence.

3.3.4　As well as discussing the general issues arising from the management of grievances (see 3.3.119), this chapter summarises the protection the law gives to workers who 'blow the whistle' on certain forms of wrongdoing (see 3.3.142) or who allege that their employer is not respecting their employment rights (see 3.3.151). It also outlines the protection that employees have from being unfairly treated or dismissed if they raise concerns about health and safety or take action in response to safety risks (see 3.3.155).

Discipline: some general principles

3.3.5　Disciplinary action should be used as a means of improving an employee's conduct or work standards rather than only as a punishment. It may not always be necessary to take formal disciplinary action to improve an employee's conduct or performance. Encouragement, guidance, counselling, instruction or a mild rebuke may be all that is required. The aim of disciplinary action should be to bring an employee's conduct or performance back into line with the standard set by the company and so enable the employee to remain in employment. However, the employee's misconduct might be so serious or persistent that it is not feasible to continue to employ him or her.

3.3.6　In some disciplinary cases, the early use of an internal or external mediator may be a helpful alternative to the use of the disciplinary procedure. Mediation involves using a neutral third party to help two or more people talk through and resolve a difference or dispute. Mediation is especially effective when used at the initial phase.

Basic ingredients of a fair dismissal

3.3.7　From a legal perspective, the fact that an employee may end up being dismissed for misconduct affects the way in which all disciplinary issues should be handled. Unfair dismissal law requires employers to act reasonably in deciding to dismiss, and the reasonableness of a decision to dismiss for misconduct may depend upon the way in which the employee's case has been handled throughout the disciplinary process. The ACAS Code of Practice on discipline and grievance is of central importance when considering the basic ingredients of a fair dismissal for misconduct. Further, this Code will be taken into account by employment tribunals in nearly all other types of tribunal proceedings (not just unfair dismissals) when the Code is considered relevant. The Code does not apply to dismissals due to redundancy or the non-renewal of fixed-term contracts on their expiry.

ACAS Code of Practice

3.3.8   An employment tribunal in an unfair dismissal claim brought by someone who has been dismissed for misconduct will be influenced by whether or not the employer has followed the guidance in the ACAS Code of Practice on discipline and grievance. A failure to follow the Code does not, in itself, make a person or organisation liable in proceedings. However, the Code will be taken into account when deciding whether the misconduct dismissal was fair or unfair. Tribunals are also able to adjust any award by up to 25 per cent for unreasonable failure to comply with any provision of the Code. Thus where the employer has failed to comply with the Code the tribunal may increase any award to an employee by up to 25 per cent and where the employee has failed to comply with the Code the award may be reduced by up to 25 per cent. This ACAS Code is supplemented by more comprehensive ACAS advice and guidance on dealing with discipline and grievance situations produced in a booklet. This guidance booklet does not have the same special status as the Code in tribunal proceedings.

3.3.9   The ACAS Code is not just a relevant document for tribunal proceedings but is mainly designed to help employers, employees and their representatives to deal with discipline and grievance issues in the workplace. The Code emphasises in its foreword that many potential disciplinary issues can be resolved informally and that a 'quiet word is often all that is required to resolve an issue'. The Code also stresses in its foreword that employers and employees should always seek to resolve issues in the workplace and where this is not possible should consider using an independent third party to help resolve the problem through mediation.

3.3.10 The Code itself says that whenever a formal disciplinary process is being followed it is important to deal with issues fairly and this involves the following elements:

> **The key elements from the Code of Practice**
>
> - Employers and employees should raise and deal with issues promptly and should not unreasonably delay meetings, decisions or confirmation of those decisions.
>
> - Employers and employees should act consistently.
>
> - Employers should carry out any necessary investigations, to establish the facts of the case.
>
> - Employers should inform employees of the basis of the problem and give them an opportunity to put their case in response before any decisions are made.
>
> - Employers should allow employees to be accompanied at any formal disciplinary meeting.
>
> - Employers should allow an employee to appeal against any formal decision made.
>
> The Code also states in its foreword employers would be well advised to keep a written record of any disciplinary cases they deal with. It also states that organisations may wish to consider dealing with issues involving bullying and harassment or whistleblowing under a separate procedure. These policies are available for download from EEF's website.

Contractual issues

3.3.11 Disciplinary rules and procedures can form part of an employee's contractual terms. They may, for example, be set out in the employee's written contract or they may be incorporated into the contract by reference to the document where they can be found.

It should be borne in mind, however, that there are distinct disadvantages in making the rules and procedure contractual. If they are contractual, the company needs the employee's consent to change them, unless they state clearly that they may be amended from time to time at the company's discretion. (The implementation of contractual changes is discussed in detail in Chapter 5.1 of this Guide.)

3.3.12   If a disciplinary procedure is contractual and an employee has been dismissed without the company following it, he or she could argue that the dismissal was wrongful, that is, in breach of contract. The employee could claim damages representing the value of the wages or salary and other benefits he or she would have received had the disciplinary procedure been followed in full. Where the employee has been disciplined in some way short of dismissal, he or she could resign and claim unfair constructive dismissal, on the basis that the company's failure to follow the procedure amounted to a serious breach of his or her contract of employment.

Disciplinary sanctions in the contract

3.3.13   Although it is inadvisable to make a disciplinary procedure contractual, it may be necessary to include some terms relating to discipline in employees' contracts. For example, if the company wants the right to apply disciplinary sanctions such as suspension without pay, demotion or disciplinary transfer, then it needs to ensure that right is included in employees' contracts. Otherwise, using these sanctions could amount to a serious breach of an employee's contract, giving rise to the possibility of a claim for damages for breach of contract or compensation for unlawful deductions from pay (see 2.1.92) or an unfair constructive dismissal claim. Likewise, a company that wishes to have the option of searching employees or their belongings for evidence of misconduct should include a term in employees' contracts giving it that power (see 3.3.53).

3.3.14   It is important to note that, even if a company's disciplinary procedure is not contractual, it is highly advisable for the company to follow it. A failure to do so may be held against the company in an unfair dismissal claim.

Discipline during probationary periods

3.3.15   Some companies make the first few weeks or months of an employee's employment a probationary period. The employee's conduct and performance is closely monitored during this period, to ensure that he or she is suitable for the job. If the employee proves unsuitable, his or her contract may be terminated during or at the end of the period.

3.3.16   Although an employee who is 'on probation' is entitled to notice of termination should it prove necessary to terminate his or her contract, it may not be appropriate to apply the full disciplinary procedure to him or her. If the company's disciplinary procedure forms part of the employee's contract, it is important to make clear that it does not apply if the employee is dismissed during or at the end of the probationary period.

3.3.17   Companies that have lengthy probationary periods should bear in mind that, once an employee has been continuously employed for one year, he or she is entitled to protection from unfair dismissal. Therefore if a company is considering dismissing a probationary employee for misconduct after one year's service or more, it needs to ensure that it acts reasonably, and that includes following a proper disciplinary procedure. Even where the probationer has less than one year's service, it may be advisable to follow a fair procedure.

Making the standards clear

3.3.18   It is essential to the fair handling of discipline that employees are not penalised for conduct or performance that they did not know was unacceptable. This is particularly important where an employee is at risk of being dismissed for alleged gross misconduct. Any rules or standards that a company wishes to enforce should therefore be made clear to all employees, and should preferably be included in any induction training that a new recruit is given. Line managers also need to be familiar with the content of disciplinary rules if they are effectively to fulfil their role in enforcing them.

3.3.19   The Code of Practice states *'Fairness and transparency are promoted by developing and using rules and procedures for handling disciplinary and grievance situations. These should be set down in writing, be specific and clear. Employees and, where appropriate, their representatives should be involved in the development of rules and procedures. It is also important to help employees and managers understand what the rules and procedures are, where they can be found and how they are to be used.'*

3.3.20   ACAS guidance suggests that, to be fully effective, the rules need to be accepted as reasonable by those covered by them and those who operate them. This means that it is best to develop the rules in consultation with employees and those who have responsibility for applying them. Also unless there are valid reasons why different sets of rules apply to different groups of employees, for example for health and safety reasons, the same rules should apply to all employees at all levels in the organisation. Usually, rules are readily accepted and so followed if people understand the reasons for them. For example, if employees are required to wear protective clothing then the reasons why should be explained.

Notifying the rules

3.3.21 Under the Employment Rights Act 1996, all employees must be provided with written information about the disciplinary rules and procedures that apply to them, within two months of starting work (see 1.2.47). The Act says that these details need not include rules about health and safety. In practice, however, it is advisable for employers to notify employees of all disciplinary rules, including those covering health and safety, in order to fulfil their duty of care under health and safety law and to avoid liability for unfair dismissal.

3.3.22 Under the Act, an employee need not be given an individual copy of the rules and procedures. He or she can be referred to some other document that is reasonably accessible, such as a set of rules displayed on a notice board or kept in the personnel office. In practice, it is preferable to supply each employee with his or her own copy of the rules and get a signed receipt to confirm that this has been done. Where practicable, the employee's manager should talk the employee through them, in order to ensure that the rules are understood.

3.3.23 Special steps may need to be taken to communicate the rules to employees who cannot read or whose first language is not English, and to employees who have a visual impairment or a learning disability. It may be unlawful under the Disability Discrimination Act 1995 to discipline a disabled employee for breach of a rule that was not made clear by making a reasonable adjustment of this kind (see 3.1.69). Special attention should also be paid to ensure that rules are understood by any employees without recent experience of working life, such as young people or those returning to work after a lengthy break.

Content of the rules

3.3.24 The content of an employer's disciplinary rules will differ according to the type of business that the company runs, the personnel policies that it has and the circumstances of the particular workplace. Unless there are reasons why different sets of rules apply to different groups they should apply to all employees at all levels in the organisation. Disciplinary rules would usually cover issues such as:

- Timekeeping
    - starting times
    - lateness
- Absence
    - authorising absence
    - approval of holidays
    - notification of absence
    - who the employee tells
    - when they tell them
    - the reasons for absence
    - likely time of arrival/return
    - rules on self-certification and doctor's certificates
- Health and safety
    - personal appearance – any special requirements regarding, for example, protective clothing, hygiene or the wearing of jewellery. (Employers should be aware that any such requirement must be solely on the basis of health or safety, and should not discriminate against either sex or on the basis of age, race, disability, sexual orientation or religion or belief.)
    - smoking policy
    - special hazards/machinery/chemicals
    - policies on alcohol, drug or other substance abuse

- Use of organisation facilities
  - private telephone calls
  - computers, email and the internet
  - company premises outside working hours
  - equipment
- Discrimination, bullying and harassment
  - equal opportunities policy
  - policy on harassment relating to age, race, sex, disability, sexual orientation, religion or belief
  - bullying and harassment policy
  - non-discriminatory clothing or uniform policies
  - any standards of written or spoken language needed for the safe and effective performance of the job
- Gross misconduct
  - the types of conduct that might be considered as 'gross misconduct' (this is misconduct that is so serious that it may justify dismissal without notice).

Rules on discrimination and safety

3.3.25   From a legal perspective, it would be advisable for disciplinary rules to specify that discriminating on the ground of race, age, sex, disability, religion or sexual orientation, including harassment on any of those grounds, amounts to misconduct and may, according to the circumstances, be viewed as gross misconduct. An employer can avoid liability for the discriminatory acts of its employees if it can prove it took such steps as were reasonably practicable to prevent the discrimination occurring (see 3.1.109). A company will have difficulty in establishing this defence if it has not adopted and enforced disciplinary rules on discrimination and harassment.

3.3.26   It is also highly advisable from a legal perspective for employers to adopt comprehensive health and safety rules. A company is under a legal duty to take reasonable care for the health and safety of its employees, which includes maintaining a safe system of work. Adopting and enforcing rules on safe working practices are an integral part of that duty, particularly where the company is operating in a physically hazardous environment.

3.3.27   In order to comply with the Data Protection Act 1998, and in particular the seventh data protection principle that personal data should be kept secure, it would be advisable to make the unauthorised disclosure of personal information a disciplinary offence.

Dress codes

3.3.28   Some employers operate rules on what employees can wear in the workplace, usually for health and safety reasons or to enhance the company's image. These employers need to bear in mind that certain religions also have rules on dress and appearance, and that it would be advisable to accommodate these traditions where practicable, in order to avoid indirect racial or religious discrimination (see 3.1.37). There is a specific provision in the law that makes it unlawful to require a Sikh who wears a turban to wear protective headgear while on a site where building operations or engineering construction is taking place.

3.3.29   Further information on the issue of religious discrimination and dress can be found in the ACAS guidance on the religious discrimination legislation (see 9.3.1). Companies can also obtain advice from us.

Gross misconduct

3.3.30   It is important for disciplinary rules to make clear the likely consequences of breaking them. In particular, employees should be given a clear indication of the type of conduct, often referred to as gross misconduct, that may lead to summary dismissal (that is, dismissal without notice). ACAS guidance suggests that the following list of acts are ones that an employer might choose to classify as gross misconduct:

- theft or fraud;
- physical violence or bullying;

- deliberate and serious damage to property;
- serious misuse of an organisation's property or name;
- deliberately accessing internet sites containing pornographic, offensive or obscene material;
- serious insubordination;
- unlawful discrimination or harassment;
- bringing the organisation into serious disrepute;
- serious incapability at work brought on by alcohol or illegal drugs;
- causing loss, damage or injury through serious negligence;
- a serious breach of health and safety rules;
- a serious breach of confidence.

Unfair dismissal and disciplinary rules

3.3.31   It is important to bear in mind that the fact that a particular form of misconduct has been described as gross misconduct in a company's disciplinary rules does not mean that it will automatically be fair to dismiss an employee for that conduct. Whether or not a dismissal is fair turns on whether the employer acted reasonably in deciding that dismissal was the appropriate sanction, and that depends on all the surrounding circumstances, not just the content of the disciplinary rules.

3.3.32   Disciplinary rules cannot cover all possible acts of misconduct. The fact that a particular act of misconduct has not been mentioned in the rules does not mean that it can never be reasonable to dismiss an employee for it. This is particularly so if it is obvious by any objective standard that it amounts to misconduct. Nevertheless, it would be advisable for companies to include a statement in their disciplinary rules that the specified acts of misconduct and gross misconduct are intended to illustrate the types of behaviour that may lead to disciplinary action or dismissal rather than being an exhaustive list.

Changing the rules

3.3.33   Many developments in a company, from the introduction of new working practices or personnel policies to a reorganisation or relocation, may make it necessary to amend disciplinary rules. Disciplinary rules should therefore be regularly reviewed and updated, to reflect developments in the company, in employment legislation and in good employment practice.

3.3.34   Provided that disciplinary rules are not part of employees' contractual terms, a company can change the rules at its discretion. Nevertheless, employees should be consulted about changes in the rules, or at least clearly notified that changes will be made, since it is likely to be unfair for a company to dismiss an employee for breaching a rule that he or she did not know existed.

3.3.35   Under the Employment Rights Act 1996, employees must be notified of any changes in the disciplinary rules at the earliest opportunity, and in any event no later than one month after the change. The Act says that an employee can be referred to some reasonably accessible document for details of the change, rather than being individually notified. In practice, it would be advisable to notify each employee individually, so that, if it becomes necessary to discipline an employee for breaking the new rule, the employee cannot argue that he or she did not know about it.

Enforcing disciplinary rules

3.3.36   Once a company has adopted a particular disciplinary rule, it should ensure that it is enforced. A failure to enforce one rule can have a knock-on effect on the authority of the rest of the rules. It may also make it difficult to enforce the rule in the future, since it may be unfair to dismiss an employee for breaking a rule that has previously been disregarded. A company therefore needs to notify its workforce if a particular rule is to be dropped or if the company intends to revert to enforcing a rule that has fallen into disuse.

Operating a disciplinary procedure

3.3.37   In order to ensure fair and effective treatment of disciplinary matters and to avoid liability for unfair dismissal, it is advisable for a company to adopt a formal disciplinary procedure that can be followed when a disciplinary rule appears to have been broken. A company should have a separate procedure to deal with cases of sickness absence, and may wish to have a separate procedure to deal with cases of poor performance that are due to lack of capability rather than lack of application. (The management of performance issues, including absence, is dealt with in Chapter 3.2 of this Guide.) Companies that are drafting a disciplinary procedure may find it useful to refer to the disciplinary procedure included at the back of this Guide.

3.3.38   The ACAS Code states: 'It is important to help employees and managers understand what the rules and procedures are, where they can be found and how they are to be used.' Those responsible for operating the rules and procedures should be trained.

3.3.39   Procedures should be kept under review, to make sure they are always relevant and effective.

3.3.40   The ACAS Code states that the keys to handling disciplinary problems in the workplace are:

- Establish the facts of each case
- Inform the employee of the problem
- Hold a meeting with the employee to discuss the problem
- Allow the employee to be accompanied at the meeting
- Decide on appropriate action
- Provide employees with an opportunity to appeal
- Special cases

The next parts of this Guide examine in greater detail these key elements in the ACAS Code.

Disciplining union officials

3.3.41 ACAS guidance points out that disciplinary action against a union official (e.g. a shop steward) can lead to a serious dispute if it is seen as an attack on the union's functions. It is unlawful for a company to penalise an employee for union activities (see 6.1.10). The Code states that, if it proves necessary to apply the disciplinary procedure to a trade union representative, the case should be discussed at an early stage, after obtaining the employee's agreement, with an official employed by the union. Companies may wish to contact us for advice if they are considering taking disciplinary action against a union official.

Criminal charges and convictions

3.3.42 The ACAS Code makes it clear that it will not be fair to dismiss an employee solely because he or she has been charged with or convicted of a criminal offence. Consideration needs to be given to what effect the charge or conviction has on the employee's suitability to do the job and their relationship with their employer, work colleagues and customers.

The employer should seek to establish the facts as far as possible and then consider whether the matter is serious enough to warrant instituting the disciplinary procedure. Where the conduct requires prompt attention the employer need not await the outcome of the criminal prosecution before taking fair and reasonable action. In circumstances where the employee cannot attend work because he or she is in prison and the alleged offence or conviction has no bearing on the employment relationship, then the employer should decide whether, in all the circumstances, especially in light of the needs of the business, the employee's job can be covered or held open until the employee is likely to be available for work. Finally, it is very unlikely to be fair to dismiss an employee for a criminal conviction that is 'spent' under the Rehabilitation of Offenders Act 1974.

Discipline and discrimination

3.3.43 Care should be taken to ensure that disciplinary action does not amount to unlawful discrimination. It would, for example, be unlawful under the Disability Discrimination Act 1995 to discipline a disabled employee for a reason relating to his or her disability, unless disciplinary action was justified in all the circumstances. It would also be a breach of the Sex Discrimination Act 1975 to discipline an employee for a reason connected with her pregnancy or maternity. If a company decides to monitor its employment practices to ensure that they are not affected by conscious or unconscious race, sex or disability bias (see 3.1.118), it may wish to include the conduct and outcome of disciplinary proceedings in that process.

Drugs and alcohol

3.3.44   Special considerations may arise where a disciplinary offence is linked to drug or alcohol abuse. Companies may find it helpful to refer to the policy on alcohol and drugs available for download from EEF's website, which covers the relevant issues, including the rules on the use of alcohol and drugs. It also suggests that where an employee has broken a disciplinary rule for reasons linked to the use of drink or drugs, it may be appropriate to suspend the disciplinary process for a time, in order to investigate whether the employee has a medical problem that is amenable to treatment.

Investigating the conduct

3.3.45   It is essential to the fair management of disciplinary issues that no disciplinary sanction is imposed upon an employee until the misconduct of which he or she is accused has been properly investigated. The facts need to be established promptly before recollections fade. Care should be taken to ensure that the investigation is conducted in a way that is as confidential as possible.

3.3.46   The ACAS Code of Practice states:

Establish the facts of each case

- It is important to carry out necessary investigations of potential disciplinary matters without unreasonable delay to establish the facts of the case. In some cases this will require the holding of an investigatory meeting with the employee before proceeding to any disciplinary hearing. In others, the investigatory stage will be the

Employment Guide 2010

> collation of evidence by the employer for use at any disciplinary hearing.
>
> - In misconduct cases, where practicable, different people should carry out the investigation and disciplinary hearing.
>
> - If there is an investigatory meeting this should not by itself result in any disciplinary action. Although there is no statutory right for an employee to be accompanied at a formal investigatory meeting, such a right may be allowed under an employer's own procedure.
>
> - In cases where a period of suspension with pay is considered necessary, this period should be as brief as possible, should be kept under review and it should be made clear that this suspension is not considered a disciplinary action.

3.3.47 It might appear unnecessary to investigate if the employee is 'caught in the act' committing some serious misconduct, such as stealing or fighting at work. However, even in this type of situation, some investigation of the surrounding circumstances will be needed, to ensure that the company has the full picture of how and why the misconduct occurred.

Suspension

3.3.48 If the employee has been accused of serious misconduct, or there are grounds for believing that the employee could commit further misconduct or impede the investigation, it may be necessary to suspend the employee from work while the investigation is carried out.

3.3.49 The employee should be suspended on full pay, since the purpose of the suspension is to preserve the status quo rather than act as a disciplinary sanction. It is advisable to confirm to the employee in writing that the suspension is not a disciplinary sanction, and to keep the suspension as short as possible.

Gathering evidence

3.3.50 The steps that are involved in an investigation depend on the nature of the alleged misconduct. It is invariably necessary to interview the employee concerned. When deciding on the eventual sanction for the misconduct, the company may want to take into account whether the employee admitted the misconduct or lied about it when interviewed.

3.3.51   Depending on the circumstances, an investigation may also involve speaking to any witnesses to the alleged misconduct and the employee's line manager, and checking documentary evidence such as attendance records, appraisal reports and correspondence. A written record should be made of what is said during any interview.

Investigatory interviews

3.3.52   Every worker has the right to be accompanied at a disciplinary hearing. An interview held as part of an investigation into an act of misconduct will not amount to a hearing for these purposes, unless it could result in a warning that forms part of the employee's disciplinary record or some other form of disciplinary sanction. If during an investigatory meeting it becomes apparent that formal disciplinary action may be needed, then this should be dealt with at a formal meeting at which the employee will have the statutory right to be accompanied.

Searching

3.3.53   Some companies may wish to have the right to search employees, their bags, lockers, desks and cars for evidence of misconduct such as theft of company property. If a company wants the option to search, it should ensure that employees are made aware when first recruited that they or their property may be searched. This should be done either by including this as a term in their contracts of employment or by stating it clearly in some other document that they are given, such as an employee handbook.

3.3.54   An employee is not obliged to submit to a search, and carrying out a personal search without consent would amount to assault. However, if an employee refuses to submit to a search when he or she has been told that a search is a possibility, or where the company has good grounds for believing that he or she may be concealing evidence of misconduct, the company is entitled to take that into account when deciding whether the misconduct has occurred and what the appropriate disciplinary sanction should be.

Monitoring and surveillance

3.3.55   Some companies use monitoring or surveillance systems to monitor performance or detect misconduct. The legal issues this raises are summarised here, but companies that are proposing to adopt monitoring or surveillance techniques may also wish to contact us for advice on whether their proposals are appropriate and lawful.

Data protection

3.3.56   If an employer's monitoring or surveillance involves processing personal information about an employee, it must comply with the principles set out in the Data Protection Act 1998 (see Appendix 8.3). 'Processing' includes obtaining, recording or holding information, so the Act applies, for example, if an employer records employees on closed-circuit television cameras, opens their e-mails or listens to their voice-mails, or examines logs of websites they have visited or telephone numbers they have called.

3.3.57   The Data Protection Code of Practice and detailed supplementary guidance explain how to comply with data protection principles when monitoring at work. (There is also a Code of Practice dealing specifically with the use of closed-circuit television.) The Code points out that employees have a legitimate expectation that they can keep their personal lives private and that they are entitled to a degree of privacy in the workplace. If employers wish to monitor their workers, they should be clear about their purpose in doing so, and be satisfied that the particular monitoring arrangement they are adopting is justified by the benefits it will deliver. This involves considering whether there are alternative ways of achieving their purpose, or less intrusive methods of monitoring that would deliver the same results. (It is also worth noting that excessive monitoring may well breach an employer's important legal obligation not, without reasonable cause, to act in a way that undermines the trust and confidence that underpins the relationship it has with its employees. It could therefore lead to employees resigning and claiming unfair constructive dismissal (see 4.1.35).)

3.3.58   The Code advises that information obtained through monitoring should be used only for the purpose for which the monitoring was carried out, unless an activity is discovered that no employer could reasonably be expected to ignore. Employers should ensure that the number of people who have access to personal information obtained through monitoring is kept to a minimum, and that arrangements are put in place to ensure that the information is kept and disposed of securely, and not retained for longer than is necessary.

3.3.59   In order to comply with data protection principles, employees should usually be told what monitoring is taking place and why. It will be lawful to monitor covertly only if the aim is to prevent or detect crime and letting employees know that the monitoring is happening would be likely to prejudice that aim.

Interception of communications

3.3.60   If an employer checks its employees' use of e-mail, fax, telephones or the internet, it must also comply with the Regulation of Investigatory Powers Act 2000 and the Telecommunications (Lawful Business Practice) (Interception of Communications) Regulations 2000. This legislation applies where an employer accesses the content of an electronic communication in the course of its transmission. The legislation is complex but, in broad summary, an employer will comply with it if it has made all reasonable efforts to tell employees that their communications may be intercepted, and ensured that any interception is carried out only for legitimate business purposes. Those purposes could include performance monitoring, the prevention or detection of crime, or the investigation or detection of unauthorised use of the system. The supplementary guidance that accompanies the Data Protection Code of Practice gives further information about this legislation.

Electronic communications policy

3.3.61   If employers decide to monitor electronic communications, the Code recommends that they first establish a policy on their use and communicate it to their workforce. Companies planning to adopt a policy may find it useful to refer to the policy available for download from EEF's website.

Involving the police

3.3.62   Some allegations of misconduct involve some form of criminal act, such as theft or assault. In these cases, the company will need to decide whether to involve the police. If the police are contacted, their decision on whether to investigate should not affect the company's handling of the case.

3.3.63   The criteria by which the police assess whether to investigate a criminal offence are very different to the factors taken into account by a company when deciding whether disciplinary action is appropriate for breach of the company's disciplinary rules. If the police do investigate and a decision is made to prosecute, the company should not usually suspend its own disciplinary procedure to await the result. Conviction for a criminal offence requires proof beyond all reasonable doubt. However, it is reasonable for an employer to discipline or even dismiss an employee on the basis of a genuine belief that the employee has been guilty of misconduct, provided that belief is based on reasonable grounds after a reasonable investigation.

Deciding how to proceed

3.3.64   Once the investigation is complete, the company will need to decide whether there are grounds for believing that the employee was guilty of misconduct and what the next step should be.

3.3.65   Even if there is evidence of misconduct, the company may consider it appropriate to deal with the matter informally, by counselling the employee or giving him or her an informal reprimand that will form no part of the employee's disciplinary record, rather than taking him or her through the formal disciplinary procedure. Even where informal action is taken, it is important for the company to make clear to the employee:

- how his or her conduct fell short of the required standards;
- what he or she needs to do to rectify this;
- how and when his or her conduct or performance will be reviewed; and
- what the consequences will be if there is no improvement – that is, that the formal disciplinary procedure may be invoked.

This should all be confirmed to the employee in writing.

Holding a disciplinary hearing

3.3.66   The ACAS Code of Practice states:

Inform the employee of the problem

- If it is decided that there is a disciplinary case to answer, the employee should be notified of this in writing. This notification should contain sufficient information about the alleged misconduct or poor performance and its possible consequences to enable the employee to prepare to answer the case at a disciplinary meeting. It would normally be appropriate to provide copies of any written evidence, which may include any witness statements, with the notification.

- The notification should also give details of the time and venue for the disciplinary meeting and advise the employee of their right to be accompanied at the meeting.

Hold a meeting with the employee to discuss the problem

- The meeting should be held without unreasonable delay whilst allowing the employee reasonable time to prepare their case.

- Employers and employees (and their companions) should make every effort to attend the meeting. At the meeting the employer should

  explain the complaint against the employee and go through the evidence that has been gathered. The employee should be allowed to set out their case and answer any allegations that have been made. The employee should also be given a reasonable opportunity to ask questions, present evidence and call relevant witnesses. They should also be given an opportunity to raise points about any information provided by witnesses. Where an employer or employee intends to call relevant witnesses they should give advance notice that they intend to do this.

3.3.67 Where informal action is not appropriate, because the misconduct is too serious, or informal action has not brought about an improvement in the past, formal disciplinary action will be necessary. A disciplinary hearing will need to be held, to give the employee an opportunity to put his or her side of the case.

Giving the employee notice

3.3.68　The company should schedule the disciplinary hearing for a date that gives the employee adequate time to prepare for it. The company must then write to the employee to let him or her know the date, time and venue of the hearing and confirm that he or she has the right to be accompanied at the hearing (see 3.3.80). The timing and location of the meeting must be reasonable: ACAS guidance suggests that, where possible, these should be agreed with the employee. It also suggests that the employee's companion should be allowed a say in the date and time of the hearing.

3.3.69　The letter inviting the employee to the hearing should also confirm what misconduct is alleged and what the potential disciplinary sanction might be, and summarise the evidence that the company has gathered during the investigation. This information needs to be sufficiently detailed to enable the employee to dispute the company's evidence, produce evidence of his or her own and argue his or her case. It may therefore be appropriate to give the employee copies of any statements that have been taken from witnesses or a summary of what they contain. The employee may want the witnesses to attend the hearing so that he or she can question them. Where witnesses have concerns about attending, companies should seek our advice.

Rescheduling and non-attenders

3.3.70　ACAS advises that, if an employee is unable to attend a disciplinary hearing, he or she should notify the employer in advance wherever possible. If the employee fails to attend through circumstances outside his or her control and unforeseeable at the time of the meeting was arranged (such as illness), the employer should arrange another meeting. The Code also states that a decision may be taken in the employee's absence should he or she fail to attend the rearranged hearing without good reason.

3.3.71　If the employee's chosen companion is not available at the time a disciplinary hearing is scheduled, the employee is entitled to have the hearing postponed to another time, provided it is reasonable and falls within five working days (excluding weekends and public holidays) of the day originally proposed. It might not be reasonable, for example, to postpone the hearing to a date when the manager responsible was away on business or holiday, unless someone else could step in to take the hearing.

Handling informants

3.3.72   In some cases, a witness may only be prepared to give evidence on the basis that he or she will not be identified. This could happen, for example, where the witness has a genuine fear of reprisals by the employee. In this situation, the company needs to balance the need to protect the informant and the need to provide a fair hearing for the employee. A detailed statement should therefore be taken from the informant and corroborative evidence should be obtained wherever possible. If practicable, the employee should be given a copy of the informant's statement with omissions that avoid the informant being identified.

3.3.73   Since the informant may have reason to fabricate evidence against the employee, enquiries may need to be made into his or her character and background, to establish the value of the evidence. The manager running the disciplinary hearing should interview the informant and be satisfied that weight is to be given to the evidence. If the employee raises a point during the hearing that needs to be put to the informant, it may be necessary to adjourn the hearing to allow the manager to do so.

Holding the hearing

3.3.74   A suitable venue will need to be found for the hearing, which is out of the way of other employees and where interruptions are unlikely. If the employee concerned is disabled, reasonable adjustments may be required under the Disability Discrimination Act 1995.

3.3.75   Ideally, the manager who conducts the hearing should be different from the manager who conducted the investigation, although this may not be practical in smaller companies. If a manager needs to give evidence to the hearing, he or she should not conduct it. A second member of management should be present to take notes and act as a witness.

3.3.76   Prior to the hearing, the manager responsible for conducting the hearing should ensure that all the relevant facts are available, such as disciplinary records and other relevant documents and, where appropriate, written statements from witnesses. The manager should also check that the standards of other employees are acceptable, and that this employee is not being unfairly singled out. As part of the preparation for the meeting, the manager should consider what explanations may be offered by the employee and if possible check them out beforehand and establish what disciplinary action was taken in similar circumstances in the past.

Structuring the hearing

3.3.77 The manager conducting the hearing should consider in advance how the hearing should be structured, and should make a note of the points to be covered. An outline structure for the hearing based on the Code might be:

> ### Outline structure of the hearing
>
> - *Open the hearing.* Introduce those present to the employee and explain why they are there. Explain that the purpose of the hearing is to establish whether disciplinary action should be taken under the company's disciplinary procedure, and explain how the hearing will be conducted and who will make the decision.
>
> - *Explore the complaint.* State the allegations being made against the employee and present the evidence. Give the employee an opportunity to state his or her case, ask questions, give evidence and call witnesses. Allow time for general questioning and discussion. If the facts are not clear and further investigation is necessary, adjourn the hearing until a later time or date. If the employee becomes upset during the hearing, adjourn the hearing temporarily to allow the employee to compose him- or herself. If the employee continues to be so upset that the hearing cannot continue, reconvene it at a later time or date.
>
> - *Sum up.* Summarise the main evidence relating to the misconduct and the main points raised by the employee and ask the employee if they have anything further to say. Explain that the company will now decide on the appropriate action and let the employee know when he or she will be informed what this is.

3.3.78 After the hearing is over, the manager who conducted it will need to take time to consider the matters raised. In particular, the manager will need to decide the facts of what took place, which may involve assessing conflicting evidence and deciding on the balance of probabilities whose version of events is true.

It is important for the manager to consider all the issues fully, and not rush to a hasty conclusion.

Overlapping grievance and disciplinary cases

3.3.79   The Code states 'where an employee raises a grievance during the disciplinary process, the disciplinary process may be temporarily suspended in order to deal with the grievance. Where the grievance and disciplinary cases are related it may be appropriate to deal with both issues concurrently.' This provision of the Code would apply, for example, when the grievance relates to a conflict of interest that the manager of the disciplinary meeting is alleged to have. The appropriate response by the employer will depend on the particular circumstances of each case, but employers need to be alert to this provision of the Code and the need to consider an adjournment. Companies in this situation may wish to contact us for advice.

The right to be accompanied

3.3.80   Workers have the right to be accompanied at disciplinary and grievance hearings if they reasonably request to be. The ACAS Code of Practice on discipline and grievance procedures states:

> ### Allow the employee to be accompanied at the meeting
>
> - Workers have a statutory right to be accompanied by a companion where the disciplinary meeting could result in
>   - a formal warning being issued; or
>   - the taking of some other disciplinary action; or
>   - the confirmation of a warning or some other disciplinary action (appeal hearings).
> - The chosen companion may be a fellow worker, a trade union representative, or an official employed by a trade union. A trade union representative who is not an employed official must have been certified by their union as being competent to accompany a worker.

> - To exercise the statutory right to be accompanied workers must make a reasonable request. What is reasonable will depend on the circumstances of each individual case. However, it would not normally be reasonable for workers to insist on being accompanied by a companion whose presence would prejudice the hearing nor would it be reasonable for a worker to ask to be accompanied by a companion from a remote geographical location if someone suitable and willing was available on site.
>
> - The companion should be allowed to address the hearing to put and sum up the worker's case, respond on behalf of the worker to any views expressed at the meeting and confer with the worker during the hearing. The companion does not, however, have the right to answer questions on the worker's behalf, address the hearing if the worker does not wish it or prevent the employer from explaining their case.

3.3.81   The right to be accompanied applies not only to employees and apprentices, but also to any other workers who have contracted to work personally for the company, such as homeworkers. Casual, seasonal and part-time workers are all also likely to qualify, as may self-employed labourers. The right does not extend, however, to the genuinely self-employed who are working for a company in the course of their own profession or business.

The companion

3.3.82   The worker can choose who accompanies him or her, provided that person falls within one of the categories laid down in the legislation. Those categories are:

- another worker who works for the company;
- a full-time trade union official;
- a lay union official whom the union has certified in writing as having experience or training in accompanying workers at disciplinary or grievance hearings.

3.3.83   Some employers may have agreed to allow their employees to be accompanied by persons other than those listed in the legislation. For example, some employees may have the right to be accompanied by their partner or legal representative.

3.3.84   The choice of companion is the worker's. However, the ACAS guidance advises workers to bear in mind that it would not be reasonable to insist on being accompanied by a colleague whose presence would prejudice the hearing or who might have a conflict of interest. Furthermore, it would not be reasonable to ask to be accompanied by a colleague from a distant location when someone suitably qualified was available on the worker's own site. The chosen companion is, of course, free to refuse to act.

3.3.85   The worker is legally entitled to choose an official from any trade union whether or not the worker is a member or the union is recognised. However, as the ACAS guidance makes clear, fellow workers and union officials do not have to accept a request to accompany a worker.

3.3.86   The ACAS guidance suggests that the worker should tell the company before the hearing who his or her companion is to be. In certain circumstances (such as where the companion is an official of a non-recognised union), it may be helpful for the company to contact the companion before the hearing.

Companion's participation

3.3.87   If the worker's chosen companion is not available at the time the disciplinary hearing is scheduled, the worker is entitled to have the hearing postponed to another time, provided the new time is reasonable and falls within five working days (excluding weekends and public holidays) of the day originally proposed.

3.3.88   Unless the worker has indicated that he or she does not want the companion to do so, the companion is entitled to address the hearing in order to put or sum up the worker's case, and to respond on the worker's behalf to any view expressed at the hearing. ACAS guidance advises that it is good practice also to allow the companion to ask questions on the worker's behalf and to participate as fully as possible in the hearing. However, the companion is not entitled to answer questions put to the employee, and must not conduct him- or herself in a way that prevents the company from explaining its case or prevents anyone else at the hearing from making their contribution. The companion must be allowed to confer with the worker during the hearing.

3.3.89 Some companies have disciplinary procedures that allow employees to chose from a wider range of companions and give the companion a fuller role. Some procedures, for example, allow the companion to speak on behalf of the employee.

3.3.90 Union officials and workers who work for the company have the right to a reasonable amount of paid time off work to accompany a worker at a disciplinary hearing.

Denying the right to be accompanied

3.3.91 It is not only unlawful for a company to deny a worker the right to be accompanied. It is also unlawful to penalise a worker for taking up the right, or to penalise the companion for carrying out the role. It is automatically unfair to dismiss a worker or his or her companion on these grounds, regardless of their age or length of service. This also covers selection for redundancy. If an employee is dismissed as a result of a disciplinary hearing at which he or she was denied the right to be accompanied, he or she could allege that the dismissal was unfair on that basis.

Accommodating disabled workers

3.3.92 Special provision may need to be made for disabled employees. The Disability Discrimination Act 1995 requires employers to make reasonable adjustments to accommodate disabled workers (see 3.1.69). It may be reasonable, for example, for an employer to allow an employee with a learning disability to be accompanied by a friend from outside work, even if the company's disciplinary procedure and the statutory right to be accompanied do not allow for this. ACAS guidance suggests that employers should also possibly cater for any disability that a companion has.

Choosing the sanction

3.3.93 Once the hearing is over, the manager will need to decide whether he or she believes, on reasonable grounds and after a reasonable investigation, that the employee was guilty of the misconduct, and what disciplinary sanction, if any, is appropriate.

3.3.94   The ACAS Code of Practice states:

> ### Decide on appropriate action
>
> - After the meeting decide whether or not disciplinary or any other action is justified and inform the employee accordingly in writing.
>
> - Where misconduct is confirmed or the employee is found to be performing unsatisfactorily it is usual to give the employee a written warning. A further act of misconduct or failure to improve performance within a set period would normally result in a final written warning.
>
> - If an employee's first misconduct or unsatisfactory performance is sufficiently serious, it may be appropriate to move directly to a final written warning. This might occur where the employee's actions have had, or are liable to have, a serious or harmful impact on the organisation.
>
> - A first or final written warning should set out the nature of the misconduct or poor performance and the change in behaviour or improvement in performance required (with timescale). The employee should be told how long the warning will remain current. The employee should be informed of the consequences of further misconduct, or failure to improve performance, within the set period following a final warning. For instance that it may result in dismissal or some other contractual penalty such as demotion or loss of seniority.
>
> - A decision to dismiss should only be taken by a manager who has the authority to do so. The employee should be informed as soon as possible of the reasons for the dismissal, the date on which the employment contract will end, the appropriate period of notice and their right of appeal.
>
> - Some acts, termed gross misconduct, are so serious in themselves or have such serious consequences that they may call for dismissal without notice for a first offence. But a fair disciplinary process should always be followed, before dismissing for gross misconduct.
>
> - Disciplinary rules should give examples of acts which the employer regards as acts of gross misconduct. These may vary according to the nature of the organisation and what it does, but might include things

such as theft or fraud, physical violence, gross negligence or serious insubordination.

- Where an employee is persistently unable or unwilling to attend a disciplinary meeting without good cause the employer should make a decision on the evidence available.

3.3.95   The appropriate sanction will depend upon all the relevant circumstances, including these issues:

Circumstances relevant to the choice of sanction

- *The nature of the act of misconduct.* An act that is categorised as gross misconduct under the employer's disciplinary rules may justify dismissal.

- *The rules of the organisation.* These may indicate what the likely penalty will be as a result of the particular misconduct.

- *The circumstances in which the misconduct was committed.* It may be reasonable, for example, to take into account that the act of misconduct was provoked by another employee or by the employee's working conditions.

- *The disciplinary sanction that the company has imposed for similar conduct by other employees.* Although no two cases are the same, it would not be reasonable for a company to impose a more severe sanction on one employee than on another for a similar offence, unless there was some significant difference between the two employees' cases. If several managers within a company have the power to deal with disciplinary issues, it is worth setting up some system for monitoring the handling of disciplinary matters, to ensure that there is a consistent approach across the company.

- *The employee's previous disciplinary record.* If the employee has already received a disciplinary warning for misconduct, the company is entitled to take that into account, provided the warning is still 'live'. (A warning should normally be disregarded, in the sense that they should not be taken into account in 'totting up' whether an employee has sufficient warnings to justify dismissal, after a period of satisfactory conduct, as mentioned in 3.3.96.) It is legitimate to take into account a previous warning even if it was for a different type of misconduct. If the employee has appealed against the previous warning and the appeal has yet to be decided, that should be borne in mind. It may be advisable to wait until the appeal has been dealt with before deciding on the sanction for the current offence, regardless of the employee's disciplinary record.

- *The employee's general employment history.* In deciding on the appropriate sanction, it would be reasonable for the company to take into account the position that the employee holds, the length of time the employee has been with the company and any relevant personal circumstances that may have contributed to the misconduct. A company should think carefully before dismissing an employee with long service and a previously unblemished record.

Possible sanctions

3.3.96 ACAS gives this guidance on choosing and applying disciplinary sanctions:

- *First formal action – unsatisfactory performance* The first step where poor performance is established is usually for the employee to be given an 'improvement note'. This should set out the performance problem, the improvement that is required, the timescale for achieving this improvement, a review date and any support, including any training that the employer will provide to assist the employee. It should be made clear that the note represents the first stage of a formal procedure and that failure to improve could lead to a final written warning and, ultimately, dismissal. A copy of the note should be kept, ACAS suggests for six months.

- *First formal action – misconduct* The usual first step is to give a written warning setting out the nature of the misconduct and the change in behaviour required. The warning should also inform the employee that a final written warning may be considered if there is further misconduct. A record of the warning should be kept, but it should be disregarded for disciplinary purposes after a specified period – ACAS suggests six months. If an employee's unsatisfactory performance or 'first offence' misconduct is sufficiently serious, it may be justifiable to move directly to a final written warning.

- *Final written warning* If the employee has a current warning about conduct or performance, then further misconduct or unsatisfactory performance (whichever is relevant) may warrant a final written warning. Such a warning should normally remain current for a specified period, for example, 12 months, and contain a statement that further misconduct or unsatisfactory performance may lead to dismissal.

- *Dismissal* If the employee has received a final written warning, further misconduct or unsatisfactory performance may warrant dismissal. In cases of gross misconduct, an employer may decide to dismiss even though the worker has not received any previous warning for misconduct. A decision to dismiss should be taken only by a manager who has authority to do so. The employee should be informed as soon as possible of the reasons for the dismissal, the date on which the employment contract will terminate, the appropriate period of notice and his or her right of appeal.

- Another penalty such as *disciplinary transfer, disciplinary suspension without pay, demotion,* or *loss of seniority* might be appropriate, but will be lawful only if the employee's contract allows for it.

3.3.97 Whichever sanction is chosen, the employer should notify the employee of it as soon as possible after the disciplinary hearing, and then confirm the decision in writing and notify the employee of his or her right to appeal including procedure and time limits. Model letters confirming written warnings are available for download from EEF's website.

Group discipline

3.3.98 After completing a reasonable investigation, a company may have reasonable grounds for believing that any one of a particular group of employees may have committed the act of misconduct. However, it may be unable to identify the particular individual who did so. In these circumstances, it may be reasonable for the company to discipline or dismiss all of the employees.

3.3.99   If a company is considering this course of action, it should contact us for advice.

Dealing with appeals

3.3.100   The opportunity to appeal against any disciplinary decision is essential to natural justice and is required by the ACAS Code of Practice. A failure to allow an employee a right to appeal against a decision to dismiss is likely to make the dismissal unfair. Further, if the employee does not pursue an appeal or if the employee tries to appeal but the employer does not allow him or her to do so, an employment tribunal has power to reduce or increase any compensation it awards by up to 25 per cent to reflect who was at fault in not complying with the Code.

3.3.101   The ACAS Code of Practice states:

> ### Provide employees with an opportunity to appeal
>
> - Where an employee feels that disciplinary action taken against them is wrong or unjust they should appeal against the decision. Appeals should be heard without unreasonable delay and ideally at an agreed time and place. Employees should let employers know the grounds for their appeal in writing.
>
> - The appeal should be dealt with impartially and wherever possible, by a manager who has not previously been involved in the case.
>
> - Workers have a statutory right to be accompanied at appeal hearings.
>
> - Employees should be informed in writing of the results of the appeal hearing as soon as possible.

Effect on contract

3.3.102   In dealing with an appeal against a decision to dismiss, the disciplinary procedure should make clear what effect the lodging of the appeal has on the employee's contract. This is important because the date the contract ends may affect whether the employee has completed the one year's service he or she needs to qualify for protection from unfair dismissal. Also, the three-month time limit for bringing an unfair dismissal claim runs from the date that the contract ends.

3.3.103 For example, a disciplinary procedure could state that if an employee successfully appeals against dismissal, he or she will be regarded as having continued in employment pending the hearing of the appeal and will be reinstated with full back pay. However, if the appeal is unsuccessful the employee's original date of dismissal will stand. Alternatively, the procedure could state that an employee who appeals against dismissal remains an employee but is suspended on full pay pending the hearing of the appeal. If the appeal is successful, the suspension is lifted; if the company decides to dismiss the appeal, the employee's contract will come to an end at the date of that decision.

Written information

3.3.104 Under the Employment Rights Act 1996, employees must be notified in writing, within two months of starting work, of the person to whom they can apply if they are dissatisfied with any disciplinary decision that relates to them, but this does not apply to any disciplinary decision that relates to health and safety at work. If there are any further steps to take after making that first application, they must also be explained, either in the written information given to the employees or in a document that is reasonably accessible to them.

EEF procedural agreements

3.3.105 The EEF national procedural agreements for the avoidance of disputes provide that employees who are dismissed can contest their dismissal, if necessary through an external conference. The intention of the agreements is that internal procedures should be completed before resort to an external conference. Where an employee seeks an external conference, the company should contact its local office, which will ensure that the conference is arranged without delay. If an employee who uses one of these procedures has been dismissed with notice, he or she remains an employee until agreement is reached or the procedure is exhausted, or until his or her notice expires, if that is later. An employee who has been summarily dismissed for gross misconduct, on the other hand, does not remain an employee while pursuing his or her rights under the procedure.

3.3.106 Those companies that observe these national procedural agreements may wish to consider whether they should be the only procedure for appealing against dismissal, or whether a separate avenue of appeal should also be provided.

Conducting the appeal

3.3.107 Disciplinary decisions may be appealed on a number of grounds. The employee may want to challenge the manager's conclusion that the employee committed the act of misconduct or may query the severity of the penalty. New evidence may have come to light since the decision was taken, or the employee may wish to argue that the disciplinary procedure was not followed. If an appeal is raised outside the time limit, the employer should consider whether the delay is unreasonable before rejecting the appeal.

3.3.108 ACAS guidance advises that a time limit should be set for lodging an appeal and suggests that five working days is usually long enough. The employee should put any appeal in writing. On being notified of an appeal, the employer should invite the employee to attend a meeting at which it will be considered. Appeals should be dealt with speedily, particularly those involving dismissal or suspension.

3.3.109 Wherever possible, the person hearing the appeal should be a more senior manager who has not previously been involved in the disciplinary procedure. In small companies this may be impractical, in which case the person dealing with the appeal should act as impartially as possible.

The employee has the right to be accompanied at the appeal hearing by a work colleague or union official of his or her choice (see 3.3.80).

3.3.110 ACAS guidance says that an appeal must never be used as an opportunity to punish the employee for appealing the original decision and good practice is that it should not result in any increase in penalty as this may deter individuals from appealing.

New evidence

3.3.111 If new evidence has come to light since the disciplinary hearing, it may be necessary to investigate further before the appeal hearing is held, and the employee should be given the opportunity to comment on the new evidence.

Appeal hearing

3.3.112 ACAS guidance says that before the appeal hearing takes place the employer should ensure that the individual knows when and where it is to be held, and of their statutory right to be accompanied. Further, the venue for the appeal meeting should be in a place which will be free from interruptions and that all records and notes of the original meeting are available for all concerned. The manager conducting the appeal hearing should begin by introducing the employee to those present and explain why they are there; the purpose of the hearing should also be stated. The employee should then be asked to say why he or she is appealing against the decision. If there is any question as to whether the original hearing was carried out properly, it is usually advisable to deal with an appeal by completely rehearing the evidence against the employee and the employee's case. The appeal hearing can then often put the earlier mistakes right. Once the relevant issues have been thoroughly explored, the manager conducting the appeal should summarise the facts and adjourn the matter to consider the decision.

3.3.113 After the hearing is over, the manager should take time to consider the proper outcome. The employee should be informed of the results of the appeal and the reasons for the decision as soon as possible, and this should be confirmed in writing. Where appropriate, the employee should also be told that this is the final stage of the disciplinary procedure.

Accommodating special circumstances

3.3.114 Special provision may need to be made in the disciplinary procedure to handle disciplinary matters amongst workers whose working hours or location causes logistical problems, such as nightshift workers and workers in isolated locations or depots. Companies may wish to contact us for advice on this.

3.3.115 Care needs to be taken to ensure that disciplinary action itself or the operation of the procedure does not amount to unlawful discrimination. This may mean that the procedure is modified to accommodate particular workers. For example, if the worker has a disability, then the normal arrangements for a disciplinary hearing may need to be adjusted. A failure to consider reasonable adjustments to the disciplinary procedure could amount to unlawful discrimination under the Disability Discrimination Act 1995 (see 3.1.69). In other cases, it may be necessary to arrange for translation facilities if the worker who is being disciplined does not have English as his or her first language. If the worker has difficulty reading, the employer may need to explain the procedure, and any letters it sends, orally.

Keeping records

3.3.116   It is advisable to keep a written record of disciplinary proceedings, not least to ensure that full and accurate evidence can be given of the way in which the proceedings were handled if a dismissal is later challenged as unfair or discriminatory.

3.3.117   The records should include:

- the complaint against the employee;
- the employee's defence;
- findings made and action taken;
- the reasons for the action taken;
- whether an appeal was lodged;
- the outcome of the appeal;
- any grievances raised during the disciplinary procedure;
- any subsequent developments; and
- notes of any formal meetings.

Data protection compliance

3.3.118 These records are personal data and so must be kept in a way that complies with the requirements of the Data Protection Act 1998. That means that they:

- must be accurate;
- should be no more extensive than is necessary;
- must be kept confidential;
- should be retained no longer than is necessary; and
- the employee has the right to have access to them, except to the extent that they reveal information about another person who does not consent to disclosure.

Dealing with grievances

3.3.119 There are practical and legal reasons why a company would wish to deal quickly and fairly with any individual grievances that its employees may have in relation to their employment. (Collective grievances affecting groups of workers are dealt with in 6.2.45.)

3.3.120 From a practical viewpoint, a contented workforce is more likely to be a productive workforce. If grievances are not dealt with, they may not only affect individuals' work performance, but also escalate into a larger problem or even a collective dispute. Further, all employees are legally entitled, under an implied term in their contract of employment, to have their grievances dealt with promptly. If a company refuses to address a serious grievance that an employee wishes to raise, it may find itself defending an unfair constructive dismissal claim. In particular, a failure to deal with a complaint that an employee is being harassed or otherwise discriminated against on one of the grounds covered by the discrimination legislation may lead to a claim of unlawful discrimination.

3.3.121 The ACAS Code of Practice on discipline and grievance sets out good practice when dealing with grievances. Employment tribunals should take into account the provisions of this Code when considering cases involving grievances.

Tribunals are able to adjust awards to individuals by up to 25 per cent for unreasonable failure to comply with any relevant provision of this Code.

The ACAS Code of Practice on disciplinary and grievance procedures

3.3.122 The Code says that grievances are concerns, problems or complaints that employees raise with their employers. It says that employees should seek to settle most grievances informally. However, where informality does not work, then the Code says that there should be a formal grievance procedure.

3.3.123 When developing rules and procedures to deal with grievances, the Code says 'Fairness and transparency are promoted by developing rules and procedures for handling…grievance situations. These should be set down in writing, be specific and clear. Employees and, where appropriate, their representatives should be involved in the development of rules and procedures. It is also important to help employees and managers understand what the rules and procedures are, where they can be found and how they are to be used.' Further, ACAS guidance suggests that management and employee representatives who may be involved in grievance matters should be trained for the task perhaps jointly.

3.3.124 In some grievance cases, the early use of an internal or external mediator can help to sort out a grievance and maintain working relationships.

Dealing fairly with formal grievances

3.3.125 When a formal process is being followed, the Code says that it is important to deal with issues fairly and that there are a number of elements which are:

- Employers and employees should raise and deal with issues promptly and should not unreasonably delay meetings, decisions or confirmation of those decisions.
- Employers and employees should act consistently.
- Employers should carry out any necessary investigations, to establish the facts of the case.
- Employers should inform employees of the basis of the problem and

> give them an opportunity to put their case in response before any decisions are made.
>
> - Employers should allow employees to be accompanied at any formal grievance meeting.
>
> - Employers should allow an employee to appeal against any formal decision made.

Key elements to handling grievances in the workplace

3.3.126   The Code of Practice states:

> ### Let the employer know the nature of the grievance
>
> - If it is not possible to resolve a grievance informally employees should raise the matter formally and without unreasonable delay with a manager who is not the subject of the grievance. This should be done in writing and should set out the nature of the grievance.
>
> ### Hold a meeting with the employee to discuss the grievance
>
> - Employers should arrange for a formal meeting to be held without unreasonable delay after a grievance is received.
>
> - Employers, employees and their companions should make every effort to attend the meeting. Employees should be allowed to explain their grievance and how they think it should be resolved. Consideration should be given to adjourning the meeting for any investigation that may be necessary.
>
> ### Allow the employee to be accompanied at the meeting
>
> - Workers have a statutory right to be accompanied by a companion at a grievance meeting which deals with a complaint about a duty owed by the employer to the worker. So this would apply where the complaint is, for example, that the employer is not honouring the worker's contract, or is in breach of legislation.

- The chosen companion may be a fellow worker a trade union representative or an official employed by a trade union. A trade union representative who is not an employed official must have been certified by their union as being competent to accompany a worker.

- To exercise the right to be accompanied a worker must first make a reasonable request. What is reasonable will depend on the circumstances of each individual case. However it would not normally be reasonable for workers to insist on being accompanied by a companion whose presence would prejudice the hearing nor would it be reasonable for a worker to ask to be accompanied by a companion from a remote geographical location if someone suitable and willing was available on site.

- The companion should be allowed to address the hearing to put and sum up the worker's case, respond on behalf of the worker to any views expressed at the meeting and confer with the worker during the hearing. The companion does not however, have the right to answer questions on the workers behalf, address the hearing if the worker does not wish it or prevent the employer from explaining their case.

Decide on appropriate action

- Following the meeting decide on what action, if any, to take. Decisions should be communicated to the employee, in writing, without unreasonable delay and, where appropriate, should set out what action the employer intends to take to resolve the grievance. The employee should be informed that they can appeal if they are not content with the action taken.

Allow the employee to take the grievance further if not resolved

- Where an employee feels that their grievance has not been satisfactorily resolved they should appeal. They should let their employer know the grounds for their appeal without unreasonable delay and in writing.

- Appeals should be heard without unreasonable delay and at a time and place which should be notified to the employee in advance.

- The appeal should be dealt with impartially and wherever possible by a manager who has not previously been involved in the case.

- Workers have a statutory right to be accompanied at any such appeal hearing.

- The outcome of the appeal should be communicated to the employee in writing without unreasonable delay.

Overlapping grievance and disciplinary cases

- Where an employee raises a grievance during a disciplinary process the disciplinary process may be temporarily suspended in order to deal with the grievance. Where the grievance and disciplinary cases are related it may be appropriate to deal with both issues concurrently.

Grievance hearings

3.3.127   For the purpose of the legal right to be accompanied, a grievance meeting is a meeting where an employer deals with a complaint about any duty owed by them to a worker. This is very broad. ACAS guidance advises that grievance meetings should be arranged ideally within five working days. In addition to complying with the requirements about grievances in the Code, it is sensible to ensure that grievance hearings are held in private without interruptions, that there is a second member of management present to act as a witness and to take notes and that the grievance is dealt with confidentially. Prior to the grievance meeting, the written statement of grievance should be considered carefully and the issue of whether similar grievances have been raised before and what happened to them should be investigated.

3.3.128   At the grievance hearing, the manager should not rush the meeting and should seek through discussions to produce an answer to the grievance. At the start of the meeting, the manager should make introductions as necessary and then invite the employee to restate their grievance and how he or she would like to see it resolved. Then the manager on behalf of the employer may wish to respond and after discussions may wish to sum up. In most cases it is good practice to adjourn the hearing before a decision is taken to decide how to deal with the employee's grievance. This allows time for reflection, proper consideration and checking any matters raised. However, at the ending of the meeting the employee should be told when he or she may reasonably expect a response from the employer if one cannot be made at the time bearing in mind any time limits set out in the employer's grievance procedure.

3.3.129 The manager should thereafter set out in writing the decision of the employer about the grievance and explain to the employee his or her right of appeal if the employee feels that their grievance has not been satisfactorily resolved. ACAS guidance suggests that the written decision should set out clearly any action to be taken and if the employee's grievance is not upheld make sure the reasons are carefully explained. The right of appeal and any time limit for appeals should also be explained.

Collective grievances

3.3.130 In some cases, a collective grievance may arise where a number of employees have the same grievance at the same time. In these circumstances it may be best to deal with the issue collectively rather than as a multitude of individual grievances. An employer's grievance procedure can explain how collective grievances will be handled by a recognised union official or employee representative. The ACAS Code does not apply to grievances raised on behalf of two or more employees by a representative of a recognised trade union or other appropriate workplace representative. The Code states that these grievances should be handled in accordance with the organisation's collective grievance process.

Adopting and publicising a grievance procedure

3.3.131 In the light of the Code of Practice requirement for a grievance procedure, it is advisable for a company to adopt a formal procedure for dealing with grievances. A model procedure is available for download from EEF's website.

Under the Employment Rights Act 1996, employers must inform all employees in writing, within two months of starting work, of the person to whom they can apply if they have a grievance, and how the application should be made. If there are any further steps after making the application, such as an appeals procedure, employers must also inform employees of those steps, or refer them to a reasonably accessible document where they can be found. There is no obligation under the Employment Rights Act to give employees details of how to raise a grievance in relation to health and safety. It would nevertheless be advisable for a company to include these details, in order to meet its duties under health and safety law to provide a safe system of working.

3.3.132 A grievance procedure can form part of an employee's contractual terms. It might, for example, be set out in the employee's written contract or might be incorporated into the contract through a reference to the document where it can be found. It is, however, inadvisable for a grievance procedure to be contractual, for two main reasons. If the procedure is contractual, the company cannot amend it without the employee's consent, unless the procedure itself makes clear that the company may amend it from time to time at its discretion. Secondly, if a company failed to follow a contractual grievance procedure, the employee could resign and claim unfair constructive dismissal (see 4.1.35), on the basis that the company had acted in serious breach of the employee's contract. As noted above, however, it is an implied term in every contract of employment that an employer will provide an employee with some means of raising a grievance, even if it has no express contractual procedure.

Special considerations

3.3.133 Special steps may need to be taken to ensure that employees whose first language is not English are able to raise a grievance effectively, possibly by providing translation facilities. Some employees may have difficulties putting their grievance in writing and they should be encouraged to seek help from a work colleague, union representative or other employee representative. It may also be necessary to modify a grievance procedure to ensure that disabled employees have effective access to it. Employers who fail to consider making reasonable adjustments for disabled employees may be acting unlawfully under the Disability Discrimination Act 1995 (see 3.1.69).

3.3.134 For example, it may be reasonable to allow an employee with a learning disability to be accompanied by a friend from outside the company at a grievance hearing, even if this would not normally be allowed under the procedure. Or it may be reasonable to provide an employee with a sight impairment with information on the grievance procedure in an alternative format, such as large print or Braille. ACAS guidance advises that employers should also cater for any disability that an employee's companion at the grievance hearing may have.

Harassment procedures

3.3.135 The ACAS Code says employers may wish to consider having a separate procedure for dealing with grievances relating to bullying or harassment, as these subjects raise particularly sensitive issues. A policy and procedure on bullying and harassment is available for download from EEF's website.

Special protection

3.3.136 As explained below, employment law gives special protection to workers who 'blow the whistle' on certain forms of wrongdoing (see 3.3.142) or who raise concerns about, or take action to deal with, health and safety hazards (see 3.3.155). Companies may wish to bear these special protections in mind when drafting or operating grievance procedures, or deal with whistleblowing separately as suggested by the ACAS Code of Practice.

The right to be accompanied

3.3.137 A worker has the right to be accompanied at a grievance hearing if he or she reasonably requests to be. Details of this right are given above (see 3.3.80).

3.3.138 For the purpose of this legal right, a grievance hearing is a meeting at which an employer deals with a complaint about a duty owed by it to a worker whether the duty arises from statute or common law. However, ACAS guidance says that it is generally good practice to allow workers to be accompanied at a formal grievance hearing even when the statutory right does not apply.

3.3.139 The companion may be a fellow worker, a union official employed by a trade union or a lay union official certified in writing by their union as a worker's companion at grievance hearings. A company, is, of course, free to operate a more generous right to be accompanied than that laid down in the statutory rules. It may, for example, allow a worker to be accompanied by their partner at formal grievance hearings.

3.3.140 Where possible, the employer should allow a companion to have a say in the date and time of the hearing. If the companion cannot attend on a proposed date, the worker can suggest an alternative time and date so long as it is reasonable and it is not more that five working days after the original date. At the formal grievance hearing or appeal hearing, the companion should be allowed to put the worker's case, sum up the worker's case and respond on the worker's behalf to any views expressed at the hearing. ACAS guidance says that it is good practice to allow the companion to participate as fully as possible in the hearing, including asking witnesses questions. However, the employer is not legally required to permit the companion to answer questions on behalf of the worker, or to address the hearing if the worker does not wish it, or prevent the employer explaining their case.

Keeping records

3.3.141 A written record should be kept of the nature of the grievance raised, the company's response, any action taken and the reasons for it, whether there was an appeal and the outcome, and any subsequent developments. Since these records are personal data, they must be kept in a way that complies with the requirements of the Data Protection Act 1998. In particular:

- they must be accurate;
- they should be no more extensive than is necessary;
- they must be kept confidential;
- they should be retained no longer than is necessary; and
- the employee has the right to have access to them (except to the extent that they reveal personal information about another person who does not consent to disclosure).

Protection for 'whistleblowers'

3.3.142 Employees who 'blow the whistle' on wrongdoing have special legal protection. This protection applies, however, only where the information they disclose relates to certain specified issues and they raise their concerns in a specified way.

3.3.143 The protection was introduced by the Public Interest Disclosure Act 1998 and is incorporated into the Employment Rights Act 1996. These provisions make it automatically unfair to dismiss an employee or select an employee for redundancy for whistleblowing, regardless of the employee's age or length of service. If an employee alleges that he or she has been dismissed for this reason, an employment tribunal may order the employer to re-employ the individual pending the hearing of his or her claim.

3.3.144 It is also unlawful to penalise a worker in any way because he or she has raised these concerns. This protection applies not only to employees and apprentices, but also to anyone else who has a contract to carry out work for the company personally, other than a genuinely self-employed worker who runs a profession or business on his or her own account. It also extends to agency workers, homeworkers, trainees and those on work experience, other than those undertaking training or work experience as part of a course run by an educational establishment. The whistleblowing legislation can also be used by individuals who are subjected to a detriment by their employer following termination of their employment.

Protected information

3.3.145 In order to qualify for protection, the worker must have reasonably believed that the information he or she disclosed indicated one of the following:

- A criminal offence has been committed.
- Someone has failed to meet a legal obligation (which could include the employer failing to meet its obligations under the worker's own contract).
- A miscarriage of justice has occurred.
- Someone's health or safety has been endangered.
- The environment has been damaged.
- Evidence of one of these things has been deliberately concealed.

The protection also applies if the worker reasonably believed that the information he or she disclosed indicated that one of these things was currently happening or would happen in the future.

Protected methods of disclosure

3.3.146 The worker is protected if he or she disclosed the information in good faith to one of the following people or bodies:

- the company, or to some other person the company had authorised to receive the information; or
- if the information related to the conduct or legal duties of some other person, that other person; or

- certain other bodies that have been prescribed as appropriate recipients of certain information. For example, the worker is protected if he or she disclosed information about income tax to HM Revenue and Customs or information about health and safety matters to the Health and Safety Executive.

The worker is also protected if the disclosure was made in the course of obtaining legal advice.

Disclosure to a wider audience

3.3.147 In certain special circumstances, the worker is protected if he or she disclosed information about the wrongdoing to someone other than those listed above. Disclosure of information to a wider audience is protected only if the worker disclosed it in good faith and not for personal gain, the worker believed the information was true, and it was reasonable for the worker to make the disclosure in all the circumstances. In addition, one of these conditions must apply:

- The worker reasonably believed he or she would be penalised in some way by the company if he or she gave the information to the company or to one of the prescribed bodies.

- There was no relevant prescribed body and the worker thought the company would conceal or destroy relevant evidence if he or she raised the issue with the company.

- The worker had already given the company or the prescribed body the information.

- The information raised issues of an exceptionally serious nature.

3.3.148 Whether it was reasonable for the employee to make the disclosure in these special circumstances depends upon the identity of the person to whom the disclosure was made, the seriousness of the wrongdoing, and whether the wrongdoing was continuing or likely to occur in the future. If the worker decided to disclose the information to a third party because he or she had already given the information to the company or a prescribed body, the reasonableness of that disclosure will depend on what action, if any, was taken by the company or the prescribed body when the information was provided to them. It is also dependent on whether the worker complied with any procedure the company had for reporting wrongdoing.

Raising concerns internally

3.3.149   This makes it important for companies to ensure that they encourage workers to raise concerns internally and inform them how to do so, assure workers that they will not be penalised for raising their concerns, and deal promptly and effectively with any concerns that are raised. If these steps are taken, the worker is unlikely to be protected if, for example, he or she discloses information about wrongdoing to the local newspaper or the local MP before raising the matter through the company's own procedure. A public interest disclosure procedure is available for download from EEF's website.

Acting in good faith

3.3.150   In most cases, whistleblowers have legal protection from victimisation only if they made their disclosure in good faith. This involves more than reasonably believing the information they disclosed was true: if their dominant motive when making the disclosure was a personal grudge against their manager, rather than a concern to address or prevent wrongdoing, they will not be protected.

Asserting legal rights

3.3.151   Employees have special protection under the Employment Rights Act 1996 from being dismissed for asserting their individual rights under employment legislation, such as, for example, their right to written information about their main terms or conditions of employment or their right to time off for union activities. The law makes it automatically unfair for a company to dismiss an employee, or select an employee for redundancy, because the employee has alleged that the company has not respected his or her rights. This is also the case if the employee has made a claim to an employment tribunal to enforce his or her rights. This protection applies regardless of the employee's age or length of service.

Good faith

3.3.152   It is unfair to dismiss for this reason even if the employee did not actually have the right he or she was claiming, and even if the company had not in fact breached the employee's rights, as long as the employee was acting in good faith. It may therefore be fair to dismiss an employee for falsely alleging that the company has not respected his or her rights, if the employee knew when he or she made those allegations that they were false. Whether the dismissal of an employee in these circumstances is fair or unfair will depend on whether the company acts reasonably in reaching the decision to dismiss, including whether it follows a proper disciplinary process.

3.3.153 In order to be protected from dismissal, the employee does not have to specify exactly what right he or she is asserting. It is enough if he or she has made it reasonably clear to the employer what the right is. For example, the employee does not have to say, 'I allege that the company has made an unauthorised deduction from my pay, contrary to Part II of the Employment Rights Act 1996.' He or she can say, 'I don't think you have paid me all the overtime you owe me.'

Other protection

3.3.154 Readers may wish to note that the discrimination legislation makes it unlawful for an employer to penalise an employee in any way for making or supporting a claim that the company has discriminated unlawfully (see 3.1.84). In addition, there are specific legal provisions making it unlawful for an employer to penalise an employee for asserting various rights, including, for example, the right to family leave (see 2.2.72, 2.2.100, 2.2.123, 2.2.148, 2.2.168), rest periods and paid holidays (see 2.3.25), and national minimum wage rates.

Responding to health and safety concerns

3.3.155 The Employment Rights Act 1996 makes it unlawful for a company to penalise an employee in any way for raising certain health and safety concerns or taking action in response to serious health and safety hazards. It is also automatically unfair to dismiss an employee or select an employee for redundancy for these reasons, regardless of the employee's age or length of service.

3.3.156 The activities that are protected are listed below. The protection applies whether the employee has already done one of these things or proposes to do so.

Protected health and safety activities

- Bringing to the company's attention, by reasonable means, circumstances that the employee reasonably believes are harmful or potentially harmful to health and safety. If there is a health and safety representative or committee at the workplace, the employee is usually protected only if he or she raises concerns by those means. If it is not reasonably practicable to raise the issue through those channels, however, or the employee reasonably believes that there is a serious and imminent threat to safety, then the employee is protected if he or she raises the issue with the employer direct, or by some other appropriate means, such as through a union representative.

- Carrying out health and safety duties allocated by the company.

- Carrying out duties as a health and safety representative or a member of a safety committee.

- Taking part in consultations over health and safety or the election of employee safety representatives.

- Leaving, or refusing to return to, the place of work because of a threat to health and safety that the employee reasonably believes to be serious and imminent, and which the employee cannot reasonably be expected to avert. This could include safety threats caused by the behaviour of fellow employees.

- Taking appropriate steps to protect the employee or other people from a threat to health and safety that the employee reasonably believes to be serious and imminent. This includes action to protect members of the public or other employees. Whether the steps the employee takes are appropriate depends in particular on the employee's knowledge and the facilities and advice that are available. It is lawful for a company to penalise or dismiss an employee if he or she has acted so negligently that any reasonable employer would have responded in that way.

section 4

Terminating employment

4.1

Terminating employment

Overview

4.1.1 This chapter of the Guide deals with the principles of law and good practice that apply when an employee leaves a company.

4.1.2 An employment relationship can end in several ways, but most commonly it ends through resignation or dismissal. This chapter outlines the mechanics of dismissal (see 4.1.6) and then goes on to examine a number of particular legal issues that arise when an employee is dismissed, such as notice rights.

4.1.3 There are also legal principles that apply to resignation, and this chapter summarises these (see 4.1.43) before moving on to examine how an employment contract can end by mutual agreement (see 4.1.53) or by the application of a legal principle known as frustration (see 4.1.58). Special considerations apply to the termination or non-renewal of fixed-term contracts (see 4.1.61) and the termination of apprenticeships (see 4.1.66), and this chapter outlines these.

4.1.4 There are other legal issues that a company may need to consider when an employee leaves. This chapter explains the rules on providing an employee with written reasons for dismissal (see 4.1.70) and references (see 4.1.72). It also sets out the legal considerations if the company wishes to restrict an employee's activities after he or she has left the company (see 4.1.79) or reach a financial settlement of any claims the employee may have against the company (see 4.1.90). An outline is given of pension rights (see 4.1.96), the tax treatment of termination payments (see 4.1.93), and social security considerations (see 4.1.95). Finally, the chapter gives some practical advice on exit interviews (see 4.1.97), labour turnover (see 4.1.102) and succession planning (see 4.1.108).

Unlawful dismissal

4.1.5   In order to put the information on dismissal in this chapter into context, it should be borne in mind that there are three main ways in which a dismissal can be challenged as unlawful:

1. A dismissal that is implemented in a way that breaches an employee's contract of employment can be challenged as a wrongful dismissal. This chapter explains the legal principles that apply here (see 4.1.21).

2. If an employer does not act reasonably in deciding to dismiss, or if the dismissal was based on certain prohibited grounds such as pregnancy or trade union membership, the employee can bring a claim of unfair dismissal. This is dealt with in Chapter 4.2 of this Guide.

3. If an employee is dismissed on grounds of sex, race, disability, age, religion or sexual orientation, then the dismissal could amount to an act of unlawful discrimination. Discrimination law is covered in Chapter 3.1 of this Guide.

Dismissal

4.1.6   A company can terminate an employee's contract by dismissing him or her. If the company terminates the contract with immediate effect, this is known as a summary dismissal. (A summary dismissal may well be in breach of the employee's contract, as discussed further below.) Alternatively, the company may give the employee notice that his or her contract is to be terminated.

4.1.7   For a notice of dismissal to be effective, it must be possible to identify the date the contract will end. The notice could specify, for example, that the contract will terminate in six months' time or on a specified date. If, on the other hand, a company informs an employee that he or she will be dismissed 'shortly' or 'by the end of the year', that amounts to a warning to the employee that he or she is soon to be dismissed, rather than a notice of dismissal. Therefore an employee who left the company in response to a warning of this nature would have resigned rather than have been dismissed.

Identifying a dismissal

4.1.8   If a company uses clear words of dismissal, the employee is entitled to view himself or herself as having been dismissed. Furthermore, once a company has given an employee notice of dismissal, it cannot usually withdraw that notice unless the employee agrees. If the words that the company uses are ambiguous, such as when a manager tells an employee to 'get out' during a heated exchange, the test is whether a reasonable employee would have understood the words used as amounting to dismissal, in the light of all the surrounding circumstances.

4.1.9   If an employer notifies an employee that he or she has been summarily dismissed in a letter, the dismissal takes effect on the date the employee reads the letter, or has had a reasonable opportunity of reading it.

4.1.10   Where a company uses disciplinary or other procedures that allow for an employee to appeal against a decision to dismiss, it should ensure that the procedures make clear what effect the lodging of an appeal has on the termination of the employee's contract. The procedures could state, for example, that the lodging of an appeal postpones the date of the dismissal until the appeal is decided. More probably, the employer will wish to confirm that the lodging of an appeal does not prevent the dismissal taking effect on the date originally notified.

4.1.11   Employers who observe the EEF national procedural agreements should note that an employee who is dismissed is entitled to call for an external conference. In cases other than summary dismissal for gross misconduct, the employee is entitled to remain in employment until agreement is reached or the procedure is exhausted, or until his or her notice expires, if that is later.

Notice rights

4.1.12   A company is usually obliged to give an employee notice of the termination of his or her contract. The exception to this is where the employee is in serious breach of his or her obligations under the contract, such as where the employee has committed an act of gross misconduct. In these circumstances, the company is legally entitled to dismiss the employee without notice. It is always advisable, however, to conduct a proper investigation before deciding to summarily dismiss an employee for misconduct, in order to confirm that he or she really is in serious breach of contract, and to avoid liability for unfair dismissal. (The management of discipline is covered in Chapter 3.3 of this Guide.)

Gross misconduct

4.1.13 It is advisable for a company to set out in its disciplinary rules the acts of misconduct that will be treated as gross misconduct justifying summary dismissal. However, disciplinary rules cannot hope to cover all eventualities, and serious acts of misconduct may well justify summary dismissal even if not specified as gross misconduct in the rules. A company should, therefore, state in its rules that they are intended to illustrate the acts that will be viewed as gross misconduct rather than amount to an exhaustive list.

Length of notice period

4.1.14 The length of notice that a company must give to terminate an employee's contract is likely to be set out in the contract itself. Under the Employment Rights Act 1996, a company must notify employees, within two months of starting work, of the length of notice that the company must give to terminate their employment. If an employee is covered by the minimum period of notice laid down in the Act (set out below), then the company can, if it wishes, refer the employee to the Act for details of his or her notice period. Alternatively, if the employee's notice period is contained in a collective agreement, the company can refer the employee to that agreement, provided it is reasonably accessible to the employee.

4.1.15 In the unlikely event that there is no express term on notice in the employee's contract, a term will be implied that the company must give a reasonable period of notice. What period is reasonable will depend on all the circumstances, including in particular the nature of the employee's job and his or her length of service. It might be reasonable, for example, for the company to give a senior executive with long service six months' or a year's notice of dismissal, but an unskilled manual employee with a few weeks' service only a week's notice.

Minimum notice periods

4.1.16 The Employment Rights Act 1996 sets down minimum periods of notice. After one month's continuous employment an employee is entitled to one week's notice. After completing two years' continuous employment, an employee is entitled to one week's notice for each complete year of continuous employment, up to a maximum of 12 weeks. These minimum notice periods effectively override any shorter notice period in an employee's contract, but do not affect any longer contractual notice period to which an employee may be entitled.

4.1.17 The statutory minimum notice periods do not affect a company's right to summarily dismiss an employee who is in serious breach of contract, nor do they prevent an employee giving up his or her right to notice or accepting a payment in lieu of notice (see 4.1.27).

Wages during notice

4.1.18 For employees who are entitled to at least one week more than the statutory minimum notice of dismissal (see 4.1.16), their rights during their notice period depend solely on the terms of their contract. For example, if such an employee is on long-term unpaid sick leave when he or she receives notice of dismissal, he or she will not be entitled to be paid during the notice period.

4.1.19 Employees who are entitled to a shorter period of notice, on the other hand, must be paid during their statutory minimum period of notice in certain circumstances, regardless of whether they are entitled to be paid under their contract. They must be paid if:

- they are ready and willing to work but no work is provided by the employer; or
- they are unable to work because of sickness or injury; or
- they are away from work wholly or partly because of pregnancy or childbirth or on parental leave; or
- they are on holiday.

4.1.20   Any payments that the company makes to the employee during the notice period, including sick pay, maternity pay, paternity pay, adoption pay or holiday pay, go towards meeting this liability.

Wrongful dismissal

4.1.21   If a company dismisses an employee in a way that breaches the employee's contract, this is termed a wrongful dismissal.

4.1.22   The most common example of a wrongful dismissal is where an employer dismisses an employee without giving him or her the proper notice of dismissal. However, a dismissal can also be wrongful if the company has disregarded other terms of the employee's contract. For example, if the company's disciplinary procedure were part of the employee's contract, it would be wrongful for the company to dismiss the employee for misconduct without going through that procedure. (This is one reason why it is advisable to ensure that disciplinary procedures are not part of employees' contractual terms.) And if the employee is entitled to sickness benefits under his or her contract, it would be wrongful for the company to dismiss the employee for ill health before those benefits were exhausted, unless the contract made clear that the company had that right.

Damages for wrongful dismissal

4.1.23   An employee who is wrongfully dismissed can claim compensation, known as damages, from the employer. This claim can be made either in the civil courts or in an employment tribunal (but a tribunal cannot award more than £25,000 in damages) (see 7.2.11).

4.1.24   When assessing the amount of damages to award, the court or tribunal aims to put the employee in the position he or she would have been in had the employer observed the terms of the contract. For example, if the employer has dismissed the employee without proper notice, the employee will be awarded his or her loss of earnings and other benefits for the notice period that should have been given, net of tax and National Insurance contributions. The employee is under a duty to minimise his or her loss by looking for another job, and any earnings that the employee receives from other employment in what should have been the notice period will reduce the damages awarded.

4.1.25   If a company wrongfully dismisses an employee, the employee is released from all his or her obligations under the contract, including any terms in the contract that restrict the employee's activities after employment has ended. This is discussed in 4.1.84.

Differences from unfair dismissal

4.1.26   It is important not to confuse the concept of wrongful dismissal with the concept of unfair dismissal. A wrongful dismissal is a dismissal in breach of contract, while a dismissal is unfair if the employer has not acted reasonably in deciding to dismiss. It is possible, though not common, for a wrongful dismissal to be a fair dismissal. And a dismissal can be unfair even if it does not breach the employee's contract.

Payment in lieu of notice

4.1.27   In some circumstances, a company may prefer to dismiss an employee with immediate effect, even though this is in breach of the employee's right to notice. If the relationship between the employee and the company has broken down, for example, the company may consider that there is no benefit in the employee working out his or her notice period.

4.1.28   If the company does not give the employee notice of dismissal, it should make him or her a payment in lieu of notice (unless the employee has forfeited the right to notice by committing an act of gross misconduct). This payment represents the damages that a court or tribunal would award the employee for the company's failure to respect his or her notice rights. It should therefore reflect not only the employee's wages or salary for the notice period but also the value of any other contractual benefits to which the employee would have been entitled during that time, such as a company car, health insurance and pension contributions.

Tax and National Insurance implications

4.1.29   Since the employee would have been paid net of tax and National Insurance contributions during the notice period, the payment in lieu can also be calculated on that basis. That is, the employer can choose to pay the net amount only, retaining the notional tax and National Insurance contributions.

Nevertheless, many employers choose to base the payment on gross pay, since that is no more than the expense they would have incurred had the employee worked out the notice period. The first £30,000 of a payment in lieu is usually tax free in the hands of the employee (see 4.1.93).

4.1.30   Some employers include a clause in their employment contracts entitling them to terminate the contract either on notice or without notice but with a payment in lieu. The advantage of a term like this is that the employer can dismiss the employee without notice and still enforce any terms in the contract that restrict the employee's activities after the employment has ended (see 4.1.83). The disadvantage from the employee's perspective is that, because the payment in lieu is made under a contract term, it is taxable in full and does not qualify for the exemption that usually applies to the first £30,000 of a termination payment (see 4.1.93).

4.1.31   Advice on termination payments and their taxation is available from us.

Garden leave

4.1.32   When a company gives an employee notice of dismissal, it may tell him or her not to come into work during the notice period. This is often described as giving the employee garden leave. A company may want to put an employee on garden leave because it fears that he or she may harm the employer's operation in some way during the notice period. Or it may prefer to put the employee on garden leave, rather than summarily dismiss him or her with a payment in lieu of notice (see 4.1.27), to prevent him or her going to work for a competitor.

4.1.33   Provided the company continues to pay the employee his or her wages or salary and other benefits during the notice period, putting the employee on garden leave is usually lawful, and the employee's employment contract continues until the notice period expires. Some employees might argue, however, that they have the right not only to be paid but also to be provided with work while their employment continues. This argument would be valid only for those employees whose pay depended on them working, or whose value in the labour market would be severely prejudiced if they were not allowed to continue to maintain their network of contacts and their visibility in the marketplace. Nevertheless, a company might wish to pre-empt the argument by including an express term in its contracts of employment entitling it to put employees on garden leave during their notice period.

4.1.34 If a company were breaching an employee's contract when it put him or her on garden leave, it would be unable to enforce any terms in the employee's contract restricting his or her right to work for a competitor after leaving the company (see 4.1.84). A company that is considering putting an employee on garden leave but is concerned about the effect this might have on these restrictive covenants may wish to contact us for advice.

Constructive dismissal

4.1.35 In some circumstances, the law views an employee who has resigned as having been dismissed. This is termed a 'constructive dismissal' and it arises where an employee resigns because the company's actions have made his or her situation untenable. An employee who has been constructively dismissed is entitled to resign without giving notice, but may decide to give the company notice of resignation. The employee may claim that the dismissal was wrongful, unfair or both.

4.1.36 In order to prove that he or she has been constructively dismissed, the employee must be able to show that the company has acted in serious breach of his or her contract, in a way that goes to the root of the employment relationship or which shows that the company does not intend to be bound by one or more of the essential terms of the contract. This is sometimes referred to as a 'fundamental' or 'repudiatory' breach of contract. A company can constructively dismiss an employee not only through a one-off single act that is in serious breach of contract, but also by a course of conduct involving several minor incidents that cumulatively amount to a fundamental breach of contract.

Breach of implied terms

4.1.37 A constructive dismissal can result from the breach of an express term or an implied term of the contract. An implied term of particular importance here is the employer's duty not, without reasonable cause, to act in a way that undermines the mutual trust and confidence that is essential to the employment relationship (see 1.2.45). A breach of this term will always be a fundamental breach of contract. A company can constructively dismiss an employee by breaching trust and confidence even if it was not aiming to force the employee out. The test is whether the company's conduct, objectively considered, was likely to damage the relationship of trust and confidence between itself and the employee.

Examples of constructive dismissal

4.1.38 Whether a company's actions amount to a fundamental breach of contract depends on all the circumstances, but courts and tribunals have accepted that these types of act are capable of leading to constructive dismissal:

- reporting an employee to the police for dishonesty without having reasonable grounds for the accusation;

- failing to give an employee reasonable support against harassment;

- downgrading an employee;

- imposing a disciplinary sanction on an employee that is grossly out of proportion to the offence he or she has committed;

- instructing an employee to transfer to another workplace when the employee's contract does not contain a mobility clause;

- instructing an employee to carry out a task that is unsafe.

Cause of resignation

4.1.39 In order to establish that he or she has been constructively dismissed, an employee must be able to show that the company's breach of contract was the effective cause of his or her resignation. For example, if an employee resigns because he or she has been offered a job with another employer and would not have left the company otherwise, he or she has not been constructively dismissed, even if the company has breached the employee's contract.

4.1.40 If the employee does not resign promptly after the company's breach of contract, the employee may lose the right to claim constructive dismissal. A court or tribunal is likely to accept, however, that an employee can take a few weeks to look for alternative work before handing in his or her resignation.

Anticipatory breach

4.1.41   It is possible for an employee to be constructively dismissed before the company has actually breached the contract. If the company has indicated clearly that it intends to breach the employee's contract in the future, this amounts to what is termed an 'anticipatory' breach. If the breach is serious enough, the employee can resign and claim constructive dismissal, without needing to wait until the breach actually occurs. For example, if the company has informed the employee that it intends to impose new shift patterns at the end of the month even though it has no contractual right to do so, or to withdraw the employee's contractual overtime premium in six months' time, the employee may be entitled to resign immediately and claim constructive dismissal. If, however, an employee 'jumps the gun' by resigning on the strength of a rumour and before the employer has indicated its clear intention to breach the contract, that amounts to an ordinary resignation and not a constructive dismissal.

Imposing a new job

4.1.42   It is worth noting that if a company unilaterally imposes radically different terms and conditions of employment on an employee, that could be viewed as the termination or withdrawal of the original contract and the imposition of a new one – that is, an express dismissal rather than a constructive dismissal. In these circumstances, the employee could claim unfair dismissal in relation to the original contract while continuing to work under the new terms. The legal issues arising from the variation of employees' contractual terms are covered in Chapter 5.1 of this Guide.

Resignation

4.1.43   An employee can terminate his or her employment by giving the company notice of resignation. If a notice of resignation is to be legally effective, it must indicate the date that the employee intends the contract to end. For example, if the employee tells a manager that he or she intends to resign 'shortly' or writes to the company stating his or her intention to resign if a particular issue is not resolved to his or her satisfaction, that does not amount to notice of resignation.

Notice of resignation

4.1.44   The employee's contract may specify how the resignation should be made, such as requiring it to be given to the employee's line manager in writing. The contract is also likely to state the period of notice that the employee should give.

4.1.45   Under the Employment Rights Act 1996, a company must notify employees, within two months of starting work, of the length of notice that they must give to terminate their employment. If the employee need only give the minimum notice laid down in the Act (see 4.1.47), then the company can, if it wishes, refer the employee to the Act. Alternatively, if the employee's notice period is contained in a collective agreement, the company can refer the employee to that agreement, provided it is reasonably accessible to the employee.

4.1.46   In the unlikely event that an employee's contract does not mention notice of resignation, a term will be implied in the contract that the employee should give a reasonable amount of notice. The length of notice that is reasonable will depend in large part on the nature of the employee's job. For example, it is likely to be reasonable for a senior executive to give six months' notice or more, whereas it may be reasonable for an unskilled manual worker to give only a week's notice.

Statutory minimum period

4.1.47   The minimum period of notice that an employee can give is fixed by the Employment Rights Act 1996: once the employee has been employed for one continuous month or more, he or she must give at least one week's notice of resignation. This minimum remains the same, regardless of the length of time that the employee has worked for the company. The minimum does not, however, prevent the company waiving its right to notice, nor does it prevent the employee resigning immediately if the company has acted in serious breach of his or her contract.

4.1.48   An employee may be entitled to be paid during the statutory minimum period of his or her notice of resignation, even if he or she is not entitled to be paid under his or her contract because, for example, he or she is on a period of unpaid leave. The circumstances in which this right applies are explained above (see 4.1.18).

Is it a genuine resignation?

4.1.49   Once an employee has given notice of resignation, he or she cannot withdraw that notice unless the company agrees. However, where an employee gives in his or her notice in a fit of pique or after a workplace altercation, the company should not immediately assume that the resignation was intended. If the resignation was given under emotional stress and the company knew or ought to have known that it was not meant to be taken seriously, or if the company was anxious to be rid of the employee and seized on the employee's resignation when it was not intended, a court or employment tribunal might conclude that it was the company that really terminated the employment. In other words, the court or tribunal could conclude that the employee was dismissed.

4.1.50   Therefore, if an employee resigns in the heat of the moment, the company should allow him or her a day or so to reflect and then ask him or her to confirm that the resignation was really intended.

Resignation under pressure

4.1.51   Courts and employment tribunals are concerned to ensure that employees have not been pressurised into giving up their employment rights. In some circumstances, they will look beyond the simple fact that an employee has resigned in order to find out whether it was the employee or the company that really terminated the contract.

4.1.52   If it is clear, therefore, that an employee has resigned under pressure from the company, that might be viewed as a dismissal. Likewise, if a company has 'invited' an employee to resign, or given the employee the option of resigning as an alternative to being dismissed, that could also amount to a dismissal. And an employee who accepts 'voluntary redundancy' is likely to be viewed as having volunteered for dismissal rather than having resigned.

Mutual agreement

4.1.53   If an employer and an employee agree that the employee's contract should terminate, then the contract ends by mutual agreement, not by dismissal. However, this applies only where both parties have genuinely and freely consented to the termination. In practice, a court or employment tribunal is more likely to accept that an employee has genuinely agreed to a mutual termination if he or she has received a favourable financial settlement on departure from the company. For example, where an employee is offered and freely accepts early retirement on a pension, that may amount to a termination by mutual agreement.

Automatic termination agreements

4.1.54   Some employers get employees to agree, either by a term in their contract or in a separate agreement, that their employment contracts will terminate automatically or by mutual agreement if the employee acts in a certain way, such as by failing to return from extended leave on the agreed date. This type of agreement is effectively an attempt to get the employee to contract out of his or her right to claim unfair dismissal, and the Employment Rights Act 1996 states that such agreements have no legal effect. Therefore, if an employer acts upon an agreement of this type and treats the individual as no longer employed, the employee has the right to claim unfair dismissal. It is advisable, therefore, for a company to deal with this type of case through its usual disciplinary or other relevant procedure.

Retirement

4.1.55   Many employees are happy to leave their employment when they reach their retirement age, especially if they have an adequate income for their retirement years. If an employee is content to retire, then their contract terminates by mutual agreement. If an employee is forced to retire against his or her wishes, on the other hand, that amounts to a dismissal, which could potentially lead to claims of unlawful age discrimination and unfair dismissal.

A company can avoid these claims by following a prescribed procedure, which involves notifying the employee of its intention to retire him or her at least six months in advance of the proposed retirement date. Since an employee may initially be happy to retire but change his or her mind closer to the retirement date, employers would be well-advised to follow the procedure in all cases. The procedure is summarised at 4.2.60.

Task or purpose contracts

4.1.56　Some employment contracts specify that they will last until a particular job or project, such as the installation of a computer system, is completed or a particular event, such as the withdrawal of funding for the post, occurs. (In practice, this type of contract is seldom used, not least because it may be difficult to define precisely when a particular task has been completed.)

4.1.57　In terms of contract law, these contracts end automatically when the task is completed or the event occurs. For the purposes of statutory employment rights, however, an employee working under this type of contract is treated as dismissed if his or her contract is not renewed when it ends (see 4.1.62). That means that, depending on the employee's length of service and the reason why the contract was not renewed, the employee may have the right to claim unfair dismissal or a redundancy payment (see 5.2.114) and to be provided with a written statement of the reasons why the contract was not renewed (see 4.1.70).

Frustration

4.1.58　In certain rare circumstances, an employment contract can be terminated by the operation of a legal principle known as 'frustration'. A contract is frustrated if some development occurs that means that the contract can no longer be performed, or it can only be performed in a way that is radically different from what was originally envisaged. The most common examples of when this might apply are where an employee is imprisoned for a criminal offence or becomes seriously ill.

4.1.59　A contract is unlikely, however, to be frustrated by events that have been catered for in the contract's terms. For example, long-term incapacity is unlikely to frustrate an employment contract that provides for long-term incapacity benefits, unless and until it is clear that the illness will outlast the period for which the benefits are payable. It can also be difficult to predict when a court or employment tribunal will conclude that a contract has been frustrated by events. For example, while a tribunal might not consider that a three-month term of imprisonment is long enough to frustrate an employment contract, it is likely to accept that a one-year sentence has that effect.

Reasonable procedures

4.1.60   If an employee's contract has been terminated through frustration, there is then no dismissal that can be challenged as wrongful or unfair. Employment tribunals are therefore reluctant to accept the argument that an employee's contract has been frustrated, because it effectively deprives the employee of the right to claim unfair dismissal. As already mentioned, there are also inherent difficulties in predicting with any certainty when a tribunal will find that the principle applies. It is therefore inadvisable for a company to rely on the principle of frustration. A safer approach would be to follow a reasonable procedure in dealing with an employee who is on long-term sickness absence or sentenced to a term of imprisonment. If that procedure eventually leads to the employee's dismissal, the company will be in a good position to show that it has acted reasonably and that the dismissal was therefore fair.

Fixed-term contracts

4.1.61   A fixed-term contract is a contract that has a precise end date. For example, a contract is for a fixed term if it states that it ends on 31 December 2008, or that it lasts six months from 1 January 2008. Fixed-term contracts commonly include terms that allow the employer or the employee to terminate the contract before the end of the fixed term. If a fixed-term contract does not include a notice clause of this type, it would be a wrongful dismissal (see 4.1.21) for the company to terminate the contract before the end date. The company would then be liable to pay the employee damages equivalent to his or her loss of pay and other benefits for the balance of the fixed term.

Right to claim unfair dismissal

4.1.62 Under principles of contract law, a fixed-term contract ends when the end date arrives, without the need for the company to terminate the contract. It is very important to note, however, that the position is different under employment legislation. For the purposes of statutory redundancy payments and unfair dismissal rights, if an employee is employed under a fixed-term contract and the term expires without the company renewing it under the same terms, the employee is treated as having been dismissed. Also the non-renewal of a task or purpose contract is treated as a dismissal for unfair dismissal and redundancy purposes. Fixed term and task or purpose contracts are sometimes described as limited term contracts. Whether the employee has the right to claim a redundancy payment or unfair dismissal depends on the reason the contract was not renewed, the length of the employee's service at the date the contract ended and whether the employer acted reasonably in deciding not to renew the contract.

4.1.63 Take, for example, the situation where a company is considering not renewing an employee's fixed-term contract because there has been a reduction in the work available for the employee. If the employee has one year's service or more, he or she has the right to claim unfair dismissal, so the company should ensure that it acts reasonably in reaching its decision not to renew. It should therefore consult with the employee about the non-renewal of his or her contract, ensure that the employee has been selected for redundancy using objective selection criteria, invite the employee to a meeting to discuss the proposed dismissal, give the employee an opportunity to appeal against dismissal and offer redeployment where possible. The employee will also be entitled to ask for written reasons for the company's decision not to renew the contract (see 4.1.70). If the employee has at least two years' service, he or she may be entitled to a redundancy payment (see 5.2.114).

Discrimination

4.1.64 It should also be borne in mind that a decision not to renew an employee's fixed-term contract on certain prohibited grounds, such as pregnancy or trade union membership (see 4.2.31), would automatically amount to an unfair dismissal, regardless of the employee's length of service. A decision not to renew could be challenged as an act of discrimination if it was taken on grounds of race, religion, sex, sexual orientation, age or disability, or if it was for a reason relating to the employee's disability and was not justified.

4.1.65   The practical upshot of these principles is that, where a company is considering not renewing an employee's fixed-term contract, it should ensure that it acts reasonably and approaches the case in the same way as it would were it considering the dismissal of an employee working under an open-ended contract.

Termination of apprenticeships

4.1.66   A traditional contract of apprenticeship usually states that it will run for a specified time or until the apprentice reaches a certain standard. The contract then ends automatically when that period ends or the standard is reached. The company is entitled to terminate the contract early only in certain very limited circumstances. These are where the apprentice has been guilty of such serious misconduct or has become so seriously incapacitated that it is impossible for the company to teach the apprentice, or the business has closed or fundamentally changed in nature, making it impossible to train the apprentice in the skills set out in the contract.

4.1.67   If a traditional apprentice's contract is terminated prematurely in breach of contract, the apprentice is entitled to compensation, or 'damages', reflecting not only his or her lost wages for the balance of the apprenticeship but also the value of his or her lost training and the reduction in his or her future employment prospects. This compensation could be substantial.

Modern apprenticeships

4.1.68   Depending on the circumstances, a modern apprentice may be working under either a traditional contract of apprenticeship or a contract of employment. A modern apprentice working under a contract of employment has the same statutory employment rights on termination of contract as any other employee. The apprentice's right to notice of termination of the contract is likely to be set out in the contract itself.

Statutory employment rights

4.1.69   It should be borne in mind that apprentices have the same statutory employment rights as employees. This means that they are entitled to claim unfair dismissal if the company acts unreasonably in terminating their contract. They may also be entitled to a redundancy payment, if they are dismissed for redundancy and have been with the company for two years.

Written reason for dismissal

4.1.70   An employee who has been employed for one year or more at the time when he or she is dismissed is entitled under the Employment Rights Act 1996 to ask for a written statement of the reason for his or her dismissal. This right also applies if the employee worked under a limited-term contract that the employer has decided not to renew. The request need not be in writing. Employees who are dismissed while pregnant or on maternity or adoption leave are entitled to written confirmation of the reason for their dismissal without having to request it, and whatever their length of service.

Setting out reasons

4.1.71   The company must provide the reasons within 14 days of receiving the employee's request. If it wishes, it can send the employee a copy of a previous statement or letter setting out the reasons for dismissal. The statement of reasons that the company gives is admissible in evidence in any legal proceedings and so it could be referred to if the employee claims that his or her dismissal was unfair.

References

4.1.72   Employers in the engineering and construction sectors are under no general legal obligation to give a reference for a current or past employee. It would, however, be a breach of the discrimination legislation for a company to refuse to provide a reference for a current or former employee because he or she had brought a discrimination claim against the company or supported someone else in doing so. On the other hand, a company would not be acting unlawfully if it refused to provide an employee with a reference in order to preserve its position in relation to a discrimination claim that the employee had brought against the company and which was still outstanding.

Taking reasonable care

4.1.73 If a company gives a reference, the employee cannot sue the company for defamation for what it says in it, even if it is inaccurate, provided the company gave the reference in good faith and was not acting with malice. The company is, however, under a duty to the employee to take reasonable care in compiling the reference and in obtaining the information on which it is based. If the company does not take reasonable care and the employee can show that he or she has suffered economic loss as a result, the employee can claim damages from the company for its negligence. For example, the employee might be able to claim for loss of earnings if an inaccurate or misleading reference causes the employee to lose the offer of a job. The company owes a similar duty of care to the recipient of the reference.

4.1.74 A company should therefore take reasonable steps to ensure not only that any reference it gives is accurate but also that the reference does not give an unfair or misleading impression overall. In order to minimise the risk of being sued for negligence, the company may also wish to make clear to the employee and to the recipient of the reference that it does not accept liability for any inaccurate or misleading information in the reference, though the value of the reference would obviously be reduced by a disclaimer of this type.

Data protection principles

4.1.75 The information contained in a reference is personal data. This means that the reference, and any copy of it that the company retains on an employee's file, must be compiled, held and released in a way that meets the requirements of the Data Protection Act 1998 (see Appendix 8.3). In order to fulfil the data protection principles, a reference must be accurate, it must be relevant and not contain unnecessary information, it must be held securely, and it must not be retained longer than is necessary.

4.1.76 The company also needs to confirm with the employee that he or she consents to the reference being compiled and sent, and to a copy being retained on file. This is particularly important where the reference contains sensitive personal data such as details of the employee's sickness absence record. It would be advisable to ask the employee to provide his or her consent in writing. The employee should also be asked to confirm whether he or she consents to references being provided to future employers or others after he or she has left the company.

Access to references

4.1.77 A reference that the company gives on a confidential basis is exempt from the subject access provisions in the data protection legislation, so the company is entitled, if it wishes, to refuse to allow the employee to see it.

4.1.78 The data protection principles relating to access to references that a company receives in the course of recruitment are covered in 1.1.84.

Post-employment restrictions

4.1.79 There are several ways in which a company might want to restrict the activities of an employee after his or her employment ends. These include preventing the employee from using or disclosing confidential information and trade secrets, going to work for a competitor, or poaching the company's customers, suppliers or employees.

4.1.80 All employees are under a legal obligation not to disclose their employer's confidential information and trade secrets or to use them for personal gain, and that obligation continues even after employees have left the company. However, if an employee is likely to have access to sensitive information in the course of his or her employment, it would be advisable to clarify and confirm the position by including an express term in his or her contract. This should identify the confidential information and emphasise the employee's obligation not to use it for personal gain or to disclose it.

4.1.81 If the company wishes to impose any other restrictions on an employee's activities after he or she leaves the company, it will need to obtain the employee's agreement to this, either by including the restrictions in the employee's contract or by agreeing them with the employee when he or she leaves. These restrictions are usually referred to as 'restrictive covenants', and can be used to limit a departing employee's ability to work for a competitor of the company, or to poach the company's customers, suppliers or employees.

Legal enforceability

4.1.82   The law starts from the assumption that any restriction that an employer places on an ex-employee's ability to participate freely in the marketplace is not in the public interest and is therefore not legally enforceable. This is the case unless the restriction is reasonable in scope and is necessary for the protection of the employer's legitimate business interests. In order to be enforceable, therefore, a restrictive covenant must be no wider than is necessary to protect the employer's legitimate interests. It must be reasonable in terms of:

- the subject matter it covers;
- the geographical area to which it relates; and
- the length of time for which the restriction lasts.

4.1.83   Restrictive covenants need to be drafted carefully if they are to be effective. Companies that wish to use restrictive covenants in their contracts of employment or as part of an agreement reached with a departing employee should therefore consider contacting us for advice.

Wrongful dismissal and enforceability

4.1.84   If a company wrongfully dismisses an employee (see 4.1.21), as where the company does not give the employee proper notice of dismissal, the employee is released from his or her own obligations under the contract. This makes any restrictive covenants in the contract unenforceable. Some employers therefore insert terms into their employment contracts giving them the right to terminate either with notice or without notice but with a payment in lieu. If this type of term is in place, the employer will not prejudice the enforceability of post-employment restrictions even if it terminates the employee's contract without notice. However, the payment in lieu that the company makes under a contract term of this type is taxable in full, as it is treated as income from the employee's employment. A payment in lieu that is not paid under a contractual obligation can benefit from the £30,000 tax exemption for termination payments. (The rules on the taxation of termination payments are outlined in 4.1.93.)

Tax considerations

4.1.85   If post-employment restrictions are agreed with a departing employee as part of a financial settlement, it is important from a tax perspective to identify the financial value of the restrictions. Payments for restrictive covenants are viewed for tax purposes as income from the employment and are taxable in full. If no separate value is attributed to the restriction, there is a danger that the whole settlement figure will be taxed in full, and the benefit of the usual £30,000 tax exemption for termination payments will be lost.

Recovering training and other costs

4.1.86   Some employers include terms in their employment contracts allowing them to recover certain costs from employees when they leave the company. These might include, for example, recovery of training costs where the employee leaves the company within a certain period after completing the training, or recovery of relocation expenses where the employee leaves within a certain period of the move.

4.1.87   These terms are likely to be legally valid provided the amount to be recovered is a genuine estimate of the loss caused to the company by the employee's departure. The amount should not, therefore, exceed the costs that the employer has incurred in providing the training or meeting the relocation expenses. It should also reduce over time, to take into account the service that the employee has provided after training or relocating and before leaving the company. Further advice on using this type of clause can be obtained from us.

4.1.88   It is worth remembering that it is unlawful for an employer to deduct any sum from a departing employee's pay unless it has authorisation to do so (see 2.1.92).

Retaining employment records

4.1.89 In order to comply with the data protection legislation, a company should not retain personal information about a former employee any longer than is necessary, and information that is no longer needed should be disposed of securely. The Data Protection Code (see 9.8.3) advises employers to establish standard retention periods for particular categories of information and gives guidance on how to identify what those periods should be.

Settlements

4.1.90 A company may wish to reach agreement with a departing employee that the employee will not bring any legal claims against the company if the company pays the employee a certain sum in settlement. Agreement may also need to be reached on practical issues such as the employee's company car, the extension of healthcare and life insurance cover, and arrangements for the recovery of any outstanding company loans.

4.1.91 In order to prevent an employee from taking a claim to an employment tribunal, any agreement must be reached with the assistance of the Advisory Conciliation and Arbitration Service (ACAS), or must meet the requirements for compromise agreements or compromise contracts set out in the employment rights legislation. These requirements are detailed and are set out in 7.1.19. The most important points to note are that the agreement must be in writing, it must identify the particular claims that the employee is agreeing to settle, and the employee must have received independent advice on the agreement before he or she signs it.

4.1.92 Financial settlements on termination of employment can raise complicated legal and taxation issues and may involve substantial sums of money. Senior employees in particular are likely to have valuable contractual rights to notice pay, bonuses, share options and pensions that may need to be taken into account in the settlement terms. We can provide advice on the terms of settlement and the wording of termination letters and compromise agreements.

Tax

4.1.93   When agreeing a termination payment with a departing employee, a company may need to take into account the rules on the taxation of termination payments. These are set out in the Income Tax (Earnings and Pensions) Act 2003 and various concessions that the Inland Revenue has made over the years. The basic principles are these:

- Any part of the financial settlement that represents a payment for the employee's work during employment is taxable in full. That will include any payment made under a term of the employee's contract, including a term giving the employer power to make a payment in lieu of notice. It may also cover a discretionary payment such as a discretionary bonus.

- Any payment made to the departing employee in return for his or her agreement to enter into a restrictive covenant is also taxable in full.

- The first £30,000 of any remaining elements of the financial settlement, such as ex gratia payments or redundancy payments, is normally exempt from tax.

4.1.94   In the case of senior employees in particular, the tax treatment of termination payments can have a substantial impact on the size of the settlement reached and the way in which it is structured. Companies may therefore wish to obtain specialist tax advice when drawing up settlements.

Social security considerations

4.1.95   Companies may find it useful to be aware of the following background information on the social security rules that apply to employees on leaving employment:

- Employees who are dismissed for misconduct may be disqualified from Jobseekers' Allowance for up to 26 weeks.

- Employees may also be disqualified from benefit for up to 26 weeks if they leave their employment voluntarily and without just cause.

- An employee who receives a termination payment may have that payment treated as income, and so may be disqualified for a period from receiving benefit.

Pensions

4.1.96　When leaving a company, an employee is entitled to an up-to-date statement of the value of his or her company pension. The employee can ask the company scheme to make a transfer payment into another occupational or personal pension scheme on his or her behalf. Alternatively, the employee may choose to leave his or her accrued rights in the company's scheme and start a new scheme with a new employer.

Exit interviews

4.1.97　Interviewing an employee who has decided to leave can provide the company with useful information on the reasons for labour turnover and help identify practices within the organisation that may need to be changed. Exit interviews can also help to identify the training and development needs of remaining employees, provide information on the marketplace and competitors, indicate whether the departing employee could be re-employed in the future and ensure that he or she leaves with a good impression of the company.

4.1.98　The information that a company may find it useful to collect from a departing employee includes:

- the reasons why the employee is leaving;
- the conditions, if any, under which the employee would have stayed;
- the compensation and benefits the employee will be receiving from his or her new employer;
- the extent to which the terms and conditions of employment offered by the company influenced the employee's decision to leave;
- whether the employee's departure was prompted by unfair treatment;
- what improvements the employee considers the organisation could make;
- the employee's forwarding address.

Methods of interview

4.1.99　An exit interview can be conducted face to face before the employee leaves. Alternatively, the company may prefer to conduct a telephone interview with the employee after he or she has left, or ask the employee to complete a questionnaire. A company may decide to interview all leavers or just a sample, such as one in every five.

4.1.100　If the personnel/human resources department conducts the exit interview, this may encourage more honesty and openness during the interview. It is important, however, that the interviewer should have a good understanding of the employee's job. Therefore if the employee retains a good relationship with his or her line manager, it may be more appropriate for that person to conduct the interview. Some companies may wish to employ the services of someone from outside the organisation to conduct exit interviews.

Guidance on conducting an exit interview

4.1.101　If the company decides to conduct a face-to-face interview, the following guidance may be helpful:

- Before the interview, explain to the employee the aims of the meeting and, if appropriate, give him or her a copy of any form or questionnaire that he or she will be asked to complete. This will enable the employee to prepare for the interview and think about the topics that will be covered.

- Draft out the content of the interview in advance, using open-ended questions.

- During the interview, engage with the employee and try to keep note-taking to a minimum.

- Create an environment that encourages the employee to be open, honest and frank.

- Encourage the employee to talk openly and freely by confirming that his or her feedback can make a positive difference for ex-colleagues and the organisation.

- Try not to react to the information being provided by the employee or to defend the organisation or individuals within it – remain neutral.

- Encourage the employee to talk about the things that he or she has enjoyed while working for the company.

- Thank the individual for his or her contribution while working for the organisation.

Labour turnover

4.1.102   The rate at which employees join and leave a company is an important indicator of the organisation's health. One of the human resource professional's key tasks is to measure the rate of labour turnover and compare it with the rate in other relevant organisations.

4.1.103   It is important to note that any organisation is constantly changing and developing and its ideal rate of labour turnover may alter over time. For example, low rates of turnover may inhibit internal progression. On the other hand, a high rate of turnover may be useful in a company that needs to reduce its size or change the mix of its workforce. Usually, however, high turnover is undesirable because of the cost of recruiting replacement employees and the loss of skill, knowledge and experience from the organisation.

Costs

4.1.104   The costs associated with turnover may include the following:

- Costs associated with the employee leaving:
  - exit interviewer's time;
  - extra administration costs of payroll and pension scheme;
  - unscheduled payments such as outstanding holiday pay.

- Vacancy costs:
  - cost of providing cover until replacement found;
  - lost knowledge, skill and experience;
  - lost sales/customers.

- Replacement costs:
    - fees of advertising/recruitment agencies;
    - extra administration costs for payroll, human resources, support functions;
    - time spent interviewing;
    - travel expenses for interviewees;
    - relocation expenses;
    - cost of induction training;
    - time spent by current employees on training new starter;
    - cost of the performance differential between an experienced employee and a new recruit.

Measures of labour turnover

4.1.105 The usual method of calculating labour turnover is:

$$\frac{\text{Number of leavers}}{\text{Average number of employees}} \times 100 = \text{separation rate}$$

This is a crude measure and will need to be refined if it is to identify the picture in particular departments, over specific periods of time or by type of leaver. It is usual to analyse only leavers who leave voluntarily rather than at the instigation of the employer.

4.1.106 Another measure is the stability index, which gives an indication of the extent to which experienced employees are being retained. It is calculated as follows:

$$\frac{\text{Number of employees with one year's (or more) service}}{\text{Total number of employees}} \times 100 = \text{stability index}$$

4.1.107 A third measure is survival rate, which is particularly useful for tracking the retention of graduate intakes. It is calculated as follows:

$$\frac{\text{Number of employees recruited in a specific period still in employment at a later date}}{\text{Number of employees recruited in a specific period}} \times 100 = \text{survival rate}$$

Succession planning

4.1.108　Any successful business needs to ensure continuity of operation and development opportunities for its people. Succession planning involves identifying successors for key posts and planning career moves and development activities for these successors, to provide them with the appropriate experience.

4.1.109　Succession planning enables a company to:

- improve internal recruitment by identifying candidates with known qualities and availability;
- actively develop longer-term successors;
- audit the available strengths within the organisation; and
- foster a corporate culture by developing a group of people with shared experiences and skills developed to meet the needs of the business.

4.1.110　Traditionally, succession planning has been an undisclosed part of the appraisal process. It has been assumed that, if the process were open, those identified as possible successors would be more aware of their marketability and those who were not seen as potential successors would be demotivated. In recent years, however, a more open approach has become common, in which the populations under consideration understand the methods used for identifying potential successors and the roles that are suitable for each individual. It is also now more common for organisations to develop a pool of individuals for a group or family of jobs. This allows the business to respond flexibly to its rapidly changing needs and acknowledges that individuals may decide to develop their careers outside the organisation.

4.1.111　Succession planning is usually focused on key roles that are often management positions. A wider view needs to be taken in times of very low unemployment and skill shortages. This is particularly important when redundancies are being made. Care must be taken not to allow rare skills to disappear from the organisation without some means of replacing them and to retain core expertise that will be needed in the future.

4.1.112　Succession planning has lost some prominence as a management tool because of the perceived bureaucratic nature of the data-gathering process, the difficulty of meeting employees' aspirations in de-layered organisations and the degree of inflexibility involved in pointing an individual in a particular direction. However, a flexible, open and developmental approach to succession planning helps organisations deliver tailored, proactive career development that is aligned to the needs of the business.

Developing a succession planning process

4.1.113   When developing a succession planning process, a company will need to address these issues:

- To what level should the process be applied and what jobs or groups of jobs require successors?

- Which managers will be responsible for the succession process?

- What methods of identification will be used?

- To what extent can the business provide appropriate development experiences to meet individual development plans?

- Is the organisation robust enough to ensure retention of the identified individuals?

- Is the process robust enough to allow for identified successors who leave the organisation?

- Does the process allow for the talents of all employees to be recognised, regardless of their age, sex, ethnic or racial origin, disability, sexual orientation or religion?

4.2

Unfair dismissal

Overview

4.2.1　Unfair dismissal is one of the longest-established areas of employment law, familiar to employers and employees alike. In interpreting and developing unfair dismissal law over the years, employment tribunals have highlighted the importance of companies following fair procedures before deciding to dismiss an employee. This chapter of the Guide explains the rules on unfair dismissal. Most unfair dismissal law is in the Employment Rights Act 1996, but unfair dismissals on trade union grounds are dealt with in the Trade Union and Labour Relations (Consolidation) Act 1992.

Eligibility and dismissal

4.2.2　This chapter begins by setting out who is eligible to claim unfair dismissal (see 4.2.10) and then goes on to look at the legal principles that govern whether a particular dismissal was fair or unfair. It is up to the employee to prove that he or she was dismissed. Dismissal is defined in a particular way for the purposes of unfair dismissal law (see 4.2.23) and includes, for example, a decision not to renew a fixed-term contract. It is then usually for the employer to prove the reason for the employee's dismissal.

Fair reason

4.2.3　Dismissals for certain reasons are automatically unfair (see 4.2.31). If the reason does not fall within one of these inadmissible categories, it must fit into one of the other categories of potentially fair reasons for dismissal recognised by the legislation. These categories are defined broadly, however, and are capable of covering all legitimate business reasons for dismissing an employee (see 4.2.34).

Retirement

4.2.4 There are complex rules that govern whether a dismissal for retirement amounts to an unfair dismissal and age discrimination. The steps that an employer should follow to ensure that a retirement dismissal is lawful are summarised at 4.2.60.

Acting reasonably

4.2.5 Once the company has established that it had a potentially fair reason for dismissing, the crucial issue is whether the company acted reasonably in treating it as a sufficient reason to dismiss the employee. Employment tribunals have definite views on what is involved in handling a dismissal reasonably, and this chapter draws on the tribunals' decisions in order to give guidance on handling different types of dismissal (4.2.36).

4.2.6 The ACAS Code of Practice on disciplinary and grievance procedures will be taken into account by employment tribunals, where relevant, when hearing unfair dismissal cases. The Code sets out the key elements in handling fairly disciplinary and grievance issues. The Code is important not only when the tribunal decides on liability (particularly whether the employer has acted reasonably) but also when deciding on unfair dismissal compensation which can be adjusted by up to 25 per cent for unreasonable failure by either party to comply with any provision of the Code.

4.2.7 Separate chapters of this Guide deal in more detail with how unfair dismissal law affects the handling of specific types of cases, such as poor attendance, sickness absence, unsatisfactory performance (see Chapter 3.2), discipline (see Chapter 3.3) and redundancy (see Chapter 5.2). The legal mechanics of how an employment contract is terminated and other legal issues that arise when an employment relationship ends, such as the obligation to provide employees with written reasons for dismissal, are covered in Chapter 4.1.

Other unlawful dismissals

4.2.8 It is also important to keep in mind that unfair dismissal law is not the only route by which a dismissal can be challenged as unlawful. A dismissal that is implemented in a way that breaches the terms of an employee's contract is a wrongful dismissal, for which the employee can recover compensation. (Wrongful dismissal is discussed in 4.1.21.) A dismissal may amount to unlawful discrimination if it is based on an individual's sex or married status or is on grounds of age, race, religion, sexual orientation or disability. It may also be discriminatory to dismiss a disabled employee if the reason for the dismissal is not the disability itself but relates to it and the dismissal is not justified, or if the employee has been dismissed before the company has met its duty to consider reasonable adjustments. Further, an employer who dismisses an employee because of his or her age, or apparent age, must be able to justify this in order to avoid unlawful age discrimination.

4.2.9 The law on discrimination is summarised in Chapter 3.1. The special rules that govern lawful retirement dismissals are dealt with below at 4.2.59.

Eligibility to claim

4.2.10 To be eligible to bring an unfair dismissal claim, an individual must have worked for the company either as an employee or as an apprentice. Workers who do not meet the legal tests of employee status (see 1.2.72) therefore do not qualify.

4.2.11 If the reason why the employee was dismissed falls within one of the categories of dismissal that are automatically unfair, as set out below (see 4.2.31), then he or she usually has the right to claim unfair dismissal regardless of his or her length of service. In all other cases, however, the individual must have worked for the company for at least one continuous year to qualify.

4.2.12 There are two anomalies here. Firstly, if an employee is dismissed for a reason connected with the transfer of a business, the dismissal may be automatically unfair but, the employee must have one year's continuous service in order to bring an unfair dismissal claim on this ground. (The employment law issues that arise on a business transfer are explained in Chapter 5.3.) Secondly, a dismissal for retirement may be unfair if the employer has not followed the procedure for lawful retirement dismissals (see 4.2.60), but only if the employee has one year's service.

Limited term contracts

4.2.13   If a company decides not to renew the contract of an employee working under a fixed-term contract, unfair dismissal law views that as a dismissal.

4.2.14   Likewise, if an employee has a contract that states it will last until a particular task is completed or a particular event occurs, and the employer decides not to renew the contract when the task is completed or the event happens, unfair dismissal law views that as a dismissal.

Industrial action

4.2.15   In certain limited circumstances, employees who are dismissed while taking part in industrial action are excluded from the right to claim unfair dismissal. These rules are complex and are explained in 6.3.42–6.3.57.

One year's continuous service

4.2.16   The rules on calculating continuous service are laid down in the Employment Rights Act 1996 and are summarised in Appendix 8.1 of this Guide. It is important to note that continuous service does not depend on the number of hours an employee works each week. Furthermore, in some circumstances, service with a previous employer can count towards an employee's continuous service with the company, and so can breaks between separate contracts with the same company.

Effective date of termination

4.2.17   An employee's qualifying service for unfair dismissal is measured up to the 'effective date of termination' of the employee's employment. Broadly speaking, this is the date when his or her contract ends. (There is an important exception to this rule, explained in 4.2.20.) Therefore, if the employee has been dismissed without notice, his or her service ends with the day on which he or she was notified of the dismissal. If the employee was dismissed with notice, then his or her service ends with the day that the notice expired, regardless of whether the employee is required to work during the notice period or is given garden leave (see 4.1.32). If the employee was dismissed with immediate effect but then appealed against the decision to dismiss, service still ends on the day he or she was dismissed, unless his or her contract states otherwise. An employee may decide to resign after being given notice of dismissal. In that event, he or she is still viewed as having been dismissed, but his or her service ends with the day the resignation takes effect.

4.2.18   A decision not to renew a fixed-term contract is viewed as a dismissal in unfair dismissal law. In this type of case, the employee's service ends with the day on which the fixed term expired. In the same way, where a contract is stated to last until a particular task is completed or a particular event occurs and it is not renewed, the employee's service ends on the day the task is completed or the event happens.

4.2.19   Where the employee has resigned in response to a serious breach of contract by the company and is alleging constructive dismissal, his or her service ends when that resignation takes effect. If the employee resigned without notice, service ends with the day on which the company learns of the resignation. If the employee chose to give notice of resignation (which he or she was not obliged to do), then service ends at the end of the notice period.

Extending the effective date

4.2.20   It is important to note that in certain limited circumstances the employee's effective date of termination is postponed beyond the end of his or her contract. This special rule applies where the employee was dismissed without notice (unless the employee had forfeited the right to notice by acting in serious breach of contract, such as by committing an act of gross misconduct) or the employee was dismissed with notice, but the notice he or she was given was less than the minimum period of notice to which he or she was entitled under the Employment Rights Act 1996 (see 4.1.16).

4.2.21   In these circumstances, the employee's service is extended to the date it would have ended if he or she had been given the statutory minimum period of notice. For example, if an employee who has been with the company since 2 June 2005 is dismissed without notice on 28 May 2006, his or her service is extended to 4 June 2006. This means that the employee qualifies for the right to claim unfair dismissal, even though he or she has not actually worked for the company for one complete year.

4.2.22   It is important to note that this special rule extends the employee's service by only the statutory minimum notice period, not by any longer contractual notice period to which he or she may be entitled. Further, the rule does not apply when deciding whether the employee has met the three-month time limit for making a claim of unfair dismissal to an employment tribunal. The time for bringing a claim runs from the date that the employee's contract actually ended.

Establishing the dismissal

4.2.23   If an individual brings a claim of unfair dismissal to an employment tribunal, it is up to him or her to prove that he or she was dismissed. The company may, for example, have expressly dismissed the employee, with or without notice. (If the company gave the employee notice of dismissal but he or she resigned before the notice expired, he or she is still viewed as having been dismissed.)

Constructive dismissal

4.2.24   It is relatively straightforward for an individual to prove dismissal if he or she was expressly dismissed. However, it may be more difficult if the employee has resigned and is alleging that he or she has been constructively dismissed. Constructive dismissal is discussed elsewhere in this Guide (see 4.1.35), but the basic rules are that the employee must be able to prove that:

- the company acted in serious breach of his or her contract of employment, in a way that went to the heart of the employment relationship or indicated that the company no longer intended to be bound by one or more of the essential terms of the contract; and
- the employee's resignation was caused by the company's actions; and
- the employee did not wait too long before resigning.

Limited term contracts

4.2.25 If an employee has been working under a fixed-term contract and the company decides not to renew the contract on the same terms, unfair dismissal law views that as a dismissal. Likewise, if an employee has been working under a contract to perform a particular task or a contract that continues until a particular event occurs, and the company decides not to renew the contract when the task is completed or the event happens, that is a dismissal.

The reason for the dismissal

4.2.26 While it is up to the individual to prove that he or she has been dismissed, the onus usually falls on the company to prove the reason for the dismissal. If there was more than one reason, the focus is on the main or principal reason for the dismissal.

4.2.27 The reason for a dismissal is simply the set of facts known to the company or beliefs held by the company that caused it to dismiss the employee. Facts that the company discovered only after deciding to dismiss cannot provide a reason for dismissal. They may, however, be taken into account by an employment tribunal when it is calculating what compensation to award the employee, if the dismissal is found unfair (see 7.2.33, 7.2.38).

Evidence of the reason

4.2.28 It is important for a company to be clear about its reasons for dismissing an employee. It must be in a position to prove the reason for the dismissal. If it cannot do so, the dismissal may be found unfair. If the company gave the employee written reasons for his or her dismissal, then that document can be used as evidence of the reason for dismissal (see 4.1.70).

4.2.29 In a constructive dismissal case, the reason for the dismissal is the reason why the company breached the employee's contract, entitling the employee to resign. A constructive dismissal is not necessarily an unfair dismissal. A constructive dismissal involves the employer acting in serious breach of contract, whereas a dismissal is unfair if the employer did not act reasonably in deciding to dismiss. An employment tribunal hearing an unfair constructive dismissal claim might accept that, even though the employer had seriously breached the employee's contract, it had acted reasonably in all the circumstances.

4.2.30 When establishing the reason for the employee's dismissal, no account can be taken of the fact that the company was pressurised into dismissing the employee through industrial action or the threat of it.

Automatically unfair reasons for dismissal

4.2.31 There are some reasons for dismissal that the law regards as automatically unfair. Some of these are dealt with in more detail in other sections of this Guide. The purpose behind many of these categories of automatically unfair dismissal is to give employees protection if they exercise certain functions or assert the rights that they have under employment legislation.

4.2.32 It is automatically unfair to dismiss an employee, or select an employee for redundancy, if the sole or main reason for the dismissal is connected with:

- The employee's pregnancy or maternity (see 2.2.72).

- The fact that the employee has taken maternity leave, paternity leave, adoption leave, parental leave or time off to care for dependants or applied for flexible working (see Chapter 2.2).

- The employee's trade union membership or non-membership or trade union activities (see 6.1.13).

- The fact that the employee is taking part in properly balloted industrial action, in certain defined circumstances (see 6.3.49).

- The employee's functions as an employee representative for the purposes of:

    - collective consultation on redundancies (see 5.2.59); or

    - collective consultation on a business transfer (see 5.3.32); or

    - negotiation or consultation under the Information and Consultation of Employees Regulations 2004 (see 6.4.80); or

    - the transnational works councils legislation (see 6.4.80);

- workforce agreements under the Regulations on working time (see 2.3.34), parental leave (see 2.2.136) or fixed-term employees (see 1.2.100); or

- consultation on pension changes (see 2.4.61).

- The fact that the employee is or has been a candidate for election as an employee representative.

- The employee's functions as a pension scheme trustee (see 2.4.75).

- The fact that the employee supported or opposed a trade union's claim for recognition under the statutory recognition procedure (see 6.2.40).

- The fact that the employee has asserted his or her rights under employment legislation (see 3.3.151), including the legislation on the national minimum wage (see 2.1.22), working time (see 2.3.25), part-time workers (see 2.3.92), fixed-term employees (see 1.2.103) and the right to be accompanied at a disciplinary or grievance hearing (see 3.3.80). It is also automatically unfair to dismiss an employee for accompanying a colleague to a hearing.

- The fact that the employee has 'blown the whistle' on certain forms of wrongdoing (see 3.3.143).

- The fact that the employee has carried out certain health and safety duties, raised safety concerns or taken steps in response to serious health and safety hazards (see 3.3.155).

- The fact that the employee is entitled to Working Tax Credit (see 2.1.105).

- The fact that the employee has been summoned for, or undertaken, jury service (see 2.3.97).

- The transfer of a business or part of a business or a service provision change (see 5.3.73).

4.2.33 Although the unfair dismissal legislation does not state this expressly, a dismissal that is in breach of the discrimination legislation is almost certain to be an unfair dismissal. Likewise, it is almost certainly unfair to dismiss an employee because he or she has a conviction that is 'spent' under the Rehabilitation of Offenders Act 1974 (see 3.1.126).

Potentially fair reasons for dismissal

4.2.34   In order for a dismissal to be potentially fair, the employer must be able to show that the employee was dismissed for a reason that fits within one of the following categories. It is important to remember, however, that the fact that the reason for the dismissal falls within one of these categories does not necessarily mean that the dismissal was fair. The fairness of the dismissal depends on whether the company acted reasonably in treating the reason as a sufficient reason to dismiss the employee, as discussed further below (see 4.2.36).

4.2.35   The potentially fair categories are these:

1. *Employee's capability*. Capability includes the employee's skill, aptitude, health or any other physical or mental quality. This category will cover, for example, the case of an employee who was dismissed for a poor sickness absence record. It would also cover a dismissal for poor performance, if this were due to the employee's lack of ability. (An employee dismissed for poor performance that was due to a lack of application or carelessness on the employee's part is likely to have been dismissed for a reason relating to the employee's conduct, another potentially fair category of reason for dismissal, mentioned below.)

2. *Employee's qualifications*. It is potentially fair to dismiss an employee for not having the qualifications for performing work of the kind he or she was employed to do. Qualifications include any degree, diploma or other academic, technical or professional qualification that was relevant to the position that the employee held. So this category could, for example, cover the case of an employee who was recruited as a health and safety adviser on the basis that he or she had, or would soon obtain, a certain safety diploma and was dismissed because it transpired that he or she did not possess that qualification, or was unlikely to be able to obtain it in the near future.

3. *Employee's conduct*. This means any conduct of the employee, whether in the course of work or outside it, that reflects in some way on the

employment relationship. This category would therefore cover cases of dismissal for misconduct and for criminal offences outside work that are relevant to the employee's job.

4. *Redundancy.* It is important to be aware that a redundancy can be challenged as an unfair dismissal if the company did not act reasonably in implementing the redundancy. The definition of redundancy and other legal and good practice issues relating to the implementation of redundancies are discussed in Chapter 5.2.

5. *The employee could not continue in his or her job without the company or the employee breaking some duty or restriction imposed by legislation.* This reason would apply, for example, if the individual worked as a driver and was dismissed because he or she was disqualified from driving. For this reason to apply, the company must be able to show that it would actually have broken some legal duty or restriction by continuing to employ the employee, not merely that it thought it would.

6. *Some other substantial reason.* The employee was dismissed for some other substantial reason of a kind that justified the dismissal of an employee doing the job that the employee did. This category is likely to cover a dismissal for any substantial and legitimate business reason that does not fall in one of the categories mentioned above. For example, it could apply to the dismissal of an employee who refused to agree to new terms and conditions of employment. It could also apply if an employee is dismissed because of pressure from a customer or because of a personality conflict with another employee. If a company recruits an employee to cover another employee's maternity leave, maternity suspension or adoption leave, and informs the replacement in writing when he or she is recruited that he or she will be dismissed when the other employee returns to work, then the legislation says that the company has a substantial reason for dismissing the replacement to make way for the returning employee.

Did the company act reasonably?

4.2.36   Once the company has established the reason for the employee's dismissal, the focus moves to the central question of whether the company acted reasonably in all the circumstances in treating the reason for dismissal as a sufficient reason for dismissing the employee. The legislation gives little guidance on what an employer must do to act reasonably. It simply states that the question of whether the dismissal was fair or unfair must be decided in the light of 'equity' (that is, general principles of fairness) and the merits of the case.

The previous decisions of employment tribunals and the higher courts are therefore the main source of guidance on the steps that companies should take in order to ensure that they have acted reasonably.

4.2.37 An important general principle that emerges from this case law is that employers must follow a fair procedure before deciding to dismiss. The steps that may be involved in a fair procedure are summarised below in relation to each category of dismissal, though many of these situations are covered in more detail in other sections of this Guide.

4.2.38 A company that does not follow a fair procedure will usually be found to have unfairly dismissed the employee. In dismissal cases involving discipline or grievance issues, the employment tribunal will have regard to the ACAS Code of Practice on disciplinary and grievance procedures which emphasises that it is essential to follow a fair process and then identifies the key elements in this process or procedure (see 3.3.40). A company that is considering dismissing an employee without implementing a fair procedure should contact us for advice.

Specified relevant factors

4.2.39 Although the legislation does not lay down detailed rules on what a company needs to do in order to act reasonably, it does specify that the size and administrative resource of the company's business should be taken into account. This means, for example, that a small employer without a separate personnel function might act reasonably in dismissing an employee for misconduct even if it followed only the basics of a fair disciplinary procedure as set out in the ACAS Code of Practice on discipline and grievance before deciding to dismiss, whereas a larger company might be expected to follow a more extensive procedure.

4.2.40 The legislation also expressly states that no account can be taken of any pressure that was brought to bear on the company to dismiss the employee by industrial action, or the threat of it.

A range of reasonable responses

4.2.41   It is important to bear in mind when considering the broad guidance set out below that there might be more than one reasonable way of dealing with a case. One employer might decide to dismiss an employee for a particular act of misconduct where another would have issued a final written warning; one company might decide to dismiss an employee for poor performance when another would have given the employee a further opportunity to improve. A dismissal is unfair only if no employer acting reasonably would have decided to dismiss.

4.2.42   The focus is, however, on the conduct of the company, not the injustice suffered by the employee. If the company has not acted reasonably, the employee's dismissal will be unfair, even if it could be said that the employee in some sense 'deserved' to be dismissed. However, if the employee contributed in some way to his or her own dismissal, then the employment tribunal that hears his or her unfair dismissal claim is likely to reflect that, by reducing any compensation it awards for unfair dismissal.

Assessment at date of dismissal

4.2.43   The reasonableness of an employer's actions is assessed in the light of the circumstances that existed up to the day on which the employee's employment ended. Therefore, if an employee is dismissed with notice, it is advisable for a company to take into account any facts that come to light during the notice period and, if appropriate, to review its decision to dismiss. The company may also need to take into account fresh evidence that comes to light on an employee's appeal against dismissal.

4.2.44   Any facts that emerge after the employee's employment is over cannot be taken into account, either to confirm the reasonableness of the company's actions or to cast doubt on whether it acted reasonably. They may, however, affect the amount of any compensation that an employee is awarded if the dismissal is found unfair.

Appeals

4.2.45   The ACAS Code of Practice on discipline and grievance specifically states that a key element in handling disciplinary and grievance issues is to provide employees with an opportunity to appeal and that their appeals should be heard without delay and ideally at an agreed time and place. It is good practice to provide for the right to appeal in all types of dismissal.

4.2.46 Wherever possible, an appeal should be heard by a more senior manager who was not involved in the original decision to dismiss. The employee has the right to be accompanied at the appeal hearing by a work colleague or trade union official of his or her choice (see 3.3.80). Completely rehearing a case on appeal can be an effective way of making good any shortcomings in the way in which the original decision to dismiss was handled.

Documenting the process

4.2.47 Companies should ensure that they have a full documentary record of the procedural steps that they took before deciding to dismiss an employee. These can prove invaluable in defending any claim that the dismissal was unfair.

4.2.48 These records are personal data and so must be kept in a way that complies with the requirements of the Data Protection Act 1998. That means that the records must be accurate, they should be no more extensive than is necessary, they must be kept confidential and they should be retained no longer than is necessary. The employee has the right to have access to the records, unless they reveal information about another person who does not consent to disclosure and it would not be reasonable to disclose them without that individual's consent.

Capability

4.2.49 The management of poor performance is discussed in Chapter 3.2. In summary, in order to act reasonably in dismissing an employee for poor performance, a company should ensure that, before deciding to dismiss, it has complied with the ACAS Code of Practice on discipline and grievance which, in summary, means the employer has:

- made clear to the employee the standard of performance that was expected and how he or she was falling short of that standard;

- cautioned the employee on what the consequences might be if he or she failed to improve;
- consulted with the employee about the reasons for his or her poor performance;
- given the employee a fair opportunity to improve;
- provided the employee with appropriate support and training to help him or her reach the required standard;
- considered whether the employee could be moved to another job that was more appropriate for someone of his or her level of ability;
- reasonably concluded that dismissal was appropriate;
- given the employee a fair opportunity to appeal against the decision.

Sickness absence dismissal

4.2.50 The management of sickness absence is covered in Chapter 3.2. In summary, a company that dismisses an employee for a poor sickness absence record should be able to show that, before deciding to dismiss, it had:

- consulted with the employee about his or her absence record, the reasons for it and the impact it was having on the company;
- made clear to the employee the possible repercussions of his or her sickness absence record for the employee's continued employment;
- gathered medical evidence on the employee's current condition and on when he or she would be fit to resume work (it may not be necessary for unfair dismissal purposes to obtain medical evidence in cases of intermittent, unrelated absences, but it is still advisable to do so in order to avoid liability for disability discrimination);
- considered whether there was any other work that it could offer the employee that was suitable for the employee to do, if the employee's condition made it impossible for him or her to return to his or her original job in the foreseeable future;

- reasonably concluded that the Impact that the employee's absence was having on the business could no longer be accepted;

- given the employee a fair opportunity to appeal against the decision.

Qualifications

4.2.51   Before deciding to dismiss an employee because he or she does not have the necessary qualifications for the job, a company should ensure that it has:

- consulted with the employee about the situation;

- supported the employee in obtaining the qualification, where this is practicable and appropriate;

- considered whether the employee could be redeployed to another job where the qualification would not be required; and

- given the employee a fair opportunity to appeal against the decision.

Conduct

4.2.52   The legal principles involved in handling disciplinary issues are covered in Chapter 3.3. In summary, before deciding to dismiss an employee for misconduct, a company should ensure that:

- It has complied with the ACAS Code of Practice on discipline and grievance.

- The disciplinary rules were clear – that is, the employee knew that the act he or she committed would be viewed as misconduct.

- It has carried out a reasonable investigation of the conduct and its surrounding circumstances to establish the facts of the case.

- Before the disciplinary hearing was held, the employee was given reasonable warning of the case against him or her, to enable him or her to prepare a response.

- At the disciplinary hearing the employee had the option of being accompanied by a colleague or trade union official, and was given a fair opportunity to put his or her side of the case.

- Dismissal was the appropriate sanction for the employee's conduct, in the light of the severity of the offence, the circumstances in which it was committed, the way in which the company treated other employees who were guilty of the same offence, and the employee's previous disciplinary record and employment history.

- The employee was given a fair opportunity to appeal against the decision to dismiss.

Redundancy

4.2.53   The management and legal principles involved in implementing redundancies are discussed in detail in Chapter 5.2. In summary, before deciding to dismiss an employee for redundancy, a company should be able to show that it has taken these steps:

- It has considered whether there are any alternatives to redundancy, such as reducing overtime working, where appropriate in consultation with trade union or employee representatives.

- It has defined fairly and objectively the group of employees from whom the redundancies were to be made, where relevant in consultation with trade union or employee representatives.

- It has given the employee as much warning as possible that redundancy was a possibility.

- It has selected the employee for redundancy on the basis of criteria that are fair and, as far as possible, objective, and that were drawn up in consultation with trade union or employee representatives where appropriate.

- It has consulted with the employee about his or her selection for redundancy.

- It has considered whether the employee could be redeployed as an alternative to dismissal.

- The employee was given a fair opportunity to appeal against the decision.

Legal restriction

4.2.54 Before deciding to dismiss an employee because of a legal restriction on his or her continued employment, a company will be expected to have:

- consulted with the employee about the situation;

- considered whether it is practicable to make temporary arrangements to cover the employee's duties if the restriction will apply only temporarily, as where an employee has been disqualified from driving for a short period; and

- considered whether there are any vacancies in the company to which the employee could be transferred that would not be affected by the restriction;

- given the employee a fair opportunity to appeal against the decision.

Some other substantial reason

4.2.55 It is not possible to generalise about the steps that an employer should take in order to act reasonably in dismissing for 'some other substantial reason', since this category of reason for dismissal can cover a variety of different situations, requiring different approaches, although the company should always ensure that it has followed a fair procedure.

Criminal offence

4.2.56 To take just one example, if the company is considering dismissing an employee who has been imprisoned for a criminal offence committed outside employment, the company might need to:

- consult with the employee about the situation and its possible impact on his or her future employment with the company;

- consider whether the nature of the offence indicates that the employee is unsuitable for continued employment by the company in his or her current job, or in any other post that may be available; and

- assess the impact that the employee's absence will have on the business and whether it is practicable to make cover arrangements.

Contract changes

4.2.57   Dismissals in order to introduce new contractual terms are also likely to fall within the category of 'some other substantial reason'. Chapter 5.1 deals with the legal principles that apply when handling this type of case, including the unfair dismissal considerations.

Retirement

4.2.58   Many employees are happy to leave their employment when they reach their retirement age, especially if they have an adequate income for their retirement years. If an employee is content to retire, then their contract terminates by mutual agreement. If an employee is forced to retire against his or her wishes, on the other hand, that amounts to a dismissal, which could potentially lead to claims of unlawful age discrimination and unfair dismissal.

4.2.59   A company can avoid these claims by following a prescribed procedure, which is explained below and involves notifying the employee of its intention to retire him or her at least six months in advance of the proposed retirement date. Since an employee may initially be happy to retire but change his or her mind closer to the retirement date, employers would be well-advised to follow this procedure in all cases.

Safe retirements

4.2.60   The rules on retirement dismissals are extremely complex, with many variables that may affect the outcome. An employer can, however, ensure that a retirement dismissal is neither an unfair dismissal nor an act of unlawful age discrimination by taking the following steps.

- Step one: Check the intended retirement date

The date at which the employee is required to retire should not be below 65. If there is an age at which employees in the employer's business who do the same kind of job as the employee are normally required to retire and that age is over 65, then the employee should not be required to retire before that date.

- Step two: Notify the employee of that date and his or her right to request to work on

Not more than one year nor less than six months before the date the employer intends the employee to retire, the employer must confirm that date to the employee in writing and inform him or her of the right to request to work on beyond that date. If the employer fails to meet this duty to notify, not only may any subsequent dismissal be unfair, but the employer will be liable to pay compensation to the employee of up to eight weeks' pay.

- Step three: Deal with any request to work on

If the employee wants to work on beyond the notified date, he or she must put that request in writing. The employee may ask for his or her employment to continue indefinitely, or for a stated period or until a stated date. The request must be made more than three months but not more than six months before the intended date of retirement. On receiving the request, the employer must either agree an extension with the employee and confirm it in writing or hold a meeting with the employee to discuss it. At the meeting, the employee has the right to be accompanied by a work colleague of his or her choice, who is entitled to address the meeting and to confer with the employee, but not to answer questions on the employee's behalf. The employer must notify the employee of the result of the meeting in writing.

- Step four: Deal with any appeal

If the employer agrees to allow the employee to work on, but not for as long as the employee requested, or if it refuses the employee's request completely and confirms the original retirement date, the employee has the right to appeal that decision. If the employee does appeal then, unless the employer and employee can agree an extension, the employer must hold a meeting to consider the appeal at which the employee has the right to be accompanied by a work colleague. The employer must notify the employee of the result of the appeal in writing.

- Step five: Implement the retirement

If the employer is not going to grant the employee an extension, the employee should be retired on the intended date of retirement as originally notified to the employee.

4.2.61 If a company is planning to retire an employee compulsorily in circumstances that fall outside this procedure, it should contact us for advice.

4.2.62 If an employee is granted an extension, the company will have to follow the same procedure when implementing his or her later retirement, unless the extension was for a fixed period of six months or less, in which case there is no duty to do so.

4.2.63 Any employee who accompanies a colleague at a meeting to discuss retirement has the right to a reasonable amount of paid time off to fulfil that duty. He or she is also protected from being subjected to any disadvantage or dismissed as a result of carrying out his or her duties, as is the employee who exercises his or her right to be accompanied.

section 5

Change and reorganisation

5.1

Changing contracts of employment

Overview

5.1.1　Any business is likely to develop or restructure its operation over time. These changes can take many forms. The most extreme might involve the selling off or closure of part or even the whole of the business, or the contracting out of part of its operation. At the other end of the spectrum, the company might simply need to make minor amendments to the way in which its employees work.

5.1.2　Whatever form business change might take, it is likely to involve some kind of alteration in the company's relationship with its workforce, and that may entail changing employment contracts. This chapter of the Guide summarises the employment law issues that arise when implementing change. Companies that are planning to implement change may find it useful to contact us for detailed advice.

Non-contractual changes

5.1.3　The flow chart at the end of this chapter summarises the contractual questions that arise when implementing business change. It may be useful to refer to this flow chart when reading this chapter, which follows the same structure. The starting point is to establish whether the implementation of the change will require any alteration in employees' contracts. No alteration will be needed if the change falls within the scope of management's right to set workplace rules and standards and working methods (see 5.1.12), or if it merely involves the company using a power it already has under a term in employees' contracts to implement change (see 5.1.18). This highlights the value of including clauses in employment contracts requiring flexibility. There is specific legal obligation on employers to consult before a decision is made to implement certain changes to their pension provision (see 2.4.61).

Contractual changes

5.1.4   In some circumstances, however, a company may be seeking to introduce change that goes beyond employees' current contractual obligations or alters employees' existing rights. In these cases, the company can implement the change if it has the employees' agreement. Agreement can be obtained either at the collective level, through negotiation with a recognised trade union (see 5.1.29), or at the individual level, through the consent of each employee (see 5.1.31).

5.1.5   If employees will not agree to a change and the company decides to impose it on the workforce, it may face legal claims. This chapter explains what those claims might be (see 5.1.42). Another option would be to terminate employees' existing contracts and offer them new ones. This chapter also explores the legal repercussions of this approach (see 5.1.44).

5.1.6   Other parts of this Guide deal with more dramatic forms of business change, such as the implementation of redundancies, which can arise through the restructuring, relocating or shedding of jobs or the closure of the whole or part of a business (see Chapter 5.2). The Guide also deals elsewhere with the principles of employment law involved in the sale of the whole or part of a business or the contracting out of its operations, including the possibility of changing terms and conditions in that context (see Chapter 5.3). The specific legal obligation on employers to consult before a decision is made to implement certain changes to their pension provision is covered at 2.4.51.

The meaning of consultation

5.1.7   This chapter makes frequent reference to the need for companies to consult with employees when introducing change. It is therefore worth noting how the courts and tribunals that enforce employment law interpret the meaning of consultation. They assume that, if a company is to consult meaningfully on a proposal, it must:

- enter into the consultation process with an open mind;
- provide employees with clear information on what is being proposed and why;
- give employees adequate time to consider that information and to prepare their responses;
- give proper consideration to employees' responses, and take them into account in finalising the proposal;
- be undertaken with a view to reaching agreement.

5.1.8 Consultation is therefore a two-way process, involving a considered exchange of views between company and workforce, rather than a one-way process of informing the workforce of what is going to happen.

Does the change affect employees' contracts?

5.1.9 When identifying the legal issues that arise in implementing a particular change, an important first step is to analyse whether the change in fact involves any alteration to employees' contracts of employment. This in turn involves establishing what the terms of employees' contracts are.

5.1.10 Terms can become part of an employee's contract in many ways, and readers may find it useful to refer to Chapter 1.2, which explains the way in which employment contracts are formed. Some terms of an employee's contract may be agreed at the recruitment interview, others may be set out in the letter offering the employee the job. Many important terms will be set out in the written statement that the company provides to the employee of the main terms and conditions of his or her employment. Or the employee may have a comprehensive written contract that contains all the terms of his or her employment.

Other documents

5.1.11 It is important to bear in mind that some of an employee's contractual terms may be found in documents such as the company's statement of its policies and procedures, job descriptions, employee handbooks, and sickness benefit scheme and pension scheme booklets. It may therefore be necessary to explore whether these documents have in fact been expressly or impliedly incorporated into the employee's contract, and whether their wording and all the surrounding circumstances indicate that the company intends to be legally bound by them.

Companies that are unclear whether the change they plan to implement affects employees' contractual rights may wish to contact us for advice.

The scope of management prerogative

5.1.12 Although contracts of employment define many important aspects of employees' rights, they do not regulate every aspect of employment conditions. Employers still have a large degree of management discretion in how they manage their workforce. In particular, management has the right to set the rules on how employees should behave in the workplace and to prescribe the way in which jobs should be done. This is the case unless its room for manoeuvre is limited in some way by the terms of employees' contracts (although consultation on any change is always advisable – see 5.1.14). This is reflected in the fact that employees are under an implied duty to co-operate with their employer and obey its lawful and reasonable instructions, provided those instructions fall broadly within the scope of the employees' duties as defined by the express terms of their contracts.

5.1.13 Companies therefore have the flexibility to meet many of their changing business needs without infringing employees' contractual rights. For example, a company is likely to be at liberty to amend or add to its disciplinary rules, since these rarely form part of employees' contracts. Likewise, it is likely to be free to require its employees to change the way they do their jobs – such as by moving to an upgraded machine or using a computer rather than a paper-based system – because working methods are rarely included in employees' contracts.

The need for consultation

5.1.14   Even if the change that is proposed falls within the scope of a company's management prerogative, it is nevertheless advisable for the company to consult with employees about the change before it is introduced. Proper consultation is a central element of good employment relations practice and is likely to be necessary to secure employees' co-operation.

5.1.15   There are also good legal reasons for consulting about change. One is that if an employee refuses to observe a new workplace rule or to follow a new method of working, the company may want to take disciplinary action against the employee, up to and including dismissal. If it has not informed employees clearly about the change and explained the rationale behind it, the company may find itself liable for unfair dismissal. This is on the basis that it is not reasonable to dismiss an employee for failing to observe a rule or reach a standard that he or she did not know about or understand.

Trust and confidence

5.1.16   Another good legal reason for consulting with employees about change is to ensure that the company meets its implied duty not to act in a way that breaches trust and confidence between itself and its employees. This is particularly relevant where the change involves new rules or working methods that are difficult for certain employees to comply with or require different skills. In order to maintain trust and confidence, it may be necessary to give employees support in meeting the new rule or to provide training in the new working methods.

Training and consultation

5.1.17   Although a company has the right to require employees to change their working methods, it also has a duty to support them in making the change, which may involve providing training. It should also be borne in mind that employers are under a specific legal duty, under the Safety Representatives and Safety Committees Regulations 1977 and the Health and Safety (Consultation with Employees) Regulations 1996, to consult with their workforce about the health and safety consequences of the introduction of new technology (see 6.4.63).

Express terms requiring flexibility

5.1.18   When drafting their employees' contracts of employment, companies have the opportunity to include a variety of express terms requiring employees to be flexible. A contract could, for example, require employees to work whatever shift pattern the company may decide, or to carry out duties that are reasonably related to their main job function even if not expressly included in their job description, or to change their place of work if the company decides to relocate. It is important that contracts are drafted clearly if they are to give the employer the flexibility it needs. Companies may therefore wish to contact us for advice on the wording of their employment contracts.

Express terms can give a company freedom to require employees to change when and where they work and what they do. That freedom is, however, limited to some degree by other legal principles, as explained below.

Indirect discrimination

5.1.19   A contract term that is indirectly discriminatory on the grounds of sex is not legally enforceable. Therefore, if a term requiring flexibility has a disproportionate impact on one sex, the company cannot enforce it unless it can show that the term is necessary to meet the company's business needs. Take, for example, terms that require employees to relocate or change their working hours at short notice. More women than men are likely to find it impossible in practice to comply with such requirements, because women are more likely than men to be the second earners in their household and to have primary responsibility for childcare arrangements. A company that uses terms like these therefore needs to ensure that it has a real business need for employees to be mobile and flexible in their working hours. Likewise, requiring employees to be flexible in their hours or days of work can interfere with some employees' religious observance, and a company should therefore be in a position to objectively justify the need for such flexibility, in order to avoid indirect religious discrimination. Indirect discrimination is explained in more detail in Chapter 3.1 of this Guide (see 3.1.37).

Health and safety

5.1.20   A company is under a legal duty to take reasonable care for the health and safety of its employees. Even if it is has a contractual right to ask employees to be flexible, it cannot use that power in a way that puts employees' health and safety at risk. This may, for example, put some limits on the company's scope for using contractual terms that allow it to ask employees to work excessive overtime or to take on onerous extra duties.

5.1.21　In relation to working hours, employees are given specific protection by the Working Time Regulations 1998 (see 2.3.20). For example, a company cannot use a contractual power to ask an employee to work overtime or to require an employee to work more than 48 hours on average a week, unless the employee has agreed in writing to work those hours. It is important to remember that the Regulations give employees' additional, specific rights in relation to working hours, rest breaks and holidays; they in no way detract from companies' overriding obligation to protect their employees' health and safety. Therefore, even if an employee had agreed in writing to work over 48 hours a week, a company would be in breach of its duty of care if it asked the employee to work such long hours that his or her health was damaged.

Trust and confidence

5.1.22　Employers have an important implied obligation not to act in a way that breaches trust and confidence between themselves and their employees. This duty operates alongside any express terms in employees' contracts. For example, even if a company had a contractual right to ask an employee to move workplace, it might be breaching trust and confidence if it asked the employee to move without notice to a new workplace beyond reasonable travelling distance from his or her home.

General flexibility clauses

5.1.23　In theory, an employment contract can include a clause giving the employer a general power to change all or any of the terms of the contract. In practice, however, courts and tribunals are reluctant to enforce a clause of this type unless the wording of the clause is very clear and there is absolutely no doubt that it covers the change the employer wants to make. Furthermore, a contract is not legally enforceable if its terms are uncertain. There is an argument that, if all the terms of an employment contract can be changed unilaterally by the employer, the contract is too uncertain to be enforceable.

5.1.24   Companies that are considering including general flexibility clauses in their employment contracts may wish to contact us for advice.

Implied flexibility

5.1.25   An employee's contract may not expressly provide for the flexibility that the company needs in order to introduce the change that it wants. In that case, the company might want to argue that it has an implied power to make the change, because the change is reasonable and in the company's business interests. However, terms are implied into employment contracts in only very limited circumstances.

Basis for implying flexibility

5.1.26   Broadly speaking, a term will be implied only if the courts have accepted that the term is a necessary part of any employment contract, or it reflects what the parties to the contract obviously intended, or it needs to be included to make the contract work. (The basis of implied terms is discussed in more detail in 1.2.37.) For example, a manufacturing employer that wanted to relocate its manual workforce could not argue that it had the implied right to require the employees to move. If it wanted the flexibility to instruct employees to move, it would need to include an express mobility clause in their contracts.

5.1.27   If employees have worked flexibly in the past and accepted changes of the type that the company is now proposing, it could be argued that this implies that they have accepted flexibility as part of their contractual terms. However, that argument would be undermined if there was evidence that the employees had accepted change in the past as a matter of goodwill towards the company, and not because they considered themselves legally bound to do so.

Change through agreement

5.1.28   The terms of an employment contract, like those of any other form of contract, can be changed if the parties agree. If a company wants to introduce a change that it currently has no express or implied power to make, it should first ask employees to agree to a change in the terms of their contract. There are two possible routes to achieve change by agreement: through bargaining with a recognised trade union or by obtaining individual employees' consent.

Change through collective bargaining

5.1.29   If a company recognises a trade union for collective bargaining, it may be able to secure the change it needs through negotiations with the union. The changes that the company agrees with the union will be binding on individual employees, provided that their contracts state that any collective agreements that the company may reach with the union from time to time will form part of their terms of employment. If an employee's contract contains an incorporation clause of this kind, any changes agreed with the union will form part of his or her contract, even if he or she is not a member of the union or is vehemently opposed to the changes. The way in which collective agreements become part of individual employees' contract terms is explained in more detail in 6.2.51.

5.1.30   The situation is different if employees' contracts do not incorporate any collective agreements, or if they do not incorporate the agreement on change that has been reached. A contract of employment is a personal contract between the individual employee and the employer. Therefore, if there is no incorporation, an employee will not usually be bound by changes negotiated and accepted by a third party such as a union. The only exception to this is where the employee has agreed that the union can act as his or her agent in the negotiations. An agency agreement of this kind is very rare, and it cannot be assumed that an employee has appointed the union to be his or her agent merely because the employee is a member of the union. In practice, however, an employee is unlikely to challenge a change that has been agreed by his or her union, even if the agreement is not binding on the employee in strict legal terms.

Individual agreement

5.1.31   If a company does not recognise a trade union, or if it recognises a union but cannot secure the union's agreement to the change it wants, it can approach employees individually for their agreement to the change. Once the end of the collective route has been reached, however, a company may well need to approach employees individually, in order to put itself in a position to defend any subsequent unfair dismissal claims, as explained below (5.1.53). In practice, employees may be prepared to agree to adverse changes if the company is able to offer them some other benefit, such as a pay increase, in compensation.

5.1.32   If an employee agrees to a change to his or her contract, it is advisable to get him or her to confirm that agreement in writing.

Notice to vary

5.1.33   It is a common misconception that an employer can alter employees' contractual terms simply by giving them a 'notice to vary' their contracts. In fact, if the employees have not agreed to the variation, a notice of this type does not alter their contract terms, but rather gives them advance warning that the company intends to breach their contracts, giving them the option of making the legal claims outlined below (see 5.1.42). Likewise, the mere fact that a company has issued employees with a written statement confirming that their contract terms have changed does not have the effect of altering those terms, if the employees have not in fact agreed to the change.

5.1.34   In practice, however, employees who are issued with a 'notice to vary', or a written statement about a change, may be prepared to go along with the change and by so doing will have implied that they have agreed to it. Nevertheless, companies that are contemplating this course of action should contact us for advice.

Imposed change and its dangers

5.1.35   It may be that a company does not have the right to implement the change it wants under the existing terms of employees' contracts, and it cannot get employees' agreement to a change. In these circumstances, the company may decide, as a last resort, to impose the change and see what happens.

5.1.36   If it decides to take this route, the company will need to bear in mind the potential practical repercussions as well as the legal ones. Imposing change may damage the goodwill between the workforce and the company, so leading to loss of productivity. It could also lead to serious industrial relations problems or even industrial action.

Implied consent and its limitations

5.1.37 If a company imposes change and employees work on without protest, the company could argue that, by their actions, the employees have shown that they accept the changed terms. In practice, employees often accept imposed change because they are unaware that they have any right to resist it or because they feel unable to enforce their rights.

5.1.38 From a legal perspective, the fact that employees have worked on without protest does not necessarily prove that they have agreed to the change. It depends on the nature of the change. If the change has an immediate practical impact, such as a cut in the employee's rate of pay, and the employee continues to work without objection, then he or she may well be taken to have implicitly agreed to the change. However, the situation is different if the change has no immediate effect – as, for example, where the company has imposed a clause requiring the employee to accept relocation but has not yet used it. The fact that the employee has not expressly rejected the new term does not necessarily mean that he or she has agreed to it.

5.1.39 In the hope of avoiding this uncertainty, a company might consider telling employees that, if they turn up to work on the day after the change has been imposed, they will be taken to have accepted it. There are drawbacks to this approach. Employees could turn up to work but still make clear that they reject the change. Or they could resign and claim constructive dismissal. They might then be able to bring one or more of the legal claims outlined below (5.1.42). Companies that are considering this option should therefore contact us for advice.

Rejection of change

5.1.40 If a company imposes a change in employees' contractual terms, the employees can reject the change simply by saying that they do so. They do not have to resign or even put their position in writing. By working on but continuing to make clear that they reject the new terms, they are effectively maintaining their right to the original terms of their contract.

5.1.41 There are various ways in which employees can enforce their contractual rights, as outlined below (see 5.1.42). There may come a point when an employee who originally protested at the imposition of a change but has not taken any action to enforce his or her rights will be taken to have agreed to the new terms. It is difficult to predict, however, exactly when that point might be.

Potential legal claims

5.1.42 If an employee does not accept changes that have been unilaterally imposed, there are various legal claims that he or she can bring. In summary:

- If the change has caused the employee some form of quantifiable financial loss, he or she can claim damages for the company's breach of contract. This claim can be made in the ordinary civil courts. It can also be made in an employment tribunal if the employee's employment has ended, but the tribunal cannot award more than £25,000.

- If the change means that the company is paying the employee less than what is 'properly payable' under his or her original contract of employment, he or she can bring a claim to an employment tribunal that the company had made an unlawful deduction from his or her pay. (The scope for unlawful deductions claims is explained in 2.1.92.)

- If the change has not yet been implemented, or if it has been implemented but does not involve financial loss, the employee can seek a court order preventing the company from implementing the change, or a declaration from the court setting out his or her contractual rights. In practice, these types of claim are rare because of the costs of legal representation.

- If the change involves a serious breach of contract that goes to the heart of the employment relationship or involves one of the more important terms of the contract, the employee can resign and claim that he or she has been constructively dismissed. The employee can then claim damages for wrongful dismissal (that is, a dismissal in breach of contract) in the civil courts or an employment tribunal, on the basis that the company gave the employee no notice that his or her contract would be terminated. The employee can also bring a claim of unfair dismissal to an employment tribunal. A constructive dismissal is not necessarily unfair, but it will be if the company has not acted reasonably in imposing the change. This issue is discussed further in 5.1.53.

- If the change that is imposed is sufficiently fundamental and wide-ranging, the employee can remain in employment and claim that the company has effectively withdrawn his or her original contract of employment and imposed a new one. That is, the employee can claim that he or she has been expressly, rather than constructively, dismissed from the original contract. Again, the employee can claim that this dismissal was wrongful or unfair.

- If the change that is imposed is fundamental and alters the nature of the work to be done, then this may give rise to a redundancy payments claim and entitlement.

5.1.43   It is important to note that some of these claims can be made while the employee is still in employment. In particular, if a company imposes a change that causes an employee immediate financial loss, it is relatively easy for the employee to bring a claim in the employment tribunal that the company has made an unlawful deduction from his or her pay. On the other hand, there are fewer legal risks involved in imposing a change that does not involve unlawful deductions from an employee's pay and is not such a significant change to an employee's terms that it would justify the employee resigning and alleging constructive dismissal.

Offering new contracts

5.1.44   A company may be unwilling, for legal or employee relations reasons, to impose the change it needs. However, it may also be unable to obtain employees' agreement to the change. In these circumstances, the company has the option of implementing the change by terminating employees' contracts of employment and offering them new contracts on the revised terms. Employees may expressly accept the new contracts. If they do not, they may by implication accept the new terms by turning up to work after their original contracts have ended.

Clean break approach

5.1.45 A company that adopts the 'clean break' approach of introducing change by dismissing its employees and offering them new contracts avoids the potential claims of breach of contract and unlawful deductions from pay that come with imposed change. The company could still, however, face claims for wrongful or unfair dismissal. It is important to note that these claims could be brought by employees who accepted the new contracts as well as by those who did not. There may also be a legal requirement to consult the affected employees' representatives and notify the Department for Business, Innovation and Skills if 20 or more employees are involved (see 5.1.55).

5.1.46 To avoid liability for wrongful dismissal, the company must give each employee proper notice of the termination of his or her original contract. If it wants to avoid allegations of unfair dismissal, the company must also ensure that it acts reasonably in terminating the employees' original contracts. The steps that an employment tribunal might expect a reasonable employer to take are discussed further below (see 5.1.53).

Avoiding unfair dismissal

5.1.47 A company may face unfair dismissal claims if it imposes significant changes in employees' contract terms or if it terminates employees' contracts and offers new terms. This section summarises how the basic principles of unfair dismissal law apply in this context and what companies can do to avoid liability for unfair dismissal. Readers who require further detail of unfair dismissal law may wish to refer to Chapter 4.2.

Establishing a dismissal

5.1.48 It is up to the employee who is alleging unfair dismissal to prove that he or she has been dismissed. Unfair dismissal law views an employee as having been dismissed if any of the following things has happened:

- The company has terminated the employee's contract in order to offer him or her new terms.

- The company has imposed a fundamental change in the employee's terms that goes to the root of the employment relationship or shows that the company does not intend to be bound by one or more of the essential terms of the contract. This is termed a 'constructive dismissal'. So where the company has imposed change rather than expressly terminated the employee's contract, the employee must be able to show that the change was sufficiently important to amount to a constructive dismissal. By way of example, any reduction in the amount that the employee gets paid is likely to be a fundamental breach of contract by the company. Putting back the start and finish times of an employee's working day by 10 minutes may not be.

- The company has decided not to renew the contract of an employee working under a limited term contract, or the company has renewed the employee's fixed-term contract but on radically different terms.

Reason for dismissal

5.1.49   If an unfair dismissal claim is made, it is up to the company to prove the reason for the dismissal. This must fall within one of the categories that the unfair dismissal legislation recognises as potentially fair reasons for dismissal (see 4.2.34).

5.1.50   If the change that the company has made relates to the particular kind of work that the employee does, then the reason for the dismissal may be redundancy. Redundancy law, including the definitions of redundancy (5.2.16), is dealt with in Chapter 5.2 of this Guide. However, it is worth noting here that although an employee who is dismissed for redundancy is usually entitled to a redundancy payment, the employee loses the right to a payment if he or she unreasonably refuses an offer of suitable alternative employment (see 5.2.105). Therefore, if the new terms that the company intends to introduce change the nature of the work that the employee does, but still amount to suitable alternative employment, the employee will not be entitled to a redundancy payment if he or she unreasonably refuses the offer of employment on the new terms.

5.1.51   If the change is not related to the kind of work that the employee does, then the reason for dismissal is likely to fall into the category of 'some other substantial reason' for dismissal. It is important to note that, in order to fall within this category, the reason for the change must be 'substantial'. In other words, the company must be able to show a real business reason for the change, such as pressing financial considerations.

Reasonableness

5.1.52   The unfair dismissal legislation does not give any detail on what is involved in acting reasonably, beyond saying that the issue must be decided in accordance with general principles of fairness and the merits of the particular employee's case. It also states that the employment tribunal must take into account the size and administrative resources of the employer. Unfair dismissal law acknowledges that there are several approaches that a company might take to introducing change, and the dismissal of an employee will be unfair only if it falls outside this range of possible reasonable approaches.

Demonstrating reasonableness

5.1.53   Although the legislation defines the test of whether a dismissal is fair in very general terms, some idea of what is expected of employers in managing dismissals arising from contractual change can be gleaned from the previous decisions of the employment tribunals and appeal courts. In order to be able to demonstrate that it has acted reasonably, a company should ensure that:

- It can show a real business need for the change.

- It has explained to the employee the nature of the change and the business need for it.

- It has consulted with the employee about the change, in order to obtain the employee's views on the change in general and its potential impact on the employee in particular.

- If the company recognises a trade union or has employee representatives, it has also consulted with those representatives about the change. (If 20 or more dismissals are involved, the company will have a specific legal duty to consult with the representatives, as explained in 5.1.55.)

- It has seriously considered any points that the employee has raised about the change and, if it has rejected them, it has sound reasons for doing so and has explained them to the employee.

- It has attempted to secure the employee's agreement to the change. (A company that has imposed change without any attempt to obtain the employee's agreement is likely to find that the employee's dismissal is found unfair for this reason.)

- If the employee did not agree, the company has explained that it may terminate the employee's contract and offer a new one on the changed terms if he or she does not agree to the change.

- It has introduced the change with a reasonable amount of warning, to enable the employee to make any practical preparations he or she may need to make to comply with it.

- It has offered the employee a new contract on terms that reflect the change required. (It would be unwise for the company to muddy the waters by using this opportunity to introduce other terms that it might ideally want included in the contract.) Compensation for unfair dismissal can be reduced if the employee has not taken reasonable steps to minimise the financial loss he or she has suffered as a result of the dismissal (see 7.2.37). It would therefore be advisable for the company to repeat its offer of a new contract on the revised terms after the original contract has ended. If the dismissal is then found unfair, the employment tribunal will take into account when assessing compensation whether the employee was acting reasonably in refusing the new contract.

Individual versus company need

5.1.54   Although the company may be introducing change that affects the whole or a major part of the workforce, unfair dismissal law concentrates on the case of the individual employee. So it may be reasonable for a company to take into account the impact that the change will have on the circumstances of a particular employee and decide not to push through the change in relation to that individual. On the other hand, the individual employee's circumstances are only one factor to be taken into account and need to be weighed against the company's need for change. If a large majority of employees had already accepted the change, that may support the argument that it was reasonable for the company to implement the change in relation to this particular employee.

Collective consultation

5.1.55   If a company is proposing to dismiss 20 or more employees at one establishment within a period of 90 days or less in order to introduce new contracts, it has an obligation to notify the Department for Business, Innovation and Skills. It must also consult about the proposals at a collective level, under the Trade Union and Labour Relations (Consolidation) Act 1992. If the company negotiates with a trade union, then it must consult with the union's representatives. If it does not negotiate with a union, then it must consult with employee representatives.

5.1.56   These duties are discussed in more detail elsewhere in this Guide (see 5.2.42 and 5.2.60).

Documenting change

5.1.57   Employers must provide employees with written information on the main terms and conditions of their employment within two months of the employees starting work. This duty is explained in 1.2.47. If there is a change in any of the terms that must be included in this information, the company must give each employee individual written confirmation of the change. This must be provided at the earliest opportunity, but in any event no later than one month after the change.

5.1.58   Employers can refer employees to other documents, the law or collective agreements for some of the details they have to provide. If they wish, they can also refer employees to the same sources for details of any changes.

Employee agreement

5.1.59   The fact that a company has issued an employee with a written statement that his or her main terms and conditions have changed does not necessarily mean that they have. If the employee has not agreed to the change, it will not become part of his or her contractual terms simply because the company has put something in writing. In particular, the fact that an employee does not protest when he or she receives notice that his or her terms have been unilaterally changed does not necessarily mean that the employee has agreed to the change.

Implementing change: the contractual issues

Cross-references are to paragraphs in this chapter of the guide.

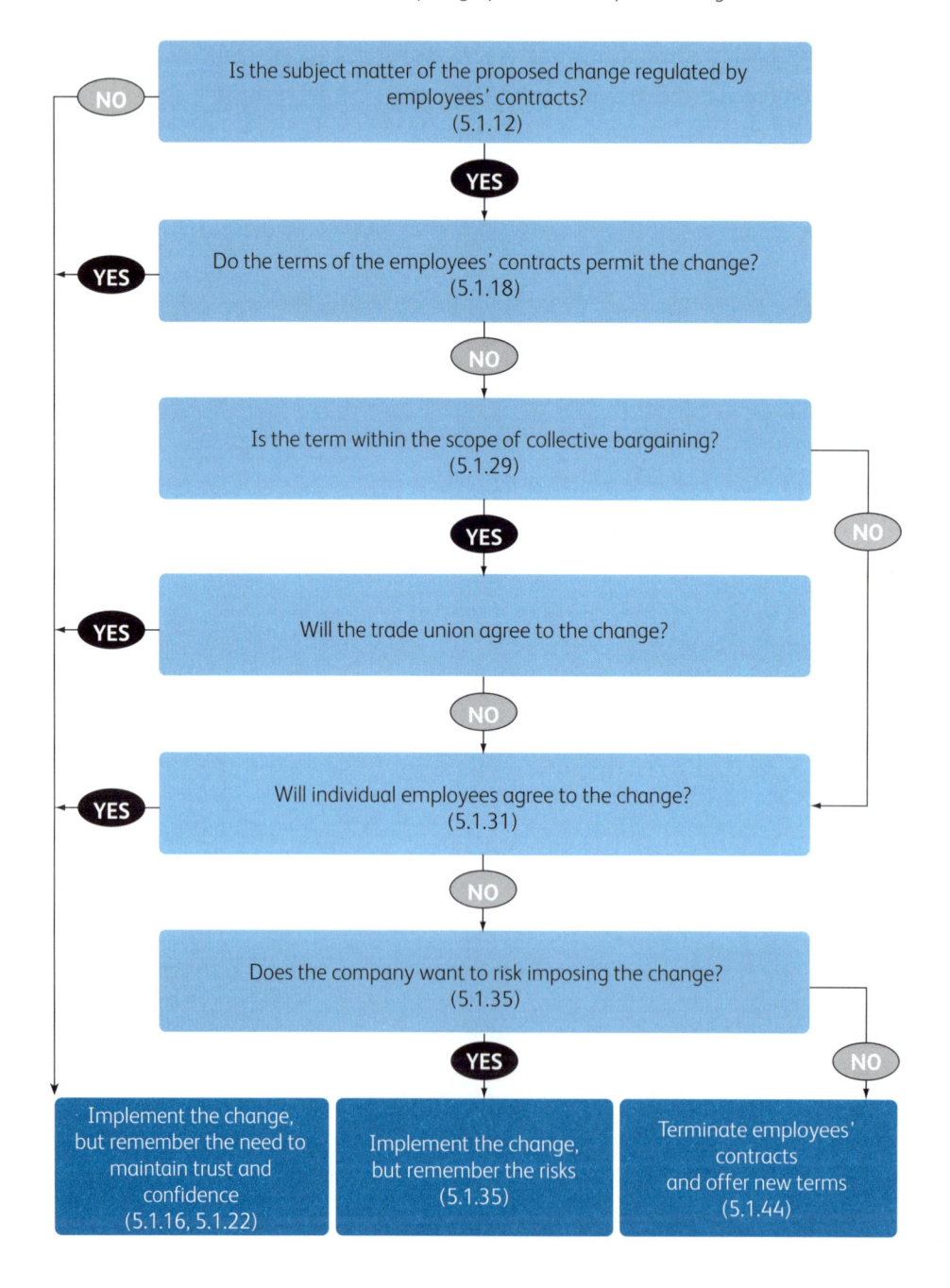

```
                Is the subject matter of the proposed change regulated by
    NO ─────────         employees' contracts?
                                (5.1.12)
                                   │
                                  YES
                                   │
                Do the terms of the employees' contracts permit the change?
    YES ────────                   (5.1.18)
                                   │
                                   NO
                                   │
                     Is the term within the scope of collective bargaining?
                                   (5.1.29)
                                   │                                    NO
                                  YES
                                   │
    YES ────────        Will the trade union agree to the change?
                                   │
                                   NO
                                   │
    YES ────────       Will individual employees agree to the change?
                                   (5.1.31)
                                   │
                                   NO
                                   │
                     Does the company want to risk imposing the change?
                                   (5.1.35)
                                   │                                    NO
                                  YES
```

| Implement the change, but remember the need to maintain trust and confidence (5.1.16, 5.1.22) | Implement the change, but remember the risks (5.1.35) | Terminate employees' contracts and offer new terms (5.1.44) |

5.2

Redundancy, lay-off and short-time working

Overview

5.2.1   Many companies will at some point need to implement redundancies, perhaps because of a downturn in demand or a need to relocate or restructure the business. This chapter of the Guide sets out the employment law framework for a redundancy exercise and also outlines the legal position if a company wishes to lay employees off or to put them on short-time working. Companies that are contemplating redundancies may wish to contact us for advice.

5.2.2   This section opens by discussing the legal definitions of redundancy and then goes on to examine the steps that are involved in implementing redundancies lawfully. A checklist summarising these steps can be found at the end of the chapter (see 5.2.143).

Consultation and fairness

5.2.3   There are several pieces to the legal jigsaw that need to be fitted together when implementing redundancies. An employer that is proposing to dismiss 20 or more employees has specific legal obligations to consult with its workforce at a collective level (see 5.2.42) and to notify the Department for Business, Innovation and Skills (see 5.2.60). In addition, unfair dismissal law requires an employer that is implementing redundancies to act reasonably. The ACAS Code of Practice on discipline and grievance does not apply to redundancy dismissals. However, previous decisions of the courts and tribunals have confirmed that acting reasonably involves:

- warning employees about the possibility of redundancy and consulting with them about the proposals (see 5.2.37);

- selecting employees for redundancy fairly (see 5.2.69);

- consulting with employees individually when they are selected for redundancy (see 5.2.85); and

- exploring the possibility of redeployment before implementing the dismissals (see 5.2.95);

- providing a right of appeal against the decision to dismiss.

Discrimination legislation

5.2.4 Discrimination legislation also needs to be borne in mind when making redundancies. The legislation that outlaws discrimination on the grounds of sex, race, age, religion and sexual orientation prohibits both direct and indirect discrimination, and this is particularly relevant when employers are deciding how to select individuals for redundancy. Likewise, a company needs to bear in mind the requirements of disability discrimination law. This means that disabled employees must not be treated unfavourably in the redundancy process because they are disabled, or for reasons linked to their disability unless this can be justified, and the company must consider whether any reasonable adjustments should be made to the process to accommodate disabled employees.

5.2.5 Part-time workers and fixed-term employees are also protected from unjustified discrimination on the ground of their part-time or fixed-term status (see 2.3.85, 1.2.89). This covers both the way they are treated during the redundancy process and the redundancy payments they receive.

Employees' rights

5.2.6 When it comes to terminating redundant employees' contracts, an employer must respect employees' contractual rights to notice of termination (see 5.2.108) and their statutory right to paid time off during their notice period to look for alternative work or be retrained (see 5.2.111). Many employees who are made redundant will also be entitled to a redundancy payment under their contract of employment, or under the statutory scheme, or both (see 5.2.114).

Lay-off and short time

5.2.7   Different legal considerations apply when an employer responds to a downturn in business by laying employees off or putting them on short-time working, rather than making them redundant. An important preliminary issue is whether the company has the right under the employees' contracts of employment to lay them off or reduce their hours and earnings (see 5.2.127). In addition, the company needs to be aware that employees who are not provided with work or have their hours reduced may be entitled to a guarantee payment or to claim a redundancy payment (see 5.2.132, 5.2.134).

Insolvency

5.2.8   Sometimes redundancies are due to a company going into liquidation. This chapter ends with a summary of the legal protection that is given to employees who have not received their redundancy payment or other sums that they are owed because their employer is insolvent (see 5.2.137).

Other aspects of reorganisation

5.2.9   The employment implications of other aspects of business reorganisations are covered elsewhere in this Guide. These include the legal issues that arise when changing contracts of employment (see Chapter 5.1) and the situation where a company transfers all or part of its business to another employer through the sale or contracting out of its operations (see Chapter 5.3).

5.2.10   The legal mechanics of how an employment contract ends and related issues such as the right to written reasons for dismissal are also covered elsewhere in this Guide (Chapter 4.1), as are the general principles of unfair dismissal law (see Chapter 4.2).

Company procedures on redundancy

5.2.11   Some companies have an established procedure on how redundancies should be handled, which may have been agreed with their recognised trade union(s). Having an established procedure can, however, limit a company's flexibility to deal with a redundancy situation in a way that meets its current business needs. As explained elsewhere in this Guide (see 1.2.17), a company's procedure can in some circumstances be part of an employee's terms and conditions of employment. If it is, the company may face breach of contract claims if it fails to follow it.

Legal status of procedure

5.2.12   Many aspects of a redundancy procedure are unlikely to be incorporated into individual employees' contracts because they deal with issues, such as collective consultation, that are not relevant to individuals' rights. There are some aspects of redundancy procedures, however, such as selection criteria and enhanced redundancy payments, that do relate to the rights of individuals and so may be capable of becoming part of individuals' contracts.

5.2.13   A redundancy procedure will not become part of employees' contracts simply because the company routinely follows it when making redundancies. Nevertheless, the fact that the company follows the procedure could be used as evidence that it considers itself legally bound to do so. In order to avoid any uncertainty about the legal status of the procedure, the company should make clear to the workforce when the procedure is first adopted whether any part of it is intended to be incorporated into employees' contractual terms and conditions.

5.2.14   If a company negotiates with a trade union, it may decide to agree a procedure for handling redundancies with the union. Before finalising any agreement, the company should decide whether it wants any part of the procedure to become part of individual employees' contractual terms. It should then check whether the wording of the collective agreement achieves the results it wants. If its employees' contracts already contain a term that incorporates collective agreements, it will also need to clarify whether and to what extent this particular agreement is covered by that term.

Failure to follow procedure

5.2.15   Whether or not a company's redundancy procedure is contractual, if it has informed its workforce about the procedure and then fails to follow it, it may face claims for unfair dismissal. This is particularly likely where the procedure has been agreed with a trade union. A company should therefore always ensure that it has good reason for departing from an established procedure, even if it is not contractual. If a company wishes to depart from a contractual procedure, it will need to change its employees' contractual terms. The legal issues that arise when changing contracts are covered in Chapter 5.1.

Defining redundancy

5.2.16　For the purposes of notifying the Department for Business, Innovations and Skills (BIS) and collective consultation with a recognised trade union or employee representatives, redundancy is defined broadly as dismissal for a reason or reasons not related to the individual concerned. For the purposes of individual statutory employment law such as entitlement to a redundancy payment and unfair dismissal, the legal definition of redundancy provides that redundancy can arise in several different ways. According to the Employment Rights Act 1996, an employee is dismissed for redundancy if his or her dismissal is wholly or mainly due to one of the circumstances described below.

Closing the business

5.2.17　An employee is redundant if he or she is dismissed because the employer has stopped, or plans to stop, running the business in which the employee was employed. This would cover a dismissal that was due to the winding up of an entire company; it would also apply to a dismissal that was due to the closure of one business within a company that ran several separate businesses.

Closing or relocating the workplace

5.2.18　An employee is redundant if he or she is dismissed because the employer has stopped, or plans to stop, running the business in the place where the employee was employed. This would cover an employee who was dismissed because the operation carried on at his or her workplace was closed. It would also cover a dismissal that was due to the employer relocating its operation from one site to another.

5.2.19　A company that closes one site may have the power to move employees to a different site, if there is a term in their contract allowing for this. If an employee refused to move, the company could deal with that as a disciplinary issue. If the employee were eventually dismissed, the reason for the dismissal would be misconduct, not redundancy.

5.2.20　An employer need not use a power to relocate an employee if it does not wish to do so. It can dismiss the employee instead. Provided the relocation or closure of the workplace is the real reason for the employee's dismissal, he or she is redundant. A company that took this route might find, however, that it faced a claim for unfair dismissal, on the basis that it was unreasonable not to offer the employee work at the other site before deciding to dismiss (see 5.2.98). In practice, therefore, the company would need to be able to show why it was reasonable not to offer the employee relocation.

'Work of a particular kind'

5.2.21　An employee is redundant if his or her dismissal is due to the fact that the business needs fewer employees to carry out 'work of a particular kind', or expects to do so. This applies whether the business needs fewer employees to do that work overall, or only in the place where the employee was employed. This type of redundancy would therefore cover the situation where work of a particular kind is transferred from one site to another, leading to redundancies at one site and recruitment at the other. (The company's power to ask employees to follow the work and the consequences if it does not do so are discussed above in the context of relocation (see 5.2.18).)

5.2.22　It does not matter whether the business's requirements for employees to do a particular kind of work have fallen permanently or temporarily. Indeed, a company may implement redundancies in one month because of a fall-off in business and find that it needs to recruit soon after because it has obtained a new customer. Provided the company made the dismissals because it genuinely believed at that time that it needed fewer employees, the dismissals were for redundancy. From a practical perspective, however, companies should avoid recruiting shortly after implementing redundancies whenever this is practical, in order to avoid the possibility of employees who were made redundant bringing unfair dismissal claims on the basis that they could not have been genuinely redundant.

The business decision

5.2.23   An employer does not need to justify why it has changed its requirements for employees. It is free to set its requirements as it sees fit, to meet the demands of the business. A company is entitled to conclude, for example, that it needs to reduce headcount in order to meet cost targets, even though the volume of work to be done has not fallen. Or the company may decide that it wants to have certain jobs done by an external contractor rather than by its employees.

5.2.24   There are two points worth noting in relation to this latter example. If a company decides to contract out a part of its operation, that may be a transfer covered by the Transfer of Undertakings (Protection of Employment) Regulations 2006. If it is, the employees involved in that part of the business should be transferred to the contractor, rather than being dismissed for redundancy (see 5.3.33). The second point relates to tax. If a company dismisses an employee for redundancy and offers the same individual re-employment on a self-employed basis, the Revenue may question whether the individual is genuinely self-employed. This type of arrangement may also prejudice the tax exemption that would normally apply to the employee's redundancy payment (see 5.2.123), since the Revenue may take the view that the payment was not genuinely due to redundancy.

Bumped redundancies

5.2.25   An employee may be redundant if his or her dismissal was due to the fact that the company required fewer employees to carry out work of any particular kind, even if not the particular kind of work that the employee did. This explains how an employee can be 'bumped' into redundancy: the employee is dismissed to make way for another employee, who does work that the company no longer requires but whom the company wishes to retain. Bumped redundancies can arise on a voluntary basis, where a company invites volunteers for redundancy from all parts of the business and moves the employees whose work is no longer needed into the vacancies that are created.

5.2.26   Because the employees who are being dismissed are not the ones doing the work that is no longer needed, compulsory bumped redundancies are often perceived by the workforce as unfair. Companies that are considering implementing bumped redundancies may therefore wish to contact us for advice.

'Fake' redundancies

5.2.27   It is not uncommon for employees whose work performance is poor or who are unable to get on with their colleagues or manager to be 'made redundant'. Using this approach has practical advantages for both employer and employee, since it means that the employee leaves the organisation without having to be taken through any disciplinary or performance management procedure and without any blame attached. From a legal perspective, however, it is unhelpful. If the employee later claims that his or her dismissal was unfair, it will be up to the company to establish the reason for the dismissal. Since the reason was not in fact redundancy, it will become apparent that the company did not adopt the appropriate procedure for dealing with the case fairly.

5.2.28   A company that is considering dismissing an employee as redundant in these circumstances may wish to contact us for advice.

Job restructuring

5.2.29   In the context of a business reorganisation or restructuring, a company may need to change the terms on which employees work. If the changes affect job content, it may be necessary to examine how substantial those changes are, in order to decide whether the definition of redundancy applies.

5.2.30   If, for example, a company decides to restructure 10 jobs within a department so that the content of the job changes substantially, it may in fact be deciding that it needs 10 fewer employees to do work of one 'particular kind' and 10 more employees to do work of a different 'particular kind'. If any of the existing 10 employees is not offered, or chooses not to accept, the new job, he or she is dismissed for redundancy and may be entitled to a redundancy payment. (As explained in 5.2.105, if the employee was offered the new job and it amounted to suitable alternative employment, the employee could lose the right to a redundancy payment if he or she unreasonably refused it.) If, on the other hand, the new jobs are not sufficiently different to amount to work of a different 'particular kind', then an existing employee who rejects or is not offered the new job is dismissed for a reason connected with the business reorganisation rather than redundancy. This means that they are not entitled to a redundancy payment.

5.2.31 Regrettably, neither the legislation nor the previous decisions of the appeal courts or tribunals gives any useful guidance on how much a job must change before it becomes work of a different 'particular kind'. Companies that are altering job content but are unclear as to whether redundancy payments may be due should contact us for advice. For the purposes of unfair dismissal law, a company that follows the procedure suggested below when restructuring jobs is likely to be able to show that it has acted reasonably if dismissals prove necessary, whether the situation falls within the definition of redundancy or not.

Considering alternatives

5.2.32 Redundancies are not only traumatic for the employees who lose their job but can also be disruptive and demotivating for the employees who remain. It is therefore clearly good business practice and good industrial relations practice for employers to avoid redundancies whenever they can. It is also advisable from a legal perspective. An employer that dismisses employees for redundancy without first consulting with its employee representatives on whether there might be alternatives may face a legal claim (see 5.2.37).

5.2.33 It is therefore important for a company to explore whether the development that has led it to consider redundancies could be addressed in some other way. If the challenge is to cut labour costs, for example, the company might be able to achieve savings by negotiating reductions in wages or other benefits with its recognised trade union or with the workforce. It might also be possible to make savings by restricting recruitment, reducing the use of agency staff and external contractors or cutting overtime working.

Temporary employees

5.2.34 If a company is considering reducing its use of temporary employees as an alternative to making permanent employees redundant, it needs to bear three legal considerations in mind. The first is that temporary employees may qualify for protection from unfair dismissal and the right to receive a redundancy payment, if they have the appropriate length of service. The company is therefore under the same obligations to act reasonably in dismissing them for redundancy as it is in relation to the permanent workforce. For employees on fixed-term contracts, this applies whether they are dismissed mid-contract or their contracts are not renewed (see 4.2.13).

5.2.35   The second consideration is that it is unlawful for an employer to treat fixed-term employees less favourably than permanent employees unless it has objective justification for doing so (see 1.2.89), meaning that a company will need to be in a position to justify a decision to make fixed-term contract employees redundant before permanent employees. The government guidance on the Regulations (see 9.1.2) suggests that where fixed-term employees have been brought in specifically to complete particular tasks or to cover for a peak in demand, the employer is likely to be justified in making them redundant at the end of their contracts.

5.2.36   The third legal consideration relates to discrimination and arises for instance where a much larger proportion of the company's temporary employees than of its permanent employees are of a particular sex or racial group. In those circumstances, it may amount to indirect sex or race discrimination to make the temporary employees redundant first, unless the company can objectively justify its strategy on the basis of a real business need. Companies can obtain advice on this issue from us.

Warning and consultation

5.2.37   Both as a matter of good industrial relations practice and in order to avoid possible liability for unfair dismissal, an employer that is contemplating redundancies should give its workforce as much warning as possible that jobs may be lost.

5.2.38   The company should also consult with the employees who may be affected by the proposed redundancies about the reasons for the proposals and how the company intends to implement them. This could be done either directly with the employees or with their representatives. (Collective consultation is discussed in 5.2.42.) Care should be taken to ensure that employees who are on maternity leave or long-term sick leave are also warned and consulted about the proposals. A failure to do so could lead to claims of sex or disability discrimination as well as unfair dismissal.

Meaning of 'consultation'

5.2.39   This section makes frequent reference to the need for companies to consult when implementing redundancies. It is therefore worth noting how the courts and tribunals that enforce employment law interpret the meaning of consultation. They assume that, in order to consult meaningfully on a proposal, an employer must:

- enter into the consultation process with an open mind on whether its proposal might need to be revised;

- provide clear information on what is being proposed and why;

- give employees adequate time to consider that information and to prepare their response;

- give proper consideration to employees' responses, and take them into account in finalising the proposal;

- undertake the consultation with a view to reaching agreement.

5.2.40   Consultation is therefore a two-way process, involving a considered exchange of views between employer and workforce, rather than a one-way process of informing the workforce of what is going to happen.

5.2.41   Because consultation and warning are central to fair redundancy dismissals, a company that fails to consult and warn is very likely to find itself liable for unfair dismissal. The company must at the very least inform the employee about the grounds on which the company is considering making him or her redundant and hold a meeting to discuss it.

Collective consultation

5.2.42   If a company recognises a trade union, then it should consult with the union about any proposed redundancies, however small the number, both as a matter of good industrial relations practice and in order to avoid liability for unfair dismissal. There may be an existing collective agreement between the company and the union setting out how the consultation process should be conducted, and how disputes over the implementation of redundancies should be resolved. Some companies may, for example, observe the engineering industry's national agreements for the avoidance of disputes in relation to manual workers and staff grades. Where the company does not recognise a trade union but does have some other means of consulting its workforce collectively, such as a works council or staff committee, it could use those channels for consultation.

5.2.43 If a company is planning large-scale redundancies, then the Trade Union and Labour Relations (Consolidation) Act 1992 imposes a specific duty on the company to consult on its proposals with either its recognised trade union or with employee representatives. Where an employer is proposing collective redundancies of 20 or more employees at the same establishment over a period of 90 days or less, then the employer should consult any appropriate trade union or other employee representatives. The employer should consult 'in good time' and at least 30 days in advance of the first dismissals. In the case of larger scale redundancies of 100 or more employees at the same establishment within 90 days then the employer must begin consultation 'in good time' and at least 90 days before the first of the dismissals. The circumstances in which this duty applies are broadly defined, to cover any situation where a company is proposing to dismiss employees for a reason that does not relate to the particular individuals concerned. It would therefore cover not only redundancy proposals but also proposals to terminate employees' existing contracts in order to introduce new terms and conditions of employment (see 5.1.45).

Less than 20 redundancies

5.2.44 This specific obligation to consult is triggered if the company is proposing to dismiss 20 or more employees at any one establishment within a period of 90 days or less. When calculating the number of employees affected by the proposal, no account need be taken of employees with fixed-term contracts of three months or less or recruited to do a specific task that is not expected to last more than three months, unless in either case the employees have in fact been employed for more than three months. It should be stressed that even if the specific obligation to consult under the 1992 Act does not apply because, for example, only 19 redundancies are proposed, it is still advisable for a company to consult with any recognised trade union or any other existing employee representatives. This would be both as a matter of good industrial relations practice and in order to avoid liability for unfair dismissal.

Definition of 'establishment'

5.2.45 Unfortunately, in setting a threshold of 20 or more employees at one establishment, the legislation does not define what 'establishment' means. In most cases, it may be synonymous with 'workplace' or local employment unit as opposed to whole of the enterprise or undertaking, but in other cases it may not. For example, where several sites are closely linked by administration and management structures, they may all count as one establishment, and the proposed redundancies at all the sites will need to be aggregated to establish whether this specific obligation to consult applies.

Who is the consultation with?

5.2.46 As a matter of good employment practice and in order to fulfil any specific legal obligation to consult on large-scale redundancies, a company should consult with all the employees who may be affected by the proposed redundancies. This includes not only those who may be dismissed but also those who may be required to move or to take on different or additional work because of the redundancies.

5.2.47 Where the specific obligation to consult applies, if the employees who are affected are covered by collective bargaining, the company must consult with the trade union's representatives. If the affected employees are not covered by collective bargaining, the company has two options:

1. To consult representatives that the employees have already appointed or elected for some purpose not specifically related to redundancies. The company can take up this option only if it is clear from the context in which the representatives were appointed or elected that they have authority to be consulted about redundancies on the employees' behalf. For example, someone appointed to a committee to organise social events is unlikely to have the relevant authority, but someone appointed to a staff committee or a works council set up to discuss major issues affecting the business may have.

2. The other option is for the company to consult with representatives who have been expressly elected by the affected employees for the purpose of consultation on redundancies. If the company takes this route, it will need to build time for the holding of the election into its timetable for implementing the redundancies. The company must also ensure that the election meets the requirements set down in the legislation. For example, there must be sufficient representatives to represent the interests of all the affected employees, who must also be entitled to vote. If no candidate comes forward for election within a reasonable period, then the company must provide each affected employee with the information about redundancies that it would have given to their elected representatives (see 5.2.52).

5.2.48　Further details on holding elections for employee representatives are given in 6.4.55. Companies can also obtain guidance on holding elections for employee representatives by contacting us.

Timing of consultation

5.2.49　Consultation needs to begin early enough for the input of employees or their representatives to be capable of affecting the result. The specific duty to consult on large-scale redundancies requires consultation to begin 'in good time'. It also lays down minimum consultation periods. If the company is proposing to dismiss 100 or more employees as redundant at one establishment within 90 days or less, then consultation must begin at least 90 days before the first of the dismissals takes effect. If the proposal by the employer is for 20 to 99 dismissals at one establishment within 90 days or less, then consultation must begin at least 30 days before the first of the dismissals takes effect. The consultation period will only begin to run once the employer has supplied in writing the required information to the appropriate representatives. If the company has invited employees to elect representatives early enough for it to meet the 30- or 90-day period but the election is not held promptly, it is sufficient if the company consults as soon as is reasonably practicable after the election has taken place.

5.2.50　Employees who are at risk of redundancy may decide to leave during the 30- or 90-day consultation period, perhaps because they find alternative employment. This may mean that the company has failed to respect the consultation period, and so it is advisable for the company to discuss the possibility of early leavers with the union's officials or employee representatives.

Content of the consultation

5.2.51   If the specific duty to consult on large-scale redundancies applies, the employer must provide certain information to the employee representatives, ensure that certain issues are covered in the consultation process and approach the consultation with the aim of reaching agreement. Companies that are proposing smaller-scale redundancies might find these requirements a useful starting point when planning their own consultation with employees or their representatives.

5.2.52   Where the specific duty to consult applies, the company must give the appropriate representatives the following information, in writing:

Required information

1. The reasons for the proposals.
2. The numbers and descriptions of the employees the company proposes to dismiss.
3. The total number of employees of that description employed at the establishment in question.
4. The way in which the company proposes to select the employees who are to be made redundant.
5. The proposed method and timing of the dismissals (covering, for example, whether the company intends to dismiss with notice or with a payment in lieu).
6. The proposed method of calculating redundancy payments, if the company intends to improve upon the payments provided for in the statutory scheme.
7. A copy of the form the company has sent to the Department for Business, Innovation and Skills, notifying it of the proposed redundancies (Form HR1) (see 5.2.60).

5.2.53   In its consultations, the company must discuss with the representatives possible ways of avoiding the dismissals altogether or of reducing the numbers to be dismissed. In the circumstances of the closure of a workplace, this duty is to be construed as an obligation to consult about the reasons for the closure. It must also discuss whether there is any way of minimising the impact of the dismissals. This could cover, for example, whether the company is able to offer employees career counselling or retraining. Although the legislation does not expressly require this, the company should consult on the specific issues contained in the information it has supplied to the employee representatives, such as redundancy selection criteria. This would also ensure that the company was acting reasonably for the purposes of unfair dismissal law.

Access to employees

5.2.54   During consultation on large-scale redundancies, the company must allow the representatives access to the affected employees, and give them whatever other reasonable facilities and accommodation may be appropriate to enable them to carry out their role effectively. Depending on the size and resources of the company, this might include, for example, the use of a telephone, photocopier and word processor.

Aim of reaching agreement

5.2.55   There is no obligation on the company to obtain the representatives' agreement to its proposals. Nevertheless, if large-scale redundancies are proposed, the company must enter into the process with the aim of reaching agreement with them. It is, therefore, advisable for the company to keep a record of the meetings that have been held and the content of the discussions, and to ensure that no announcements are made that indicate that an irreversible decision to implement the redundancies has already been made before the end of consultation.

Redundancy notice

5.2.56   Notices dismissing employees for redundancy should not be sent out until the consultation has been completed. In the case of large-scale redundancies, this could be earlier than the 30- or 90-day period set down by the legislation, provided agreement has been reached on the company's proposals or it is clear that no further meaningful discussion is likely. It is possible that employees who are at risk of redundancy will leave before the consultation period has ended, by obtaining another job. It would be advisable to discuss the possibility of early leavers with the employee representatives.

Special circumstances

5.2.57 If there are special circumstances that make it not reasonably practicable for a company to comply with its specific duty to consult on large-scale redundancies, it must still do what it can to comply. For example, if the redundancies have been precipitated by the unexpected and sudden loss of its only customer, the company may not be able to consult for the usual 30- or 90-day minimum period. However, it may still be possible for the company to keep the employee representatives informed about the situation and hold an emergency meeting to obtain their views. The fact that the decision that gave rise to the redundancies was made by the employer's parent company, which failed to pass that information on to the employer, does not amount to special circumstances justifying a failure to consult.

Rights of employee representatives

5.2.58 The representatives involved in collective consultation on large-scale redundancies are entitled to reasonable paid time off during working hours in order to perform their functions and to undergo relevant training. Employees are also entitled to reasonable paid time off to stand for election as representatives.

Protection from detriment and dismissal

5.2.59 It is unlawful for a company to treat an employee unfavourably, dismiss an employee or select an employee for redundancy on the grounds that the employee has carried out his or her role as a representative. This protection also extends to employees who stand as candidates for election or participate in an election. It applies regardless of the employee's age or length of service with the company.

Notifying BIS

5.2.60 If a company is proposing to dismiss 20 or more employees within a period of 90 days at one establishment, it has a duty to give the Department for Business, Innovation and Skills certain basic information about its proposals. The Department provides a standard form for this purpose, form HR1 (see 9.5.2) which should be used.

5.2.61 The obligation to notify applies whenever an employer is proposing to dismiss 20 or more employees for a reason that is unrelated to the individuals concerned. An employer would therefore need to notify the Department if it was, for example, considering dismissing employees in order to introduce new terms and conditions of employment.

5.2.62 The company must provide the appropriate employee representatives with a copy of the completed form HR1.

Timing of notification

5.2.63 If 100 or more redundancies are proposed, a completed form HR1 must be filed by the employer before giving notice to terminate employees on grounds of redundancy and at least 90 days in advance of the date when the first of those dismissals takes effect. If 20 to 99 redundancies are involved, form HR1 must be filed before giving notice to terminate employees on grounds of redundancy and at least 30 days in advance of the date when the first of those dismissals takes effect.

Volunteers and early retirement

5.2.64 In order to act reasonably for the purposes of unfair dismissal law, an employer should consider whether it could achieve the redundancies it needs by inviting volunteers for redundancy, unless there are good reasons for not doing so.

Criteria for acceptance

5.2.65 Before asking for volunteers, however, a company needs to bear in mind that it may receive applications from employees whom it does not want to lose, and that the number of volunteers may exceed the number of redundancies needed, particularly if attractive financial terms are on offer. Employees who apply for redundancy but are not accepted may conclude that they have been treated unfairly and so become demotivated. It is therefore advisable for the company to clarify in advance the criteria that it will be using to decide whether an application for redundancy will be accepted, and to ensure that employees are aware both of those criteria and of the fact that they are not guaranteed to be made redundant if they volunteer.

5.2.66 An employee who volunteers for redundancy is not resigning: he or she is volunteering to be dismissed. Although he or she is unlikely to do so, a volunteer could theoretically claim unfair dismissal. A company should therefore ensure that, before volunteers are dismissed, the employees are aware of the options available to them and are sure that they want to volunteer.

Early retirement

5.2.67 An employer may be in a position to offer employees who volunteer for redundancy an early retirement option that includes enhanced pension benefits. Depending on the circumstances, an employee who opts for early retirement may be terminating his or her contract by agreement with the company, rather than being dismissed. This means that he or she is not entitled to a redundancy payment under the statutory scheme or to claim unfair dismissal. In practice, however, the financial package that the employee is offered is likely to take account of the value of the statutory redundancy payment.

5.2.68 Because of the uncertainty that can surround whether an employee is genuinely agreeing to a mutual termination of his or her contract, it would be advisable for a company to treat an employee who is opting for early retirement as if he or she was being dismissed for redundancy. The company should follow its own redundancy procedure and consult with the employee fully about the redundancy and his or her options, in order to be in a position to show that it has acted reasonably should the employee later bring an unfair dismissal claim.

Identifying the pool for selection

5.2.69   Depending on the reason for the redundancies, it may be clear that all employees doing a particular job or working in a particular location need to be made redundant. In other cases, however, the company may need to identify the section of the workforce from which the redundancies are to be made, sometimes referred to as the 'redundancy selection pool', and then choose individuals from within that pool for dismissal. The pool is one of the issues that should be covered in the consultations an employer has with employee representatives.

Defining the pool

5.2.70   Under unfair dismissal law, an employer has a large degree of discretion in how it defines the pool, provided it acts reasonably and there is a clear business rationale for the pool it chooses. Unfair dismissal claims are most likely to arise if the pool is drawn too narrowly. Take, for example, a company that needs to contain or reduce the labour costs for Department A. It decides that this can best be achieved by shedding administrative staff. It has employees doing similar types of administrative work in Department A and in Department B. It may be reasonable for the company to include administrative staff in both departments in the selection pool, rather than limit the pool to Department A alone. This is particularly true where Department A has employees with substantially more service than those in Department B. We can provide advice on identifying an appropriate selection pool.

Indirect discrimination

5.2.71   It is also important to avoid defining the redundancy selection pool in a way that involves indirect discrimination. Indirect discrimination is discussed elsewhere in this Guide (see 3.1.37). In summary, it makes it unlawful for employers to adopt practices that work to the particular disadvantage of people of a particular sex, race, age, religion or sexual orientation, unless they can show a clear business need for the practice. For example, if a company decided to make redundancies from among staff on temporary contracts only, and a larger proportion of its temporary employees than its permanent employees were women, it would need to consider whether it was justified in limiting the pool in that way. Limiting the redundancy selection pool to fixed-term employees only would also be in breach of the Regulations on fixed-term work, unless the use of that pool could be objectively justified (see 1.2.89). Companies can obtain advice on the issue of justification from us.

Choosing the selection criteria

5.2.72 An employer has a large degree of discretion in the criteria it adopts to select the individuals who are to be made redundant. In order to meet the requirements of unfair dismissal law, an employer need only ensure that the criteria it uses are reasonable and, as far as possible, capable of objective measurement, and that it consults about them with its appropriate employee representatives.

5.2.73 Criteria that are commonly used include length of service, attendance record, job performance, adaptability and disciplinary record. Many employers now use matrices for redundancy selection, scoring employees against several factors. However, if you use length of service as the selection criterion you risk unlawfully discriminating on grounds of age, unless you can justify doing so. It may be easier to meet the test of justification, therefore avoiding unlawful discrimination, where length of service is used as only one of several factors. Companies can obtain advice on appropriate selection criteria from us.

Redundancy procedures

5.2.74 A company may already have a redundancy procedure or a redundancy agreement with its recognised trade union that lays down certain selection criteria. If that part of the procedure or agreement has been incorporated into employees' contracts of employment and the company decides to use different criteria, the company could face breach of contract claims from individuals who would not have been selected for redundancy had the original criteria been used. Even if the criteria are not contractual, a company could face unfair dismissal claims if it departed from them without good reason for doing so. A company that is considering departing from an established selection procedure should therefore contact us for advice.

Inadmissible criteria

5.2.75   It is important to note that it is automatically unfair to select an employee for redundancy for certain inadmissible reasons, regardless of the employee's age or length of service. These reasons are listed in full in 4.2.32. One of the inadmissible reasons, for example, is pregnancy and maternity. It would be automatically unfair to select an employee for redundancy on the basis of her poor attendance record, if she would not have been selected had she not been absent on pregnancy-related sick leave or maternity leave. Pregnancy- and maternity-related absences should therefore not be taken into account in scoring absence in a redundancy selection matrix.

Avoiding discrimination

5.2.76   Before finalising its selection criteria, a company should ensure that they are not discriminatory. Selection criteria that discriminate directly or indirectly on the grounds of sex, race, age, religion or sexual orientation are unlawful. If an employee was selected for dismissal for reasons relating to her pregnancy, for example, she could claim direct sex discrimination as well as unfair dismissal. (Avoiding discrimination against disabled employees is discussed separately in 5.2.89.)

Indirect discrimination

5.2.77   Employers are unlikely to choose selection criteria that are directly based on sex, race, age, religion or sexual orientation; indirect discrimination is the greater danger. The concept of indirect discrimination is explained elsewhere in this Guide (see 3.1.37). In essence, it means that a company must be able objectively to justify the use of a selection criterion that puts people of a particular age, sex, race, religion or sexual orientation at a particular disadvantage. For example, using a criterion such as ability to be flexible in hours or place of work is likely to work to the disadvantage of more women in the workforce than men. The company would therefore need to show why it had a business need to retain employees with that degree of flexibility. Using 'last in, first out' might also have a disproportionate impact on women, if the jobs that are being cut have traditionally been seen as 'men's jobs' and the company has recently been successful in attracting women into them.

Likewise, a length of service criterion would be likely to have a bigger adverse impact on younger employees than older employees. If it had this impact, then it would need to be justified, and this is possible where the length of service criterion is part of a redundancy selection criteria agreement with a trade union.

Part-time and fixed-term employees

5.2.78   A company that decides to select part-timers for redundancy before full-timers will need to be in a position objectively to justify its decision. Unjustified discrimination against part-timers is not only likely to be indirect discrimination against women but is also expressly outlawed by the Part-time Workers (Prevention of Less Favourable Treatment) Regulations 2000 (see 2.3.85). Likewise, the Regulations on fixed-term work make it unlawful to select fixed-term employees for redundancy before permanent employees because of their fixed-term status, unless the employer can objectively justify this (see 1.2.89). The government guidance on the Regulations (see 9.1.2) suggests that where fixed-term employees have been brought in specifically to complete particular tasks or to cover for a peak in demand, the employer is likely to be justified in selecting them for redundancy, if this happens at the end of their contracts.

Inviting applications

5.2.79   In some circumstances, a company may wish to invite all the employees who are within the redundancy selection pool to apply for the jobs that will remain. If the company adopts this approach, it should bear in mind that the employees who do not apply, or who apply but are not successful, will effectively have been selected for redundancy. It must therefore be confident that it will be able to demonstrate that it has acted reasonably in selecting those employees.

Job restructuring

5.2.80   Redundancies can arise where a company decides to cut jobs involving work of one particular kind and create new jobs doing work of a different particular kind, as discussed above (see 5.2.21). In these circumstances, the company is effectively making all the employees in the old jobs redundant, and so it is, in theory, free to fill the new posts as it sees fit. It may decide, for example, to fill the new posts by inviting employees in the old jobs to apply for the new posts, or by external recruitment.

In practice, however, if the company does not offer the new posts to the employees who are being made redundant from the old jobs, it is likely to face claims for unfair dismissal. These can be made on the basis that it would have been reasonable to consider those employees for alternative employment before deciding to dismiss them (see 5.2.95). Therefore, if the company decides not to offer the new jobs to the existing employees, it should be prepared to show why the individuals were not considered suitable for the new posts.

Applying the selection criteria

5.2.81 In order to avoid liability for unfair dismissal and unlawful discrimination, an employer that is implementing redundancies must not only adopt fair selection criteria, it must also apply those criteria objectively. This makes it advisable for a company to ensure that it has documented evidence of the way in which employees were assessed against the criteria it used. It would also be advisable for managers who are involved in the assessment to be given training or guidance on the meaning of the selection criteria and how to assess employees objectively against them.

5.2.82 Any documentary evidence used in redundancy selection – such as attendance, appraisal and disciplinary records – needs to be accurate and up to date. This is necessary not only to ensure that any selection based on this information is fair, but also to meet the requirements of the Data Protection Act 1998 (see Appendix 8.3). Data protection principles require that employees should have been told in advance that this personal information might be used for redundancy selection purposes.

5.2.83 It is also advisable to bear in mind that if an employee is selected for redundancy on the basis of poor performance or an unsatisfactory attendance record but has never previously been told that he or she is not meeting the required standards, this could lead to an unfair dismissal claim.

5.2.84 Where resources permit, companies should monitor the results of the redundancy selection process, to ensure that it is being carried out objectively and that there is no evidence of bias on the grounds prohibited by the discrimination legislation. If several managers are involved in applying selection criteria, monitoring also enables the company to identify and address any inconsistencies of approach, which might otherwise lead to unfair dismissal claims.

Consultation

5.2.85   Once an individual employee has been provisionally selected for redundancy, the company should consult with him or her about the provisional selection (or, as it is sometimes known, of being 'at risk' of redundancy dismissal) before deciding whether to confirm the selection decision. This is not only a matter of good employment practice but is also essential to avoid liability for unfair dismissal.

5.2.86   It would be good practice for a manager to hold a preliminary meeting with the employee to break the news that he or she has been provisionally selected for redundancy. Whether or not a preliminary meeting is held, the employer should write to the employee confirming that the company has provisionally selected him or her for redundancy and the basis for the selection, and invite the employee to a meeting to discuss the situation. It is good practice to allow the employee to be accompanied at that meeting. The employer must notify the employee of the result of the meeting and his or her right to appeal if the provisional selection for redundancy is confirmed.

5.2.87   Consultation gives the employee an opportunity to raise any issues that may be relevant to the selection decision. It may be, for example, that the employee has been selected for redundancy because of his or her poor work performance. The employee may be able to bring to the company's attention events in his or her personal life or in his or her working relationships that explain the poor performance and may cause the company to reassess the selection decision. This is also an opportunity to discuss with the employee whether he or she is interested in being redeployed within the business or in an associated company, what work would be suitable, and what vacancies might be available.

5.2.88   It is advisable to keep a record of the content of consultation meetings.

Disabled employees

5.2.89   The Disability Discrimination Act 1995 makes it unlawful for a company to select a disabled employee for redundancy on the ground of his or her disability. The Act also puts employers under a duty to make reasonable adjustments to accommodate disabled employees (see 3.1.69).

5.2.90   A company may therefore need to consider whether it should make any adjustments to the way in which it applies selection criteria to disabled employees. The disability Code of Practice states, for example, that it is likely to be reasonable to discount disability-related sickness absence when applying a selection criterion related to attendance.

5.2.91   Even after the company has made reasonable adjustments to the way in which it applies its selection criteria, it may still end up selecting a disabled employee for redundancy for a reason that is linked to his or her disability. If this happens, the employer will not be acting unlawfully, provided it can justify its decision on relevant and substantial grounds (3.1.66).

Appeals

5.2.92   In redundancy exercises, whether large or small, employees should be offered the right to appeal against their selection for redundancy. This is not only to show that the dismissals have been handled fairly but also it will give the company a final opportunity to review the process, including selection where relevant, and to correct any mistakes that have been made. Whenever possible, the appeal should be conducted by someone not involved in the original process and, as a matter of good practice, the employer should allow the employee to be accompanied at the appeal hearing by a work colleague or union representative if he or she wishes to be.

5.2.93   The EEF national procedural agreements for the avoidance of disputes provide that employees who are dismissed can contest their dismissal, if necessary through an external conference, and remain employees until agreement is reached or the procedure is exhausted or their notice of dismissal expires, whichever comes last. Those companies that observe these national agreements may wish to consider whether this should be the only procedure for appealing against redundancy, or whether a separate avenue of appeal should also be provided.

Disclosure of others' scores

5.2.94 An employer is not under any general obligation to let an employee see the scorings of other employees who were not selected for redundancy. Indeed, disclosing that information without those individuals' consent would breach the company's duty to maintain the confidentiality of their personal information and would also be contrary to the principles of the Data Protection Act 1998 (see Appendix 8.3). If, however, an employee makes a specific allegation of unfairness in the way in which he or she was scored compared with colleagues, the company may need to consider whether it is possible to address the allegation by disclosing the scorings without revealing the identities of the employees.

Considering alternative employment

5.2.95 As a matter of good employment practice and in order to avoid liability for unfair dismissal, a company should not dismiss an employee for redundancy until it has explored whether the employee could be redeployed. If the company belongs to a corporate group, the possibility of employment with another company in the group should be explored.

5.2.96 When looking for alternative jobs, the company need consider only work that the employee is capable of doing, or would be capable of doing with whatever training and support the company might reasonably be expected to provide. If the employee is disabled, the company will also be under a duty under the Disability Discrimination Act 1995 to consider whether any jobs that seem unsuitable for the employee because of his or her disability could be made suitable through reasonable adjustments (see 3.1.69). When considering redeployment of potentially redundant employees, the company should bear in mind that, under the Regulations on fixed-term work, fixed-term employees must be given the same opportunity to obtain permanent work in the company as permanent employees, unless treating them differently can be objectively justified (see 1.2.89). The government guidance on the Regulations (see 9.1.2) suggests that it may be justifiable not to give fixed-term employees the same support in finding alternative work when their contract expires, if they knew when they were recruited that their employment would last only as long as their contract.

Available work

5.2.97 Possible alternative work should not be discounted because it demands less skill and experience than the employee has. If that is the only work that is available, then it should be offered to the employee, leaving him or her to decide whether to accept it.

5.2.98 Efforts to find alternative work for an employee should continue until his or her contract ends. If an employee is dismissed with notice, the company should monitor the situation during the notice period, to ensure that he or she is considered for any vacancies that arise during that time.

Refusal of alternative work

5.2.99 When a company is discussing suitable alternative work with an employee, it would be good practice to explain to him or her the legal repercussions of accepting or rejecting any job that is offered. As explained further below, an employee can work for a trial period in such a job without prejudicing his or her right to a redundancy payment, but may lose the right to a payment if he or she unreasonably refuses the offer (see 5.2.105).

Employees on maternity or adoption leave

5.2.100 An employee who is on maternity or adoption leave at the time he or she is made redundant is entitled to be offered any suitable alternative employment that is available. The legislation does not define what 'suitable' means. It can be safely assumed, however, that the closer the alternative work is to the employee's current job, in its content and level of skill required, terms and conditions, and status, the more likely it is to be suitable.

5.2.101 If an employee on maternity or adoption leave is made redundant without being offered a vacancy that was suitable for the employee and available at the time, his or her dismissal is automatically unfair. This means in effect that employees on maternity or adoption leave have first refusal on any vacancies that are suitable for them. If they unreasonably refuse the offer of suitable alternative work, however, they lose the right to a redundancy payment, as explained in 5.2.105.

Trying the new job

5.2.102   In order for the company and the employee to have an opportunity to decide whether an alternative job is suitable, the employee is entitled to a trial period of four weeks in the new job. The company and employee can agree a longer trial period if the employee needs to be retrained, although this agreement should be confirmed in writing. If the employee resigns during the trial period for any reason, or the company dismisses the employee during the trial period for a reason connected with the change in job, the employee is still viewed as dismissed for redundancy. The employee therefore does not lose any right to a redundancy payment that he or she may have. If, on the other hand, the employee resigns unreasonably during the trial period, he or she is not entitled to a redundancy payment. Whether or not it was reasonable for the employee to resign will depend on all the surrounding circumstances, including the employee's personal situation.

Extending the trial period

5.2.103   The four-week trial period provided for in the statutory redundancy payment scheme may well not be long enough for the company properly to assess whether the employee is suitable for the new job, and for the employee to decide whether he or she wants it. The company may therefore decide to agree a longer trial period with the employee. If it does so, it would be advisable to confirm the terms of the agreement in writing, since the employee's right to a redundancy payment then depends on the terms of the agreement rather than on the statutory redundancy payment scheme.

Unfair dismissal

5.2.104   Employees who work on in their new job beyond the end of their trial period are no longer entitled to a redundancy payment as a result of their dismissal from their original job. They can, however, still bring an unfair dismissal claim if the company acted unreasonably when making them redundant. They are also entitled to claim unfair dismissal if the company acts unreasonably in dismissing them from their new jobs, whether during their trial period or later. A company that has given an employee alternative work should therefore ensure that it acts reasonably and, where relevant, follows the ACAS Code of Practice on discipline and grievance if the employee proves to be unsuitable for the new post. Before deciding to dismiss, it should make the employee aware of his or her shortcomings, give him or her the opportunity to improve, and provide appropriate support and training. (The management of performance is discussed in Chapter 3.2 of this Guide.)

Unreasonably refusing alternative work

5.2.105   In certain narrowly defined circumstances, an employee who refuses an offer of alternative employment from his or her employer may lose the right to a redundancy payment. This applies only where the offer of alternative work is made before the employee's original contract ends, the new contract is to begin within four weeks of the original contract ending, and the work is suitable for the employee. The legislation does not define what makes alternative work 'suitable', but the closer the work is to the employee's current job, in its content and level of skill required, terms and conditions, and status, the more likely it is to be suitable.

5.2.106   If these conditions are met, then the employee has no right to a redundancy payment if he or she unreasonably refuses the offer. Whether an employee is reasonable to refuse an offer depends on the employee's individual circumstances. There may be personal reasons, such as caring commitments, that make it reasonable for an employee to refuse an offer of work that otherwise would appear to be suitable.

Offers from associated employers

5.2.107   The rules discussed above on trial periods in alternative employment and refusing suitable alternative work apply whether the job on offer is with the employee's original employer or with an associated employer. Two employers are associated if one is a company over which the other has direct or indirect control, or both are companies over which a third company has direct or indirect control. The rules therefore apply to an offer of work with a company within the same group of companies as the original employer.

Terminating employment

5.2.108 If an employee's provisional selection for redundancy is confirmed after the process of consultation is completed and he or she is to be dismissed, the company will need to ensure that it gives the employee the notice of termination to which he or she is entitled (see 4.1.12). If the company would prefer the employee not to attend work during the notice period, it may be in a position to ask him or her to take garden leave. Alternatively, it may decide to bring the employee's contract to an end immediately and make a payment in lieu of notice. (Garden leave and payments in lieu of notice are discussed in 4.1.32 and 4.1.27.)

Early leavers

5.2.109 An employee who is told that redundancies are likely or who has been provisionally selected for redundancy may well decide to resign before being given formal notice of dismissal, perhaps because he or she has found a job elsewhere. As the employee has resigned, he or she is not entitled to a statutory redundancy payment or to claim unfair dismissal.

5.2.110 If, on the other hand, the employee resigns after being given notice of dismissal, he or she is still viewed for unfair dismissal purposes as having been dismissed for redundancy. So the employee can still claim unfair dismissal if the company has acted unreasonably in dismissing him or her. An employee who resigns after being given notice of dismissal may also be entitled to a redundancy payment. The company can, however, write to the employee asking him or her to work until the end of the notice period given by the company, and can refuse to make the employee a redundancy payment if he or she does not do so. If the employee is refused a payment in these circumstances, he or she can apply to an employment tribunal, which will decide whether the company should pay the whole or part of the payment, according to what it considers to be fair in the circumstances.

Time off during notice period

5.2.111 An employee with two years' service who has been given notice of dismissal for redundancy is entitled under the Employment Rights Act 1996 to a reasonable amount of paid time off during working hours, in order to look for work or arrange training.

'Reasonable' time off

5.2.112   The legislation does not define what is meant by a 'reasonable' amount of time off. There is a limit, however, on the amount of time for which the company has to pay the employee, which is 40 per cent of the employee's weekly pay. Therefore, an employee who works a five-day week is entitled to two days off with pay, but may be entitled to further time off on an unpaid basis, so that the paid and unpaid periods amount to a reasonable total.

Increasing time off

5.2.113   It would be good practice for a company to allow all employees who have been given notice of redundancy reasonable time off during their notice period to look for alternative work or retrain, even if they do not have two years' service. A company might also wish to consider increasing the amount of time off for which it is prepared to pay above the statutory two days.

Redundancy payments

5.2.114   Most employees who are dismissed for redundancy are entitled to a redundancy payment under the Employment Rights Act 1996, provided they have been continuously employed for two years or more. (The rules on calculating continuous service are explained in Appendix 8.1.)

5.2.115   Where an employee is working under a contract that states that it will expire on a specified date, after a specified period or on completion of a specified task, and the employer decides not to renew the contract when it expires, the law views that as a dismissal. So, if the reason that the employee's contract was not renewed falls within the definition of redundancy (see 5.2.16), the employee will be entitled to a redundancy payment, if he or she has two years' service.

Payment calculation

5.2.116 A statutory redundancy payment is calculated by reference to the employee's age, length of service and weekly pay. There are complex rules for calculating an employee's week's pay, which are summarised in Appendix 8.2. There is also an upper limit on the amount of a week's pay that can be taken into account. This is usually reviewed annually in line with the Retail Prices Index and stands at £380 from October 2009.

5.2.117 Reckoning backwards from the end of the employee's employment, a redundancy payment is:

- one and a half weeks' pay for each complete year of employment in which the employee was aged 41 or over; plus

- one week's pay for each complete year in which the employee was under 41 but not under 22; plus

- half a week's pay for each complete year in which the employee was aged 21 and under.

5.2.118 The maximum number of years that can be taken into account is 20. This means that the maximum statutory redundancy payment is currently £11,400 (from October 2009). A ready reckoner is included at the end of this chapter to help with the calculation of redundancy payments.

5.2.119 The company must give the employee a written statement showing how his or her statutory redundancy payment was calculated. It is a criminal offence to fail to provide this statement without reasonable excuse.

Enhanced payments

5.2.120 Many companies give employees more generous redundancy payments than those provided for in the statutory scheme. These commonly base the payment on the employee's actual week's pay, without limit, or apply a higher multiplier for years of service than the statutory scheme. Employees may be legally entitled to these enhanced redundancy payments under a term in their contract of employment, perhaps incorporated from a redundancy procedure or a collective agreement that the company has reached with a trade union. Or the company may simply decide to offer the payments, without legal obligation, in the course of a particular redundancy exercise.

5.2.121   To the extent that they are based on age and length of service, redundancy payments, whether made under the statutory scheme or under an enhanced employer's scheme, could potentially amount to age discrimination. The age discrimination legislation, however, provides exceptions so that redundancy payments made under statute do not involve unlawful discrimination. Enhanced payments are not unlawful either, provided they are calculated in broadly the same way as statutory payments – that is, they are based on an employee's week's pay and length of service, but they do not cap the employee's week's pay and/or they use a multiplier of more than one for each year's employment. Enhanced payments are also lawful if they are calculated by using exactly the same formula as the statutory scheme but then multiplying that figure by more than one. Enhanced payments that are based on age and/or service but are not calculated in the same way as statutory payments will need to be justified (see 5.2.77).

5.2.122   Under the Regulations on fixed-term work (see 1.2.89), fixed-term employees must not be treated less favourably than permanent employees unless there is objective justification for doing so. The government guidance on the Regulations (see 9.1.2) suggests that where companies offer enhanced redundancy payments to compensate employees for the unexpected loss of their jobs, it may be possible to justify excluding those on fixed-term contracts, if they were recruited on the basis that there was no reasonable prospect of their contracts being renewed.

Taxation

5.2.123   The first £30,000 of a redundancy payment is exempt from income tax, whether it is a statutory or a non-statutory payment, provided it is genuinely and solely due to redundancy. Other payments made in the context of a redundancy exercise may, however, be taxable in full, as income from employment. For example, payments made for meeting production targets or doing extra work in the period leading up to the redundancies are likely to be taxable in full, as are payments that are conditional on an employee continuing in employment for a specified time after receiving his or her redundancy notice. If companies are in any doubt about the tax status of the payments they intend to make to employees who are to be made redundant, they can contact the Inland Revenue for advance clearance of the payments.

5.2.124   The rules on taxation of termination payments are summarised in 4.1.93.

Exclusions and reductions

5.2.125 In some circumstances (summarised in 5.2.126), employees are not eligible for a statutory redundancy payment, or are entitled to only a reduced payment. Most of these cases are complex, and companies that are considering refusing to pay a redundancy payment or reducing a redundancy payment in these circumstances are advised to contact us for guidance.

5.2.126

Exclusions from and reductions to statutory redundancy payment

1. Employees lose the right to a redundancy payment if they have unreasonably refused an offer of suitable alternative employment (see 5.2.105), or unreasonably terminated their contract during a trial period in suitable alternative employment (see 5.2.102).

2. An employee who has committed an act of gross misconduct may lose his or her right to a redundancy payment. However, if the employee is dismissed for gross misconduct after receiving notice of dismissal for redundancy, he or she can apply to an employment tribunal, which may order the company to pay the employee the whole or part of the payment, if it considers that fair in the circumstances.

3. An employee who takes part in strike action after being given notice of dismissal for redundancy does not lose his or her right to a redundancy payment. The company may, however, write to the employee asking him or her to extend his or her employment by the same number of days as were lost through the strike action. If the employee does not agree, the company may refuse to make a redundancy payment. However, the employee can then apply to an employment tribunal, which may order the company to make the payment if it considers that the employee was unable to meet the company's request to make up the lost days, or it was reasonable in the circumstances for the employee not to comply with it.

4. If an employee resigns after being given notice of dismissal for redundancy but the company asks the employee to work on until the end of the period of notice given by the company, the employee may lose the right to a payment if he or she does not do so.

Alternatives to redundancy

5.2.127 If an employer is facing only a temporary dip in its need for labour, it may prefer to lay employees off temporarily or reduce their working hours for a limited period, rather than make them redundant. Three legal questions are raised here. Can the employer take these steps without breaching its employees' contracts of employment? What right do employees have to be paid in these circumstances? And in what circumstances can an employee who is laid off or put on short time claim a redundancy payment?

Contractual issues

5.2.128 If a company anticipates that it may want to lay employees off or reduce their working hours, it should ensure that their contracts of employment give it the power to do so. The power might be contained in an express term set out in the contracts themselves or in a collective agreement that has been incorporated into the contracts by reference. Or it might be an implied term based on custom and practice. (It is sometimes difficult to establish an implied term based on custom and practice, and it is therefore advisable for companies to ensure that their contracts give them an express power to lay off or reduce hours.)

5.2.129 Even if an employer has no contractual power to lay employees off or reduce their working hours, it may not be breaching their contracts if it does so, provided it continues to pay them the wages or salary they would normally receive. This is because most employees have the right to be paid if they are ready and willing to work, but no right to insist on working. For most employers, however, the aim of laying employees off or reducing their hours is to save labour costs, and so they would not want to maintain employees' pay.

Constructive dismissal

5.2.130 An employer that lays an employee off or reduces his or her working hours without maintaining his or her pay and without having the contractual power to do so, is acting in serious breach of the employee's contract. The employee is therefore entitled to resign and claim that he or she has been constructively dismissed and that the dismissal was unfair. Whether or not the employee

Payment for workless days

5.2.131   An employee who is not provided with work on any day may nevertheless be entitled to be paid for that day, under his or her contract of employment. For example, employees who receive an annual salary or a set weekly wage are likely to be entitled to their usual pay even if they are not provided with work, unless their contract provides otherwise. Employees who are covered by the engineering industry's National Guarantee of Employment Agreement for hourly-rated manual workers are guaranteed to receive pay at their time rate for 39 hours a week even if no work is available, provided they are ready and willing to work. Payment is reduced where short-time working has been approved as an alternative to redundancy. Any hourly-paid worker who is required to be available for work at or near the workplace for any period may be entitled to be paid the national minimum wage for that time, even if no work is actually provided (see 2.1.34).

Guarantee payment

5.2.132   If an employee has no right to be paid during a workless day under his or her contract or the minimum wage legislation, he or she may still be entitled to a guarantee payment under the Employment Rights Act 1996. A statutory guarantee payment is calculated on the basis of the employee's normal hourly rate for working his or her normal working hours in that day, but is subject to a limit. The limit is adjusted each year in line with the Retail Prices Index, but currently (from February 2010) stands at £21.20. An employee is entitled to only a limited number of days' guarantee pay in any three-month period. The limit is the number of days in the employee's normal working week, up to a maximum of five.

5.2.133

> **Employees who are not entitled to statutory guarantee payment**
>
> 1. Employees who have been employed for less than one continuous month.
>
> 2. Employees whose workless day is due to a strike or lock-out or some other industrial action involving any employee of their employer or of an associated employer.
>
> 3. Employees who have unreasonably refused an offer of suitable alternative work or have not complied with the company's reasonable requirements to ensure that they are available to work.

Claiming a redundancy payment

5.2.134   If an employee has been laid off or put on short-time working for an extended period, he or she may be entitled to claim a statutory redundancy payment from the company. This applies only to employees whose right to be paid depends on them being provided with work. An employee is viewed as laid off for a week if he or she has not been paid because there has been no work that week. An employee is viewed as being kept on short time for a week if his or her pay is at less than half the usual amount because the employer has provided less work than normal.

5.2.135   An employee can claim a redundancy payment if he or she has been laid off or kept on short time for 4 or more consecutive weeks, or for any 6 or more weeks in a period of 13 weeks. In order to claim, the employee must resign. The company may be able to resist the claim for a payment if it is reasonably likely that the employee will, within 4 weeks of claiming the payment, have 13 weeks' work without being laid off or put on short time.

5.2.136   The rules on entitlement to a redundancy payment through lay-off or short-time working are complex. Companies that wish to resist a claim for a redundancy payment in these circumstances should therefore consult us for advice.

Redundancy and insolvent companies

5.2.137 Some redundancies are precipitated by a company becoming insolvent. Whether insolvency has the effect of terminating contracts of employment depends on the way in which the company has become insolvent, and companies that are facing insolvency will therefore need to obtain specialist advice on this issue.

National Insurance Fund

5.2.138 Under the Employment Rights Act 1996, employees who work for a company that becomes insolvent may be entitled to have their redundancy payment paid from the National Insurance Fund, a central government fund administered by the Department for Business, Enterprise and Regulatory Reform. The Fund will pay only if the employee has taken all reasonable steps to recover the payment, including taking employment tribunal proceedings, but the company has failed to pay up, or if the company is insolvent. For these purposes, a company is insolvent only if one of the following events has happened:

- a winding up order or administration order has been made;
- a resolution for voluntary winding up has been passed;
- a receiver or manager has been appointed, or possession has been taken, of company property subject to a floating charge; or
- a voluntary arrangement has been approved under Part I of the Insolvency Act 1986.

Other sums owed

5.2.139 An employee who is owed certain other sums by a company that becomes insolvent is also entitled to a payment from the National Insurance Fund, but only if the company is insolvent as defined above. The Fund will cover, for example, up to eight weeks' arrears of pay, notice pay for the employee's statutory minimum notice period (see 4.1.16) and up to six weeks' holiday pay. The amount that the Fund will pay for each week is capped at an amount that is usually reviewed annually but currently (from October 2009) stands at

£380. The Fund will also pay an apprentice a reasonable sum in reimbursement of any fee or premium that the apprentice has paid. In addition, the government will pay up to 12 months' unpaid pension contributions owed by an insolvent company, under the Pension Schemes Act 1993.

Apprentices

5.2.140 A traditional contract of apprenticeship usually states that it will run for a specified length of time or until the apprentice reaches a certain standard. The contract then ends automatically when that period ends or the standard is reached.

5.2.141 The contract may include an express term allowing the company to terminate the contract early in certain circumstances, which could include redundancy. If there is no such term, the company is entitled to terminate the contract for redundancy only where the redundancy has arisen because the business has closed down completely or has fundamentally changed in nature. If an apprentice's contract is terminated prematurely in breach of contract, the apprentice is entitled to damages reflecting not only his or her lost wages for the balance of the apprenticeship but also the value of his or her lost training and the reduction in his or her future employment prospects. (For a summary of the employment status of modern apprentices, see 1.2.86.)

Statutory employment rights

5.2.142 It should be borne in mind that apprentices, whether traditional or modern, have the same statutory employment rights as employees. This means that they are entitled to claim unfair dismissal if the company acts unreasonably in terminating their contract for redundancy, provided they have one year's service. They may also be entitled to a redundancy payment if they have been with the company for two years or more.

5.2.143

Checklist for handling redundancies

1. Identify the business reason for the proposed redundancies and check whether they will fall within the legal definition of redundancy (see 5.2.16).

2. Consider whether the business's needs could be met in some way that avoids redundancies (see 5.2.32).

3. Draft proposals on:
   - the number of employees who need to be dismissed;
   - the sections of the business from which they will be drawn;
   - the criteria that will be used to select employees for redundancy;
   - the payments that will be made to employees who are dismissed; and
   - the steps that the company can take to minimise the impact of the dismissals through redeployment, retraining and assistance with obtaining work outside the company.

4. Announce the proposed redundancies to the workforce (see 5.2.37).

5. If 20 or more employees are likely to be dismissed at one establishment within a period of 90 days, consider whether all the affected employees are covered by collective bargaining or, if they are not, whether they are represented by appointed employee representatives. If not, arrange for the election of employee representatives (see 6.4.55).

6. Where 20 or more dismissals are proposed at one establishment within a period of 90 days, consult with recognised trade union representatives or, where the affected employees are not covered by union recognition, employee representatives on the company's proposals (see 5.2.42) and notify the Department for Business, Enterprise and Regulatory Reform (see 5.2.60).

7. Finalise the proposals, including, where necessary, appropriate selection criteria (see 5.2.72).

8. Consider whether to invite volunteers for redundancy (see 5.2.64).

9. Apply the selection criteria (see 5.2.81) and begin consultation with the individuals who are provisionally selected for redundancy as a result (see 5.2.85). Where fewer than 20 are to be made redundant, write to each of those employees explaining the background to his or her provisional selection and invite the employee to a meeting to discuss his or her proposed redundancy. Discuss their selection and the possibility of alternative employment (see 5.2.95).

10. Finalise selection decisions and issue notices of termination (see 5.2.108).

11. Offer confirmed redundant employees an appeal, and deal with any appeals.

12. During any notice period, continue efforts to redeploy and allow employees time off to find alternative work or to retrain (see 5.2.111). Make redundancy payments (see 5.2.114).

Ready Reckoner for calculating the number of weeks' pay due for redundancy pay purposes
To use the table:
Read off employees' age and number of complete years' service. The table will then show how many weeks' pay each employee is entitled to. The maximum week's pay used to calculate a payment is £380.

Age (years) \ Service	2	3	4	5	6	7	8	9	10	11	12	13	14	15	16	17	18	19	20
18*	1																		
19	1	1½																	
20	1	1½	2																
21	1	1½	2	2½															
22	1	1½	2	2½	3														
23	1½	2	2½	3	3½	4													
24	2	2½	3	3½	4	4½	5												
25	2	3	3½	4	4½	5	5½	6											
26	2	3	4	4½	5	5½	6	6½	7										
27	2	3	4	5	5½	6	6½	7	7½	8									
28	2	3	4	5	6	6½	7	7½	8	8½	9								
29	2	3	4	5	6	7	7½	8	8½	9	9½	10							
30	2	3	4	5	6	7	8	8½	9	9½	10	10½	11						
31	2	3	4	5	6	7	8	9	9½	10	10½	11	11½	12					
32	2	3	4	5	6	7	8	9	10	10½	11	11½	12	12½	13				
33	2	3	4	5	6	7	8	9	10	11	11½	12	12½	13	13½	14			
34	2	3	4	5	6	7	8	9	10	11	12	12½	13	13½	14	14½	15		
35	2	3	4	5	6	7	8	9	10	11	12	13	13½	14	14½	15	15½	16	
36	2	3	4	5	6	7	8	9	10	11	12	13	14	14½	15	15½	16	16½	17
37	2	3	4	5	6	7	8	9	10	11	12	13	14	15	15½	16	16½	17	17½
38	2	3	4	5	6	7	8	9	10	11	12	13	14	15	16	16½	17	17½	18
39	2	3	4	5	6	7	8	9	10	11	12	13	14	15	16	17	17½	18	18½
40	2	3	4	5	6	7	8	9	10	11	12	13	14	15	16	17	18	18½	19
41	2	3	4	5	6	7	8	9	10	11	12	13	14	15	16	17	18	19	19½
42	2½	3½	4½	5½	6½	7½	8½	9½	10½	11½	12½	13½	14½	15½	16½	17½	18½	19½	20½
43	3	4	5	6	7	8	9	10	11	12	13	14	15	16	17	18	19	20	21
44	3	4½	5½	6½	7½	8½	9½	10½	11½	12½	13½	14½	15½	16½	17½	18½	19½	20½	21½
45	3	4½	6	7	8	9	10	11	12	13	14	15	16	17	18	19	20	21	22
46	3	4½	6	7½	8½	9½	10½	11½	12½	13½	14½	15½	16½	17½	18½	19½	20½	21½	22½
47	3	4½	6	7½	9	10	11	12	13	14	15	16	17	18	19	20	21	22	23
48	3	4½	6	7½	9	10½	11½	12½	13½	14½	15½	16½	17½	18½	19½	20½	21½	22½	23½
49	3	4½	6	7½	9	10½	12	13	14	15	16	17	18	19	20	21	22	23	24
50	3	4½	6	7½	9	10½	12	13½	14½	15½	16½	17½	18½	19½	20½	21½	22½	23½	24½
51	3	4½	6	7½	9	10½	12	13½	15	16	17	18	19	20	21	22	23	24	25
52	3	4½	6	7½	9	10½	12	13½	15	16½	17½	18½	19½	20½	21½	22½	23½	24½	25½
53	3	4½	6	7½	9	10½	12	13½	15	16½	18	19	20	21	22	23	24	25	26
54	3	4½	6	7½	9	10½	12	13½	15	16½	18	19½	20½	21½	22½	23½	24½	25½	26½
55	3	4½	6	7½	9	10½	12	13½	15	16½	18	19½	21	22	23	24	25	26	27
56	3	4½	6	7½	9	10½	12	13½	15	16½	18	19½	21	22½	23½	24½	25½	26½	27½
57	3	4½	6	7½	9	10½	12	13½	15	16½	18	19½	21	22½	24	25	26	27	28
58	3	4½	6	7½	9	10½	12	13½	15	16½	18	19½	21	22½	24	25½	26½	27½	28½
59	3	4½	6	7½	9	10½	12	13½	15	16½	18	19½	21	22½	24	25½	27	28	29
60	3	4½	6	7½	9	10½	12	13½	15	16½	18	19½	21	22½	24	25½	27	28½	29½
61†	3	4½	6	7½	9	10½	12	13½	15	16½	18	19½	21	22½	24	25½	27	28½	30

*It is possible that an individual could start to build up continuous service before age 16, but this is likely to be rare, and therefore we have started Table 2 from age 18.

†The same figures should be used when calculating the redundancy payment for a person aged 61 and above.

5.3

Transfer of undertakings

Overview

5.3.1 Any restructuring or reorganisation of a business inevitably brings some changes for the workforce. Employees' terms and conditions of employment may need to be altered to reflect the new needs of the business, as discussed in Chapter 5.1. On occasions, substantial changes in job content or reductions in staffing levels may be involved, raising the redundancy issues covered in Chapter 5.2. This chapter of the Guide deals with the situation where the reorganisation involves the business, or the part of it in which some employees work, being sold or contracted out, resulting in a change in the identity of their employer.

5.3.2 Under general principles of contract law, if a business changes hands and a new employer is put in the old employer's place, an important term of the employment contract of the business's employees is fundamentally changed. This change means that, effectively, they are constructively dismissed (see 4.1.35). In order to avoid this result and give some protection to the interests of employees caught up in business transfers, employment law has intervened, in the form of the Transfer of Undertakings (Protection of Employment) Regulations 2006 (often referred to as 'TUPE'). This chapter explains how the Regulations operate.

5.3.3 One of the most important effects of the Regulations is that the new owner of the business automatically inherits the employees who work in it, together with almost all their existing contractual and other legal rights (see 5.3.33).

The Regulations therefore require the old employer to give the new employer certain information about the employees who transfer in this way (see 5.3.41). The Regulations also make it automatically unfair for the old or the new employer to dismiss an employee for a reason connected with the transfer, unless there is some economic, technical or organisational reason for the dismissal (see 5.3.60).

5.3.4 Because the transfer of a business has important repercussions for the workforce of both the old and the new employer, the Regulations require the employers to give certain information to their workforce representatives about the transfer. If they are considering taking any steps in connection with the transfer that may affect their employees, the employers must also consult with their workforce representatives about the measures they are proposing (see 5.3.17).

5.3.5 These considerations arise, however, only if the business transfer falls within the scope of the Regulations. This chapter therefore opens with an explanation of the types of transaction covered by the Regulations (see 5.3.7).

5.3.6 It will be clear from this introductory summary of the Regulations that they can have substantial financial and practical consequences for the commercial viability of any transaction to which they apply. They are also likely to affect the terms of the commercial agreement under which the transaction is made. Companies that are considering entering into a transaction to which the Regulations might apply may therefore wish to contact us for advice at an early stage.

When do the Regulations apply?

5.3.7 Many businesses change hands through the sale of shares in the company. This type of transaction does not have any effect on the employment rights of the workforce, since it does not involve any change in the identity of the employer, which was and remains the company itself. Although a change in the identity of the person or organisation that owns the shares in a company may have great practical significance for the future terms and conditions and job security of its workforce, the Regulations do not apply.

5.3.8   The Regulations do potentially apply in two types of situations. The first is where the whole or part of a business is sold. The second is where a business contracts out or contracts in some of its activities, or changes the contractor it uses to provide those services, which the Regulations refer to as a 'service provision change'. The Regulations can apply regardless of the size of the transferred business or service provision change. (Additional considerations apply to government contracts, as summarised at 5.3.72.)

Sales of the whole or part of a business

5.3.9   It is important to note that not all sales of the whole or part of a business are necessarily covered by the Regulations. The Regulations will apply only where the sale involves an identifiable 'economic entity' that retains its identity. An economic entity is an organised grouping of resources that has the objective of pursuing an economic activity. The resources could be tangible ones, such as employees, buildings and machinery, or intangible ones, such as goodwill and know-how.

5.3.10   In order to find out whether the Regulations apply to a proposed sale, a useful first step is to decide whether it is possible to identify an economic entity that will be the subject of the transaction. It does not matter whether the entity has a separate existence prior to the time of the transfer, provided it can be identified as a separate entity at the point of the transfer. The entity could be, for example, 'the heavy duty plastics division of ABC plc'. In order to identify the entity, it will be necessary to identify the people and assets that are involved in it. These could include, for example, employees, premises, buildings, equipment, work-in-progress, know-how, goodwill and customer base. If the proposed sale will involve the new employer taking over all or the major part of these tangible and intangible assets, then that is a strong indicator that the transaction is covered by the Regulations.

Transfer as a going concern

5.3.11   In order for the Regulations to apply to a sale of the whole or part of a business, the transaction must involve an economic entity being transferred as a going concern. The more similar the activities of the entity are before and after the transaction, the more likely it is that this condition will be met. Likewise, if the operation of the entity is continued or resumed by the new employer with little or no interruption, that points towards there being a transfer covered by the Regulations. On the other hand, if the operation stops for a substantial period, that could indicate that there has not in fact been a transfer of an economic entity as a going concern, but rather a closure of a business or part of one, and the launch of a new business.

5.3.12 If the economic entity retains its identity at the point it is transferred, the Regulations will apply, even if the entity is subsequently integrated into the new employer's business.

Contracting out, contracting in and changing contractors

5.3.13 As mentioned above, the Regulations also apply to a service provision change. This is where a business that had been carrying on an activity 'in-house' decides to contract with another business to carry out that activity on its behalf (often called 'contracting out'), or to change the contractor that carries out that activity on its behalf, or to bring the activity 'in-house' (usually referred to as 'contracting in').

5.3.14 A service provision change is covered by the Regulations, if there exists, immediately before the change, an organised grouping of employees (which could be only a single employee) which has as its main purpose the carrying out of the activities concerned on behalf of the client business. The contract must involve more than a single specific event or task of short-term duration. The grant of a one-off contract to provide catering services for a promotional event would not, for example, be covered, whereas a contract to run a company canteen might well be.

5.3.15 Contracts that are wholly or mainly concerned with supplying goods for the client's use, such as a contract to provide raw materials, are not covered.

Further advice

5.3.16 In most cases it will be clear whether the Regulations apply, but there may be some where it is difficult to decide. Companies that are in any doubt as to whether the transaction they are contemplating making is covered by the Regulations may wish to contact us for advice.

Informing and consulting the workforce

5.3.17   Before a transaction covered by the Regulations takes place, both the old employer and the new one must provide representatives of their workforces with certain information about the transfer. If they intend to take any steps in connection with the transfer that affects their employees, they must also consult with the representatives.

5.3.18   When giving its employees information about a transfer, the old employer is under a legal duty to take reasonable care to ensure that the information is accurate, especially where the employees are relying heavily on the information in order to decide whether to object to the transfer. This duty applies whether or not the employer is providing the information to meet the requirements of the Regulations.

5.3.19   Any employees who may be affected either by the transfer itself or by any steps connected with it are entitled to be consulted through their representatives. It is important for employers to bear in mind that a transfer and its consequences may well affect many, if not all, of its employees, even if they do not work in the part of the business that is being transferred. For example, a company that is planning to sell part of its business may need to reorganise the job duties of its remaining employees as a result. If it does, it must give information about the transfer to representatives of all its employees and consult with representatives of the employees whose work will be reorganised.

Identifying the appropriate representatives

5.3.20   The identity of the workforce representatives depends on whether the employer recognises a trade union for collective bargaining. If the affected employees are covered by a collective bargaining arrangement, then the employer must inform and consult the union's representatives. If the affected employees are not covered by collective bargaining, the company has two options.

5.3.21   The first is to inform and consult representatives that the employees have already appointed or elected for some purpose not specifically related to business transfers. The company can take up this option only if it is clear from the context in which the representatives were appointed or elected that they have authority to be consulted about the transfer on the employees' behalf. For example, someone appointed to a committee that only organises social events is unlikely to have the relevant authority, but someone appointed to a staff committee or a works council set up to discuss major issues affecting the business will have.

Electing representatives

5.3.22 The other option is for the company to inform and consult representatives who have been elected by the affected employees for the express purpose of being consulted on business transfers. If the company takes this route, it must ensure that the election meets the requirements set down in the Regulations. For example, there must be sufficient representatives to represent the interests of all the affected employees and all the affected employees must be entitled to vote. The candidates must themselves be employees who are affected by the transfer or measures that may be taken in connection with it. Further details on holding elections for employee representatives are given in 6.4.55.

Information for representatives

5.3.23 Both the old employer and the new employer must provide their workforce representatives with certain information about the transfer. The Regulations say that the information must be provided long enough before the transfer to enable proper consultation to take place (although, as explained below, an employer is not under any duty to consult if it does not propose to take any measures in connection with the transfer).

5.3.24 This is the information that must be given (see overleaf):

> ### Information for workplace representatives
>
> - The fact that the transfer is to take place, when it is likely to happen and the reasons for it.
>
> - The legal, economic and social implications of the transfer for the affected employees. This would include, for example, explaining the protection they have under the Regulations.
>
> - Any measures that the company envisages it will be taking in connection with the transfer, or if it is not planning any measures, that fact. If the company is the old employer, it must also tell the representatives about any measures that the new employer plans to take in relation to the employees who will be transferred. The new employer must provide the old employer with the information it needs to meet this duty.

Consulting with representatives

5.3.25   If either the old employer or the new employer envisages that it may be taking any measures in connection with the transfer that relate to its employees, it must consult with the workforce representatives. A company is legally obliged to consult only about those measures that it is taking itself. This means that the old employer has no duty to consult about measures that the new employer proposes to take in relation to the employees who will be transferred.

5.3.26   In order to fulfil its duty to consult, a company should take the steps set out in the following box.

> **Steps to fulfil duty to consult**
>
> 1. The company should enter into the consultation process with an open mind on whether its proposal might need to be revised. Although the Regulations do not require the employer to negotiate and reach agreement with the workforce representatives, they do say that the employer must enter the consultation process with a view to seeking the representatives' agreement to the measures it is proposing.
>
> 2. The company should ensure that it has provided clear information on what is being proposed and why.
>
> 3. The company should give the employee representatives adequate time to consider that information and to prepare their response.
>
> 4. The company should give proper consideration to the representatives' responses, and take them into account in finalising its proposals. The Regulations require the company to reply to any responses made by the employees' representatives, and if it rejects the representatives' arguments, explain why.

5.3.27 Consultation by the employer should be with a view to seeking agreement and therefore needs to be a two-way process, involving a considered exchange of views between the company and the workforce representatives, rather than a one-way process of telling the representatives what is going to happen. It is advisable for the company to keep a record of the meetings it has held with the representatives and the content of the discussions. It should also ensure that no announcements are made that indicate that an irreversible decision to implement the measures under discussion has already been made.

5.3.28 During the consultation, the company must allow the representatives access to the affected employees, and give them whatever other facilities and accommodation may be appropriate to enable them to carry out their role effectively. Depending on the size and resources of the company, this might include, for example, the use of a telephone, photocopier and word processor.

Exceptional circumstances defence

5.3.29 The Regulations acknowledge that in some exceptional circumstances it may not be reasonably practicable for a company to comply fully with its duty to consult. In that event, the company must still do what it can to comply. If, for example, the company needs to take certain steps urgently in order to secure the sale of part of the business, it may not have enough time to go through a full consultation process. However, it may still be able to keep the workforce representatives informed about the situation and hold an emergency meeting to obtain their views.

5.3.30 The Regulations also acknowledge that the possibility of consultation will be limited if the employer has asked its workforce to elect representatives but the election is delayed by the employees. In these circumstances, the employer will meet its legal obligations if it consults as soon as is reasonably practicable after the election has taken place. If the workforce fails to elect representatives within a reasonable time, the company must give each affected employee the information it would have given to the representatives, as set out above (see 5.3.24).

Rights of representatives

5.3.31 The workforce representatives involved in the information and consultation process are entitled to reasonable paid time off during working hours in order to perform their functions and to undergo relevant training. Employees are also entitled to reasonable paid time off to stand for election as representatives.

5.3.32 It is unlawful for a company to treat an employee unfavourably, and automatically unfair to dismiss an employee or select an employee for redundancy, on the grounds that the employee has carried out his or her role as a representative. This protection also extends to employees who stand as candidates for election or participate in an election. It applies regardless of the employee's age or length of service with the company.

Transfer of employees

5.3.33   When a business is transferred, the Regulations state that the employees who work in the business must be viewed as if they are employed, and have always been employed, by the new employer. In effect, the new employer steps into the shoes of the old one and there is an automatic transfer of the employment contracts.

5.3.34   This means that the new employer must respect the pre-existing terms of the contracts of employment of the transferred employees and their length of service with the old employer. The employees in their turn continue to be bound by the terms of their contracts of employment. (There are special rules on how employees' pension rights are protected on a transfer (see 5.3.56) and where the old employer is insolvent (see 5.3.68).)

Transfer of contract terms

5.3.35   The new employer needs to be aware of the possible legal and practical problems that may be raised by the wording of the employment contracts it inherits.

5.3.36   For example, an employee may have a contractual term restricting his or her ability to work for a competitor after leaving the company. After the transfer, this restriction will not change in scope, so it will continue to relate only to the competitors of the business that is transferred. It may therefore be inadequate to protect the new employer's interests.

5.3.37   Problems can also arise in relation to pay. The employee may be entitled to a bonus, commission or profit share that is calculated in a way that is integral to the old employer's financial systems or working arrangements. A profit share scheme might, for example, involve allocation of shares in the old employer's company, making it impossible in practice for the new employer to apply it. Where insuperable practical problems of this sort arise, it is sufficient if the new employer provides a benefit that is substantially equivalent to the old one. If the employee's contract states that his or her rate of pay is set by negotiation between certain parties, such as a national negotiating committee, the new employer must respect that term, even if it is not one of the negotiating parties. It may therefore be obliged to pay rates that it has not set itself. Case law suggests that the obligation does not extend to increases negotiated subsequent to the transfer. For more information contact us.

5.3.38   As explained below, it may be difficult and costly for the new employer to change the terms of transferred employees' contracts, even if they are obviously inappropriate in the changed circumstances.

Transfer of other liabilities

5.3.39   As well as inheriting the employees' contractual terms, the new employer takes over any legal liabilities that the old employer had towards them, other than liabilities under the criminal law. The new employer could find itself legally responsible, for example, for equal pay claims or claims for unlawful discrimination to which the employee was subjected before the transfer or for personal injuries the employee sustained at work. The new employer does, however, inherit the benefit of any employer's liability insurance policy the old employer held that covered the employee.

5.3.40   The law is currently unclear on whether the new employer inherits any liability that the old employer had for failure to consult on large-scale redundancies (see 5.2.42), although the prevailing view appears to be that liability does transfer. A company that may be affected by this issue should contact us for advice. If the old employer failed to consult on the transfer itself (see 5.3.17), then both the old employer and the new employer are legally liable for that failure.

Employee liability information

5.3.41   Because of the employee liabilities that a company may inherit if it acquires a business or secures a contract where the Regulations apply, the law requires the old employer to provide it with certain information about each employee who will be transferring. With regard to the disclosure of personal data, there is a Data Protection Good Practice Note on the disclosure of employee information under TUPE produced by the Information Commissioner's Office.

5.3.42   The information that must be provided is set out in the box below. The information must be accurate at a specified date not earlier than 14 days before it is supplied. If any of the information changes, the old employer must notify the new employer in writing.

> **Employee liability information**
>
> - The identity and age of the employee.
>
> - The main terms and conditions of the employee, as required by Section 1 of the Employment Rights Act 1996 (see 1.2.53).
>
> - Information about any disciplinary procedure taken against the employee or grievance procedure taken by the employee within the past two years.
>
> - Information about any court or tribunal claim the employee has brought against the old employer in the past two years, or which the old employer has reasonable grounds to believe the employee may bring against the new employer, arising out of his or her employment with the old employer.
>
> - Information about any collective agreement that will transfer under the Regulations (see 5.3.67).

5.3.43   The information must be provided in writing or be made available in a readily accessible form, and be given no less than 14 days before the transfer, or, if that is not reasonably practicable, as soon a reasonably practicable after that. It may also be provided indirectly through a third party, as where an outgoing contractor provides the information to the client business, which passed it on to the incoming contractor.

5.3.44   If the old employer fails to provide the required information in relation to one or more of the employees transferred, an employment tribunal may award the new employer compensation of whatever sum it considers just and equitable. In assessing compensation, the tribunal will have regard to any loss the new employer suffered as a result of not receiving the information, and the terms of any contract between the old employer and the new providing for compensation for failure to give the information. Compensation will not, however, be less than £500 in relation to each employee involved, unless the tribunal considers it just and equitable to award a smaller sum.

Due diligence

5.3.45   In practice, a company that is thinking of purchasing the whole or part of a business or tendering for a contract would be well advised to ask the existing employer for this employee liability information, in advance of a sale or contract being agreed. If these enquiries reveal that the new employer might inherit costly legal liabilities, it will then have the opportunity to include provision for this in the terms of the sale agreement or contract. The new employer might, for example, be able to negotiate a change in the price of the sale or contract, or get the old employer to agree to meet the costs of any legal claims that might materialise.

Liability for breach of duty to consult

5.3.46   Although there is currently uncertainty as to whether the new employer inherits legal liability for the old employer's failure to inform and consult its workforce about large-scale redundancies, the prevailing view is that liability does transfer. Further, the Regulations provide that the new employer shares legal responsibility with the old employer for any failure by the old employer to consult about the transfer. It would therefore be advisable for the new employer to check that the old employer has taken adequate steps to meet all its information and consultation obligations.

Transfer-related contract changes

5.3.47   In normal circumstances, an employer can effectively change the terms of its employees' contracts provided they agree to the change. However, the Regulations try and ensure that employees are not penalised when they are transferred by being placed on lower terms and conditions. Therefore not only do employees transfer on their pre-existing terms and conditions but employees cannot validly waive their acquired rights. The Regulations do this by imposing limitations on the ability of the new employer and employee to do this. The Regulations provide that a contractual variation is not valid (i.e. it is rendered void) where the main reason is the transfer itself or a reason connected with the transfer which is not 'an economic, technical or organisational reason entailing changes in the workforce'. The same restrictions apply to the old employer where it tries changing terms and conditions of those employees who will transfer to the new employer in anticipation of the transfer happening. However, BIS guidance says that 'as the underlying purpose of the Regulations is to ensure that employees are not penalised when a transfer takes place', then 'changes to terms and conditions agreed by the parties which are entirely positive are not prevented by the Regulations'.

5.3.48 Unfortunately, the decisions of the courts and employment tribunals have not given a clear picture of what amounts to an ETO reason. They have confirmed, however, that it must entail changes in the size and make-up of the workforce, rather than merely changes in employees' contractual benefits. For example, the need to make major changes to the content of employees' jobs may be an ETO reason, but harmonisation of a workforce's terms and conditions after a transfer would not.

5.3.49 This can pose considerable problems for a company that wants to change the terms and conditions of the employees it has inherited after a business transfer. There could be a variety of reasons why the company needs the change. The current terms may, for example, be too expensive, or not appropriate to the new employer's circumstances, or the company may want to harmonise the transferred employees' terms with those of its existing workforce.

Introducing valid contract changes

5.3.50 One possible answer to this problem would be for the company to introduce the changes when it next reviewed and revised all of its employees' contracts. It could then argue that the general review, rather than the transfer, was the reason for the changes. Another option would be to dismiss the transferred employees and offer them fresh contracts on new terms. If the employees accepted the new contracts, the terms would be legally enforceable, but at a price. Dismissing an employee in these circumstances could be automatically unfair as being for a reason connected with the transfer (see 5.3.60). The company would therefore end up paying the employee compensation for unfair dismissal. If the reason for introducing the new terms was to save costs, this would defeat the point of the exercise. A company considering this course of action may therefore wish to contact us for advice.

Which employees transfer?

5.3.51   It is only those employees who are part of the business or work on the contract that is transferred who go over to the new employer. If the transfer involves the sale of part of a business, it will be only those employees who are assigned to that part who will transfer, and in the case of a service provision change, it will be only those employees who are assigned to the organised grouping of employees involved in carrying out the activity concerned who will go over to the new employer. This covers all the employees who normally work solely in that part of the business or on those activities, or who do only a minimal amount of work elsewhere. Employees who are only temporarily assigned to the part or activity will not transfer. If a company wants to retain some employees who would otherwise transfer, it should ensure that it moves them out of the part of the business to be transferred or off the contract that is changing hands before the transfer takes place, assuming that it has the right to do so under their contract of employment or can obtain their agreement to the move.

5.3.52   The new employer also inherits legal responsibility for any employees who were dismissed by the old employer before the transfer took place but for a reason connected with it, unless there was an economic, technical or organisational reason for their dismissal. As explained below (5.3.60), it is automatically unfair to dismiss an employee for a reason connected with the transfer, so the new employer inherits liability for the employees' unfair dismissal as well as any other legal liabilities that the old employer had towards them.

Objecting to the transfer

5.3.53   The employees who work in the business or on the contract that is being transferred cannot be forced to work for the new employer. If an employee indicates clearly to the new employer or to the old one that he or she refuses to be employed by the new employer, then his or her contract ends when the transfer takes place. The employee can object by word or deed, but it must be clear that he or she is refusing to work for the new employer rather than merely being unhappy about the transfer. An employee who refuses to transfer is in the same legal position as if he or she had resigned. That means that the employee cannot claim a redundancy payment from the old or the new employer, or bring a claim of unfair dismissal.

5.3.54   The position is different if the employee decides to resign because the transfer will involve, or has involved, a substantial change for the worse in his or her working conditions. In these circumstances, the employee is entitled to claim unfair dismissal and, as explained below (see 5.3.60), the dismissal may well be automatically unfair.

5.3.55   The employee's claim will be against whichever company was employing him or her when he or she resigned. Therefore, if the employee resigned before the transfer took place, his or her claim would be against the old employer, even if the change that prompted the resignation was made by the new employer.

Pensions

5.3.56   There is one exception to the principle in the Regulations that employees retain their rights with the new employer: any rights the employees have to belong to an occupational pension scheme do not transfer (although any rights they have accrued under the old employer's scheme are protected under the Pension Schemes Act 1993). This exception relates only to benefits paid at the end of an employee's normal working life, as defined in the scheme rules. So, for example, if the old employer's scheme gave employees the right to an early retirement pension if made redundant before normal retirement age, that right transfers to the new employer. Any pension rights that do not relate to membership of an occupational pension scheme, such as the right to have the employer make contributions towards a personal pension, also transfer.

5.3.57   While transferred employees may have no protection for their pension rights under the Regulations, they may have some rights under the Pensions Act 2004, if they were in, or eligible to join, the old employer's occupational pension scheme. The Act does not require the new employer to match the old employer's pension arrangements, but it does require the new employer to make a certain minimum standard of pension provision.

5.3.58   The new employer can do this in one of three ways. The first is to offer the employees access to a stakeholder pension scheme and, if the employees take this up, match their contributions to the scheme, up to a maximum of 6 per cent of pay. Alternatively, the new employer may choose to provide a money purchase occupational pension scheme and match the employees' contributions up to a maximum of 6 per cent. The third option is to provide a final salary occupational pension scheme that satisfies the Reference Standard Test in the Pension Schemes Act 1993 (which qualifies the scheme for HM Revenue and Customs approval) or meets a minimum standard specified in regulations.

5.3.59   Even if the transferred employees had no pension rights with the old employer, the new employer may be obliged to offer them access to a stakeholder pension in any event, if it is required to do so by the stakeholder pension legislation (see 2.4.79).

Protection from dismissal

5.3.60   The Regulations make it automatically unfair for an employer to dismiss an employee if the only or main reason for the dismissal was the transfer or a reason connected with it. This principle applies whether the employee was dismissed by the old employer or the new, and extends to all employees of both employers, whether or not they work in the part of the business that is transferred or under the contract concerned. In order to be entitled to bring an unfair dismissal claim on these grounds, an employee must have been continuously employed for one year or more.

Economic, technical and organisational reasons

5.3.61   There is an exception to the principle that dismissals relating to a transfer are automatically unfair. If an employee has been dismissed for an economic, technical or organisational reason entailing changes in the workforce of the old employer or the new one (an 'ETO' reason), the dismissal will not be automatically unfair.

5.3.62   Instead, the reason for the dismissal will either be redundancy, if the statutory definition of redundancy applies (see 5.2.16), or some other substantial reason justifying the employee's dismissal. The question of whether the dismissal was fair or unfair will depend on the normal tests, namely whether the employer acted reasonably in all the circumstances in treating the reason as a sufficient basis for dismissing the employee.

5.3.63   As yet, the decisions of the courts and employment tribunals have not given a clear picture of what amounts to an ETO reason. They have confirmed, however, that it must relate to the way in which the business is conducted, not its attractiveness to a potential buyer. It will not, therefore, apply if employees have been dismissed in advance of the transfer at the request of the new employer. An ETO reason must also entail changes in the size and make-up of the workforce, rather than merely changes in employees' contractual terms. For example, the courts have confirmed that it would cover dismissals to reduce staffing levels or effect major changes in the content of employees' jobs, but not dismissals to harmonise a workforce's terms and conditions after a transfer.

Whose liability for unfair dismissal?

5.3.64   As discussed above (see 5.3.60), if the old employer dismisses an employee before the transfer for a reason connected with it that is not an ETO reason, that dismissal is automatically unfair. Furthermore, liability for it passes to the new employer, even though the employee was no longer employed at the time of the transfer. For example, if the old employer dismisses employees at the request of the new employer, the new employer will inherit liability for those unfair dismissals.

5.3.65   If, on the other hand, an employee is dismissed for an economic, technical or organisational reason, or for a reason unconnected with the transfer, whether before or after the transfer occurs, the employer who dismissed the employee is legally responsible for the dismissal. The dismissal may be fair or unfair, depending on whether the employer acted reasonably in deciding to dismiss.

Effect on collective bargaining

5.3.66   If the old employer recognised a trade union for collective bargaining in relation to the employees who are transferred, the new employer must recognise the union to the same extent – but only if the economic entity that is transferred remains distinct from the rest of the new employer's business. If the new employer inherits union recognition in this way, there is nothing to prevent it derecognising the union, unless the union was recognised by the old employer as a result of the statutory recognition procedure. In that case, the new employer can derecognise the union only by following the statutory procedure for derecognition. (The law on recognising and derecognising a union is summarised in Chapter 6.2 of this Guide.)

Transfer of collective agreements

5.3.67   If the old employer reached any collective agreements with a trade union in relation to the employees who are transferred, the new employer inherits those agreements as they apply to those employees. The new employer can, if it chooses, withdraw from any collective agreements that it inherits, since collective agreements are not in themselves legally binding. However, it will still be bound by any terms of the agreements that are part of employees' contracts. (An explanation of how collective agreements can be incorporated into individual employees' contracts can be found in 6.2.51.)

Special rules for insolvent employers

5.3.68   The usual principles of the Regulations are modified in various respects if the old employer is insolvent. Which special rules apply depends upon whether the employer is subject to bankruptcy proceedings or other insolvency proceedings that are aimed at liquidating the business's assets and winding it up, or whether the aim of the insolvency proceedings is to ensure the survival of the business.

5.3.69   If the aim is to liquidate the business's assets, then the Regulations will apply only where that involves selling off part of the business as an economic entity transferred as a going concern. Where there is such a sale, all the usual rules apply, save that the employees do not automatically transfer to the new owner and transfer-related dismissals are not automatically unfair.

5.3.70   On the other hand, if the aim of the insolvency proceedings is to ensure the survival of the business, there are two different special rules. The first is that not all of the old employer's liabilities towards its employees transfer to the new employer: the National Insurance Fund picks up liability for any statutory redundancy payments it owes and for any other sums, such as up to eight weeks' arrears of pay, that would normally be payable from the Fund in the event of an employer's insolvency (see 5.2.138, 5.2.139).

5.3.71　The other special rule is that either the old employer (or the insolvency practitioner dealing with the insolvency proceedings) or the new employer can make legally binding changes to the terms and conditions of the employees that transfer, even if the reason for the change is related to the transfer and is not an ETO reason, provided two conditions are met. The first is that the change is designed to save jobs by ensuring the survival of the business; the second is that the change has been agreed by the employees' representatives (whose identity is determined in the same way as employee representatives for the purpose of information and consultation – see 5.3.20). If the appropriate representatives are not union representatives, then the agreement must be in writing and the employer must provide all employees with a copy of it, and guidance on what it means, before it is signed.

Government contracts

5.3.72　When granting contracts, central and local government require the successful contractor to observe the principles of the Regulations, even in cases where there may be some doubt as to whether, on the usual legal tests, they actually apply (see 9.5.3). That means that the successful contractor will inherit the employees currently working in the area concerned, and must honour their existing terms and conditions. Further, the company will be required to make a specified standard of pension provision for the transferred employees, even though pension benefits are not transferred under the Regulations themselves (see 5.3.56). A company awarded a government contract must also ensure that any new recruits it takes on to work on the contract are given terms and conditions that are, overall, no less favourable than those of the transferred employees and make a specified level of pension provision for them.

5.3.73　Companies that are considering tendering for government contracts and so may be affected by these special rules can obtain further details on them from us.

section 6

The collective dimension

6.1

Trade union members

Overview

6.1.1 This chapter of the Guide deals with the rights that workers and job applicants have in relation to trade union membership. These are all set out in the Trade Union and Labour Relations (Consolidation) Act 1992. Perhaps the most important is the right not to be discriminated against for being a union member or taking part in union activities (see 6.1.7). The law acknowledges that individuals who do not wish to join a union should also be protected from discrimination. It is therefore unlawful for an employer to discriminate against an individual because he or she is not a union member (see 6.1.22).

6.1.2 If a company recognises a trade union for the purposes of collective bargaining, the union's officials and members have certain rights to time off work if they are the company's employees. The union's officials, including shop stewards and learning representatives, are entitled to reasonable paid time off to carry out their functions and to undergo related training (see 6.1.30 and 6.1.33), and the union's members are entitled to reasonable unpaid time off for union activities, including using the services of their learning representatives (see 6.1.38 and 6.1.44).

6.1.3 Companies that employ a significant number of union members may be prepared to deduct union membership subscriptions from employees' pay and forward them to the union. There are some legal requirements that 'check-off' arrangements of this type must meet (6.1.46).

6.1.4   A check off agreement is available for download from EEF's website.

6.1.5   Other aspects of the law that are of importance in relation to trade union membership are dealt with elsewhere in this Guide. Employees may join a trade union in the hope that the union will secure improved terms and conditions of employment for them, through negotiations with the employer. This will be possible, of course, only if their employer bargains with the union, and it may choose not to do so. However, there is a legal procedure that a union can use to secure recognition if it has sufficient support among the workforce (see 6.2.16).

6.1.6   Even if their employer does not bargain with unions, employees may decide to join a union for other reasons. One of the most important of these is the assistance the union may provide if an employee is facing disciplinary proceedings or wishes to raise a grievance. Information on the legal right that workers have to be accompanied at disciplinary and grievance hearings by a union official of their choice is provided in 3.3.80.

Discrimination on trade union grounds

6.1.7   The law makes it unlawful for an employer to discriminate against an individual on trade union grounds in three main areas: in recruitment, during employment and in dismissal.

6.1.8   The employment tribunals that hear claims of trade union discrimination are aware that there is unlikely to be any direct evidence that an employer has discriminated on trade union grounds. They may, therefore, take into account the surrounding circumstances, including any anti-union statements that managers may have made, in order to decide whether it is appropriate to infer that the employer acted on union grounds.

Discrimination during recruitment

6.1.9   It is unlawful for an employer to refuse to employ a person because he or she is a union member. On the face of it, this does not protect an individual from being refused a job because of his or her past involvement in union activities. Nevertheless, it would be inadvisable for a company to turn down a job applicant because of his or her past activities. The company's real concern in these circumstances is likely to be that the individual might continue those activities in its employment, indicating that the company is in fact basing its recruitment decision on the individual's current union membership.

6.1.10　When advertising a job, it is important not to suggest that the post is not open to union members. If an advertisement indicates that not being a union member is a pre-condition for employment and a union member unsuccessfully applies for the job, the law views that person as having been refused the job on union grounds, regardless of the real reason for the decision.

Discrimination during employment

6.1.11　It is unlawful for an employer to put a worker under any form of disadvantage in order to prevent or deter him or her from being a union member, or penalise him or her for union membership. It is also unlawful to prevent, deter or penalise a worker's participation in the activities of a union, or use of union services, provided those activities take place at an appropriate time (see 6.1.20). (Removing an individual's accreditation as a shop steward can amount to penalising him or her for union membership. Companies that are considering 'derecognising' a shop steward should therefore contact their local office for advice.) Likewise, it is unlawful for an employer to offer a worker any inducement to give up union membership or activities or not to use union services.

6.1.12　This protection from discrimination covers only members of independent trade unions. A union is not independent if it is under the employer's control or vulnerable to interference by the employer, whether through financial or practical support or in some other way. A union can apply to the Certification Officer for a certificate confirming that it is independent.

Dismissal on union grounds

6.1.13　If an employer dismisses an employee for being a union member or for taking part in union activities or using union services at an appropriate time, the dismissal is automatically unfair. It is also automatically unfair to select an employee for redundancy on union grounds. This rule applies regardless of the employee's age or length of service. It should be noted, however, that this protection from dismissal, like the protection from discrimination during employment, extends only to members of independent unions (see 6.1.12).

6.1.14 If an employee alleges that he or she has been dismissed on union grounds, an employment tribunal may order the employer to re-employ the individual pending the hearing of his or her claim (see 7.2.21).

Collective bargaining

6.1.15 Although it is unlawful for an employer to deter a worker from being a union member or using union services, union membership and services do not carry the right to be covered by collective bargaining. So if an employer refuses to recognise, or derecognises, a union, that does not amount to deterring its employees from being members of that union or using its services.

6.1.16 An employer may, however, be required to recognise a union under the statutory recognition procedure, summarised in Chapter 6.2. Once this procedure is in operation, it is unlawful for an employer to put an employee under a disadvantage, to dismiss the employee, or to select the employee for redundancy on the ground that the employee has supported or opposed recognition or derecognition of the union.

6.1.17 Further, and more generally, it is unlawful for an employer to offer any worker who is a member of an independent trade union that is recognised, or seeking to be recognised, by the employer, any inducement to give up or forgo the right to be covered by collective bargaining.

Past union activities

6.1.18 The law does not expressly prohibit discriminating against a worker on the grounds of his or her past union activities, rather than his or her current membership and activities. However, if there is evidence that an employer's treatment of a worker was influenced by the fact that he or she had been involved in union activities in the past, that could indicate that the employer was in fact discriminating against the worker because of his or her current union membership or activities.

6.1.19 Some examples of the union activities that might be protected include recruiting to the union, organising its activities, obtaining advice from the union, attending formal or informal union meetings, and participating in ballots and elections.

Activities at an 'appropriate time'

6.1.20   An individual is protected from discrimination for taking part in union activities or using union services only if the activities took place at an 'appropriate time'. Any time when the worker is not required to be actually working is an appropriate time. For example, activities during rest breaks are covered. If the employer has agreed to union activities taking place at certain times within working hours, then those times also count.

Blacklisting of trade unionists

6.1.21   The government intends to introduce regulations in 2010 that prohibit the compilation, dissemination and use of blacklists of trade unionists and to make it unlawful for organisations to refuse employment to, dismiss or otherwise cause a detriment to an individual for a reason related to a blacklist. The online version of the *Employment Guide* will be updated when full details are available.

Protection for non-members

6.1.22   The law also prohibits employers from discriminating against those who choose not to join a union. It is therefore unlawful for a company to refuse to recruit an individual because he or she is not a union member.

Advertising jobs

6.1.23   When advertising a job, it is important not to suggest that the post is open only to union members. If an advertisement indicates that being a union member is a pre-condition for employment and a non-member unsuccessfully applies for the job, the law views that person as having been refused the job on union grounds, regardless of the real reason for the decision.

Pressure on non-members

6.1.24   An employer is also acting unlawfully if it puts a worker under any form of disadvantage in order to compel him or her to become a union member or offers the worker any inducement to join a union. And it is automatically unfair to dismiss an employee or to select him or her for redundancy on the grounds that he or she is not a union member or refuses to become one.

6.1.25   It is unlawful for an employer to discriminate against an individual for not being a union member even if it was pressurised into doing so by a union taking or threatening to take industrial action. In those circumstances, however, an employment tribunal may order that the union should join the employer in defending any discrimination claim that the individual then makes, and should pay all or part of any compensation that is awarded.

'Closed shop'

6.1.26   As a result of these legal provisions, the operation of 'pre-entry' or 'post-entry' closed-shop arrangements, whereby an employer recruits or employs only trade union members, is very likely to be unlawful, as are union-only labour supply arrangements and practices.

Rights to time off

6.1.27   If a company bargains with an independent trade union, employees who are members or officials of that union are entitled to a reasonable amount of time off to carry out their activities and duties. This includes their activities as, or using the services of, union learning representatives.

ACAS Code

6.1.28   The Advisory, Conciliation and Arbitration Service (ACAS) has produced a Code of Practice on time off for union duties and activities including guidance on time off for union learning representatives (see 9.6.1). This detailed Code gives practical guidance on the management of requests for time off. The Code is not in itself legally binding, so it is not necessarily unlawful not to follow it. Nevertheless, the content of the Code will be taken into account by an employment tribunal when hearing a claim that an employer has unlawfully refused to allow time off.

6.1.29   It is automatically unfair to dismiss an employee, or to select an employee for redundancy, for enforcing his or her right to time off for union duties or activities, or for alleging that the employer has failed to allow him or her the right to time off. This applies regardless of the employee's age or length of service.

Time off for union duties

6.1.30   Employees who are officials of an independent recognised union have the right to a reasonable amount of paid time off to carry out their duties. This covers union officers as well as shop stewards elected or appointed at workplace level.

6.1.31   The right to paid time off covers any of the official's duties that are concerned with:

- negotiations with the company over issues that are covered by the recognition agreement the company has with the union (recognition agreements are discussed in 6.2.7);

- the performance of any other function that the company has agreed the official should perform; or

- the receipt of information and consultation under the legislation for instance on large-scale redundancies (see 5.2.42) and business transfers (see 5.3.17).

6.1.32   The ACAS Code suggests that duties concerned with negotiations with the employer could include preparing for the negotiations and informing members of their progress and outcome.

Time off for training

6.1.33   Officials are also entitled to a reasonable amount of paid time off to undergo training in aspects of industrial relations that are relevant to the duties for which they are entitled to time off. The training must, however, be approved by the Trades Union Congress (TUC) or the officials' own union.

6.1.34   The amount, purposes and timing of the time off that should be allowed, and any conditions that may apply, are whatever is reasonable in the circumstances. The ACAS Code is relevant here. The Code suggests, for example, that an official requesting time off should take into account the employer's operational circumstances, including its size and the need to maintain the production process, and give as much notice as possible. For its part, when considering a request for time off, the employer should take into account possible difficulties that the official may have in communicating with members who work part-time or on shifts or at distant locations.

Training courses

6.1.35   If the official is asking for time off to attend a training course, the ACAS Code suggests that he or she should provide a copy of the syllabus or prospectus indicating the content of the course.

6.1.36   Employers should bear in mind that it is reasonable to expect officials to spread their absences for training over a period, particularly where the course at issue is repeated regularly and a number of officials have asked to attend the same course. A company may wish to consider running a training course jointly with the union on the company's premises and making the course more relevant to the company's business. The company could even arrange for its own management staff or external experts, such as from us, to contribute to the course.

Payment during working hours

6.1.37   Under the trade union legislation, officials have the right to be paid only for time off that falls during their working hours. However, the law requires, and the ACAS Code acknowledges, that officials who work part-time are entitled to be paid for time spent on their duties and training in the same way as officials who are full-time employees. So, for example, a part-timer who is given time off to attend a full-time training course connected with his or her union's duties should be paid for the full duration of the course, and not just for his or her part-time hours.

Time off for union activities

6.1.38   Employees who are members of an independent recognised union are entitled to a reasonable amount of unpaid time off to take part in the union's activities. The ACAS Code gives some examples of the activities that could be covered: attendance at meetings to discuss and vote on the outcome of negotiations; meeting with union officials to discuss workplace issues; and voting in union elections.

6.1.39   If an employee is acting as the union's representative by, for example, attending a union conference as representative of a particular branch, he or she is entitled to reasonable unpaid time off to carry out his or her activities in that role. The ACAS Code suggests that a representative's activities might include attending branch, area or regional meetings of the union, the union's annual conference and meetings with union officials to discuss workplace issues.

6.1.40   The amount, purposes and timing of the time off that should be allowed, and any conditions that may apply, are whatever is reasonable in the circumstances. The ACAS Code gives guidance on this. It suggests, for example, that the amount of time off that an employee has already had can be taken into account when deciding whether a request for further time off is reasonable.

Union learning representatives

6.1.41   If an independent recognised union has appointed or elected a learning representative from among the workforce, the representative is entitled to reasonable paid time off to carry out certain activities in relation to those of the union's members who are covered by the recognition agreement. The activities are: analysing the members' learning or training needs; providing them with information and advice about learning or training matters; arranging learning or training for them; and promoting the value of learning and training. The representative is also entitled to time off to consult with the employer about these activities, to prepare for them and to undergo relevant training.

6.1.42   In order for the representative to qualify for time off, the union must have notified the employer in writing that the employee is its learning representative, and the individual must have had, or shortly be about to receive, sufficient training to carry out the activities. The ACAS Code on time off for trade union duties and activities includes guidance on time off for union learning representatives and it advises on what amounts to sufficient training.

6.1.43   Under the trade union legislation, learning representatives have the right to be paid only for time off that falls during their working hours. However, the law requires, and the ACAS Code acknowledges, that representatives who work part-time are entitled to equal treatment with representatives who work full-time. This effectively means that they should be paid for any time they spend on their activities outside their part-time hours but within full-time working hours, if a full-time employee would have been entitled to time off for those activities.

6.1.44   Members of the union are entitled to a reasonable amount of unpaid time off in order to use the learning representative's services. The amount, purposes and timing of the time off that should be allowed for learning representatives and members using them, and any conditions that may apply, are whatever is reasonable in the circumstances. The ACAS Code gives guidance on this.

Time off agreements

6.1.45   The ACAS Code encourages employers to reach a formal agreement with their recognised unions on time off. The existence and content of an agreement may be relevant to whether it is reasonable for time off to be granted in a particular case. Time off issues may be included in the general recognition agreement that an employer has with its recognised union. Recognition agreements are discussed in 6.2.42.

Check-off arrangements

6.1.46   Where a company employs a number of union members, it may agree to deduct membership subscriptions from employees' wages and pay these over to the union. There are advantages and disadvantages of operating a 'check-off' system of this kind:

- A check-off system can provide the employer with information on the extent of union membership, although it will give only a partial picture, as many members choose to pay their subscription by other means, such as direct debit.

- An employer can offer a check-off arrangement as a positive concession to the union in the collective bargaining process.

- Setting up a check-off arrangement involves administrative costs, including the expense of making computer payroll changes. On the other hand, the union might agree to contribute towards the costs of operating the system.

- A check-off system could potentially halt or reverse a decline in union membership levels.

- Check-off contributions are a regular flow of money into union funds, some of which may be used for purposes that do not benefit the employer, such as strike pay.

Legal regulation of check-off

6.1.47   A company cannot lawfully deduct union subscriptions from a worker's pay unless it has the worker's written authorisation to do so. If a worker writes to the employer withdrawing his or her authorisation, the employer must stop making the deductions as soon as it is reasonably practicable to do so. A check-off agreement and authorisation form are available for download from EEF's website.

6.1.48   The protection from unauthorised deductions applies to 'workers'. It therefore covers not only employees but also those who work under any other form of contract personally to perform any work. Only those who are genuinely in business on their own account are excluded. Some casual workers or homeworkers who do not have employee status (see 1.2.72) may therefore be covered.

6.1.49   If an employer operates check-off, it should ensure that the deduction is mentioned on the employee's pay statement (see 2.1.20).

Political levy

6.1.50   If a union wants to spend money on political objectives, it must set up a separate political fund. Its members can opt out of making contributions to this fund, sometimes referred to as the 'political levy'. If an employer that operates a check-off arrangement is told by a union member that he or she does not contribute to the union's political fund, the employer must ensure that no political levy is deducted from that member's pay.

6.1.51   It is automatically unfair to dismiss an employee, or to select an employee for redundancy, for enforcing his or her right not to have unauthorised union subscriptions or the political levy deducted from his or her pay, or for alleging that the employer has failed to respect this right. This applies regardless of the employee's age or length of service.

6.2

Collective bargaining

Overview

6.2.1 This chapter of the Guide deals with the practical and legal issues relating to bargaining between employers and trade unions.

6.2.2 An employer may choose to deal with, or 'recognise', a union on a number of different levels. It may decide, for example, to recognise the union as the appropriate representative for its employees in disciplinary and grievance hearings – although workers have the legal right to be accompanied by the union official of their choice, regardless of whether that union is the one their employer recognises (see 3.3.80). Alternatively, or in addition, the employer may recognise the union as a channel through which it can disseminate information to, or consult with, the workforce. Some companies recognise unions for the purposes of collective bargaining, and negotiate with them on terms and conditions of employment or other issues of relevance to the workforce.

6.2.3 This chapter opens with a discussion of some of the considerations that employers will need to bear in mind when deciding whether to recognise a union (see 6.2.7). In some circumstances, an employer may be compelled to recognise a union for bargaining purposes. Where a union has sufficient support among the workforce, it can use a legal procedure to secure recognition. That procedure is outlined in this chapter (see 6.2.16).

6.2.4	If a company recognises a union, it is advisable for the employer and the union to reach a formal recognition agreement that sets out the way in which the relationship will work and the issues that will be covered. This chapter gives some suggestions on what such an agreement might include (see 6.2.42).

6.2.5	When negotiations are concluded between an employer and a union they may result in a formal collective agreement. Collective agreements are not, as a rule, legally binding on the employer and the union that make them. They can, however, create legal rights for the employees they cover, if they are incorporated into individual employees' contracts of employment. This chapter explains how incorporation works (see 6.2.51).

6.2.6	A trade union recognised for collective bargaining purposes has certain rights. This chapter outlines one of them, namely the right to receive information for the purposes of bargaining with the employer (see 6.2.58). The main other rights are described elsewhere in the Guide:

- the right to information on the employer's occupational pension scheme (see 2.4.55);
- the right to appoint safety representatives (see 6.4.61);
- the right to be informed and consulted in the event of large-scale redundancies (see 5.2.43) or a business transfer (see 5.3.17); and
- union officials' and members' right to time off for union duties and activities (see 6.1.27, 6.1.38).

Recognition considerations

6.2.7	If a company receives a request from a trade union for recognition, it should contact us for advice on how to respond. The company's main considerations are likely to be whether recognition will lead to an improved relationship with its employees or help achieve its business objectives. For some employers, employee relations are better managed through some other employee involvement mechanism. (Employee involvement is discussed in Chapter 6.4.) The company will also need to decide what degree of recognition is appropriate – that is, whether it should recognise the union for bargaining purposes (and if so, on what issues) or only for the purposes of providing information to, representing or consulting with the workforce.

Voluntary agreement

6.2.8   Since there is a legal procedure by which a union can secure recognition for bargaining purposes if it has sufficient support (see 6.2.16), the company will need to consider whether it is likely to be able to resist such a claim. Where there is a strong likelihood that recognition could be imposed, the company may prefer to reach a voluntary agreement on recognition with the union. A company that recognises a union voluntarily has more control over the recognition process and its outcome than a company that has recognition forced upon it through the legal procedure. This gives the company greater control over which union it bargains with, which workers are covered by the bargaining arrangement, and the way that bargaining is conducted.

One union or more?

6.2.9   Two or more unions may approach a company for recognition. Recognising more than one union can have disadvantages. Separate negotiations make for a more time-consuming and complicated bargaining process. There is also the possibility of inter-union disputes on bargaining priorities and recruitment issues. These potential problems can be avoided by the use of single-table bargaining, where the employer agrees to negotiate with two or more unions on condition that the unions act on a joint basis when bargaining and on all other collective issues. The employer may agree to the unions acting separately when dealing with their members' individual disciplinary issues and grievances.

6.2.10 If an employer decides to bargain with only one among several unions seeking recognition, it may be able to secure some concessions from that union in return. The union may, for example, be prepared to agree to some form of dispute-resolution mechanism that avoids the use of industrial action.

Which level?

6.2.11 It is possible for collective bargaining to take place at several different levels. Negotiations may happen at national level, with several employers and several unions bargaining jointly and the resulting collective agreement covering many workplaces in a particular sector or industry. National-level agreements of this type are now rare, but there is, for example, a national agreement in the engineering construction industry.

6.2.12　Within a company, bargaining can take place at several levels. It may cover the whole company, or one division or region of the company, or one establishment or plant within the company. A company might consider it appropriate for different issues to be covered at different levels. For example, negotiations on the company's pension scheme might most effectively be carried out at company level, while negotiations on productivity bonuses might be dealt with at establishment level.

Bargaining units

6.2.13　When deciding whether to recognise a union, an employer will need to consider which employees should be covered by the recognition agreement. The group or groups of employees to whom a recognition agreement on collective bargaining relates are normally referred to as the 'bargaining unit'.

6.2.14　The scope of the bargaining unit will usually depend upon the employer's organisational structure and the areas in which the union has sufficient membership or support to make recognition appropriate. A bargaining unit is commonly defined by the type of work that employees do or the location of their workplace or both.

Data protection considerations

6.2.15　A union may ask an employer for the names and contact details of employees, to enable it to recruit them to the union. The Data Protection Code (see 9.8.3) advises employers to provide this information only if the union is recognised by the employer, the information is necessary to enable the union to recruit, and the employee has been told that his or her information will be released for this purpose and has been given an opportunity to object. The information can also be released to the union if the employee has expressly agreed to this.

Statutory procedure for recognition

6.2.16 If a trade union has sufficient support among a company's workforce, it may be able to secure recognition from the company for collective bargaining purposes under a procedure set down in the Trade Union and Labour Relations (Consolidation) Act 1992. This procedure is extremely complex and a summary only is provided here. A flow diagram illustrating the operation of the procedure can be found at the end of this chapter. Companies that are facing a legal claim for recognition should contact us for advice.

6.2.17 The statutory procedure has been designed to encourage employers and unions to reach voluntary agreements on recognition wherever possible: employers and unions are provided with opportunities throughout the procedure to reach a voluntary agreement on recognition rather than move on to the next stage. If they wish, they can call on the services of the Advisory, Conciliation and Arbitration Service to help them reach agreement.

6.2.18 The procedure does not apply to small employers, that is, those that employ 20 or fewer people. In deciding whether a company meets this figure, the numbers employed by the company and by any associated employer are taken into account. (Employers are associated if one is a company controlled by the other or they are both companies controlled by another body, so companies within the same corporate group are likely to be associated.)

Union approach

6.2.19 The first step in the statutory procedure is for the union to approach the employer formally, to ask for recognition. If the employer does not agree to recognition, the union can apply to a body called the Central Arbitration Committee (CAC) for it to decide whether the union should be recognised. The CAC will accept applications for recognition only from independent trade unions, that is, unions that are not under the employer's domination or control or liable to interference by the employer. Joint application from two or more unions will be considered, provided they can show that they will co-operate in the bargaining process and, if the employer wants it, that they will agree to single-table bargaining (see 6.2.9).

6.2.20 The CAC will not accept an application for recognition if the employer already recognises a union in respect of any workers covered by the application. This ensures that established collective bargaining relationships with one union are not disrupted by an application for recognition by another union.

Need for reasonable support

6.2.21 The CAC will consider a union's application for recognition only if it is satisfied that the union has reasonable support from the workers in the proposed bargaining unit. (The bargaining unit is the group of workers who are to be covered by the bargaining arrangements. If the union and employer have not agreed the unit, the CAC may have to decide what the appropriate unit is, as explained in 6.2.23.) A union will be viewed as having reasonable support if at least 10 per cent of the workers in the bargaining unit are members of the union and the CAC thinks a majority of the workers in the unit are likely to favour recognition.

6.2.22 The CAC may receive competing applications from unions seeking to represent the same group of workers. If only one of the unions has at least 10 per cent of the workers as members, its application will be accepted. If both unions pass this test or neither one does, then neither application will be accepted. The unions then have the option of making a joint application if they wish.

Defining the bargaining unit

6.2.23 If the employer does not agree to the union's proposed bargaining unit, the CAC will decide whether that unit is in fact appropriate. In reaching its decision, the CAC will apply certain criteria laid down in the legislation. The overriding criterion is that the unit must be compatible with effective management. This is, in practice, a low hurdle for the union to cross. Provided the union proposed bargaining unit does not conflict with that criterion, the following factors will also be taken into account:

- the views of the employer and the union;
- existing national and local bargaining arrangements;
- the desirability of avoiding small, fragmented bargaining units;

- the characteristics of the workers falling within the proposed unit and of any other employees the CAC considers relevant; and

- the location of workers.

If the CAC concludes that the union's proposed unit is appropriate, it will confirm it, even if it is not the best or most effective unit that could have been put forward. However, if the CAC concludes that the proposed unit is not appropriate, it will decide what unit is appropriate.

Automatic recognition

6.2.24   If it is satisfied that the majority of the workers in the bargaining unit are members of the union, the CAC will automatically grant recognition, unless one of the conditions requiring a ballot (see 6.2.25) applies. If the majority of the workers are not members of the union, a ballot will always be held.

Ballot on recognition

6.2.25   If the majority of the workers in the proposed bargaining unit are not members of the union, the workers will be balloted for their views on whether the union should be recognised. Even if the majority of the workers are members, a ballot will be held if:

- the CAC considers that a ballot should be held in the interests of good industrial relations; or

- the CAC has evidence, which it considers to be credible, from a significant number of the union's members in the bargaining unit that they do not want the union to bargain on their behalf; or

- evidence is produced on the length of time the workers in the unit have been union members, or on the circumstances in which they became members, that leads the CAC to doubt whether a significant number of union members want the union to bargain on their behalf. This might apply, for example, if new members were offered free membership as part of the union's campaign for recognition.

6.2.26   The ballot is conducted by an independent third party appointed by the CAC. It is a secret ballot, conducted at the workplace, or by post, or by a combination of those methods, as the CAC considers appropriate. The cost of the ballot is shared equally by the employer and the union.

Employer co-operation and fair play

6.2.27 The employer must co-operate generally with the ballot and provide the CAC with the names and home addresses of the workers in the proposed bargaining unit, so that these can be passed on to the person running the ballot. The employer must also allow the union reasonable access to the workers in the proposed bargaining unit, so that the union can let them know what the ballot is about and seek their support or their opinions. This may involve allowing the union to hold a private meeting with the workers, if the union requests one, to discuss the ballot and the issues involved. If such a meeting is held, the employer must not try to dissuade workers from attending it or penalise them if they do so, nor attempt to find out what went on at it.

6.2.28 Both the employer and the union are under a duty not to engage in unfair practices aimed at influencing the ballot result. This means, for example, that neither employer nor union must offer workers money or any other benefit to encourage them to vote in a particular way, or pressurise them to disclose how they intend to vote or have voted, or threaten them with any sanction. There is a Code of Practice on access and unfair practices during union recognition and derecognition ballots, which gives further detail and practical guidance on these duties (see 9.6.2).

6.2.29 If an employer refuses to co-operate with the ballot or either side engages in unfair practices, the CAC has a range of powers, including power to cancel the ballot, make the ballot result void, and order the employer to recognise the union.

Ballot result

6.2.30 If a majority of those voting in the ballot and at least 40 per cent of the workers in the unit vote in favour of recognition, then recognition will be ordered. For example, if the proposed bargaining unit contains 200 workers and 75 vote in favour of recognition and 50 against, recognition will not be awarded, as fewer than 40 per cent of the electorate voted in favour. On the other hand, if 85 vote in favour and 60 against, recognition will follow.

Method of bargaining

6.2.31 If recognition is awarded but the employer and the union are unable to reach agreement on how bargaining should be conducted, the CAC can impose a method. This will be based on the model method set out in the Trade Union Recognition (Method of Collective Bargaining) Order 2000. The model method requires the employer and union to establish a Joint Negotiating Body, made up of at least three employer representatives and at least three union representatives. The Body must negotiate at least annually on pay, hours and holidays.

6.2.32 If an employer refused to bargain in accordance with the imposed method, the union could apply to the court for an order that the company should comply with it. If the employer still failed to comply, it would be in contempt of court.

Subject matter and legal effect of bargaining

6.2.33 If a union achieves recognition under the statutory procedure, the company must negotiate on pay, hours and holidays. Negotiations can also extend to other matters if the employer and union agree that they should be covered. If a bargaining method has been imposed (see 6.2.31), the employer will also be required to consult with the union on training matters.

6.2.34 Once a collective agreement is reached, the legal effect it has depends on whether it is incorporated into individual employees' contracts of employment. The incorporation of collective agreements is discussed below (6.2.51).

New applications

6.2.35 If the union fails to secure recognition, it cannot apply again for the same bargaining unit for three years.

Derecognition

6.2.36   If a union has been recognised under the statutory procedure, there is a separate procedure by which the employer or one or more of the workers in the bargaining unit can apply to the CAC for the union to be derecognised. The application for derecognition cannot be made earlier than three years after recognition was awarded. The union will be derecognised if a majority of those who vote and at least 40 per cent of the workers in the bargaining unit favour derecognition in a secret ballot.

6.2.37   If an employer recognises a union voluntarily, it is free to derecognise the union whenever it wishes. Any employer that derecognises a union, whether under the statutory procedure or otherwise, should bear in mind that it is bound by the terms of any collective agreements that it reached with the union that have been incorporated into individual employees' contracts (see 6.2.51).

6.2.38   The legislation also lays down procedures that allow an employer to apply for the union to be derecognised if:

- the employer no longer employs more than 20 workers; or
- the bargaining unit no longer exists; or
- recognition was awarded without a ballot on the basis that 50 per cent of the workers in the unit were union members, but membership has now fallen below 50 per cent.

Revising the bargaining unit

6.2.39   If the employer changes its structure, nature or size, the bargaining unit covered by the original recognition award may become inappropriate. The legislation therefore lays down a procedure whereby either the employer or the union can apply for the bargaining unit to be amended to reflect the changed circumstances.

Protection for employees

6.2.40   It is automatically unfair for an employer to dismiss an employee or to select an employee for redundancy because he or she has supported or opposed the recognition or derecognition of a union under the statutory procedure. This protection applies regardless of the employee's age or length of service. It is also unlawful for an employer to put a worker under any other form of disadvantage on these grounds. More generally, it is unlawful for an employer to offer any worker who is a member of an independent trade union that is recognised, or seeking to be recognised, by the employer, any inducement to give up or forgo the right to be covered by collective bargaining.

6.2.41 If an employee alleges that he or she has been dismissed for a reason relating to union recognition, an employment tribunal may order the employer to re-employ the individual pending the hearing of his or her claim (see 7.2.21).

Recognition agreements

6.2.42 If a company decides to recognise one or more trade unions, voluntarily or under the statutory procedure (see 6.2.16), it would be well advised to reach a formal recognition agreement with the union or unions. Companies may wish to contact us for advice on the content of the agreement.

Content

6.2.43 When drafting a recognition agreement, the company might consider including the following:

- *Definitions*. In order to make the agreement clear and easy to read, any terms that are used frequently, such as 'the Company' and 'the Union', should be defined at the outset.

- *Aims*. The agreement could open with a summary of its aims and the responsibilities that the employer and union have to make the relationship work.

- *Extent of recognition*. The agreement should state the purposes for which the employer recognises the union. If the company recognises the union for the purposes of bargaining, but only on certain aspects of employees' terms and conditions, the agreement should make clear which issues are covered.

- *The bargaining unit*. The employees that are covered by the agreement should be clearly defined. This could be done, for example, by reference to job title, or work location, or both.

- *The union's representatives*. The agreement should specify who will represent the union in its dealings with the company. Depending on the size and structure of the company and the number of employees involved, the company may wish to consider having a separate official for each section, shift, skill group or geographical location represented in the bargaining unit. The agreement could also state how the union will notify the company of the identity of its officials. It would be advisable for the union to confirm the identity of its officials periodically, after elections have taken place or on an annual basis.

- *Facilities*. If the company is prepared to provide facilities for union officials, such as the use of telephones, copying facilities or a notice board, the agreement could confirm what these are.

- *Time off*. The agreement could also cover how union officials' and members' requests for time off for union duties and activities will be handled. It would be advisable for these arrangements to reflect the guidance in the Code of Practice on time off for union duties and activities (see 9.6.1). (The right to time off for union duties and activities is explained in 6.1.27 and 6.1.38.)

- *Recruitment*. If the company is willing to promote union membership, the agreement could set out what arrangements the company will make to facilitate the union in recruiting new employees as members. The agreement should not, however, suggest that union membership will be required of new recruits, as union membership requirements are unlawful (see 6.1.9).

- *Check-off*. Some employers are prepared to deduct union members' membership subscriptions from their pay and forward them to the union, perhaps in return for the union paying an administration fee. If that is the case, the agreement could confirm those 'check-off' arrangements (see 6.1.46).

- *Procedure for negotiations*. The agreement should outline the procedure for negotiations, including their timing and any further procedure for disclosure of information to the union. (The union's right to receive information for the purposes of negotiations is discussed further in 6.2.58.)

- *Resolution of disputes.* The agreement should contain some procedure for the resolution of disputes between the employer and the union. This is discussed further in 6.2.44.

- *Review.* It would be advisable for the agreement to provide for its contents to be reviewed once it has been in place for a year or so, so that both parties can consider whether any amendments are necessary.

- *Termination.* The agreement should specify what length of notice a party should give to terminate the agreement.

Resolution of disputes

6.2.44   It is important for the health of the relationship between an employer and its recognised trade union that an effective agreed procedure should be available to resolve disputes between them. Companies may wish to obtain advice from us on the content of such a procedure.

Collective grievances

6.2.45   Commonly, dispute resolution procedures provide for collective grievances to be raised in writing to or by a specified level of management, and then dealt with by negotiation. It may also be advisable to include an external stage to cover the possibility that the dispute cannot be resolved internally. This might involve a meeting between a representative of the employer's Association and a full-time official of the union, or some form of mediation or arbitration by a third party such as the Advisory, Conciliation and Arbitration Service. There could even be provision for an unresolved dispute to be referred to compulsory arbitration, the results of which would be binding on both parties.

It is advisable for any dispute resolution procedure to include a 'peace clause'. This requires the union not to resort to industrial action before the procedure is exhausted. For its part, the company agrees not to implement any change that is being challenged until the procedure has run its course.

Individual grievances

6.2.46   It is usually appropriate for individual employees' grievances to be dealt with through the company's grievance procedure. (The handling of individual grievances is discussed in Chapter 3.3.) It could be useful, however, to provide that individual grievances that raise issues common to many employees will be dealt with through the dispute resolution procedure.

Collective agreements

6.2.47   When an employer and a trade union successfully conclude their negotiations, they may confirm the results of their efforts in a formal collective agreement.

6.2.48   Collective agreements can broadly be divided into two main types. One type regulates the relationship between the employer and the union, and deals with mainly procedural issues such as how and when negotiations will be conducted and the facilities the employer will provide to the union's officials. A recognition agreement falls within this category. The other type covers substantive issues such as pay, holidays and sickness benefits. Some collective agreements are a hybrid of the two. An agreement on redundancy, for example, may deal with issues such as consultation with the union, as well as the size of the redundancy payments that individual employees will receive.

Form and content

6.2.49   It is advisable for a collective agreement to be in writing. It should be clearly drafted to avoid disputes over its meaning. If the agreement will be renegotiated from time to time, then it should state how long it is intended to last and when negotiations will begin again.

Legal status

6.2.50   According to the Trade Union and Labour Relations (Consolidation) Act 1992, a collective agreement is legally enforceable by the parties to it only if it is in writing and states that the parties intend it to be legally enforceable. These conditions are rarely, if ever, met. As a result, neither employer nor union has any legal redress if the other party decides to ignore the terms of the agreement or withdraw from it.

Collective agreements may, however, create legal rights if they form part of the contracts of employment of the employees they cover, as explained in 6.2.51.

Incorporation

6.2.51 The terms of a collective agreement can become part of an individual employee's contract by a process known as 'incorporation'. A collective agreement can be incorporated into an employee's contract even if the individual is not a union member. A contract can even incorporate the terms of a collective agreement that the employer had no part in negotiating. However, any terms of a collective agreement which prohibit or restrict the right of workers to engage in industrial action ('no strike clauses') are not to be incorporated into employment contracts unless a number of conditions are satisfied in the collective agreement itself. These conditions are seldom, if ever, met.

6.2.52 In order to be capable of being incorporated, an agreement must cover issues that are suitable and appropriate for inclusion in an individual's contract. For example, an agreement dealing with collective bargaining arrangements between the employer and the union would not be capable of incorporation, but an agreement on working hours or rates of pay would be. Some agreements deal with a combination of procedural and substantive issues, and the terms dealing with substantive issues may be capable of being incorporated even if the terms covering procedural issues are not.

Express incorporation

6.2.53 If an agreement is appropriate for incorporation, the next question is whether the whole or part of it has actually been incorporated into an individual employee's contract. The clearest mechanism for doing this is a term in the employee's written contract of employment, offer letter or written statement of terms and conditions that expressly states that the agreement is part of the individual's terms and conditions. As explained in 1.2.47, an employer is required to provide its employees with written information on their terms and conditions of employment. This must include a statement of whether there are any collective agreements that directly affect the individual's terms and conditions. If the employer is not party to those agreements, the employee must also be told the bodies by whom the agreements were made.

Incorporation by implication

6.2.54   It is also possible, however, for a collective agreement to be incorporated into an individual's contract by implication. This can happen if the employer intends the agreement to be part of its employees' contracts, even if it has not expressly stated anywhere that this should be so. If an employer observes the terms of a collective agreement in practice, this may be viewed as evidence that the employer intends to be bound by them.

Incorporation and variation

6.2.55   If it is intended that a collective agreement that is incorporated into an individual's contract will be reviewed and renegotiated from time to time, any incorporation clause in the employee's contract should reflect the fact that the terms of the agreement may change. In that way, the employee will be bound by any change, even if he or she has not individually consented to it. The clause could read, for example: 'Your basic rate of pay will be as set down in the Pay Agreement as negotiated by the Company and the XYZ Union from time to time.'

6.2.56   Once the whole or part of a collective agreement has been incorporated into an individual employee's contract, the incorporated terms become part of that individual's enforceable legal rights. An employer that departed from the terms of the agreement could therefore face a variety of legal claims, including breach of contract, unlawful deductions from pay and unfair constructive dismissal. Further, the terms of the agreement remain part of the employee's contract even if the employer decides to withdraw from the agreement because, for example, it has derecognised the union. Therefore, the employee remains entitled to the terms and conditions set by the agreement before the employer withdrew.

Other legal repercussions

6.2.57   The content of a collective agreement may have legal implications even if it is not incorporated into individual employees' contracts. Where, for example, an employer disregards a collectively agreed disciplinary or redundancy procedure when dismissing an employee, that could possibly lead to a finding of unfair dismissal, on the basis that the employer did not act reasonably when deciding to dismiss.

Right to bargaining information

6.2.58   An independent trade union that is recognised by a company for the purposes of collective bargaining is entitled to be supplied, on request, with certain information about the company to assist it in the bargaining process. A union is independent if it is not under an employer's domination or control or liable to interference by the employer. The right to information is set out in the Trade Union and Labour Relations (Consolidation) Act 1992.

Information covered

6.2.59   The union is entitled to information if all the following conditions are met:

- the information relates to the company's business and is in the possession of the company or an associated employer (employers are associated if one is a company that is controlled by the other or both are companies that are controlled by a third party, so companies in the same corporate group are likely to be associated employers);

- the information relates to issues and categories of workers covered by the company's recognition agreement with the union;

- the union would be impeded in the bargaining process if it did not have the information;

- it would be good industrial relations practice for the company to disclose it; and

- the information is not covered by one of the exclusions set out in 6.2.64.

Code of Practice

6.2.60   There is an ACAS Code of Practice (see 9.6.2) that gives guidance on what information should be disclosed, and the Central Arbitration Committee takes this Code into account when deciding whether the employer has met its legal obligations. The Code states that it would be good industrial relations practice for an employer to give the union any information that would influence the way in which it formulated, presented or pursued its claim, or how it reached agreement at the end of the negotiations.

6.2.61   As the Code points out, the information that is relevant to collective bargaining depends on the subject matter of the negotiations and the level at which they are carried out. The Code gives some examples of information that could potentially be relevant. Information on pay and benefits, it suggests, could include:

- the principles and structure of payment systems;
- job evaluation systems and grading criteria; and
- earnings and hours analysed according to work-group, grade, plant, sex, out-workers and homeworkers, department or division.

6.2.62   The Code suggests that relevant financial information could include:

- gross and net profits;
- sources of earnings;
- assets;
- liabilities and allocation of profits.

6.2.63   When supplying information, the company is not obliged to let the union see or have a copy of the original documents from which the information may have been compiled. Nor does the company have to provide information if compiling or assembling it would involve effort or expense out of reasonable proportion to its value to the union in negotiations. The Data Protection Code (see 9.8.3) advises employers to ensure that, when supplying a union with information on staffing in the course of bargaining, individual workers are not identified: aggregated or statistical information should suffice.

Excluded information

6.2.64   A company does not have to disclose information if any of the following circumstances apply:

1. Disclosing the information would substantially damage the employer's business for some reason other than its effect on collective bargaining, such as loss of customers or damage to the company's ability to raise funds. The Code of Practice gives these examples of information that might cause substantial damage if disclosed:

- cost information on individual products;
- detailed analysis of proposed investment, marketing or pricing policies;
- price quotas or the make-up of tender prices.

2. The company received the information in confidence.

3. The information relates specifically to an individual and the individual has not consented to its disclosure.

4. The company obtained the information for the purpose of legal proceedings.

5. Disclosing the information would be against the interests of national security.

6. Disclosing the information would involve the company breaking a prohibition imposed on it by legislation.

Collective bargaining

Union applies for recognition

```
                              ↓
                        21 or more
                          people          ──no──→
                         employed
                              │yes
                              ↓
     Agree to recognise ←─no─ Does employer refuse
         union?                or fail to respond to
                                    request?
     yes│    no│                      │yes
        │      ↓                      ↓
        │   Employer willing  ──no──→ CAC  ──10 days*──→ Evidence of  ──no──→
        │   to negotiate?                                 sufficient
        │        │yes                                      support?
        │        ↓                                           │yes
   yes  │    Negotiations  ──no──→                           ↓
    ←───┤    successful?
                                                      Bargaining unit  ←─no── Voluntary  ←─no── CAC decides
                                                         agreed?                agreement?         bargaining unit
                                                           │yes                                         │
                                                           ↓                                            ↓
        Are over half the  ──yes──→ Is the unit the same  ──no──→ Evidence of
        bargaining unit union      as originally sought?           sufficient support?
            members?       ←─yes──
          yes│    no│                                                │yes
             │      ↓                                                 │
             │   Does CAC believe  ──yes──→ Recognition
             │   a ballot should be           ballot
             │   held anyway?                   │
                   │no                       20 days*
                   ↓                            ↓
               Union         ←──yes── Majority of voters  ──no──→ Union not
             recognised               and more than 40%           recognised
                                      of all employees
                                    support recognition?
```

days* = working days

Source: based on the Explanatory Notes to the Employment Relations Bill, 13 April 1999 [HL Bill 48]

497

6.3

Industrial action

Overview

6.3.1   Industrial action can have very serious consequences for a business. This chapter of the Guide opens by describing the types of industrial action that may be used by workers who are in dispute with their employer (see 6.3.5). It then outlines ways of avoiding industrial action (see 6.3.9) and summarises the practical considerations that employers need to bear in mind when formulating their response to it (see 6.3.12).

6.3.2   The chapter then goes on to deal with the law. This is a complex area, and companies that are facing industrial action may wish to contact us for advice.

6.3.3   In calling employees out on strike, a trade union and its officials are not only asking their members to break their obligations under their employment contract but also interfering with the employer's ability to fulfil its obligations under its commercial contracts with its customers and suppliers. On the face of it, these actions are unlawful and, if legislation did not intervene, the employer would be able to ask a court to order the union to stop calling the action and award the employer compensation for any economic loss the action had caused. The law does, however, give unions some leeway to organise industrial action without being sued, provided that the action meets certain conditions. This chapter explains what those conditions are (see 6.3.16), the most important being the need for the action to be supported by a properly conducted secret ballot.

6.3.4　Industrial action has important legal consequences for the individuals who take part in it, as well as for the union that organises it. This chapter explains how employees who take industrial action are very likely to be breaking their contractual obligation to be ready and willing to carry out their duties (see 6.3.58). The chapter also explains how employees may in certain limited circumstances lose their protection from being unfairly dismissed (see 6.3.42). Drawing on these legal rules, the chapter ends with a discussion of the options that are open to an employer in dealing with individuals who take industrial action (see 6.3.61).

Types of industrial action

6.3.5　Industrial action can take a variety of forms, but the common characteristic of all of them is that workers are acting together in order to put pressure on their employer. Commonly, the aim is to secure the employer's agreement to the employees' claim for improved terms and conditions or to persuade the employer to accept the merits of the employees' collective grievance.

Examples of industrial action

6.3.6　Industrial action can range from minor restrictions on the work that employees are prepared to do through to complete and prolonged stoppages of work. The following are examples of industrial action:

- A 'go slow', where employees deliberately reduce their productivity.
- A 'work to rule', where employees do no more than the minimum required of them under the express terms of their contract.
- An overtime ban, where employees refuse to undertake overtime working, whether or not they are obliged to work overtime under their contract.
- 'Blacking', which entails employees refusing to work with particular customers, suppliers, articles, machines or people.
- Picketing, which involves workers standing outside a particular location, usually a workplace, in order to publicise their case, often with the aim of dissuading their fellow employees or the employees of suppliers or customers from entering.

- Strike action, which involves a complete withdrawal of labour. It can be a continuous stoppage that lasts for days or weeks, or a periodic stoppage, where employees strike for an hour or a day in certain weeks.

Mass meetings

6.3.7   A mass meeting may amount to industrial action if it is held in order to disrupt the employer's business or to put pressure on the employer by demonstrating support for the union's position in a dispute. It is important to bear in mind, however, that employees have the right to a reasonable amount of unpaid time off to carry out union activities (see 6.1.38) and the right not to be discriminated against on the grounds that they have taken part in union activities at an appropriate time (see 6.1.11). Union activities do not include taking part in industrial action, but they can include organising or campaigning for it. In practice, it may be difficult to establish whether a meeting amounts to industrial action or a union activity. Employers may therefore wish to seek advice from us before taking action in response to the holding of a mass meeting.

Lock-outs

6.3.8   There is one form of industrial action that is taken by employers rather than workers. An employer that wishes to bring pressure to bear on its workers to accept certain working conditions or practices may decide to close the workplace or suspend them from work until they agree. This is termed a lock-out.

Avoiding industrial action

6.3.9   The most effective means of avoiding industrial action is to adopt good employment relations practices that reduce the likelihood of industrial disputes arising. Efficient and fair procedures for dealing with the resolution of grievances and effective channels of communication between management and workforce are particularly important.

Dispute resolution mechanism

6.3.10   Employers that have established relationships with trade unions are likely to have agreed some form of dispute resolution mechanism with the unions in order to avoid or reduce the risk of industrial action. The national procedural agreements between the EEF and the unions in engineering, for example, set out procedures for resolving disputes. They also provide that there will be no stoppage of work until the procedure has been exhausted, and that whatever practice or agreement existed prior to the dispute arising will continue to apply while the procedure is under way.

'Unconstitutional action'

6.3.11   Industrial action that is taken before these agreed procedures have been exhausted is termed 'unconstitutional action'. When industrial action is taken after procedures have been exhausted it is termed 'constitutional action'. Whether or not action is constitutional within the terms of an agreed procedure does not, however, affect whether it can be legally challenged. That depends on the legal rules explained in 6.3.16. However, it is, of course, easier to persuade a trade union official to call off unconstitutional action than constitutional industrial action.

Responding to industrial action

6.3.12   An employer's response to industrial action will vary according to the nature of the action and the employer's business situation. In formulating its response, however, the employer should bear in mind that its overriding objective is to resolve the underlying dispute as speedily as possible, rather than to aggravate it.

Assessing the action

6.3.13   An employer facing industrial action will need to assess the degree of support the action has among the workforce and the union's officials. It will also need to assess the legal position. If the action does not meet the requirements of the law (see 6.3.16), the company may be able to get the union to repudiate the industrial action or obtain a court order requiring the union to call off the action. It may also be able to take action against individuals to dissuade them from taking part in the action (see 6.3.41).

Planning ahead

6.3.14   From a practical perspective, it is important for a company to plan ahead if industrial action is threatened. It needs to decide how it will:

- minimise the disruptive effect that the action will have on its operations;

- communicate with customers and suppliers about the action and the company's plans for minimising the disruption it causes;

- maintain effective channels of communication with its workforce during the dispute;

- ensure that the company's strategy for handling the dispute is clearly communicated to all management staff;

- communicate effectively to and through the media.

Record of dispute

6.3.15   It would be advisable for the company to keep an accurate and complete record of the dispute, including the content of meetings and other developments, in case this is needed for the purpose of legal proceedings or negotiations to end the dispute.

Union liability for industrial action

6.3.16   If legislation did not intervene, an employer would be able to ask a court to order the trade union or its officials to call off the action and pay the employer compensation for the economic loss the action had caused. This is because, in calling for industrial action, a trade union and its officials are usually encouraging their members to break their contractual obligations towards their employer. In doing so they are also interfering with the employer's ability to fulfil its obligations under its commercial contracts with its customers and suppliers. It is a civil wrong (known in England and Wales as a 'tort' and in Scotland as a 'delict') to encourage people to break their contracts or to interfere with the performance of contracts in this way.

6.3.17 The law accepts, however, that a union should have some leeway to organise industrial action without the risk of being sued, provided that the industrial action meets certain conditions. These conditions are complex, and are set out in the Trade Union and Labour Relations (Consolidation) Act 1992. This chapter refers to action that meets these conditions as *'protected' industrial action*. Because of the complexity of the law, companies that are considering challenging industrial action through the courts should contact us for advice.

Is the union legally responsible?

6.3.18 A union can be held legally responsible for industrial action only if it has authorised or endorsed the action. This means that the action must have been approved by whoever has the power to do so under the union's rules, or the union's principal executive committee, president or general secretary, or any other committee or official of the union.

6.3.19 An 'official' includes anyone elected or appointed to represent members under the union's rules, so it covers lay officials such as shop stewards as well as full-time officials. If the action was approved by a group whose purpose was to organise or coordinate industrial action and the official was a member of that group, then the official is viewed as having approved it.

6.3.20 A union can authorise action by a formal, minuted decision. It can also authorise action in an informal way by, for example, giving approval by a 'nod and a wink'.

Repudiating the action

6.3.21 If action has been approved by an official or committee of the union other than the principal executive committee, the union has the opportunity to disown or 'repudiate' it. This involves the union's principal executive committee, president or general secretary writing to the official or committee as soon as reasonably practicable after they learn of the action. The union must also do its best to notify all its members who are taking part or might take part in the action that it has repudiated it, and give the date of the repudiation. The notice must be sent to each member individually and must contain this statement:

Your union has repudiated the call (or calls) for industrial action to which this notice relates and will give no support to unofficial action taken in response to it (or them). If you are dismissed while taking unofficial industrial action, you will have no right to complain of unfair dismissal.

(The effect of unofficial action on employees' right to claim unfair dismissal is discussed in 6.3.46.) The union must also give the employer involved in the dispute written notice that it has repudiated the action, and the date of repudiation.

6.3.22 Repudiation will be ineffective if the executive committee, president or general secretary of the union then acts in a way that is inconsistent with that position, such as informally indicating they support the action.

Purpose of the action

6.3.23 In order to be 'protected', industrial action must be taken 'in contemplation or furtherance of a trade dispute'. A dispute is a trade dispute only if it relates to issues such as terms and conditions of employment, allocation of work, and disciplinary issues. Action that was taken for political purposes would therefore not be protected.

6.3.24 Certain action taken to enforce union membership or union recognition is not protected. An employer could challenge action that was organised:

- to force the employer to employ only union members; or
- to force the employer to require its customers or suppliers to employ only union members or to recognise a union; or
- to disrupt the employer's relationship with a supplier that does not recognise a union.

6.3.25 However, action taken against an employer to pressurise it to recognise a trade union may be protected if it meets the other legal requirements for protected action.

Secondary action

6.3.26 Workers who are not in dispute with their own employer may be prepared to take action in support of another group of workers who are in dispute with theirs. This is referred to as 'secondary action' or 'sympathy' or 'solidarity' action. Secondary action is generally not protected.

Support for unofficial action

6.3.27 A union can also be sued for organising action in support of employees dismissed while taking part in unofficial industrial action. The meaning of 'unofficial' industrial action in this context is explained in 6.3.44.

Ballots

6.3.28 In order to be protected, industrial action must in almost all circumstances have the support of a ballot that meets certain conditions. There is a Code of Practice (see 9.6.3) on the conduct of industrial action ballots and notice to employers that summarises the legal rules and gives practical guidance on the fair conduct of ballots. This Code will be taken into account by a court if it is asked to decide whether a proper secret ballot has been held.

6.3.29 The conditions that must be met by the ballot are complex, but in summary:

1. All the members that the union reasonably believes at the time of the ballot will be taking part in the action must be given a vote, and nobody else. This includes not only employees but also those working under any other form of contract to perform work personally, so it may cover self-employed and casual workers. If the union accidentally fails to include some members in the vote, this can be disregarded if the numbers involved are unlikely to affect the outcome of the ballot.

2. Ballot papers must be sent out to members by post and members must be entitled to vote by post, without interference from the union and at no direct cost to themselves. A union campaigning for a 'yes' vote does not amount to interference.

3. If the members who are to be called upon to take action work in different workplaces, it may be necessary to hold separate ballots for

each workplace. A single ballot covering more than one workplace is permissible, however, if:

- there is at least one union member at each workplace who is directly affected by the dispute; or

- the union is balloting every member in a particular occupational category who is employed by a particular employer involved in the dispute; or

- the union is balloting every member who is employed by a particular employer involved in the dispute.

4. At least seven days before the ballot, the union must notify the employer that a ballot is to be held and when the first ballot papers will be sent out. The union must also give the employer certain information about the individuals it will be balloting, namely: the total number to be balloted; the categories of employees involved and the total number in each category; the workplaces involved and the number at each workplace; and an explanation of how those numbers have been arrived at. If the employer deducts union subscriptions from wages, the union has the alternative option of providing the employer with information that will enable it to deduce the relevant information by reference to the employees covered by the check-off arrangement. The union is under no obligation, however, to give the employer the names of the individuals who are being balloted.

5. At least three days before the ballot is due to open, the union must provide the employer with a sample of the voting paper.

6. If the union is assessing support for strike action and action short of a strike, the voting paper must have a separate question on each. For these purposes, an overtime ban and a call-out ban amount to action short of a strike. The paper must also contain certain information, details of which are given in 6.3.31.

7. A majority of those voting in the ballot must vote in favour of the question that relates to the type of action that the union intends to call.

8. As soon as reasonably practicable after the ballot, the union must let the employer and those entitled to vote know the number of votes cast, the number of 'yes' and 'no' votes cast for each question on the ballot paper, and the number of spoiled papers.

9. If more than 50 people are to be balloted, the union must appoint a qualified independent person to scrutinise the ballot. Within four weeks of the ballot, the scrutineer must prepare a report on whether it met the statutory requirements. The union must supply a copy of the report to any of the people who were balloted and to the employer, if they request a copy within six months of the ballot.

6.3.30 If a union official or committee has authorised or endorsed unballoted industrial action, the union cannot escape legal liability for it simply by holding a ballot. It must first repudiate the action in the way explained in 6.3.21 and then hold a ballot.

Ballot paper contents

6.3.31 These are the required contents of a ballot paper:

- One or both of the following questions (which can be framed in any way provided they require a 'yes' or 'no' answer):
    - Are you prepared to take part in or continue to take part in a strike?
    - Are you prepared to take part in or continue to take part in action short of a strike?
- The following statement, unqualified or commented upon:

    If you take part in a strike or other industrial action, you may be in breach of your contract of employment. However, if you are dismissed for taking part in a strike or other industrial action which is called officially and is otherwise lawful, the dismissal will be unfair if it takes place fewer than twelve weeks after you started taking part in the action, and depending on the circumstances may be unfair if it takes place later.

- The address to which the paper must be returned.
- The date by which the paper must be returned.
- The person or persons authorised to call for industrial action if the vote is in favour of industrial action.

- The number of the paper. (The papers must be numbered with consecutive numbers.)
- If an independent scrutineer has been appointed, the name of the scrutineer.

Organising the action

6.3.32   In order to be protected, industrial action must not only be approved in a ballot. It must also be organised in a way that meets the following conditions:

Conditions for the organisation of industrial action

1. The union must not call for the action, or authorise or endorse it, before the ballot has been held.
2. The action must be called by whoever was named as the person authorised to do so on the ballot paper.
3. Workers who were not balloted must not be called on to take action, unless they were not members of the union at the time of the ballot or it was not reasonable for the union to believe at the time of the ballot that they would be called on to take part. This means, for example, that the union can call out members who have joined the union since the date of the ballot or who have changed jobs since the ballot and moved into a category of workers that the union intends to call out. The union can also call out workers who were not balloted because it was not reasonably practicable to give them a vote. This could include, for example, workers who had only recently joined the employer and had not told the union of the change in their employment.
4. The action must take place within four weeks of the ballot. (If votes are cast on more than one day, the date of the ballot is the last of those days.) If the employer and the union agree, this can be extended to up to eight weeks, giving them more time to reach a negotiated settlement of the dispute. (The period can be further extended in

> certain circumstances if the action was initially prohibited by a court order but the order has since expired or been overturned.)
>
> 5. At least seven days before the action is due to begin, the union must write to the employer with certain information about the employees that the union intends to call on to take action, namely: the total number involved; the categories of employees involved and the number in each category; the workplaces involved and the number at each workplace; and an explanation of how those numbers have been arrived at. If the employer deducts union subscriptions from wages, the union has the alternative option of providing the employer with the relevant information by reference to the employees covered by the check-off arrangement. The union is under no obligation, however, to give the employer the names of the individuals who will be taking action. The notice must also say whether the action is intended to be continuous or discontinuous. If it is to be continuous, the employer must be given the start date. If it is to be discontinuous, the employer must be told the days on which it will happen.

Temporary suspension

6.3.33   Generally, if the union has notified the employer that the action will be continuous, the action must continue without substantial interruption if the ballot is to remain effective. The employer and the union can, however, agree a temporary suspension of the action while negotiations take place, and can agree to extend that suspension. If the union suspends the action without agreement with the employer, it must give the employer seven days' notice that the action is to resume.

6.3.34   It may be that during the course of negotiations the nature of the dispute changes. If it changes to such a degree that it has effectively become a new dispute, the union must organise a fresh ballot.

Picketing

6.3.35   There is a specific rule that a union cannot be sued for organising a peaceful picket in contemplation or furtherance of a trade dispute. Two conditions must, however, be met. The first condition is that the pickets must be picketing at or near their own place of work. Pickets who are union officials may picket at or near the place of work of any union member they are accompanying and represent. Some employees, such as drivers, may not have one particular place of work. Others may find it impracticable to picket at their normal place of work, perhaps because of its location, such as an offshore oilrig. These employees may lawfully picket at the premises from which their work is administered. A former employee who was dismissed in connection with the dispute or whose dismissal gave rise to the dispute may picket at his or her former place of work.

6.3.36 The second condition for a lawful picket is that the purpose of the picket must be to obtain or communicate information peacefully, or peacefully to persuade any person to work or not to work. A picket would therefore not be lawful if its purpose were physically to prevent the passage of people or vehicles.

6.3.37 There is a Code of Practice (see 9.6.3) that gives guidance on the conduct of picketing. The content of the Code will be taken into account by the court if picketing is challenged as unlawful. The Code advises that there should normally be no more than six pickets at any workplace entrance. It also gives details of the criminal offences that can be committed during picketing, and which may lead to prosecution of the offenders under the criminal law.

Bringing a claim to court

6.3.38 If industrial action is unprotected because it does not meet the rules outlined above, an employer can apply to a court for an order (known as an 'injunction' or, in Scotland, an 'interdict'), requiring the union to call off the action. If the union fails to respect the order, it is in contempt of court, and may be fined or have its assets taken out of its control.

6.3.39 The employer can also claim compensation, or 'damages', from the union, to compensate it for the economic loss it has suffered because of the action. There is a limit on the amount of damages that a court can award, which depends on the size of the union. For unions with fewer than 5,000 members, for example, the limit is £10,000, whereas for unions with 100,000 members or more, it is £250,000.

6.3.40　If the action has not been authorised by a properly conducted ballot, a member of the union can also apply for a court order requiring the union to call off the action. Further, if the action is not protected, a member of the public can apply for a court order to have it called off. In order to be entitled to apply, the individual needs to be able to show that the action has disrupted, or reduced the quality of, the supply of goods or services he or she has received, or it is likely to do so.

The position of individual employees

6.3.41　In formulating their response to employees who take industrial action, employers need to be aware of the legal position of those individuals. The steps that an employer can lawfully take depend on two legal questions:

- Does the employee have the right to claim unfair dismissal (see 6.3.42)?

- Is the employee breaking his or her contract of employment (see 6.3.58)?

Unfair dismissal protection

6.3.42　An individual's right to claim unfair dismissal when involved in industrial action depends on whether the action has been authorised or endorsed by a union and whether the action is 'protected' because it meets the legal requirements, including the balloting requirements outlined above (see 6.3.17). An employee's right to claim unfair dismissal may also depend on the timing of the dismissal and the reason for the dismissal. These rules, which are set out in the Trade Union and Labour Relations (Consolidation) Act 1992, are summarised in the flow diagram at the end of this chapter.

6.3.43　In most cases, the effect of the legal rules is that it is unfair to dismiss a striking employee. Companies that are considering this course of action should therefore contact us for advice.

Official or unofficial?

6.3.44　An employee's right to claim unfair dismissal depends on whether the action was 'official' or 'unofficial'. If an employee is a union member, the industrial action is official in relation to that employee only if it has been authorised or endorsed by his or her union. (The way in which a union authorises or endorses industrial action is explained in 6.3.18.) If an employee is not a union member, the action is official if it has been authorised or endorsed by a union that has at least one member taking part in the action. In the unlikely event that none of the employees taking part in the action is a union member, the action is viewed as being official.

6.3.45   Action may become unofficial if the union repudiates it. (The way in which action can be repudiated is explained in 6.3.21.) The action does not become unofficial, however, until the end of the working day after the repudiation takes effect, which gives employees time to consider their position. If the union repudiated the action on a Monday, for example, an employee would lose protection from unfair dismissal only if he or she were still participating in the action on the following Wednesday.

Unofficial action

6.3.46   As a general rule, an employee who is dismissed while taking part in 'unofficial' action has no right to complain of unfair dismissal, regardless of the reason for the dismissal and even if others taking part in the action were not dismissed. (It should be borne in mind, however, that most action is official.)

6.3.47   There are limited exceptions to this rule. These exceptions are where the reason for the employee's dismissal is related to his or her right to:

- maternity, paternity, adoption or parental leave or time off for dependants or apply for flexible working (see Chapter 2.2);
- protection on certain health and safety grounds (see 3.3.156);
- act as an employee representative or a candidate or voter in an election of employee representatives for the purpose of consultation on large-scale redundancies (see 5.2.43) or business transfers (see 5.3.15) or concluding a workforce agreement under the Working Time Regulations (see 2.3.34); or
- make a protected disclosure (see 3.3.142)

or if the employee's dismissal relates to the fact that he or she has been summoned for or undertaken jury service (see 2.3.96).

6.3.48   In these circumstances, it is automatically unfair to dismiss the employee, even if he or she is taking part in unofficial action, and regardless of his or her age or length of service.

First twelve weeks of official, protected action

6.3.49   If action is official and protected, then it is automatically unfair to dismiss an employee if the reason for the dismissal is the fact that he or she is taking part in the action and the dismissal occurs in the twelve weeks after the employee first participates in the action. (The meaning of 'official' action is explained in 6.3.44.) This principle applies regardless of the employee's age or length of service. It is also automatically unfair to dismiss an employee for redundancy in the first twelve weeks of official, protected action if the employee was selected for redundancy because he or she was taking part in the action. If the employer conducts a lock-out (see 6.3.8) in the 12-week period, then protection is extended by the length of the lock-out.

6.3.50   In two sets of circumstances it is also automatically unfair to dismiss an employee for taking part in the action even after the initial twelve-week period is over. One is where the employee stopped taking part in the action within the first twelve weeks. The other is where the employee is still taking part in the action after the first twelve weeks but the employer has not taken reasonable procedural steps to resolve the dispute that led to the action.

6.3.51   In deciding whether the employer has taken reasonable steps, an employment tribunal will take into account whether the employer or the union has followed any agreed dispute-resolution procedures, pursued a negotiated resolution to the dispute, or unreasonably refused conciliation or mediation. If either side agreed to conciliation or mediation, then the tribunal will also take into account whether they co-operated in setting up meetings, sent an appropriate person to the meetings, answered reasonable questions put to them there, and fulfilled any commitments to take action that they gave during the process. It is important to note that it is the way in which the employer and the union conducted themselves during the dispute that is relevant here, not the merits of the dispute itself.

Other cases of official action

6.3.52   Some categories of employees are not covered by the rules mentioned above. These include:

- employees who are dismissed because they are taking part in protected official action, but their dismissal occurs more than twelve weeks after they began to participate, they have not stopped participating in those first twelve weeks and their employer has taken reasonable procedural steps to resolve the dispute;

- employees who are dismissed during the twelve weeks after first taking part in protected official action but who are not dismissed for taking part in the action; and

- employees who are dismissed while taking part in official action that is not protected (because, for example, it is not covered by a ballot).

6.3.53   An employee in one of these situations has no right to complain of unfair dismissal if the following two conditions are met: 1) all those taking part in the action at the establishment where the employee worked were dismissed; and 2) none was offered re-engagement within three months of the employee having been dismissed.

6.3.54   If the employer has selectively dismissed or re-employed, then the employee will be entitled to claim unfair dismissal, provided he or she meets the usual eligibility requirements, including at least one year's service. If the employer dismissed the employee for an automatically unfair reason, such as support for the union's claim for recognition under the statutory recognition procedure (see 6.2.16), then the dismissal will be automatically unfair.

6.3.55   If the employer dismissed the employee for a potentially fair reason, such as conduct or redundancy, then the fairness of the dismissal will depend on whether the employer acted reasonably in all the circumstances, including whether it followed a fair procedure before deciding to dismiss. If, for example, the employer dismissed the employee for misconduct in taking part in the action but did not follow its usual disciplinary procedure, the dismissal may well be unfair. (Unfair dismissal is discussed in Chapter 4.2.)

6.3.56 There are limited exceptions to the rule that unfair dismissal protection depends on selective dismissal or re-engagement. A dismissal will be automatically unfair if the reason for the employee's dismissal related to his or her right to:

- take maternity, paternity, adoption or parental leave or time off for dependants or apply for flexible working (see Chapter 2.2);
- protection on certain health and safety grounds (see 3.3.156);
- act as an employee representative or a candidate or voter in an election of employee representatives for the purpose of consultation on large-scale redundancies (see 5.2.43) or business transfers (see 5.3.17) or concluding a workforce agreement under the Working Time Regulations (see 2.3.34); or
- make a protected disclosure (see 3.3.142)

or if the employee's dismissal relates to the fact that he or she has been summoned for or undertaken jury service (see 2.3.96).

6.3.57 This is so regardless of the employee's age or length of service, and even if everyone else who participated in the action was dismissed and none was offered re-engagement.

Contractual issues

6.3.58 Every employee is under an implied obligation to serve his or her employer faithfully and to be ready and willing to perform the duties set out in the express terms of his or her contract of employment. An employee who takes part in industrial action is therefore likely to be acting in serious breach of the express or implied terms of his or her contract.

6.3.59 The clearest example of this is where an employee withdraws his or her labour completely by going on strike, whether for a continuous period or at occasional times or on occasional days. An employee may also be acting in breach of contract if he or she refuses to carry out certain parts of his or her contractual duties by, for example, 'blacking' a particular machine or customer. An employee involved in a 'go slow' or 'work to rule' or a withdrawal of goodwill may be breaking his or her implied obligation to serve his or her employer faithfully, even if the employee is not breaching any express term of his or her contract.

No breach of contract

6.3.60   There are some limited forms of industrial action that may not involve the employee breaking his or her contract. For example, an employee who refuses to work overtime may not be breaking his or her contract if the overtime is purely voluntary and the employer has no right to require the employee to work it.

Employer responses

6.3.61   There are a number of possible responses that an employer might make to individuals who take part in industrial action, ranging from dismissal through to deductions from pay or claims for compensation. However, as discussed in 6.3.42, most dismissals connected with industrial action are unfair. Further, an employer that makes a deduction from an employee's pay without being entitled to do so may find that the employee resigns and claims unfair constructive dismissal. Companies are therefore strongly advised to obtain advice from us before deciding on an appropriate course of action.

Dismissal

6.3.62   As discussed in 6.3.58, an employee who takes part in industrial action is likely to be in serious breach of his or her contract of employment. If an employee is in serious breach of contract, his or her employer is contractually entitled to dismiss the employee without notice or any payment in lieu of notice. However, as explained in 6.3.42, it may nevertheless be unfair to dismiss the employee, unless the situation falls within the limited circumstances in which the employee has no unfair dismissal protection. Companies that are considering dismissing employees who are taking part in industrial action should therefore contact us for advice.

Non-payment of wages or salary

6.3.63   If an employee is refusing to do any work, as would be the case in a strike, his or her employer is not obliged to pay for the days or hours on which he or she does not work. However, it may be that the employee is refusing to perform only part of his or her contractual duties. In these circumstances, the employer has a choice. It can accept the work that the employee is prepared to do, and pay him or her a reduced wage or salary to reflect the fact that the employee is not carrying out his or her full duties (an option discussed further in 6.3.68). Or it can reject the employee's part-performance of his or her duties and refuse to pay the employee any wages or salary at all.

6.3.64   If it chooses the latter approach, however, the employer must clearly reject the employee's part-performance. That will normally involve sending the employee home until he or she is prepared to work normally. In suspending the employee from work, the employer must ensure that the employee knows that he or she is not being disciplined or dismissed, and that any work that he or she does will be voluntary work for which the company will not pay. Further, the company should be aware that it may be viewed as locking the employee out (see 6.3.8), in which case the employee's protection from unfair dismissal will be extended by the length of the lockout (see 6.3.49). Companies considering this course of action should contact us for advice.

Amount of withheld pay

6.3.65   The amount of pay that an employer can withhold if an employee is on strike or if it refuses to accept part-performance depends on how the employee's contract defines his or her pay period or rate of pay. If the strike or part-performance lasts for the whole of a pay period, such as a complete week or month, the employer can withhold all the pay due for that period. If the employee's contract specifies an hourly rate, the employer can withhold pay for the contractual hours that the employee failed to work.

6.3.66   The calculation becomes more complicated if the strike or part-performance does not last for a whole pay period and the employee's pay is not expressed as an hourly rate, as is the case, for example, with salaried staff paid monthly. In these cases, companies should contact us for advice on the appropriate deduction.

6.3.67   The legal rules that normally regulate deductions from wages (see 2.1.92) do not apply to deductions made in respect of strikes or other industrial action. The employer should, however, ensure that the deduction is itemised on the employee's pay statement (see 2.1.20). Time during which an employee is involved in industrial action does not count for the purposes of calculating his or her entitlement to the national minimum wage (see 2.1.22).

Reduction for part-performance

6.3.68   As explained above (see 6.3.63), if an employee is refusing to carry out part of his or her contractual duties, the employer is entitled to refuse to accept that part-performance. If the employer chooses instead to accept the work that the employee does, it is entitled to reduce the employee's usual wages or salary to reflect the fact that the employee is not carrying out his or her full duties. It may, however, be difficult to calculate what the appropriate reduction should be, and companies considering this course of action should contact us for advice. The factors that are likely to be most relevant are the proportion of total working time that the employee usually spends on the duties that he or she is refusing to do and the value of those duties to the company.

6.3.69   The legal rules that normally regulate deductions from wages (explained in 2.1.92) do not apply to deductions made in respect of strikes or other industrial action. The employer should, however, ensure that the deduction is itemised on the employee's pay statement (see 2.1.20). Time during which an employee is involved in industrial action does not count for the purposes of calculating his or her entitlement to the national minimum wage (see 2.1.22).

Claim for damages

6.3.70   In theory, if an employee engages in industrial action that involves breaking his or her contract, the employer can sue the employee for compensation for the economic loss the employee's action has caused. In practice, this type of legal claim is almost unheard of, for two reasons. The first is that it would be very difficult to prove that the particular employee's breach of contract caused the employer's loss. Secondly, even if that link could be established, the employee would be unlikely to have the funds to pay the compensation awarded.

Lay-off and redundancy

6.3.71   The disruption to production caused by industrial action may mean that a company has to lay employees off or make them redundant. The law on lay-off and redundancy is explained in Chapter 5.2 of this Guide. Here we explain, in outline, how those rules are affected by industrial action.

Lay-off

6.3.72   As explained in 5.2.128, it is lawful for an employer to lay an employee off if it has no work for the employee to do, provided that it has the power to do so under the employee's contract of employment. An employee who is laid off would normally be entitled to a guarantee payment under the Employment Rights Act 1996. This right does not apply, however, if the employer cannot provide work because of industrial action involving the employer or an associated employer. Similarly, hourly-rated manual workers covered by the EEF National Guarantee of Employment Agreement will have their guarantee of a minimum amount of weekly pay suspended if production has been disrupted as a result of industrial action in their own or any other federated establishment.

Redundancy pay

6.3.73   The law on redundancy payments is set out in the Employment Rights Act 1996. Special rules apply in relation to employees who are involved in industrial action. These rules are complex, and companies that are considering their impact on a redundancy exercise they are planning may wish to contact us for advice. In summary:

- If an employee has taken industrial action that amounts to gross misconduct and is then dismissed for redundancy, the company may not be obliged to pay a redundancy payment. In order to avoid liability to pay, the company must dismiss the employee:
    - without notice; or
    - with shorter notice than he or she would normally be entitled to; or

- by giving the employee notice but including a statement that the company would be entitled to terminate the contract without notice because of the employee's conduct.

- If an employee has already been given notice of dismissal for redundancy and then takes part in industrial action involving a stoppage of work (such as a strike or an overtime ban) and is dismissed for that reason, the employee is still entitled to a redundancy payment.

- If an employee is given notice of dismissal for redundancy and then takes part in action that does not involve a stoppage of work and is dismissed for that reason, the employee may still be entitled to the whole or part of his or her redundancy payment, if an employment tribunal considers it just and equitable that the employee should receive it.

- If an employee takes part in a stoppage of work after receiving notice of dismissal for redundancy, the company may ask the employee to extend his or her contract for the number of working days lost by the strike. If the employee refuses, he or she loses the right to a redundancy payment, unless he or she was unable to extend the contract for some reason such as sickness or injury, or it was reasonable in the circumstances for the employee not to agree to the extension. In that case, an employment tribunal may award the employee the whole or part of the redundancy payment, according to what it thinks fit.

Unfair dismissal protection for employees taking industrial action

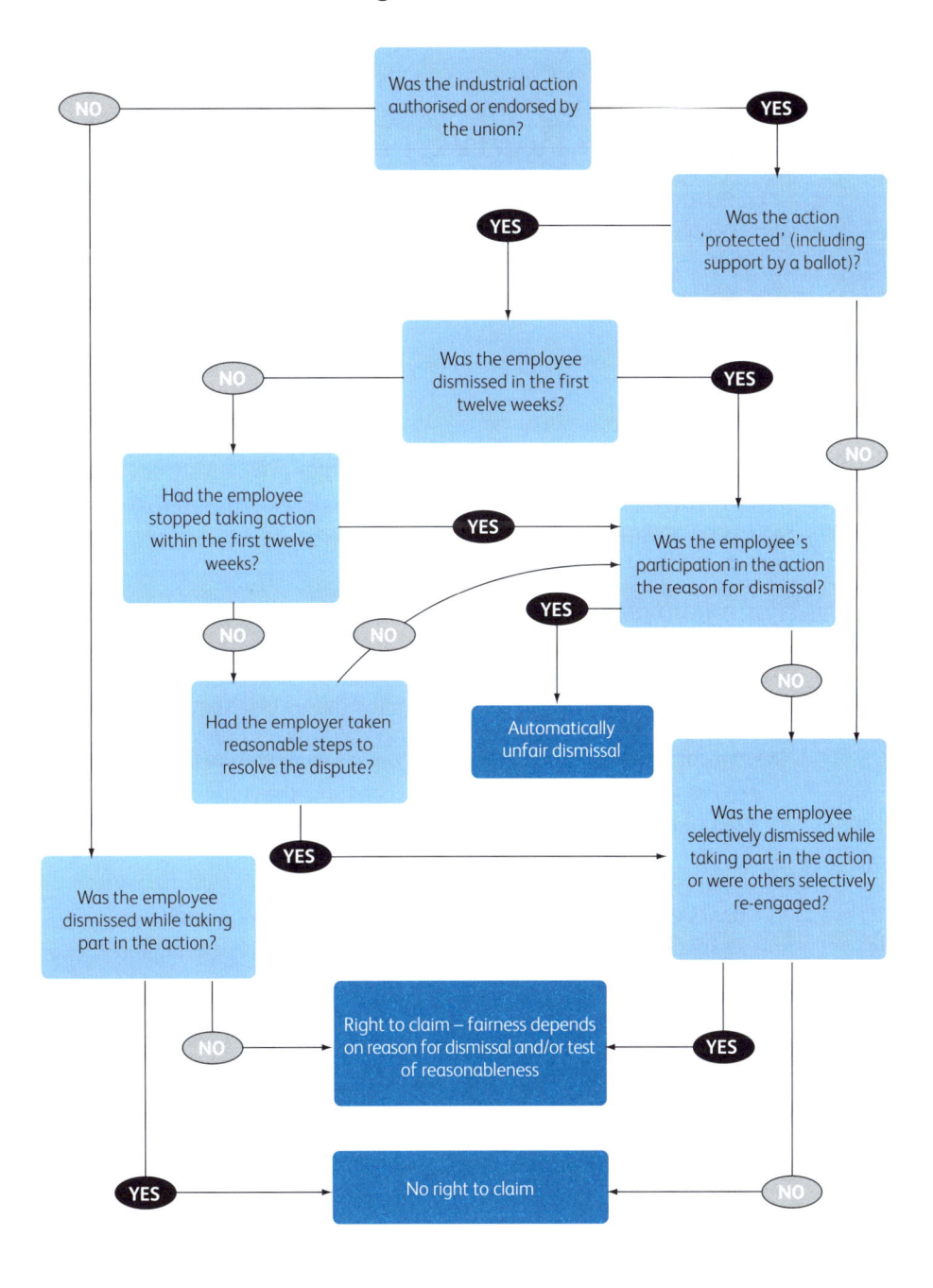

- Was the industrial action authorised or endorsed by the union?
  - NO → Was the employee dismissed while taking part in the action?
    - YES → No right to claim
    - NO → Right to claim – fairness depends on reason for dismissal and/or test of reasonableness
  - YES → Was the action 'protected' (including support by a ballot)?
    - YES → Was the employee dismissed in the first twelve weeks?
      - YES → Was the employee's participation in the action the reason for dismissal?
        - YES → Automatically unfair dismissal
        - NO → Was the employee selectively dismissed while taking part in the action or were others selectively re-engaged?
          - YES → Right to claim – fairness depends on reason for dismissal and/or test of reasonableness
          - NO → No right to claim
      - NO → Had the employee stopped taking action within the first twelve weeks?
        - YES → Was the employee's participation in the action the reason for dismissal?
        - NO → Had the employer taken reasonable steps to resolve the dispute?
          - NO → Was the employee's participation in the action the reason for dismissal?
          - YES → Was the employee selectively dismissed while taking part in the action or were others selectively re-engaged?
    - NO → Was the employee selectively dismissed while taking part in the action or were others selectively re-engaged?

6.4

Employee involvement

Overview

6.4.1 This chapter of the Guide deals with 'employee involvement', a phrase that is used to cover a wide range of ways in which employees can be involved in the business in which they work.

Methods of employee involvement

6.4.2 In some circumstances, employee involvement is required by law, in others it is wholly voluntary. The main methods of employee involvement are these:

- providing information to the workforce, either directly or through their representatives or both, on matters relating to the current and future operation of the company;

- consulting with employees or their representatives or both, to gather their views on issues relating to the company's current and future operation so that these can be taken into account in the company's decision-making;

- negotiating with a trade union on issues of relevance to the employees the union represents, from terms and conditions of employment through to broader issues such as job security and equal opportunities;

- facilitating employees' financial participation in the company's performance by, for example, offering them shares in the company.

6.4.3　Involving employees by negotiating with a union is covered in Chapter 6.2. This chapter concentrates on how employees can be involved through information provision and consultation. The chapter summarises the benefits of employee involvement (see 6.4.9) and the ways in which it might be promoted (see 6.4.10), and then examines the legal requirements.

Legal duties to inform and consult

6.4.4　Employers have various general and specific legal duties to inform and consult with their workforce. Starting with the general duties: a company that employs more than 50 employees may be obliged to negotiate and operate an information and consultation procedure, if it has been asked to do so by 10 per cent or more of its workforce (see 6.4.21). The other general duty applies only to trans-European employers, that is, companies or groups of companies that employ at least 1,000 people overall and have at least 150 employees in two or more countries in the European Economic Area. These employers may be obliged to set up a mechanism to inform and consult their workforce on transnational issues of concern to their employees (see 6.4.36).

6.4.5　All employers are under a specific legal obligation to consult their workforce if they are proposing to make large-scale redundancies or to take measures in connection with a business transfer. Other chapters of this Guide explain when these obligations to consult are triggered and what the consultations must cover (see 5.2.43, 5.3.15). This chapter explains what options employers have in terms of the consultation mechanism they use (see 6.4.52).

6.4.6　All employers must also consult on health and safety issues. This chapter outlines employers' obligations in this area, which differ between those employers who have union-appointed safety representatives (see 6.4.61) and those who do not (see 6.4.66).

6.4.7　Where an employer has been ordered to recognise a trade union under the statutory recognition procedure (see 6.2.16) and a method of collective bargaining has been imposed, the employer is under a duty to consult with the union about training issues. This chapter explains that duty (see 6.4.73).

6.4.8　Employers also have a duty to provide employees with information about pensions (see 2.4.52) and to consult before certain pension changes are made (see 2.4.61).

Benefits of employee involvement

6.4.9   Promoting employee involvement makes good commercial sense because of the benefits it brings to the business. For example:

- By increasing employees' awareness of the business and the environment in which it has to operate, employee involvement can make the workforce more able to adapt to and meet the changing requirements of the market.

- By drawing on employees' experience and knowledge, employee involvement can improve the company's decision-making, performance and ability to develop.

- By fostering employees' commitment to the success of the business and increasing their job satisfaction, employee involvement can increase employees' productivity and willingness to accept change.

Methods of employee involvement

6.4.10   In order to be effective, employee involvement must have the full support of the company's management team. Ideally, it should be part of a wider strategy for improving the performance of the business.

Planning an involvement strategy

6.4.11   When a company is planning its employee involvement strategy it will need to decide whether its aim is merely to communicate information to employees about certain company matters or whether it intends to go further and consult with the workforce on some issues. If the company is to consult meaningfully on a proposal, it must be prepared to:

- enter into the consultation process with an open mind on whether its proposal might need to be revised;

- provide clear information to employees on what is being proposed and why;

- give employees adequate time to consider that information and to prepare their response;

- give proper consideration to employees' responses, and take them into account in finalising the proposal.

6.4.12 Consultation is therefore a two-way process, involving a considered exchange of views between employer and workforce, rather than a one-way process of informing the workforce of what is going to happen.

Company circumstances

6.4.13 The most effective form of employee involvement will depend on the circumstances of the particular company. It could include, for example, production of company newsletters or videos, team briefings, quality circles or project improvement teams. A company may also wish to consider establishing a works council or staff committee, either on a permanent basis to discuss general company matters or on a temporary basis to discuss a particular issue facing the company.

Works councils and consultative committees

6.4.14 Many workplaces have some form of permanent company or works council or consultative committee. As these bodies are primarily concerned with consultation rather than negotiation, the range of issues discussed is usually broader than in traditional collective bargaining. Discussion topics could include, among others: company performance and business results, operational changes and future strategy. Where a company has in place consultative arrangements that:

- are in writing;
- cover all the employees in the undertaking;
- have been approved by the employees; and
- set out how the employer is to give information to the employees or their representatives and to seek their views on the information

it is relatively difficult for employees or their representatives to remove the voluntary arrangement and replace it with the statutory system (see 6.4.25). Employers considering putting in place such arrangements should contact us.

6.4.15   Many company councils work in non-union contexts and individuals are commonly elected as employee representatives answerable to a particular department, shift, or workplace area. The number of representatives must be large enough to allow genuine representation of all areas of the workforce but not so large as to impede the effectiveness of the committee or council. Typically the number of representatives will be between 10 and 20 but can be more or less, depending on the size of the organisation. It is usual for managerial representatives to be appointed to the council or committee, but it is normally appropriate for there to be more elected representatives than appointed ones.

6.4.16   It is worth noting that the statutory obligations to consult on large-scale redundancies and business transfers can be met through consultation with representatives who were elected or appointed for some other purpose, provided the method and purpose of their election or appointment gives them the authority to be consulted (see 6.4.53). Therefore a company may be able to consult with an established works council or staff committee rather than have to organise an election of employee representatives, should redundancies or a business transfer be proposed.

Employee share ownership schemes

6.4.17   These schemes have been developed to encourage employee participation and commitment and to aid retention. With a tangible stake in the success of the business, employees may have a greater level of commitment to its continuing growth and development.

6.4.18   HM Revenue and Customs regulates these schemes and can provide further guidance on them.

Other mechanisms

6.4.19   Other forms of employee involvement include employee suggestion schemes, attitude surveys (whether by structured questionnaire, interview or focus group), performance appraisal and quality initiatives such as total quality management, kaizen and lean manufacturing.

Reporting on employee involvement

6.4.20 There is no general legal obligation on employers to promote employee involvement. However, the Companies Act 2006 requires companies that employ more than 250 people to state in their annual reports what action, if any, they have taken in that year to promote employee involvement. This can be through information provision, consultation or financial participation in order to increase employees' awareness of the financial and economic factors affecting the company.

General duty to inform and consult

6.4.21 A company may be under an obligation to inform and consult its employees about work-related issues, under the Information and Consultation of Employees Regulations 2005. The Regulations currently cover only those employers that have a workforce of 50 or more.

6.4.22 Because the Regulations are complex, this Guide only summarises their content. The Department for Business, Innovation and Skills has produced detailed guidance on the Regulations (see 9.6.4). We can provide you with advice on how the Regulations apply to your organisation, and there is an EEF model information and consultation agreement that reflects the Regulations' requirements.

Triggered by request

6.4.23 The thrust of the Regulations is to require an employer to negotiate and operate a procedure for informing and consulting with its workforce, if it has received a written request to do so by at least 10 per cent of its workforce or 2,500 employees, whichever is the lesser. The request may be a single request from at least 10 per cent of the workforce, or a number of separate requests totalling at least 10 per cent of the workforce and made within any rolling six-month period. Employees may submit their request through the Central Arbitration Committee, if they would prefer the employer not to know their identity.

6.4.24 Because the application of the Regulations is triggered by a request from the workforce, a company that receives no request, or receives a request that is not endorsed by the requisite number of employees, need take no action. There are good reasons, however, for an employer to take the initiative in setting up an information and consultation arrangement, even if does not currently anticipate receiving a request, as explained in 6.4.27.

Pre-existing arrangements

6.4.25   A company that receives a request to negotiate an information and consultation procedure may already have an arrangement for informing and consulting. Whether that pre-existing arrangement affects the company's legal duty to enter negotiations on a new procedure depends on a number of factors. First, in order to have any legal effect, the pre-existing arrangement must be in writing, it must set out the way in which the employer will inform and consult, it must cover all employees and it must have been approved by the workforce (through a ballot, for example, or by being agreed with a union that represents a majority of the workforce). The Regulations provide a degree of flexibility here: the arrangement can meet these conditions even if it covers employees in more than one company, or provides for different arrangements in different parts of the business, or consists of several agreements covering different parts of the business.

6.4.26   If the pre-existing arrangement meets the conditions, then its legal effect depends on how many employees requested negotiations on a new procedure. If 40 per cent or more of the workforce made the request, then the employer must negotiate. If fewer than 40 per cent made the request, the employer has two options: it can decide to negotiate or it can conduct a secret ballot of the entire workforce on whether they want to endorse the request. If the employer opts for a ballot, then it must negotiate on a new procedure if the request is endorsed in the ballot by at least 40 per cent of the employees and a majority of those who voted.

Benefits of a proactive approach

6.4.27   Although it is possible for a company to take no action on an information and consultation procedure unless and until it receives a request to negotiate, it may be advisable for the company to adopt a proactive approach, and put in place an agreement that meets the conditions in 6.4.25 before any request is received. By putting in place a pre-existing agreement, an employer can demonstrate a positive commitment to keeping its workforce involved in the business, with all the benefits that brings (see 6.4.9), rather than seeming to be coerced into the process reluctantly by an employee request. Further, the legal enforcement mechanisms that apply to procedures reached under the Regulations (see 6.4.32) do not apply to pre-existing agreements.

Negotiating the procedure

6.4.28   If it receives a valid employee request, the employer's first step is to arrange the election or appointment of negotiating representatives. These employees will represent all the employees of the undertaking in negotiations with the company on what form the procedure for information and consultation will take. All employees must be eligible to take part in the election or appointment of the negotiating representatives.

6.4.29   The Regulations lay down few requirements for the agreement that results from the negotiations. They simply say that the agreement must:

- cover all the employees in the business;

- set out the circumstances in which the employer will inform and consult; and

- either provide for the appointment or election of employee representatives with whom the employer will inform and consult, or provide for the employer to give information directly to, and consult directly with, the workforce, or provide for both methods.

It is therefore up to the negotiators to decide the method, frequency, timing and subject-matter of the information and consultation process. (The Department for Business, Innovation and Skills guidance on the Regulations and the EEF model agreement may be of assistance here.)

Standard fall-back provisions

6.4.30   If the company and the negotiating representatives are unable to reach agreement after six months of negotiation (or whatever further period the parties may agree), or if the employer fails to negotiate at all, then the Regulations set out standard information and consultation provisions that will automatically apply.

6.4.31   In summary, these are:

- The employer must arrange for the election of information and consultation representatives. The ballot must meet detailed requirements, the most important being that all employees must be entitled to vote, the employer must consult with employee representatives about the ballot arrangements and the ballot must be independently supervised. There must be one representative for each 50 employees, subject to a maximum of 25. (If fewer people than this stand as candidates for election, then those candidates become the representatives without the need for a ballot.)

- The employer must provide the representatives with information in these three areas:

    1. The recent and probable development of the business's activities and economic situation.

    2. The situation, structure and probable development of employment within the business, and any measures planned, including in particular any threat to employment.

    3. Decisions likely to lead to substantial changes in work organisation or in the employer's contractual relations with its employees, including large-scale redundancies and changes connected with the transfer of the business or part of it.

- The employer must consult with the representatives on the second and third of these areas, unless it already has a duty to consult as a result of the specific legislation on large-scale redundancies, business transfers and pension changes (5.2.43, 5.3.17, 6.4.51, 2.4.61) and has notified the representatives in writing that it will be meeting its duties under those provisions instead.

- The employer must ensure that the timing, method and content of the consultation are such as to make the process meaningful. The consultation will be based on the information the company has supplied and the representatives' own views. The consultation will need to be conducted by the level of management that is most relevant to the subject under discussion, and the company must provide the representatives with a reasoned response to their opinions. In relation to the third area listed above, consultation must be entered into with a view to reaching agreement on any decisions that fall within the employer's powers.

Penalty for not complying

6.4.32   An employer who negotiates an agreement under this statutory procedure but then fails to observe it, or is covered by the fall-back procedure and fails to follow it, is liable to a penalty of up to £75,000, payable to the government and imposed by the Employment Appeal Tribunal. The size of the penalty will depend on the gravity of the failure and the reason for it. No penalty will be imposed if the Tribunal is satisfied that the reason for the employer's failure to inform and consult was beyond its control, or that it had some other reasonable excuse for its failure. The fact that a person by which the employer is directly or indirectly controlled (such as a parent company) has failed to provide it with the relevant information does not amount to a valid excuse.

Duty to co-operate

6.4.33   Whether they are negotiating or implementing a negotiated agreement or operating the fall-back provisions, employers and employees are under a duty to work in a spirit of co-operation and with due regard for their respective rights, obligations and interests.

Preserving confidentiality

6.4.34   The Regulations require employee representatives not to disclose any information or documents that the employer has given them on a confidential basis (unless the employee reasonably believes this would be a protected public interest disclosure – see 3.3.142–3.3.150). An employer is not required to disclose any information or documents that, on an objective assessment, would prejudice the business or seriously harm its functioning.

Three-year moratorium

6.4.35   There is generally a moratorium on further employee requests for negotiation for three years after a negotiated agreement on an information and consultation procedure has been reached, or the fall-back provisions apply, or a ballot has failed to endorse fresh negotiations where a pre-existing arrangement exists. On the other hand, if there have been material changes in the business that mean that the negotiated agreement no longer covers all the employees, or pre-existing arrangements no longer cover all employees or are no longer approved by the employees, then another request for negotiations may be made.

Consultation by trans-European employers

6.4.36　Employers with a presence in more than one European country may be under an obligation to set up a European Works Council or some other information and consultation procedure to discuss issues that relate to the business and affect employees in more than one country. This obligation is contained in the Transnational Information and Consultation of Employees Regulations 1999 (the TICE Regulations). It applies to companies that employ at least 1,000 people in the European Economic Area (EEA) and at least 150 in two or more countries in that area. It also applies to groups of companies that meet these thresholds. The EEA is the 27 Member States of the European Community plus Norway, Liechtenstein and Iceland.

Application of TICE Regulations

6.4.37　The TICE Regulations apply only to:

- companies or groups of companies whose central management is in the UK; or

- whose central management is outside the EEA but whose representative agent is in the UK; or

- who have neither central management nor a representative agent in the EEA but employ more people in the UK than in any other EEA country.

6.4.38　However, the TICE Regulations were adopted to implement the requirements of a European Community Directive and other countries in the EEA will also have legislation reflecting the Directive's requirements. Therefore trans-European companies or groups of companies are likely to have similar obligations to consult their workforces, wherever their central management is located.

6.4.39   The TICE Regulations may not apply to companies or groups that had already established transnational information and consultation arrangements on a voluntary basis, or were already covered by transnational information and consultation arrangements established under the law of another EEA country, when the TICE Regulations came into force in January 2000. Companies that consider that they may be excluded from the Regulations for this reason should contact us for advice.

6.4.40   The TICE Regulations are very detailed, and this section only summarises their content. Companies that are approached to set up a consultation mechanism under the Regulations should contact us for advice.

Special negotiating body

6.4.41   A company can meet its obligations under the TICE Regulations by establishing a European Works Council or by adopting an information and consultation procedure. Whichever mechanism is adopted, it must be agreed with a special negotiating body representing the employees, it must be capable of delivering information and consultation on transnational questions that significantly affect employees' interests, and it must cover at least those of the company's businesses that are located in EEA countries.

6.4.42   The company may decide on its own initiative to begin negotiations with the special negotiating body on the appropriate consultation mechanism. Otherwise, it need negotiate only if it is asked to do so by at least 100 employees, or the representatives of at least 100 employees, who work in at least two Member States. Employees or their representatives have the right to ask a company for information that will help them establish whether the company or its group is covered by the TICE Regulations.

6.4.43   The special negotiating body must have at least one member from each EEA country in which the company or group is represented, and additional members from countries in which the largest numbers are employed. The UK members may be elected by a secret ballot in which all the UK employees are entitled to stand as candidates and to vote. Alternatively, if the company already has an independent committee of elected employee representatives that it consults on issues that may significantly affect employees, that committee can nominate the UK members.

Agreement with special negotiating body

6.4.44   The aim of the negotiations between the company and the special negotiating body is to agree the scope, composition, functions and term of office of a European Works Council, or arrangements for the information and consultation procedure.

6.4.45   An agreement to establish a European Works Council must set out:

- the businesses that are covered by the agreement;
- how the Council is to be composed, the number of members, the allocation of seats and the term of office of members;
- the functions of the Council and the procedure for information and consultation;
- the venue, frequency and duration of the Council's meetings;
- the financial and material resources that the Council will have; and
- the duration of the agreement and the procedure for its renegotiation.

6.4.46   If the company and the special negotiating body decide to establish an information and consultation procedure instead of a European Works Council, the agreement they reach must specify a method by which the information and consultation representatives are to meet to discuss the information provided to them. The information they receive must cover in particular transnational questions that significantly affect the interests of the employees.

Fallback provisions

6.4.47   The TICE Regulations set out fallback provisions that will apply if the company and special negotiating body agree that they should, or if the company refuses to negotiate, or if negotiations do not lead to an agreement. The fallback provisions provide for the establishment of a European Works Council with between 3 and 30 members, with at least one member from each EEA country and additional members from the countries where the largest numbers are employed.

6.4.48   Under the fallback provisions, the Council meets with central management at least once a year to be informed and consulted on the progress of the business and its prospects. The meeting covers, in particular:

- the structure, economic and financial situation;
- the probable development of the business and of production and sales;
- the situation and probable trend of employment;
- investments;
- substantial changes relating to the organisation;
- introduction of new working methods or production processes;
- transfers of production;
- mergers;
- cut-backs or closures; and
- collective redundancies.

6.4.49   Where exceptional circumstances arise, such as with relocations, closures or redundancies, the Council can ask for a special information and consultation meeting with management.

Protection for sensitive information

6.4.50   The TICE Regulations contain specific provisions to protect sensitive and confidential information. The company need not disclose information that may prejudice or seriously harm the business to the special negotiating body, the European Works Council or employee representatives under any information and consultation procedure. If the company does decide to give them confidential information, they are under a legal duty not to disclose it, unless it qualifies as a 'protected disclosure' (see 3.3.143).

Redundancies and business transfers

6.4.51 A company has an obligation to consult with its workforce if it is proposing to dismiss 20 or more employees at one establishment within 90 days or less for redundancy or for some other reason unconnected with the individuals concerned, such as the introduction of new contract terms. This obligation is discussed in 5.2.43. An employer must also provide information to its employees if it is involved in the transfer of the whole or part of a business or a service provision change, and must consult on any measures that it is proposing to take in connection with that transfer or change, as explained in 5.3.17.

Mechanism to meet obligations

6.4.52 The mechanism that an employer can use to meet these obligations depends on its circumstances. If the affected employees are covered by a collective bargaining agreement, the employer must consult with the recognised trade union. If any of the affected employees are not covered by collective bargaining, either because the employer does not bargain with a union at all or because the recognition agreement does not cover all the affected employees, then the employer has two options.

6.4.53 The first option is to consult representatives that those employees have already appointed or elected for some purpose not specifically related to redundancies or transfers. The company can take up this option only if it is clear from the context in which the representatives were appointed or elected that they have authority to be consulted about redundancies or transfers on the employees' behalf. For example, someone appointed to a committee whose sole function is to organise social events is unlikely to have the relevant authority, but information and consultation representatives elected or appointed under the Information and Consultation of Employees Regulations 2004 (see 6.4.21) would.

6.4.54 The other option is for the company to consult with representatives who have been expressly elected by the affected employees for the purpose of consultation on the particular redundancies or transfer. If the company takes this route, it will need to ensure that the election meets the requirements set down in the legislation, set out in 6.4.56.

Election requirements

6.4.55 The law lays down detailed requirements for the election of representatives for the purposes of consultation on business transfers or redundancies. These requirements are set out in the Trade Union and Labour Relations (Consolidation) Act 1992 and the Transfer of Undertakings (Protection of Employment) Regulations 2006.

6.4.56 The company's overall obligation is to make whatever arrangements are reasonably practical to ensure that the election is fair. The election must also meet these more specific requirements:

> ### Election requirements
>
> - *Number of representatives.* The company can decide how many representatives are to be elected and whether there should be general representatives for everyone, or specific representatives for specific classes of employees, such as particular operational categories. In making these decisions, however, the company must ensure that there are sufficient representatives to represent the interests of all the employees who are affected by its proposals.
>
> - *Length of office.* Before the election, the company must decide how long the representatives will hold office. This must be long enough to ensure both that the representatives receive all the information to which they are entitled and that meaningful consultation can take place.
>
> - *Eligibility of candidates.* Candidates for election must be employees who are affected by the company's proposals on the date of the election. No affected employee should be unreasonably excluded from standing for election. If only one candidate comes forward, that person can be appointed without an election being needed.
>
> - *Electorate.* All employees who are affected by the proposals on the date of election must be entitled to vote.

> - *Number of votes.* Each employee must be entitled to vote for as many candidates as there are to be representatives. If particular classes of employees are to have separate representatives, then each employee must be entitled to vote for as many representatives as there are to be for his or her class.
>
> - *Conduct of the election.* So far as reasonably practicable, employees must be able to vote in secret. Votes must be accurately counted.
>
> - *Vacancies.* If an employee stops acting as a representative for some reason, such as the fact that he or she has resigned or been dismissed, another election must be held to fill the vacancy.

6.4.57   If the employer invites the affected employees to elect representatives but they fail to do so within a reasonable time, it must give the employees the information it would have given to the representatives (see 5.2.52, 5.3.24).

Health and safety

6.4.58   Effective management of health and safety requires the commitment and involvement of the entire workforce. In recognition of this, health and safety law requires employers to involve their employees in health and safety issues, through information provision and consultation.

Employers' general duty

6.4.59   Employers have a general duty under the Health and Safety at Work etc Act 1974 to provide their employees with the information, instruction and training that are necessary to ensure, so far as is reasonably practicable, their health and safety at work. More specifically, the Management of Health and Safety at Work Regulations 1999 oblige employers to provide their employees with certain health and safety information, including the risks to health and safety that have been identified in the workplace and the preventive and protective measures that are being taken to avoid those risks. Many health and safety regulations dealing with specific issues, such as work equipment, noise at work and manual handling, also require employers to provide employees with information.

6.4.60 In addition, the law imposes a general obligation on employers to consult their workforce on health and safety issues. The way in which consultation occurs depends on whether the employer recognises a trade union for the purposes of collective bargaining. If the employer does bargain with a union, it must consult with union-appointed safety representatives, who can ask for a safety committee to be formed (see 6.4.61). If employees are not covered by a union representative, either because no union is recognised or because the union's safety representatives do not represent the entire workforce, the employer must consult with them either directly or through elected health and safety representatives (see 6.4.66).

Safety representatives and committees

6.4.61 If a company bargains with a union, the union is entitled to appoint safety representatives from among the company's employees, in accordance with the Safety Representatives and Safety Committees Regulations 1977. Safety representatives have extensive functions. These include:

- investigating potential hazards and dangerous occurrences at the workplace;
- examining the causes of accidents;
- investigating employees' complaints about health and safety; and
- making representations to the employer about these issues.

6.4.62 Safety representatives also have the right to carry out safety inspections and to represent employees in consultations at the workplace with health and safety inspectors. The employer must provide safety representatives with whatever facilities and assistance they reasonably require to enable them to carry out their functions.

Consultation with union safety reps

6.4.63 An employer is obliged under the Health and Safety at Work etc Act 1974 and under the Safety Representatives Regulations to consult with its safety representatives about certain issues. These include:

- how the employer and the workforce can work together to promote a safe and healthy workplace;

- how any changes, including the introduction of new technology, may affect employees' health and safety;

- the employer's arrangements for appointing competent persons to assist it with meeting its health and safety duties; and

- any health and safety information and training the employer is legally required to provide to its workforce.

6.4.64 Under the Safety Representatives Regulations, the employer must provide the representatives with the information they need to fulfil their functions, such as information about changes that may affect health and safety, and technical information about hazards and safety precautions. Representatives also have the right to inspect and copy any health and safety records the employer is legally required to keep, other than individuals' health records.

6.4.65 If at least two safety representatives request it, the employer must establish a safety committee to review its health and safety measures. The Health and Safety Commission has issued a Code of Practice on safety representatives and guidance on the operation of safety committees (see 9.6.4). Although it is not unlawful in itself for an employer to disregard the Code, its contents may be taken into account by a court or tribunal when deciding whether the employer has met its obligations under health and safety law.

Consultation with employees not represented by a union

6.4.66 As discussed above (see 6.4.61), where an employer negotiates with a union, the union has the right to appoint safety representatives. However, employees will not have access to a safety representative if:

- their employer does not recognise a union; or

- a union is recognised but it does not represent the entire workforce; or
- the union has not appointed safety representatives.

6.4.67 In these circumstances, the Health and Safety (Consultation with Employees) Regulations 1996 apply. These Regulations require the employer to consult with any employees who are not covered by union-appointed safety representatives on matters relating to health and safety at work and, in particular, on:

- how any changes, including the introduction of new technology, may affect employees' health and safety;
- the employer's arrangements for appointing competent persons to assist it with meeting its health and safety duties; and
- any health and safety information and training the employer is legally required to provide to its workforce.

Consultation methods

6.4.68 An employer can choose to carry out this consultation directly with its employees, or through those of its employees who have been elected as representatives of employee safety, or a combination of both. The Health and Safety Executive has issued a guide to the Consultation Regulations (see 9.6.4), which suggests that an employer that wishes to consult with its employees direct could do so through a variety of methods, including:

- briefing meetings;
- quality circles;
- staff councils;
- notice boards;
- newsletters;
- e-mail; or
- surveys.

6.4.69 The employer must provide the employees, or their elected representatives, with the information that is necessary to enable them to participate fully and effectively in the consultation, such as information on workplace risks and hazards and measures the employer is taking to eliminate or reduce them.

Election of representatives

6.4.70 Unlike elections of employee representatives in the context of large-scale redundancies and business transfers, there are no detailed legal requirements for the election of representatives of employee safety. The Health and Safety Executive's guide to the Consultation Regulations does, however, give some guidance on holding a fair election. It suggests, for example, that when deciding how many representatives there are to be, an employer should take into account:

- the number of employees involved;
- the different occupational or geographical groups into which they are divided;
- the nature of their work; and
- the health and safety risks to which they may be exposed.

Representatives' other functions

6.4.71 In addition to their role in consultation, elected representatives of employee safety have other functions. They can make representations to the employer on potential hazards and dangerous occurrences and on general health and safety matters, and they can represent employees in consultations at the workplace with health and safety inspectors. The employer must provide them with the information that is necessary for them to carry out these functions, and any information contained in records of injuries, disease and dangerous occurrences that the employer is legally required to keep. The employer must also provide the representatives with a reasonable amount of training in their functions and whatever other facilities and assistance they may reasonably require. This could include, for example, a list of the employees they represent and where they work, and communication, distribution and photocopying facilities.

Training

6.4.72   Where a trade union has sufficient support in a workplace, there is a legal procedure that it can use to secure recognition from the employer, as explained in 6.2.16. If an employer is ordered to recognise a union but cannot agree a method of bargaining with it, the Central Arbitration Committee will prescribe a method.

Obligation to consult

6.4.73   If a bargaining method is imposed in this way, the employer is obliged to consult with the union on training issues. The detail of this obligation is set out in the Trade Union and Labour Relations (Consolidation) Act 1992. In summary, the employer must meet with union representatives at least once every six months, in order to consult with them on its training policy and the training it has planned for the period up to the next meeting, and to report on the training carried out since the previous meeting.

6.4.74   At least two weeks before each meeting, the employer must provide the union representatives with the information they need to participate fully in the meeting and any additional information that it would be good industrial relations practice to disclose. The employer must also take into account any written representations the union makes in the four weeks after the meeting.

Legal rights of representatives

6.4.75   All the legislation on employee involvement, whether dealing with general or transnational information and consultation, large-scale redundancies, business transfers or health and safety, gives employees who act as representatives legal rights and protection. In summary, employees have the right to paid time off from work to stand as candidates for election and to carry out their functions as employee representatives. They are also protected from being unfavourably treated, dismissed or selected for redundancy because they have carried out their functions as candidates or representatives. All of these rights apply regardless of the employee's age or length of service with the employer.

Time off

6.4.76 The Information and Consultation of Employees Regulations 2004 give employees who act as negotiating representatives or information and consultation representatives the right to a reasonable amount of paid time off to carry out their functions.

6.4.77 Under the Transnational Information and Consultation of Employees Regulations 1999 (see 6.4.36), employees have the right to a reasonable amount of paid time off to carry out their functions as a member of a special negotiating body or a European Works Council or as an information and consultation representative. Employees who are standing for election to these positions are also entitled to reasonable paid time off to perform their functions as candidates.

6.4.78 Under the Safety Representatives and Safety Committees Regulations 1977, safety representatives have the right to as much paid time off work as is necessary to perform their functions and to undergo related training. The Health and Safety Commission has issued a Code of Practice (see 9.6.4) that gives guidance on this right. While it is not unlawful in itself for an employer to disregard the Code, its contents will be taken into account by an employment tribunal when hearing a claim that the employer has failed to respect a representative's right to time off. Similarly, elected representatives of employee safety are entitled to whatever paid time off is necessary to perform their functions, under the Health and Safety (Consultation with Employees) Regulations 1996. Employees standing for election as representatives are entitled to a reasonable amount of paid time off to perform their functions as candidates.

6.4.79 Employee representatives, and candidates for election as representatives, involved in consultation on large-scale redundancies (see 5.2.43) and business transfers (see 5.3.17) have similar rights to paid time off work to perform their functions.

Detriment and dismissal

6.4.80 It is unlawful for an employer to treat an employee unfavourably, dismiss an employee or select an employee for redundancy because the employee:

- performed his or her functions as a negotiating representative or an information and consultation representative, or as a candidate or voter in an election of representatives, under the Information and Consultation of Employees Regulations 2004;

- performed his or her functions or activities as a member of a special negotiating body or a European Works Council, an information and consultation representative, or a candidate for election to one of those positions, under the Transnational Information and Consultation of Employees Regulations 1999;

- asserted his or her rights under those Regulations or took certain other steps, including supporting or opposing the establishment of a European Works Council or an information and consultation procedure;

- took part in consultation with the employer on health and safety, under the Health and Safety (Consultation with Employees) Regulations 1996;

- participated in an election of representatives of employee safety under those Regulations, whether as a candidate or as a voter;

- carried out functions as a safety representative or member of a safety committee; or

- asserted his or her right to time off work to carry out the various representative functions outlined above.

6.4.81 Similar protection applies to employees carrying out their functions as representatives, or candidates for election as representatives, in relation to consultations on large-scale redundancies and business transfers.

6.4.82 In some cases, employee representatives who are dismissed for carrying out their functions may be able to obtain an order from an employment tribunal that they should be re-employed pending the hearing of their unfair dismissal claim (see 7.2.21).

section 7

Employment tribunals and remedies

7.1

Employment tribunals

Overview

7.1.1 Most employment rights created by legislation are enforced by bringing a claim to an employment tribunal. The table on pages 567–71 lists the main statutory employment rights, together with qualifying periods of employment, the time limit for bringing a claim and the legal remedies available. Employment tribunals also have the power to deal with breach of contract claims in certain circumstances (see 7.2.10).

7.1.2 This chapter explains briefly how employment tribunals work. It begins with an explanation of who sits on tribunals (see 7.1.5). It then goes on to outline how a claim is brought (see 7.1.8), and how an employer may either defend a claim (see 7.1.12) or settle it (see 7.1.16) and the evidence that will need to be gathered (see 7.1.23). On occasion, the tribunal may hold a preliminary hearing (see 7.1.26) before the main hearing of the claim (see 7.1.30), and this chapter explains why. It also outlines the circumstances in which a tribunal may restrict the publicity given to a case (see 7.1.43) or award costs and expenses (see 7.1.46). The chapter concludes with a summary of the grounds on which a tribunal's decision can be reviewed or appealed (see 7.1.50).

7.1.3 Tribunal claims can be costly, not only in terms of the compensation that tribunals may award but also in terms of the management time taken to deal with them and the adverse publicity they may cause. Companies are therefore strongly advised to contact us for advice as soon as they receive notice of a tribunal claim.

Parties to the claim

7.1.4   The person bringing a claim to tribunal is known as the 'claimant' and the employer against whom the claim is brought is known as the 'respondent'. The claimant and the respondent are referred to as the 'parties' to the claim.

The membership of employment tribunals

7.1.5   Employment tribunals are made up of three people: an Employment Judge and two lay members.

Lay members

7.1.6   The lay members, sometimes referred to as 'wing members', are intended to bring practical employment relations experience to the tribunal's decision-making process. Although they will have been appointed because of their experience of a particular side of industry, they are under a duty to deal with cases impartially and objectively. The views of all three members of the tribunal have equal weight when reaching a decision. A decision can be reached on a majority vote, so it is possible for the lay members to outvote the Employment Judge. If the parties agree, the tribunal can be made up of the Employment Judge and only one lay member.

Lone Employment Judge

7.1.7   Certain types of case, including breach of contract claims and claims that an employer has made an unlawful deduction from a worker's pay, may in certain circumstances be heard by an Employment Judge sitting alone.

Bringing a claim

7.1.8   There are strict time limits for bringing a claim to an employment tribunal. Tribunals have limited discretion to allow late claims, which they exercise sparingly (see 7.2.5).

Employment tribunals

Claim form

7.1.9 There is a standard form, known as an ET1, which must be used for making a claim to a tribunal. A claimant should send his or her claim to an office of the employment tribunals in England and Wales or in Scotland, as appropriate. Applications can also be made online, by completing the form on the employment tribunals website (see 9.7.1).

7.1.10 When it receives the claim, the tribunal office will check whether it should be accepted. The claim will not be accepted for example if it does not contain all the required information, or the claim is not one the tribunal has power to deal with.

Responding to a claim

7.1.11 If the claim is accepted, the tribunal office sends a copy of it to the respondent. Companies are strongly advised to contact us as soon as they receive a claim. Prompt action is essential because of the strict time limit for entering a defence to a claim. We are able to provide advice and representation in defending or settling tribunal claims.

Response form

7.1.12 If a company wishes to defend the claim, it must return its response form within 28 days of the claim being sent to it. If a company intends to appoint a representative, such as us, to deal with the claim on its behalf, it should ask the representative to complete and send off the response form, rather than send one in itself.

7.1.13 The response form is a standard form, known as an ET3, which the tribunal will have sent out to the employer with the copy of the claim. Responses can be sent online, by completing the form on the employment tribunals website (see 9.7.1). If the company cannot meet the 28-day deadline for some reason, it must apply for an extension of time within that period. The tribunal will grant an extension only if it is satisfied that it would be just and equitable to do so. If the company does not send in a response, it is effectively barred from taking any part in the case, and the tribunal may rule in the claimant's favour.

Clarification

7.1.14   If the nature of the claimant's claim is unclear, the respondent can ask the claimant to provide clarification or further details. If the claimant fails to do so voluntarily, the tribunal can order him or her to do so. A respondent can also be ordered to provide further details of its defence.

Settling a claim

7.1.15   When a company receives a tribunal claim, it must decide whether to defend the claim or explore the possibility of settling it. In order to be legally binding on the claimant, a settlement needs to meet certain conditions, as explained in 7.1.18 – 7.1.20.

7.1.16   The advisability of seeking a settlement depends on several factors, including:

- the strength of the claim;
- the potential monetary value of the claim compared with the cost of the management time and expenses likely to be involved in defending it;
- the employment relations repercussions of defending or not defending the claim; and
- the potential adverse publicity for the company if the claim continues to a hearing.

7.1.17   Because of the legal technicalities involved in drafting an agreement to settle a claim, companies are strongly advised to contact us for advice on this. It may be advisable, for example, to make it a condition of the settlement that its terms will remain confidential. If the claimant wants the company to provide a reference, the terms of the reference may also need to be negotiated.

ACAS involvement

7.1.18   When the tribunal office accepts a claim, it sends a copy to the Advisory Conciliation and Arbitration Service (ACAS). ACAS then appoints a conciliation officer to the case, whose job is to contact the claimant and the respondent to explore whether there is any possibility of the claim being settled. Discussions with an ACAS officer are confidential, and cannot be referred to in any subsequent tribunal hearing. If a settlement is reached through ACAS involvement, the claimant will be barred from pursuing the claim in the tribunal. An ACAS settlement is usually recorded on a standard form, known as a COT3.

Compromise agreement

7.1.19 The other possible channel for reaching a legally binding settlement of a tribunal claim is through a compromise agreement. A compromise agreement can be reached without ACAS involvement, but it must meet certain stringent conditions. The agreement must be in writing and relate to the particular claim being made. Before signing the agreement the claimant must have received independent advice on its terms and effect, including the fact that signing it removes the right to go to a tribunal. The adviser may be:

- a qualified lawyer;
- a union official, employee or member whom the union has certified as competent and authorised to give advice;
- an advice centre worker whom the centre has certified as competent and authorised to give advice ; or
- a legal executive employed by a firm of solicitors.

The adviser must be covered by insurance or a professional indemnity against the risk of providing negligent advice and must be named in the agreement. The agreement must also state that it meets the conditions regulating compromise agreements.

7.1.20 It is possible to reach a legally binding settlement of a breach of contract claim without ACAS involvement and without meeting the conditions for a compromise agreement.

Mustering the evidence

7.1.21 If a company intends to defend a tribunal claim, it needs to begin gathering the evidence to support its case as soon as possible. If the claim is one of discrimination, the company may also need to respond to a questionnaire that the employee has sent (see 2.1.64 and 3.1.36).

Written statements

7.1.22   Written statements should be taken from those who were involved in the case. We can assist in this. The information in these statements will help in assessing the strengths and weaknesses of the company's case and in identifying who will need to be called as a witness at the tribunal hearing. The tribunal is likely to order that the claimant and the respondent should, in advance of the hearing, exchange copies of the statements of the witnesses they intend to ask to give evidence at the hearing. The tribunal has the power, on its own initiative or on the application of one of the parties, to order a person to come to the hearing to give evidence, if that person has relevant evidence to give and would not attend the tribunal hearing voluntarily.

Relevant documents

7.1.23   Documentary evidence may also need to be collected. In an unfair dismissal claim arising from a disciplinary dismissal, for example, the relevant documents are likely to include any letter sent to the employee inviting him or her to a meeting, the notes of disciplinary and appeal hearings, a copy of the company's disciplinary rules and procedure, and copies of any written warnings. The employment tribunal is likely to ask the parties to agree, in advance of the hearing, the contents of a single bundle of the documents they wish to refer to at the hearing. The tribunal can also order one party to disclose and provide copies of relevant documents to the other party.

Preliminary hearings

7.1.24   In some cases, the tribunal may decide to hold a hearing in advance of the main hearing, to deal with preliminary procedural or legal issues.

Case management discussion

7.1.25   In a complex case, the tribunal may hold a hearing to decide how the case should be handled. The tribunal will use this hearing, known as a case management discussion, to clarify the legal issues, decide how much time should be allocated for the hearing, identify what witness orders may be needed, and decide whether any documents should be disclosed by one party or the other. This discussion is conducted by an Employment Judge alone.

Pre-hearing review

7.1.26   An Employment Judge may also decide, on his or her own initiative or on application by one of the parties, to hold a pre-hearing review. The purpose of this hearing is for the Judge to consider preliminary legal questions. In an unfair dismissal claim, for example, the Judge may decide that a pre-hearing review is necessary to decide whether a late claim should be allowed, whether the claimant is an employee or whether the claimant has the necessary qualifying service to bring the claim. In addition, the Employment Judge can look at the written claim and response, hear from the parties on what their case is about and then decide whether the claim or the defence has any reasonable prospect of success.

7.1.27   If the Employment Judge concludes that a party has little reasonable chance of success, he or she can order that party to pay a deposit of up to £500 as a condition of being allowed to continue. A tribunal chaired by a different Judge will then conduct the main hearing. At the conclusion of the case, the party's deposit may be refunded. If the party is ordered to pay the other party's costs or expenses (see 7.1.46), however, the deposit will go towards meeting those costs. If the Judge concludes that a party has *no* reasonable chance of success, he or she can strike out the claim or, as the case may be, the response.

The main hearing

7.1.28   The tribunal sends out a notice of the hearing date at least 14 days in advance. If the date is unsuitable for some reason, such as an important witness being ill or out of the country, the tribunal may be prepared to postpone the date of the hearing.

7.1.29 Employment tribunal hearings are more informal than hearings in the ordinary civil courts, and tribunals have a broad discretion as to how their hearings should be run. In particular, tribunals are not bound by the usual technical rules of what evidence is or is not admissible. There is still, however, a degree of formality to the proceedings. Witnesses will, for example, be asked to give their evidence under oath or affirmation and will be cross-examined.

Overriding objective

7.1.30 According to legislation, a tribunal's overriding objective is to deal with the case justly. That includes, as far as practicable:

- ensuring that the parties are on an equal footing;
- saving expense;
- dealing with the case in a way that is proportionate to the complexity or importance of the issues; and
- ensuring that the case is dealt with quickly, efficiently and fairly.

Tribunal's process

7.1.31 The parties may choose to represent themselves at the hearing. Alternatively, they may appoint a representative of their choice, who might be a friend, a trade union official, a lawyer or some other adviser such as an EEF official. The tribunal will indicate which party should present its case first. In a discrimination claim it is usual for the claimant to go first, whereas in an unfair dismissal claim the company usually puts its case first, if it concedes that it dismissed the claimant.

7.1.32 A witness will be asked to take an oath or affirm before giving evidence. Once a party's witness has given his or her main evidence, the other party may ask the witness questions, and so may the tribunal.

7.1.33 After it has heard all the evidence, the tribunal usually asks the parties briefly to sum up their case before it retires to consider its decision.

The decision

7.1.34   Before reaching its decision, the tribunal will need to decide what the facts of the case are, in the light of the evidence that it has heard. That may involve it deciding which of two conflicting accounts it believes. The tribunal will then apply the relevant legislation or other principles of law to those facts.

EC and human rights legislation

7.1.35   When deciding what the UK's employment legislation means, the tribunal must take into account any relevant European Community legislation. It is also under a duty, under the Human Rights Act 1998, to interpret the legislation in a way that is compatible with the rights set out in the European Convention on Human Rights. In the field of employment rights, the most relevant parts of the Convention are those that deal with:

- the right to respect for private and family life;
- the right to freedom of thought, conscience and religion;
- the right to freedom of expression; and
- the right to enjoy the rights set out in the Convention without discrimination.

The tribunal's judgment

7.1.36   The tribunal may have time to reach its decision on the day of the hearing, in which case it will announce its judgment and the reasons for it to the parties. After the hearing, a written copy of the judgment will be sent to the parties. Written reasons for the judgment will also be sent to the parties, if either of them has requested this at the hearing or within 14 days of the date the judgment was sent to the parties.

7.1.37   If there is no time to reach a decision on the day, the tribunal will meet at a later date to reach its decision. This is termed a 'reserved judgment'. The parties will then be sent a copy of the judgment and the reasons for it by post.

Remedies

7.1.38 If the tribunal upholds a claim but does not have time to decide what compensation or other remedy should be awarded, the case will be adjourned to a later date, when a further hearing will be held to deal with remedies. The parties may be able to settle the claim before that date and so avoid the expense of a further hearing.

Recoupment

7.1.39 If a claimant has been claiming Income Support or Job Seekers' Allowance, the Department for Work and Pensions can in some cases recover those benefits from the compensation that the claimant is awarded by the tribunal. This is known as 'recoupment'. Since the recoupment rules do not apply to sums paid under a negotiated settlement, there is a strong incentive for claimants who have been claiming benefits to settle their claim before the tribunal hearing, or before the hearing on remedies. Where recoupment applies, the respondent will be required to pay part of the award to the claimant and part to the Department for Work and Pensions.

Liability for interest

7.1.40 If compensation is awarded by the tribunal, it should be paid promptly to avoid liability for interest. Interest becomes payable 14 days after the judgment is sent to the parties in discrimination cases and 42 days after the judgment is sent out in other cases.

Enforcement

7.1.41 If the respondent does not pay the compensation the tribunal has awarded, the claimant can apply to the county court or, in Scotland, the sheriff court, to convert the tribunal's award into a court judgment. The claimant can then use the court's enforcement mechanisms to obtain payment.

Restrictions on publicity

7.1.42   Tribunal hearings are normally open to the public, including the press. Cases involving national security issues may be held in private, and the tribunal may also hear evidence in private in some other limited circumstances. These include where the witness may reveal information that he or she was given in confidence and where the business in which the witness works would be substantially damaged if his or her evidence were made public.

Restricted reporting order

7.1.43   If a case involves allegations of sexual misconduct, including sexual harassment, the tribunal may order that the people involved in the allegations should not be identified in any publication, including the press. This is known as a 'restricted reporting order'. The restriction is lifted once liability and remedy have been decided, or earlier if the tribunal so decides. If a case involves an allegation of a sexual offence under the criminal law, a restricted reporting order may be made and the tribunal's judgment will also be altered to remove anything that might identify the person affected by or making the allegation.

7.1.44   A restricted reporting order can also be made in a disability discrimination case, if evidence of a personal nature is likely to be heard by the tribunal.

Costs and expenses

7.1.45   The general rule is that employment tribunals do not award costs or, in Scotland, expenses. The parties therefore have to meet their own costs of bringing or defending the claim. However, the tribunal can in some limited circumstances order one party to pay the other party's costs, including time spent by parties who are not legally represented in preparing their case.

7.1.46   The tribunal has the power to award costs if it considers that the party has acted 'vexatiously, abusively, disruptively or otherwise unreasonably' in bringing or conducting the case. It can also award costs if it considers that the bringing or conducting of the case was misconceived, which includes where the claim or response had no reasonable prospect of success.

7.1.47 Costs can be awarded against a party if the party's representative has acted unreasonably in conducting the case. The tribunal can also order a party's representative to pay costs if he or she has acted improperly, unreasonably or negligently, but only if the representative was acting in pursuit of profit in representing the party.

7.1.48 The tribunal office will pay out-of-pocket expenses to those attending hearings as witnesses or parties. This covers travel and accommodation expenses and loss of earnings, up to certain limits. The tribunal system will also meet the cost of professional interpreters and fees for medical reports in some circumstances.

Reviews and appeals

7.1.49 In some limited circumstances, a tribunal may review its own decision, either on its own initiative or on the application of a party. An application for a review must be made within 14 days of the date the tribunal's decision was sent to the parties. The grounds for a review are narrowly drawn. They include where the decision was wrongly made as a result of a mistake by the tribunal's administrative staff, or where new and relevant evidence has come to light since the tribunal hearing that could not reasonably have been known or foreseen at the time. On reviewing its decision, the tribunal can confirm or amend it, or overturn it entirely and order a re-hearing of the claim.

Lodging an appeal

7.1.50 A losing party may want to appeal against the tribunal's decision. There is no right to appeal against the tribunal's findings of fact. If the tribunal has made an error of law, on the other hand, it is possible to appeal to the Employment Appeal Tribunal (EAT). A party has six weeks to lodge an appeal with the EAT from the date on which the tribunal sent out the reasons for its decision or, if written reasons were not given, from the date on which the written record of the judgment was sent out. If the EAT concludes that the tribunal did not make a mistake on the law, it will confirm the tribunal's decision. If, on the other hand, it does identify an error of law, the EAT will overturn the whole or part of the tribunal's decision, or send the case back to the same or a different tribunal to be reconsidered.

7.1.51   It is possible to appeal against a decision of the EAT on a point of law, to the Court of Appeal in England and Wales and the Inner House of the Court of Session in Scotland. A further appeal is then possible to the Supreme Court.

7.2

Enforcing employment law

Overview

7.2.1 This chapter of the Guide outlines how employment rights are enforced. The table at the end of the chapter, on pages 567–71, lists the main employment rights, together with qualifying periods of employment, the time limit for bringing a claim and the legal remedies available. Some aspects of enforcement are explained further.

Table of Employment Rights

7.2.2 The table on pages 567–71 lists the main employment rights and how they are enforced. It gives cross-references to where further details of the rights or remedies can be found. Almost all claims are brought to an employment tribunal. The exception is breach of contract claims, which can be dealt with either by an employment tribunal or by the ordinary civil courts, as explained in 7.2.10. An explanation of how tribunals operate is given in Chapter 7.1.

7.2.3 Where a right depends on a qualifying period of service, the length of an employee's service is calculated according to the rules on continuity of employment, which are explained in Appendix 8.1. Some time limits for bringing a claim run from the 'effective date of termination' of the employee's contract. An explanation of how to identify an employee's effective date of termination is provided in 4.2.17. An employee's effective date of termination is postponed in some circumstances when calculating his or her length of continuous employment (see 4.2.20). This rule does not apply, however, when calculating the time limit for bringing a tribunal claim.

Employees working overseas

7.2.4   There are complex rules on the employment rights of employees who work overseas temporarily or permanently, and on where they are entitled to enforce their rights. The rules differ according to whether the employee is claiming breach of contract, discrimination, unfair dismissal or breach of some other statutory right. A company that is facing a legal claim from an employee who works overseas some or all of the time is therefore strongly advised to contact us for advice before entering a response to the claim.

Late claims

7.2.5   Each employment right listed in the table contains a reference to its time limit for bringing a claim to a tribunal. In general, the time limit for bringing a claim is usually three months or six months. The tribunals apply the time limits strictly, but in certain circumstances allow a late claim. The rules allowing late claims are different under discrimination law, including discrimination against part-time workers and fixed-term employees and so are dealt with separately in 7.2.9.

7.2.6   In cases other than discrimination, a tribunal can allow a late claim only if it is satisfied that it was not reasonably practicable for the claim to be made within the time limit and that the claim was brought within a further reasonable period. Therefore, even if a tribunal accepts that it was not reasonably practicable for the claimant to have met the time limit, it will not allow a late claim if it was not made as soon as it reasonably could have been after the time limit expired.

Reasons for late claims

7.2.7   Tribunals are reluctant to allow late claims unless there are very good reasons for the delay. Each case will turn on its own particular facts, but previous tribunal decisions indicate that a tribunal will not necessarily allow a claim that was late because the claimant's advisers gave him or her poor or inaccurate advice or because the claimant misunderstood the law. On the other hand, a late claim may well be accepted if the reason for the delay was the claimant's illness or a postal strike.

7.2.8   A tribunal may also allow a late claim if the claimant discovered facts that indicated he or she had a claim only after the time limit had expired – provided the claimant could not reasonably have been expected to know those facts earlier. For example, a tribunal may allow a late claim of unfair dismissal for redundancy if the claimant discovered over three months after being dismissed that there were suitable alternative vacancies for which he or she could have been considered but was not.

Late discrimination claims

7.2.9   A late claim may be allowed under the discrimination legislation and the legislation on part-time workers and fixed-term employees if the tribunal considers that, in all the circumstances of the case, it is just and equitable to do so. This gives the tribunal much wider discretion than it has in relation to other claims, where the question is whether it was reasonably practicable to bring the claim in time. For example, a tribunal might allow a claimant to bring a late discrimination claim because he or she reasonably misunderstood the law, whereas it would be unlikely to accept a late unfair dismissal claim on that basis.

Breach of contract

7.2.10   As explained in 1.2.59, an employee who alleges breach of contract may claim damages or an injunction or interdict. The employee may have a choice as to where to bring the claim. It is always possible for the claim to be brought in the ordinary civil courts. Depending on the size and complexity of the claim, the appropriate court will be either the county court (in Scotland, the sheriff court) or the High Court (in Scotland, the Court of Session).

Tribunal claim

7.2.11   If the employee's employment has ended, he or she has the alternative option of bringing a damages claim in an employment tribunal, provided the claim either arose or was outstanding on the termination of the individual's employment. A tribunal cannot deal with certain types of claims. These are claims relating to damages for:

- personal injury;
- breach of a term that relates to living accommodation;
- intellectual property (such as copyright, patents and trade marks);
- confidentiality obligations; or
- restrictive covenants (see 1.2.32).

Further, a tribunal cannot award more than £25,000 in damages. Therefore an employee who is bringing one of the above types of excluded claim or is seeking to recover more than £25,000 will need to bring his or her claim in the ordinary civil courts.

Making a counter-claim

7.2.12 If an employee brings a claim for breach of contract, the employer can make a counter-claim if the employee was himself or herself in breach of contract. In order for this to be possible in the employment tribunal, however, the counter-claim must have arisen or been outstanding on the termination of the employee's employment.

Remedies for discrimination

7.2.13 If a tribunal upholds a claim of discrimination, it can take whichever of the following steps it considers just and equitable:

- The tribunal can declare what the rights of the claimant and the respondent are in relation to the matters to which the claim relates.
- The tribunal can order the respondent to pay the claimant compensation.
- The tribunal can recommend that the respondent should take steps to avoid or reduce the adverse effects on the claimant of the matters to which the claim relates. For example, if the claimant has been refused promotion because of discrimination, the tribunal may order the

employer to review and revise its promotion procedures, to ensure that future decisions are made on an objective, non-discriminatory basis. If the employer fails to comply with a recommendation without reasonable justification, the tribunal can either increase the amount of compensation it has awarded or, if it has not yet made an award of compensation, make one.

Calculating compensation for discrimination

7.2.14   When a tribunal awards compensation for discrimination, its aim is to put the employee in the position he or she would have been in had the discrimination not occurred. There is no limit on the amount that it can award. The employee's main losses are likely to be loss of earnings and other benefits, both past and future, and injury to feelings. The employee will, however, be expected to take reasonable steps to minimise his or her loss. For example, if the employee has lost his or her job as a result of discrimination, he or she will be expected to make reasonable efforts to find a new one.

7.2.15   The tribunal may, if it considers it just and equitable, increase compensation to an employee by up to 25 per cent if it appears to the tribunal that the employer has unreasonably failed to comply with the ACAS Code of Practice on discipline and grievance (see 3.3.8). Further, the tribunal may, if it considers it just and equitable, decrease any award to an employee by no more that 25 per cent if it appears to the tribunal that the employee has unreasonably failed to comply with the ACAS Code of Practice.

Compensation for injury to feelings

7.2.16   The amount of compensation that a tribunal awards for injury to feelings will depend on the effect that the discrimination has had on the employee. It is very unlikely that less than £750 will be awarded for even the most minor injury to feelings. Serious cases of discrimination that have affected the employee deeply can lead to awards running into five figures, although awards are unlikely to exceed £30,000 other than in the most exceptional cases. The aim is to compensate the employee, not to punish the employer.

7.2.17   If the employer has acted in a high-handed, malicious, insulting or oppressive manner, the tribunal may increase the compensation it awards to reflect that.

If, on the other hand, the employer has admitted that it has acted in breach of the discrimination legislation, that may help reduce the employee's hurt, and so may reduce the award.

Personal injury

7.2.18　In extreme cases, where the discrimination has caused the employee personal injury, compensation may be awarded for that. This might arise, for example, where the claimant has suffered physical injury from a sexual assault or has become mentally ill because of a sustained campaign of harassment.

7.2.19　The tribunal will also award interest on awards in respect of the claimant's past financial losses and injury to feelings.

Remedies for unfair dismissal

7.2.20　If a tribunal upholds a claim of unfair dismissal, it may order the employer to re-employ the employee (7.2.24). If the tribunal decides not to order re-employment, it will award the employee compensation (7.2.27).

Interim relief

7.2.21　In certain cases, an employee who considers that he or she has been unfairly dismissed can apply to an employment tribunal for an order that the employer should continue to employ him or her until the claim is heard or settled. This remedy, known as 'interim relief', is available if the employee alleges that he or she was dismissed because of his or her trade union membership or activities (see 6.1.13) or because of his or her activities as:

- a health and safety representative;
- a workforce representative under the Working Time Regulations or a candidate for election as a workforce representative;
- an occupational pension scheme trustee; or
- an employee representative for the purposes of collective consultation on large-scale redundancies or business transfers or as a candidate or taking part in an election of employee representatives.

7.2.22   Interim relief is also available if the employee was dismissed for making a protected disclosure (see 3.3.142) or for supporting or resisting an application for union recognition under the statutory recognition procedure (see 6.2.16).

7.2.23   The employee must apply for interim relief either before being dismissed or in the seven days following his or her effective date of termination (see 4.2.17). If the tribunal that hears the application considers it likely that the employee's claim will succeed, it can order the employer to reinstate the employee into his or her old job or to re-engage the employee in another job on broadly similar terms and conditions, until the claim is heard or settled. If the employer is unwilling to reinstate or re-engage the employee, the tribunal will order that the employee's contract should continue. This means that the employee will have the right to be paid and receive all his or her other contractual benefits until the claim is heard or settled.

Re-employment

7.2.24   If a tribunal upholds an unfair dismissal claim, its first consideration will be whether the claimant wishes to be re-employed by the employer. This could involve either reinstatement into his or her original job or re-engagement in a comparable alternative post. If the claimant does not want to be re-employed, the tribunal will go on to award compensation, as outlined below (7.2.27). If the claimant does want to be re-employed, the tribunal will consider whether it should make a re-employment order. In deciding whether to order re-employment, the tribunal will take into account whether it would be practicable for the employer to re-employ and, if the claimant caused or contributed to the dismissal, whether it would be just to order re-employment in those circumstances.

7.2.25   If the employer is ordered to re-employ the claimant but fails to do so, the tribunal will award the employee compensation, as outlined in 7.2.27. It will also award the employee an additional award of compensation of between 26 and 52 weeks' pay, unless the employer can prove that it was not practicable for it to comply with the re-employment order. For these purposes, a week's pay is calculated in the way set out in Appendix 8.2 and is subject to a limit. This limit is usually updated annually in line with the Retail Prices Index. From 1 October 2009 it stands at £380.

7.2.26   In practice, re-employment orders are rarely made.

Basic award

7.2.27 Compensation for unfair dismissal is made up of two elements: the basic award and the compensatory award. Under the Employment Act 2008, the tribunal may, if it considers it just and equitable, increase compensation to an employee by up to 25 per cent if it appears to the tribunal that the employer has unreasonably failed to comply with the ACAS Code of Practice on discipline and grievance. Further, the tribunal may, if it considers it just and equitable, decrease any award to an employee by no more that 25 per cent if it appears to the tribunal that the employee has unreasonably failed to comply with this ACAS Code. These provisions provide a clear incentive for the parties to follow the recommendations in the Code.

7.2.28 The basic award is calculated by reference to the employee's age, length of service and week's pay. The employee is entitled to:

- half a week's pay for each complete year of service in which he or she was under 22;

- one week's pay for each year of service in which he or she was 22 or over but under 41; and

- one and a half weeks' pay for each complete year of service in which he or she was 41 or over.

7.2.29 The maximum number of years' service that can be taken into account is 20. A week's pay is calculated in the way set out in Appendix 8.2. There is a limit on the amount of a week's pay, which is adjusted each year in line with the Retail Prices Index. From 1 October 2009, the limit was raised to £380 and the maximum basic award is £11,400.

Minimum basic award

7.2.30 If the dismissal was unfair because the employer failed to notify a retiring employee of his or her right to request to work on (see 4.2.59), the basic award will be increased, if necessary, to a minimum of four weeks' pay, unless the tribunal considers that increasing it would result in injustice to the employer.

7.2.31 There is a minimum basic award of £4,700 in certain other cases. These are where the employee has been dismissed, or selected for redundancy, for:

- acting as a health and safety representative;
- acting as a workforce representative under the Working Time Regulations or as a candidate for election as a workforce representative;
- acting as an occupational pension scheme trustee;
- acting as an employee representative for the purposes of collective consultation on large-scale redundancies or business transfers or as a candidate or taking part in an election of employee representatives; or
- reasons relating to union membership or activities.

7.2.32   The basic award will be two weeks' pay if the employee has been unfairly dismissed for redundancy but has been re-employed or has unreasonably refused an offer of re-employment.

Reductions to basic award

7.2.33   There are various circumstances in which a basic award may be reduced. The tribunal may reduce the award if the employee has unreasonably refused an offer of reinstatement or if the tribunal considers that it would be just and equitable to reduce the award because of the employee's conduct before dismissal. Any redundancy payment that the employee has received will also be offset against the basic award.

Compensatory award

7.2.34   The second element of unfair dismissal compensation is the compensatory award. This is whatever sum the tribunal considers it just and equitable to award in the circumstances, having regard to the loss the employee has suffered as a result of the dismissal, in so far as that loss is due to the employer's actions. The aim of the award is to compensate the employee, not to penalise the employer. As mentioned above, the compensatory award may be adjusted by the tribunal by up to 25 per cent if it appears to the tribunal that either party has unreasonably failed to comply with any relevant provisions of the ACAS Code of Practice on discipline and grievance.

7.2.35   There is a limit to the compensatory award, which is adjusted annually in line with the Retail Prices Index. For the year from February 2010, it stands at £65,300. In some limited cases the limit does not apply. These are where the employee was dismissed or selected for redundancy for certain reasons relating to health and safety (see 3.3.155) or for making a protected disclosure (see 3.3.142).

Calculating the award

7.2.36 The bulk of a compensatory award is likely to be made up of compensation for earnings and other financial benefits, such as pension rights, that the employee has lost as a result of the dismissal. The tribunal will first calculate the employee's loss up to the date of the hearing, based on the net wage or salary of the old job less any income the employee has received from the old employer, such as pay in lieu of notice, or from new employment. If the employee has not secured another job by the date of the hearing, or has another job that is paid less than the one from which he or she has been dismissed, the tribunal will then need to assess how long the employee's loss is likely to continue into the future. If the employee has been unemployed since the dismissal, for example, the tribunal will need to decide how long it will take for him or her to secure another job, in the light of the employee's skills and experience and the conditions in the relevant job market.

7.2.37 The employee is under a duty to minimise his or her loss, and so will be expected to make reasonable efforts to secure another job. If he or she does not do so, the tribunal may decide to award loss of earnings only up to the date by which it considers the employee could have found other work. If the employee has incurred expenses in finding another job, these can be included in the compensatory award.

Reducing the award

7.2.38 In some circumstances, the tribunal may limit or reduce the compensatory award. If the tribunal has found the dismissal to be unfair because the employer failed to follow the proper procedure, but is satisfied that it is likely that the employee would have been dismissed even if a fair procedure had been followed, it may decide to reduce the award by a percentage to reflect that. The tribunal may reduce the compensatory award by whatever proportion it considers just and equitable if the employee caused or contributed to the dismissal by some form of blameworthy or culpable conduct. Any redundancy payment that the employee has received in excess of the basic award will be offset against the compensatory award.

Recoupment

7.2.39 The Department for Work and Pensions (DWP) is entitled to recover any Job Seekers' Allowance or Income Support that an employee has received in respect of a period for which a tribunal has awarded the employee compensation for lost earnings. When the tribunal makes the award, it will order the employer to withhold a specified sum and pay the employee the balance only. The DWP will then notify the employer of the amount of benefits that the employee has received. The employer must then pay the DWP that sum and pay the employee the balance of the amount it had withheld.

7.2.40 This procedure, known as 'recoupment', applies only where a tribunal makes an award of compensation. It does not apply to settlements. It therefore provides a major incentive for an employee who has been claiming benefits to settle a claim in advance of a tribunal hearing.

The ACAS arbitration scheme

7.2.41 If employer and employee agree, an unfair dismissal claim can be dealt with by arbitration, through a scheme administered by the Advisory, Conciliation and Arbitration Service (ACAS), rather than by an employment tribunal. The arbitrator, appointed by ACAS, decides whether the dismissal was fair or unfair according to general principles of fairness and good employment relations practice, rather than by applying legal tests or rules from legislation or case law. The arbitration hearing is held in private, where possible at a location that is convenient to both sides, and is conducted more informally than a tribunal hearing. ACAS anticipates that most hearings will last for only half a day. The arbitrator's decision is confidential and can be appealed against only in very limited circumstances. If the arbitrator decides that the dismissal was unfair, he or she has power to award the usual remedies for unfair dismissal. The scheme also applies to claims under the flexible working legislation and aims to provide a speedy, informal, private and generally less legalistic alternative to an employment tribunal hearing.

ACAS administers a similar scheme to arbitrate on claims for flexible working (see 2.2.153).

We can provide details of the ACAS arbitration schemes, and advice on the advantages and disadvantages of opting for arbitration.

Enforcing employment law

Nature of claim/right	Qualifying period of service	Time limit	Legal remedy
Adoption leave (see 2.2.103)	26 weeks by the week match notified	Enforcement is via protection from detrimental treatment (see below) or unfair dismissal (see below)	Remedies are as for detrimental treatment (see below) or unfair dismissal (see below)
Adoption pay (see 2.2.113)	As above	Three months beginning with date of non-payment	Amount not paid
Breach of contract (see 1.2.59)	None	Tribunal claim: three months beginning with the effective date of termination (see 4.2.17). Employer's counter-claim: six weeks beginning with date of receipt of the employee's claim. Civil court claim: within six years of breach of contract	Civil court claim: injunction (see 1.2.63) or damages of a sum that will put the party in the position he or she would have been in had the breach of contract not occurred Tribunal claim: limit of £25,000 that can be ordered
Collective consultation on business transfer (see 5.3.17)	None (claim usually brought by employee representative)	Three months beginning with date of transfer	Up to 13 weeks' pay (see Appendix 8.2) for each affected employee, according to what the tribunal considers just and equitable in the light of the seriousness of the breach, i.e. punitive
Collective consultation on large-scale redundancies (see 5.2.43)	None (claim usually brought by employee representative)	Before dismissal or within three months beginning with date on which the last dismissal takes effect	Up to 90 days' pay for each employee dismissed as redundant or proposed to be dismissed as redundant, according to what the tribunal considers just and equitable in the light of the seriousness of the breach, i.e. punitive
Deduction or payment from wages, unlawful (see 2.1.92)	None	Three months beginning with date of last deduction or payment	Amount of unlawful deduction or payment plus such amount as the tribunal considers appropriate to compensate the worker for any financial loss sustained by him which is attributable to the matter complained of
Detrimental treatment relating to health and safety (see 3.3.155), occupational pension scheme trustees (see 2.4.75), employee representatives (see 6.4.80), representatives of employee safety (see 6.4.80, 2.4.80), working time (see 2.3.25), time off for study or training (see 2.3.102), protected disclosures (see 3.3.144), maternity, paternity, adoption and parental leave and time off for dependants (see Chapter 2.2), trade union recognition, trade union membership (see 6.2.40), right to be accompanied in disciplinary and grievance hearings (see 3.3.80), or at meetings to discuss retirement (see 4.2.59) national minimum wage (see 2.1.22) and payment of tax credits (see 2.1.105)	None	Three months beginning with date of act or failure to act	Compensation of whatever sum the tribunal considers to be just and equitable in the light of the treatment and the loss it caused to the employee
Disability discrimination (see 3.1.51)	None	Three months beginning with date of act complained of	Declaration, recommendation and/or unlimited compensation for loss caused, including injury to feelings (see 7.2.16)
Equal pay (see 2.1.53)	None	Within six months of termination of employment	Difference between applicant's and comparator's terms, for six-year period preceding date of claim (or five-year period preceding date of claim in Scotland)
Fixed-term employee, failure to inform of vacancy (see 1.1.23)	None	Three months beginning with the date on which others were informed of the vacancy	Declaration, recommendation and/or compensation of whatever sum the tribunal considers just and equitable in the light of the employer's fault and the loss caused to the employee

Employment Guide 2010

Nature of claim/right	Qualifying period of service	Time limit	Legal remedy
Fixed-term work, discrimination on grounds of detrimental treatment (see 1.2.92 and 1.2.103)	None	Three months beginning with the date of the act complained of	Declaration, recommendation and/or compensation of whatever sum the tribunal considers just and equitable in the light of the employer's fault and the loss caused to the employee
Flexible working, right to request (see 2.2.153)	26 weeks by date of request	Within three months beginning with date employee notified that appeal rejected or breach of procedure occurred	Declaration, order to reconsider application and/or compensation of whatever sum the tribunal considers just and equitable in all the circumstances, up to a maximum of 8 weeks' pay
Guarantee pay (see 5.2.132)	One month	Three months beginning with day for which payment claimed	Amount that should have been paid, up to maximum of £21.20 per day; maximum of five days' pay in any three-month period
Health and safety – breach of common law duty of care	None	Claim in negligence: broadly, three years from illness or injury. Claim for breach of contract: within six years of breach	Damages to put the employee in the position he or she would have been in had the duty not been breached, including compensation for pain and suffering
Holidays under the Working Time Regulations (see 2.3.71)	None	Three months beginning with day on which leave should have been permitted (or first day of period of leave that should have been permitted) or payment should have been made	Refusal to allow: compensation of whatever sum the tribunal considers just and equitable in the light of the employer's fault and the loss caused to the employee. Failure to pay: amount that should have been paid
Inducements relating to union membership or collective bargaining (see 6.1.11 and 6.1.17)	None	Within three months beginning with date when offer was made	Declaration, compensation of £3,100
Marital and civil partnership discrimination (see 3.1.43)	None	Three months beginning with the date of act complained of	Declaration, recommendation and/or unlimited compensation for loss caused, including injury to feelings
Maternity leave, ordinary (see 2.2.25)	None	Enforcement is via protection from detrimental treatment (see above) or unfair dismissal (see below)	Remedies are as for detrimental treatment (see above) or unfair dismissal (see below)
Maternity leave, additional (see 2.2.25)	None	Enforcement is via protection from detrimental treatment (see above) or unfair dismissal (see below)	Remedies are as for detrimental treatment (see above) or unfair dismissal (see below)
Maternity pay, statutory (see 2.2.47)	26 weeks by 15th week before the expected week of childbirth	Three months beginning with date of non-payment	Amount not paid
Maternity suspension: right to be offered alternative work before suspension (see 2.2.21)	None	Three months beginning with first day of suspension	Compensation of whatever amount the tribunal considers just and equitable in the light of the employer's fault and the loss caused to the employee
Maternity suspension: right to be paid (see 2.2.22)	None	Three months beginning with day in respect of which the claim is made	Amount that should have been paid
National Minimum Wage (see 2.1.22)	None	As for breach of contract (see above) or deductions from wages (see above) Note: Inland Revenue may also enforce – criminal sanctions available	Amount due
Parental leave (see 2.2.128)	One year at beginning of leave	Time limits are as for detrimental treatment (see above) or unfair dismissal (see below)	Remedies are as for detrimental treatment (see above) or unfair dismissal (see below)

Enforcing employment law

Nature of claim/right	Qualifying period of service	Time limit	Legal remedy
Part-time work, discrimination on grounds of/or detrimental treatment (see 2.3.85 and 2.3.91)	None	Three months beginning with date of act complained of	Declaration, recommendation and/or compensation of whatever sum the tribunal considers just and equitable in the light of the employer's fault and the loss caused to the employee
Paternity leave (see 2.2.85)	26 weeks by the 15th week before the expected week of childbirth/ week match is notified	Enforcement is via protection from detrimental treatment (see above) or unfair dismissal (see below)	Remedies are as for detrimental treatment (see above) or unfair dismissal (see below)
Paternity pay (see 2.2.95)	As above	Three months beginning with date of non-payment	Amount not paid
Pay statement, itemised (see 2.1.20)	None	Three months beginning with date employment ended	Amount of unnotified deductions, for the 13-week period prior to the application to the tribunal
Race discrimination (see 3.1.7 and 3.1.16)	None	Three months beginning with date of act complained of	Declaration, recommendation and/ or unlimited compensation for loss caused, including injury to feelings (see 7.2.16)
Redundancy payment (see 5.2.114)	Two years	Within six months beginning with date of dismissal, employee must make written claim to employer or claim to tribunal for redundancy payment or unfair dismissal (or take one of these steps within a further six months and the tribunal considers it just and equitable that the employee should receive a payment)	Redundancy payment calculated by reference to age, length of service and week's pay (see 5.2.117), subject to maximum of £11,400 plus such amount as the tribunal considers appropriate to compensate the worker for any financial loss sustained by him which is attributable to the non-payment of the redundancy payment
Refusal of employment on trade union grounds (see 6.1.9)	None	Three months beginning with date of conduct complained of	Compensation for loss caused, including injury to feelings, up to maximum of £65,300
Religious discrimination (see 3.1.7 and 3.1.24)	None	Three months beginning with date of act complained of	Declaration, recommendation and/or unlimited compensation for loss caused, including injury to feelings (see 7.2.16)
Rest breaks – in-work, daily, weekly, compensatory (see 2.3.61)	None	Three months beginning with day (or first day) on which rest should have been allowed	Compensation of a sum that the tribunal considers just and equitable in the light of the employer's fault and the loss caused to the employee
Right to be accompanied at a disciplinary or grievance hearing (see 3.3.80)	None	Three months beginning with date of failure to respect right, or threat to do so	Up to two weeks' pay (see Appendix 8.2), subject to maximum of £760
Sex discrimination (see 3.1.7 and 3.1.11)	None	Three months beginning with date of act complained of	Declaration, recommendation and/or unlimited compensation for loss caused, including injury to feelings (see 7.2.16)
Sexual orientation discrimination (see 3.1.7 and 3.1.22)	None	Three months beginning with date of act complained of	Declaration, recommendation and/or unlimited compensation for loss caused, including injury to feelings (see 7.2.16)
Time off during notice of redundancy (see 5.2.112)	Two years	Three months beginning with day time off should have been allowed or paid	Failure to allow: amount that would have been paid had time off been allowed, up to a maximum of 40% of a week's pay (see Appendix 8.2). Failure to pay: amount that should have been paid, up to a maximum of 40% of a week's pay (see Appendix 8.2)

Employment Guide 2010

Nature of claim/right	Qualifying period of service	Time limit	Legal remedy
Time off for trade union duties and activities (see 6.1.27), negotiating representatives and information and consultation representatives (see 6.4.76), union safety representatives (see 6.4.78), pension scheme trustees (see 2.4.74) and representatives of employee safety (see 6.4.78)	None	Within three months of day time off should have been allowed or paid	Refusal of time off: compensation of whatever sum the tribunal considers just and equitable in the light of the employer's fault and the loss caused to the employee. Failure to pay: amount that should have been paid
Time off for dependants (see 2.2.161) and for public duties (see 2.3.92)	None	Three months starting with day time off should have been allowed	Compensation of whatever sum the tribunal considers just and equitable in the light of the employer's fault and the loss caused to the employee
Time off for antenatal care (see 2.2.12), employee representatives (see 6.4.77), study or training (see 2.3.104)	None	Three months from day on which time off should have been allowed or paid	Failure to allow time off: amount that would have been paid had time off been allowed. Failure to pay: amount that should have been paid
Unfair dismissal under general principle of reasonableness (see 4.2.36)	One year	Three months beginning with effective date of termination (see 4.2.17)	Re-employment or compensation of up to £76,700 (£11,400 maximum basic award and £65,300 maximum compensatory award) (see 7.2.20)
Unfair dismissal for taking part in official industrial action (see 6.3.50)	None	Six months beginning with date the applicant was given notice of dismissal or, if dismissed without notice, six months beginning with the applicant's effective date of termination (see 4.2.17)	Re-employment or compensation of up to £76,700 (£11,400 maximum basic award and £65,300 maximum compensatory award) (see 7.2.20)
Unfair dismissal for reason connected with a business transfer (see 5.3.61)	One year	Three months beginning with effective date of termination (see 4.2.17)	Re-employment or compensation of up to £76,700 (£11,400 maximum basic award and £65,300 maximum compensatory award) (see 7.2.20)
Unfair dismissal for reason connected with pregnancy, maternity or family rights (see Chapter 2.2)	None	Three months beginning with effective date of termination (see 4.2.17)	Re-employment or compensation of up to £76,700 (£11,400 maximum basic award and £65,300 maximum compensatory award) (see 7.2.20)
Unfair dismissal for health and safety reason (see 3.3.141)	None	Three months beginning with effective date of termination (see 4.2.17)	Re-employment or unlimited compensation (see 7.2.20). Interim relief (see 7.2.21) available for health and safety representatives
Unfair dismissal for reason connected with the Working Time Regulations (see 2.3.26)	None	Three months beginning with effective date of termination (see 4.2.17)	Re-employment or compensation of up to £76,700 (£11,400 maximum basic award and £65,300 maximum compensatory award) (see 7.2.20). Interim relief (see 7.2.21) available for workforce representatives
Unfair dismissal for acting as a pension fund trustee (see 2.4.72) or for a reason relating to consultation on pension changes	None	Three months beginning with effective date of termination (see 4.2.17)	Re-employment or compensation of up to £76,700 (£11,400 maximum basic award and £65,300 maximum compensatory award) (see 7.2.20). Interim relief (see 7.2.21) available for pension scheme trustees
Unfair dismissal for acting as an employee representative in collective consultations on large-scale redundancies (see 5.2.61) and business transfers (see 5.3.31)	None	Three months beginning with effective date of termination (see 4.2.17)	Re-employment or compensation of up to £76,700 (£11,400 maximum basic award and £65,300 maximum compensatory award) (see 7.2.20). Interim relief (see 7.2.21) available
Unfair dismissal for making a protected disclosure (see 3.3.129)	None	Three months beginning with effective date of termination (see 4.2.17)	Re-employment or unlimited compensation (see 7.2.20). Interim relief (see 7.2.21) available
Unfair dismissal for asserting a statutory right (see 3.3.137) or for a reason relating to jury service	None	Three months beginning with effective date of termination (see 4.2.17)	Re-employment or compensation of up to £76,700 (£11,400 maximum basic award and £65,300 maximum compensatory award) (see 7.2.20)

Enforcing employment law

Nature of claim/right	Qualifying period of service	Time limit	Legal remedy
Unfair dismissal for reason relating to the national minimum wage (see 2.1.22)	None	Three months beginning with effective date of termination (see 4.2.17)	Re-employment or compensation of up to £76,700 (£11,400 maximum basic award and £65,300 maximum compensatory award) (see 7.2.20)
Unfair dismissal for reason relating to the Part-time Workers Regulations (see 2.3.91)	None	Three months beginning with effective date of termination (see 4.2.17)	Re-employment or compensation of up to £76,700 (£11,400 maximum basic award and £65,300 maximum compensatory award) (see 7.2.20)
Unfair dismissal for reason relating to the Fixed-term Employees Regulations (see 1.2.103)	None	Three months beginning with the effective date of termination (see 4.2.17)	Re-employment or compensation of up to £76,700 (£11,400 maximum basic award and £65,300 maximum compensatory award) (see 7.2.20)
Unfair dismissal for reason relating to a claim for union recognition (see 6.2.40)	None	Three months beginning with effective date of termination (see 4.2.17)	Re-employment or compensation of up to £76,700 (£11,400 maximum basic award and £65,300 maximum compensatory award) (see 7.2.20). Interim relief (see 7.2.21) available
Unfair dismissal for reason relating to European Works Councils (see 6.4.80) or acting as a negotiating representative or information and consultation representative (see 6.4.80)	None	Three months beginning with effective date of termination (see 4.2.17)	Re-employment or compensation of up to £76,700 (£11,400 maximum basic award and £65,300 maximum compensatory award) (see 7.2.20)
Unfair dismissal for trade union reason (see 6.1.13)	None	Three months beginning with effective date of termination (see 4.2.17)	Re-employment or compensation of up to £76,700 (£11,400 maximum basic award and £65,300 maximum compensatory award) (see 7.2.20). Interim relief (see 7.2.21) available
Union subscriptions, unauthorised or excessive deduction of (see 6.1.47)	None	Three months beginning with date of payment	Amount of unauthorised deduction or amount by which deduction exceeds authorised amount
Written reasons for dismissal (see 4.1.69)	One year (none if dismissal during pregnancy or maternity or adoption leave)	Three months beginning with effective date of termination (see 4.2.17)	Two weeks' pay (see Appendix 8.2)
Written statement of main terms and conditions of employment (see 1.2.47)	One month	Three months beginning with date employment ended	Tribunal determines terms and conditions. Two or four weeks' pay if other successful claim

Appendices

appendix 8.1

Calculating qualifying periods

Overview

8.1.1 Many of the employment rights that employees and other workers have are given to them by legislation. Some of these rights, such as the right to claim unfair dismissal and the right to a redundancy payment, depend on the employee or worker having completed a specified period of continuous employment.

8.1.2 This appendix explains the rules for calculating continuous employment. A table setting out the main employment rights together with their qualifying periods of service can be found in the table on pages 567–71.

Calculating continuous employment

8.1.3 The rules for calculating continuous employment are set out in the Employment Rights Act 1996. The main principles are these:

- Continuity is calculated in weeks ending with a Saturday.

- A week counts towards an employee's period of continuous employment if the employee has a contract of employment with the company for the whole or part of the week. The employee does not have to do any work in that week, as long as the contract exists. Therefore weeks when the employee is on sick leave or maternity leave will count.

- Continuity continues even if the employee is employed on a succession of different jobs under different contracts. Therefore, an employee working under a series of fixed-term contracts continues to build up continuity of

581

employment unless and until there is a complete week's break (Sunday to Saturday) between the contracts.

- There is a statutory presumption of continuity of employment, i.e. the onus is on the party seeking to establish a break in continuity to establish the break relied on.

Gaps between contracts

8.1.4　In some circumstances, gaps between contracts with the same employer can count towards an employee's continuous employment.

8.1.5　These include weeks between contracts when the employee is absent from work because of a temporary cessation of work. This rule might apply, for example, if a company makes an employee redundant because of a downturn in orders and re-employs the individual as soon as demand picks up again. (It should be noted that, if an employee in these circumstances were paid a redundancy payment at the end of the first period of employment, that would break the employee's period of continuous employment for the purpose of calculating entitlement to any future redundancy payment. It would not, however, affect the individual's continuity for any other purpose, such as unfair dismissal protection.) A cessation is temporary if, judged with hindsight, it is relatively short compared with periods when the employee was in work. For example, even a break of several months between contracts might be viewed as temporary if the employee has been employed for upwards of 10 years.

8.1.6　For the temporary cessation rule to apply, the employee's absence must be due to the fact that there is no work available. So it will not apply if work is available but the company has simply chosen not to give it to the individual.

8.1.7　Weeks between contracts can also count towards continuity if, by arrangement or custom, the employee is regarded as continuing in employment for all or any purposes during those weeks. For this rule to apply, the arrangement must be made at the beginning of the break. The rule could, for example, apply where a company maintains a pool of casual workers and offers them permanent vacancies by reference to how long they have been members of the pool. The rule could also cover a situation where an employee resigns to go on a career break but is kept on the payroll or in the pension scheme and is then re-employed. Therefore, if a company does not want an individual to build up continuous employment during such a break in employment, it should make clear to the individual at the outset that he or she will not be regarded as continuing in employment during the break.

Change of employer

8.1.8   In some circumstances, a change of employer will not break an employee's period of continuous service. An important example of this is where the employee works for a company or part of a company that is the subject of a transfer of undertakings (see 5.3.33).

8.1.9   Another example is where the employee goes to work for an *associated employer*. Two employers are associated if one is a company of which the other has direct or indirect control, or both are companies of which a third company has direct or indirect control. This rule is therefore likely to preserve the continuity of employment of employees who move between companies in the same corporate group.

Industrial action

8.1.10 If an employee takes part in a strike for the whole or part of any week, that week does not count towards the length of an employee's continuous service. On the other hand, the strike week does not break the employee's continuity of service.

appendix 8.2

Calculating a week's pay

Overview

8.2.1   Many of the employment rights that are given to workers by legislation are linked in some way to their 'week's pay'. The Employment Rights Act 1996 lays down detailed rules on how to calculate a week's pay. The rules refer to a calculation date, which differs according to the purpose for which the calculation is being made. The table at 8.2.14 gives the main calculation dates.

8.2.2   When calculating a basic or additional award of compensation for unfair dismissal or a redundancy payment, the amount of a week's pay is capped. The limit is usually reviewed annually in the light of movements in the Retail Prices Index. For the year from 1 October 2009 it stands at £380 for the purposes of awards of unfair dismissal and redundancy pay as well as payments made by the Secretary of State out of the National Insurance Fund where an employer is insolvent.

Normal working hours

8.2.3   The rules for calculating a week's pay differ according to whether or not the employee has normal working hours. Whether or not an employee has normal working hours will depend on all the circumstances, but the terms of his or her contract are likely to be the most important indicator. For example, an employee's contract may specify that his or her normal working hours are 37 hours a week. Employees are also viewed as having normal working hours if they are entitled to overtime pay if they work more than a fixed number of hours in any period. The normal working hours are those fixed hours. If an employee is both contractually entitled to be offered and contractually obliged to work a fixed amount of overtime in any period, then his or her normal hours include those overtime hours.

12-week average

8.2.4   In some cases, as mentioned below, a week's pay is calculated by averaging the pay the employee has received over a 12-week period. If this entails taking into account payments that are attributable to a longer period, such as annual bonuses, those payments must be fairly apportioned. If in any of the 12 weeks over which an average is calculated the employee was not paid, earlier weeks are taken into account instead. In particular, any weeks when an employee was on maternity, paternity, parental or adoption leave and receiving no pay, or less than his or her normal pay, are disregarded and earlier weeks are used.

Employees with normal working hours

8.2.5   If an employee's pay for working normal working hours does not vary with the amount of work he or she does in that period, then the employee's week's pay is the amount the employee is paid for working normal working hours in a week.

8.2.6   If the employee's pay does vary with the amount of work done, then a week's pay is the amount the employee is paid for working normal working hours in the week, calculated at the employee's average hourly rate of pay over the 12 weeks prior to the calculation date (8.2.14). This means, for example, that employees who are paid a bonus when they reach a certain level of productivity are entitled to have that bonus taken into account when working out their average hourly rate of pay.

8.2.7   There is a slightly different calculation if the employee works his or her normal hours on different days of the week, or at different times of day, and gets paid different amounts as a result. The employee's week's pay is then what he or she is paid for the average number of weekly normal working hours at the average hourly rate of pay, both calculated over the 12-week period prior to the calculation date (8.2.14).

8.2.8   It is important to note that, when calculating an average hourly rate of pay, only hours when the employee was working, and what he or she was paid for those hours, should be taken into account. Further, the premium element of any voluntary overtime payment should be discounted.

Employees without normal working hours

8.2.9   If an employee does not have normal working hours, then his or her week's pay is his or her average weekly pay in the 12-week period before the calculation date (8.2.14).

New employees

8.2.10   Where an employee is a new recruit, so that it is not possible to apply the usual rules on calculating a week's pay, the employee's week's pay is the amount that fairly represents a week's pay. What is fair is determined in the light of the usual rules and what other people doing comparable work are paid.

8.2.11   In making these calculations, employment with a previous employer that counts as part of the employee's period of continuous employment (see 8.1.3) is taken into account.

Appropriate hourly rate

8.2.12   Under some statutory rights to time off, such as for union duties (see 6.1.30) or antenatal care (see 2.2.12), employees are entitled to be paid during their time off.

8.2.13   Payment should be at the employee's 'appropriate hourly rate'. This is normally the employee's week's pay divided by the number of normal working hours in a week. If the employee's normal working hours differ from week to week or over a longer period, the week's pay is divided by the employee's average normal working hours over the past 12 weeks.

The calculation date

8.2.14

Right	Calculation date
Holiday pay under the Working Time Regulations 1998	First day of period of leave in question
Rights to time off (other than time off during notice of redundancy)	Day time off was taken/should have been given
Guarantee payment	Normally, the day in respect of which the guarantee payment is payable
Redundancy – time off during notice of	Day employer gave notice of dismissal for redundancy
Maternity suspension	Where day before suspension falls during maternity leave, day before that leave began. Otherwise, day before suspension began
Notice period – right to pay during	Day before first day of statutory minimum notice period
Short-time – definition of	Day before period of four/six weeks' short-time working began
Redundancy payment	Broadly, day on which statutory minimum notice period began, or would have begun had notice been given

appendix 8.3

Data protection

Overview

8.3.1   When employers process information about individuals, they must comply with the eight data protection principles laid down by the Data Protection Act 1998. Processing covers all forms of handling information, including:

- obtaining and recording it;
- using and manipulating it;
- holding it; and
- passing it on.

8.3.2   The data protection principles reflect good practice in the handling of personal information. Broadly speaking, employers can meet the main requirements of the Act by ensuring that:

- they have individuals' consent to the holding of information about them;
- the information is used only for the purposes for which it was obtained;
- the information is accurate and retained only for so long as is necessary; and
- the information is not passed on to anyone else without the individuals' consent.

Further information

8.3.3   The Data Protection Act is a very complex piece of legislation and this appendix does no more than outline its main principles as they relate to employment. Readers who require more detailed information on data protection may wish to consult the Information Commissioner's Legal Guidance (see 9.8.3). It is also worth being familiar with the Employment Practices Data Protection Code, which gives benchmarks on how to comply with the Act (see 9.8.3). The Code is in four parts, dealing with: recruitment and selection; employment records; monitoring at work; and information about workers' health. Although employers are under no express legal obligation to comply with this Code, it could be referred to as evidence should the Information Commissioner decide to take legal action against an employer for failing to comply with the legislation. Advice on implementing the Act can also be obtained from us and the Information Commissioner's information line (9.8.3).

8.3.4   The checklist at 8.3.31 may assist employers to ensure that their employment practices comply with the Act. There is a British Standard for Data Protection: Specification for a personal information management system (BS 10012: 2009).

The information covered

8.3.5   The Data Protection Act 1998 applies to information about any living individual. It therefore covers information about job applicants and former employees as well as an employer's existing workforce, whether they are employees, contractors or agency workers.

Personal information

8.3.6   In order to be covered by the legislation, the information at issue must be 'personal data'. Information is not personal data simply because it names an individual or records that the individual was involved in an event with no personal connotations. Information will be covered, on the other hand, if it consists of personal details about the individual and has the individual as its focus.

8.3.7   The Act covers all personal information that is held on computer. It also covers any information held in manual files that are structured so that specific information relating to a particular individual is readily accessible. This is likely to cover, for example, personnel files that are divided into sections on different aspects of an individual's employment, such as attendance record, holiday entitlement and employment history, but will not include a personnel file containing documents arranged solely by chronological order. Health records produced by a health professional in connection with the care of an individual are also covered by the Act, whether or not they are in a structured filing system. This could cover, for example, the records kept by an occupational health adviser.

8.3.8 Some information, such as information held in unstructured personnel files, may not be covered by the Act. But in practice it may be simpler and safer for a company to base its working practices and procedures on the assumption that the data protection principles apply to all the personal information it holds. This means that data protection principles should be observed in relation to:

- application forms;
- recruitment documentation, including interview notes and assessments;
- personal details such as addresses, telephone numbers, dates of birth and emergency contact numbers;
- payroll information;
- equal opportunities monitoring forms;
- medical records;
- sickness absence records;
- attendance records, including clocking cards;
- records of disciplinary and grievance proceedings, including notes of hearings; and
- personnel files relating to former employees.

Conditions for fair and lawful processing

8.3.9 The first data protection principle is that information must be processed fairly and lawfully. In particular, one of the conditions for fair and lawful processing set down by the Act must be met. These conditions are set out in the following box:

Conditions for fair and lawful processing

- The individual has consented to the processing.

- The processing is necessary for the performance of the individual's employment contract or in order to enter into an employment contract with the individual. This could apply, for example, to the processing of information given on a job application form.

- The processing is necessary for the employer to comply with a legal obligation, other than a contractual obligation. For example, this could cover processing that is necessary in order for the employer to deduct income tax from an employee's pay.

- The processing is necessary to protect the vital interests of the individual. This covers life and death situations, such as where an employer may need to give information about an individual's medical history to a hospital if he or she has had an accident at work.

- The processing is necessary for the purposes of the employer's legitimate interests and does not unduly prejudice the individual. This broadly phrased condition will cover many types of processing that a company must carry out in the course of employing an individual.

Additional conditions for sensitive data

8.3.10 The Act imposes additional requirements in relation to the processing of sensitive personal data. Sensitive data are information relating to an individual's racial or ethnic origin, political or religious beliefs, trade union membership, physical or mental health, sex life or criminal record. If this information is to be processed, one of the conditions set out above must be met, and at least one of the following additional conditions must also apply:

> **Additional conditions for sensitive data**
>
> - The individual has given his or her explicit consent to the processing.
>
> - The processing is necessary in order for the employer to exercise or perform any legal right or obligation connected with employment.
>
> - The processing is necessary to protect the vital interests of the individual or another person, and the individual cannot give consent or the employer cannot reasonably be expected to obtain the individual's consent.
>
> - The processing is necessary for the purposes of legal proceedings.
>
> - The processing is necessary for medical purposes, provided it is undertaken by a health professional or someone who owes a similar duty of confidentiality.
>
> - Where the processing relates to information about an individual's racial or ethnic origin, religious beliefs or physical or mental condition, the processing is necessary to monitor equal opportunities.

Fair processing information

8.3.11 In order for information to be fairly processed, the employer must provide the individual with certain information at the time when the information is obtained. This fair processing information should usually include:

- the identity of the employer;

- if the employer has nominated a representative for the purposes of meeting the requirements of the Act, the identity of that person;

- the purposes for which the information is intended to be processed;

- the likely consequences of the processing;

- whether the employer anticipates that it will disclose the information to anyone else.

Processing for a lawful and specified purpose

8.3.12 The second data protection principle is that information must be obtained only for a specified purpose, and must then be dealt with in a way that is compatible with that purpose. The individual should have been notified of the purpose for which the information was to be held when it was first obtained, under the first data protection principle (8.3.9).

8.3.13 This principle means, for example, that an employer that has obtained an employee's home address for the purpose of personnel administration should not then use that address for marketing purposes.

Information must not be excessive

8.3.14 In order to meet the third data protection principle, an employer must ensure that the information it obtains and holds is relevant for the purpose for which it was intended. It must be full enough to meet that purpose but must not be excessive.

Information must be accurate

8.3.15 The fourth data protection principle requires that information should be accurate and kept up to date. Employers therefore need to have a system in place to check the accuracy of personal information periodically. An employer cannot be held accountable for any inaccuracies in information supplied by the individual or a third party, provided it has taken reasonable steps to ensure the accuracy of the information.

Obsolete information should not be retained

8.3.16 Under the fifth data protection principle, employers should ensure that they do not retain information for any longer than they need to in order to meet the purpose for which it was held. For example, employers will need to establish a system for reviewing the information they hold on ex-employees, to ensure that the information is kept only for as long as is necessary to cater for specific purposes. An example of this might be the possibility of needing to defend a legal action or satisfy the Inland Revenue that the correct tax deductions were made.

Respecting the rights of individuals

8.3.17　The sixth data protection principle is that employers must ensure that, in processing information about individuals, they observe the rights those individuals have under the Act. These rights, including individuals' right to have access to the information that is held on them, are explained further in 8.3.21 and 8.3.24.

Safeguarding information

8.3.18　Under the seventh data protection principle, employers must take steps to ensure that personal information is not processed in an unauthorised or unlawful way, and is not lost, destroyed or damaged. This is likely to involve setting up systems to ensure that those who have access to personal information, such as employees who work in a management, personnel or payroll function, are aware of their responsibility to keep the information confidential and not to disclose it in an unauthorised way. The Data Protection Code (9.8.3) gives guidance on how employers should deal with requests they receive from outside parties for information on employees.

8.3.19　If an employer uses a third party to process information on its behalf, such as an individual contractor or company that provides payroll or personnel services, it must ensure that the third party also has effective security measures in place. The employer must have a written agreement with the third party that it will comply with those measures.

Transferring information outside the EEA

8.3.20　Under the eighth data protection principle, if an employer transfers personal information outside the European Economic Area, it must ensure that the country to which the information is transferred has adequate data protection measures in place. The EEA consists of the 27 Member States of the European Community together with Iceland, Liechtenstein and Norway. This principle does not apply if the individual has consented to the transfer of the information or if the transfer is necessary for the performance of the individual's employment contract.

Subject access rights

8.3.21 The Data Protection Act gives various rights to individuals whose personal information is processed. One of the most important is the right to know what information their employer holds on them. In order to have access to this information, an individual must make a request in writing. The employer has 40 days to comply with the request, and is entitled to ask for a fee of up to £10. The most straightforward way for an employer to meet a request is to supply the individual with a copy of the information that is held, and an explanation of any information that would not otherwise be intelligible. The employer must also let the individual know the source of the information, the purposes for which it is being processed, and the people or organisations to whom it may be disclosed. The Data Protection Code (9.8.3) gives guidance on handling subject access requests. In particular, it advises employers to check the identity of the person making the request, to ensure that information is given only to the person entitled to it.

Exemptions from disclosure

8.3.22 An employer does not have to disclose information that includes information about another individual or that identifies a particular person as the source of the information, unless the other person consents to the disclosure, or it is reasonable in all the circumstances to comply with the request without the other person's consent. This may mean, for example, that the employer need not disclose a confidential reference that it has received from a current or former employer. The Data Protection Code (9.8.3) gives detailed guidance on this. Confidential references that the employer has itself given are exempt from disclosure.

8.3.23 An employer need not disclose information that is processed for the purposes of management forecasting or management planning, if that would be likely to prejudice the conduct of the business. This means that information about proposed redundancies, mergers, promotions or reorganisations may be exempt. Likewise, there is no obligation to disclose information that records the employer's intentions in relation to negotiations with the individual, if disclosure would be likely to prejudice the negotiations. An employer may therefore not need to disclose information about its negotiating position on a salary increase or a severance package.

Automated decision-making

8.3.24   The Data Protection Act gives individuals certain rights if a decision is made about them on an automated basis. An automated decision would include, for example, a decision on whether to offer an individual a job interview based solely on automatic CV scanning. The employer must inform the individual when an automated decision has been made.

8.3.25   On the individual's written request, the employer must provide a written explanation of the logic involved in the decision-making process. Further, it must take steps to safeguard the individual's interests by, for example, allowing him or her to make representations about the way in which the decision was reached.

Enforcement

8.3.26   If an employer contravenes the data protection principles and an individual suffers damage or damage and distress as a result, he or she can apply to a court for compensation. (Compensation is not available if the individual suffers only distress.) The employer has a defence to the claim if it can show that it took such care as was reasonable in all the circumstances to comply with the Act.

Court order

8.3.27   A court can also order an employer to correct, block, erase or destroy information that is inaccurate, or which contains an expression of opinion that is based on inaccurate information. An order of this type can also be made if the individual has suffered damage because the employer has failed to comply with the data protection principles and the court considers that there is a substantial risk that further contraventions of the Act will occur.

Enforcement notice

8.3.28   An individual may also ask the Information Commissioner to assess whether the employer is complying with the Act. Depending on the result of that assessment, the Commissioner may decide to bring enforcement action against the employer. The Commissioner has the power to serve an enforcement notice on an employer, requiring it to comply with the Act. Failure to comply with an enforcement notice is a criminal offence, unless the employer can show that it exercised all due care to comply.

Notification

8.3.29   Organisations that process personal information by computer may have to notify the Information Commissioner, so that their details can be entered in a public register. There is a fee for notification, which currently stands at £35, and notification must be renewed annually. An organisation has no duty to notify if it processes personal information only for one or more of these purposes:

- staff administration;
- advertising;
- marketing and public relations; or
- accounts and records.

8.3.30   The Information Commissioner has produced a guide to the notification procedure (9.8.3).

Compliance checklist

8.3.31   In order to ensure that they are complying with the data protection principles, employers may wish to consider taking the steps in the checklist on the following page:

Data protection checklist

- Investigate what personal information is currently held, for what purposes and by whom.

- Review the way in which information is currently processed to assess whether it complies with the data protection principles.

- Appoint someone to be the company's representative for the purposes of data protection.

- If necessary, notify the Information Commissioner (8.3.29).

- Establish a policy and procedure or guidelines for handling personal information.

- Consider whether consent is needed in order to process any personal information that the company holds and, if it is, how consent should be obtained.

- Identify and mark sensitive information.

- Ensure that the company has adequate arrangements to keep personal information secure (8.3.18).

- Ensure that a system is in place to dispose of outdated, inaccurate and irrelevant information (8.3.16).

- Train all staff who process information on the requirements of the Data Protection Act.

- Consider whether any information is sent outside the EEA and, if it is, whether consent is required to send it (8.3.20).

- Consider putting in place a procedure for dealing with subject access requests (8.3.21)

appendix 9

Useful information

General

Recruitment and Induction, ACAS advisory booklet
ACAS
Helpline: Tel: 08457 474747
Website: **www.acas.org.uk**

Criminal records

Recruiting ex-offenders: the employer's perspective
National Association for the Care and Resettlement of Offenders
Park Place
10–12 Lawn Lane
London SW8 1UD
Tel: 020 7840 7200
Website: **www.nacro.org.uk**

Criminal Records Bureau (England and Wales)
Information Line: 0870 909 0811
Website: **www.crb.gov.uk**

Disclosure Scotland
Website: **www.disclosurescotland.co.uk**
Helpline: Tel: 0870 609 6006

Independent Safeguarding Authority
Information Line: 0300 123 1111
Website: **www.isa-gov.org.uk**

Data protection

The Employment Practices Code
Information Commissioner
Wycliffe House
Water Lane
Wilmslow
Cheshire SK9 5AF
Tel: 01625 545745
Website: **www.ico.gov.uk**

Discrimination

Equality and Human Rights Commission
Tel: 020 3117 0235
Helpline: 0845 604 6610
Website: **www.equalityhumanrights.com**

Age and the Workplace – Employer's Guide to putting the Employment Equality (Age) Discrimination Regulations 2006 into practice
Helpline: 0845 474747
Website: **www.acas.org.uk**

Code of Practice: Employment and Occupation (on disability discrimination)
Website: **www.equalityhumanrights.com**

Statutory Code of Practice on Racial Equality in Employment
Equality and Human Rights Commission
Website: **www.equalityhumanrights.com**

Code of Practice on Sex Discrimination: Equal opportunity policies, procedures and practices in employment
Website: **www.equalityhumanrights.com**

Sexual Orientation and the Workplace
ACAS
Helpline: 08457 474747
Website: **www.acas.org.uk**

Religion and Belief and the Workplace
ACAS
Helpline: 08457 474747
Website: **www.acas.org.uk**

Recognition of qualifications

Recognition of European Union qualifications
Website: **www.dfes.gov.uk/europeopen**

Right to work in the UK

Code of Practice for All Employers on the Avoidance of Race Discrimination in Recruitment Practice while Seeking to Prevent Illegal Working
Website: **www.homeoffice.gov.uk**

Guidance on right to work in the UK
Employer's helpline: 0300 123 4699
Website: **www.ukba.homeoffice.gov.uk**

Certificates of Sponsorship
Tel: 0114 207 4074
Website: **www.ukba.homeoffice.gov.uk**

EHRC are committed to producing updated guidance and codes on discrimination issues before October 2010.

9.1.2 Contracts of employment

Producing a Written Statement, ACAS self-help guide
ACAS
Tel: 08457 474747
Website: **www.acas.org.uk**

Example form of a written statement
Department for Business, Innovation and Skills
Website: **www.bis.gov.uk**

Fixed-term Work: a Guide to the Regulations, Ref: URN 06/535
Department for Business, Innovation and Skills
Website: **www.bis.gov.uk**

9.2.1 Pay and related matters

General

Appraisal-related Pay, ACAS advisory booklet
Pay Systems, ACAS advisory booklet
ACAS Publications
Tel: 0870 242 9090
Website: **www.acas.org.uk**

Attachment of earnings

Attachment Orders: A handbook for employers
Court Service
Tel: 0845 456 8770
Website: **www.hmcourts-service.gov.uk**

Income tax and National Insurance contributions

Employer's Annual Pack and detailed information on all aspects of PAYE and National Insurance contributions
HM Revenue and Customs Employer Orderline
Tel: 0845 764 6646
Website: **www.hmrc.gov.uk**

Job evaluation

Job Evaluation: An introduction, ACAS advisory booklet
ACAS Publications
Tel: 0870 242 9090
Website: **www.acas.org.uk**

Job Evaluation Check
Equality and Human Rights Commission
Tel: 020 3117 0235
Helpline: 0845 6046610
Website: **www.equalityhumanrights.com**

National minimum wage

HM Revenue and Customs
National Minimum Wage Helpline
Tel: 0800 917 2368

A Detailed Guide to the National Minimum Wage, Ref: URN 04/1253
Department for Business, Innovation and Skills
Publications Orderline
Tel: 0845 015 0010
Website: **www.bis.gov.uk**

Part-time workers

Employing part-time workers
Website: **www.businesslink.gov.uk**

Sex discrimination

Code of Practice on Equal Pay
Equality and Human Rights Commission
Helpline: 0845 6046610
Website: **www.equalityhumanrights.com**

Equal Pay Resources and Audit Toolkit
Equality and Human Rights Commission
Helpline: 0845 6046610
Website: **www.equalityhumanrights.com**

Equal Pay, Fair Pay: A small business guide to effective pay practices
Equality and Human Rights Commission
Tel: 020 3117 0235
Helpline: 0845 6046610
Website: **www.equalityhumanrights.com**

Student loans

Collection of Student Loans: Employer's guide
HM Revenue and Customs Employer Orderline
Tel: 0845 764 6646
Website: **www.hmrc.gov.uk**

9.2.2 Family rights

General

Business Link Employing People
Website: **www.businesslink.gov.uk**

Work and families

Website: **www.businesslink.gov.uk**

Flexible working

The right to apply for flexible working, ACAS advisory leaflet, ACAS publications.
Website: **www.acas.org.uk**

Health and safety

New and Expectant Mothers at Work: A guide for employers
Health and Safety Executive
HSE Books
PO Box 1999
Sudbury
Suffolk CO10 2WA
Tel: 01787 881165
Website: **www.hsebooks.co.uk**

Statutory maternity and paternity pay

Pay and Time Off Work for Parents, Ref: E15
HM Revenue and Customs
Employer Orderline
Tel: 0845 764 6646
Website: **www.hmrc.gov.uk**

Useful information

Time off for dependants

Time Off for Dependants: A guide for employers and employees
Website: **www.businesslink.gov.uk**

9.2.3 Working time

Jury service

Court Service Customer Service Unit
Tel: 020 7202 6800
Website: **www.hmcourts-service.gov.uk**

Part-time workers

Employing Part-time Workers
Website: **www.businesslink.gov.uk**

Public holidays

Information about bank holidays in England and Wales
Department for Business, Innovation and Skills
Tel: 020 7215 5000
Website: **www.bis.gov.uk**

Information about bank holidays in Scotland
Tel: 0131 244 2180
Website: **www.scotland.gov.uk**

Time off for study or training

Time Off for Study or Training, Ref: TfST/EL1
Department for Children, Schools and Families
Tel: 0845 600 9506
Tel: 0131 556 8400 (for how the rights apply in Scotland)

Employee requests for time off for training

Website: **www.businesslink.gov.uk**

Volunteer Reserve Forces

National Employer Advisory Board for the Armed Forces
Website: **www.sabre.mod.uk**

Working Time Regulations 1998

Workplace (Health, Safety and Welfare) Regulations 1992 and Approved Code of Practice
Health and Safety Executive
HSE Books
PO Box 1999
Sudbury
Suffolk CO10 2WA
Tel: 01787 881165
Website: **www.hsebooks.co.uk**

Working Time
Website: **www.businesslink.gov.uk**

9.2.4 Pensions

Dispute resolution

Pensions Advisory Service Helpline
11 Belgrave Road
London SW1V 1RB
Tel: 08456 012923
Website: **www.pensionsadvisoryservice.org.uk**

Pensions Ombudsman
11 Belgrave Road
London SW1V 1RB
Tel: 020 630 2200
Website: **www.pensions-ombudsman.org.uk**

General information on pensions

The Pension Service
Department for Work and Pensions
Tel: 0845 60 60 265

Information on the register of stakeholder pension schemes

Decision tree on whether employers are obliged to offer stakeholder pensions
The Pensions Regulator
Tel: 0870 606 3636
Website: **www.thepensionsregulator.gov.uk**

Stakeholder Pensions: A guide for employers, Ref: PME1
The Pension Service
Department of Work and Pensions
Tel: 0845 60 60 265

9.3.1 Equal opportunities

General

Equality and Human Rights Commission
Website: **www.equalityhumanrights.com**

Age discrimination

Age and the Workplace – Employer's Guide to putting the Employment Equality (Age) Regulations 2006 into practice
ACAS Publications
Tel: 0870 242 9090
Website: **www.acas.org.uk**

Useful information

Codes of Practice

*Code of Practice: Employment and
   Occupation* (on disability discrimination)
Equality and Human Rights Commission
Helpline: 0845 6046610
Website: **www.equalityhumanrights.com**

*Statutory Code of Practice on Racial
   Equality in Employment*
Equality and Human Rights Commission
Helpline: 0845 6046610
Website: **www.equalityhumanrights.com**

*Code of Practice on Sex Discrimination:
   Equal opportunity policies, procedures
   and
   practices in employment*
Equality and Human Rights Commission
Helpline: 0845 6046610
Website: **www.equalityhumanrights.com**

Disability

*Guidance on matters to be taken into
   account in determining questions relating
   to the definition of disability*
Equality and Human Rights Commission
Helpline: 0845 6046610
Website: **www.equalityhumanrights.com**

Ex-offenders

National Association for the Care and
   Resettlement of Offenders
Website: **www.nacro.org.uk**

Criminal Records Bureau (England and
   Wales) Information Line
Tel: 0870 909 0822
Website: **www.crb.gov.uk**

Disclosure Scotland
Information line
Tel: 0870 609 6006
Website: **www.disclosurescotland.co.uk**

Gender reassignment

*Gender Reassignment – A Guide for
   Employers*
Website: **www.equalities.gov.uk**

Religious discrimination

*Religion or Belief and the Workplace:
   Putting the Employment Equality
   (Religion or Belief) Regulations 2003 into
   practice*
ACAS Publications
Tel: 0870 242 9090
Website: **www.acas.org.uk**

Sexual orientation discrimination

*Sexual Orientation and the Workplace:
   Putting the Employment Equality (Sexual
   Orientation) Regulations 2003 into
   practice*
ACAS Publications
Tel: 0870 242 9090
Website: **www.acas.org.uk**

Absence management

*Managing attendance and employee
   turnover*, ACAS advisory booklet
ACAS Publications
Tel: 0870 242 9090
Website: **www.acas.org.uk**

9.3.2 Managing performance

Appraisal

Employee Appraisal, ACAS advisory booklet
ACAS Publications
Tel: 0870 242 9090
Website: **www.acas.org.uk**

Disability discrimination

Code of Practice: Employment and Occupation
Equality and Human Rights Commission
Helpline: 0845 6046610
Website: **www.equalityhumanrights.com**

Statutory sick pay

E14 *Employer helpbook on Statutory Sick Pay*, Ref: CA29
Ref: CA 35
Employer Orderline
Tel: 0845 764 6646
Website: **www.hmrc.gov.uk**

9.3.3 Handling discipline and grievances

Alcohol and drugs

Alcohol Concern
64 Leman Street
London E1 8EU
Tel: 020 7264 0510
Website: **www.alcoholconcern.org.uk**

Alcoholics Anonymous
General Service Office of AA
PO Box 1
10 Toft Green
York YO1 7NJ
Website: **www.alcoholics-anonymous.org.uk**

Drug Misuse at Work
Health and Safety Executive
HSE Books
PO Box 1999
Sudbury
Suffolk CO10 2WA
Tel: 01787 881165
Website: **www.hsebooks.co.uk**

DrugScope
Prince Consort House
Suite 204 (2nd Floor)
109/111 Farringdon Road
London EC1R 3BW
Tel: 020 7520 7550
Website: **www.drugscope.org.uk**

Useful information

Discipline and grievance

ACAS Code of Practice on discipline and grievance procedures
ACAS publications
Tel: 0870 242 9090
Website: **www.acas.org.uk**

ACAS Guidance handbook on discipline and grievance
ACAS publications
Tel: 0870 242 9090
Website: **www.acas.org.uk**

9.5.1 Changing contracts of employment

Varying a contract of employment, ACAS advisory leaflet
ACAS Publications
Tel: 0870 242 9090
Website: **www.acas.org.uk**

9.5.2 Redundancy, lay-off and short-time working

Form HR1
Department for Business, Innovation and Skills
Website: **www.bis.gov.uk**

Redundancy Handling, ACAS advisory booklet
ACAS Publications
Tel: 0870 242 9090
Website: **www.acas.org.uk**

9.5.3 Transfer of undertakings

Code of Practice on Workforce Matters in Public Sector Service Contracts
Website: **www.dwp.gov.uk**

Code of Practice on Workforce Matters in Local Authority Service Contracts, Annex D to ODPM Circular 03/2003 *Local Government Act 1999: Part I Best value and performance improvement*
Website: **www.odpm.gov.uk**

Cabinet Office Statement of Practice on Staff Transfers in the Public Sector
Website: **www.hm-treasury.gov.uk**

9.6.1 Union members

Time Off for Trade Union Duties and Activities, ACAS Code of Practice
ACAS Publications
Tel: 0870 242 9090
Website: **www.acas.org.uk**

9.6.2 Collective bargaining

Disclosure of Information to Trade Unions, ACAS Code of Practice
ACAS Publications
Tel: 0870 242 9090
Website: **www.acas.org.uk**

Statutory Recognition: A guidance document for the parties
Central Arbitration Committee
Tel: 020 7904 2300
Website: **www.cac.gov.uk**

Code of Practice: Access and unfair practices during ballots for trade union recognition or derecognition, Ref: URN 05/1463
Department for Business, Innovation and Skills
Website: **www.bis.gov.uk**

9.6.3 Industrial action

Code of Practice: Industrial action ballots and notice to employers, Ref: URN 05/1462
Code of Practice: Picketing, Ref: URN 96/618
Department for Business, Innovation and Skills
Website: **www.bis.gov.uk**

9.6.4 Employee involvement

Employee Communications and Consultation, ACAS Advisory Booklet
ACAS Publications
Tel: 0870 242 9090
Website: **www.acas.org.uk**

For further information on share schemes
IFS ProShare
IFS House
4/9 Burgate Lane
Canterbury
Kent CT1 2XJ
Tel: 01227 818609
Website: **www.ifsproshare.org**

The Information and Consultation of Employees Regulations 2004: DTI guidance, Ref: URN 06/657
Department for Business, Innovation and Skills
Website: **www.bis.gov.uk**

A Guide to the Health and Safety (Consultation with Employees) Regulations 1996
Safety Representatives and Safety Committees, 3rd edn, 1996 (Includes Health and Safety Commission Codes of Practice on safety representatives, safety committees, and time off for safety representatives)
Health and Safety Executive
HSE Books
PO Box 1999
Sudbury
Suffolk CO10 2WA
Tel: 01787 881165
Website: **www.hsebooks.co.uk**

9.7.1 Employment tribunals and remedies

Employment Tribunals enquiry line,
  Tel: 0845 795 9775
Website:
  www.employmenttribunals.gov.uk

Employment Appeal Tribunal (England and Wales)
Audit House
58 Victoria Embankment
London EC4Y 0DS
Tel: 020 7273 1041
Website:
  www.employmentappeals.gov.uk

(Scotland)
52 Melville Street
Edinburgh EH3 7HS
Tel: 0131 225 3963
Website:
  www.employmentappeals.gov.uk

9.8.3 Data protection

Information Commissioner's information line
Tel: 01625 545745

The Data Protection Act 1998: Legal guidance

The Employment Practices Code and Supplementary Guidance

Notification Handbook: A complete guide to notification

All publications available from:
Information Commissioner's Office
Wycliffe House
Water Lane
Wilmslow
Cheshire SK9 5AF
Tel: 08456 306060
Website: **www.ico.gov.uk**

9.8.4 Other organisations and government bodies

Department for Business, Innovation and Skills
1 Victoria Street
London SW1H 0ET
Tel: 020 7251 5000
Website: **www.bis.gov.uk**

The Department for Children, Schools and Families
Sanctuary Buildings
Great Smith Street
London SW1P 3BT
Tel: 0870 000 2288
Website: **www.dfes.gov.uk**

The Department for Work and Pensions (DWP)
The Adelphi
1–11 John Adam Street
London WC2N 6HT
Tel: 020 7723 2171
Website: **www.dwp.gov.uk**

Health and Safety Executive (HSE)
Head office: (19) Redgrave Court
Merton Road
Bootle
Merseyside L20 7HS
Website: **www.hse.gov.uk**

Publications: HSE Books
PO Box 1999
Sudbury
Suffolk CO10 6FS
Tel: 01787 881165
Fax: 01787 313995
Website: **www.hsebooks.co.uk**

appendix 10

Model documents

All the model documents referred to in the *Employment Guide 2010* (and many more) are available for download from EEF's website, in Essential HR Documents.

About EEF

EEF is the manufacturers' organisation. We transform our members' ability to work, innovate and respond to climate change.

Manufacturing, engineering and technology industries are helping to design, build and shape the future. They are the bedrock of the UK economy. We work on behalf of over 6000 companies, together employing close to a million people.

We understand the challenges they face, provide them with high-quality services and represent their interests to government. Whether they are cutting-edge global leaders or niche SMEs, we make a real difference to their business.

We help get our members ready for the challenges ahead. The ones they know about – and the ones they don't.

EEF regional and affiliated Associations

East Anglia
32 High Street, Hadleigh, Ipswich IP7 5AP
Tel: 01473 827894
Fax: 01473 824218

Bridgend
Waterton Technology Centre,
Waterton, Bridgend CF31 3WT
T: 01656 641790
E: bridgend.hse@eef.org.uk

Bristol
Engineers' House, The Promenade,
Clifton Down, Bristol BS8 3NB
T: 0117 603 4800
E: bristol.hse@eef.org.uk

Birmingham
St James's House, Frederick Road,
Edgbaston, Birmingham B15 1JJ
T: 0121 456 2222
E: birmingham.hse@eef.org.uk

About EEF

Hadleigh
32 High Street, Hadleigh,
Ipswich, Suffolk IP7 5AP
T: 01473 827894
E: hadleigh.hse@eef.org.uk

Hook
Station Road,
Hook, Hants RG27 9TL
T: 01256 763969
E: hook.hse@eef.org.uk

Leamington Spa
Woodland Grange, Old Milverton Lane,
Leamington Spa, Warwickshire CV32 6RN
T: 01926 336621
E: info@wgrange.com

Leeds
Fieldhead, Thorner,
Leeds LS14 3DN
T: 0113 289 2671
E: leeds.hse@eef.org.uk

Oakham
Barleythorpe, Oakham,
Rutland LE15 7ED
T: 01572 723711
E: oakham.hse@eef.org.uk

Sandy
54 High Street,
Sandy, Bedfordshire SG19 1AJ
T: 01767 681722
E: sandy.hse@eef.org.uk

Sheffield
Broomgrove, 59 Clarkehouse Road,
Sheffield S10 2LE
T: 0114 267 0671
E: sheffield.hse@eef.org.uk

Warrington
Glazebrook Lane, Glazebrook,
Warrington, Cheshire WA3 5BN
T: 0161 777 2500
E: warrington.hse@eef.org.uk

Washington
Derwent House, Town Centre,
Washington, Tyne & Wear NE38 7SR
T: 0191 416 5656
E: washington.hse@eef.org.uk

Belonging to EEF means that we can offer you business advice, resources and support services, helping you operate more effectively. Our unique structure means we are owned by our members, allowing us to focus on delivering excellent value.

Index

Absence
    data protection, 253–4
    defining the problem/causes, 252
    disability adjustments, 255
    disciplinary issue, 255
    flexible working practices, 251
    intermittent, 266–7
    managing, 251–5
        legal framework, 262–3
    monitoring, 253
    poor attendance, 254
    procedures on, 254, 264–72
    reducing, 252–3
    sickness, 255–72
        ACAS Code of Practice, 264
        alterations/redeployment, 270
        data protection, 261
        disabled employees, 260
        discrimination and, 262–3
        dismissal, 262–3, 271–2, 372–3
        frustration of contract, 263
        legal framework, 262–3
        long-term benefits, 259–60
        managing, 260–4
        pay during, 255–60
        procedure, 264–72
    unauthorised, 251
ACAS
    Arbitration Scheme, 572
    Code of Practice
        appeals, 305
        collective bargaining, 494–5
        discipline/grievance, 247, 264, 275–6, 287–8, 292–3, 297–8
        employment tribunal claims, 552–3
        investigations, 287–8
        time off for union duties/activities, 472–6
Adoption leave
    continuous employment, 128
    entitlement, 125
    holidays, 128
    keeping in touch days, 128–9
    length, 125
    notice
        pay, 130
        requirements, 126
    paternity leave, in addition to, 121
    pensions, 127
    redundancy during, 130, 428–9
    return from, 127, 129
    rights during, 127
    statutory adoption pay (SAP), 127–8
    temporary cover, 110–11
    timing, 126
    transfer of, 100
    unfavourable treatment and dismissal, 129–30

Index

Advertising
 content, 10
 drafting, 10
 internal, 9
 jobs, 471
 placement of, 9
 word of mouth, 9
Age discrimination
 definition, 207
 exceptions, 228, 230
 job applicants over 65, 228
 pay rates, 69, 89
 recruitment, 3, 7, 10
 redundancy, 402, 422–3
 retirement, 376–7
Agency workers
 adjustment for disabled, 223–4
 employer's liability, 232
 national minimum wage, 75
 protection of, 58–9, 82
Alcohol and drugs
 abuse, 287
Appeals
 conduct, 307–8
 disciplinary decision, from, 305–9
 dismissal, against, 306, 370–1
 Employment Appeal Tribunal (EAT), in, 560–1
 hearing, 308
 redundancy, 426–7
Application
 data protection and, 13
 forms, 12
  adjustment for disabled applicants, 8, 12
  content, 13
  information
   applicants, for, 14
   supporting, 18–24
  on-line, 13
  submission, 11–13
Apprenticeships
 modern, 344–5
 national minimum wage, 76
 protection, 60–61
 redundancy, 440

 statutory rights, 345
 termination, 344–5
Assertion of legal rights
 protection for, 321–2

Breach of contract
 anticipatory, 337
 claim for, 518, 562, 564–5
 effect of, 52–5, 335–6
 fundamental, 335
 industrial action, 516
 repudiatory, 335
Bullying and harassment
 breakdown in relationships, 246
 bullying and, 227–8
 discriminatory grounds, 226–7

Calculations
 qualifying periods, 581–3
 week's pay, 583–7
Change and reorganisation
 agreement, through, 388–90, 398–9
  collective, 389
  individual, 389–90, 397–8
 clean break approach, 394
 consultation
  collective, 397
  meaning, 382–3
  need for, 385
  training and, 385
  trust and confidence, 385, 387
 contract, effect on, 337, 383–5
 contractual, 382, 400
 documentation, 384, 398–9
 express terms requiring flexibility, 386–8
 implementation, 400
 implied consent, 391
 imposed, dangers of, 337, 390–3
 individual versus company need, 397–8
 management prerogative, scope of, 384
 new contract
  imposing, 337
  offering, 393–4
 non-contractual, 381–2
 notice to vary, 390
 potential legal claims, 392–3

615

redundancy, 403, 408–9, 424–5
rejection of, 391–2
transfer of undertaking, 456–7
unfair dismissal, avoiding, 394–8
Check-off
arrangements, 96, 476–7
legal regulation, 477
political levy, 477
Children
protection of, 23–4
Collective agreements
form and content, 491
incorporation, 492–3
express, 492
implied, 493
variation and, 493
status, 491–2
Collective bargaining
ACAS Code of Practice, 494
bargaining unit, 481
defining, 483–4
revising, 487
change through, 389
data protection considerations, 481
derecognition, 487
discrimination, 470
dispute resolution, 490–1
effect of, 486
employer co-operation/fair play, 485
generally 478–9
information, right to, 494–6
method, 486
protection for workers, 487–8
recognition
agreements, 480, 488–90
application, 482–4, 486, 497
automatic, 484
ballots, 484–6
considerations, 479–81
level of, 480–1
of more than one union, 480
statutory procedure, 482–8
voluntary agreement, 480
subject matter, 486
transfer of undertaking, 461–2

Consultation
change and reorganisation,
collective, 398
meaning, 382–3
need for, 385
training and, 385
trust and confidence, 385, 387
duty, 523, 527–32
employee representatives, 450–1, 452
liability for breach, 456
health and safety, 538–43
meaning, 382–3, 411–3
methods, 541–2
pensions, on, 193–6
redundancy, 425
access to employees, 416
aim of, 416
business transfers and, 536–8
collective, 411–2
content, 415–6
employee representatives' rights, 417
less than 20 employees, where, 412–3
meetings, 425
notice, 416–7
parties, 413–4
special circumstances, 417, 452
timing, 414–5
sickness absence, 265
Trans-European employers, by, 532–5
transfer of undertaking, 448–52, 536–8
employee representatives' rights, 452
union safety representatives, with, 540
warning and, 410–7
works councils/consultative committees etc., 525–6
Continuity of Service
adoption leave, 128
maternity leave, 108–9
parental leave, 135
unfair dismissal, 361
Contract of employment
appeal against dismissal, effect on, 305–6
company sick pay, status of, 257–9
content, 34–43
changing, 38
confidential information, 41–2

disciplinary issues, 276–7, 305–6
flexibility clauses, 387–8
holiday entitlement, 41
job, description/location, 39–40
lay-off/suspension, 40–1
management prerogative, 43
notice of termination, 42–3
pay conditions, 40, 69
redundancy, 436
restrictive covenants, 42
sick pay, 40, 257–9
working time, 41
discretionary benefits, 35–6
discrimination, effect of, 36
documenting, 47–52
enforcing, 52–5, 568
fixed-term, 59, 61–5
formation of, 26, 27, 32, 33–4
frustration, 264, 341–2
incorporation,
   constraints on, 36–7
   documents, of, 36, 72
   part, of, 38–9
   reference, by, 37–8
   suitability for, 39
   terms, of, 37–9
industrial action, 515–6
overtime, 1447
prior conditional, 33–4
statutory rights prevail, 32
task or purpose, 341
termination of, 42–3
terms,
   express, 34–43
      breach, 335
      flexibility, requiring, 147, 386–8
      legal constraints , 36–7
      trust/confidence requirement, 387
   implied, 36–7, 43–7, 148
      breach of, 335–6
      custom and practice, 44–5
      employees' obligations, 46–7
      employers' obligations, 45–6
      filling gaps, 43–4
      flexibility, requiring, 388
   incorporation of, 37–9

limited, 364
transfer, 453–4, 456–7
variation
   effect of, 337, 381
   notice, 390
working time, 41, 147–8
   Regulations, 163–8
written, benefits of, 32–3, 34, 47–52, 64

Criminal convictions
access rights, 23
certificates, 23
check on, 22
discipline, 286
disclosure, 13, 23–4
discrimination, 239–40
dismissal procedure, 375–6
investigation of conduct, 287–92
records, 22, 29
spent, 13, 22–3, 239–40, 286

Damages
breach of contract, 52–3, 518
unprotected industrial action, 510
wrongful dismissal, 332–3

Data protection
access rights of subject, 595
automated decision-making, 596
compliance checklist, 261, 597–8
enforcement, 596
exemptions from disclosure, 595
generally, 588–9
health, 20–1
information covered, 589–90
   fair/lawful processing, 590–1, 592–3
   obsolete, 593
   requirements, 593
   respect for individual rights, 594
   safeguarding, 594
   sensitive data, 591–2
   transfer outside the EEA, 594
notification, 597
pensions, 192
record-keeping, 29, 253–4, 261, 290–1, 310, 350
recruitment, 5, 11, 13, 18–19, 20, 30
references, 23–4, 346–7

trade union members, 481
Dependants
  contractual rights, 143
  definition 142
  time off for, 141–3
Directors
  employees, may be, 57
Disability
  benefits, 260
  definitions, 215–7
    guidance on, 218
    impairment, assessing, 217–8
    medical treatment/aids, 216
    mental conditions excluded, 216
    normal day-to-day activities, 216–7
  discrimination
    adjustments, duty to make, 12, 14,
      220, 255, 270–1, 300
        agency workers, 223–4
        potential, 221–2
        reasonable, 220, 222–3
    Codes of Practice, 188–9, 219, 271
    direct, 218
    exceptions, 226–9
    justification, 219
    reason relating to, 219
    pay, 90
    pensions, 187–8, 260
    recruitment, in, 4, 6, 8, 13, 19–20
    redundancy, 402, 426
    working time, 149
  Government assistance, 224
  health and safety requirements, 223
  justification, 219
  poor performance, 250
  statutory authority, 230–1
  underperformance and, 246
Disciplinary hearing
  ACAS Code of Practice, 292–3, 297–8
  accompanied, right to be, 265, 297–8
    choice of companion, 298–9
    companion's participation, 299–300
    denying, 300
  conduct of, 292–3
  definition, 265
  disabled workers, 300

holding/structuring, 295–6
informants, handling, 295
new evidence, effect of, 308
notice, 292–3, 294
overlapping grievances, 297
rescheduling/non-attenders, 294
structuring, 296–7
Discipline
  ACAS Code of Practice, 275–6, 278, 285–6,
    287–8, 292–3, 297–8, 305, 312–4
  appeals, 305–9
  contractual issues, 276–2, 305–6
  criminal charges/convictions, 286
  data protection, 310
  decisions, appeal against, 305–9
  discrimination and, 286–7
  drugs and alcohol, 287
  general principles, 274–8
  group, 304–5
  hearing, 265, 292–300, 308, 314–5
  investigation of conduct, 287–92
  procedure, 284–7, 306–7, 310–8
  record-keeping, 309–10
  rules, 278
    changing, 284
    clarity of, 278–9
    content, 279–81
    discrimination, 281–2
    dress codes, 282
    enforcing, 284
    gross misconduct, 282–3
    notification, 279, 306
    safety, 281–2
    unfair dismissal, 283
  sanctions
    ACAS guidance, 301–2
    choice of, 300–4
    contract, in, 277
    probationary period, during, 277–8
    union officials, of, 286
    special circumstances, accommodating,
      308–9
Discrimination
  acts covered, 226–8
  age *see* Age discrimination
  assertion of legal rights, 321–2

civil partners, against, 89, 187, 206
claims, bringing, 83
    late, 29, 564
    victimisation for, 224–5
Codes of Practice, 28, 235–6
compensation, 566–7
criminal records, people with, 239–40
defence, 232
defining, 204–9
direct, 209–11
disability *see* Disability
discriminatory acts, 226–8
employer liability, 231–7
Equality and Human Rights Commission role, 235
fixed-term contracts, 93, 343–4
grounds, 204–9
indirect *see* Indirect discrimination
liability, 231–2
like for like comparison, 209–105
married people, against, 206
monitoring, 18, 28, 236–7
motive irrelevant, 210
non-discrimination principle
    exceptions to, 90–92, 228–31
part-time workers, 69, 82, 90–2, 149, 170
paternity leave, 124
pay, as to, 69–71, 82–93
pensions, 184–9, 260
positive, 10, 237–9
preventing, 233–5
proving, 210–11
questionnaires, 211
racial *see* Racial discrimination
recruitment, 4–5, 6, 8, 12, 16, 25–6, 28
redundancy, 402, 420–1, 422–3
references, 345–7
religion/belief *see* Religion/belief discrimination
remedies, 565–7
safety and, rules on, 281–2
sex *see* Sex discrimination
sickness absence, 262–3
trade union grounds, on, 468–72
victimisation 224–5

workers covered, 225
working time, 148–9
Dismissal
actions, 55
adoption leave, during, 129–30
appeals, 305, 370–71
assertion of legal rights against, 321–2
automatically unfair, 365–7
contractual issues, 276–7, 376
constructive, 55, 335–6, 363, 436–7
definition, 358, 363
employee representatives, 417, 543
entitlement on, 272
establishment, 363–4, 394–5
exit interview, 328, 352–4
express, 337
fair,
    ACAS Code of Practice, 275–6
    acting reasonably, 359
    basic ingredients, 274–5
    potentially, 367–8
    reason, 358–9
frustration 341–2
garden leave, 334–5, 431
gross misconduct, 330
identifying, 329
industrial action, 361, 516
limited term employees, 361, 364
maternity leave, during, 116, 365
notice, 328–9, 329–30
    minimum, 331, 338–9
    payment in lieu, 333, 425
    period, 330
    rights, 329–30
    time off during, 431–2
    wages during, 331–2
parental leave, during, 136–7
paternity leave, during, 124
pension rights, 327
post-employment restrictions, 347–9
probationary period, during, 31, 277–8
procedures,
    ACAS Code of Practice, 278–9
    documentation, 371
reasonableness of, 358–9, 359, 396
    demonstrating, 368–9, 396–7

responses, 370
specified relevant factors, 369
reason for, 364–8, 395–6
   automatically unfair, 321, 365–7
   capability, 371–2
   conduct, 373–4
   contract changes, 376
   criminal offence, 375–6
   economic/technical/organisational, 460–1
   evidence, 364
   fair, 358–9, 367–8
   legal restriction, 375
   potentially fair, 367–8
   qualifications, 373
   redundancy, 374–5
   sickness absence, 271–2, 372–3
   some other substantial, 375
   trade union grounds, on, 469–70
   written, 117, 130, 345
record-keeping, 350, 371
recovery of training costs etc., 349
redundancy, 374–5, 402, 417, 432–5
references, 345–6
resignation, 327, 336, 337–9
summary, 55, 328
tax and NI implications, 333–4, 349
trade union members, 469–70, 471
transfer of undertaking, 460–1
unfair, distinguished, 55, 333 *and see* Unfair dismissal
unlawful, 328, 360
wrongful, 55, 328, 332, 360
   damages for, 332–3
   enforceability and, 348–9
   unfair distinguished, 333

Electronic communications
policy, 291

Employee
discrimination liability 232–3
industrial action of, 511
involvement
   benefits, 524
   health and safety, 538–43
   information/consultation duties, 523, 527–35
   methods, 522–3, 524–6
   redundancy/business transfers, 536–7
   report on, 527
   training, 543
share ownership, 526
status, 55–7
transfer of, 453–60
   liability information, 454–6
   objection to, 458–9
   selection for, 458
union learning, 475–6

Employee representation
access to employees, 416, 451
consultation with *see* Consultation
election of, 449, 537–8, 542
functions, other, 542
identifying, 448–9
information for, 415–6, 449–50
rights of, 417, 452, 543–5

Employment tribunals
appeals, 560–1
claims in the
   bringing, 550–1
   costs and expenses, 559–60
   defence, 551–2
   evidence, 553–4
   forms, 551
   late, 29, 563–4
   parties, 550
   response to, 551–2
   settlement of, 552–3
compromise agreement, 553
decision, 557
   review of, 560
EC and Human Rights legislation, 557
enforcement, 558, 562–3, 573–7
generally, 549
main hearing, 555–6
membership, 550
preliminary hearing, 554–5
procedure, 556
publicity restrictions, 559
remedies, 558, 573–7

Index

Enforcement
    contract of, 52–4, 564–5
    employment rights table, 558, 562–3, 573–7
    overseas employees, 563
    post employment restrictions, 348
    tribunal claims,
        breach of contract, 564–5
        late, 29, 563–4
        table of, 562–3, 573–7

Equality and Human Rights Commission (EHRC)
    Codes of Practice, 203, 235–6
    role, 235

Equal opportunities
    checklist, 233–5
    generally, 203–4
    and see Discrimination

Establishment
    definition, 413

Family rights in the workplace
    contractual, 100–1, 143
    generally, 99–100
    health and safety, 101–4
    see also Adoption leave, Dependants, Maternity leave, Parental leave, Paternity leave

Fixed term employees
    discrimination, 149, 343–4
    equal treatment principle, 62, 189
        basis of comparison, 62
        objective justification, 62–3
        pensions, 189
        statement of reasons, 63
    pay discrimination, 69, 82, 93
    pensions, 189
    protection of, 61–2
    redundancy, 402, 423
    successive, 63–4
    termination of contract, 342–4
    unfair dismissal, 343, 361
    vacancies, right to be informed of, 9
    victimisation, 65
    working time, 149
    written statement, 64

Flexible working
    basis for change, 140
    express terms requiring, 386–8
    general clauses, 387–8
    health and safety, 386–7
    implied, 388
    indirect discrimination, 386
    managing absence and, 251
    procedure, 138–9
    qualifying for, 138
    refusal grounds, 139–40
    request for, 137–40
    right to, 138
    sex discrimination, 137–8
    trust and confidence, 387
    working time, 147, 153–4

Frustration
    contract, of, 264, 341–2

Grievances
    ACAS Code of Practice, 311–4
    appeals,
        ACAS Code of Practice, 305
        conducting, 307
        contract, effect on, 305–6
        EEF procedural agreements, 306–7
        hearing, 308
        new evidence, 308
        special circumstances, accommodating, 308–9
        written information, 306
    collective, 315, 490
    data protection, 310
    dealing with, 310–11
    harassment procedure, 317
    hearing, 314–5
    individual, 491
    procedure
        adopting/publicising, 315–6
    record-keeping, 309–10, 318
    responding to, 310–18
    right to be accompanied, 317–8
    special considerations, 316
    whistleblowers, protection for, 274, 317, 318–21

Harassment
 breakdown in relationships, 246
 bullying and, 227–8
 discriminatory grounds, on, 226–7
 policy and procedure, 317
Health and safety
 assessment, 102
 concerns, responding to, 322–23
 consultation, 539–42
 disabled workers, 223
 employees' involvement, 538
 employers' duty, 538–9
 flexibility and, 386–7
 implied duties as to, 47
 pregnant woman/new mother, 101, 104
  alternative work, 103
  antenatal care, 101–2
  guidance, 99, 104
  night workers, 103–4
  risks to, 102–3
 safety representatives/committees, 539–40
 time off, 102
 working time, 145–6, 159–60
Holidays
 contract terms, 163–8
 family leave, impact of, 107–8, 168
 illness, and, 166
 non-statutory leave, 169–70
 Working Time Regulations, 107–8, 128, 135, 163–8
Homeworkers
 national minimum wage, 75
 protection of, 60, 94, 150

Immigration
 Codes of Practice, 4
 points-based system, 22
Indirect discrimination
 accommodating differences, 213–4
 barrier, identifying, 212
 effect, 36
 examples, 212
 flexible working, 137, 386
 generally, 211
 impact, assessment of, 213
 justification, 214–5
 part-time workers, 90–1, 170
 pay, 86–7, 89
 recruitment, 7
 redundancy, 420–1, 422–3
 re-organisation, 386
 sexual orientation, 206
Induction
 data protection requirements, 30
 programmes, 30
 special needs, 30
Industrial action
 assessment of, 501–2
 avoiding, 500–1
 ballots, 505–8
 claim, bringing, 510–11
 contractual issues, 515–6
 dispute resolution mechanism, 501
 examples, 499–500
 generally, 498–9
 individual employees, 511
 lay-off, 519
 liability, 502–11
 lock-outs, 500
 mass meetings, 500
 official, 511–2, 513–5
 organisation, 508–9
 pay during, 95–6
 picketing, 509–10
 planning, 503
 purpose, 504
 recording, 502
 redundancy, 519–20
 repudiating, 503–4
 responding to, 501–2, 516–8
 secondary, 505
 temporary suspension, 509
 types, 499–500
 trade union liability, 502–11
 unconstitutional action, 501
 unfair dismissal, 361, 511–5, 521
 unofficial, 505, 512–3
Injunction
 breach of contract, 54
 unprotected industrial action, 510

Index

Insolvency
  redundancy and, 403, 439–40
  transfer of undertaking and, 462–3
Interview
  exit, 328, 352–4
  investigatory, 289
  recruitment, 14–17
Investigation of conduct
  ACAS Code of Practice, 287–8
  communications,
    electronic, policy as to, 291
    interception of, 291
  data protection, 290–1
  evidence gathering, 288–9
  interviews, 289
  monitoring and surveillance, 290
  police, involving, 291–2
  procedure, deciding on, 292
  searches, 289
  suspension during, 288

Job
  description
    content of, 6, 39
    drawing up, 5–6
  evaluation schemes, 84–6
  location, 39–40
  new
    imposing a, 337
    trying, 429
  offer
    applicant's conditions, 27
    conditional, 21, 27
    content of, 26
    existing employer's rights, 28
    legal implications, 26
    making, 26–8
    record keeping, 29
    telephone, by, 27
    unconditional acceptance, 27
  restructuring, 408–9, 423–4
  share
    justification for, 8
    refusal to consider, effect of, 7
Jury service
  time off for, 173–4

Labour turnover
  costs, 354–5
  effect of, 354–5
  measures, 355

Maternity
  checklist, 117–20
  dismissal during, 116
  leave *see* Maternity leave
  pay (SMP), 100, 101, 109–10
    during notice, 117
    see also Statutory pay
  protection for, 114–7
  redundancy, 115–6
  sex discrimination, 115, 206, 230
  unfair dismissal, 115, 116
  unfavourable treatment, 114–12, 206
Maternity leave
  continuous employment, 108–9
  entitlement protection, 106–7
  generally, 104
  holidays, 107–8
  keeping in touch during, 111–2
  length, 105
  notice requirements, 105–6
  pensions, 107
  redundancy, 116, 428–9
  return from, 112–3
    date of, 106
    early, 112
    failure to, 113
    job on, 103
  rights during, 107
  sex discrimination, 108
  statutory maternity pay (SMP), 109–11
  temporary cover, 110–11
  timing, 104–5
Medical information
  alterations/redeployment considerations, 270–1
  assessment of, 159, 266, 270
  dismissal on, 271–2
    entitlement on, 272
  obtaining, 265–6
    consent to, 267
    intermittent absence, 266–7

623

questionnaires, 19–20, 159
reports, 20, 265–6
    access to, 268
    data protection, 261
    employee's comments, 269
    requesting, 269–70
    withholding, 268

Misconduct
ACAS Code of Practice, 287–8
gross,
    disciplinary rules, 282–3, 330
    examples of, 282–3
investigating, 288
meaning, 273
police, involving, 291–2
searching employees, 289
surveillance/monitoring, 290

Monitoring
absence, 253
data protection, 290–1
disciplinary procedure, 290–1
discrimination, 18, 28, 236–7
probationer's performance, 31
recruitment, 28–9
staff performance, 245, 290

National Insurance
Fund, 439–40

National minimum wage (NMW)
access request, 82
apprentices, special rules for, 76
calculation, 81
exclusions, 76
introduction, 69
legislation underpinning, 75
rates, 76–7
record-keeping, 81
workers qualifying for, 75–6

Night work
calculating average hours, 157–8
definition, 157
health and safety duty, 156, 159–60
limits, 157
regulation of, 156–7
special hazards, 158
transfer to day work, 160

young workers, 158

Notice
adoption leave requirements, 126
dependants, time off for, 142
dismissal, 328–9, 329–30
maternity leave, 105–6, 112
paternity leave, 122–3
pay
    during, 117, 130, 331–2, 334–5, 431–2
    in lieu, 333
redundancy, 116, 402, 416–7, 435
resignation, 337–8
termination of contract, 42–3, 329–32, 402, 431
time off during, 402, 431–2
vary contract, to, 390

Parental leave
collective agreement, 134
continuous employment, 135
default rules, 133–4
dismissal, 136–7
holidays, 135
length, 131
mechanics, 132
pensions, 135
purpose, 131
qualifying for, 131
return from, 136
rights during/after, 134–5, 136
temporary cover, 110–11
timing, 132
unfavourable treatment, 136–7

Part-time workers
comparable full-timers, 90–1
disadvantage, protection from, 171–2
discrimination, 69, 82, 90–1, 149, 170
equal treatment, 91–2, 171, 187
growth in, 172
pay, 69, 82, 90–2
pensions, 187
Regulations, 170–1
redundancy, 172, 402, 423
victimisation, 92, 172
working time, 149
written reasons, 92, 172

Paternity leave
   additional, 100
   discrimination, 124
   dismissal, 124
   entitlement, 121
   length, 121–2
   notice requirements, 122–3
   pensions, 123
   return from 124
   rights during, 123
   statutory paternity pay (SPP), 124
   timing, 122
   unfavourable treatment, 124

Pay
   breach of rights, 73
   company sick pay, 257–9
   contractual issues, 71–3
   deductions from, 70, 94–8
      contract terms, 70, 96–7
      fixed, 75
      industrial action, 95–6, 517–8
      lawful, 96
      part performance, 518
      trade union subscription, 96
      unlawful, 54–5
   discretionary, 72–3
   discrimination, 69, 82–93
   documenting, 73–5
   industrial action during, 95, 517–8
   itemised statement, 69, 74
   legislation, 70
   methods, 71
   national minimum wage, 69, 75–82
   non-payment, 517
   notice period
      during, 117, 130, 331–2, 431–2
      in lieu, 333
   recovery,
      overpayments, 95
      training costs, 97, 349
   redundancy, 41, 402, 432–5, 519–20
   reviews, 71
   statutory sick (SSP), 255–7
      adoption (SAP), 127–8
      maternity (SMP), 109–10
      paternity, (SPP). 124

   systems, 72
   trade union members, 474
   withheld, 517–8

Pensions
   additional voluntary contributions, 179
   adoption leave, 127
   basic state, 180–1
   benefits, 181–2
   changes, consultation on, 193–6
   contractual issues, 183–4
   data protection, 192
   defined benefit/contribution schemes, 179
   discrimination in, 184–9, 260
   dispute resolution, 197
   drafting terms, 183–4
   employee
      rights, 196
      trustee, 196–7
   employer's duty, 198–9
   equal treatment claims, 186–7
   fixed term employees, 189
   generally, 177–8
   information on, 190–3, 199
   legal framework, 182–3
   maternity leave, 107
   parental leave, 135
   part-timers, 187
   paternity leave, 123
   personal, 180
   Regulator, role of, 196
   Second State Pension,
      contracting out, 181
   spouse, restricting to, 187, 231
   stakeholder, 180, 198–9
   taxation, 183
   termination of employment, on, 327, 352
   transfer of undertaking, 459–60
   trust deed, 182
   types of schemes, 178–81
   written statements, 184

Performance
   absence, managing, 251–5
   appraisal, 241–2
      adopting formal system, 242–4
      documenting, 240–4

monitoring and surveillance, 245, 290
breakdown in working relationships, 246
part, reduction in pay for, 518
poor,
   dealing with, 247–50
   disability discrimination, 246, 250
   disciplinary issue, 255
   reasons for, 245
   sex discrimination, 250
underperformance and disability, 246

Person
shortlist criteria linked to, 14
specification, 6–8

Pregnancy
dismissal during, 116
pay, during notice, 117
protection for, 114–7
redundancy, during, 115–6
sex discrimination, 115, 206, 230
unfair dismissal, 115, 116
unfavourable treatment, 114, 206

Probationary period
dismissal during, 31, 277–8
failure, effect of, 31
monitoring performance, 31
purpose, 31

Public duties
time off for, 172–5

Questionnaires
employee, 87, 211
health, 19–20, 159

Racial discrimination
definitions, 206–7
dress codes, 282
exception, 230
indirect, 211
pay, 88
recruitment, 3, 6
redundancy, 402, 422
statutory authority, 230–1

Recruitment
applications, inviting, 8–11
candidate assessment, 11, 25–6
children, protection of, 23–4

Codes of Practice, 4, 28
conditional offers, 21
contractual repercussions, 17
data protection, 5, 11. 13, 18–19, 20–21, 30
defining
   job, the, 6–7
   person, the, 6–8
disabled applicants, 12, 14
discrimination during, 468–9
external agencies, briefing, 9
induction programmes, 30
interview, conduct of, 15–17
job offer, making, 26–8
medical questionnaires, 19–20
monitoring, 18, 28–9
probationary periods, 31
record-keeping, 16–17, 29
references 24–5
restrictions, 3
security clearance, 18
selection tests, 17–18
shortlisting criteria, 14
small businesses, 5
succession planning, 356–7
training managers, 4–5
unsuccessful candidates, 26
vulnerable adults, protection of, 23–4

Redundancy
adoption leave, during, 130, 428–9
alternatives to, 409–10, 427–30, 436–8
appeals, 426–7
apprenticeship, 440
BIS, notifying, 401, 418
bumped, 407–8
checklist, 441–2
constructive dismissal, 436–7
consultation, 401–2, 405–11, 410–7, 425, 536–7
   collective consultation, 411–12
contractual rights, 402, 436
definitions, 405–9, 420
disabled employees, 402, 426
discrimination, 402, 420–1, 422–3
early retirement, 419
employee rights, 402, 417

fake, 408
fairness, 401–2
fixed-term employees, 402, 423
generally, 401
identifying pool for, 420–1
industrial action, 519–20
insolvency, 403, 439–40
inviting applications, 423
job restructuring, 408–9, 423–4
lay-off and short-time, 403, 519–20
less than 20 employees, where, 412–3
maternity leave, during, 115–6, 428–9
notice, 402, 416–7
    time off during, 402, 431–2
part-timers, 172, 402, 423
payment, 402, 432–5, 519–20
    calculation, 433, 443
    claiming, 438
    early leavers, 431
    enhanced, 433–4
    exclusions and reductions, 428, 435
    guarantee, 437–8
    industrial action, 519–20
    taxation, 434
    workless days, 437
pregnancy, during, 115–6
procedures, 403–5, 421
reasons for, 374–5
record-keeping, 425
re-organisation, 403, 408–9, 423–4
selection for,
    applying the criteria, 424–5
    choosing the criteria, 421–4
    identifying the pool, 420–1
    inadmissible criteria, 422
temporary workers, 409–10
terminating employment, 374–5, 431
unfair dismissal, 374–5, 401, 425, 429–30
voluntary, 413–19
warning, 410–17

References
data protection, 346–7
employer's duty, 24, 345–6
individual's access to, 24, 347
taking up, 24–5, 36–7

Religion/belief discrimination
definitions, 208
dress codes, 282
exception, 230
indirect, 211, 386
pay, 69, 88
recruitment, 3, 6, 10
redundancy, 402, 422
working time, 148–9

Remedies
compensation, 558, 570
    calculating, 571
    basic award, 569, 570
    compensatory award, 570
    minimum award, 569–70
    reducing, 571
enforcement, 558
interest liability, 558
interim relief, 567–8
recoupment, 558, 572
re-employment, 568

Resignation
cause of, 327, 336
genuine, whether, 339
notice, 337–8
redundancy, 431
under pressure, 339

Retirement
age, 7, 228
dismissal, 359
early, 259, 419
non-discrimination exception, 228
safe, 376–8
termination of contract on, 340–1, 376
voluntary, 418–9

Right to work in UK
recruitment of person not having, 21–2

Self-employed people
protection of, 57, 82, 94, 150, 232

Sex discrimination
civil partnership status, 206
definition, 205
equal treatment claims, 186
indirect, 386
flexible working, 137–8, 386

gender
  genuine occupational qualification
    (goq), 228–30
  reassignment, 208–9
married status, 206
maternity/pregnancy, during, 108,115,
  206, 230, 263
pay, 69, 82–9
  bringing a claim, 83
  Code of Practice, 87
  comparator, choosing, 83
  employer's defence, 86
  equal work/value, 83–4
  review, 87–8
  indirect, 86–7
  job evaluation schemes, 84–6
  questionnaires, 87
parental rights, 125
part-time workers, 69, 82, 90–92, 149,170
pensions, 185–6
poor performance, 250
pregnancy, during, 108, 115, 206, 230,
  263
recruitment, 3, 6
redundancy, 402, 422
working time, 148

Sexual orientation discrimination
  definition, 207–8
  exception, 230
  pay, 69, 88
  pensions, 187
  recruitment, 3, 6
  redundancy, 402, 422

Statement of employment particulars
  content, 48–52
  failure to provide, effect of, 47
  format, 51
  status of, 48
  time limits, 47–8

Statutory pay
  adoption (SAP), 127–8
  maternity (SMP), 109–10
    features, 109
    notice, during, 117
    rate and payment period, 110
    recouping, 110

  paternity (SPP), 124
  sick, 255–7

Study and training
  recovery of costs, 97, 349
  time off for
    right to, young workers', 175
    right to request, all employees', 176

Taxation issues
  payment in lieu, 333–4
  post-employment restrictions, 349
  termination payments, 351

Temporary workers
  protection of, 59–60
  redundancy, 409–10

Termination of employment
  apprenticeships, 344–5
  automatic, 340
  costs, 354–5
  dismissal, by, 328–37
  effective date of, 361
    assessment at, 370
    extending, 362–3
  employment records, retention of, 350
  exit interview, 328, 352–4
  fixed term contracts, 342–4
  frustration, by, 264, 341–2
  labour turnover, 354–5
  mutual agreement, by, 340
  notice of, 42–3, 329–32, 402, 431
  pensions, 327, 352
  post-employment restrictions, 347–8
  probationer, of, 31, 277–8
  redundancy, 374–5, 431
  references, 327, 345–7
  resignation, 327, 337–9
  restrictive covenants, 21, 42, 347–8
  retirement, 340–1, 376–8
  settlements, 350
  social security issues, 351
  succession planning, 356–7
  task or purpose contracts, 341
  tax issues, 333–4, 349, 351
  training and other costs, recovery of, 349

Trade Union
  ACAS Code of Practice, 472–6

activities at an 'appropriate time', 471
blacklisting, 471
check off arrangements, 476–7
closed shop, 472
collective bargaining, 470, 478–97
consultation, 539–40
disciplining officials, 286
discrimination, 468–71
dismissal, 469–70
employment, 469
industrial action, liability for, 502–11
generally, 467–8
learning representatives, 475–6
membership, 467–8
non-members, protection for, 471–2
officials, disciplining, 286
past activities, 470–1
payment, 474
recruitment, 1, 11, 468–9
subscriptions, 96, 476–7
time off, 472–6, 474, 476
training, 473–4
unfair dismissal, 469–70, 487–8

Trainees
national minimum wage, 76
protection of, 60–61
recovery of costs, 97, 349

Transfer of undertakings
business decision, 407
collective bargaining, 461–2
consultation, 448–52, 456
contract terms, 453–4, 456–7
contracting in and out, 447
dismissal, protection from, 460–1
due diligence, 456
employees, transfer of, 453–60
generally, 444–5
going concern, as, 446–7
Government contracts, 463
information, 448–52, 454–6
insolvent employers, 462–3
pensions, 459–60
redundancy, 405–6, 536–8
regulations, application of, 445–739–41
sale of whole/part of business, 446
unfair dismissal, 460–1

UK Border Agency
Code of Practice, 235–6
right to work in UK
documentation required, 21–2
Worker Registration Scheme, 22

Unfair dismissal
avoiding, 394
change and reorganisation, 394–8
disciplinary rules and, 283
dismissal, 358
eligibility, 360–3
fixed term contracts, 343, 361
industrial action, 361, 511–5, 521
interpretation, 358
limited term contracts, 361
one year's continuous service, 361
pregnancy/maternity, during, 115
reasonableness, 359–60, 368–71, 396
 appeals, 370–1
 assessment at dismissal date, 370
 demonstrating, 396
 documenting process, 371
 redundancy, 420
 responses, 370
 specified relevant factors, 369
reason for, 364–8, 371–8, 395–6
 automatically unfair, 358–9, 365–7, 469–70, 472
 capability, 371–2
 conduct, 373–4
 contract changes, 376
 criminal offence, 375–6
 evidence, 364–5
 fair, 358–9
 legal restrictions, 375
 new terms imposed, 337
 potentially fair, 367–8
 qualifications, 373
 redundancy, 374–5
 retirement, 359, 376–8
 sickness absence, 263 372–3
 some other substantial, 375
record-keeping, 371
redundancy, 374–5, 420, 425, 429–30, 431
remedies, 567–71

retirement, 359, 376–8
trade union
    grounds, 469–70
    recognition, 487–8
transfer of undertakings, 460
wrongful distinguished, 333

Victimisation
discrimination complaint, for bringing, 224–5
fixed term employees, 65
part-time employees, 92, 172

Volunteer Reserve Forces
time off for, 174–5

Whistleblowers
protection of, 274, 317, 318–21
    disclosure methods, 319–20
    good faith, acting in, 321
    information, 319
    raising concerns internally, 321

Work
alternative, 427–30
experience,
    protection for those on, 60, 61
fit for, 19
particular kind, of a, 406
place
    closing/relocating, 405–6
    employer's liability outside, 231
status, 57–8
unmeasured, 80

Working time
compassionate and extended leave, 169
contract terms, 41, 147–8
definition, 152
discrimination issues, 148–9, 170
flexibility
    by agreement, 153–4

over hours, 147
health and safety, 145–6
holidays, 163–8
implied terms, 148
night work, 156–60
non-statutory leave, 169–70
overtime, 147
part-time work, 170–2
pension
    employee trustee, time off, 196–7
public duties, time off for, 172–5
regulations, 144–5, 149–54
    compensatory rest, 150–1
    contract terms and, 163–8
    disadvantage/dismissal, 151
    entitlement/obligations, 151
    excluded workers, 152
    family leave, impact, 168
    further rights, 144–5
    keeping records, 151
    principle behind, 154
    scope, 150
    special cases, 152–3
rest breaks and periods, 160–2
study and training, time off for
    right to request, 176
    young people, 175
working week limit, 154–6
    average, calculating, 154–5
    opting out, 155
    reasonable steps, 154
    young workers, 146, 150, 156

Young workers
night work, 158
working time, 146, 150, 156